329

William E. Martin   PURDUE UNIVERSITY

Celia Burns Stendler   UNIVERSITY OF ILLINOIS

under the general editorship of
WILLARD B. SPALDING, *Chairman,*
Division of Education, Portland State College

child
behavior and
development

REVISED AND ENLARGED EDITION OF CHILD DEVELOPMENT

Harcourt, Brace & World, Inc.   *New York / Chicago / San Francisco / Atlanta*

Photographs on pages 1, 159, 303, and 437 were taken by
Louis B. Schlivek.

Library of Congress Catalog Card Number: 59-7736

Printed in the United States of America

editor's foreword

It has been said—erroneously—that the best way of coming to understand child behavior and development is to study a child. This method undoubtedly yields much valuable information, but surely a better method is to study many children, and from many points of view. Yet few parents have an opportunity to observe numbers of children with the meticulous care and attention—or the objectivity—that are required, and even most teachers deal with only a restricted sample of that widely varied species. A fundamental purpose of this book, therefore, is to present in systematic fashion the known facts about children—all children—as these facts have been discovered by educators, psychologists, pediatricians, anthropologists, and many others who have devoted themselves to the scientific study of child behavior. Thus the book gives the reader a reliable framework within which to evaluate the behavior of a given child, or group of children. By knowing what can reasonably be expected of a child at a given age, adults can realistically adjust their aspirations and their methods of child training.

But the book does more than describe what we know about child behavior. For the authors believe that teachers, parents, doctors, psychologists—everyone who contributes to or is concerned with the fascinating process by which a child becomes an adult—must understand the process as well as its results at various stages. That is, they not only must know what children in general are like at various stages of growth but must recognize and understand the many forces and influences that make each child unique in some respects. Only by understanding the process as well as its results can adults guide child development intelligently and constructively. Only by understanding the social, cultural, physical, emotional, and intellectual factors that affect the child's behavior can adults hope to change that behavior. And behavior change—what the authors call socialization—is the broad goal of all adults in their relation to children, whether the adult is an educator who wishes to change the child's behavior in response to the question "How much are two and two?" by teaching him how to add, a parent who wishes to teach the child "proper" table manners, or an advertiser who wishes to inculcate certain buying habits in impressionable youth.

We do not, of course, know everything there is to know about child behavior and development; perhaps we never shall. It is to the authors' credit that this book raises almost as many questions as it answers—and that the answers it provides are based on sound and thorough research. Readers of this book who do not intend to pursue further the formal study of child behavior and development can find no more authoritative or readable guide to the subject, and none that explores a complex field so thoroughly within a limited space. For those who wish to probe the subject more deeply, the book has still greater treasures in its meticulous bibliography of current and "classic" research, in its carefully chosen and annotated suggestions for further reading, and in the provocative questions interspersed throughout the text. It is a pleasure to recommend this new and expanded edition of a fine and useful book.

WILLARD B. SPALDING

introduction

The subject of this book is the area of study known as child behavior and development. By "the area of child behavior and development" we mean not a single "subject" but a field which draws upon such varied sciences as biology, physiology, pediatrics, sociology, anthropology, and psychology in an attempt to understand children. Specifically, students of this field attempt to answer two questions: In what ways do children grow and develop and behave? Under what conditions do they grow and develop and behave in any particular way?

"The area of child behavior and development" therefore represents a body of knowledge, culled from many sources. As a body of knowledge, it does not directly answer the question "How should children be trained and educated?" But it does provide a basis for making decisions concerning this very practical and necessary endeavor. The facts that we accept as part of the body of knowledge, and the interrelationships of those facts, determine in large part the nature of the training and educational programs that we select as desirable for children.

Consider the case of Betty, a six-year-old, who is just learning to ice skate. She puts on her skates and stands at the edge of the rink, hanging on to the surrounding rail. Then she takes those first few steps onto the ice. But her right foot goes in one direction, her left foot in another. She falls. She is obviously unhurt, but she is frightened. She has lost her confidence. She lies there for a moment.

What would you, an adult, do at this point? You want to help Betty learn to skate. Will you help her more by picking her up and encouraging her to try again? Or would it be better in the long run for her to pick herself up? If you help her too much, won't you be encouraging her to depend upon you? Eventually she must skate alone. Why not encourage her to be independent of others from the beginning? Your answers to these questions are influenced by what you believe to be true of the developmental process.

Further, the facts that we accept help to shape our attitudes toward children. This has been demonstrated in a recent study by Costin (1958), who found significant changes in the attitudes of his students toward parent-child relationships after the students had taken an undergraduate course in child psychology.

A DESCRIPTIVE APPROACH

Our decision about how best to help Betty depends in part upon our knowledge of six-year-olds in general. What are children like at this age? How much help do six-year-olds need? What kinds of problem can they be expected to solve without help, and to what extent must they rely upon adults?

To help us in answering questions about the normal expectations for children in any given age group, we have available a considerable body of information derived from research. In fact, in the past, most students of child development concentrated their attention on description of the child—or parts of the child—as he is at various age or maturity levels under a variety of environmental conditions. As a result of this emphasis, we now know a great deal about the physical, social, emotional, and intellectual development of children. We know, for example, that the body length of the average newborn child is twenty inches, that the fifth carpal bone appears in boys at an average age of five years, that most children have their first tooth before eight months, that the vocabulary of the average eighteen-month-old child contains five words. On the basis of these and many other facts of similar nature, we have formulated standards for evaluating the development of children. We can decide whether a child is retarded, accelerated, or normal in the rate and quality of his growth.

Descriptive studies have attempted to determine not only

what children are like at a particular age in respect to a particular characteristic but also how they change with time in respect to this characteristic. Thus an investigator of cognitive behavior might be interested not only in describing the quality of thinking characteristic of four-year-olds but also in identifying the sequence of stages in the development of this form of behavior. Sometimes the sequence of development is investigated by means of longitudinal studies, in which the same children are studied over a period of years. Sometimes the studies are cross-sectional; that is, they compare the development of one age group—say, four-year-old children—with that of a different group—say, six-year-old children. The samples selected for study, of course, must be fairly representative of four-year-olds and six-year-olds in the population at large.

Some studies have gone beyond mere description to investigate whether the development of a particular characteristic might be related to the development of some other characteristic. Is Pete's unusual independence the result of a particular training experience early in his life? Is Joan's superiority in language development related to her birth order—and will other first-born children tend to be more advanced in this respect than their siblings? Is the social acceptance of children (that is, their popularity among their agemates) related to the rate at which they mature?

Relatedness, of course, must not be confused with causality. The finding that first-born children are superior in language development does not mean that being born first is in itself the *cause* of that superiority. We must look further to see what factors that might facilitate language learning are present in the family situation for a first-born and not present for his brothers or sisters. Descriptive studies may tell us the extent to which two or more variables are related, but they do not say that one is the necessary antecedent of the others.

Because of what descriptive studies have revealed to us, our expectations of children have undoubtedly become much more realistic. If we know that most children go through a period of negativism at about two or three years of age, we shall not be greatly disturbed to encounter negative behavior in a particular two-year-old, for we know that this is normal behavior at this age level. Similarly, we do not expect a five-year-old to be a very effective group member because we know that the ability to participate effectively in groups requires certain skills and a level of general maturity that develop later in life for most children. Effective group behavior is not normal for five-year-olds.

Also, since some descriptive studies emphasize a developmental point of view, we gain a picture of the interrelationship of the past, the present, and the future. We are told that, if we become too discouraged by the brashness, combativeness, hesitancy, indecision, and "strangely contradictory spurts of affection and of antagonism" of the six-year-old, we can look back to the stability, friendliness, and self-containedness of the five-year-old or forward to the dependability, social sensitivity, and "inwardized consolidation" of the seven-year-old (Gesell & Ilg, 1946, pp. 60-68, 88-99, 131-38). The present is always an outgrowth of the past and a precursor of the future. We see development as a sequence of behavioral stages through which every child must pass, one stage following another in fairly systematic fashion. Seven-year-old stability follows six-year-old instability as permanent teeth follow baby teeth and as night follows day. The differences that we observe among children of the same chronological age can be attributed to differences in the rate at which they go through this sequence. For, of course, not all six-year-olds behave like six-year-olds. Some are developing at a faster than normal rate and are beginning to act more like seven-year-olds. Others are developing at a slower than normal rate and are still acting more like five-year-olds. As we learn more about the sequence of development, we can arrange the environment so as to prepare the child for next stages; but the implication of descriptive-developmental studies is that we cannot eliminate or alter the major steps in that sequence or effect any significant change in their timing.

Even so brief a discussion as this reveals some of the contributions that the descriptive approach has made to the study of child development: (*1*) it has resulted in a great amount of information about children and how they grow and develop; (2) it has provided norms or standards against which we can evaluate the behavior of children at any given stage of development; (3) it has given us a picture of the total developmental sequence which has important implications for those who are concerned with the training and educating of children.

A CROSS-CULTURAL APPROACH

There is a temptation to regard commonly observed behavior as "normal" behavior. Negativism is normal behavior in the two-year-old in the sense that it is very common behavior. But investigators have found that boys generally are more negativistic than girls. Can we say, therefore, that this type of behavior is "more normal" in boys than it is in girls? Studies also indicate that boys from homes of high socioeconomic status tend to be more negativistic than girls from similar homes. But if we observe children from homes of low socioeconomic status, we find the girls more negativistic than the boys. What is "normal" behavior now? It seems to vary with the situation.

Studies of children in societies other than our own lend further confusion to the problem of defining normality. For what we, in the United States, observe to be typical behavior is often found to be unusual behavior in other societies.

What a contrast we find between a child who is born and reared in one of our cities and a child who is born and reared in Samoa. The two children speak a different language: the American refers to "house" or "apartment"; his counterpart in Samoa speaks of a "fale." Moreover, the two youngsters differ in dress: an American boy would be socially ostracized if he appeared on the streets of Chicago, even in the warmest weather, in a "lava-lava," the loin cloth or skirtlike garment worn by every Samoan boy. In addition, cultural anthropologists tell us that these two youngsters differ in temperament or personality. The American typically strives, wants to get ahead, is concerned with what others think of him. The Samoan child, on the other hand, is characterized by an attitude of "not caring":

The Samoan background which makes growing up so easy, so simple a matter, is the general casualness of the whole society. For Samoa is a place where no one plays for very high stakes, no one pays very heavy prices, no one suffers for his convictions or fights to the death for special ends. Disagreements between parent and child are settled by the child's moving across the street, between a man and his village by the man's removal to the next village, between a husband and his wife's seducer by a few fine mats. Neither poverty nor great disasters threaten the people to make them hold their lives dearly and tremble for continued existence. No implacable gods, swift to anger and strong to punish, disturb the even tenor of their days. Wars and cannibalism are long since passed away and now the greatest cause for tears, short of death itself, is a journey of a relative to another island. No one is hurried along in life or punished harshly for slowness of development. Instead the gifted, the precocious, are held back, until the slowest . . . have caught the pace. And in personal relations, caring is as slight. Love and hate, jealousy and revenge, sorrow and bereavement are all matters of weeks. From the first months of its life, when the child is handed carelessly from one woman's hands to another's, the lesson is learned of not caring for one person greatly, not setting high hopes on any one relationship [Mead, 1928, pp. 198-99].

The behavior of the Samoan youngster clearly differs from that of the American city child. Which is "normal" behavior? We can only conclude that they both are. That is, "striving" is normal under the conditions we find in a typical urban center in America; but "not caring" is normal under the conditions we find in Samoa. These differences in the behavior of the children can be attributed directly to the differences between the societies in which they grew and developed.

Development, then, is more than the unfolding of a predetermined design, as is implied in some descriptive studies. It is a process that is influenced to a considerable extent by the social conditions under which it takes place. What a child is **and does** is determined largely by the nature of those conditions. The Samoan and the American differ because they have learned to be different. And they have learned to be different because the conditions under which they learned were different.

In the past thirty or forty years, anthropologists have collected a great deal of information about child rearing in other societies. Most of their studies have been of primitive societies; a few have focused on industrial societies other than our own. All have emphasized the relationship between the kind of society in which the child grows up and the course of his development. Thus they have helped us to see that the child's personality is molded as he learns the accepted ways of behaving in his society. As a result, we have become more objective about the behavior we observe. Now we no longer naïvely assume that all the ways of behaving which we observe in our children can be attributed to human nature. Nor do we assume that the ways of behaving accepted in our society are necessarily superior to those in other societies.

We know not only that ways of behaving differ from society to society but also that subgroups within a society may develop characteristics which set them apart from the rest of that society. Sociologists who have studied various subgroupings within American society have told us, for example, that lower-class children in America develop differently in some respects from children of the upper class. Once we acknowledge the influence of society in the development of behavior, we can begin to ask which training experiences specifically influence which behaviors.

THEORIES OF BEHAVIOR AND DEVELOPMENT

Cross-cultural studies have helped us to understand child development as a social process. As such, it involves an intimate interaction between the child and others who act, more or less consciously, as the agents of the society. What takes place in this interaction is *socialization,* which we can define, for the moment, as the process by which the child learns the ways of his society and thus becomes able eventually to take his place as an adult member-in-good-standing of that society. His teachers are socializing agents: parents, friends, acquaintances, school teachers, and all the other members of society with whom the child interacts as he grows and develops.

When a mother weans her baby, she is socializing him. When a father tells his five-year-old son that boys do not cry when they are hurt, he is socializing him. When a fourth-grade teacher shows his pupils ways of working together as a group toward a common goal, he is socializing them. When a thirteen-year-old tells her friend, "But *nobody* wears ankle socks any more; surely you don't want to," she is socializing her. Through these and other socializing experiences, the child's character and personality, as well as his behavior, are shaped.

But what actually takes place in the socializing process? What are its dynamics? To answer this question, it is not enough merely to describe behavior or even to compare the behavior of one group with that of another; we must develop a theory to explain all the facts as we know them.

Psychoanalytic theory provides one explanation of the process of socialization. This body of theory, derived largely from the work of Sigmund Freud, describes stages in the unfolding of human personality according to a rather fixed biological pattern. Much emphasis is placed upon the influence of the unconscious and the importance of early childhood experiences. This theory, as we shall see, has been enormously fruitful of hypotheses for scientific investigation. Because of its great influence, we include in this text a description of the developmental process and the structure of personality according to Freudian doctrine.

Learning theory provides a second explanation of the process of socialization. According to this body of theory, socialization is a learning process. Most of the child's behavior is seen as learned behavior, acquired as his original biological drives become modified. The process of learning takes place in accordance with certain principles which have been verified in many investigations.

Investigators have applied learning theory to a number of problems of human development. They have tested hypotheses derived from both Freudian theory and cross-cultural studies. They have used the findings from descriptive studies in setting up hypotheses to explain the behaviors observed by earlier research workers. This scientific approach to the study of behavior has shed new light on how motives are learned and what variables influence the learning. A major part of current psychological research is being carried on within the framework of learning theory, and it is upon this theory of socialization that we draw most heavily in this book.

Emphasis upon learning theory does not overlook the facts of biology. Because of the physical nature of human beings and because of certain universal distinctive characteristics of the human environment, all children are alike in some ways. They are born with the same biological needs and they grow and develop in accordance with known principles. We must understand the ways in which children are alike, the nature of their human inheritance, before we can turn to the question of how this basic similarity is modified by learning.

We also know that children are different when they come into the world. Each child is unique with respect to certain constitutional characteristics. Each has certain genotypes which make the learning of some forms of behavior easy and that of other forms more difficult. Some individuals always operate in high gear because they have learned to do so, but the learning was easy for them because of the way in which their bodies are constituted. We must understand constitutional differences as well as similarities to understand the socialization process.

METHODS OF STUDYING CHILDREN

Observation

Whether their approach is purely descriptive, comparative, developmental, or cross-cultural, investigators of child behavior and development use a variety of techniques for collecting data. Actual observation of the child is basic to many of them. Very careful controls must be set up to make the evidence collected as reliable as possible.

Suppose that an investigator wished to study the incidence of quarreling among young children during a free-play period. He would first have to define "quarreling," describing very precisely the items of behavior to be interpreted as quarreling. Then he would have to plan his observations, making sure that certain variables are held constant. For example, frequency and duration of observations and the time of day at which they are made should be the same for each child; the space and toys available should be the same for each play period. To ensure greater accuracy in recording data, he would work out a standard form, perhaps preparing a list of specific behaviors to be observed, which an observer could easily and quickly check. If several observers are participating, the investigator must take steps to determine and improve consistency in recording. He might do this by having all the observers watch and record the behavior of the same child simultaneously; then he would compute the percentage of agreement. (The higher the percentage of agreement, of course, the more faith he could have in his data.) If agreement among observers is low, the investigator might provide more practice for his recorders or might revise the observation schedule.

Sometimes an investigator uses rating scales to collect evidence. He might have an observer rate a child on a five-point continuum with respect to a particular behavior. Again, he must control other variables in the situation and determine the reliability of the observers who are making the ratings.

Interviews

Students of the socialization process often interview parents to discover information about the child's early experiences, his reactions to certain situations, and the parents' methods of child training. Teachers are also an excellent source of information about child behavior. Interviews with teachers have been successfully employed to ascertain the child's adjustment as revealed in the school situation. And, since teachers are socializing agents as well as observers of child behavior, the investigator is also interested in information, obtained through interviews, about their methods of discipline and attitudes toward children.

The investigator might design a completely structured questionnaire or interview schedule—that is, one which calls for "restricted" answers ("Would you say that your methods of discipline are about as strict as, less strict than, or more strict than those employed by your parents?"). Or he might plan a partially structured interview, with "open" questions ("How would you say that your methods of discipline compare in strictness with those used by your parents?"). The first type of interview has the advantages of being more carefully controlled and of yielding data that can be tabulated without further processing. However, it is not always possible to present a clearly defined choice of answers to the respondent. When this is the case, the open (or open-ended) question must be used.

The open-question type of interview is a potentially richer source of information than the closed-question type. It provides an opportunity to discover attitudes and feelings that might never be revealed in a completely structured interview. It presents more difficulties in processing data, however, for the replies are not such that they can be neatly tabulated. Usually the investigator devises rating scales for analyzing the interviews and trains judges to rate the data obtained.

Interviews have obvious limitations. There is always the danger that the respondent will answer a question as he thinks the investigator wants it answered, or that he will distort information to protect his feelings about himself. Investigators try to word questions to take care of this possibility. Stating or implying that "some" parents report a particular kind of difficulty before asking a respondent whether he has encountered it may encourage the respondent to be freer in his answers.

Interviews are also hampered by the limitations of human memory. Not many parents keep diaries of their children's development, and few are likely to be accurate when asked to recall, several years later, at what age a particular behavior appeared or at what age they instituted a particular discipline. Investigators try to avoid questions about specific behaviors that probably occurred long before the interview. When such questions are included, respondents are rarely asked to pinpoint the time for a past event; instead, they are asked to indicate, for example, whether the event occurred during the first three months, before six months of age, or during the first two years.

Projective Techniques

An investigator can infer certain things about a child's personality structure from observational and interview data. But much of a child's motives and needs are hidden from us—indeed, often from himself—and can be brought to light only through the use of indirect techniques. Some of these techniques are projective in nature; that is, they are such that the child is encouraged to put (or project) himself into the situation.

Doll play is a projective technique that has been extensively used to probe the personality depths of preschool children. The investigator works with the child in a room where such toys as a family of miniature dolls, blocks, and housekeeping equipment are available. The child is encouraged to play freely with the toys. Usually children verbalize as they play, and in their conversation as well as their play reveal things about themselves that would otherwise be hidden from the investigator. A young child may not feel free in his home to express hostility toward a baby brother, but he may safely direct this hostility toward the baby doll in a family of dolls, spanking the doll, trying to destroy it, or hiding it from view. Or he may reveal some facets of his relationship with his parents that are impossible for him to verbalize. He may, for example, take good care of the child doll, but continually complain while doing so about how much work the child is creating for him. He may dramatize a situation in which the father doll is disposed of and the boy doll has undisputed claim to the mother doll's attentions.

Pictures are also used as a projective device in child study. The investigator may show a series of pictures to a child and encourage him to tell a story about each picture. Often the child is really talking about himself as he relates his story.

A widely used test of this sort is the Thematic Apperception Test (TAT), a series of pictures of which some can be used with young children. One of the pictures, for example, shows a young boy seated at a table on which a violin rests. One child may explain: "He's thinking about when he'll be grown up and how he'll be famous as a great musician. All the people will come to hear him and stand up and clap when he finishes playing. He'll make lots and lots of money." Another may read into the picture: "He's got a real strict mother. She's always after him to practice and do his homework and then she gets mad because he doesn't do it right. He's thinking he'd like to bust that violin right over her head, but he doesn't dare do it." The TAT has been used extensively in personality studies, particularly those concerned with motivation.

Another widely used projective device is the Rorschach Ink-Blot Test. The Rorschach Test consists of a series of cards on each of which appears a blot of the kind that would result from dropping ink on a piece of paper and then creasing the paper down the center. Just as different people see different things in a cloud, so people differ in their associations to the ink blots. Most find resemblances to things in their physical environment in each blot. The way in which they respond is quite significant. Some people use all the blot material on the card within the framework of a single concept. Some begin at the top right and work around each blot systematically, giving an interpretation to every tiny portion. Some give a considerable number of movement responses. Some include many texture and color responses. Some confine themselves entirely to form, spending considerable time and effort on the accuracy and correctness of their responses. In these ways do they reveal their personality.

Much research has been done on the Rorschach Test at both the adult and the child level in order to standardize methods of scoring responses. In the hands of a psychologist trained to administer and score the test and to interpret results, it can provide insights into a child's creativity, emotional balance, impulse control, and intellectual processes. It probes deeper into the personality than other projective tests.

Other picture tests have been designed to get at more limited aspects of the child's personality. The reader will find reference in this text to several attitude studies, and particularly to studies of prejudice, which employ a projective type of picture test. Although all these tests are useful in supplying an investigator with information not otherwise obtainable, because so much depends upon interpretation, they must be carefully designed and skillfully used to minimize the possibility of error.

THE PLAN OF THE TEXT

This book draws upon developmental, comparative, and cross-cultural studies, using material obtained by means of all the techniques discussed above. It begins with a discussion of the human nature of the child. In Part One we examine some of the ways in which children are alike the world over because they are human beings. In successive chapters we answer these questions:

1. What characteristics do all children possess because they are human beings?

2. What fundamental drives are present in all children at birth?

3. What differences among children can be ascribed to biological inheritance rather than to the influence of society?

4. In what ways is the process of growth and development similar for all children, regardless of the particular society in which they are born and reared?

5. What characteristics describe the beginnings of life for all children?

In Part Two we turn our attention to the socialization process. We first examine the basic similarities in character and personality among various ethnic groups and discuss some possible explanations for these similarities. Then we analyze theories of socialization, derived from both psychoanalytic theory and learning theory. A separate chapter deals with early experiences and their highly significant impact upon later socialization. We ask:

6. How does growing up in a particular society influence the socialization process?

7. How does psychoanalytic theory explain the process of socialization?

8. Can we look upon socialization as learning, with the content and conditions of that learning defined by society?

9. What are the effects of early experiences upon later behavioral development?

In Part Three we analyze the contributions of several agents of society to the process of socialization.

10. How does the family influence the socialization?

11. What is the role of the teacher and the school?

12. To what extent does the peer culture influence the socialization of the child?

13. What aspects of the community at large are important for the socialization of the child?

In the final section, Part Four, we consider the outcome of the socialization process as revealed in three major areas of development—physical, cognitive, and motivational. We review what is known about the normal course of development in each area. We ask:

14. What facts, principles, and generalizations are known about the physical and motor development of the child?

15. How does the child acquire language? How does he form concepts? How is intelligence assessed? To what factors can we attribute variability in intelligence?

16. How does the child acquire new drives in the process of socialization?

Readers of this book who are acquainted with its predecessor, *Child Development* (1953), will find the framework a familiar one. However, two major changes in organization have been made. The reader is now introduced at an early stage (Part Two) to the psychological and cultural theories that will contribute to his understanding of the socialization process. And because of the increasing recognition of and wealth of research on the impact of early experiences upon later development, a new chapter (Chapter 9) has been written on this topic, incorporating the findings of psychologists who are following up the pioneering work of Lorenz, Tinbergen, and others.

The second major change is the addition of a completely

new section (Part Four) dealing with the physical, cognitive, and motivational aspects of normal development. Research in these three areas during the past five years has helped to crystallize thinking on a number of issues and has made a fresh approach to reporting findings possible.

Of the chapters retained from the original edition, the one on constitutional differences among children (now Chapter 4) has been completely rewritten, and all the others have been revised and expanded to include the significant research of recent years.

Like all textbooks, regardless of their subject, this book is essentially a summary of what the authors and others have discovered. Students who wish to enrich their understanding by examining for themselves the significant research will find these studies reprinted in convenient form in *Readings in Child Development,* edited by the authors and published by Harcourt, Brace in 1954. *Observation and Analysis in Child Development,* by J. Richard Suchman (Harcourt, Brace, 1959), is also recommended. This laboratory manual of exercises is designed to clarify concepts, to sharpen powers of observation, and to provide actual research experiences for students of child development.

The authors are indebted to several individuals for help and advice in revising *Child Development.* Chief among them is Robert R. Sears, of Leland Stanford University, for his constructive criticism of the first edition and of the manuscript of the present book. We also acknowledge our appreciation to Willard B. Spalding, of Portland State College, for his comments on the manuscript.

WILLIAM E. MARTIN

CELIA BURNS STENDLER

contents

xxi

PART FOUR

the course of normal development

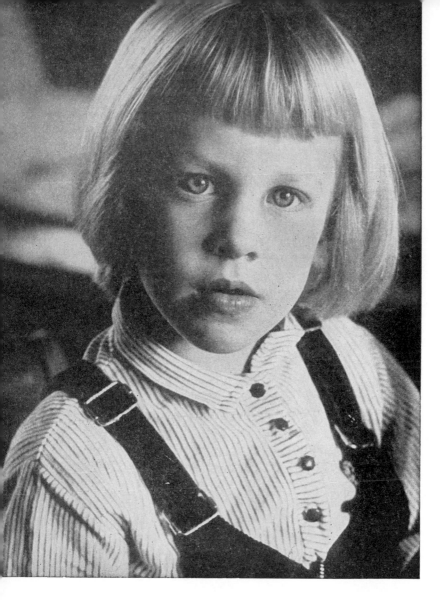

the child

1
the child
as a
human being

The child is the object of our study. It is about him and his behavior that we ask such questions as these: How does he act under certain specified conditions? Why does he behave in those particular ways? In what respects and for what reasons does his behavior change as he grows and develops?

Before we can undertake to answer such questions, we need to define the object of our investigation. What is a child? What can we say about him that will distinguish him from the many other objects in the world that might be studied? We can note that he has two legs, two arms, a head with two eyes, two ears, and one nose, all attached to a trunk or body stem. In other words, we can describe the child as a physical structure. On the basis of such a description, we can eliminate many classes of objects which are not children.

But it will be even more helpful if we picture the child as a living organism. He behaves. He grows and develops. But so does a tree or a radish, although in a more limited fashion. How can we differentiate the child from the various forms of plant life?

3

Unlike them, he sees; he feels; he hears. He gets excited. He has significantly greater freedom of movement. His behavior is more varied. He belongs to the animal, rather than to the plant, world of living creatures.

But he is a very special kind of animal. He is a human being. Unlike other animals, he speaks, reads, remembers, thinks, cooperates, competes, aspires, anticipates, generalizes. All these characteristics are part of his nature, his human nature.

A description of the child is, in effect, a description of human nature. It is a statement both of what the child is and of what he is capable of becoming. In part, a description of the nature of the child is a statement of his potentialities. It therefore determines what we expect of the child. If we say that every child has within him the potentiality of becoming an adult, we are saying, in effect, that we expect him to be an adult some day. In every case in which that turns out not to be true, whether for reason of injury, deprivation, malfunction, or even death, that individual has failed to live up to our expectations.

Let us consider a more specific example of the relationship between our conception of human nature and our expectations of human behavior. Some people have concluded that there is an element of aggressiveness in all human beings, that aggressiveness is part of the nature of a human being. Under certain conditions, this particular potentiality is realized in the form of overt behavior, aggressive behavior. People who believe that aggressive behavior is a universal characteristic expect this kind of reaction. The appearance of aggressive behavior is consistent with their definition of the human being. They are not surprised, then, if one child attacks another without provocation. They expect it. Nor are they surprised to find groups of individuals indulging in aggressive behavior.

Our conception of human nature also determines in large part what we do *to* and *for* individuals as they grow and develop. Imagine a society in which a majority of the members believes that every individual is potentially aggressive. Suppose, further, that this society holds an essentially pacifistic attitude toward other societies. In each succeeding generation, it would have the task of curbing the aggressive predisposition in individual members and replacing it with a desire for peace, harmony, and concord. The society, through its agents in the home, the school, the church, and the neighborhood, would have the task of modifying human nature. These agents would have to make the pursuit of harmony as attractive as aggression. On the other hand, a militaristic society with the same view of human nature would do everything possible to encourage aggressiveness in its people, precisely as the Spartans of ancient Greece and the Germans under Hitler in modern times, among others, did do.

A well-known essay by William James, entitled "The Moral Equivalent of War" (1911),* further demonstrates the point. In it, James concluded, rather pessimistically: "Our ancestors have bred pugnacity into our bone and marrow, and thousands of years of peace won't breed it out of us." He did not believe that we could, or even should, eliminate the martial aspect of man's nature. But he did think that we could put this aggressive tendency to more productive uses. He suggested that we could declare war on the miseries and injustices in our society—a foe truly worth vanquishing. We would thus retain the "military ideals of hardihood and discipline," but we would put them to better use than the killing off of our fellow men. We would satisfy the need to conquer without destruction. This was to be the "moral equivalent of war."

James had in mind a particular conception of human nature, and he expected human beings to behave accordingly. He then outlined what we would have to do with each individual in the light of this potentiality and the related expectations.

Consider one further example of the significance of our view of human nature. Some people seem to think of the individual, at least at the beginning of his development, as an "empty organism." In a sense, they look upon him as having no resources. They expect little or nothing of him. The job,

* Dates in parentheses refer to references listed in full in the bibliographical index which begins on page 583.

as they see it, is literally to fill him up—with skills, with knowledge, with attitudes, with motives. They don't "pour it on"; they pour it *in*. According to this view, what the individual becomes depends entirely upon factors in his social and physical environment.

There are others who look upon each individual not as "empty" but as "full" of possibilities. A given individual may be aggressive; he may be unaggressive. He may be dominant; he may be submissive. He may be a good reader; he may be a poor one. He may be a leader; he may be a follower. He may turn out to be a good citizen; he may turn out to be a bad one. These are all potentialities which may or may not exist in a given child. Persons who believe that such potentialities are inborn concern themselves not so much with implanting as with drawing out characteristics that are latent in the child. They permit or foster the development of those potentialities which they believe to be good for the individual and the society; they discourage or suppress the development of those potentialities which they believe to be bad for the individual and the society. What the individual becomes, according to this view, depends upon factors within himself—his resources—as well as upon factors in his environment. (It will be clear in the discussion that follows that the authors hold to this view of human nature.)

Our conception of human nature, then, determines what we expect of the individual and how we train and educate him. The point of view we adopt, therefore, has great significance and far-reaching consequences.

The first section of this book is devoted to a study of the nature of the child. In this chapter we shall give our attention to the characteristics of the child which define his nature as a human being. Some he has in common with all animal life; others he shares only with all other human beings.

> 1. Can you think of other examples of how our conception of human nature determines what we expect of the child? What would we expect if we viewed human beings as inherently lazy or inquisitive or good?

2. How does a democratic society differ from an authoritarian one in its conception of human nature?

THE CHILD AS A
LIVING ORGANISM

The Child Is a System

The child begins life as a system, not as a mere collection of isolated parts. The parts that make up this system are organized in structure and coordinated in function. Any one part has meaning only as it is related to other parts and to the system as a whole. For example, it would be difficult to describe meaningfully a structural part of the body, such as an arm, without relating it to the total structure. Similarly, to describe the function of that arm, it would be necessary to place it in its proper relation to the function of the total system.

In any activity of this system, the total organism is involved. Of course, in any given activity some parts may be involved to a greater degree than others. What happens when a child reads a book? He certainly uses his eyes and certain parts of his nervous system. But he also uses his hands to hold the book and turn the pages. He changes his posture frequently, first sliding down in his chair, then pushing himself up and moving from one side to the other. He swings his feet in some irregular rhythm.

His reading efficiency may be affected by the fact that he has just eaten a meal or is sleepy or has recently quarreled with his best friend. These activities and experiences involve parts of the system that seemingly have no relationship to the act of reading. Nevertheless, they are present and do influence that act. In any situation, we must deal with *the whole child,* although our interest may be focused on but one aspect of him. Alfred North Whitehead, in one of his essays on *The Aims of Education,* wisely cautions: "I lay it down as an educational axiom that in teaching you will come to grief as soon as you forget that your pupils have bodies" (1929, p. 78).

Since he is a system, the child begins life as an organization. He does not arrive, like a jigsaw puzzle, as a collection of unassembled pieces. We cannot rightfully look upon development, therefore, as progress from no organization to some organization. Development can only be from some to more organization or from one kind to another kind of organization. In what we do to guide the developmental process, we can help the child to a higher level or a better type of organization. In this sense, the child, from the very start, possesses integrity. Whenever we lose sight of the child as a whole, we violate that integrity.

As a system, the child is productive. If we provide him with food, he converts it to energy. If we provide him with both food and stimulation—light striking the eye, sounds impinging upon the ear, objects in contact—he gives out with energy in the form of behavior. Thus, we may properly speak of the child as an energy system, in which the raw materials are food and stimulation, and behavior is one of the products. One of the most important contributions that teachers and parents can make to the development of the child is helping him to utilize his energy in individually and socially constructive ways.

A remarkable feature of this energy system that is the child is that it is capable of adjusting its operations to variations in the supply of raw materials. If we furnish the child with a great deal of stimulation or food, he produces energy at a high level. If we stimulate him only a little and give him meager food rations, he produces energy at a low level. Stuart (1944) demonstrated this point in his study of the adjustment of French children to inadequate nutrition during World War II. These children had been existing on a daily diet of fewer than 1000 calories for a period of at least six months. They adjusted to this state of subnutrition by reducing their output of behavior, becoming more docile, less energetic, and less concerned with the world about them. This lessening of energy display happens to be a very sensible solution to the problem that they faced. But they were not given the solution by their elders. Nor did they consciously formulate it themselves. As energy systems, they automatically adjusted to the change in nutritional supply.

Although the child is capable of adjusting to variations in the supply of raw materials for conversion to energy, he is not always willing to do so. Or he may be willing to do so, but only within relatively narrow limits. The reason is that, as a system, the child is striving to achieve some degree of internal constancy. His adjustment to variations in external conditions is always an attempt to maintain a steady internal state, a state that Cannon (1939) has referred to as "homeostasis."

The child's striving for stability in physiological functioning is a significant aspect of his development. For example, the variation in body temperature that characterizes the infant and the very young child gives way to the relatively steady temperature typically found in older children and adults. This achievement of physiological stability comes about as a result of what Shock (1944) has called "physiological learning."

As stability in internal functioning increases, so does consistency in behavior. Variability is to be expected in the young child; in the older child, it is a sign of immaturity. The two-year-old can walk, but his progress is unsteady. The child of five can talk, but how wasteful he can be of words; how involved he gets in the simplest of explanations! Only the passage of time will bring stability in behavior, a condition which involves not only efficiency but consistency.

Once this stable pattern of behavior is achieved, the child attempts to maintain it without change despite variations in external conditions. It is only when the external variation is extreme in amount and prolonged in time—as was the case with the French children described above—that the individual is forced to make significant changes in his way of behaving.

Recognition of this characteristic of the child as an energy system may help to explain the seeming failure of some efforts in training and education. Consider, for example, Kirk, who is exceedingly active; in fact, his parents and teachers are inclined to consider him overactive. For a given intake of food and stimulation, a high level of activity seems to be optimal for him. His brother Evan, with the same intake of food and stimulation, has a contrasting pattern of activity, not nearly so intense, not nearly so versatile. His parents decide to augment Evan's diet and to increase the frequency and variety of stimulation to which he is exposed.

The resulting changes in his behavior are so slight that his parents are both frustrated and mystified. Because Evan is striving to maintain a steady internal state, he assimilates the increased intake in such a way as to maintain his previous output.

Changes in variety and quantity of food and stimulation are not always reflected in changes in behavior. We must keep in mind the system's resistance to change. The child is a conservative system.

As the child grows older and attains ever-greater stability of functioning, his resistance to change increases. Thus, the adult persists in using old patterns of functioning and behavior in the face of new and different circumstances. Note his difficulties when he faces the problem of gaining or losing weight, more frequently the latter (Olson, 1949). If he is dieting, it is difficult enough for him to accustom himself to a relatively meager quantity of food. But then he usually finds that the resulting decrease in weight is small indeed when compared with the amount of reduction in intake. The organism, in its attempt to maintain constancy, utilizes the smaller supply of food more efficiently. Similarly, the person who is trying to gain weight finds that his increases are not commensurate with the increase in intake. In this case, the body reduces its efficiency in utilizing food in an attempt to maintain its original weight.

The child finds himself in an environment in which there is almost constant change in some amount and kind. Yet, as a living organism, he is a system which is continually striving to achieve constancy of functioning in this changing environment. To the extent that he succeeds, he makes these "external fluctuations . . . a matter of indifference" (Dempsey, 1951) and thus preserves a measure of personal freedom and integrity.

3. Is there any kind of functioning in which *the whole child* **is** not involved?

4. Does the concept *the whole child* mean that teachers and parents should never concentrate on specific functions or aspects of behavior?

5. On the basis of the concept of the child as an energy system, how would you criticize methods of discipline based largely on repression?

6. J. E. Anderson, in *The Psychology of Development and Personal Adjustment,* says this: "The problem of a living organism is not one of doing or not doing, but one of *what* to do in a world in which there are better and poorer ways of doing" (1949, p. 31). Would you agree? What are the implications in this statement for controlling and guiding children's behavior?

7. Does an individual ever achieve absolute homeostasis? Explain your answer.

8. Observe a child at work or at play. Can you see any relationship between the amount of stimulation present and the intensity and kind of his behavior?

9. How do reactions to external temperature changes illustrate the striving to maintain internal constancy?

10. Is there any basis in human nature for saying, "You can't teach an old dog new tricks"?

The Child Seeks Stimulation

The child, as a living organism, is sensitive to his surroundings. He is equipped by nature to see, to hear, to feel, to taste, and to smell. It is by these means that he becomes acquainted with the world in which he lives.

But he is not content merely to let this world come to him. He seeks it out. The infant does not wait until an object is placed directly in front of his eyes. He turns his head from side to side, now to see this, now to see that. Many of his waking hours he spends in exploring visually the people and objects around him.

Not only does he want to see things, he also wants to feel them. It is not enough for him to see the red ball dangling from the top of his crib; he reaches out to touch it. He tries to

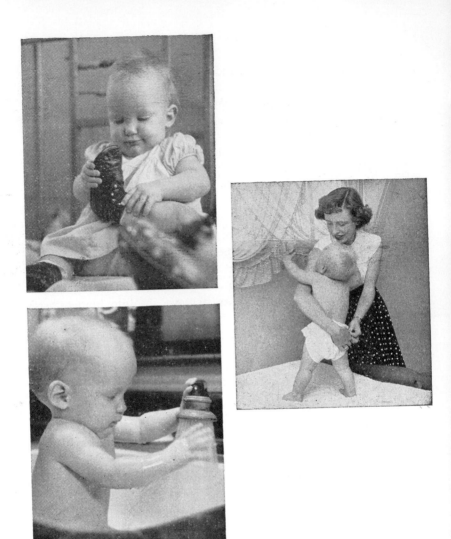

FIGURE 1-1. The child continually seeks stimulation. At seven months curiosity impels him to explore nearby objects—including his own foot. He discovers the properties of these objects not only by feeling but also by tasting and chewing. At times his quest for stimulation is downright dangerous, and his curiosity must be restrained until he has a more realistic perception of depth and awareness of gravity. But the child's desire for stimulation leads eventually to a greater understanding and mastery of his environment.

put it into his mouth. As Forest expresses it, "The young baby is 'stimulus-hungry' " (1954, p. 35).

The child is positively oriented. He is capable of putting himself in contact with the outside world. Moreover, he seeks to do so. In this sense, we can say that he is an inquisitive animal. It is fortunate that he is so, for he can develop only as he is able and willing to interact with his environment. He begins life so constituted. We do not have to concern ourselves with interesting him in the elements of that environment. In the beginning, at least, we have only to put them within his reach. If something is there for him to see, he will look at it. If something is there for him to touch, he will touch it.

As the child grows and becomes able to crawl and then to walk, his physical world steadily expands. The number of things that attract his attention steadily increases. It seems to most mothers that a young child wants to get acquainted with every single one of them. In a family with a toddler, the fragile and dangerous objects of the house are put away, out of reach of little fingers. To those that cannot be moved, such as electrical outlets and lamp cords, are attached the magic words "No! No!"

For the child seeks all kinds of stimulation. He is ready to make friends with everything and everyone. He does not discriminate. Only through experience does he establish preferences, acquire likes and dislikes, become interested or uninterested. When the experience he seeks is a dangerous one, adults step in. We do not let him burn himself so that he may learn the danger that lies in a hot stove. We do not let him eat mud pies—at least, not very many of them—so that he may learn that his interior does not tolerate such a diet. Early in the child's life, we begin to admonish him. We direct his attention to some things; we divert his attention from others. Thus we begin his training and education.

The child not only seeks stimulation but also seeks to prolong it, except when it is painful. He cannot see enough of a given object. If he can get it in his hands, he will play with it for long periods of time. It is true that the young child has a short span of attention. But it is also true that it sometimes seems as if he cannot get enough of one experience. He wants to have it over and over again. Thus he keeps old toys and possessions long after they have lost their original form and substance. To describe this tendency of the child to seek to continue stimulation psychologists have formulated the "principle of adience," which Murphy defines as the "tendency to immerse oneself ever more deeply in the present situation" (1947, p. 979).

11. What are the implications of the principle of adience for educators?

12. Observe a classroom activity. What demonstrations of the principle of adience do you find?

13. Seeking stimulation is a characteristic of all animal life. In what ways does the child differ from other animals in this respect?

14. Since the child is presumably interested in everything, how can you explain the specific interests which develop as he grows older?

15. How important do you think the early interests of a child are? Should we concern ourselves with the nature of stimulation in the environment of the infant and the young child? Explain.

16. Assume for the moment that, instead of being "positively oriented," the child is "negatively oriented" toward his environment; that, instead of seeking stimulation, he tries to avoid it. How would he grow and develop? How could we help him to grow and develop?

The Basic Dilemma of Life

We have seen, on the one hand, that the child, as a system, is always attempting to maintain a state of internal constancy. He is trying to maintain his equilibrium. His task is made difficult by the fact that he is constantly being bombarded from all sides by stimulation, most of which tends to challenge the sought-for equilibrium. The pattern of that stimulation is never quite the same from one moment to the next. He must continually seek some kind of adjustment to this ever-changing pattern of stimulation. He does this by utilizing different kinds and amounts of stimulation in such a way that his behavioral output remains the same. In the midst of a changing environment, he tries to achieve constancy in both internal and external functioning. This is his adjustment. To the extent that he achieves it, he experiences satisfaction.

Knowing this characteristic of the child as a system, we might expect that he would avoid stimulation as much as possible, for it is stimulation that intensifies the problem of adjustment. The less stimulation, the less intense the problem. If the child could shut himself off from all but a minimal amount of stimulation, his task of achieving homeostasis would be relatively simple.

Yet we find, instead, that it is the child's nature to seek, rather than avoid, stimulation. It is almost as if he deliberately makes the problem of adjustment more difficult. He intentionally risks change and modification. Desiring contentment, he simultaneously seeks discontentment. Wanting to remain the same, he nevertheless courts change. He actively seeks experiences which stimulate development.

This is the dilemma that every child faces. It is intrinsic in his nature as a form of animal life. In one sense, the dilemma is more apparent than real. Contentment and discontentment, satisfaction and dissatisfaction, adjustment and development— these are all relative terms. To experience satisfaction, the child must first experience dissatisfaction. He cannot be contented unless he is first discontented. He never achieves the goal of complete satisfaction or contentment or adjustment; he merely approaches it. It is the approach to the goal that brings whatever degree of satisfaction the child will enjoy.

For example, Mary sees a wonderful doll in a shop window. She has never seen anything like it. She wants it more than anything in the world. But her mother tells her that it is much too expensive. Mary accepts her mother's word but cannot resist thinking about that doll. Repeatedly, she seeks excuses for passing the store window to gaze at this marvelous object. She deliberately makes herself discontented. By doing so, however, she creates the possibility of satisfaction—not necessarily through getting the doll, but through imagining how she would feel and what she would do if she did obtain it.

All of us, children and adults alike, experience satisfaction to the extent that we are able and willing to tolerate dissatisfaction. There cannot be achievement without ambition. There can be no pleasure without first displeasure. What is the fun of riding a roller coaster? It consists of intentionally exposing ourselves to the thrills and terrors of the ride and, at the same time, looking forward to the feeling of relief and achievement that comes when the ride is over.

Although the dilemma may be more apparent than real, it still constitutes a problem for the child. Sustained or intense dissatisfaction may make it impossible—or at least difficult—to achieve satisfaction. The child must seek out that kind and amount of stimulation with which he can cope. His wants, interests, yearnings, and desires must be reasonable ones in the sense that there is some chance that he will realize them and that when they are realized he will feel some degree of satisfaction. For Mary to want a doll is perfectly reasonable. There is always some chance that she will get a doll, although perhaps not the exact one she wants. For Johnny to want to touch a hot iron is not reasonable; for, even if he were allowed or were able to do so, more dissatisfaction than satisfaction would result.

Furthermore, neither satisfaction nor dissatisfaction is an all-or-none affair; rather, it is a matter of more or less. In order to experience the pleasure of eating ice cream for dessert, many a child undergoes the displeasure of eating his vegetables. It is noteworthy, in this example and in others, that the dissatisfaction precedes the satisfaction. As the time lapse between the dissatisfaction and the satisfaction—between the promise and the realization of pleasure—lengthens, the situation becomes more difficult for the child to handle. For the dissatisfaction is here and now and certain, while the satisfaction is there and later and only possible. Moreover, anticipation of a pleasant future, even a highly probable one, can never completely remove the sting of an unpleasant present.

The real problem that the child faces, then, is one of

choice. Of all the possible kinds of stimulation available, in which ones shall he interest himself? To which shall he respond? And to what extent? In which ones will an interest have some chance of being satisfied? In which ones will an interest arouse just the amount of disequilibrium and imbalance that can be handled? In other words, what kinds and amounts of stimulation will eventually bring relative pleasure and contentment?

The infant and the young child are not able to make these choices by themselves. But neither are they completely helpless. The child tends to choose, from all the possibilities in a situation new to him, those which are best for him in the sense that they tend to enhance his development and eventual adjustment. He displays what has been called "wisdom of the body."

The concept of "wisdom of the body" underlies the adoption of various kinds of self-demand schedules for infants and young children. To some extent, we let them sleep when they want to sleep. We let them eat when they want to eat. We even let them choose, within limits, what they want to eat. C. M. Davis (1939) has demonstrated, in a now-famous study, that infants and young children, when allowed to make their choices from a rather wide variety of foods, tend to choose those which, over a period of time, constitute as adequate and proper a diet as adults could select for them. Olson (1949) has reported encouraging results from the practice of allowing youngsters some freedom of choice in educational situations. They tend to undertake those tasks which seem to be "wisest" for them at that particular point.

But wisdom of the body is not infallible. The child cannot be left completely to his own devices in any situation, even one from which we have carefully removed the possibility of choices that might harm him in some way. He needs the help of adults. But we need always to respect and consider his choices; for they may represent, in some cases, better ones than we can make for him.

However, there are times when adult choices are superior

to those which the child makes. We must remember that his choices are made with respect to the particular pattern of adjustment he is trying to maintain. By some standards, that pattern of adjustment may not be acceptable. The adjustment of the juvenile delinquent is sometimes amazingly stable. But it is not a good one from the standpoint of the society or of the child who lives in that society.

The poor reader may be well adjusted to the fact that he cannot read. He may have formed an image of himself as a poor reader. His inability to read only supports the validity of that image. He maintains "good" adjustment by choosing not to read. According to the goals of education in a literate society, this "solution" is too high a price to pay for adjustment. As teachers, we deliberately set out to upset this pattern of adjustment. We may first try to change the child's image of himself. As soon as we plant some seeds of doubt in him that he is necessarily a poor reader, he loses confidence in that particular picture of himself. Soon, we hope, he is saying to himself: "Maybe I could read. Maybe I could learn to read just as well as the others." At this point, his behavior—still poor reading—is no longer consistent with his picture of himself. He is developing aspirations. He is beginning to entertain the thought of change. For a while, he may be relatively discontented. For a time, his adjustment may take a turn for the worse. But, with help, he can hope to bring his behavior into line with his ambitions and his new image of himself. Eventually, he attains a stable adjustment once more, but at a higher level and of a better quality than before. For he now is able to experience the satisfactions that come with being able to read. Through his reading he is able to solve problems which he has previously been unable to recognize or admit existed. We have helped him to develop. But we have also helped him to adjust to that higher level of development.

Learning is a source of both dissatisfaction and satisfaction. It is a means of enhancing both development and adjustment. Properly planned, a learning program helps the child to choose situations which may be temporarily discontenting but which, in the long run, with help, make for greater contentment as well as for greater maturity.

17. One entry in the diaries of Franz Kafka reads: "Like everyone, I too have my center of gravity inside me from birth, and this not even the most foolish education could displace" (1948, p. 19). Discuss this statement as it relates to what we have called the basic dilemma of life.

18. Can we make children too discontented? Do we ever do so in the home or in the classroom? What are the dangers of extreme discontent?

19. Do we also fail by letting children become too contented? What are some examples of "good" adjustment which the society does not accept as good?

20. J. E. Anderson says that a person "selects from . . . [his] environment whatever is congruent or consonant with . . . [his] own make-up" (1949, p. 408). Is this statement consistent with the concept of the wisdom of the body?

THE CHILD AS A HUMAN BEING

In the foregoing section, we have discussed those characteristics which the child, as a form of animal life, possesses in common with all other animals. But the child is a special form of life, a human being, and therefore possesses additional qualities which are unique to man. These qualities are unique because they have been developed to a superior degree in man or because they are present only in man.

Such qualities can best be identified by describing briefly the position that man as a particular species holds in the total scheme of life, particularly animal life. Zoologists, who have classified animal life according to structural similarity, have successively limited the group to which the human belongs to the point at which the species of Homo sapiens, with its attendant peculiarities, can be identified.

For example, Simpson (1950) first locates man by dividing the existing kinds of animal life—more than a million of them—into twenty major groups, or phyla, and placing man in a particular phylum, known as the Chordata; therefore, the original specification is that man is a chordate. How does a chordate differ from the members of the other phyla? Chordates, including man, have highly complex tissue and organ differentiation. In fact, they are the most complex of all forms of life. This greater degree of complexity in organization is made possible, in part, by the fact that the chordate is multicellular. Contrast the organizational possibilities of the child, who is made up of hundreds of billions of cells, with those of the amoeba, a single-celled animal which is a member of another phylum, the Protozoa. Even were the amoeba to exist under the most favorable environmental conditions, it could never become so complex an organism as a chordate.

The chordates are also distinguished in that they are members of the phylum in which bilateral symmetry in structure is most highly developed. Paradoxically, it is his bilateral symmetry in structure as a chordate that makes possible man's asymmetry in function. He can and does develop an orientation toward the world; he becomes monolateral—right-handed or left-handed, right-eyed or left-eyed, right-footed or left-footed, and so on. The degree to which such monolateral dominance is attained and maintained varies from individual to individual and, for a given individual, from situation to situation. Some degree of bilaterality is always present, but perfect bilaterality— true ambidexterity, for example—is rare, perhaps even nonexistent. Man is a positionally directed organism.

Gesell has observed the appearance of asymmetric behavior in the infant: the tonic neck reflex, or t-n-r, in which the head is turned to the right or left, the arm on the side toward which the head is turned is extended, and the opposite arm is bent (see Fig. 1-2). Gesell found this response to be "a ubiquitous, indeed a dominating, characteristic of normal infancy in the first three months of life" (1954, p. 349). Only later do bilateral symmetrical behavior patterns appear; only later will the infant hold his head in midposition and bend both his arms.

Finally, chordates, and therefore human beings, differ from

other forms of life in that they have an internal skeleton, the most noteworthy feature of which is a longitudinal rod along the back, called the notochord. Here is the genesis of part of man's ability to assume an upright posture (see Fig. 1-3). How

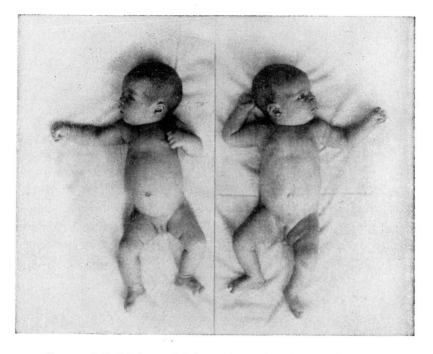

FIGURE 1-2. Right and left tonic neck reflex in six-week-old infants.

(From A. Gesell. The ontogenesis of infant behavior. In L. Carmichael, *Manual of Child Behavior*, Wiley, 1954, p. 351)

differently the world looks to man from this position than it would were he still on all fours!

But man is a very special kind of chordate; he belongs to the division called the Vertebrata, a classification which includes fishes, amphibians, birds, reptiles, and mammals. The vertebrate differs most significantly from other chordates in that he has a backbone, or jointed notochord, which represents a further step

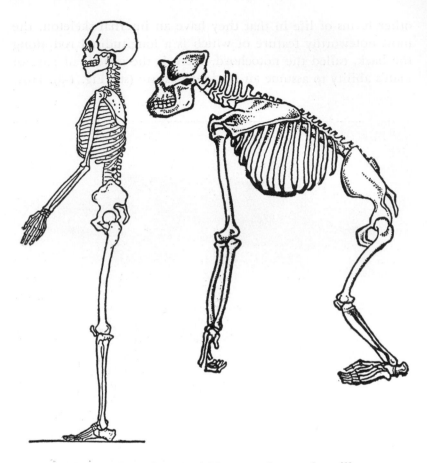

FIGURE 1-3. Skeletons of Homo sapiens and gorilla.

(From W. Howells. *Mankind So Far,* Doubleday, 1944, p. 74)

along the way to the assumption of an adaptive upright posture. "Man is the only vertebrate, perhaps the only animal, that stands and moves fully erect . . ." (Kroeber, 1948, p. 72).

Furthermore, man is a particular kind of vertebrate; he is of the class of Mammalia, which is distinguished by the following features, among others:

1. Special care of the young for a period prior to birth, during which they are nourished within and from the body of the mother. It is during this long period of gestation under such

carefully controlled conditions that the organism develops the capacity to survive in the external world without a repertoire of specific inborn habits (Howells, 1944).

2. High level of activity. No other class of vertebrates, with the exception of birds, is generally characterized by such energy display, made possible in the mammal because it is warm-blooded. As Howells says:

> The mammals are, above everything, warm-blooded. It is simply not possible to overrate this, because it is what gives them their power and activity. Activity comes from a high efficiency in feeding the muscles with energy derived from food, and in being able to release this energy suddenly and in large amounts in response to a nervous command, and it also requires a fullness of nervous coordination and development. All of the involved biochemical processes back of this seem to function best in a constant temperature not far from a hundred degrees Fahrenheit [1944, pp. 32-33].

3. Stability and flexibility of the skeleton during growth. Again, from Howells:

> In lower vertebrates the working bones of the limbs and the spine take their shape (ossify, as bone) within a cartilaginous "form" which takes shape first, so that the center of the shaft or body is bone, expanding outward toward the ends, which remain cartilage. But the growing mammal has centers of ossification at the ends of the bone as well as for the shaft, with cartilage between, so that the caps or joint surfaces (epiphyses) are of bone like the shaft, giving the active animal the advantage of a more completely formed skeleton during his development while still allowing the bone to go on growing in cartilage in the space between; the parts unite to become a single piece *only* at maturity [1944, p. 29].

Thus, firm bone joints are maintained even as they are growing. The child, as a mammal, is not handicapped in his motor behavior even though his skeleton is not completely formed until he is some twenty years of age.

4. Efficient utilization of food. Although it is difficult to generalize in these matters, we might conjecture that man, as a

mammal, must make exceptionally good use of his food in order to support the metabolism associated with the high level of activity he maintains. Simpson notes this as a mammalian feature and suggests that this particular function is made possible in part by a specialization in structure of the teeth by area: "nipping incisors in front, then larger, pointed, piercing or

"Remember now, you got the brains."

(Reproduced by permission. Copyright 1941 The New Yorker Magazine, Inc.)

tearing canines, and then a row of cheek teeth (premolars and molars), diversely fashioned for seizing, cutting, pounding, or grinding the food before it is swallowed" (1950, p. 65). This description may not be true of all mammals, but it certainly is of men.

The uniqueness of man may be further identified by noting that he is a special kind of mammal—a primate. The members of this order are sometimes called the "brainy" animals; they are characterized by a less rigid form of adaptation to specific external conditions than the members of other mammalian orders. Not only is the brain of the primate larger with respect to the body dimensions, but it is characterized by a greater degree of differentiation in structure.

As a special kind of primate, man belongs to the genus Homines, of which there is a single species, Homo sapiens. Simpson, in a discussion of man's place in nature, speaks of four interrelated features of Homo sapiens: (*1*) intelligence, (*2*) flexibility, (*3*) individualization, and (*4*) sociality,† all of which "occur rather widely in the animal kingdom as progressive developments . . . [but] in man all four are carried to a degree incomparably greater than in any other sort of animal" (1950, p. 284).

The preceding remarks are summarized briefly in Table 1-1, which indicates the successively more limited groups to which man belongs and the identifying characteristics of each.

We now turn to a consideration of the unique attributes which man possesses by reason of the special position he occupies in the animal world.

Intelligence

However intelligence may be defined, man possesses it in amount, if not in kind, superior to all other forms of life. He is better able to learn new things, to grasp broad and subtle facts, especially abstract facts; he is more alert; he is better able to see relationships; he can foresee and plan for the future, and can remember and profit by past experience. This high level of functioning is, of course, made possible by the relatively great size and complexity of his brain. According to Gillin, the distinctive features of this superior brain are: greater brain surface, or cerebral cortex; "greater convolution and folding"; "expansion of the visual, auditory, tactile, and motor functions of the cortex at the expense of the olfactory functions"; and "an increasing amount of . . . behavior . . . controlled by the cortex

---

† Simpson (1950) uses the term *socialization* rather than *sociality*. But the former term is given a somewhat different meaning in this book (see pp. xi-xii), and is therefore not used in this context. The meaning attributed to *sociality* and to the three terms taken from Simpson is that of the writers.

Table 1-1

The Place of Man in the Animal World

Classification	Designation	Identifying Characteristics
Phylum	Chordata	High degree of complexity of tissue and organ differentiation; well-established bilateral symmetry; notochord (dorsal stiffening rod).
Division	Vertebrata	Backbone (jointed notochord).
Class	Mammalia	Special care of the young before birth; high level of activity; stability and flexibility of skeleton during growth; efficient utilization of food.
Order	Primates	Brain large in relation to body size and differentiated in structure.
Genus	Homines	Relatively large size; more advanced development of brain and associated structures.
Species	Homo sapiens	Intelligence; flexibility; individualization; sociality.

rather than by lower brain or spinal centers" (1948, p. 36). With regard to the last feature, it can be said that man is more intelligent because he is more sensitive. Not only are the cortical areas of the brain which are involved in perception more highly developed in man, but the sense organs themselves, with the exception of the organ of smell, are more sensitive to stimuli in general. The structure and function of the eye especially is such that man has an advantage over other forms of life, actually and potentially. According to Howells:

. . . The eye of man and his higher primate relatives . . . is intricate and highly developed. Not only is vision in the optical sense excellent and flexible, but it is the only eye which sees fully in three dimensions and in color. Of course any eye is specialized for sight, being useless for anything else. But the human eye, for all its intricacy, is not specialized beyond this for a particular purpose, nor does it give the impression that it might not continue evolving to undreamed-of capacities. Its improvements to date have been basic patents, so to speak, which would hardly seem to have confined its evolutionary possibilities [1944, p. 12].

It is, of course, difficult to evaluate the optical power of man except as it is related to his brain functioning. Man almost has to be of superior intelligence in order to perceive and adjust

"My man don't wrestle till we hear it talk."

(Reproduced by permission. Copyright 1934 The New Yorker Magazine, Inc.)

to all he sees. Without that superiority, potential advantages in visual functioning could hardly be realized.

But the intelligence of man is reflected largely in his ability to use symbols, especially those verbal symbols which constitute language. Man is capable of both articulating and understanding words, whereas other primates are not. It is difficult to think of man except as a talking, conversing, verbal animal. But a "talking" animal of any other kind is a curiosity, and a rare one

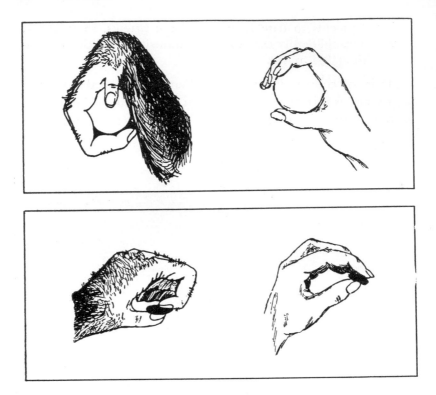

Figure 1-4. Hand grasp of a chimpanzee and of a human. *Top:* The chimpanzee grasps with its fingers and rolls its wrist to push the ball against the surface of the arm. The human opposes his thumb and fingers to hold the ball in his hand. *Bottom:* The chimpanzee takes the pellet between its fingernails because it cannot rotate its thumb. The human, who *can* rotate his thumb, takes the pellet between the ball of the thumb and the ball of the forefinger.

(After W. N. Kellogg & L. A. Kellogg. *The Ape and the Child,* McGraw-Hill, 1933)

at that, even in cases in which considerable training has been given. Even were other animals "intelligent" enough to acquire a symbolic language, there is some question of their structural capacity to do so. Gillin has called attention to the "lighter construction and the greater roominess of the human jaw" and to "hindrances to free movement of the tongue in the apes" as factors to consider in explaining the superior speech ability of man (1948, pp. 47-48).

Add to these qualities the ability of man to use his hands and fingers in manipulating the objects of his environment, especially that made possible by the functional opposition of the thumb to the fingers, as shown in Figure 1-4. In their comparative study of the development of a chimpanzee and a boy, seven and a half and five months of age, respectively, the Kelloggs (1933) found that, even at these early ages, the boy was clearly superior to the ape in the ability to bring the tips of the thumb and fingers together. What may seem to be an insignificant difference underlies the child's greatly superior capacity to explore his environment tactually and to examine and manipulate objects in it. According to Whitehead:

> The connections between intellectual activity and the body, though diffused in every bodily feeling, are focused in the eyes, the ears, the voice, and the hands. There is a coordination of senses and thought, and also a reciprocal influence between brain activity and material creative activity. In this reaction the hands are peculiarly important. It is a moot point whether the human hand created the human brain, or the brain created the hand [1929, p. 78].

Flexibility

Another functional attribute distinctive to man is flexibility. Man is the most accommodating of all forms of life; that is, he can survive and even develop under a wide variety of conditions. Thus, the child can flourish anywhere in the world, given half a chance, whether he be an Eskimo at the North Pole or a Hottentot in some African jungle. What other species of life can be found to exist at so advanced a level of development under such varying conditions! Further evidence of the human's flexibility is seen in the maintenance of viability when he is transplanted from one set of conditions to another. An individual reared in the temperate climatic zone can adjust, with time, to both the heat of the tropics and the cold of the polar areas. Few other animals can approach this level of adaptability.

It is his flexibility that makes it possible for the child to withstand and even to profit from pressures of the external world. The fact that he is able to survive the experience of birth is in itself evidence not only of his hardihood but also of his pliability. In today's complex world, observers are somewhat prone to emphasize the breakdown of man. Although his vulnerability to excessive demands upon his energies and integrity cannot be denied, it can reasonably be argued that no other form of animal life could withstand so much and survive.

By virtue of his flexibility, man can tolerate not only variety but also complexity. He can adjust to conditions as they vary from one time to another. He can also adjust to a variety of conditions all present in a given situation. He is therefore superior to all other forms of life in his susceptibility to training. The child tends to learn to read whether he is taught by the phonetic, the alphabet, the phrase, the word, the sentence, the kinesthetic, the visual, the auditory, or the experience method. But he also tends to learn when he is taught by a combination of these methods. It is true, of course, that he may learn to read by one method or by one particular combination of methods more efficiently than by any other. However, it is sufficient for our present purposes to note his ability to accommodate and profit to some degree under a wide range of conditions.

Similarly, the child tends to learn whether he is taught by good or poor teachers, by blondes or brunettes, by young or old, by men or women. He tends to learn whether he goes to school in a one-room building or in a veritable tower of learning; in fact, the child tends to learn even when he is not taught. Because, by his nature, he responds to pressures from within and without, he learns much even before he goes to school, before he is subjected to formal education. For example, Baruch has observed: "Most little boys proudly imitate Daddy in standing up to urinate. They do this quite of their own accord. We don't have to insist that this is what custom demands" (1949, p. 74).

Howells discusses similar qualities of man under the heading "generalization," as opposed to "specialization," and illustrates what he means by the following comparison:

> The specialization of the horse has made him one of nature's most admirable open-country runners, but in spite of being a bright animal as well, he has no other capacities; moreover, he will never turn into anything but a horse. And when a race meeting is held, who is it that runs, and who takes the profit? Almost any thoroughbred horse can run a mile in a minute and three quarters. No man can do it in twice the time. But while the horses run, it is only a race meeting by virtue of a horde of generalized men, who feed, rub, train, ride, judge, rake, ush, play in the band, and sell tote tickets and pop, none of which can be done by the best horse who ever lived [1944, pp. 14-15].

The moral of this sad story is, of course, that while a horse can never be anything but a horse, a man can be many things. This is the real challenge to those who set the conditions under which the child develops. No other group of trainers has such excellent material with which to work. With this potentiality in human nature, we should be very much surprised to find any great degree of uniformity in men. There are so many possibilities that variation should be almost unlimited. But this point leads us to a discussion of the third of man's unique characteristics.

Individualization

Because he is a higher form of life, because he is so complex an organism, because he is of superior intelligence and characterized by flexibility, man has almost unlimited potentialities; the possible variation in the outcome of growth and development is almost infinite. New varieties are constantly appearing; the pattern is ever changing. We might conclude that the potentialities of man have been realized at any point in time to the extent that there is maximal heterogeneity and minimal homogeneity.

This quality of individualization, as it exists in the child, has been called multiple potentiality. When we look at a six-year-old on his first day of school, we cannot help but wonder what he will be twenty years from now. Will he be a bricklayer, a lawyer, a merchant? Will he be a Republican or a Democrat? Will he play bridge or will he prefer canasta? Will he attend church on Sunday morning or will he be playing golf? Will he play the piano or only the radio?

We cannot answer these questions. We can only admit all the alternatives they suggest as possibilities. Because a child is capable of doing so many things, of becoming so many things, he needs help in making choices. He can be either a Republican or a Democrat; he cannot be both. He can spend his Sunday mornings playing golf or attending church; he cannot do both. In a free society, he will make his own choices. But we can help him. We can point out the advantages and disadvantages of any one choice. We can provide a variety of situations in which he will have a chance to try out several alternative decisions.

Sooner or later, he must make up his mind. He cannot ride off in all directions at once. The nature of our society is such that everyone must become specialized to some degree. No one can be a Jack-of-all-trades and a master of none. Because the child as a human being is characterized by individualization, he requires guidance as he grows and develops.

Sociality

Man, as a unique form of life, has a fourth characteristic, which we may term sociality. The human being is, in fact, a social being. He lives, not as a hermit, but as a member of society.

The origins of this characteristic are not clear. Psychologists of an earlier day spoke of a gregarious instinct in man, an inherited (and thus unlearned) adaptive response, the presence of which was presumably the result of selective breeding. That is, those people who cooperated with one another in the past were the ones most likely to survive and to reproduce their kind. It is their descendants who inhabit the earth and who constitute the greater proportion of the human race.

But today we are disinclined to think of responses, as such, as being inherited in man as they seem to be in other organisms.

Social life in an ant colony may well be instinctive; that social life in human groups is also instinctive is highly doubtful. A more plausible explanation of man's social proclivities lies in the childhood experience of "biological helplessness," common to all men, which virtually compels him to be social, to be dependent upon others, if he is to survive.

Man has the potentialities for effective and productive relationships with his fellow men. His physical dependency requires that he develop these potentialities to some extent. As a human being, he both can and must be sociable.

The necessity does not disappear as he grows older. For, even in the years of his maturity, the world is so complex that he cannot live independently of others. They, in turn, must depend upon him. Even were the individual not to acquire social habits with increasing age, he would still not be free of the need to be social. As a matter of fact, most of us do develop such habits, and thus do what we have to do, unaware of the fact that our human nature gives us little choice in the matter.

We see the beginning of this development early in life, first as an awareness of, then as an interest in, and finally as a desire for the presence of others. Initially, the infant's concern is with the attention of others, with what they can do for him; before long, it is also with the other persons themselves. Before long, a preference for social living, quite apart from any biological necessity, is clearly apparent. We look askance at any five-year-old who persistently chooses to play or work by himself; for we do not consider voluntary isolation, as opposed to enforced isolation (used as a form of punishment), "normal" or "natural" behavior.

Men are thus influenced by their nature to formulate and establish ways of living together, to form a society with beliefs, values, standards, and approved modes of behavior—in short, a society with a culture. They transmit that culture to succeeding generations through a program of education. It is important to note, therefore, that the nature of man is not incompatible with society; it is, in fact, responsible for the development and continued existence of society. For society is a realization of one of the unique potentialities in human nature.

It is the possession of these characteristics of intelligence, flexibility, individualization, and sociality, the possession of them in superior amount, that makes man the creature he is. Because of his unique nature, he produces a culture and organizes a society appropriate to that nature. Because of his complex nature, he lives in complex and variable societies with complex and variable cultures. A given society with its culture may call for the greatest or the least of the potentialities resident in man. If that society makes it possible to realize more and more of these potentialities, man will, in turn, build a better and better social world—at least as measured by his own standards.

21. What is there in the everyday behavior of a child that might be offered as evidence of his human nature?

22. What aspects of training and education are made necessary by the nature of the human being?

23. In view of what we have said about the flexibility of man, can it be argued that any one method or technique of teaching is best?

24. Is it not true that the flexibility of the human being must always be in conflict with his tendency toward individualization?

25. Is there anything in the nature of man that might make one form of society superior to all other forms?

26. In what ways do we fail to take advantage of the multiple potentiality of the child? How could we realize more of this potentiality?

27. Observe a young child. What evidence do you find of a tendency to be sociable?

SUGGESTED READINGS

DAVIS, CLARA M. Results of the self-selection of diets by young children. In William E. Martin & Celia Burns Stendler (eds.), *Readings in Child Development,* Harcourt, Brace, 1954, pp. 69-74. A dramatic example of "wisdom of the body" in operation.

FRANK, LAWRENCE K. *Nature and Human Nature,* Rutgers University Press, 1951. A modern conception of man by one of the most able and thoughtful students of human development.

HAYES, CATHY. *The Ape in Our House,* Harper, 1951. A fascinating story of the first three years in the life of a chimpanzee reared in the home of a young psychologist and his wife. Particularly interesting is a description of the limits which "chimpanzee nature" places upon development.

HOWELLS, WILLIAM. *Back of History: The Story of Our Own Origins,* Doubleday, 1954. An anthropologist's account of the history of man, with some acute observations on human nature. Of particular relevance are four chapters in Part 1: "The Nature of Human Life"; "The Coming of Mankind"; "The Meaning of Society"; "Culture: How We Behave"; and "Language: How We Talk."

LABARRE, WESTON. *The Human Animal,* University of Chicago Press, 1954. Still another examination of human nature by an anthropologist, this one emphasizing the relationship between man's biology and his culture.

MONTAGU, M. F. ASHLEY. *On Being Human,* Henry Schuman, 1951. A view of man especially concerned with his potentialities for cooperative behavior.

PFEIFFER, JOHN. *The Human Brain,* Harper, 1955. A popularly written but reliable account of the development and operation of the structure that makes it possible for humans to behave intelligently.

STAGNER, ROSS. Homeostasis as a unifying concept in personality theory. In Martin & Stendler, *op. cit.,* pp. 3-14. A review of the uses which psychology has made of the concept of homeostasis in the study of human personality.

2

the foundations
of human
motivation

No parent or teacher needs to be told that the child is an active organism. He is constantly behaving in one way or another; he is never completely at rest. Even when he is asleep, he continues to act and react. A leg moves; an eye twitches. In addition, dreams of imagined activity appear and disappear, one after the other.

DRIVES AS THE EXPLANATION
OF BEHAVIOR

How can we explain this constant stream of behavior? What is its cause? Since every child, regardless of the particular conditions under which he lives, is an active organism, we might reasonably assume that the explanation lies within the child. The particular behavior, of course, varies with the environment. A Kwoma child in far-off New Guinea spends hours searching the forest for a grub or beetle. When he finds it, he roasts it and devours it with great relish (Whiting, 1941). An American child, on the other hand, spends his time begging his mother for a piece of bread and jelly. When he gets it, he eats it with as much pleasure as his Kwoma brother does the roasted beetle. Although the behavior is hardly the same in the two cases, the reason for the behavior is. Both children are hungry and are behaving because they are hungry. They have not learned to be hungry; but they have obviously learned how to satisfy that hunger, and to do so in different ways.

Hunger is only one of the many conditions within the organism that predispose a child to activity or change in activity. There are also thirst, fatigue, excitement, jealousy, ambition, curiosity, fear, revenge, love, and many others. We can refer to all these conditions as drives, using Murphy's definition of a drive as a "basic tendency to activity" (1947, p. 984).

Some drives are present, at one time or another, from birth. These are called primary, or basic, drives. Others are learned as the child grows older; they are known as secondary, or acquired, drives. The discussion of these acquired drives we shall postpone until Part Two. For the present, our concern is with drives that are found in all children and are not a product of learning. We shall see, however, that experience alters the nature of these primary drives and of the objects and situations that gratify them. Thus our discussion of the general characteristics of primary drives and their modification through experience will provide a foundation for the later examination of secondary drives.

We can think of a drive as a state of disequilibrium or instability. When such a state exists within an individual, he is temporarily "out of kilter." Tension increases within the organism. The longer this state continues, the greater is the accumulation of tension.

When Johnny comes in from play, he is hungry. Internally, he is upset. He wants something to eat. But his mother isn't quite ready for lunch. Johnny must wait until she finishes her morning's work. The longer he waits, the more upset he gets. He complains, "Gee, Mom! I'm starved. Can't we eat now?" He runs back and forth to the kitchen; he searches for a cracker or a cookie. He sits down to look at a comic book but is soon up moving about again. He turns on the television set but doesn't stay around to watch it. Johnny is an aroused organism. He is in a state of disequilibrium.

The individual is thus susceptible to increases in tension. But, as we have seen in Chapter 1, he also tends to behave in such a way as to reduce that tension and attain some degree of equilibrium. In the example above, Johnny behaves because he is in a state of tension. He is in a state of tension because he is hungry. At least part of his behavior is designed to obtain food and thereby to eliminate the cause of his tension. His behavior is *instrumental* in achieving his goal; it is *goal-seeking* behavior. The *goal* is food. The *goal response* is obtaining food or perceiving that it is available to him.

But Johnny will succeed in reducing the tension associated with hunger only to find himself confronted with disequilibrium emanating from some other source. Thus life might be described most succinctly as a succession of cycles of tension-production–tension-reduction. The primary purpose of behavior is to minimize tension and to maximize equilibrium—if not at the moment, then over a period of time or ultimately.

But how do these states of disequilibrium arise? Why does tension increase within the organism? For the very young child and, to some extent, for the older child as well, the answer is found in certain primary or innate needs within the organism. Some of these are tissue needs; for example, the body must have food. Others are the need to regulate body temperature and the need to avoid unlimited distention of the bladder and the colon. We refer to such needs as visceral, since they originate in those parts of the body constituted of smooth muscle tissue and commonly known as the viscera.

But tension also emanates from so-called kinesthetic sensations within the striped muscles of the body—the skeletal musculature. The organism has a need, in a somewhat different sense, for activity or change in activity. Tension within the body is also produced by sensations in the external sense organs—the eye, the ear, the skin, and so forth. For example, light falling on the eyes of the neonate brings about an increase in overt activity (Pratt, 1954). The infant must adjust to the disturbance which that stimulation creates. He "needs" to approach or withdraw from such stimuli; we say that he has sensory needs. Finally, there is the tension associated with emotional states. The excitement characteristic of such states requires some form of readjustment, involving behavior, explicit or implicit. Thus, the child may be said to have emotional needs.

These categories of needs and resulting tension states, or drives, are clear cut, but they are by no means mutually exclusive. The unity of the organism in structure and function, described in Chapter 1, makes it improbable that any given tension state involves only one need or one type of need.

In Johnny's case, we assumed that the need was for food and that the drive was hunger. But Johnny was probably a bit tired from his play. If so, his actions were also the result of fatigue and the need for rest. Perhaps his need was not so much for rest as for a change of activity, from active and vigorous play to a more sedentary type of behavior, or from one kind of play to another. In this case, in our attempt to explain Johnny's behavior, we should have to take into account an activity drive. It would be virtually impossible to determine how much of the existing tension was due to need for food, how much to need for rest, and how much to need for change in activity. We can only say that all three drives may have been operating.

We know, then, that the reasons for behavior can seldom, if ever, be found in any single drive or in any single type of drive. Nevertheless, for purposes of discussion, we shall treat, in turn, four distinct classes of needs and their associated tension states, or drives. They are: visceral, activity, sensory, and emotional (Murphy, 1947).

1. The following drives are commonly found in the human being: thirst, fatigue, excitement, jealousy, ambition, curiosity, fear, revenge, love. Which of these would you classify as primary (innate) drives? Which as secondary (acquired) drives?

2. We have not mentioned the sex drive. Is it present at birth? If not, must we therefore consider it a secondary drive?

3. We have said that the child is behaving even when he is asleep. What primary drives might be operating then?

Throughout the discussion which follows, we should keep in mind that the language is usually that of the observer, rather than of the agent, of behavior. The child is hungry and is driven to some form of behavior long before he knows that he is hungry. After continued experience, he learns to associate certain inner conditions or signs of hunger—stomach contractions, in this case—with food-getting behavior and with the food which brings about the disappearance of such conditions; he will thereafter know when he is hungry. Furthermore, he will be able to say so, when he has developed adequate linguistic ability. But hunger does not delay its appearance until the child is mature enough to comprehend and name its existence. So it is with the other drives.

VISCERAL DRIVES

If the organism is to remain viable, and, more importantly, if it is to grow and develop, certain organic needs arise which must be satisfied. The existence of some of these needs is first made known by physiological changes, which ultimately raise the level of tension throughout the entire organism. This increased internal tension then manifests itself in increased sensitization to external stimulation and in increased output of behavior. The hungry infant cries, throws his body around, and kicks his legs. Murphy, Murphy, and Newcomb describe how "the touch of the finger on the cheek of some infants causes them, if hungry, to turn the head suddenly in the direction of the finger, whereas much greater pressure has to be applied to cause this behavior in a satiated child" (1937, p. 77). Children—and even adults—are more likely to lose their tempers when hungry (Goodenough, 1931a). In short, inner tension is associated with heightened irritability.

At the same time, certain internal signals are produced which enable the organism to learn what its need is at a given time and what behavior is appropriate to satisfy that need. Thus the changes in blood chemistry which are due to the need for food also produce the contractions in the stomach which the individual learns to accept as the sign of hunger. It should be emphasized in this case that the muscular contractions of the stomach constitute only the sign for hunger, not hunger itself. For a given person, the sign may not appear or may not be perceived, for one reason or another. Whatever the reason, a person who does not perceive the sign may nevertheless be very hungry; he just doesn't know it. This state of disequilibrium, together with the hunger contractions, continues in the organism until the need is satisfied, either by food or, later in life, by the thought or anticipation of food.

The cycle of tension-production–tension-reduction associated with such visceral drives as hunger, thirst, oxygen deprivation, and sexual tension can be delineated by such a sequence as this: (*1*) need; (*2*) physiological changes; (*3*) increase in tension throughout the system; (*4*) internal reactions specific to a given need that constitute a sign of that need; (*5*) heightened level of activity, in part because of increased susceptibility to external stimuli; (*6*) behavior which attempts to satisfy the need; (*7*) need-satisfaction; (*8*) restoration of physiological equilibrium; (*9*) reduction of inner tension; (*10*) disappearance of sign of need; (*11*) reduction in activity.

This is a logical sequence, but it is not necessarily what is perceived by the subject, especially after step 6. The individual eats and almost immediately experiences a state of relaxation, both inner and outer; his hunger pangs disappear almost with the first bite of food. This happens long before the food he eats can possibly be assimilated and put into a form that will meet the nutritional needs of his body tissues. Apparently, he learns to anticipate the restoration of physiological equilibrium that he knows will eventually result from eating. Psychological satisfaction precedes physiological satisfaction.

This ability to "jump the gun" perhaps explains why many persons are unable to stop eating when they have had enough to satisfy the original organic need. Physiological satisfaction comes long after they have left the dinner table—too late to check excesses in eating. The organism can then respond only by fat deposition.

Psychologically, the sequence beginning with step 6 must be amended: (*6*) behavior which attempts to satisfy the need—the procuring of food, for example; (*7*) disappearance of inner tension and any sign of need; (*8*) reduction in activity—that feeling of relaxation, even drowsiness, after a meal; (*9*) need satisfaction and restoration of physiological equilibrium. Of course, the last step occurs without the knowledge of the individual.

We have used the example of but one visceral drive to illustrate the cycle of tension-production–tension-reduction. The same basic sequence applies, with only minor modifications, to other visceral drives, such as thirst, oxygen deprivation, fatigue, sex, regulation of body temperature, and elimination.

The satisfaction of visceral needs is, of course, essential to the preservation of life and occupies much of the young child's attention and that of the persons who care for him. Therefore, these needs and their associated drive states deserve further comment.

Hunger

Hunger is perhaps the first uncomfortable experience after birth. Fortunately, we do not have to worry about determining whether the baby is hungry; he can tell us so from the beginning. He cries. He is restless. We find that feeding quiets him.

X rays of the digestive tracts of infants show that it takes from one to four hours for the stomach to empty (Bartram, 1954). Thus a baby in the first week of life may require as many as ten feedings in a period of twenty-four hours. As he grows older, the necessary number of feedings decreases markedly until, by the time he is nine to twelve months of age, three major feedings during the day will suffice. This decrease reflects, in part, a change in infant physiology which makes the recurrence of hunger less frequent; in part, it is due to the fact that, with increasing maturity, the infant learns to postpone gratification of his need for food and thus adjusts to the eating schedule of other individuals in the household. (See Chap. 5 for further discussion of infant feeding.)

It is the baby who decides when he is hungry. It is also the baby who determines when he is no longer hungry and decides to stop feeding. We are not certain how he knows, whether through sensation arising from distention of the stomach or through some chemical control related to the fat or sugar content of the blood (Aldrich & Aldrich, 1954).

Although the baby is a relatively helpless creature, we cannot help but be impressed with the fact that he likes to eat and knows when to eat, how to eat (using the sucking and swallowing reflexes), and when to stop eating. He needs help only in obtaining food. When he is hungry and food is not available, he will act to obtain food and thereby relief from hunger. Even though he grows less dependent on others as he grows older, behavior will continue to be elicited by the need for food; the greater the need, the greater the amount and intensity of that behavior.

Of the energy provided by the food that the infant consumes, approximately half is utilized in maintaining him as a living organism, a third in building body tissue (growth), and somewhat less than a tenth in behavior (Hansen, 1954). Thus he behaves in order to get food which provides energy which enables him to live, to grow, and to behave.

If the first discomfort after birth is associated with hunger, so is the first pleasure associated with the reduction or elimination of this drive. Thus feeding is important, not only because it is essential for survival, but also because it is one of the first satisfying experiences in the individual's life. It has both physiological and psychological significance. Fortunate is the infant who has a relatively satisfying feeding history, for his first experience with the outside world is a gratifying one (Brody, 1956; Erikson, 1950'

Thirst

Thirst is a primary drive associated with the need for liquid. When the water content of the body tissues falls below a certain level, a thirst center in the lower brain causes the pharynx to contract. The resulting sensation is that of a dry throat, the sign of thirst. The resulting behavior in the infant may be crying or some other behavior indicating distress.

The need for fluid is greater in the infant than in the adult. The water content of the body of a baby is 75 to 80 per cent of his body weight; that of the adult is 60 to 65 per cent. As anyone who has handled babies knows, they are damp creatures.

To maintain this relatively high water content, the young baby must consume proportionately more fluid than the adult— approximately one quart per day. This is equivalent, pound for pound, to about fifteen to twenty quarts in the adult (Aldrich & Aldrich, 1954). With advances in age, the amount of water required per unit of weight gradually decreases, as does the water content of the body.

In view of this fluid requirement, it is fortunate that the natural diet of infants and children is high in water content. Most of their solid food contains 60 to 70 per cent water, and fruits and vegetables have as much as 90 per cent (Hansen, 1954). Partly because much of the need for liquid is met through normal feeding, and partly because the need is not a regularly recurring one, as is the need for food, thirst never assumes the same importance as hunger in the life of the individual and in his care. However, fluid intake is directly related to frequency of the need for elimination of urine, as well as to the maintenance of physical well-being. It is, therefore, of concern to all who are charged with the supervision of infants and children to provide, on the one hand, water and juices and, on the other hand, toileting facilities.

Elimination

To satisfy his needs for food and for fluid and thus to reduce his hunger and thirst drives, the baby requires the help of others. But elimination, whether by evacuation of the bowel or by voiding of urine, is an automatic process. The infant accomplishes it without assistance.

Mass movement of the lower intestine periodically deposits waste material with a certain degree of suddenness into the rectum. The resulting pressure activates straining of the abdominal muscles and relaxing of the muscles which close the rectum, and a bowel movement takes place. The frequency of bowel movements varies with feeding schedule, with diet, with age, and with the individual. By the time he is six months old, however, the infant typically has one or two movements per day with some regularity.

Fluid wastes collect in the bladder. As these wastes accumulate, the bladder expands to the point at which pressure is sufficient to cause the sphincter muscles to relax and permit the voiding of urine. We have already seen that the fluid intake of the infant is relatively high. Almost half of this intake is eliminated through the kidneys and voided as urine (Hansen, 1954). Because the child's intake is great and his bladder small, there must be frequent fillings and frequent emptyings. After the first or second day of life, the daily frequency of elimination ranges widely from four or six to thirty or forty. By the age of two years, however, the typical child needs to urinate only five or six times in a period of twenty-four hours (Aldrich & Aldrich, 1954). The growth of the bladder, the decrease in intake, and the increase in the amount voided at one time are responsible for the decrease in frequency with age.

We may infer, from the behavior of the infant in the period prior to elimination, that the mass movement of the lower intestine and the pressure on the rectum and the bladder are not pleasant experiences. Because elimination brings a relief of discomfort, it must be counted a satisfying experience.

It will continue to be a pleasant experience as the child grows older. However, the inevitable requirement that elimination be brought under conscious control and that it be accomplished under prescribed conditions of time and place cannot help but complicate the experience for the child. The parent, who is the facilitator in the feeding situation, is the inhibitor in the toilet-training situation. It is not surprising that a certain degree of maturity is necessary before children will accept this interference with the pleasurable process of elimination and will exchange reflex for conscious regulation. The psychological significance of elimination, as a primary drive, lies in the fact that it brings the child face to face, perhaps for the first time, with a world which is clearly not going to accept him as he is (Erikson, 1950).

Fatigue

Fatigue is a primary drive associated with the need for rest, or some degree of sustained reduction in activity and consciousness. Again, regulation is automatic. The baby sleeps when he needs to sleep. Adults need only provide the conditions under which he can obtain rest as he requires it.

In the beginning, the difference between being asleep and being awake is a tenuous one. The baby lives much of the time in a twilight zone between these two states. He is neither wide awake nor sound asleep. Instead he drowses. Frequently his eyes open, his eyelids flutter, shut, and then open again. He cries, yawns, snuggles, stretches, rubs his face, kicks, starts, moves his arms and legs. In other words, his sleeping behavior is his waking behavior in a lower key.

As he grows older, the states of sleeping and being awake become more differentiated. He falls rather than drifts into sleep. Sleep deepens; behavior during sleep lessens in amount and in intensity. When he is awake, he is more alert and more vigilant. We begin to see signs that he resists going to sleep. He seems to enjoy being awake. His awakening from sleep is a sharper and more definite event. Four distinct stages develop: going to sleep, staying asleep, waking, and staying awake (Gesell, 1945).

In the first few weeks of life, the individual seems to rest or sleep much of the time. A typical four-week-old baby will so spend nineteen hours per day. There may be as many as a dozen sleeping periods daily. At first, the baby seems to awaken only when he is hungry. "He wakes to eat, he eats to sleep" (Gesell, 1945, p. 147). But, as we have seen, the frequency of feeding decreases with age, thus tending to bring about a decrease in the number of sleep periods. When the baby gives up his early-morning feeding, at about six weeks, he also eliminates the waking period at that time. At four months, he foregoes the late-evening feeding and sleeps through the night for about twelve hours. The midmorning nap may persist even after the infant has been taken off the midmorning bottle. But, by the end of his first year, when he is on a three-meal-a-day schedule, he generally meets his need for rest with an afternoon nap and a longer night's sleep.

Figure 2-1 depicts the daily patterns of sleep, awakeness, and feeding for a child from two weeks to four years of age, based on the mother's observation in the home, as reported by Gesell (1945). In general, the observations are in accord with our description, except for the interruption in the night's sleep noted at one year.

There are presumably many schedules of sleeping which would provide the rest needed by a growing child. The particular one established in the case of any given child is the resultant of several factors besides his need: his awareness of and interest in being awake; the level of stimulation in his environment; his feeding schedule; conditions which facilitate or interfere with his sleep, in the individual and in his surroundings; the customs of his family. As he grows older, he will undoubtedly need some help in resisting the temptation to stay awake too long and become too tired. We do not need to teach him how to sleep, but we must provide conditions that will enable and encourage him to sleep in response to moderate rather than extreme need and thus avoid the irritability and ill health which are the results of inadequate rest. Sleep is essential to the child's physical well-being; it can also be one of his most satisfying experiences.

Oxygen Deprivation

Oxygen deprivation is a very powerful drive, but one which most children do not experience to any marked degree. We do not have to teach the infant how to breathe, nor do we have to tell him when to breathe. When the blood lacks oxygen, a respiratory center in the lower brain activates certain muscles which cause the infant to breathe more rapidly and deeply. In addition, the baby has certain respiratory reflexes: he coughs; he sneezes; he yawns. All these behaviors affect the amount of air breathed and the rate of breathing. He also has some de-

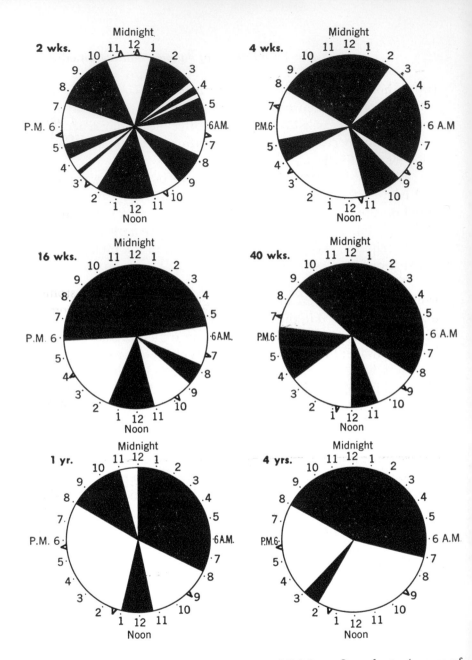

FIGURE 2-1. Daily cycle of behavior for a child from 2 weeks to 4 years of age, based on observations by the mother in the home. Sleep is indicated by black segments; awakeness, by white segments. Feedings are noted by small triangles on the edge of each clock dial.

(From A. Gesell, in collaboration with C. S. Amatruda. *The Embryology of Behavior*, Harper, 1945, p. 158) fensive reactions which ensure a sufficient supply of oxygen: for example, he reacts vigorously to any threat of suffocation.

With experience, there is a refinement in the child's respiration, an example of the "physiological learning" to which we referred in Chapter 1. In fact, the lungs do not function completely in the first ten days or two weeks of life. Fortunately, the infant's blood is especially rich in red cells, with a count of about six million, or one or two million more than will be present later, when the fully expanded lungs are at work (Aldrich & Aldrich, 1954). Even after the first two weeks, the infant's breathing is relatively shallow and rapid. It will gradually undergo change in the direction of greater depth and diminished rate.

Regulation of Body Temperature

Physiological disequilibrium results unless the temperature of the body is constant within relatively narrow limits. To maintain such stability, the metabolic processes of the body must produce more energy as heat than the body loses from its surface to the surrounding air. There are three problems involved: conserving heat; facilitating the loss of heat, or keeping cool; and producing heat, or keeping warm.

The body is provided with a thermostatic control system. Small changes in the temperature of the surrounding air are detected by sense organs in the skin. Impulses are transmitted by these sense organs to the hypothalamus at the base of the brain, which, through its control of the autonomic nervous system, varies heat production and loss to accommodate to these external changes (Langley & Cheraskin, 1958). To conserve heat, the surface blood vessels are constricted to reduce radiation loss and perspiration is reduced. To lose heat, perspiration is increased, leading to surface cooling by evaporation; the blood vessels in the skin are dilated; body activity is reduced; the rate of oxidation of body tissues is decreased. To produce heat, oxidative processes are stepped up; shivering is initiated; body activity is intensified; blood flow at the surface is decreased; and respiration is increased in rate and depth. Activity level is especially important in maintaining body temperature since three fourths of the energy used by the skeletal muscles is released as heat (Breckinridge & Murphy, 1958).

These regulatory mechanisms do not work perfectly in the young infant, in part because of his relatively large surface area, the immaturity of his sweating and shivering reflexes, and his "delicate skin and meager subcutaneous fat" (C. A. Smith, 1951, p. 167). Special care must be taken to keep him warm or cool, as circumstances require.

Voluntary measures by other persons, and by the child himself as he grows older, supplement these autonomic controls. In hot weather, we bathe to augment the natural cooling effects of perspiration, reduce clothing to a minimum, imbibe cool liquids, and in general "take it easy." In cold weather, we increase our food consumption, dress warmly, and engage in intensified activity—swinging arms, stamping feet, and jumping about.

Through a combination of these involuntary and voluntary processes, body temperature remains remarkably constant despite large fluctuations in the environmental temperature. However, body temperature does vary from one normal, healthy individual to another, and within the same individual. In a study of children from their first to their thirty-sixth month, Bayley and Stolz found that rectal temperatures, on the average, increased in the first seven months, remained relatively constant from the seventh to the twenty-fourth month, and declined thereafter. Their data also showed that readings below 99° were rare between the sixth and the twenty-first month, and that readings of 100° or more were comparatively frequent during this time. Temperatures of the children in any one age group varied rather widely, as did the temperatures of individual children from one age to another, somewhat less so after the age of two years. There was "some evidence that healthy children may have consistent tendencies toward high temperatures or toward low temperatures which are normal for them" (1937, p. 205). It seems clear that "normal" temperature is specific to a given child at a given time. The commonly cited figure of 98.6° for "normal" oral temperature is only a statistical average. However, normal variation is confined to rather narrow limits.

It is difficult, if not impossible, to determine how much behavior can be explained as reflecting the child's need to regulate body temperature. We do know that this is a potent and ever-present need. But, since gratification is so frequently accomplished autonomically, the individual is not so aware of the existence of the drive or of the measures taken to reduce it as he is in the case of other visceral drives.

Sex

The sex hormones, the androgens and the estrogens, play an important part in sensitizing the individual to stimulation of an erotic character and in giving rise to sexual tensions. Since these hormones are not present in appreciable amounts until the period of middle childhood (eight to ten years of age), or in significant amounts until adolescence (Tanner, 1955), it may be that sex, as a primary drive, is not present to any marked degree until the individual has reached or is approaching physical maturation.

But we must take cognizance of the incontrovertible evidence that genital sensitivity, stimulation, and activity exist from birth (R. R. Sears, 1943). Halverson (1940) observed tumescence and detumescence of the penis in nine infants between the ages of three and twenty weeks. During a ten-day period, the frequency of tumescence was at least once a day for seven of the subjects; for the total group the median number per day varied from three to eleven. Tumescence was accompanied by behavioral signs of restlessness much more often than was detumescence, leading to the inference that the latter event was pleasurable and thus associated with some kind of drive reduction. Tumescence occurred when there was abdominal pressure on the bladder, whether from hampered feeding, fullness of the viscera, or straining in eliminative acts; detumescence very often occurred after the restriction to feeding had been removed, after feeding had stopped, or after elimination had occurred. Whatever the related factors, the important point is the genital responsiveness at this early age and the ensuing experience of pleasure.

Masturbation in young children, particularly males, is not uncommon (Levy, 1928; Koch, 1935). Some of this behavior, Kinsey (1948) suggests, is merely tactile stimulation rather than activity leading to some erotic reward and inspired by anticipation of that reward. Nevertheless, Kinsey's data, based on actual observation of 317 males, show that nearly one third of the boys in the age range from two to twelve months experienced orgasm (without ejaculation, of course); the figure for the two- to five-year-olds was 57.1 per cent. In the population as a whole, the percentage of males reaching climax at such early ages would presumably be much smaller; these data indicate only that capacity for orgasm is present in a substantial number of young boys. Finally, there must be noted the occurrence of social sex play among young children, involving exhibition, exploration, and manipulation.

Some of this behavior can undoubtedly be attributed to curiosity; any sexual meaning attached to it is in the eye—and mind—of the beholder. Yet, the amount of activity of a sexual nature that brings satisfaction to the young child and that he therefore initiates, quite apart from any adult instigation or reaction, makes it difficult to reject completely the existence of sex as a primary drive in infancy and childhood. Indeed, Freud looked upon early sensual pleasures as "infantile sexuality" and believed them to be the roots of adult sexual behavior and motivation. (For a discussion of psychoanalytic theory, see Chap. 7.)

It must be concluded that some need for sexual gratification does exist in the young child. Although activity of young children leading to sexual gratification may have no immediate undesirable consequences, we are confronted with the fact that our society places explicit and relatively severe restrictions upon the expression of sexual drives in youth and adults. Parents and teachers cannot be indifferent to sexual activity in the preadolescent years unless they believe that early license provides, as seems unlikely, a foundation for the later acquisition of control. If adults do not completely inhibit sexual impulses in children, at least they attempt to divert the expression of these impulses and to minimize stimulation and opportunity for gratification (Sears, Maccoby, & Levin, 1957).

Thus we see that the primary experiences of life are the discomforts associated with visceral needs and the pleasures associated with satisfying them. As these needs are modified in kind and amount by time and training, so are the kind and amount of pleasures that come with their satisfaction. These experiences undoubtedly have a significant influence on the growth and development of the child. We are not yet in a position to specify the nature and extent of that influence.

4. What behavior of a child during a typical school day might be ascribed in part to the operation of visceral drives?

5. Consider the drive to regulate body temperature. Describe the sequence of events beginning with the need and closing with need-satisfaction, according to the steps outlined in the text.

6. How is the planning of the school day for children affected by a knowledge of the nature of visceral drives? How does an informed parent take visceral drives into account when making plans for the day of a three-year-old?

7. Does a period of time always elapse between the behavior which satisfies the need and the actual need-satisfaction, as it does in the operation of the hunger drive? What about the eliminative drive, for example?

8. Describe the instrumental, or goal-seeking, behavior and the goal responses for each of the visceral drives as you might observe them in a typical infant. Observe an infant, if you have the opportunity, to test the accuracy of your descriptions.

ACTIVITY DRIVES

In the drives discussed thus far, the respective needs arise in the viscera of the organism. But needs also originate in those muscles of the body that are attached to the skeleton and involved in any movement of that skeleton. These are actually needs for activity. We therefore call the corresponding drives "activity drives." We need to examine the nature of these drives and the part they play in the behavior of the individual. What state of tension or disequilibrium is properly called an activity drive? What does an individual do in order to reduce this tension?

Except in the completely relaxed organism, stress always exists within the skeletal muscles. For the body to maintain any one position or posture is an effort involving stress because it requires an asymmetrical functioning within the muscular system. What happens, for example, when a person stands in casual conversation with a friend? A photograph of the skeletal muscles would indicate that some muscles are extended while others are flexed. Stress is not distributed equally throughout his muscle system.

We notice that, after a time in his original position, the person bends his right knee slightly and straightens his left leg so that his weight is balanced on the left side. But, before long, he straightens his right leg and bends the left, thus redistributing his weight. At the same time, he puts his hands in his pockets; then he places them behind him; finally, he folds his arms across his chest. Any one position seems to be comfortable for only a limited period of time. The discomfort he feels when he maintains one posture too long stems from the fact that any sustained pattern of stress in the skeletal muscles increases tension to some critical point. At that point, a change in the pattern becomes desirable in the interests of tension reduction.

The individual is constructed in such a way that he must be active. He is not made to be still. Nor is he made in such a way that any particular activity will be comfortable indefinitely. There is a point at which any activity becomes monotonous; the individual gets tired of it.

But he is not "tired" in the sense that he is fatigued. He does not need cessation of activity. He needs change of activity. That change does not necessarily mean a different kind of activity; it may mean less or more activity of whatever kind he has been engaged in. Thus activity drives lead to changes in the amount or kind of activity. Since the organism is never in a completely inactive state, there is always some inequality in stress distribution which, when maintained, produces tension; thus, drives to activity are always present.

Elsworth by Seeg.

Some patterns in the skeletal musculature are more comfortable than others. They involve less increase in tension and can therefore be maintained for longer periods of time. Finding and adopting them undoubtedly require experience, practice, and maturation. Certainly, the champion athlete, who can perform his specialty over and over again without experiencing either fatigue or monotony, seems to be an example of an individual who has discovered and refined those patterns of flexion and extension which involve minimal tension and maximal equilibrium. We commonly apply such terms as "poise" and "balance" to his performance. It looks so easy—until we try it ourselves.

But the child, of course, has not yet identified and perfected such patterns. He can only change from one activity to another as he is driven to do so. But we can help him. We can provide a variety of activities. We can select those activities which involve least stress when continued over a period of time. We can also terminate an activity before the point of discomfort is reached. In those activities in which sustained practice is necessary if the child is eventually to master them, we space that practice. We provide intervals with contrasting activities between the practice periods. A real problem in systematic training and instruction is how to avoid stress and yet, at the same time, give adequate and sustained practice in a given skill.

In any program of education and training, we need to recognize the importance of activity drives and the part they play in the behavior of the child. We need to know the sequence of events initiated by this type of drive. We can describe that sequence as follows: (*1*) need, arising in intolerance for the continuation of any one pattern of distribution of stress in the skeletal musculature; (*2*) resultant spread of tension throughout the system, with a decrease in the precision of performance; (*3*) kinesthetic sensations within the muscles, interpreted as fatigue or strain; (*4*) change in behavior, in amount or kind; (*5*) reduction of tension, together with disappearance of those muscular sensations perceived as strain or fatigue; (*6*) need-satisfaction. This sequence of events underlies such qualities of child behavior as perseveration and rhythm and the pattern of activity in general.

9. What effects has the awareness of activity drives and their nature had upon classroom programs and management in recent years?

10. Explain the difference between the visceral drive of fatigue and activity drives. Can both kinds of tension state be present simultaneously? Give an example.

11. To what extent can school children be expected to sit quietly? How do you think the introduction in recent years of classroom furniture better suited to the anatomy of the child might affect our expectations in this respect? Why?

12. Observe a fellow student at work in the library. Keep a record of the frequency and type of his movements in a fifteen-minute period. Make the same kind of record for a child in a classroom as he works at his desk. Can you find any rhythm in their behavior? Do they move every few seconds? Or every few minutes? Can you identify any pattern in their respective behaviors?

13. Might restlessness in the young child be a result of activity drives? Under what conditions? How about stretching in an individual of any age?

SENSORY DRIVES

In the drives we have discussed thus far, the corresponding states of disequilibrium originate within the organism, either in the viscera or in the skeletal musculature. But inner stability can also be threatened and upset by forces arising outside the organism.

At times the child behaves, not because he is hungry or tired, but because he is aroused by external stimulation. For he is a sensitive organism. He can see; he can hear; he can touch and feel; he can smell; he can taste. Such sensations disturb his inner adjustment. The result is an increase of tension within the system which can be reduced only by some kind of behaving. Sensations and the states of disequilibrium they produce are drives, sensory drives.

A baby lies quietly in his crib. His mother approaches and leans over him. At the sight of her, the baby kicks his feet, extends his arms toward her, and smiles. She speaks to him. He becomes even more active. He laughs. He tries to sit up. He behaves because he is stimulated. The stimulation is external—in this case, the appearance of the mother and the sound of her voice. But the disturbing effects of that stimulation are internal.

The physical energy associated with these external stimuli has been transformed into nervous energy which invades the organism. What was previously a relatively quiet, relaxed state becomes an aroused one. The organism must deal in some way with this invading energy and the tension that it has produced. It does so by behaving. In effect, it utilizes this excess of energy in behavior. Once it does so, the source of disturbance is re· moved. Equilibrium is restored.

But the child is always being stimulated in one way or another. He takes care of the instability resulting from one kind of stimulation only to be confronted with another. In fact, as we saw in Chapter 1, the child seeks stimulation in spite of the fact that it leads to increase of tension which he must reduce through some kind of behavior.

The sequence of events initiated by the sensory drives, from instability to stability, from disequilibrium to equilibrium, is similar to that caused by the visceral and activity drives. The only significant difference is that the need arises, not within the body, but in the boundary between that system and its environment. It is here, in the sensory organs of the body, that the organism is first affected by objects in the external world.

Thus the signs of sensory needs would seem to be the sensations and the stimulus objects which give rise to these sensations. Light falling upon the eye and the corresponding sensation are a sign to look; the subsequent behavior serves to resolve the resulting disequilibrium. Ironically, the very behavior that reduces the tension often exposes the child to more stimulation, which, in turn, tends to increase tension. The child sees; he looks; in looking, he sees some more; he looks some more; and so forth. This kind of circular reaction underlies the principle of adience, which we stated in Chapter 1, according to which the child tends to persist in his behavior in a given situation. Theoretically, the child in our example might keep on looking indefinitely.

But how is this circular reaction ever broken? For we know that it is. The child does not keep on looking indefinitely. He shifts to some other kind of behavior. He does so because he must deal with other sensory drives. As a result of seeing, he may tend to persist in looking. But he may also hear, and, therefore, he must listen. He may both look and listen, but he cannot do either to the exclusion of the other. Looking will not reduce the increase of tension associated with hearing; listening will not reduce the increase of tension associated with seeing.

In addition, visceral and activity drives are always present. The child may tend to persist in looking, but he also needs a change in activity. Or he may become tired and need rest. Sooner or later, other needs become pre-eminent to any particular sensory need. The circular reaction is broken. The cycle is ended.

With time, of course, the child learns to prefer to see certain things, to hear certain sounds, to feel certain objects. That is, he develops tastes. It is thus the sensory drives which make possible the later development of what Murphy, Murphy, and Newcomb (1937) have called the esthetic drives.

14. Concerning sensory drives, what do we mean when we say that a child is overstimulated or understimulated? Can you give some examples of overstimulation in the classroom? Of understimulation?

15. In what sense are activity drives and sensory drives in opposition?

16. Try to trace the development of an esthetic drive—such as a taste for good food—back to its origin in sensory experience.

EMOTIONAL DRIVES

There are times when the organism finds it very difficult to arrive at the optimal tension-free distribution of energy within the system. Several sources of disequilibrium may be operating simultaneously. Drives of all three types—visceral, activity, and sensory—may be present at the same time. Tension increases to a critical level.

The whole organism is involved, and intensely so; it proceeds on an emergency basis. All of its reserve forces are called up. Increased quantities of adrenalin are secreted. As a result, more sugar, a source of quick energy, is released to meet this critical situation. The walls of the blood vessels contract; the heart beats faster. The rate of circulation of the blood therefore increases. Sugar is carried more quickly to all parts of the body. Nonessential activities of the body are inhibited. Digestion of food, for example, is delayed. These physiological changes are involuntary, automatic, and under the control of the autonomic nervous system. Cannon (1929) has aptly named them "emergency reactions." They put the organism into a state of excitement. It is this state of excitement which is the essence of emotion.

The Causes of Emotional Reaction

But why does the organism react to some situations with excitement and not to others? There is no single explanation for this phenomenon, and not all explanations are logical. Some situations arouse excitement by chance. It just happens that, at a time when a child is hungry and upset physiologically in the sense already described, he is made to persist at a somewhat routine task. After a period during which neither the visceral nor the activity need is met, he may "lose his temper." The tension has built up to such a point that it has spread through his entire system.

Similarly, a child may be extremely fatigued; he has a need for rest. Yet he is in a play situation in which the stimulation is both intense and varied. There comes a time when tension builds up to the breaking point. Without provocation, he may attack another child. Or he may burst out crying for the slightest of reasons. When the organism reaches the limits of its tolerance for tension, it goes into an emergency state. Thus, if the child gets hungry enough or tired enough, or if life becomes too monotonous for him, he gets "emotional" or excited.

There are other situations which, by their strangeness or the intensity of their demands, place the child in the position of not knowing what to do. He cannot act. The resulting damming up of the tension which is always being produced within the organism, for a variety of reasons, leads to excitement.

Faced with situations that put him into a state of excitement, the child can take action of three types: (*1*) he can approach the situation; (*2*) he can attack the situation; or (*3*) he can withdraw from the situation (cf. Horney, 1937). If the situation is a relatively unfamiliar one for him and he has no help in meeting it, the behavior he tries originally may be selected at random from the three possibilities. Consider the situation of a dog for a young child who has never seen one before. He is alone. He is excited. What shall he do? He may step up to the dog and pat it on the head. The dog wags his tail and indicates his desire for more of the same. This behavior on the part of the dog serves to drain off some of the tension which has produced the exciting state in the child. The child associates this reduction in tension with the approaching kind of behavior. He may use this behavior in other similar situations. Approach may become a generalized form of behavior with which to cope with exciting situations. This is "loving" behavior. The exciting state that the child experiences in situations in which he uses or wants to use approaching behavior he eventually perceives as a particular kind of exciting state, a particular emotion, which he—and others—may call "love."

A second child meeting a dog for the first time may have a quite different experience. He, like the first child, approaches the dog. In this case, the dog bites him. He withdraws. If the withdrawal is fast enough and great enough, he escapes further attack and pain. But, thereafter, the exciting state aroused by the sight of a dog causes him to withdraw. This is the behavior that he has found serves to reduce the excitement and the associated tension. He may use this behavior in other situations. This is "fearful" behavior. The exciting state that he experiences in situations in which he uses or wants to use withdrawing behavior he eventually perceives as a particular kind of exciting state, a particular emotion, which he—and others—may call "fear."

Finally, a third child in the same situation may decide to attack this strange object. The dog runs away. Tension, aroused by the strangeness, is reduced. Attacking behavior is reinforced. The child tends to use it in other situations. This is "angry" behavior. The excitement which he associates with success in the use of attacking behavior he learns to know as a special form of excitement, an emotion, which he finds is generally called "anger."

As the child undergoes a greater number and variety of experiences, as he has the opportunity to try out the several basic responses to them, as he learns to discriminate among those experiences and responses, he builds an emotional repertory (see Chap. 16). There is not just love, there is love for parents, for teachers, for friends, for lovers. The extensity of that repertory depends upon the extensity of experience. In societies in which the consequences of any particular behavior are not serious, in which the differences in the results of different kinds of behavior are not significant, only the most limited of emotional repertories could be expected. Almost anything seems to relieve tension; it is difficult to know when one is angry or fearful or in love. Such shallow emotional behavior has been described by Margaret Mead (1928) as characteristic of the Samoans.

As situations lose their strangeness with continued experience, they lose their ability to bring about excitement. Thus, the child learns to be unemotional in situations which do not threaten him, which do not call for more than he can give.

But this discussion has gone far beyond a description of primary emotional drives. For our present purposes, it can be said that the only emotion which the child possesses by reason of his nature is what might be called "excitement." This is nothing more than an intensification of the interference in the energy distribution of the system which, as we have already seen, underlies all drives. The child can be said to be afraid only in the sense that he has learned by consequence or by imitation or by heeding his parents' verbal warnings that, in certain situations in which excitement is aroused, the appropriate behavior is withdrawal. The child who is protected, but not overprotected, may adopt an attacking approach toward his environment; he may be said to have a need for or a drive toward independence or adequacy. From certain exciting situations, however, he may tend to withdraw to points previously established as safe—home, parents. This may be described as a drive or need for dependence or security. But these are learned drives; they merely issue from and are not identical with the undifferentiated drive of excitement with which the child is endowed. A child by nature may be prone to excitement; but he is not predisposed to be fearful or aggressive or affectionate.

From this point of view concerning the nature of the emotional drive, it is what the child does in an exciting situation, not what the state of the organism is, that determines what the emotion is. This view is compatible with the claim that there is little or no differentiation in visceral state for the various emotions (Cannon, 1929). This view also considers emotion to be a drive to constructive activity rather than a disorganized response (Leeper, 1948). It is a strength, not a weakness, in the nature of the child.

17. What part do emotional drives play in training and education? How can a program be designed to make the best use of this reservoir of energy?

18. What arguments could be advanced against the proposition that education and learning should be unemotional or de-emotionalized?

19. In what circumstances might emotion be considered disorganizing?

20. To what extent can you agree with the statement: The source of all behavior can be located within the organism? In what sense can we say that we motivate a child?

21. In his book *Organization of Behavior,* Hebb (1949) makes

a distinction between the terms "emotion" and "emotional behavior." Is such a distinction compatible with our discussion
of emotional drives?

These drives—visceral, activity, sensory, and emotional—
constitute the spurs to activity which are an inherent part of
the nature of the child. In this sense, they have been called the
primary drives. Depending upon the conditions which sur-
round the child as he grows and develops, one type of drive
or one particular drive may become more important than
others in explaining his behavior. One child's activity might
be ascribed more often to visceral drives; another's, more often
to sensory drives. Whatever the character of the drive state or
states, we use a general term, "motivation," to refer to all such
states. To say that a child is motivated is to say that some drive
state exists.

As the child grows older, he learns which kinds of behavior
are most effective in reducing tension and restoring equilibrium. He learns that a certain kind of behavior is appropriate
when one drive is operating but that another kind is appropriate when another drive is present. Thus, he learns to seek
food when he is hungry, to seek rest when he is tired, and to
change activities at the sign of muscular stress.

In addition, by means to be discussed later (Chap. 8), he
acquires secondary drives, some of which may be more socially
useful than those with which he is originally endowed. But primary drives will continue throughout life to account for much
of his behavior and provide the foundations for his later motivational development.

SUGGESTED READINGS

ALDRICH, C. ANDERSON, & ALDRICH, MARY M. *Babies Are Human
Beings: An Interpretation of Growth* (2nd Ed.), Macmillan,
1954. A delightful account of the nature and nurture of infants. The authors write with authority and understanding of
the needs and satisfactions of the first year.
FRANK, LAWRENCE K. *Feelings and Emotions,* Doubleday, 1954. A

thoughtful and thought-provoking examination of our modern point of view toward emotions and the part they play in the life of every child.

MURPHY, GARDNER. *Personality,* Harper, 1947. An excellent and thorough discussion of motivation is presented in Chapter 5, "The Elementary Biology of Motivation," and in Chapter 6, "The Biology of Motive Patterns."

WISHIK, SAMUEL M. *Feeding Your Child,* Doubleday, 1955. A book devoted entirely to the problems of feeding children from birth through adolescence. Although it is written primarily for parents, all those with an interest in children and their behavior and development will find this book worthwhile.

3
the biological
basis of individual
differences

Thus far, we have emphasized those characteristics which all children, as human beings, have in common. Can we, then, assume that any differences among children which appear later are a consequence of differences in the environments in which they grow and develop? To answer "yes" to this question, we should have to assume that the starting point is the same for all children. Even casual observation tells us that this is not a valid assumption.

At a rather high level of generality, we can say that all children are self-maintaining, sensitive, and intelligent organisms; that they are all motivated by the same basic drives; and that they grow and develop according to a common pattern (see Chap. 4). But as we try to describe individual children more specifically, we are forced to recognize differences among them. From the time of birth, individuals differ in many ways— and noticeably so. Some babies are fat and husky; some are slender and frail looking. Some infants have blue eyes; some have brown. Some are active and some passive. In fact, as any parent can and does tell you, his particular baby is unique. He is right. No one infant is exactly like any other one. Even "identical" twins differ in some respects, such as in the pattern of their fingerprints.

Each individual has his constitution: his make-up, his biological individuality, his unique structure and function. It provides the substance and, to some extent, the direction for his later growth and development. To the degree that there are constitutional differences among children which persist over time, we may expect differences in the quality, quantity, and rate of development and in structure and function at any given point in time.

In this chapter we shall discuss the nature and magnitude of these constitutional differences, their origin, and their significance, in general, for the developmental process. In later chapters we shall consider their contribution to individual differences in specific aspects of development: physical (Chap. 14), cognitive (Chap. 15), and motivational (Chap. 16).

THE NATURE AND MAGNITUDE OF CONSTITUTIONAL DIFFERENCES

Constitutional differences, as we have said, exist at birth: "At no point in the cycle of human life do otherwise comparable individuals present such a wide array of differences as at the moment when they are born" (Gesell, 1945, p. 13). Differences in external body structure and form are present, immediately observable, and measurable. Differences in internal body structure, form, and function are present but not immediately observable, nor are they measurable except through the use of special procedures and tests. Differences in growth potential are present but are neither observable nor measurable at the moment of birth, for they become manifest only with the passage of time.

Unfortunately, our knowledge of constitutional differences in infancy is extremely limited. Such information as we do have concerns, for the most part, those differences which are present, immediately observable, and measurable, such as differences in weight, length, eye color, amount and type of hair, and general body conformation, all of which are aspects of external structure. We know much less about differences in internal structure and function and still less about differences in potentiality for later growth and development.

Differences in External Body Structure

Infants differ greatly in their external body structure, not only with respect to mass, as measured by weight, but also with respect to size, or body dimensions. Some of these dimensions are of especial importance for what they contribute to general body configuration or form and to behavioral capabilities. Others, such as length of nose or of fingers or size of ears, are certainly of interest but are of less significance. It is understandable, then, that most of the available information concerns general body dimensions. Table 3-1 presents the percentiles for weight, body length, pelvic breadth, head circumference, and chest circumference, all at birth, as reported by Stuart and Stevenson (1954) on the basis of data collected in the Department of Maternal and Child Health, Harvard School of Public Health. Since boys are somewhat larger in all respects than girls, on the average, two sets of figures are given.

Body form is the resultant or combination of a given weight, body length, head circumference, chest circumference, and pelvic breadth, together with given amounts of many other body dimensions. It is not unlikely that two infants will have the same birth weight, but it is less likely that they will have the same birth weight *and* the same body length, and even less likely that they will be identical with respect to three or more dimensions. In fact, considering the multitude of body dimensions, we should expect to find that each infant has a unique body form or constitution. But a given child will resemble some infants in body form more than he will others. Thus, we speak of body types.

We have no precise way of describing different types of body form for infants, such as we have for older children and

Table 3-1

Percentiles for Selected Body Measurements at Birth *

Percen- tiles	Weight (kg.)		Length (cm.)		Pelvic Breadth (cm.)		Head Cir- cumference (cm.)		Chest Cir- cumference (cm.)	
	B	G	B	G	B	G	B	G	B	G
3	2.63	2.63	46.3	47.1	7.1	7.0	33.0	32.5	29.8	30.0
10	2.86	2.81	48.1	47.8	7.4	7.2	33.5	33.4	30.6	30.8
25	3.13	3.13	49.3	49.0	7.7	7.4	34.4	33.9	31.8	31.8
50	3.40	3.36	50.6	50.2	8.1	7.7	35.3	34.7	33.2	32.9
75	3.76	3.67	52.0	51.0	8.4	8.2	36.2	35.4	34.4	34.0
90	4.13	3.90	53.3	51.9	8.7	8.5	37.0	36.0	35.7	35.0
97	4.58	4.26	54.6	53.6	9.0	8.9	37.5	36.6	36.8	36.0

* Data from H. C. Stuart and S. S. Stevenson. Physical growth and development. In W. E. Nelson (ed.), *Textbook of Pediatrics* (6th Ed.), Saunders, 1954, pp. 54-65.

adults (see pp. 451-55). Nevertheless, on the basis of casual inspection, we are accustomed to label or type one infant as "stocky," another as "slender," and still another as "average" in build (see Fig. 3-1). How these infant body types are related to later physical growth and status is as yet undetermined. For the moment, it is enough to recognize that differences in body type do exist from birth.

Infants differ with respect to many other external body characteristics: skin color, finger- and footprints, length of arms and legs, trunk or stem length, facial profile, and so on. Together with the body dimensions that we have already discussed, these characteristics provide for each infant an individuality in form, size, and appearance that is readily observable.

1. According to Table 3-1, are females superior to males in size of any body dimension?

2. What do the data in Table 3-1 tell us about the body form and proportion of the newborn? Consider a male infant who is average in all dimensions. Note particularly the relation between his head and chest circumferences.

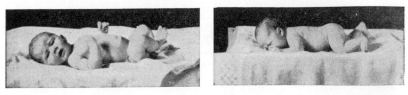

One month

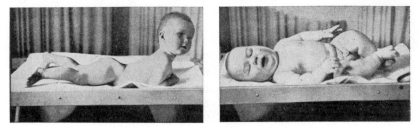

Five months

FIGURE 3-1. A "slender" child (*left*) and a "stocky" child (*right*) aged one month and five months.

(From N. Bayley & F. C. Davis. Growth changes in bodily size and proportions during the first three years: a developmental study of 61 children by repeated measurements, *Biometrika*, 1935, *27*, 26-87)

Differences in Internal Structure

All available evidence indicates that newborn infants differ in internal structure as well as in external structure. Although these differences are not apparent to the naked eye, they can be measured through the use of X rays. For example, we know that there is variation in the size and placement of the various organs of the body, such as the heart, the stomach, the liver, and the lungs (see, for example, Bakwin & Bakwin, 1935).

Infants differ also with respect to the stage of development reached at time of birth by a given organ or structure. Some infants are accelerated in their physical maturation; some are relatively retarded. X rays provide a picture of maturational differences in the skeleton of infants.

One measure of the maturity of the skeleton is the presence or absence of centers of ossification, at which points the replacement of cartilage by bone begins. Their presence indi-

cates a fairly advanced status; their absence indicates the contrary. Table 3-2 gives the percentages of white and Negro boys
and girls of various birth weights in which each of several ossification centers was present at birth. It can be seen that the degree of skeletal maturity varies, not only with birth weight,
but also with sex, with race, and with the specific ossification
center. Thus girls are generally advanced with respect to boys,
and Negroes with respect to whites. The latter difference is
particularly interesting in view of findings that Negro infants
are accelerated in gross motor behavior and development (Pasamanick, 1946; Williams & Scott, 1953).

A further example of the many aspects of internal structure
in which infants differ is blood type. Among white children,
approximately 45 per cent belong to Group O, 40 per cent to
Group A, 10 per cent to Group B, and 5 per cent to Group AB
(Vaughan, 1954).

3. Is body build a function of external structure, of internal
structure, or of both?

4. Two individuals may have the same body weight and yet
differ markedly in body build. How can this be?

Differences in Internal Function

Differences in structure, external or internal, can be determined by direct means. Some differences in internal function are also observable in this sense. Pulse rate can be measured
directly; for the average infant, it is 120 beats per minute, but
it may increase to 170 beats under stress or with activity and
decrease to 70 beats during sleep (Lyon & Kaplan, 1954). It
fluctuates so much and so rapidly in early infancy that it is
difficult to say what range of variation we should expect to find
under normal conditions in any group of infants. That there
is some, there can be no doubt.

Similarly, blood pressure is measurable. Typically, the sys-
tolic figure is 85, but the middle two thirds of a distribution of
infants may range from 77 to 90, the middle 95 per cent from
69 to 101. Diastolic pressure is, on the average, 60, but it may
range from 52 to 68 for the middle two thirds and from 44 to

Table 3-2

Presence of Ossification Centers in Newborns *

Ossification Center	Birth Weight (gm.)					
	under 2000	2000-2499	2500-2999	3000-3499	3500-3999	4000 or more
Calcaneous						
White boys	100	100	100	100	100	100
girls	100	100	100	100	100	100
Negro boys	100	100	100	100	100	100
girls	100	100	100	100	100	100
Distal femoral epiphysis						
White boys	9	75	85	100	100	100
girls	50	92	98	100	100	100
Negro boys	18	89	91	94	100	100
girls	50	94	99	100	100	100
Cuboid						
White boys	0	6	15	40	44	60
girls	0	38	57	65	70	76
Negro boys	0	23	44	58	68	100
girls	21	38	68	78	82	75
Hamate						
White boys	0	7	6	6	10	11
girls	0	0	11	13	21	33
Negro boys	0	16	16	18	44	29
girls	0	9	23	41	55	67
Cuneiform, third						
White boys	0	0	0	3	2	3
girls	0	0	0	0	6	10
Negro boys	0	4	8	15	14	14
girls	0	6	14	17	18	25

* Data from A. Christie. Prevalence and distribution of ossification centers in the newborn infant. *Amer. J. Dis. Child.*, 1949, 77, 355-61. The original data are reported to the nearest tenth; here they have been rounded off to the nearest whole percentage.

76 for the middle 95 per cent of the distribution (Lyon & Kaplan, 1954).

Other differences in internal function could be, but as yet have not been, measured. Mirsky (1953) has suggested that infants differ with respect to the amount of their gastric secretions, some being hypersecreters and thus fast digesters, others being hyposecreters and thus slow digesters. Such differences, if they exist, could explain why infants vary in the frequency with which they demand feeding, although other factors, such as size of stomach and rate of metabolism, would also be involved.

Some differences in internal function are measured in terms of behavioral rather than physiological responses. In any group of infants, there are noticeable differences in, for example, reactivity, or sensitivity. Some are "tough" in that they are relatively unaffected by either external or internal factors. They do not seem to get upset or overwrought easily. They have a certain placidity or even indifference to events. Other infants are "tender." They not only react; they tend to overreact. They are easily disturbed. They are more animated. They cry more often. When Aldrich, Sung, and Knop (1945) studied the amount of crying in a group of newborn infants in a hospital setting, they found a range from 48.2 to 243 minutes in a twenty-four-hour period.

In her study of twenty-five babies during the first two years of life, Shirley (1933b) obtained ratings of the irritability of her subjects in response to various examinations (anthropometric, physical, and psychological) during the first year. The results for twenty-one of the babies are shown in Figure 3-2. It is interesting to note that, for each child, the amount of irritability varied with the type of examination. Without exception, the greatest amount was elicited by the anthropometric tests; with two exceptions, the least amount was elicited by the psychological tests. But of more interest are the differences among children, without regard to type of examination. Virginia Ruth is clearly a very "irritable" child as compared with James. Other highly reactive children are Maurice, Quentin, and Carol; placid children, other than James, are Fred, Doris, Harvey, Larry, and Peter.

How can we explain these differences in reactivity? Obviously, external factors play a part. It was Shirley's examina-

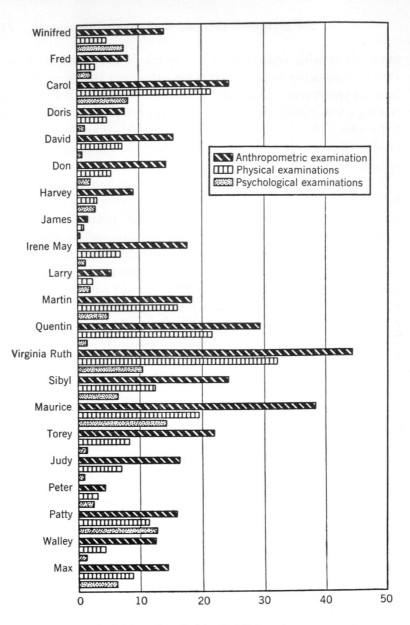

FIGURE 3-2. Irritability of individual children in response to various examinations during the first year (percentage of total possible irritability score).

(From M. M. Shirley. *The First Two Years*, Vol. III. Personality Manifestations, University of Minnesota Press, 1933)

the biological basis of individual differences 75

tions that produced the irritability. But the point is that they produced different amounts of irritability in different children. Students of infant behavior and development suggest that the answer lies, in part, in constitutional factors. Escalona discusses two such characteristics, skin sensitivity and strength of impulse. Concerning the former, she observes:

> Some babies respond markedly to the slightest touch. If it is sudden, however gentle, they may startle. Otherwise, depending on their general state and the nature of the stimulation, it may soothe or irritate, animate or provoke, cause comfort or discomfort. Slight provocation, like a harsher soap or slightly rough material, wetness or heat, will cause prickly skin irritation in some and not in others. Gentle handling and holding will leave pressure marks which may not disappear for five minutes or more in some; the reddening of the skin will disappear before the observer's eye within five seconds in others. There can be no doubt that something like skin awareness, or sensations of the kind generated by the skin, are sharp and frequent throughout the day for some babies but less intense for others [1953, p. 17].

Escalona's observations of infant behavior also support the hypothesis that there are constitutional variations in the strength of impulse. Infants differ in the strength and frequency of bodily movement toward which they seem to be impelled. They also vary in the "strength of other impulses such as those related to oral needs (sucking, biting, etc.) . . . [and] the intensity with which hunger is felt . . ." (1953, p. 20).

Sex differences in muscular reactivity, reflecting perhaps both differential sensitivity and impulsivity of a constitutional origin, have been noted in the young infant. Gatewood and Weiss (1930) found newborn males more reactive than females to stimulation as measured by increases in respiration rate.

It also appears that each individual may have his own personal tempo of functioning. Balint (1948) observed the sucking behavior of bottle-fed infants and found that each baby, once he began to suck, did so with a certain well-defined characteristic rhythm (or rhythms). He tended to maintain this rhythmic pattern despite the imposition of a different rhythm by the nurse as she assisted him in feeding and despite changes in his state of health. The appearance of such persistent idiosyncratic response patterns at so early an age suggests the existence of constitutional differences in personal rhythm.

Some students have suggested that there are constitutional types of internal functioning. Thus the "internalizing" type of infant tends to respond viscerally. Under stress, he is characterized by digestive and eliminative disturbances and by increase in heart rate and blood pressure. His opposite is the "externalizing" type of infant, who reacts to distress with overt behavior involving the striped muscles and the skeleton. H. E. Jones (1930) has furnished some evidence that there is a predisposition toward one or the other type of response early in life.

5. What nonconstitutional factors might have contributed to the differences in crying among newborns reported on page 73?

6. Arrange the children named in Figure 3-2 from highest to lowest irritability on each type of examination. How much consistency do you find in the infants' relative position from list to list?

7. If the opportunity permits, observe, with a fellow student, the behavior of an infant. Can you infer anything from that behavior about the child's internal functioning? Do you and your co-observer agree on what is typical of the internal functioning of this particular infant? How sensitive does he seem to be? How impulsive? Is he "internalizing" or "externalizing"?

8. Studies of older children and adults indicate that males have greater stability of bodily function than females (Terman & Tyler, 1954). Can these findings of sex differences be taken as evidence of constitutional differences? What other explanation might there be for them? (See pp. 86-87.)

Differences in Growth Potential

From the time of birth, it is clear that individuals differ with respect to many characteristics of structure and function. Observation of subsequent changes in both structure and function has led to the conclusion that they differ in their potential for growth as well. Each child has his own individual pattern (Bayley, 1956a), which is influenced only slightly and temporarily by normal environmental variation. However, severe and prolonged malnutrition, among other factors, may have a lasting effect on growth; just how severe the circumstances must be before profound changes are effected is as yet undetermined (Tanner, 1955).

From what has already been said, it is to be expected that our knowledge of constitutional differences in growth potential, inferred as it must be, is restricted largely to changes in external structure, particularly as they are revealed in repeated measurements of height and weight on the same children over a period of time. We shall defer the presentation of these data until Chapter 14. For now, it is sufficient to note that newborns differ, not only in body dimensions, but also in the rate at which they will increase in these dimensions in the years to come. They will differ in the length and the timing of periods of rapid, average, and slow growth. So orderly is this process for a given individual in the case of growth in height that it has been found possible to predict adult height from height at earlier ages with considerable accuracy after the age of eight years (Tanner, 1955), and with even greater accuracy when the prediction is based on assessments of the skeletal maturity of the individual rather than on his height at earlier ages (Bayley & Pinneau, 1952). For weight, prediction cannot be nearly so accurate since environmental factors, particularly the individual dietary, are so much more potent than early status.

9. Of what practical importance is the ability to predict the future structure and function of an individual from measurements at earlier ages?

THE ORIGIN OF
CONSTITUTIONAL DIFFERENCES

Since differences in biological structure and function are present at birth, there is a tendency to think of them as innate or genetically determined. But to do so ignores the fact that the newborn has been growing and developing, and even responding, for a period of some nine months *in utero*. Events during this period may have profound and lasting effects upon the child (see Chap. 5).

In addition, during the early postnatal period, the vulnerability of the young organism is so great that the nature and amount of the care he receives may well influence his biological structure and function. Even in the later years of growth and development, environmental effects may be significant. Perhaps the most dramatic example is the substantial acceleration of growth in height and the equally substantial increase in adult stature among the peoples of Western Europe and the United States over the past century. Both boys and girls today reach puberty and attain their adult stature at earlier ages than did their grandparents. Regarding secular changes in adult height, Tanner (1955) reports that the average gain between 1880 and 1950 was about 1½ cm. per decade for the age period five to seven years, about 2 cm. per decade for the adolescent period, and 1 cm. per decade for the adult. On logical grounds, these changes are attributed—in part, at least—to the steady improvement of diet over these years (Tanner, 1955; Greulich, 1958).

But nutrition is not the only factor that influences the course of biological development. It is now well established that there is a seasonal effect on growth; increases in height are most pronounced in spring, and increases in weight are greatest in autumn, regardless of the dietary (Tanner, 1955).

It is clear, then, that structure and function are not biological "givens." They emerge over a period of time in an environmental setting. The nature of that environment influences both the course and the outcome of the developmental process. In one sense, the individual acquires everything. In another sense, he inherits everything, not only his form and function but also his environment.

But even geneticists no longer concern themselves with the question of heredity-*vs.*-environment. Muller, one of the world's foremost geneticists, has said: "The heredity-environment controversy, which had been raging for a long time in my student days a half century ago, is an excellent example of wishful thinking by two sets of fanatical opponents, both of whom ought to know better" (1956, p. 277).

Dobzhansky has offered a simple equation, which reads:

$$\text{Genotype} \times \text{Environment} = \text{Phenotype}.$$

By "genotype" he means "the sum total of [the individual's] hereditary properties." "Phenotype" is defined as "all external and internal structures and functions of the organism" (1950, p. 161). The phenotype is, then, the outcome of development. But what determines the outcome? What is the cause of development? Is it the genotype? Is it the environment? The answer is neither. As the equation clearly indicates, it is the interaction between them.

According to this formulation, it is inaccurate to say that we inherit any characteristic, whether it be stature or hair color or energy level. What do we inherit? Properly speaking, we inherit a given genotype which responds in a given way to a given environment; the result is a given outcome, or phenotype. In the words of Dunn and Dobzhansky: "It is not the . . . [trait] but the response to the environment that is inherited" (1946, p. 17).

What are the implications of this point of view for those concerned with the growth and development of the child? Since the genotype is fixed, there is little that we can do about it. Our real job is to discover that environment which will elicit the most favorable responses from a fixed genotype. Dunn and Dobzhansky point out that the diabetic has a fixed genotype. But, by furnishing him with an environment containing insulin, we modify the outcome tremendously. His genotype responds differently to this environment than it does to an insulin-free environment. The challenge to teachers, parents, and all others concerned with child development is to make the most out of whatever capacity an individual possesses. We accomplish this not by changing his genotype—which we cannot do—but by manipulating his environment—which we *can* do.

In too many cases, the same environment is furnished to all children, although they differ greatly in their hereditary properties. The importance of the genotype, of course, increases as the environment becomes more standardized; when each child is exposed to the same environment, most of the differences in outcome can be attributed to heredity. On the other hand, to the extent that we design the environment to fit the child, we help him to realize his unique potentialities and enhance the differences among individual children. We are still in the early stage of development of a science which Dobzhansky has called the "management of the human phenotype" (1950, p. 162).

> Nature provides a great variety of locks, and Nurture many different keys. Each trait has its own class of locks and will respond to a limited number of keys. Some locks do not at present respond to any keys provided by the existing variety of environments [Dunn & Dobzhansky, 1946, p. 24].

Constitutional differences are basic and persisting differences in phenotype. The task before us is to analyze the significance of these differences for behavioral and personality development.

THE SIGNIFICANCE OF CONSTITUTIONAL DIFFERENCES

We may agree that constitutional differences exist. But these questions remain: What is their significance for the growth and development of children? What is the relationship between biological individuality and psychological individuality, or individuality in behavior and personality?

The influence of constitutional characteristics varies with the particular psychological function. In some instances, it appears that biological structure and function determine, or are prepotent in determining, the type or quality of behavior and personality. For about two thirds of all Americans, the taste of a weak solution of phenylthiocarbamide (P.T.C.) is intensely bitter; for the remaining third, the same solution has no taste. This difference persists in the face of any known changes in the environment (Dunn & Dobzhansky, 1946).

A more significant example of the prepotency of constitutional factors comes from studies of locomotor development, particularly the ability to walk. Shirley found that each of the babies she studied developed according to the same general pattern, but that they differed markedly in the rate of development as well as in certain qualities of their locomotor behavior. Although she was unable to establish any one-to-one correspondence between these developmental and behavioral traits and any particular constitutional characteristic, she did conclude: "The least that can be said is that there are anatomical trends in development that vary along with the broad motor trends. Individual idiosyncrasies in rate of motor development . . . , which are relatively constant, probably have their origin in permanent physical factors . . ." (1931, pp. 126-27). Norval (1947) found that so small a difference as one inch in length between two newborn babies of the same weight can significantly influence motor development: the longer child will walk, on the average, twenty-two days earlier than the shorter child. It appears that differences in locomotor development and behavior, particularly in walking, reflect differences in biological structure and function. A child acquires—he is not taught—his particular ability to walk in his particular way, largely as a result of his particular constitution.

However, in few other aspects of behavior and personality does constitution have the determining influence that it exerts in the cases of taste and locomotion. More frequently, it exerts itself as a predisposition. Sontag (1946) has called our attention to the importance of the energy level. A high energy level predisposes a child to be active in his reactions to his environment; a low energy level predisposes a child to be passive. Aldrich and Aldrich have vividly described the manifestation of differences in activity level in infants:

If we take a few babies out of their cribs and place them side by side on a table in the hospital nursery, it is easy to see the differences in their behavior as they respond to the imposition of outside force. . . . All of them lie with their arms and legs folded up, never relaxing their extremities asleep or awake. What happens when we attempt to change this posture by straightening out their legs?

As we try it out down the line, many of them offer little or no resistance and allow their legs to be pumped up and down, placidly awaiting the end of this curious exercise. But every once in a while an upstanding individualist is encountered who by no means will allow his legs to be pulled with impunity. Heel against thigh, he will resist this imposition of adult force with every ounce of his amazing strength. Some newborn babies will fight with such persistence that they can be suspended by one heel, the leg still rigidly doubled on the thigh. Not only do they resist with leg muscles, but by crying and by violent jerks of the entire body they register acute distress.

It is possible to show that this reaction is not the result of a passing, cantankerous mood, because these same babies will respond in the same manner repeatedly, day or night. . . . They seem to be affected more acutely by the disturbing things in their routine, as though they were more aware of themselves as individuals. They lie poised like hair triggers and demonstrate the startle reflex even when we roll them over gently in bed. We might say that the violent or hair-trigger reactors were "more" babies, as far as their infant behavior is concerned. The term "sparklers" has seemed to describe them quite accurately to me [1954, pp. 49-50].

Undoubtedly, more than energy level is involved in these behavioral differences; we must also consider such factors as strength, size, sensitivity, and impulsivity. On the basis of his thorough studies of general motility in the newborn over twenty-four-hour periods, Irwin (1930, 1932a, 1932b) concluded that the amount of activity was related, in large part, to events in the alimentary tract. This theory explains both variations from one time to another in the same infant and differences among infants at any one time. From the beginning, biological characteristics give direction and substance to the individual's reactions to environmental stimulation. Differences in biological characteristics give rise to differences in reactions to such stimulation.

Whether these constitutional predispositions manifest themselves and how they do so depend to a great extent upon whether environmental circumstances are demanding, encouraging, permitting, neutral, discouraging, or prohibiting of a given response or response pattern. A high-energy-level child with a restrictive parent will respond differently from one with a permissive parent. A low-energy-level child with an inhibiting mother will probably be more passive than one with a challenging mother. A "sparkler" can be extinguished; a "dim light" can be stimulated to respond with greater vigor and intensity.

To emphasize the importance of constitutional predispositions is not to depreciate environmental factors. We may be able to identify the predisposition. We cannot accurately and fully predict its manifestation without a knowledge of the environmental conditions under which it takes place.

There is a third and quite different way in which constitutional factors exert an influence: by the expectations they produce and the demands they make on other individuals. Wishik has presented a striking example of the latter type of influence in his description of burping positions in the feeding of infants:

> Now what do I mean by the "burping positions"? The purpose of the burp is to get up the air in the stomach when there are milk and air in the stomach together. Naturally the air is lighter and rises to the top of the stomach in the form of a bubble. In the upper side of the stomach there is an opening into the tube which connects the stomach with the throat. In order for a bubble to come up easily, it has to be located just at that upper opening [Fig. 3-3a].
> Most babies have the bubble at this favorable position when the baby is held upright over the mother's shoulder. Not all babies' stomachs are the same, however, as the diagrams show. A baby may have a stomach that is shaped in such a fashion

that the bubble rises to one side of the opening instead of straddling it [Fig. 3-3b]. If this baby is held in the usual position, the bubble will rise into a sort of pocket and will not be able to get out. But if this baby is tilted in a different position, as in the drawing [Fig. 3-3c], then the bubble will straddle the opening and will come out more easily when the baby burps [1955, pp. 44-45].

FIGURE 3-3a.   FIGURE 3-3b.   FIGURE 3-3c.

(Drawings by Alvin Pimsler, from S. M. Wishik. *Feeding Your Child,* Doubleday, 1955, p. 45)

Obviously, differences in constitutional characteristics of structure may require differences in maternal handling (see Fig. 3-4). So may differences in biological function. In their study of early phases of personality development, Escalona, Leitch, and others report that "mothers' feelings toward their infants, and their management of them, is in part a function of what the infants are actually like" (1952, p. 24). They ask the question: "Do mothers of active and robust infants choose child-rearing methods characteristically different from those chosen by the mothers of sensitive, physically fragile infants?" (p. 23). "Goodness of mothering" involves the skill and intelligence of the mother, but it also depends upon the constitution of a particular child. With some children, it may be easy to be a "good" mother; with others, it may be difficult, even impossible.

FIGURE 3-4. Babies vary in the position in which they burp most easily.

(Drawings by Pimsler, from Wishik, *op. cit.*, p. 46)

The influence of infant constitutions further complicates the parent-child relationship. But, in this age of emphasis upon the effects of child-rearing practices on the development of the child, it may be of some reassurance to mothers (and to all those who like to think that even infants are human beings) to note that the influence is not all in one direction. Perhaps we shall some day study the effects of child rearing upon maternal personality.

An individual's constitution, as manifested in his appearance and behavior, elicits reactions in other persons. Differences in constitution elicit differential reactions in other individuals. The nature of those reactions, of course, depends partly upon the values and beliefs of the other individuals. If one believes that red-haired individuals tend to have a "temper," then one expects a particular redhead to be quick to anger.

We have a tendency to expect an individual who achieves adult physical proportions relatively early in his growth period to behave in accordance with his size rather than his years. Conversely, scarcely anyone is surprised to find a slow-growing youngster behaving somewhat childishly for his age. The impact of constitutional characteristics upon the expectations of others explains—in part, at least—the significant differences in behavior and personality found by Mary Cover Jones and Bayley (1950) between early- and late-maturing boys at seventeen years of age. The finding that there were similar personality differences among the same individuals at thirty-three years of age, some sixteen years later, although differences in physical size and maturity had virtually disappeared by then and could therefore no longer be immediately responsible for the differences observed, demonstrates the potency and persistence of the influence of constitutional differences in rate of maturation (M. C. Jones, 1957).

The importance of rate of maturation as an influence upon behavioral and personality development is further demonstrated by the report that, for the men in the Oakland Growth Study, skeletal maturing in adolescence was a better predictor of occupational success and leadership activities in adulthood than were measures of leadership and social behavior at earlier ages (H. E. Jones, 1958). Such findings suggest that even those who are exclusively concerned with behavioral development cannot ignore biological variables.

Sex is a constitutional characteristic which has both a direct and an indirect influence. Interestingly enough, the two types of influence may be in contradiction. For example, as we have already noted, the male is somewhat more reactive than the female; yet in many societies, including the United States, he is expected, as a male, to be somewhat less emotional and expressive. In most cases, however, the two influences are congruent. In general, the greater strength and size of males, together with their greater reactivity, predispose them to be more overt, more energetic, and more capable of sustained activity, and also lead to expectations in other individuals that their behavior will manifest these characteristics.

The consequences of some constitutional characteristics, particularly those that affect appearance, are somewhat more capricious and unpredictable. Standards of ideal form and beauty change from time to time. Beauty in the female is defined differently today than in the 1920's; at any given time, it is defined differently in one part of the world than in another. Gentlemen may prefer blondes; whether they actually do or not depends upon the gentlemen, where they live, and the age, historically speaking. Fortunate is the girl whose particular endowment fits the spirit of her times; she will be considered a beauty. Born in another era, she may appear quite ordinary, even unattractive.

The inescapable conclusion is that constitutional characteristics play an important role in individual growth and development, sometimes prepotent, sometimes predisposing, sometimes only as they create expectations or make demands upon other individuals. That role is often quite clear in the case of relatively simple and specific aspects of growth and development. In the case of more complex psychological qualities, such as intelligence, the biological basis is still so obscure that we can only speculate about it. The problem is further complicated by the fact that the newborn child does not display intelligence as it is ordinarily defined (Irwin, 1942). "It simply possesses a repertory of motor responses, whereas intelligent behavior must await further maturation" (Pratt, 1954, p. 271). In fact, we are unable to obtain a valid measure of intelligence before the age of two or three years (see Chap. 15). But, obviously, such factors as reactivity, alertness, and sensitivity are involved in the level and quality of what we think of as intelligent behavior in older children and in adults. To the extent that these factors are constitutional and are related to the structure of the organism, particularly that of the nervous system, intelligence may be said to have some constitutional basis.

The very early manifestation of personality differences in children indicates that constitutional factors are not unimportant in this complex aspect of development. Before her twenty-five subjects reached the age of six months, Shirley (1933b) was able to differentiate among them on the basis of personality. Figure 3-5 shows four of these "real persons" as seen by those who studied them.

> 10. Every child has a characteristic way of walking. In fact, his walk may identify him for us before we can make out his face or other aspects of his appearance. What specific differences in body structure might explain these observed differences in quality of locomotion?
>
> 11. In their discussion of "sparklers," Aldrich and Aldrich write: "People are apt to call the vigorous reactors 'bad children' and the more placid ones 'good children' " (1954, p. 51). It appears that constitutional differences in energy level have both a direct and an indirect influence. Explain.
>
> 12. What constitutional differences might underlie the personality differences among the four infants shown in Figure 3-5?
>
> 13. Observe a mother's handling of her infant. What aspects of the mother's behavior seem to be in response to the infant's constitutional characteristics?
>
> 14. Inspect, in Figure 3-2 (p. 74), the "irritability scores" of the four children shown in Figure 3-5. Are these scores consistent with the personalities of these individuals?

In a dynamic society such as is found in much of Europe and North America, the individual who constitutionally is characterized by a high energy level has an advantage. The same individual would be at a disadvantage in Bali, where the way of life is static and behavior is devoid of emotional expression (M. Mead, 1954).

Nutritional deficiency may be expected to have some effect on the growth of all children, as we have previously mentioned.

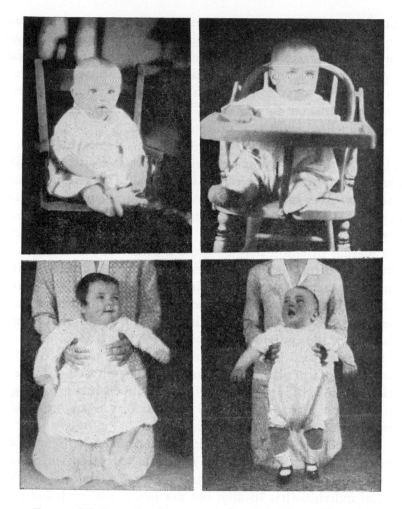

FIGURE 3-5. Four "real" persons: shy Quentin at 33 weeks (*upper left*); bored Peter at 33 weeks (*upper right*); independent Virginia Ruth at 38 weeks (*lower left*); affable James Dalton at 38 weeks (*lower right*).

(From Shirley, *op. cit.*)

The amount and persistence of that effect, however, depends not only on the nature and degree of the deficit but also on the degree of vulnerability of each individual as defined by his constitution. The "goodness" or "badness" of an environment can be assessed and its influence predicted only in terms of the constitutional characteristics of a given individual. One man's meat is another man's poison. Similarly, the significance of a given constitutional characteristic can be assessed and its consequences predicted only in terms of the environment in which and through which it is manifested.

Constitutional and environmental factors are ineluctably related. For the environment itself is determined, in a sense, by the constitutional nature of the individual. Two children may find themselves in the same physical environment. But, to the degree that they differ in constitution, their environments are psychologically different. For a very sensitive child, an overstimulating situation may be quite a problem; for an insensitive child, it may be no problem at all. A biologically passive child is no match for a domineering parent; a biologically active child is likely to try to resist such a parent. Thus we see that the nature of the environment is defined in terms of the constitution of the individual. What *he* sees, hears, feels, touches, smells, tastes—that is *his* environment. And it is in this environment that he will acquire, not only his adult physical characteristics, but also, in interactions with others, his adult psychological characteristics. Psychological individuality is an inevitable consequence of biological individuality.

How much psychological individuality results is another question. The answer depends upon the extent to which environmental circumstances permit the manifestation of biological individuality. Ideally, but not practically, each individual would have his own unique environment, designed especially for, and even perhaps by, him. Living together, as humans must and as they are predisposed to do, exacts a price in the form of some sacrifice of individuality by everyone. Each individual learns to do some things which it is not "natural" for him to do; he also learns not to do some things which it is "natural" for him to do. Men acquire tastes, values, responses, and ideas in common. They learn to perceive similarly the world in which they live, despite constitutional differences in sensory experiences, and they learn to react similarly to that world, despite differences in predisposition.

This similarity does not become identity, however; within limits, each individual persists in his efforts to construct and maintain that particular environment which best suits his particular constitution or to order any environment in which he finds himself so as to enhance its congeniality for him. He tries to mold the environment to fit him; he resists attempts to change him to fit an environment. Of course, the level and intensity of his aspirations and his resistance to change are functions, in part, of his constitution. Thus we observe again the integrity of the organism which we first considered in our discussion of homeostasis (pp. 9-10).

Perhaps this biological conservatism, derived from constitutional characteristics, explains a certain consistency over time in the behavior and personality of an individual. As the child grows up, he is exposed to variation of many types: in people, in places, in situations. But, from the standpoint of personality development, we can overemphasize the magnitude and significance of these changes and their influence upon the individual. An old French proverb is relevant: *Plus ça change, plus c'est la même chose* (The more things change, the more they remain the same). A child moves to a new community and enters a new school with adults and children who are strangers to him. How does he meet this new situation? Does he develop a new personality? Does he exhibit new responses? No. He tends to maintain previously learned behavior patterns. He carries on the same routines as before. He seeks out the same kind of friend that he had in the former community. He reconstructs the new environment, insofar as possible, in the image of the old.

We see in the child, then, a kind of psychological or behavioral conservatism which parallels or reflects his biological conservatism. He tries to maintain things as they are. Much as he may be interested in the new and unusual, he does not cut loose from the moorings of the past. He accepts and assimilates the new and the unusual only to the extent that he finds them congruent in one respect or another with the old and the familiar. He is always attempting to meet the future with the equipment of the past.

In order to change personality in any basic way, it is necessary to confront the individual with an environmental challenge which cannot be met with any past learning and which cannot be modified to resemble previously met challenges. Relatively few individuals experience discontinuities of such magnitude in their life histories. Thus, for most of us, personality, even as it develops, remains relatively constant in many of its basic aspects.

Perhaps the most spectacular example of constancy in personality lies in Neilon's demonstration (1948) that Shirley's personality sketches of twenty-five babies, based on data for the first two years, could be matched, with rather extraordinary accuracy, with sketches based on data collected on the same subjects at seventeen years of age.

15. How would you explain differences in behavior and personality among children of the same parents who have grown up in the same family environment? Do constitutional differences play any part?

16. Can you think of some instances in which two or more persons may agree in their definitions of an experience that has probably been unique for each of them?

17. How do our educational methods and materials take into account constitutional differences among children? Do they do so to a sufficient extent?

18. Confucius once said: "Men's natures are alike; it is their habits that carry them far apart." Considering our discussion of constitutional differences among children, to what extent would you agree or disagree with this statement?

19. Examine the contents of a book on infant care and training written for parents. What recognition is given to constitutional differences among babies?

From biological individuality to psychological individuality is the course of development. The interplay of constitutional and environmental factors is, indeed, complex. And, as the child grows older, we are confronted, not only with the complex interaction of constitution and environment, but also with the influence of past history—the interactions of constitution and environment that have taken place previously and have left their impress on the individual—thus making the pattern even more intricate and masking still further the influence of each contributing factor.

But, although we cannot delineate the particulars, we can be sure that they exist. We cannot hope to understand the growth and development of the individual without recognizing the influence of his biological structure and function. We cannot hope to understand differences in growth and development without recognizing the influence of constitutional differences among children.

SUGGESTED READINGS

GLUECK, SHELDON, & GLUECK, ELEANOR. *Physique and Delinquency,* Harper, 1956. A report of some of the findings from a study of five hundred delinquents and five hundred nondelinquents, indicating that different body types respond differently to the same environmental factors.

HALL, CALVIN S. The inheritance of emotionality. In William E. Martin and Celia Burns Stendler (eds.), *Readings in Child Development,* Harcourt, Brace, 1954, pp. 59-68. A constitutional basis for temperamental differences in animals is suggested by this report of a successful attempt, by means of selective breeding, to produce "emotional" and "nonemotional" rats.

SENN, MILTON J. E. (ed.). *Problems of Infancy and Childhood,* Josiah Macy, Jr., Foundation, 1953. Two discussions from the Sixth Conference on Problems of Infancy and Childhood, sponsored by the Josiah Macy, Jr., Foundation Conference Program, are related to the early manifestation of individual differences. The first, conducted by Sibylle Escalona, concerns "Emotional Development in the First Year of Life" (pp. 11-92). The second, with Katherine M. Wolf as discussion leader, is devoted to "Observation of Individual Tendencies in the First Year of Life" (pp. 97-137).

WILLIAMS, ROGER J. *Biochemical Individuality*, Wiley, 1957. A systematic treatment of the implications of biological individuality, in which the author, an eminent biochemist, defines and discusses his "genetotrophic concept," according to which each organism has unique nutritional needs that must be met if he is to grow and function with maximal efficiency and capacity.

———. *Free and Unequal: The Biological Basis of Individual Liberty*, University of Texas Press, 1953. An impassioned appeal for human individuality (and an equally impassioned attack on the concept of the "average man").

4

principles of growth and development

The child has more in common with children everywhere than the human attributes discussed in Chapter 1 and the basic drives discussed in Chapter 2. Because of his nature, the child's growth and development takes place in an orderly fashion, according to certain known principles. We know, for example, that the newborn baby will lie prone for many weeks, that little by little he will gain control of the muscles supporting his head, and that soon he will be able to lift it up, erect and steady. Slowly but surely, in the next few months he will gain control of his spine and sit up, first with and then without support. Soon his control over his body will extend to his legs; he will creep, if creeping is permitted in his society, and eventually walk. From the head downward, his development will proceed in a sequence which is predictable.

Yet there will be times when the walking baby again resorts to creeping. There will be periods in the developmental span when the child who has a vocabulary of a dozen words seems to stand still in his speech development or even to revert to an earlier babbling stage. There will be times when the child who appears to be on the brink of being toilet trained suddenly is incontinent most of the time. Repetition of behavior characteristic of an earlier stage of development is to be expected of the child as part of the growth rhythm.

These and many other things are true of children in any society. All human beings grow and develop in ways we can predict on the basis of certain principles of growth and development. It is to these principles that we shall now turn our attention.

THE CONCEPT OF
DEVELOPMENTAL DIRECTION

We can predict the direction of development in the infant in the light of two developmental trends: (*1*) growth tends to proceed in a cephalocaudal, or head-to-foot, direction; (*2*) growth tends to proceed in a proximodistal, or center-to-periphery, direction. Thus, in accordance with the first principle, the head develops weeks in advance of the lower extremities in prenatal life; arm buds form before leg buds. After the child is born, he attains control of the muscles which hold his head erect before he can sit up, and he sits up before he can walk. Both growth and function tend to follow this head-to-foot direction.

According to the second law, growth and function proceed "from near to far." From shoulder to finger tip, from hip to toes, the limbs mature, accompanied by the development of control in the same order.

These trends have been noticed in the human infant since the time of Aristotle, and they have been subjected to proof over the course of many years by experimental embryologists working with embryos of fish, birds, and infrahuman mammals. Coghill's work (1929) on the *Amblystoma,* a type of salamander, is classic in this area. From his observations, he concluded, not only that development proceeds in a head-to-foot direction, but also that early behavior is generalized and diffuse and that specific responses develop out of early mass behavior by a process of individuation. That is, the salamander does not learn control of his body by moving one part and then another before finally moving all parts together; rather, he begins with mass movements out of which specialized movements gradually emerge. Coghill reasoned that human beings develop in similar fashion. However, although the theory of head-to-foot direction in development has been widely accepted, Coghill's description of the process of individuation has not. Later investigators have indicated that development after birth consists of *both* gradual specialization of movements from mass behavior *and* a knitting together of movement patterns not previously integrated (Carmichael, 1951). Thus the child, in response to a pinprick on his arm, gradually comes to move his arm rather than his whole body; at the same time, however, he may also come to coordinate leg movements and arm movements that have not previously been integrated.

The principles associated with the concept of developmental direction have influenced our selection of the experiences and materials provided for young children in our society. Fat pencils, crayons, and paint brushes, large sheets of paper, big blocks—all of which emphasize mass movements—have replaced the peg boards and sewing cards of yesteryear, with their emphasis upon finer coordination. Much of this change in emphasis, however, is based upon an exaggerated application of developmental trends. Before his first birthday, the infant is quite capable of picking up tiny pellets and placing them in a cup; the two-year-old likes to carry pebbles or other tiny objects clutched in his palm; young Chinese children are taught to do intricate puzzles and embroidery. "Small muscle" activity does not wait for all "big muscle" activity to be perfected before it begins. We must justify activities for children on some other basis than which muscles of the body are involved; activities that require mass coordination should not be provided to the exclusion of those requiring finer coordination because of a faulty notion of how development proceeds. Big pencils and paint brushes are good for children, but for other reasons than that they furnish "big muscle" activity. Actually, it is during the early years of the child's life that we see the cephalocaudal and proximodistal trends most clearly illustrated. The nursery-school and elementary teacher will be more concerned with other concepts of development, treated below.

THE CONCEPT OF MATURATION

An infant lying on his back and moving from side to side one day achieves the ultimate: he turns completely over. A few months later he raises himself from a kneeling position to completely upright posture, using a nearby object for support. Still later there comes the day when he abandons all support and strikes out on his own for the first time, with a few halting steps. In our society, he may sit in his baby swing while his mother or the wind pushes him gently to and fro. Eventually he graduates to a regular swing, but he still must be pushed because he hasn't learned the art of pumping. He practices daily, and finally legs and arms and back and head all coordinate and he is able to move the swing by his own power.

What is at work here? Those who have had daily association with children know that these new skills which appear are not the result of direct teaching. Few if any parents attempt direct instruction in the method of walking; they may take the baby's hands and let him practice the skill with their support, but they do not say, "Now put one foot out, now the other," or use other words or gestures to teach walking except the force of example. When they do try to teach the child, say, swinging by giving such instructions as "Push with your legs and bend back with your back," even though the child is eager to learn and does his best to follow directions, his back, legs, and arms do not work together properly. Similarly, adults may give oral instruction on how to beat a rhythm on the tom-tom or they may demonstrate the skill, but the child, despite his desire to learn, apparently is unable to catch on and the teaching appears to be wasted.

So it is in a typical classroom situation in our society. Over and over again, the first-grade teacher patiently calls attention to the visual characteristics of the printed words "Dick" and

"Jane," yet day after day some children appear unable to distinguish between the two. Then, seemingly all of a sudden, they not only can distinguish between "Dick" and "Jane" but can make many other distinctions which they have not been taught.

The Meaning of Maturation

The concept of maturation has been developed to explain the appearance of those phenomena which do not seem to be influenced by direct teaching but rather seem to be the product of an innate process of growth. When we see certain abilities appear without benefit of training, when we observe new behaviors before the organism is mature enough for habit formation to take place, when we note the same behavior patterns emerging in all children, it becomes clear that some internal mechanism must be at work. This is not to say that there is a particular part of the organism that decides when it is time for a particular child to get up on his two legs and walk, but rather that certain structural changes, influenced chiefly by inheritance, must occur before a certain behavior can appear. The term "maturation" is used to describe those structural changes involving the coordination of numerous relationships within the neural system. The principle that has emerged to explain phenomena which seem to result from an innate process is that maturation is essential to learning.

Maturation and Learning

The maturation-learning area is a controversial one. Some writers contend that environment has no influence at all upon maturation. Gesell, for example, distinguishes between those traits which are constitutional and which develop through the process of maturation, and those which are social and are acquired through the process of acculturation. "Environmental factors support, inflect, and modify; but they do not generate the progressions of development. . . . The glove goes on the hand; the hand determines the glove." Acculturation can never transcend maturation (1954, p. 358).

Other writers, including Carmichael in his earlier works,

have taken the position that "from the moment growth has begun in the fertilized ovum until senescence or death, development consists in the alteration of existing structures and functions in an organism living in a continually changing environment. That is, it is not possible . . . to say at any point that growth has stopped and learning has begun . . . the environment plays a part in all 'maturation' and maturation plays a part in all learning" (McGraw, 1946, p. 338).

An illustration at this point may clarify the two positions. Six-year-old Jack receives a new two-wheeler for his birthday. His father takes him out and runs around the block holding onto the bike, so that Jack can "get the hang" of it. Jack doesn't, and the tired father has to give up. Every day for a week he has a practice session with Jack, but the boy is unable to ride the bike. The father abandons the job of teaching Jack and Jack temporarily abandons the bike. Two months later, Jack gets out the bike and, without further coaching or help, manages to mount the wheel and ride off.

According to the Gesell position, what was operating in Jack's case was a ripening of the organism, involving the coordination of many different relationships within the neural system. According to the Carmichael position, we would have to ask whether the ripening was due only to the kind of genes with which Jack was born. To what extent did his previous experiences with baby walker, tricycle, and scooter affect structure? To what extent did his parents' expectancy and encouragement of gross motor ability influence his choice of activities and, in turn, affect structure? To shed light on these questions, we turn to the studies which have been done on the problem of maturation and learning.

THE EFFECTS OF PRACTICE. One approach to the problem of maturation and learning has been to attempt to determine whether intensive training can speed up the appearance of a skill or can appreciably improve performance. Gesell and Thompson (1929) worked with a pair of identical twins, forty-six weeks old, who were on the threshold of stair-climbing and cube-building behavior. Twin T was given a ten-minute training period each day for eight weeks on stair climbing and cube building. Six weeks after Twin T's training had begun, Twin C was given a two-week training session covering the same activities. After two weeks of work, Twin C's performance was as good as her sister's, although her sister had had the benefit of six additional weeks of instruction and practice. The authors concluded that training does not hasten such activities as stair climbing and cube building but that the time of their appearance is determined by the ripeness of the neural structures.

We do not know the exact nature of the changes occurring within the neural system as the organism matures. We do know that the cells of the nervous system, by a process of differentiation, form a multitude of neuron types, each with a highly specialized function to perform. Because they are specialized in function, their advancing tips form synapses only with certain other of the neurons that they encounter in their outgrowth. Then there follows an orderly assembling of various nerve cells into appropriate patterns, making it possible for the infant to lift his head, turn over on one side, or perform some other new behavior. The basic patterns of synaptic association which build up throughout the nervous system are dependent upon innate forces and not upon learning (Sperry, 1951).

J. R. Hilgard's findings (1932) support the maturational thesis, but she adds a qualifying phrase. She experimented with two groups of ten children each in a nursery-school situation. The experimental group was given twelve weeks of practice in buttoning, cutting with scissors, and climbing; then the control group was given four days of practice in the same three skills. Before the experiment began, there were no reliable differences between the groups. Thirteen weeks later, after the practice group had had twelve weeks of practice and the control group less than one week, the two groups were equally proficient. Hilgard concludes that "factors other than specific training contributed to the development of these three skills, factors which may be partly accounted for by maturation and partly by general practice in related skills."

Two studies by McGraw need to be mentioned here. One is her famous study of fraternal twin boys, Johnny and Jimmy (1935). Johnny was given extensive practice at a tender age in crawling and standing and in climbing, skating, and swimming; Jimmy was not. Johnny was taught to swim when he was less than a year old; tricycling practice was begun at eleven months, and roller skating at slightly less than a year of age. Jimmy's practice periods began at twenty-two months and lasted for two and a half months. McGraw's findings, while unfortunately marred because the twins turned out to be fraternal rather than identical, indicate that there are critical periods for learning skills which are dependent upon maturation. Johnny, trained in roller skating at eleven months, was a skilled skater at sixteen months; no improvement was noted in tricycling until he was nineteen months old, some eight months after practice had begun. Jimmy, at twenty-four and a half months, after two and a half months of practice, was still not so good at roller skating as his brother, perhaps because fear of falling is greater in a two-year-old than in a twelve-month-old infant. He learned trike riding, however, in a shorter time than his brother. In other words, speeding up the learning of roller skating was apparently effective, but speeding up the learning of trike riding was not; in fact, it may even have been detrimental, for Johnny apparently suffered from his long and futile practice periods. Although maturation is a basic factor, according to McGraw, other factors, such as the child's attitude, appear to influence learning.

> 1. Observe a group of kindergarten children in running and skipping activities. Disregarding the maturational factor, what experiences might account for the individual differences you observe?
> 2. Parents are frequently concerned about the question of when a child should begin piano lessons. List some of the factors that should be taken into account in reaching a decision for a particular child.

McGraw's experimental work on toilet training (1940) contributes additional evidence of a maturational factor. Two sets of identical male twins were studied to see whether systematic toilet training could speed up development. During the second month of life, one member of each pair of twins was placed on the chamber at hourly intervals for seven hours of the day. The others were started at fourteen and twenty-four months of age, respectively. At twenty-eight months, the achievement of the boys who were trained late approximated that of their brothers. McGraw concludes that toilet training should be delayed until the child's behavior indicates that he has conscious control over the muscles which regulate micturition.

THE EFFECTS OF RESTRICTING ACTIVITY. A different approach to the study of maturation has been to restrict activities beyond the supposed ripening period. Here the problem is to see what happens to a particular skill when restrictions are imposed during the period of normal maturation. The Dennises conducted a study of fraternal twins to see the effects of restriction upon sitting alone, standing with support, and reaching for a dangling object (Dennis, 1941). The twins were confined to their cribs until the thirty-sixth week and continued to spend most of the day there until the fifty-second week. Some kinds of behavior, such as smiling and vocalization, raising the head when on the back, and turning toward one side while supine, appeared without any stimulus, lending support to the maturation theory. Reaching, sitting, and standing did not appear at the "normal" time. As the author points out, most parents prop their babies up with pillows before they can sit up; the environment supports neural ripening. However, when training was instituted, these forms of behavior developed quickly According to these specialists, environment can influence the rate of development, but only within the limits set by heredity.

The Hopi Indians are frequently cited as another example of restriction of activity (Dennis, 1940). The Hopi child is bound to a board, with only its head free to move, all day from birth until three months of age, and part of the day after that. Despite these restrictions, when the infant is free, he exhibits the same kinds of behavior as unrestricted infants, and his fundamental development is not significantly different.

Some of the most interesting evidence bearing on the effects of restriction comes from experimental work on animals. This evidence tends to show that when some subjects are *visually* restricted early in life, certain behaviors which might normally appear in the developmental timetable either are delayed in appearance or do not appear at all. In one investigation, chicks were reared in darkness, fed artificially from a spoon for two weeks, and then placed in the light. Once in the light, even though they were given plenty of food and grit for pecking, these chicks did not develop the pecking response and consequently starved surrounded by food. Other birds, whose stimulation to peck apparently was touched off by other signs, were more fortunate; pecking appeared in ringdoves reared in darkness after only a brief delay (Beach & Jaynes, 1954).

Restricting early visual experiences also has an important influence upon the appearance of certain behaviors in chimpanzees. In one experiment (Riesen, 1949), chimps were reared in darkness for the first sixteen months. When first brought into the light, they were roughly equivalent in behavior to newborn animals. Even after six months, their perceptions were immature as compared with those of normally reared chimps of the same age. They did not blink when threatened with a blow in the face, and they made no effort to grasp a feeding bottle extended to them. Apparently, visual perception in the chimp is something that depends not on neural ripening alone but on early experiences as well.

Restricting tactile experiences also has an influence upon later development. A chimpanzee was reared with his hands and feet encased in mailing tubes so that manual exploration was prevented (see Fig. 4-1). When the tubes were removed, the grooming behaviors which typically appear in normally reared chimps were not in evidence. Also, the ape showed forced grasping, which normally disappears in chimps during the first postnatal month (Nissen *et al.*, 1951).

Although studies of animals suggest that restricting activity may delay or prevent the appearance of behaviors which nor-

FIGURE 4-1. Rob's sitting posture at 31 months, cylinders in place. What kinds of perceptual experience are possible for Rob? What kinds are not?

(From H. W. Nissen *et al.* Effects of restricted opportunity for tactual, kinesthetic, and manipulative experience on the behavior of a chimpanzee. *Amer. J. Psychol.,* 1951, *64,* 488)

mally appear as part of the maturation process, studies of human infants tend to minimize the effects of restricting activity. One explanation for this apparent inconsistency may be that the particular stimulus which sparks a particular response has yet to be located for certain behaviors. It has been found, for example, that the pecking response can be produced in the herring gull by presenting the proper stimulus. The herring-gull chick, shortly after being hatched, pecks at the parent's bill tip and so receives food from the parent's bill (see Fig. 4-2). This response can be released in chicks hatched in an incubator merely by showing them something red. Apparently, the red spot on the parent's bill tip is the stimulus that releases this response (Tinbergen, 1953).

FIGURE 4-2. A herring-gull chick pecking at its parent's bill tip. The red patch on the bill tip, because of its color and its contrast with the rest of the bill, acts as a stimulus to the pecking response.

(From N. Tinbergen. *Social Behaviour in Animals,* London, Methuen, 1953, p. 78)

We know from the Dennises' research that the human infant does not need to see another human being smile in order for the smile response to appear. We know, then, that a smiling adult is not the stimulus for this response, but we do not know whether some other stimulus is necessary. When we talk about restricting activity, we must be careful in making claims that a particular response appears without any environmental stimulation. It may be that in our experiments we simply have not restricted the kind of stimulus that triggers the response we are studying.

Although there are inconsistencies in these studies of intensive training and restricting of activity, they lead us to certain conclusions. They illustrate the difficulty of separating the maturational factor from learning after birth. But they also show that an innate factor is at work which determines whether or not a certain learning is neurally possible. However, it should be pointed out that without environmental stimulus, certain kinds of behavior for which the organism is ripe may not appear. Thus the twins in the Dennis experiment did not sit up at the time when the organism is usually mature enough for sitting; a sitting posture was achieved only after a training period had been inaugurated. Our conclusion is that maturation is essential to learning, but that proper environmental conditions will ensure the development of those kinds of behavior for which the organism is ripe.

As children grow older, it becomes increasingly difficult to separate out the influence of the maturational factor upon development, for the child's environment and previous experiences more and more determine what and whether he will learn. An older girl in Samoan society learns to weave intricate fish baskets, but her skill is only partly dependent upon neural ripening; it is also partly dependent upon the fact that she has had many weaving experiences before she tackles a fish basket. A child in the first grade in an American school learns to read, but this learning depends not only on his being "mature" enough, but also on his having enough native intelligence plus previous experiences with words as symbols, plus a desire to learn to read. This has certain implications for the kinds of experience we provide for children prior to basket weaving or reading, or any other learning which is dependent partly upon new learning and partly upon prior experience. The good teacher in Samoan society or in an American school will not wait for certain behaviors to spring full-blown from the child but, rather, will attempt to provide experiences suited to each child's level of development. In Samoan society she will see that the child has had successful weaving experiences at a simpler level before introducing basket weaving; in American society she will plan activities that will provide the necessary foundation for learning to read. A good teacher will not introduce intricate basket weaving before the child has mastered the preliminary steps, for the resulting failure on the child's part will negatively affect his future attempts at basket weaving. Nor will a good teacher keep the child too long in the beginning stages of reading, for the child may be so "mature" that he becomes bored with the process and loses his motivation.

Maturation and Developmental Sequence

Still another principle stemming from the concept of maturation is that *development follows a sequence.* This principle is readily apparent in such areas as motor development; it is obvious that the child sits before he stands and stands before he walks. The step-by-step progress of the child in this area has been carefully studied and described in minute detail, as Table 4-1 shows. But it is not so simple to describe a sequence due to maturation in other areas.

Consider, for example, so complex an area as causal thinking. As children mature, do they go through progressively higher stages in ascribing reasons to certain phenomena? On the basis of innate development, can we expect the older child to give a more satisfactory explanation of, for example, why he sees himself in a mirror?

Early evidence favored the maturational factor, indicating that, merely in the process of growing older, children learn to give better answers. Piaget (1929), for example, originally described seventeen levels of causal thought and theorized that causal thinking evolves steadily from level to level. According to him, the preschool child, when asked to explain why a pebble thrown into water sinks to the bottom, will give an explanation in terms of phenomenalistic causality; that is, he will answer that the pebble sinks because it is white. The child has no true conception of the relationship between pebble and water; he saw that pebble and whiteness occurred together and so he explains one in terms of the other. Older children, according to Piaget, give more mechanistic and logical explanations.

Table 4-1

The California Infant Scale of Motor Development *

Test Items	Age (in months)
Head erect—vertical	1.9
Head erect and steady	2.9
Turns from side to back	3.4
Sits with support	3.5
Holds head steady	3.6
Beginning thumb opposition	4.1
Sits with slight support	4.6
Turns from back to side	5.0
Partial thumb opposition	5.1
Sits alone momentarily	5.7
Pulls to sitting position	6.2
Rolls from back to stomach	7.0
Complete thumb opposition	7.6
Partial finger prehension	7.8
Sits alone with good coordination	8.5
Fine prehension with pellet	9.3
Raises self to sitting position	9.4
Pulls to standing position	10.5
Stands up	10.6
Walks with help	11.6
Sits down	12.5
Stands alone	12.5
Walks alone	13.0
Walks upstairs with help	20.3
Walks downstairs with help	20.5
Walks upstairs alone; marks time	24.3
Walks downstairs alone; marks time	24.5
Jumps off floor; both feet	28.0

* From N. Bayley. The development of motor abilities during the first three years. *Monogr. Soc. Res. Child Develpm.,* 1935, *1*:1, 3. By permission of the publisher, Society for Research in Child Development, Purdue University, and of the author.

Later work in this same area, however, raises questions regarding Piaget's conclusions. In an experimental situation (Deutsche, 1937), children ranging in age from eight to sixteen years were asked to explain why a lighted candle goes out when a jar is placed over it, how it is that one can see oneself in a mirror, and similar phenomena. Contrary to Piaget, Deutsche found that children's thinking did not proceed in developmental stages. She found examples of "magical thinking" even at the oldest age levels. Although phenomenalistic explanations decreased and mechanistic explanations increased with age, Deutsche's outstanding finding was that there was a great deal of overlapping at all age levels. Most types of answers were found over the entire age range and no kind of answer was found at but a single age.

Perhaps the safest conclusion we can draw from the evidence is that there is an orderly and predictable sequence which is followed in the development of phylogenetic skills—that is, those skills that the child must acquire as a member of the human race. All children will learn to sit, to stand, and to walk, and in doing so will follow approximately the same sequence. But, in areas as strongly influenced by the culture as causal thinking, it seems unlikely that sequence in development can be attributed to the maturational factor alone. When children are not exposed to experiences that will help them to move to a higher level of development, progress does not occur.

THE DEVELOPMENTAL SPIRAL

As a result of their findings, Gesell and Ilg (1943) have developed a concept related to the maturational factor and allowing for both upward and downward gradients. The mechanical model used to illustrate this concept is the spiral. According to Gesell and Ilg, development proceeds, not in a slanting line which goes onward and upward, but, rather, in spiral fashion: The child makes progress upward in a particular line of development only to revert downward to an earlier stage of development before going upward again to a new and higher level. Plateaus on the spiral may occur at either the upward or the downward gradient.

The spiral helps to explain certain behaviors which we can observe in the child. Observation of infants' feeding behavior indicates, as we have previously pointed out, that the time between feedings gradually increases and that night feedings gradually disappear. However, at the point at which it appears that an infant has almost completed the adjustment to sleeping all night, he may revert to an earlier way of behaving and wake up regularly at 2 A.M. Following this downward gradient in the feeding spiral, he may then move upward to a higher level of adjustment and sleep peacefully through night after night. The same thing is true with regard to walking. Shortly after the onset of this skill, the young baby may revert to creeping and do little or no walking before proceeding to a higher level of development, walking almost to the exclusion of creeping.

Gesell and Ilg attribute the downward gradient to internal forces which operate to give the organism a chance to consolidate gains. It differs from regression in the psychiatric sense (see pp. 228-29) in that it does not represent a return to an earlier mode of adjustment because of a failure to conquer reality problems. Rather, it is an important and necessary part of development because it enables the child, by repeating behavior characteristic of a previous stage, to build up enough strength to forge upward to higher levels of achievement.

THE INTERRELATEDNESS OF
VARIOUS FORMS OF DEVELOPMENT

A Salteaux Indian regains his physical well-being after he has publicly confessed to a sin. A six-year-old child who has been complaining about his substitute teacher loses his breakfast before going off to school and begs to stay home for the day. A frightened ten-year-old comes in for an intelligence test and the examiner reports that she can give no accurate picture of the boy's intelligence; in her judgment his test score is much lower than it should be. A kidney ailment sends the blood pressure up and the sufferer is excitable and short-tempered.

These are examples of how one's physical well-being and intellectual functioning can be affected by one's emotions and how, conversely, one's emotional behavior can be affected by one's physical well-being. They are commonplace incidents presented to illustrate the principle that all forms of development are interrelated. This principle seems so obvious that the reader may wonder why it should even be mentioned. Yet much of the thinking in the past with regard to how children develop has not taken full account of it.

Part of the difficulty is that our research on children has focused on separate areas, such as "physical development," "mental development," "emotional development," and the like. Each area of development has been studied without reference to other areas. Consequently, we have little evidence on how development in one area affects development in others.

Part of the difficulty, too, lies in the fact that it has been fashionable to place the blame for all irregularities in behavior first in one area of development and then in another. In the 1930's, for example, it was common practice to relate the behavior difficulties of American children to a physical cause. Thus, if a child of normal intelligence could not learn to read, his tonsils were to blame; if he indulged in temper tantrums, it was because he needed a tonic; if he developed a tic, involuntarily blinking his eyes all the time, this was an indication that he should wear glasses; if a girl didn't have any dates, it was because of halitosis. In the 1940's, on the other hand, all behavior was explained in terms of the emotions. Thus, a listless, daydreaming child was so because he was jealous of his baby brother; a child's many attacks of tonsillitis were caused by his anxiety over being separated from his mother; a boy's poor coordination on the baseball field was a sign that his aggression was directed against himself.

Both the approach that treats each area of development separately and the approach that explains behavior always in terms of one area would seem to be faulty. A sounder approach to explaining behavior would be one which recognized the possibility of interrelationships among various areas of development and acknowledged that the interrelationships might shift from time to time.

Emotional Development and Physical Well-being

From the field of psychosomatic medicine come some illustrations of relationships between physical well-being and the
emotions which indicate that one's health can be affected by
one's emotional state and vice versa. Indeed, extremists in psychosomatic medicine would attribute all forms of sickness to the
emotions. It may be that, as we learn more about the chemistry
of the human body, we will find more relationships than are
admitted at the present time. Today, such ailments as tics,
eczema, asthma, constipation, and enuresis are generally recognized as frequently psychosomatic in origin. Tics, for example,
may develop in children because of tensions which they cannot
master in any integrated form and so express through the muscular system. Studies of children with tics have shown that such
children, while outwardly controlled—indeed, rigid—in their
behavior, often have a deep underlying resentment or hostility toward adults. Because they dare not release their tension
through aggression, it is discharged through motor movement.
(Gerard, 1946).

But while we recognize the importance of the emotions as
a basis of physical ailments, we also recognize that physical well-
being may influence emotional development. Take, for example,
a sixteen-year-old boy whose sex organs are retarded in their
growth. It is difficult to say whether the original hormone deficiency stemmed from some unknown physiological phenomenon or was due to an identification dilemma; that is, whether
the boy's system failed to generate the proper amount of hormones for physiological reasons or because he did not want to
be a man and consequently was unable to think and act like a
man. Hormonal treatments are used to speed up the development of his sex organs and he begins to look, talk, and act more
like a man. And because he looks, talks, and acts in a more
mannish fashion, he is not so anxious about himself and his
emotional outlook improves. Mind influences body, but body
also influences mind.

From one point of view, all serious illnesses of childhood

are "psychosomatic" in that they affect the emotional well-being of the child. A growing boy who has rheumatic fever which necessitates a long convalescence and leaves him with a damaged heart is likely to be affected psychologically. Illnesses which impose continuing restriction of activity, and which result in overanxiety on the part of the parents, may bring out feelings of self-depreciation on the part of the sufferer and anxiety in competitive relations with other children (Mohr, 1948).

Motor and Social Development

From a different context comes other evidence of interrelationships, this time between motor and social development. The problem for study was to see whether a child's social behavior might change as a result of building up skill in a motor area. Can we reasonably expect, for example, that an Indian boy who masters an intricate dance step will differ in his social behavior in subsequent dance ceremonies as a result of this learning? Will a fifth-grader whose baseball-playing skills are deficient improve in his social adjustment if he is trained to be proficient in baseball? To answer this kind of question, five young children in an American nursery school were taught certain competencies. These children, the least ascendant in their dealings with others, were given special training in fitting mosaic blocks together to form a design, putting together a picture puzzle, and telling a story. Then the children were paired with others in situations in which these skills might be observed. The five children showed a significant change in their behavior in the direction of asserting themselves, giving directions, and otherwise being more ascendant (Jack, 1934).

The study rightly does not attempt to claim radical changes in every phase of the children's social development; changes took place only in those areas in which training had been given. It does, however, help to illustrate how a vicious cycle can be broken. An adolescent who finds social contacts with the opposite sex difficult and who is also a poor dancer is made more insecure upon the occasion of a school dance; learning to dance expertly may help him to overcome his insecurity with girls, at least on the dance floor. Classroom teachers have frequently made use of the principle of interrelatedness in trying to build up a child's strength in a physical or intellectual area in order to help him socially and emotionally.

Erikson (1950) has attempted to explain, in his discussion of ego-identity, the manner in which physical and emotional development come to be related. He points out that mastery of a skill such as walking helps to make the child a part of his culture; the child becomes "one who can walk" and acquires a cultural status different from that of one who cannot walk. Physical mastery of walking plus the resulting cultural recognition contribute to the child's self-esteem. Parents and teachers have noted a similar increase in self-esteem on the part of children as the result of mastering physical or intellectual skills which have cultural value. Becoming "one who can ride a two-wheeled bicycle" or "one who can throw a spear" or "one who can read" brings with it cultural approval and affects emotional well-being in a positive manner.

Interrelationships between the physical and the social or emotional areas are more dependent upon the society in which one lives than upon one's physiology. We should expect a person with an overactive thyroid to be continually working and highly excitable. But some aspects of physical development affect social and emotional development because of the *meaning* this physical development comes to have in a particular society. Consider the case of Ben, who was carefully and thoroughly studied from the time he was in fifth grade through the adolescent period (Stolz & Stolz, 1951). Ben was precocious in his physical development, big and fast growing. This tended to make his parents and teachers expect much more of him in the way of performance than they would have if he had been small and slow growing. His precocity in one area established a role which he struggled to achieve. There were times during the adolescent period when he could not measure up either to the goals he set for himself or to the expectations of adults. During such times, his social and emotional behavior was adversely affected; when he made progress toward his goals and those of others, he was a better

integrated individual. Had Ben been reared in a different society, however, in which expectancies for children were based
on factors other than how grown-up they looked, his physical
development might have affected his social and emotional development in quite different ways.

INDIVIDUAL PATTERNS OF GROWTH AND DEVELOPMENT

Rate of Maturation

Every society abounds with illustrations of individual
differences in rate and pattern of growth. These are clearly
discernible in public school classrooms in our society, where
children are grouped according to age. Indeed, as the kindergarten or high school teacher surveys his group, differences
among the children may appear to be greater than similarities.
Five-year-old George, a big, husky youngster who is forty-six
inches tall and weighs sixty-two pounds, already the proud possessor of three permanent teeth, sits beside his pal Ray, also
aged five. Ray is a slight child who measures only thirty-eight
inches and weighs forty pounds. His deciduous teeth are still
firm in his mouth, and it will be more than a year before he
loses his first baby tooth. George is a "fast-growing" child as
compared with Ray, a "slow-growing" child.

A group of young girls, members of a primitive tribe, are
working together. One is a mature, buxom youngster of thirteen
who first menstruated at nine years of age and is now in the
later adolescent period. Another girl of the same chronological
age is a slight, immature-looking child who has not yet entered
puberty. The first is already a woman, accelerated by four years
in menarcheal age as compared with the second girl.

But not all children maintain the same rate of growth
throughout their childhood and adolescence. Indeed, Bayley
(1956b) has stated that it is a rare child whose growth pattern
is entirely stable. In the Berkeley Growth Studies, norms of
development based upon averages of healthy children were set

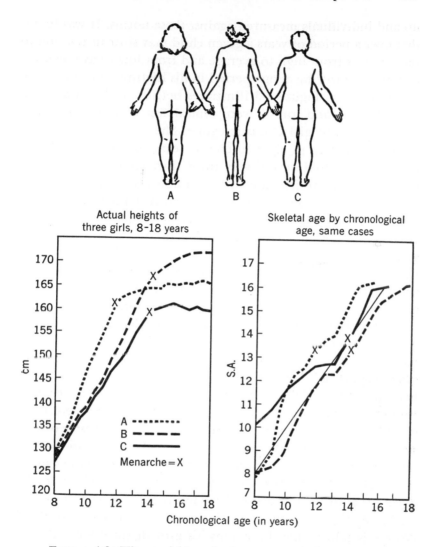

FIGURE 4-3. Three girls, each shown at age 18, who matured differently. A's growth was accelerated; B's was retarded; C's was irregular. Curves of height are shown at lower left; at lower right, skeletal ages according to chronological ages are plotted for the same cases. Age at menarche for each girl is indicated by an X.

(From N. Bayley. Individual patterns of development. *Child Develpm.*, 1956, 27, 52) up and individuals measured against these norms. It was found that over a period of years a given child may shift in relation to these norms from high to average and from low to average. He may be fast growing at one period in his lifetime but slow growing at another. Figure 4-3 illustrates both typical and atypical cases. Girl A and girl B were typical fast and slow growers, respectively, but girl C was irregular. She was very accelerated in skeletal age from eight to eleven years, as the graph shows, but then matured very slowly until thirteen years, when her growth once more fell into line with norms of development.

These variations in individual growth patterns are better understood in the light of the factors that control growth. During the childhood years, the functioning of the pituitary gland is of the greatest influence. Between ages eight and eleven, the release of hormones from the gonads stimulates fresh growth activity (Goldberg, 1955). These factors may vary in intensity and timing, with corresponding changes in rate of growth.

Observations such as these are of more than casual interest. Knowing a child to be fast growing or slow growing enables us to make certain predictions about him. All children have a growth spurt before entering adolescence, but George will have his spurt at an earlier age than will Ray. George, however, will stop growing before Ray does, for fast growers complete their growth at an earlier age. (See Fig. 4-4 for a comparison of two such children.) Whether George will exceed Ray in height, however, depends not so much upon his rate of growth as upon the height of his parents. George, as a fast-growing child, might reach his adult height before Ray, but if Ray comes from taller stock, he might eventually catch up with or surpass George. If George is taller when he begins his growth spurt than Ray is when he begins his, chances are that George will be taller as an adult; for there is a high correlation between the height of boys at the onset and at the end of the puberal period.

Rate of Maturation and Other Aspects of Growth

Rate of maturation and certain types of body build appear to be related (Bayley, 1943). The child who is a fast grower is likely to be broadly built, large, and strong, whereas the slow grower is likely to be slender, long-legged, weak-muscled, and small. The fast grower is also more likely to reach his maximal

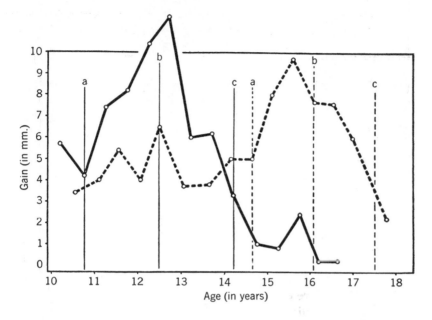

FIGURE 4-4. Height-growth curves for two boys, illustrating early and late development. The beginning, midpoint, and end of each boy's period of puberal growth are indicated by the vertical lines labelled, respectively, *a*, *b*, and *c*. Case 216 (*solid lines*) was one of the most precocious in beginning and ending the puberal growth period. Case 130 (*broken lines*) was the most delayed of the 67 cases studied.

(From H. R. Stolz & L. M. Stolz. *Somatic Development of Adolescent Boys*, Macmillan, 1951, p. 61)

height at an early age; the slow grower will probably continue growing for a longer period of time.

Figure 4-5 shows typical examples of a physically retarded and a physically accelerated boy. The two figures at the left show a slow-growing boy at age thirteen and again at age seventeen.

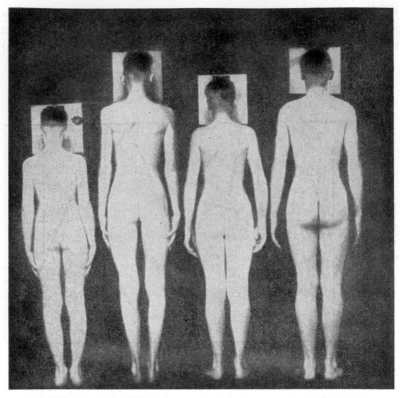

A 13.1 yrs.   A 17.1 yrs.   B 13.2 yrs.   B 17.2 yrs.

FIGURE 4-5. A comparison of two boys who differ in skeletal maturity. At age 13, the late-growing boy (A) is slender in build and much shorter than the husky accelerated boy (B) at the same age. Note that the late grower at age 17 is slightly taller than the accelerated boy at the same age.

(From N. Bayley. Size and body build of adolescents in relation to rate of skeletal maturing. *Child Develpm.*, 1943, *14*, 81)

Note that at age thirteen he reaches only to the shoulder of his seventeen-year-old height. The two figures at the right are of a fast-growing boy at ages thirteen and seventeen, respectively. Note that this boy has almost attained his maximal growth at the age of thirteen. Note also that the "little" boy of thirteen is a bit taller at age seventeen than his formerly "big" contemporary. Differences in body proportions are also evident in the photographs. The slow grower at age seventeen has more of his height in his legs; the fast grower at seventeen is actually shorter than the other boy, but his sitting height is greater.

Possible relationships between rate of maturation and behavior have been explored in an interesting study by M. C. Jones and Bayley (1950). These authors compared two groups of boys who were of the same average chronological age but two years apart in skeletal age. The fast-growing boys were significantly different from the slow growers in a number of ways. At the junior high and high school levels, the physically accelerated boys seemed much more mature in their behavior, presented a better appearance, were more popular, and were more apt to be leaders of their group. The slow-maturing boys were rated by their classmates as attention-seekers, restless, talkative, bossy, less good-looking, less grown-up. It should be noted that these are not traits which are highly regarded by high school students. Indeed, they reflect a childish activity pattern which most adolescents have abandoned and which they regard as undignified. The more childish behavior of the slow growers may be in part a reaction to the physical disadvantage under which they labor; their greater activity or striving for attention may be their way of counteracting the lack of status they are experiencing.

But not all slow growers are at a disadvantage, and not all fast growers have an advantage. A boy who is receiving good psychological support in the home does not suffer so much as a result of his slow growth as one who lacks this support. Some early-maturing boys have severe acne, which offsets their advantage in rapid growth. But, by and large, the findings from this study show rather clearly that physical maturing does affect behavior and that the early-maturing boy has an advantage over his late-maturing contemporary.

Whether an individual's physical rate of growth is related to other aspects of growth is not quite clear. Will the child who weighs the most and gets his second teeth earliest also learn to read most quickly? Are measures of physical growth related to mental growth? To academic achievement? Can we assume, from the principle of interrelatedness, an underlying unity for all growth?

Some findings indicate a "going togetherness" of physical growth, mental growth, and school achievement. Olson and Hughes (1943) kept longitudinal records of such items as mental capacity, reading, height, weight, strength of grip, ossification of hand and wrist, and dental eruption for a number of children. They translated their data for each child into a height age, weight age, dental age, grip age, and so on, and averaged these various ages to find what they called the "organismic age." Table 4-2 gives the data for a nine-year-old girl. Her average, or "organismic," age was eleven and a half years. Olson and Hughes point out that, although there is variation in growth within this child, the variation is not so great as that typically found within a group. They conclude that there is an underlying unity in growth which applies to intellectual as well as physical growth. According to this point of view, a child is ready to read when he has reached a certain maturity with respect to height, eruption of second teeth, and other physical factors.

Other writers have questioned the concept of organismic age. Blommers and others (1955) point out that measures of physical growth are related to mental growth and academic achievement, but in only a spurious way. Growth takes time, and during the childhood years we expect growth to occur; we expect children to grow in height, in weight, in number of teeth, in reading ability, and in many other ways. According to these writers, if we plot children's growth in yearly increments on a curve, we would expect to find relatedness because elapsed time is common to all the functions measured. These writers have also raised doubts with respect to the statistical soundness of the concept of organismic age. They found in their analysis that organismic-age scores do not constitute a meaningful basis for discriminating among children.

Furthermore, the usefulness of the concept of organismic age has been questioned. Tyler (1953) doubts that an average computed from such diverse statistics as reading age and dental

Table 4-2

**Cross-sectional Data for Girl Aged
Nine Years (108 Months) ***

Function Measured	Raw Score	Age Equivalent (in months)
Height	60.4 in.	160
Reading	28 items correct	130
Weight	96 lbs.	156
Strength of grip	19.7 kg.	130
Ossification of hand and wrist	X ray	135
Mental capacity	Tests passed	134
Dental eruption	16 permanent teeth	119
Organismic age		138
Variability		11.7

* From R. G. Barker, J. S. Kounin, & H. F. Wright, *Child Behavior and Development*, McGraw-Hill, 1943, p. 203. Reprinted by permission of the publisher.

age can have any psychological meaning. It is not so helpful, for example, for a teacher to know that Philip has an organismic age of 11.7 years as it is for him to know that the child has a reading age of 10.3 and a mental age of 11.4. The organismic age obscures differences which it is important to recognize.

At this point in our research knowledge, we cannot say that there is a push for growth which will affect all aspects of growth uniformly. A child who is fast maturing in terms of skeletal growth will not necessarily be fast maturing in all aspects of his growth. Precisely what is the nature of growth within the individual is still to be determined.

Measuring Rate of Growth

One approach to measuring rate of growth is through a measure of skeletal growth. An accurate assessment of the maturation of the skeleton can be made from X-ray films of the hand and wrist (Greulich, 1950). The skeleton of the healthy, adequately nourished child develops as a unit; therefore, the developmental status of the bones of other parts of the body can be inferred from that of the hand and wrist alone. A girl, for example, whose first menstruation occurred when she was seven years old was found to have had a skeletal age of thirteen and a half years as measured by hand X ray when she was only six years old chronologically.

It is conceivable that there are relationships between skeletal maturity and forms of behavior which we do not know about at the present time. However, on the basis of what we do know, we can use skeletal age, when it is available over a period of years, to find the growth rate of an individual child and to note unusual shifts in rate. When the rate drops off alarmingly, a physical check-up would be advisable; when it is accelerated, a careful planning of daily activities is indicated.

A less complex method of measuring rate of growth as far as schools are concerned is for school physicians, guidance workers, or others to obtain careful measurements of many phases of growth. One research team (Stolz & Stolz, 1951) suggests measuring height, stem length, leg length, weight, and muscular strength at six-month intervals. If these measurements are plotted in terms of rate of change, individual growth profiles can be derived. Stolz and Stolz suggest some very practical uses for such profiles. The question of whether a particular boy should engage in interscholastic football competition could be decided partly on the basis of his previous growth pattern. In reaching a decision, we need to ask such questions as: Has he shown great or small fluctuations in growth rate? Has his development in muscular strength lagged behind growth in weight? Does his pattern tend toward synchrony or asynchrony of development? George may have the build of a football player, but if he has shown great fluctuations in growth rate, if his muscular strength has lagged behind growth in weight, or if his pattern tends toward asynchrony, he will be better off not engaging in strenuous competitive sports.

Developmental direction, the concept of maturation, the interrelatedness of development, individual patterns of growth—

these are the broad principles which apply to all children regardless of their culture. When we know more about these and possibly other principles of growth and development, we may be better able to evaluate what we do with children. It may be that in some societies child-rearing practices are geared to only one growth rhythm, thus working a hardship on children who do not conform to the accepted constitutional type. As Mead (1949b) points out, there are societies in which a new step of development is enforced when the calendar or the clock dictates, rather than when an individual is ready for it. Thus initiation ceremonies for adolescents in a primitive tribe may include eight-year-old children. Pediatric dictum in our society used to be that infants weighing seven pounds or more should be fed at four-hour intervals, whereas infants weighing one ounce less than seven pounds should be fed every three hours. So, also, there are societies in which precocity or slow development is culturally disapproved; in which a child may be protected or not protected during such critical periods as weaning, birth of a sibling, and puberty. Evaluating cultural practices in the light of known principles of development may help us to be more successful in transmitting cultural learnings to children.

3. Expert help in accurately plotting individual growth curves is not available in most schools at the present time. What kinds of observation might a teacher make in the course of a year that would give some insight into an individual pupil's growth rate?

4. If possible, examine the records of a group of upper-grade children covering a number of years. Select three children at random for study. Find the rate of growth for the various measurements given from year to year. What differences in growth rate do you find among these children? Does the same child consistently show the most gain on the average from year to year? Are the children consistent within themselves? Suggest factors that might explain any inconsistencies that you find.

SUGGESTED READINGS

GESELL, ARNOLD, & ILG, FRANCES L. *Infant and Child in the Culture of Today*, Harper, 1943. Part 1, "Growth and Culture," discusses the growth process, as well as some principles of development, in very readable fashion. Practical suggestions for putting these principles into operation are included.

GREULICH, WILLIAM W. The rationale of assessing the developmental status of children from roentgenograms of the hand and wrist. In William E. Martin & Celia Burns Stendler (eds.), *Readings in Child Development,* Harcourt, Brace, 1954, pp. 42-47. In this paper, the author explains and illustrates the use of X rays of the hand and wrist in assessing the skeletal maturity of the child.

JERSILD, ARTHUR T., & ASSOCIATES. *Child Development and the Curriculum,* Bureau of Publications, Teachers College, Columbia University, 1946. Chapter 2 considers some principles of growth and development based on research findings and suggests some implications of these principles for the education program.

JONES, MARY COVER, & BAYLEY, NANCY. Physical maturing among boys as related to behavior. In Martin & Stendler, *op. cit.,* pp. 48-58. This paper presents evidence collected on the question: Is there a relationship between an individual's behavior and his rate of physical maturation?

STOLZ, HERBERT R., & STOLZ, LOIS M. *Somatic Development of Adolescent Boys,* Macmillan, 1951. Chapter 18 contains a very thorough and readable report of the somatic development of a young boy. The data presented are used to show the interrelationships among various phases of development. The case of Ben is particularly interesting because it illustrates the problems of an early-maturing boy.

5
the beginnings
of life

Because of his nature, because he is a human being, we can make certain predictions about every child, regardless of the society in which he lives. We know that all children will be born with the primary drives discussed in Chapter 2 and that they will grow and develop in accordance with the principles presented in Chapter 4. In addition, we can describe, as we shall do in this chapter, the ways in which children everywhere resemble one another at different age levels. For example, a child anywhere in the world will have spent approximately 280 days *in utero* before he is born; during his first year of life he will attain the capacity to sit up and to stand; by eighteen months he will be capable of uttering a few words; around six years of age his second teeth will appear; just before adolescence he will grow very rapidly; during puberty his voice will deepen. These and many more things we can predict about any child because of his nature. In this chapter we describe those characteristics of all human beings that apply to the prenatal period and to the first month after birth—the neonatal period. These months—ten in all for most human beings—constitute a period of phenomenal growth, from a tiny fertilized cell, indistinguishable to the naked eye, to a highly complex organism, over twenty inches in length.

PRENATAL DEVELOPMENT

The prenatal period of development has long been shrouded with mystery. As is so often the case with things that man does not understand, many superstitions have arisen in all societies to explain later development in terms of events during the months before birth. In our society, there are those who hold that a baby whose mother is frightened by a rat during pregnancy may develop a birthmark resembling a rat; similarly, strawberry birthmarks are thought to be caused by an expectant mother's eating of too many strawberries. Among the Yurok, a tribe of fishermen and acorn-gatherers on the Pacific coast, it is believed that if the fetus is not kept awake when daylight is waning, he may see the "wise people" as an infant and become a behavior problem. (The "wise people," the Yurok believe, are a race of small beings which preceded the human race. Their magic is dangerous; it may make a child have temper tantrums or lose his appetite or become sickly and die.)

Another group of superstitions has to do with prenatal influence upon personality. Thus some people in our society believe that a woman who wants her child to be musical should listen to good music during pregnancy; an expectant mother who desires a happy child is admonished to think only happy thoughts. In Samoan society it is held that any wrong deed committed by a pregnant woman will injure her child in temperament or in some other way. Physical deformities, too, are sometimes explained in terms of a simple one-to-one relationship between the mother, or even the father, and the fetus. A one-armed adult in our society reports her father's lifelong conviction that his habitual driving of a horse and buggy with only one arm was responsible for her deformity in that it caused his other arm to be weak, which weakness, he believed, was passed on to his daughter in the genes.

Fortunately, knowledge of prenatal development accumulated in recent years has dispelled many of these superstitions. We now know considerably more than we did of prenatal development, although the difficulties of studying this period are obviously tremendous. The scientist has two kinds of subject with which he can work in his search for knowledge in this area. One is the embryo of animals, including fish, frogs, salamanders, and birds and mammals of all varieties. The other type of subject is the human embryo or fetus which has had to be removed surgically from the mother's body before it is old enough to survive outside the womb. (If the fetus is less than six months of age, chances are that the mechanisms later involved in respiration will not be sufficiently developed to enable it to obtain oxygen outside the mother's body.) Upon removal, the fetus is placed in a physiological salt solution, where limited experimentation and observation are possible before the onset of asphyxiation (Carmichael, 1954). In addition, some observations, necessarily of a short duration, have been made of the fetus *in utero* before it has been removed by Caesarean section (see p. 148). Such studies of surgically delivered fetuses have enabled scientists to increase our understanding of prenatal behavior, although the number of human fetuses it has been possible to study in such circumstances has been small—a total of fewer than 250 (Munn, 1955).

Early Stages in Development

A human being begins existence when an ovum, the female germ cell, is penetrated and fertilized by a spermatozöon, the male germ cell, while the ovum is in the uterine tube on its way from ovary to uterus. Most women produce only one mature ovum every twenty-eight days; this occurs during the middle of the menstrual cycle, which is defined as beginning with the onset of one menstrual period and ending with the beginning of the next. It is estimated that the fertilized ovum takes about three days to progress through the tube to the uterus and four or five days more to become implanted there. Cell division, however, begins even before the fertilized egg reaches the uterus; cells begin to cleave together, and the cluster becomes a blastocyst.

As the number of cells in the blastocyst increases, some of the cells move outward and mass at one end, or pole, leaving in

PATTERNS OF DEVELOPMENT

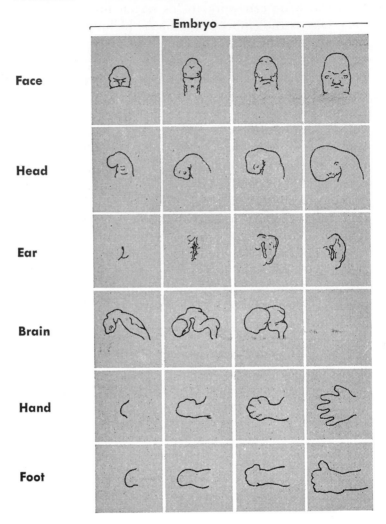

(From *The Miracle of Growth,*

the center of the mass a cavity which fills up with amniotic fluid. This tiny cavity becomes surrounded by a layer of thin cells. During the period when the amniotic cavity is being formed, a second and initially larger cavity arises—the primary yolk sac.

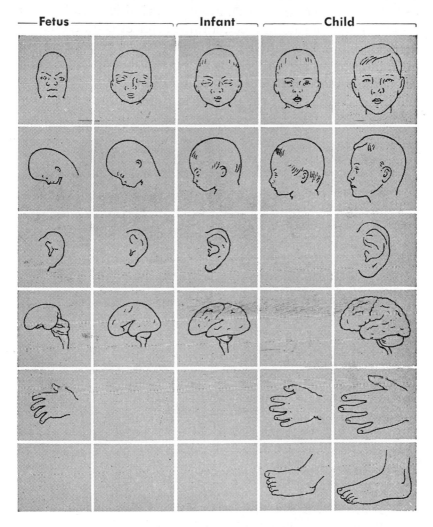

University of Illinois Press, 1950, pp. 18-19)

(The quantity of yolk in the sac is small, for the human mammal obtains its food from the mother; little or no nourishment need be derived from the yolk sac.) Between the amniotic cavity and the yolk sac, the embryonic disk forms. This disk is made up of a layer of cells called the ectoderm (upper layer) and a layer of endodermal cells (lower layer). From the primitive streak where ectoderm and endoderm meet, a third layer of cells, the mesoderm, develops. From these three primary germ layers, cells are differentiated which will fashion different body tissues. The ectoderm is the point of origin for the skin, the sense organs, and the nervous system; the mesoderm is the point of origin for

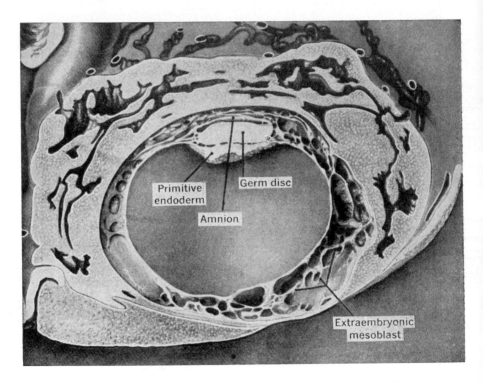

FIGURE 5-1. A schematic representation of a human implantation of estimated age 12 days.

(Adapted from W. J. Hamilton, J. D. Boyd, & H. W. Mossman. *Human Embryology*, Baltimore: Williams and Wilkins, 1952, p. 47)

the muscular, circulatory, and skeletal systems; from the endoderm are derived some of the future glands of internal secretion and the alimentary canal.

The Embryonic Period

During the second week of its existence, the blastocyst becomes imbedded in the uterus; the organism is then referred to as an embryo. The embryonic period extends to the beginning of the third lunar (twenty-eight-day) month of pregnancy, when the so-called fetal period begins. It is during the embryonic period that the body takes form and all main systems and organs are laid down. In fact, the rate of growth is most rapid in the earlier stages of pregnancy and decreases as pregnancy advances (Hamilton *et al.,* 1952).

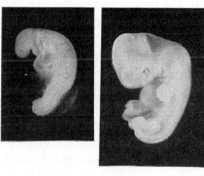 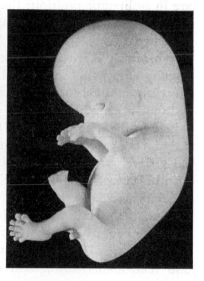

FIGURE 5-2. An embryo of 28 days (*left*), 40 days (*center*), and 60 days (*right*). Magnifications are, respectively, 6, 2, and 2.

(Carnegie Institution of Washington)

By the end of the first month, the embryo has become elongated in shape and markedly curved. The head fold is distinct, and contained in it are swellings that mark the arches of the lower jaw and the pharynx, while tiny cavities indicate the location of the eyes- and ears-to-be. To the side of and below the head fold is a bulge due to the developing heart. Both the umbilicus and the umbilical cord can be recognized, as can a tiny tail. The embryo is about one-fifth inch in length.

During the second month, paired arm and leg buds appear. The head region becomes elevated from the heart region, and a ridge appears between them. The olfactory pit becomes visible, and the rudiments of the external ear appear. By the thirty-seventh day, the upper limb bud shows a differentiation into arm, forearm, and hand. By the fortieth day, the outlines of future digits have appeared and the leg bud has divided into thigh, leg, and foot regions. At the end of the second month, the embryo, although barely more than an inch long, has assumed a distinctly human appearance. The neck region has become established, the eyelids are discernible, the external ear is apparent, the tail has almost completely disappeared. The limbs are in embryonic position; that is, the legs are characteristically bent at the knees and the arms are bent at the elbow and held close to the body.

Meanwhile, internal organs have been developing and have already begun their work. All parts of the growing organism must have nourishment and wastes must be carried away. These tasks are accomplished in the placenta, to which the embryo is joined by the umbilical cord. They can be carried on, of course, only by the cardiovascular system of the body, and the embryo early develops its own blood system. During the third week primitive blood cells and vessels appear and the embryonic heart becomes active. By the fourth week circulation of the blood has started. By the sixth week the heart has acquired a definite form; although primitive in structure, it is nevertheless differentiated from the rest of the tiny organism. There are further changes and refinements throughout the period of gestation, but the general plan of the circulatory system is laid down early.

The nervous system is also developmentally precocious. The basis of the nervous system is a thickened band of ectoderm which early appears down the middle of the embryo. This thickened band is folded into a neural groove which is apparent by the nineteenth day. The groove continues to deepen and the thickened neural folds meet and fuse over it to enclose a hollow tube. From the upper end of this tube, three primary vessels of the brain develop by the fourth week, and at the same time nerves and ganglia begin to form. The remainder of the tube slowly undergoes change; by the tenth week it has the definite internal structure of the spinal cord. Meanwhile, growing nerve fibers reach out to the periphery of the body and make connections with the proper receptors. By the end of the embryonic period, cerebral hemispheres have appeared and the cerebral cortex has acquired typical cells. By the twelfth week the brain has attained its general structural features.

The embryonic period also sees amazing growth in other organs of the body. The rudiments of the internal organs of digestion make their appearance in the first month. Liver and pancreatic buds are present; there is a tubelike intestine, a spindle-shaped stomach, and the beginnings of a gall bladder. By the end of the embryonic period, these structures have developed further and others have emerged. In the respiratory system, lung buds are apparent in the fourth week; by the eighth week they become glandlike. The bronchi, larynx, and pharynx have also appeared by the end of the embryonic period.

Our résumé does not cover all the major aspects of growth during the embryonic period. There is parallel development in other parts of the embryo; the organism does not develop one system at a time but is characterized, instead, by correlated development in all body parts. And once functional nervous connections are established between receptors and effectors, responses which are neurally mediated appear, even though the body part may be in a primitive stage of development. Thus, by eight weeks of age, there is clear evidence of response to tactual stimulation; when the upper or lower lip of a surgically removed embryo is lightly stroked with a hair, there is flexion of the neck and trunk of the body (Hooker, 1952). A "wormlike" movement of arms, legs, and trunk has also been observed (Carmichael, 1954). These early movements are generalized, with neck, trunk, and limbs moving in combination rather than separately.

During the early embryonic period, other membranes are also forming, which serve to protect and nourish the growing organism. From the early stages of pregnancy, the embryo is suspended in clear fluid in the amniotic sac; this fluid acts as a protective water cushion which absorbs jolts, equalizes pres-

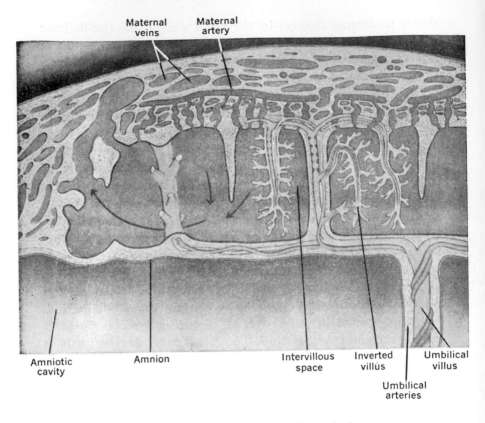

Maternal
veins

Maternal
artery

Amniotic
cavity

Amnion

Intervillous
space

Inverted
villus

Umbilical
arteries

Umbilical
villus

FIGURE 5-3. A schematic representation of the mature placenta, showing the circulation of the maternal blood in the intervillous spaces and the circulation of blood in the villi.

(Adapted from Hamilton, Boyd, & Mossman, *op. cit.*, p. 73)

sures, and permits change of fetal posture. At childbirth, these membranes rupture, and some of the fluid escapes as the "waters." (If the amnion fails to burst, the head is delivered enveloped in a "cap," known popularly as the "caul" [Arey, 1946].) The amniotic sac is surrounded by another, rather shaggy, sac, which is called the "chorion." The chorion has minute, hairlike branching outgrowths called "villi," filled with blood vessels. From some of these chorionic tissues, plus maternal tissue, the placenta is formed. At birth, this is a thick circular disk averaging seven inches in diameter, one inch in thickness, and a little more than a pound in weight. The umbilical cord extends from the abdominal region of the embryo to the placental membrane.

The blood of the mother and that of the fetus circulate independently, in totally separate channels. Maternal blood fills the spaces between the villi of the placenta, which contain blood from the embryonic system. There is no direct contact or intermingling between the external fluid and the blood of the villi; their only communication is through diffusive interchange. Nutritive substances, inorganic salts, and oxygen in solution pass from the mother's blood to the fetus, while waste products from the embryo are transferred in the reverse direction (Arey, 1946).

The Fetal Period

The term "fetus," as we have said, is used for the embryo from the commencement of the third lunar month of pregnancy to the end of the period of gestation. This change in terminology emphasizes the fact that the organism has now taken on an unmistakably human appearance. The fetal period marks the beginning of the stage at which the generic identity of a mammalian embryo can readily be recognized.

By the end of the third lunar month, the fetus is almost three inches long. Its head is still relatively large, and its rump region and legs are relatively small. The forehead is high and prominent; the nose looks like a giant snout; the external ear lies level with the lower jaw. Hair has begun to appear in the eyebrow and lip region, and a fine crop of fetal hair shows itself in the region of the forehead. Nails are indicated by furrows on the back of the finger tips. The external genitals undergo marked changes, and by the end of this period it is possible to identify the sex of a fetus by external inspection (Hamilton *et al.*, 1952).

During the fifth lunar month, fetal movements ("quickening") are first detected by the mother. The fetus has developed a varied repertoire of movement; the earlier generalized pattern of responses is breaking up and many separate reflexes are appearing. Arms and legs show some mobility, and the fingers can close in a weak but effective grasp—strong enough to hold a thin glass rod (Hooker, 1952). Stimulation of one foot may arouse a response in the other and also in the opposite hand (Carmichael, 1954), a reflex which is thought to underlie the crawling activities of the infant. Fine fetal hair now covers most of the body, and secretions from the sweat glands appear on the skin.

During the sixth lunar month, respiratory movement begins, making it theoretically possible for an occasional fetus to survive outside the mother's body. The fetus is now a foot long and weighs about a pound and a half. The face is more infant-like, with eyebrows and eyelids well defined, but the skin is characteristically very wrinkled, owing to the fact that it is growing more rapidly than the underlying connective tissue.

From the seventh lunar month on, fetuses removed from the womb more frequently survive, if they are given adequate care. However, such fetal infants, as they are called, are skinny and wizened in appearance; at twenty-eight weeks they weigh about two and a half pounds and are about fifteen inches long. At this time, an audible sucking response is present and a startle response has appeared—roughly the same response made by an adult who is startled as he dozes off to sleep. The behavior of the fetus—and, indeed, the behavior of full-term babies as well— appears to be controlled subcortically; apparently, the cerebrum exerts little if any influence over activity until some time after birth (Munn, 1955).

The last two months of fetal life (the ninth and tenth lunar months) are devoted more to a general building up of tissue than to the establishment of any new tissue or organ. During this period, subcutaneous fat is deposited so that the contours of the fetus become rounded. The fetal hair disappears. The fingernails reach the finger tips and the toenails lengthen. The lower extremities grow rapidly.

At birth the average full-term infant weighs a little more than seven pounds, although any weight between five and ten pounds is within the normal range. Heredity appears to be more significant in determining weight than does the amount of food the mother eats, provided that the diet is adequate. A diet that is nutritionally inadequate can result in infants who are abnormally small or defective in some other respect, as we shall see later. It can even cause fetal mortality. A full-term infant is about twenty inches long. The normal term of pregnancy is generally taken to be 280 days; 180 days is the average lower limit for survival and 334 days is the longest period, legally considered, during which an infant who is delivered alive may be said to have lived in the mother's body (Carmichael, 1954).

INFLUENCES OF THE PRENATAL ENVIRONMENT UPON DEVELOPMENT

It often happens in the world of ideas that a widely accepted theory is discarded because it has been "proved" false, and then is accepted again, with some modification, when new evidence becomes available. With respect to our theories of prenatal influences upon later development, the pendulum has swung from overly simple and superstitious beliefs about the ways in which an infant might be marked physically and psychologically before he was born to a complete rejection, by the layman, at least, of the notion that such influences exist. Recent research, however, has made it clear that the prenatal environment *can* influence development and is reflected in behavior after birth in certain predictable ways. (This, of course, in no way implies a return to the superstitions of the past.)

Maternal Infections

Research on factors in the prenatal environment has led to the conclusion that certain maternal infections may be transmitted across the placental barrier, enter the fetal bloodstream, and affect the developmental process. German measles (*rubella*) is perhaps the best-known offender; a review of the literature shows a clear relationship between maternal rubella and certain congenital abnormalities (cataracts, deafness, mental deficits, heart disease, etc.) that were formerly attributed to defective genes (Swan *et al.*, 1947). Other viruses and some bacterial toxins can also cross the placental barrier. Some of these, such as smallpox, chicken pox, mumps, malaria, and syphilis, may infect the fetus so that the disease is present in the newborn. If the noxious substance is virulent enough, an abortion may ensue; if the dose is sublethal and occurs early in pregnancy, a congenital defect may appear in the infant.

Apparently, the timing of the disturbance is a crucial factor in determining whether an abnormality will appear and, if so, of what kind it will be. As we have seen, there is a special period in the prenatal timetable for the development of each organ. If an organ does not develop at the proper time, it will never be able to develop fully (Stockard, 1931). Particular defects are apparently caused by growth disturbance at a particular time during pregnancy, and *at that time only*. Thus, if development is interrupted while the internal ear is being formed (seventh to tenth week), deafness may result. If the disturbance occurs during the period when the brain is being formed (third to twelfth week), a mental deficit may ensue. These interruptions do not affect the organs that have already developed or those that have not yet appeared. Since the first three months of pregnancy are critical for differentiation of the body organs, infections occurring during this time produce most of the defects originating in the prenatal period.

The precise manner in which environmental disturbances affect fetal growth is not yet known. Ingalls (1950), on the basis of his experiments with mice, has suggested that the cause of anomalies may be anoxia, or insufficiency of oxygen, resulting from a disease suffered by the mother during pregnancy. He was able to induce specific defects in newborn mice by cutting down the oxygen supply of the mothers. Each of twenty litters of mice was deprived of sufficient oxygen on one of the first seventeen days of pregnancy. On the eighteenth day the young were surgically delivered. Analyses of defects in the litters showed that they were affected by the strength, duration, and timing of anoxia. For example, harelip was produced after anoxia on the twelfth day of pregnancy, and incompletely formed skulls resulted from anoxia on the eighth day. From knowledge of when a particular fetal organ was to appear, it was possible to produce a specific deformity by cutting down the oxygen supply at the critical time.

Other Prenatal Environmental Influences

Severe maternal nutritional deficiencies during pregnancy also affect the child. Deficiencies in vitamins B, C, and D have been known to cause fetal abnormalities and even mortality (Hamilton *et al.*, 1952). Deficiencies in certain vitamins and minerals at the time when the teeth are developing may affect the structure of the teeth and their dentine, making them more liable to caries in postnatal life. A maternal diet low in protein also affects the infant adversely. In one study, infants whose mothers' diet during pregnancy was rated high in protein were compared with infants whose mothers' diet had been low in protein. Pediatricians rated 95 per cent of those children born to mothers on the good diet in excellent or good health, whereas only 8 per cent of those born to mothers on the poor diet were so rated. The investigators also found a positive correlation between infant length and weight and the protein intake of the mother during pregnancy (Burke *et al.*, 1949).

Maternal malnutrition also affects the birth weight and length of the newborn. Babies born in occupied countries during World War II to mothers on substandard diets were found to be shorter and lighter in weight than babies born before the occupation. Investigators also found that the number of premature births and stillbirths increased during this period (C. A. Smith, 1947).

The old popular notion that the fetus will take what it needs from the mother and that a malnourished mother will consequently suffer more during pregnancy than the fetus, and more than an adequately nourished mother, is now open to question. Some investigators report, rather, that it is the fetus who suffers more as a result of inadequate maternal nutrition. Of 120 women in a poor-diet group whose infants were affected adversely, not one showed the slightest sign of a deficiency disease (Montagu, 1950). Although the question of which suffers more cannot yet be answered conclusively, one thing is clear: it is highly important that pregnant women maintain an adequate diet.

Blood incompatibilities may also affect the newborn. If the father is Rh positive and the mother Rh negative, certain antigens (substances which produce antibodies) may be present in the fetal blood as a result of inheritance from the father but absent from the maternal blood. It is possible, in a manner as yet unknown, for these antigens to pass into the maternal blood, resulting in the production of anti-Rh substances in the mother's red blood cells. These anti-Rh substances may then cross the placental barrier and affect the fetal blood. Changes in the mother's blood, however, occur so slowly that the fetus in a first pregnancy is not injured. In a second pregnancy, the newborn may be so affected that an exchange transfusion is necessary at birth. However, there have been several instances of pregnancies with an Rh incompatibility in which the blood system of the infant was not injured.

Some investigators hypothesize a "continuum of reproductive casualty" (Lilienfeld & Pasamanick, 1956). A study of birth certificates and hospital records of children born in Baltimore between 1935 and 1952 showed significantly more abnormalities during the mothers' pregnancy and the delivery of children later found to be mentally defective than were found in the records of a control group of normal children. Continuing maternal abnormalities during pregnancy may also result in cerebral palsy, epilepsy, and behavior disorders, or may be severe enough to cause stillbirths and neonatal deaths.

The work of Pasamanick and his group extends the earlier work of Benda (1949). This investigator, who concentrated on mongolism, found that mental defectives of this type were born following a pregnancy marked by many abnormal maternal conditions, such as bleeding, uterine and ovarian anomalies, and impaired hormonal regulation. Mongolism also occurred in children born to mothers who had a history of menstrual difficulties, early menopausal symptoms, abortions, and difficulty in becoming pregnant. It may be that the endocrine system of some women responds poorly to pregnancy.

Students frequently ask about the effects of maternal smoking upon fetal development. It is known that the fetal heartbeat increases when the mother smokes a cigarette (Sontag & Wallace, 1935), but no studies have been reported on the effects of continued and heavy smoking by the mother.

Considerably more research is needed on prenatal environmental influences and particularly on the causes and prevention of infant anomalies. But enough has been done to show that many of the defects formerly attributed to heredity are due, rather, to disturbances during the prenatal period. Fortunately, such anomalies are rare. Lest the prospective parent be frightened by this review of the research, he should remember that nature has provided a very protective environment for the human fetus and that most babies are "normal" in every respect at birth. The studies do, however, point up the importance of good prenatal care and of avoiding exposure to contagious diseases and accidents during pregnancy.

EMOTIONAL STATES. Studies of prenatal influences upon later development have gone beyond the physiological aspects. Research workers interested in the psychosometric aspects of medicine have theorized that the emotional state of the mother during pregnancy has an influence upon the personality development of the child. This theory may seem to be an echo of the old superstition that a mother who is frightened during pregnancy will produce a fearful baby, but it is actually very different. Modern psychosomatic theory recognizes that, since there are no nerve connections from the mother to the fetus and no intermingling of maternal and fetal blood, there is no possibility of establishing a one-to-one relationship between a particular emotional state of the mother and a particular characteristic of her child. But it also recognizes that a mother's emotional state can bring about chemical changes in her body, and that some maternal hormones may cross the placental barrier to produce changes in the fetus. According to Sontag, infants whose mothers were emotionally disturbed during pregnancy frequently exhibit signs of an irritable and hyperactive autonomic nervous system:

> Early feeding difficulties based on motor and sensory abnormalities of the gastro-intestinal system are, in many instances, of autonomic origin. The presence of feeding difficulties of a motor or secretory nature from birth must presume their etiology and basic disturbances during intra-uterine life. In prenatal development of such a condition, prolonged nervous and emotional disturbances of the mother during the later months of pregnancy seem to be important [1941, p. 1001].

Indeed, he goes so far as to say that a child may be "to all intents and purposes a neurotic infant when it is born." However, whether the emotional disturbance of the mothers whose children he studied continued after childbirth and was reflected in their relationship to the newborns is not known. An emotionally disturbed mother may behave in such a way toward her child that his development after birth is adversely affected.

PREMATURITY. It is difficult to isolate the effects of premature birth from those of other environmental influences upon development. The premature child, because he is premature, is often treated differently by his parents; he is protected and babied and as a result may develop personality characteristics that differ from those of children who were full-term babies. Shirley (1939), in an intensive study of prematures, found that they experience an initial arrest in development during the first few weeks after birth, but that they grow at an accelerated rate thereafter and eventually overtake their full-term contemporaries, both physically and intellectually. However, she also found, in a comparison of the personality traits of premature and full-term children during the preschool years, that many prematures had speech difficulties and were overdependent and distractible. Some positive traits were noted as well. Shirley concluded that family environment rather than prematurity *per se* accounts for the differences she found.

FETAL BEHAVIOR

We should also consider certain other aspects of the prenatal period which have more to do with normal development. Fetal behavior is one of these. We have already mentioned some of the developmental changes in fetal behavior in the month-by-month discussion of prenatal growth. Here we report some of the experimental evidence on behavior.

It is known that the fetus responds to sound; one teacher-mother reported that the fetus was particularly active during the mother's noon-hour duty in a noisy school cafeteria. Other mothers report that the sound of an automobile horn, a loud buzzer, or banging and hammering will cause the fetus to kick. Their observations have been substantiated by the research of Sontag and Wallace (1934). It is doubtful whether the fetus truly "hears," however, since the Eustachian tube is filled with fluid; it is more likely that the fetus responds to vibration.

There is some evidence that a conditioned response can be established before birth. Spelt (1948) worked with women twenty-six to thirty-four weeks pregnant. When his apparatus made a loud sound and at the same time applied a tactile vibration to the mother's abdomen, the fetus responded with movement. After fifteen to twenty contiguous presentations, the fetus responded to the tactile vibration applied without the sound. Such conditioning is governed primarily by the spinal cord and lower brain centers; as we have said, the cerebral cortex is not functioning at this time.

Spontaneous movements can be detected with a stethoscope when the fetus is only four months old; mothers generally feel "life" during the fifth month of pregnancy. These spontaneous movements increase in number (up to two hundred daily) and in vigor until the time of birth. There is some evidence that the activity of the mother may affect fetal activity, with the fetus less active immediately following exercise on the mother's part. The amount of spontaneous fetal activity may have some predictive value; one study of twelve six-month-old infants found that those who were most active as fetuses had the highest scores on the Gesell Developmental Schedule (Richards & Newberry, 1938). However, it may be that mothers vary in their sensitivity to fetal activity. More work needs to be done on the problem before we can safely conclude that there is a correlation between amount of fetal activity and motor development after birth.

For the reader's information, it might also be noted that crying and hiccuping occur in fetal life and that the thumbs of some neonates indicate that thumbsucking occurred before birth.

Before we turn to other matters, we should make some mention of how women feel about pregnancy. In one study of 379 middle-class mothers who had five-year-old children, more than half reported that they had been delighted to find themselves pregnant (R. Sears *et al.*, 1957). By the time the baby arrived, more were content, and only 4 per cent acknowledged that they were still displeased. Interestingly enough, women who enjoyed working also looked forward to motherhood, while those who were indifferent to their jobs expressed little delight at the prospect of giving birth. And pleasure at becoming pregnant was found to be correlated with affectional warmth toward the child in infancy and later years.

THE BIRTH PROCESS

The authors of *The Miracle of Growth* have described the birth of a baby so well that we quote from them in detail:

> Ten of the regular twenty-eight day cycles of woman have been completed.
>
> The time of ten full moons is sufficient to establish a new individual on the earth. By that time the fetus in his protected prenatal existence is fully equipped to make the postnatal adjustment.
>
> In all the rest of his life there will never be such a sudden and complete change of locale. No other journey will ever start from such profound seclusion. Even in his deepest sleep he will not be so thoroughly hidden as he is at birth.

At a given moment on the final day of uterine existence, there will be a sharp and sudden signal that the term is over. The placenta and umbilical cord can no longer supply sufficient food and oxygen. Escape, as it were, becomes imperative. Through the events that follow, the commencement of life is made possible. Significantly, the transition is known as labor.

Labor consists of a series of spontaneous exertions by the muscles of the uterus. They create a force. The force sends the fetus downward through the pelvis. The passages slowly widen and the infant emerges.

The first flexings of the uterine muscles begin, for a first child, about seventeen and a half hours before birth. For subsequent children the average is twelve hours. Contractions increase in power as the time between contractions diminishes. At the beginning, contractions are usually fifteen to twenty minutes apart. The time between contractions decreases slowly. When they are only three minutes apart, the birth is imminent. When they are two minutes apart, the fluid-filled sac which enclosed the baby in the uterus is broken. The entrance to the uterus (or cervix) is sufficiently wide for the infant to emerge. Although there are a great many variations to this pattern, the basic principle is usually the same.

The head of the baby usually presents itself first. The shoulders slowly rotate in the birth canal as the entire body of the baby emerges. The umbilical cord is clamped, cut, and tied. At this moment, for the first time, the baby exists independent of the mother. From this time onward, it is the world with which he must cope [1950, pp. 21-23].

Not all deliveries, however, proceed in normal fashion. In a breech delivery the buttocks appear first, then the legs, and lastly the head. Such deliveries are dangerous since the infant may suffocate before the head emerges. Deliveries necessitating extensive use of instruments are also potentially dangerous, for permanent damage to the brain centers may occur. Doll and others (1932) report that feeble-mindedness, in 5 to 10 per cent of the children so afflicted, is the result of birth injuries, and that poor motor coordination and even paralysis are also in part attributable to the same cause.

Some babies are delivered surgically, by Caesarean section. When the mother is too small for the size of the fetus, or when waiting for labor to occur might endanger the life of mother or child, or when the position of the fetus is abnormal, delivery may be made by surgery. Such a technique is obviously easier on the baby, but it has the possible disadvantage of limiting the size of the mother's family, since the abdominal wall cannot sustain very many operations of this kind.

Again we remind prospective parents, lest they become unduly frightened by the foregoing remarks, that most babies are born in normal fashion. Where abnormal conditions exist, the hazards to both mother and child can be reduced by good obstetrical care.

BIRTH RITUALS

Birth is a natural process, but in every society it is accompanied by certain rituals. Our own society is no exception. Perhaps we can better evaluate our own rituals if we look first at some of the procedures which accompany childbirth in primitive societies.

First we note that each society assigns particular roles to both father and mother. Among the Comanches, for example, the mother goes to a special tepee where a professional midwife delivers the baby. The mother goes through the birth pangs kneeling and holding on to the ridge-pole of the tepee while the midwife presses down on the abdomen. In case of an extremely difficult birth, medicine men are called in. The lying-in period is ten days. The father is excluded from the scene of birth and may not even touch food served by a woman who has been present at the delivery. He is not permitted to see the child, although he is informed of its sex. If the child is his first, he is given gifts by his wife's parents.

Among the Alorese, the mother goes to the home of a female relative, where the baby is delivered. During the lying-in period of five or six days, the father stays away and refrains from vigorous work for fear of affecting the health of the child.

In other societies, the father assists with the delivery, pushing down on his wife's abdomen with each labor pain. In societies in which couvade is practiced, the father goes through the motions of labor, even to moaning and groaning and being assisted by friends and relatives. Meanwhile his wife crawls unnoticed to the bushes and delivers the baby with little or no help.

In our society the ritual has changed several times during the past fifty or sixty years. During the early 1900's, most babies were born at home, with a midwife or family doctor in attendance. Older children were sent to the home of friends or relatives during delivery, and although the father remained close at hand he customarily did not assist in the delivery. The mother stayed in bed for the better part of a week and performed only light household work for another week.

With the growth of the hospital movement, a whole new set of rituals came into being. Now father was assigned the role of pacing up and down the hospital corridor, chain-smoking while nurses and doctors assisted mother in the labor and delivery rooms. Despite the increased use of anesthetics, it was customary for mothers to portray the first delivery as a long, painful, and dangerous process. Each story of delivery sounded as if both baby and mother had been saved by sheer miracle. It was believed that only peasant women or women in primitive societies had babies easily and that childbirth was a much more difficult and painful process in civilized societies because women were built more fragilely. The period of hospitalization was ten days in length, during which time husband and friends were expected to be extremely solicitous. A period of recuperation at home followed. The father customarily distributed cigars and candy to friends and relatives, who, in turn, were expected to give gifts to the baby.

Today, however, doctors are advising mothers that childbirth can be less painful if it is not accompanied by fear. Many mothers, encouraged by a "natural" childbirth movement, are having their babies with little or no anesthesia. Delivery has become a family affair, with father present in the delivery room. Partly as a result of the increased birth rate and hospital over-crowding, and partly because medical science today believes that a shorter period in bed speeds recovery, the lying-in period has been shortened to five days, and women are encouraged to get up soon after delivery.

Another innovation of recent years has been a rooming-in arrangement, under which plan the newborn is kept in the same room as the mother rather than in a hospital nursery. For many new mothers this arrangement is a particularly happy one, for it gives them the opportunity to become accustomed to neo-natal behavior under guidance. They learn firsthand that er-ratic breathing and considerable crying characterize the neo-nate and they are less nervous when they first return home with the baby. They also feel more secure about their baby. The advantages to the infant of rooming-in are obvious; he enjoys more natural and diverse stimulations under rooming-in conditions, and he is spared unnecessary crying (Gesell & Ilg, 1943).

The meaning the birth process has for the child has been a matter for speculation among many psychoanalysts in our society. Otto Rank (1929) has postulated a "birth trauma"; he believes that the shock of being born is so great that its effects may endure throughout one's lifetime. This raises the very in-teresting question as to whether a baby born by Caesarean section will differ significantly in personality from a baby whose coming into the world has been a long-drawn-out and difficult affair. However, we have no conclusive evidence that birth is a psychological shock to the child or that an easy delivery is less shocking as measured in terms of later personality development.

1. Poll your friends regarding superstitions surrounding the prenatal period. What evidence has been presented in this chap-ter to refute such superstitions? Are there some folk-beliefs for which the evidence is not clear-cut or for which we have no evidence?

THE NEONATE

The reader's first reaction to a newborn infant may be amazement. Here is a red-faced, screaming piece of humanity, completely helpless, yet so "finished" in his appearance. "He has everything," as one mother put it, "even to tiny fingernails and toenails that are perfectly formed." Yet the neonate is not perfect in his physiological adjustment to life outside the uterus. Having left a sheltered environment where temperature was constant and food intake automatic, he now must breathe, take food through the mouth, and adjust to temperature change.

The neonate's early attempts at breathing are apt to be imperfect. Breathing begins when the first column of air hits his lungs; the birth cry occurs simultaneously with the onset of respiration. Thereafter, he does not take in air regularly but gasps, yawns, sneezes, and coughs in his effort to regulate the amount of air he needs. Both heart and breathing rate are almost twice that of adulthood: 120 beats and 33 breaths per minute (Landreth, 1958). Breathing is of the abdominal type; the thorax becomes more involved as the child assumes an upright posture. Breathing and sucking are related, as Peiper has shown (Pratt, 1954). The infant can suck, swallow, and breathe at the same time—truly a remarkable skill, which is lost as the child matures.

Feeding, too, presents difficulties. Upon birth the alimentary canal must take over the job of ingesting food, digesting it, and egesting what it cannot use. Defecation occurs an average of 4.7 times (Halverson, 1940) and urination an average of 18 times, as we have indicated in Chapter 2. The quantity secreted at one time may be very small, however; prospective parents need not think that diapers will need changing twenty or more times a day. The transition to autonomy in digestion is accompanied by a loss of birth weight until about the middle of the first week. Then the infant begins to gain, but he still has digestive difficulties. He may regurgitate his food, or his hiccups may be long and loud, for the first few months, until the alimentary tract becomes more efficient.

Although studies report that the newborn sleeps twenty out of twenty-four hours for the first ten days (Pratt, 1954), no new mother will believe them. The difficulty is that neonatal patterns do not suit the adult; the baby may fall asleep several times during a feeding and then awake to cry lustily as soon as he is put down. Fortunately, he makes rapid strides toward stability of functioning and even during the first month extends his periods of wakefulness and unbroken sleep.

When the neonate is placed on his back, the tonic neck reflex, to which we have referred earlier (p. 21), may appear. The t-n-r, an early example of asymmetric behavior, may be a predictor of hand preference; according to Gesell, it is probable that "emphatic, constitutional left-handedness is correlated with a strong, infantile, left t-n-r" (1954, p. 351).

The amount of crying done by the neonate has been shown to be related to nursing care. From a study of fifty infants in a hospital nursery, Aldrich (1946) concluded that when nursing care improves, crying decreases. Before changes in care were made, the babies being studied cried for an average of 117 minutes a day, with a range of individual differences from 48 to 243 minutes. When more nursing time was made available, and when babies were wrapped in a cotton blanket to give them a feeling of support, crying averaged only 55 minutes a day.

Hunger in the Neonate

Of particular interest to parents is the fact that the neonate experiences certain muscular contractions of the stomach even before his stomach is emptied. These contractions, which are more vigorous than those experienced by adults, are known as "hunger contractions" and are accompanied by restless behavior and eventually the "hunger cry." In normal full-term neonates, these may occur as soon as two hours and fifty minutes after nursing during the first two postnatal weeks, and as early as three hours and forty minutes after meals during the next six weeks (Taylor, 1917).

Studies of feeding practices in societies other than our own lend some weight to Taylor's finding. Among the Navaho, for example, where infants are fed in response to restless behavior or the hunger cry, neonates are nursed an average of eight and a half times a day and twice during the night (Kluckhohn, 1947). As hunger contractions decrease in frequency, the number of nursing periods declines. Gesell's studies show that American infants who are fed on a self-demand schedule may vary considerably in the spacing of their feedings, both as compared with other infants and from feeding to feeding (Gesell & Ilg, 1937). Thus the same infant may sleep for only two hours between some feedings and for as long as five hours between others. As his alimentary tract becomes more stable, or as he learns to wait for food, variations tend to disappear. These reports have implications for the feeding of infants; they clearly suggest that the rigid four-hour feeding schedule used for so long by American mothers probably was suited to few, if any, neonates.

Functions of the Neonate

What the neonate can do—other than breathe, cry, feed, burp, and eliminate—and what he is capable of experiencing has long intrigued specialists in the field. How well his senses function at birth has been of particular interest. The infant does not "see" in the sense of being able to focus upon an object. His eyes move about, sometimes describing an arc, sometimes "crossing" in an alarming fashion. Yet he is sensitive to light; when a light is flashed into his eyes, he closes his lids or twitches them if they are already closed (Pratt, 1954). By the time the child is four weeks old, he shows some control over eye movement, and observers can also note eye fixations. The infant stares, although blankly, at lights and even, apparently, at faces that are close to him.

The neonate can also "hear"; that is, he is sensitive to sound. He does not make discriminations in pitch, but he modifies his responses to sound according to the duration and intensity of the stimuli. Short, intense sounds may produce a variety of responses, from closing the eyelids to gross muscular activity. One response is so typical as to be considered a reflex— i.e., the Moro reflex. At a sudden noise the infant throws out his arms and then brings them together as if in an embrace, while the legs show similar activity. This reflex disappears after a few months.

Other sensory mechanisms gradually begin to function. With respect to smell, the neonate responds to such stimuli as ammonia and acetic acid. It is uncertain whether he differentiates all four taste qualities; sugar and, to a lesser extent, acid solutions encourage a sucking response, while salt solutions break it up and quinine solutions seldom elicit any response. It has been demonstrated that the normal newborn has some sensitivity to pain, although the degree is in doubt, and that this sensitivity increases during the first week after birth (Carmichael, 1954).

Experiments have been conducted to see whether the neonate can learn. In one study (Marquis, 1931), attempts were made to condition food-taking responses in the neonate to the sound of a buzzer by presenting the bottle immediately before the buzzer was sounded. After a number of presentations of bottle and buzzer together, only the buzzer stimulus was presented. Some infants responded to the buzzer with food-sucking responses, indicating that conditioning had occurred. Although not all attempts to establish conditioned responses in the neonate have been so successful (Wenger, 1936), conditioning of older infants can be accomplished with stable results. This is important to remember, for it indicates that simple learning, at least, can be expected quite early in life.

Tumescence of the penis has been noted in the male neonate and enlargement of the uterus accompanied by secretion in the female. There is also a secretion from the breast of the female. It is not clear, as we pointed out in Chapter 2, whether these phenomena have a sexual significance. Halverson (1940) concludes that tumescence is caused by pressure stimulation of the bladder. It has a frequency of three to four a day, ranging in duration from a half minute to sixty-six minutes each. The cause of the phenomena in the female is not known.

The reflex activities of the neonate—his automatic responses to external stimuli—have also received considerable attention in the literature. Put something on the palm of the neonate and he will react by gripping firmly, even to the point of sustaining his own weight with one or both hands. Stroke the sole of the neonate's foot and plantar responses (extension of the big toe and fanning of toes) will appear. Produce a strong, sudden stimulus and the Moro reflex will occur. A related startle pattern may also occur, beginning with an eye blink, a thrusting forward of the head and neck, and a flexion of other parts of the body. These reflex activities have been interpreted by some laymen as evidence of biological recapitulation. According to this theory, every individual goes through a series of changes which repeat or are analogous to stages in the evolution of man. The grasping reflex, for example, has been cited as evidence that man's ancestors originally lived in trees and needed a strong grasp in order to swing from a limb. The Moro reflex supposedly originated in early man's need for safety; when startled, presumably he would clasp his mother or a tree trunk or some other protective object for safety.* These theories are no longer acceptable to psychologists since they are not supported by the data of embryology.

By four weeks of age, the baby has made considerable progress. His body muscles have more tone; he seems less limp when he is picked up. His breathing is deeper; his temperature regulation is steadier. All his body functions are under better control; he has come a long way in his adjustments to a postnatal environment.

* The theory of recapitulation was originally developed by G. Stanley Hall (1904) as an extension of Darwin's conclusions regarding the evolution of man. According to Hall, human beings pass not only through earlier stages of biological evolution (as exemplified by the grasping reflex) but also through cultural epochs of development. The creeping baby is reliving the time when his ancestors moved about on all fours; the child playing Indian is reliving the period when man was a hunter and fighter. Although Hall made many noteworthy contributions and, indeed, was a pioneer in the child-development field, his recapitulation theory has no basis in fact.

2. If possible, observe a neonate for a two-hour period. Record as much of his behavior as you can. Is he relatively still much of the time? What movements seem to be characteristic? Are most of his movements generalized or specific?

3. Interview parents who have recently had their first baby. What personal adjustments did father and mother have to make? How do these adjustments differ from those of parents whose newborn is their second or third child?

4. It may be possible for your class to gather some interesting data on changes in attitudes toward the birth process. Interview your own parents to find out what they remember about your birth, including their feelings and the length of labor and the lying-in period. Interview parents who have recently had a child, asking them the same questions. Pool your findings with those of your classmates and see if any trend is apparent. (Gather data only on attitudes toward the birth of children who have appeared in the same birth order.)

SUGGESTED READINGS

DENNIS, WAYNE (ed.). *Readings in Child Psychology,* Prentice-Hall, 1951. Part 1, "Behavior of the Fetus and the Neonate," contains abbreviated reports of research which has bearing on the material in this chapter.

GESELL, ARNOLD, & ILG, FRANCES L. *Infant and Child in the Culture of Today,* Harper, 1943. Chapter 8, "A Good Start," discusses the advantages of rooming-in practices in some detail. Chapter 9, "Four Weeks Old," is a delightfully written account of the behavior day of a four- to six-weeks-old infant.

MONTAGU, M. F. ASHLEY. Constitutional and prenatal factors in infant and child health. In William E. Martin and Celia Burns Stendler (eds.), *Readings in Child Development,* Harcourt, Brace, 1954, pp. 15-29. In this stimulating paper, Montagu discusses the various ways in which conditions of the prenatal environment may influence later development.

PRATT, KARL C. The neonate. In L. Carmichael (ed.), *Manual of Child Psychology,* Wiley, 1954, pp. 215-91. The advanced student will find a wealth of material in this scholarly review of research on the neonate. A section on physiology contains many details on the functioning of the newborn child: circulation, respiration, alimentation, and endocrinology.

SEARS, ROBERT R., MACCOBY, ELEANOR E., & LEVIN, HARRY. *Patterns of Child Rearing*, Evanston, Ill.: Row, Peterson, 1957. Chapter 2, "Background for Parenthood," describes the attitudes of 379 mothers, mainly middle class, toward becoming pregnant, and how much warmth and affection these mothers felt toward their children.

the process
of socialization

6
the impact of
society and
culture

In Part One we have been examining ways in which we can expect children the world over to resemble one another because of their biological inheritance. We found that, because he is a member of the human race, each child has many aspects of growth and development in common with all other children. This fact is not difficult for us to accept, because we can find illustrations all about us of the aspects of growth and development that we have been discussing. We can see, in children whom we know, examples of maturation, of different body types, of the prepubertal growth spurt, and so we can readily accept the fact that *all* children are like this by reason of their nature.

But we know that children are not alike in *all* ways; we know that there are important differences from society to society. American children are like Japanese children in some ways, but they also differ from the Japanese; they are like Norwegian children in many ways, but they also differ from the Norwegians. Similarly, Norwegians differ from the Japanese and from all other ethnic groups—including the Danes and the Swedes—in some ways.

If we were to poll our readers about what they regard as the outstanding characteristics of certain nationalities, we would probably find a high degree of consensus. If we were to ask what the Dutch are like, for example, the typical adjectives used to describe them would be "clean" and "neat." If we were to ask about Germans, many readers would reply "sober," "industrious." "Careful with money" and "taciturn" might be the words used in describing the Scots. Many of the characteristics that we associate with these and other nationalities are stereotypes; that is, they are conventional ideas which have not been subjected to research, and some of which would probably not stand up under the close scrutiny of research. These stereotypes or trait names represent an oversimplification of the problem, for societies and their members cannot be described so succinctly. However, the trait-name approach does reflect a popular appreciation of the similarities that are found among the people of the same society.

These similarities are not inborn; we are not born with American ways of behaving, or Mexican ways, or Hindu ways. We *learn* American characteristics as we grow up in American society with American culture. From the moment of birth we are exposed to the influence of culture. All normal children learn to walk as part of their biological inheritance and in so doing follow a certain sequence; but children of some Indian tribes turn their toes inward as they walk, whereas in white society children toe straight ahead or outward. All children can creep before they walk, but creeping is not permitted in Japanese households; the Japanese baby learns to walk without going through the creeping stage. All children need to eat, but many American babies are fed a scientific formula from a nursing bottle at regular intervals during the day, whereas the Samoan baby nurses at will from his mother's breast and the Alorese baby has premasticated food fed to him from a papaya leaf. That our tastes in food are learned is illustrated by the story of visitors to the Southwest who were fed rattlesnake-meat sandwiches without knowing what the meat was. When they were told what they were eating, one man promptly vomited.

In this chapter, which draws heavily upon cultural anthropology, we shall present material on growing up in many different parts of the world to help the reader understand how the fact of growing up in a particular society influences the course of development.

SOCIETY AND CULTURE

Society Makes Us Human

The first thing we note about the influence of society is that *it is growing up in a society that makes us human.* From time to time we see newspaper accounts of unfortunate children who have spent their formative years locked in dark closets or attics, prevented by deranged mothers from having any contact with other human beings. When found by the police, typically these children are more animal-like than human. Some of them do not walk upright; they "speak" only a few gutturals; they wolf their food and have few of the attributes we usually associate with human beings.

We also hear stories of children who, during their formative years, allegedly lived completely removed from other humans, in isolation or with only animals for company. Such "wolf" children are generally inhuman in behavior—and sometimes in appearance as well—and few of them exhibit much improvement even after several years in society, although the precise reason for their failure to develop after returning to society is not known. Two such cases are abstracted here (Dennis, 1951a):

A Wolf-Boy of India

Estimated age at isolation: three years.

Estimated age at discovery: nine years.

Behavior at isolation: was led by his mother to the field from which he was stolen; no other data.

Behavior at discovery: ferocious, bit at captors, ate nothing but raw flesh, dipped face in water to drink, went on all fours, tore off his clothes.

Recovery: never learned to speak, very little improvement [p. 154].

A Bear-Girl of India

Estimated age at isolation: exact age unknown, but less than three years.

Estimated age at discovery: three years.

Behavior at isolation: no data.

Behavior at discovery: ferocious, attempted to bite and scratch, ran on all fours, growled like a bear, ate and drank like a bear.

Recovery: learned to walk, eat, and drink like a human being, laughed often and loudly, did not learn to use or to understand language [p. 156].

These data are difficult to substantiate; they rely heavily upon circumstantial evidence. But if there is any validity to them, they show what can happen to children who grow up outside of society. They illustrate the fact that man's fate is bound up with the fate of a group and that a man who has been denied human association early in life survives, if he does so at all, as something hardly recognizable as a member of our species.

The Categories of Culture

It is not the mere presence of other human beings that makes man human. The child brought up in an isolated attic knew of the presence of the mother who from time to time thrust food inside the door. It is only as these other human beings teach us the ways of their society that we become human. Each society has its culture, its own body of "knowledge, belief, art, morals, law, custom, and any other capabilities and habits acquired by man as a member of society" (Tylor, 1871, p. 1). As we learn the culture of the society to which we belong, we become socialized beings.

The term "culture" includes *all* the learned behaviors of the members of a particular society. One grouping of these behaviors, proposed by the Institute of Human Relations at Yale University (Murdock *et al.*, 1950), includes the following categories.

language	drink and indulgence
communication	dress
exploitative activities	daily routine
technology	labor
implements	specialization
housing	exchange
food	finance
transportation	family
travel	kinship
numbers and measures	social organization
lore and learning	government
reaction to nature	social control
religion	ingroup conflict
ethics	war
property and contract	art
social stratification	recreation

Customs and institutions dealing with:

human organism	youth
sex	marriage
reproduction	adulthood
infancy	old age
childhood	sickness
death	socialization

Because man everywhere faces the same basic problems, these same categories apply to all cultures, from the most primitive to the most highly industrialized. In fact, they are common denominators in the hundreds of studies that have been made of societies all over the world. Take the category "language," for example. Every society teaches its children what to say, when to say it, how to say it, and whom to talk to. Similarly, children in every society must learn what and what not to wear, when to wear it, how to put on clothing, how to take care of clothing, what parts of the body must be covered, and many other customs of dress. Learning the accepted ways of behaving for each of these categories makes the child a member of society. This learning process begins at birth and continues throughout the lifetime of every individual.

The Diversity of Cultural Practices

Although societies resemble one another with respect to the categories of culture, the ways of behaving appropriate to each category differ tremendously from one society to another.

*"One thing I'll say for him, he's always
been a good provider."*

(Reproduced by permission. Copyright 1952 The New Yorker Magazine, Inc.)

If, for example, we consider, in the category "socialization," the question of who takes care of the young, we find many different answers. In our society infant care is almost entirely the mother's responsibility; the father and other relatives have little to do with it. In Alorese society the mother returns to the fields to work when the baby is three months old, and older women in the tribe or older siblings look after the infant. In our society we have institutionalized the baby sitter, often a stranger, who is hired to come in during the parents' absence. In pre-Communist Chinese society, mothers never had to worry about baby sitters, for there were enough relatives living in the same household to care for the infant should the mother be absent temporarily. The Sioux have no problem with baby sitters either; the baby is strapped on the mother's back and carried with her wherever she goes.

In the "socialization" category we also find diversity with regard to who punishes the baby, and how the punishment is inflicted. In our society the mother is generally the chief punishing agent, although she may threaten the child with later reprisal by the father as well, when he returns from work. Among the Hopi Indians, a Pueblo tribe, parents do not punish their child by striking him but once a year call in Kachinas, masked creatures dressed in terrifying costumes, who frighten the child into at least promising to be good. (The Kachinas, of course, are actually adult male relatives.) In our society a parent may spank the child's buttocks, slap his hands, or convey to him by words or actions that she no longer loves him or will not love him if he persists in a certain behavior. Navaho women say of us that we do not love our children because we slap them and make them cry.

Every society provides some set of social arrangements which comes under the category of "family," but the form the family takes differs from society to society. It may differ with respect to who lives in a household. The arrangement with which we are most familiar is that of husband and wife and their children; accepted variations may include relatives of the husband or wife, or children by adoption or former marriage. Among the Mentowie, children are adopted by their mother's father, and their mother's brothers feed them. Among the Zuni, a man lives in and works for his mother's household. Among the Comanche, the family group consists of a man and wife, or a man and his brothers with their wives, living together with sons, daughters, and their spouses and children. A married man may allow his younger unmarried brother to have sexual relations with his wife in the expectation that, when the younger brother marries, he will reciprocate the favor. Indeed, the term "brother" in this society includes all those who share the same woman, whether or not the men are "blood relatives." In other societies the household may contain husband and wife (or wives), their children, and the child-wives of their sons.

In our own society, we can find evidence that these family patterns are learned. Among American Negroes of the lower socioeconomic group, the primary unit may be mother, child, and mother's mother, a pattern which was established in the days of slavery. The slaves were encouraged by their owners to have children, regardless of legitimacy, so that the owners could sell the offspring. This pattern has been dramatically described in *His Eye Is on the Sparrow,* the moving autobiography of the Negro singer Ethel Waters. Such Negroes have never had the opportunity to learn a family pattern that includes a father who shares the responsibility for raising the family; consequently, men may attach themselves to the mother-child-mother's-mother unit on a very temporary basis. This is not true among middle-class Negroes, whose family pattern is the typical American one, and who may be exceedingly strait-laced with regard to accepted family morality in our middle-class culture. Middle-class Negroes *learn* a different family pattern from that of Negroes in the lower socioeconomic group.

Within the family in every society there are basic incest rules governing relationships between father and daughter, mother and son, and brother and sister. Yet, beyond these basic relationships, incest is defined differently in different cultures. It may be extended to mean all the members of one's own clan, several hundred in number, or to include first cousins or certain household groups. Incest rules of some sort are apparently necessary in every society, for they help to preserve the family unit by keeping related men and women from fighting over the same sexual object. The way in which a society defines its incest rules, however, depends upon cultural factors peculiar to that society.

"BASIC PERSONALITY TYPES"

We can see, then, that men everywhere face the same basic problems because of their nature as men, but that they solve these problems differently in different societies. It is because

"Rotten shame that cheetah making off with Sir Roger's dinner jacket."

Once learned, our cultural behaviors tend to be carried with us, even though they may not be well suited to a new environment.

(Reproduced by permission. Copyright 1937 The New Yorker Magazine, Inc.)

the members of a particular society learn the same ways of behaving that they come to resemble one another in personality. Members of a group who practice the same culture tend to develop some of the same characteristics. These basic similarities are so pervasive that they are sometimes described by such terms as "basic personality," "national character," and the like. That is, people who share the same culture resemble one another to the extent that we can describe a "basic personality type" to which most people in that society conform. To understand the concept of "national character" or "basic personality type," we turn first to examples in the literature.

Basic Similarities Among the Balinese

The Balinese have been described for us by many writers, including Belo (1949), who discusses the Balinese "temper," as she calls it, or basic personality type, as we have used the term. Among the patterns that she finds in Balinese personality is one that has to do with the amount of tension in Balinese life. She describes the Balinese as a careful and deliberate people; they move slowly, never hurrying, for they conceive hurrying to be unnecessary and stupid. In contrast to the typical American, the Balinese is quiet, relaxed, and peaceful in his daily life. He works hard and steadily, but with no feeling of the pressure of time. Because of his unconcern over the passage of time, he can wait for long periods without showing impatience. Because of his lack of tension, he can enjoy an eight-hour dramatic performance crouched in a press of bodies comparable only to one of our subway jams.

Balinese temper, however, does have another side. The workaday existence of the Balinese is broken from time to time by joyous festivals and celebrations in which all Balinese participate intensely and feverishly. On these occasions they change from their usual steady selves and their behavior becomes wild and frenzied.

Another important dimension of Balinese personality has to do with the order in their lives. There are few choices open to the Balinese with regard to behavior; they live according to a rigid code which governs all phases of their lives. The rules governing language, for example, are rich and complex, with special versions for High and Low Balinese and for intermediate castes. A Balinese in talking with others must choose expressions that are suited to the caste of his listeners. As Belo puts it, it is as if we had to choose among the expressions "he has eaten," "he has dined," and "he has partaken of his repast," with the most formal phrase reserved for members of the highest caste. There are, in addition, strict rules prescribing ways of sitting, manner of eating, age-sex roles, and religious behavior. Even the facial expressions permitted the Balinese are prescribed by custom. Thus the individual Balinese knows exactly what behavior is correct on every occasion and is relieved of the responsibility of making decisions with regard to right and wrong. All he has to do is to learn the rules and follow them.

The Balinese, then, are a well-balanced people who seem to lead lives relatively free from excessive tension. In their daily behavior, love and affection are manifested more frequently than anger and hostility.

Basic Similarities Among the Tepoztecans

From the primitive society of the Balinese, we turn next to a small agricultural village in Mexico—the village of Tepoztlán. Here are people whose standard of living is low but who nevertheless enjoy some of the "benefits" of Western civilization in the form of radios, phonographs, steel plows, aspirin, colas, sewing machines, and flashlights. The people of Tepoztlán represent a fusion of Indian and Spanish culture and resemble in important respects other groups in Middle America. What kind of people are they? Lewis describes them for us in terms of their interpersonal relations:

> . . . Tepoztecans value hard work, thrift, practicality, restraint, submission to authority, and the ability to conform. In interpersonal relations, Tepoztecans are detached, individualistic, and sensitive to status differences, with a generalized readiness to be suspicious, negativistic, and even hostile. Gossip, complaint, envy, and criticism are common. Tepoztecans are a constricted people, as seen in their lack of warmth and limited expression of affection, in their attitudes toward sex, and in their general absence of self-expression. Fantasy, imagination, and creativity are at a minimum; although Tepoztecans are

turned within themselves, they are not dreamers. They are an indirect people; they frequently rely upon the use of intermediaries and upon formality. Deception also is a sanctioned form of indirection, and the direct expression of aggression is strongly discouraged. Competition between individuals is rare. When competition occurs, it is between groups, thereby giving it a quality of impersonality. Finally, the aspiration level of most Tepoztecans does not place an undue burden on them and does not lead to any marked anxiety [1951, p. 418].

How Basic Personality Types Develop

Earlier in this chapter we saw that children growing up in different societies learn different patterns of behavior in connection with the same category of culture. The fact that they learn different behavior patterns for the same cultural category, however, explains only superficially why an American child differs from a Balinese child, a Tepoztecan child, or any other kind of child. The culture patterns governing eating, for example, are interesting but do not account for the basic personality differences among children who grow up in different societies. Eating escargots or smørrebrød or pizza does not make a child *basically* different from any other child. Wearing a sari instead of a dress is not a fundamental distinction between an American girl and an Indian girl.

Consider the following description of two Parisian children—a boy of five and his sister, aged seven:

Both children are dressed in the elegant (to our eyes) fashion of French children. They wear fitted gray-flannel leggings or slacks, high white shoes, beautifully tailored gray jackets, white string gloves, and attractive little hats. It is hard for the American observer to detect boy-girl differences in the way in which they are dressed, although these differences exist. It is also hard to believe that these beautifully dressed children are going to the Bois for recreation; Americans have a concept of special clothes for play which is not common among the French, except, of course, the special clothes for certain sports.

As these children emerge from the apartment house, they meet friends, a girl of six and her mother. They stop; the children shake hands with their friend's mother and say, "Bonjour, Madame." Then they shake their friend's hand and say, "Bonjour, Michèle." They grin in friendly fashion at one another while their mothers shake hands and exchange pleasantries, and then their friends go on. The formal shaking of hands and the insistence upon a formal greeting—not just "Bonjour," but "Bonjour, Madame"—again appear very different from the casual American greeting of "Hi" to young and old alike.

These two children with their mother await the appearance of the grandfather, who now drives up in his car. He gets out, kisses both children warmly, first on one cheek, then on the other, and greets the mother in similar fashion. All get in the car and they drive off. Again the American observer is struck by this demonstration of affection in public and also by the overt affection expressed by the grandfather toward his grandson. One is reminded of the letter in the *New Yorker* from a seven-year-old at camp to his aunt, instructing her to bring candy when she came to see him and adding "DO NOT kiss me" [Stendler, 1954a, p. 196].

The differences in behaviors between French and American children are important, of course, not in and of themselves, but only as expressions of differences in values between the two cultures. The French custom of shaking hands is important psychologically as a reflection of a drive which French parents help their children to acquire—the drive to be courteous. And although the picture of a father or grandfather kissing a boy on both cheeks may be interesting or funny depending upon the observer's cultural sophistication, it is important psychologically only because it is an indication of the warmth and closeness of relationships within the French family.

The fundamental differences among children in different societies and the basic similarities among children of the same society can be explained in two ways. First, different societies have different *goals* in mind in rearing their children, and they teach their children certain behaviors that are consistent with these goals. Secondly, societies differ in their *methods* of socialization, and these varying methods also influence the basic personality. We turn now to a consideration of the goals of socialization and how they influence basic personality.

HOW GOALS OF SOCIALIZATION
INFLUENCE BASIC PERSONALITY

A traveler newly returned from England furnishes us with a simple example of how societal expectations or goals for children influence behavior. The traveler noticed English children playing comfortably outdoors on cold September days dressed in thin cotton dresses or shorts and light wool sweaters. She knew that American children on similarly cold days shivered in heavy winter coats. Part of the difference in reaction, of course, can be explained in terms of adjustment to climate. But part of the explanation goes somewhat deeper. In an English textbook on health for primary school children, the traveler found a picture of a child who, the text claimed, was improperly dressed for play—bundled into a warm jacket, muffler, and leggings, much as American children might dress for winter play. This child, the reader was told, could not enjoy playing because of his heavy clothing. The text also showed a child properly dressed for play—in light sweater, shorts, and high socks—and thoroughly enjoying himself as a result. Because the English child is expected to withstand the rigors of the cold, he learns his Spartan ways. Because the American child is expected to bundle up when the weather turns cold, he does not learn to *want* to be Spartanlike in this particular respect.

The expectations that societies have for their children influence child rearing in various other ways. For one, they help to determine the kinds of model that will be held up to the child to emulate. He may be told to be like the Jones boy down the street; but is the Jones boy a friendly, outgoing, independent lad, or is he a shy, reserved, and dependent child? What are the characteristics of the television and motion-picture heroes he sees? What kinds of behavior are rewarded in the books he reads and the folk-tales he is told? What kinds are punished?

Children are continually exposed to models of behavior which conform to the expectations adults in their society have for them.

Also, parents and teachers themselves reward or punish certain behaviors depending upon their goals of child rearing. An American five-year-old plays noisily on the living room floor with his toy jeep. He pretends that the jeep is charging an enemy and sends it with a terrific push in and out of furniture while his mother attempts to carry on a conversation with a visitor. When the noise reaches a high decibel level, she hushes the child, but in an indulgent fashion that surely must communicate to him her feeling that his behavior is really pretty cute. American parents affectionately refer to their children as "little monsters"; Dennis is expected to be a menace.

The French child, in contrast, knocks on the living room door when his mother is entertaining a guest. When he is given permission to do so, he enters the room and shakes hands with the guest. He converses politely for a short time, speaking only when he is spoken to, and then is excused to return to his room for play. If he were to behave as the American child does, he would be punished. Conversely, if the American child were to behave like the French, his mother would scold him later for being too shy and for "standing there like a dolt."

The expectations or goals that a society has for its children help to shape what children learn to want and what ways of behaving they learn to value. We may think of these goals as *drives* which are learned by children and which motivate their behavior. As goals of socialization differ from society to society, so also do the acquired needs of children and the personalities they develop. The process by which new drives are learned is discussed in Chapter 8. An important part of socialization is learning to want to be the kind of person our society wants us to be.

1. How might the goals of Americans brought up in an era of prosperity differ from those of Americans reared in the depression years?

2. The practice of regarding our own ways of living as

superior to those of others is called ethnocentrism. Can you think of some examples of ethnocentrism?

3. Select a single category of culture from the list on page 165. Describe the behavior patterns for this category which are prevalent in American society. Try to find descriptions of how other societies behave in relation to this category.

The Goals of Socialization in American Society

It is difficult in a society as complex as ours to describe a set of goals of socialization which are accepted by all segments of the population. We could do this accurately only if we carefully studied a representative sample of Americans and identified those characteristics which appear to some degree in all of them. No one has yet made such a study, but a number of social scientists have considered the question of "the American character," or basic personality. On the basis of these studies, we can make some tentative statements about the kind of adult the American child is expected to become. These goals of socialization apply, of course, only to a "typical" American. In kind, degree, and number, goals vary from person to person, from group to group. We cannot assume that any particular adult, or any particular subgroup of adults, accepts these goals, or that all who accept them do so to the same degree and define the behavior that satisfies them in the same way. For example, a particular group may or may not accept "friendliness" as a goal; it may consider this trait a highly important or a minor objective; it may encourage the elimination of all competitive behavior as a means of achieving the goal or it may see no incompatibility between friendliness and rivalry.

Thus our description can serve only as a benchmark; we can describe the goals of particular members of American society by determining the extent to which they agree with or depart from this standard. The reader should bear in mind that the characteristics discussed below are not necessarily those that are considered ideal by the writers; they are, rather, the characteristics that seem to be considered ideal by many Americans. They constitute the "social character" of Americans—that is, the way in which the members of American society tend to resemble one another. Each particular American, of course, has an individual character, consisting of aspects of the social character plus characteristics unique to him.

GETTING ALONG WITH OTHERS. High on a list of American goals of socialization is the goal of getting along with others, of working or playing with them without friction.

This goal is so highly regarded in American society that schools sometimes evaluate the mental health of children in terms of their adjustment to other children. In some classrooms teachers apply sociometric techniques, asking children to name those near whom they would like to sit or with whom they would like to play. The results of these sociometric surveys (see Fig. 6-1) reveal the children who are "popular"—i.e., chosen by several others—and, usually, one or two pupils who are "isolates"—i.e., chosen by no one. All too often teachers assume that the most frequently chosen children are the best adjusted, with the fewest problems. Yet the price of their adjustment may be the relinquishment of considerable individuality or the acceptance of questionable values. After all, there are some individuals with whom we should *not* get along; perhaps none of our readers would accept getting along well with Nazis as a desirable goal, since getting along with others also indicates a willingness to accept or condone their values.

The goal of getting along with others has many facets. One of them is friendliness. Few observers have failed to note that Americans are a friendly people, although some do not entirely approve of the ways in which we demonstrate our friendliness. The tremendous sale of Dale Carnegie's *How to Win Friends and Influence People* is an indication of the need Americans feel for skills and techniques to be used in social situations. It is not enough to be oneself; that will not automatically result in friendships. One must be a social self; one must know the right things to say at the right time and the right things to do at the right time. This is more than a matter of social manners,

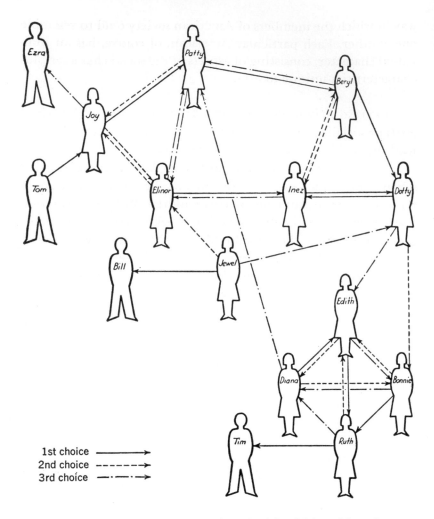

FIGURE 6-1. A sociogram showing the friendships of fourth-
and fifth-grade girls.

(From R. Cunningham. *Understanding Group Behavior of Boys and
Girls,* Columbia University Press, 1951)

patterns of which can be found in other societies. One must
develop a social personality.

Another facet of this goal of getting along with others—or
perhaps a result of it—is sociability, seeking out the companion-

ship of others to avoid being by oneself. The American child seems lost when he has to play by himself; when he has no play-mate or companion, he tends to turn on the radio or the tele-vision set to escape being alone. As an adult, he is a "joiner"; he may belong to a number of organized groups in his com-munity. (In this connection we note the tremendous number of clubs even in quite small communities. In one city of 15,000 population, more than four hundred social organizations were counted; "successful" adults in this city might participate in ten or twelve of them.)

How does this goal of sociability affect children? The child, particularly if he is a member of the middle class, becomes part of many different organizations while he is still in the elemen-tary school. Sunday school is likely to be a social group with parties, picnics, and other social affairs; the child is encouraged to join the Cubs and then the Scouts; he may also be a 4-H member, a member of a neighborhood club, and a member of the country club or some other social set. This tendency to join organized groups is less characteristic of the lower-class child (Stendler, 1949).

Gorer points out some of the consequences of our emphasis on the companionship of others:

> It is these feelings which make loneliness intolerable to well-adjusted Americans, and account for the numerous social fea-tures which are designed to obviate it: the absence of doors in all but the most private parts of most houses, the wedged-open doors of offices and studies, the shared bedrooms in col-leges and boarding houses, the innumerable clubs and fraternal and patriotic associations, professional organizations, and con-ventions, the club cars on trains, the numberless opportunities and facilities given for casual conversation, the radio piped into every hotel bedroom, into many railway cars and automobiles, left on incessantly in the house (for even the voice of the radio is better than silence). "I should go mad if I had to spend a week (or shorter period) alone" is a constantly reiterated remark which conceals real psychological truth under its surface exag-gerations. Americans, psychiatrists as well as laymen, consider that there is something odd, something suspect, in a young

person who deliberately eschews company and chooses privacy or loneliness [1948, pp. 107-09].

Still another facet—or outcome—of this goal of getting along with others is conformity. Many observers of the American scene have been struck by what one writer (Fromm, 1941) has called our "compulsive conformity." Every society, of course, teaches conformity to a certain extent. Every member must observe the mores of his society to some degree or the society would disintegrate for lack of a common culture.

But some social scientists have noted a tendency toward *undue* conformity in American society. Our children not only feel the need to wear the same kinds of clothes as others, use the same slang, watch the same television programs, sing the same songs, keep the same hours, and the like; they also accept the values of their peers with respect to their behavior toward others. They may go along when the gang rejects a certain classmate, expresses intolerance toward those who are "different," worships a certain actor or singer, or indulges in delinquent behavior. They become so sensitive to the opinions of others that what others think becomes their most important guide for behavior.

INDEPENDENCE. Another objective that parents have in mind in socializing their children is the goal of independence or self-reliance. Every American dreams of some day being "independent." By that term, he most often means financial security—a home paid for, a new car in the garage, paid-up annuities, money in the bank. He looks forward to the time when he doesn't have to take orders from anybody. A man wants to own his business or his farm. The unconditional possession of material things is a clear sign of independence. The strength of these aspirations lies in the fact that they have so often been realized throughout American history. That the gaining of such "independence" brings with it many responsibilities, that many who achieve it do not know what to do with it—these do nothing to dispel the dream.

Not only financial security but the ability to "stand on one's own feet," to take care of oneself in all aspects of life, is part of this goal of socialization. During the great depression of the 1930's, the ideal man was one who refused to accept government aid or "made" work but who, instead, set up his own little apple-stand or made his own little mousetraps and independently supported himself or even amassed a small fortune as a result. Even today, many people oppose social-security measures on the ground that too much reliance on the government will result in too little initiative and self-reliance.

Training for this aspect of the ideal personality begins early in our society. Many young mothers defend the practice of going out occasionally and leaving their child with a baby sitter by saying that it teaches the child to get along without his mother. The American mother is likely to be proud of the fact that her three-year-old no longer cries when she leaves him. In contrast, in French society, where dependency rather than independence is stressed, mothers would not regard this as an accomplishment. It is expected that babies will want to be with their mothers and vice versa. The child is not consciously trained to bear separation as a step in growth toward independence (Stendler, 1954a).

"Standing on one's own feet" with respect to defending one's rights and possessions is also encouraged by American parents. American parents teach their children to keep an eye out for their fire truck, doll, or sand toy in group play, and even preschool-age children are sharply rebuked if a toy disappears in play. Children are taught not to let others infringe upon their rights; if someone snatches his toy, the child must be sure to get it back. Again we note a contrast with the French. When young French children are engaged in play with others in the park, it is expected that the mothers will look out for the toys of their offspring and will settle disputes among the children (Wolfenstein, 1955a).

Our schools also encourage self-reliance and independence. Tattling is frowned upon, and children are frequently told to settle grievances among themselves. Pupils are expected to learn to work independently, without relying upon others for help. Even report cards reflect our emphasis upon this goal. The report forms used in many school systems consist of a list of traits on which teachers grade children as satisfactory or unsatisfactory. "Gets along well with others" and "Works independently" are behaviors typically found on such lists.

One of the goals of every society obviously must be the eventual independence of adults; if all adults were dependent, there would be no one to rear the young. But we might question the early and rather extreme emphasis upon this goal in our society. Strong dependency upon the parents when children are young can be a very powerful socialization tool. The child learns to expect direct help from his parents, but he also learns to depend upon and accept their guidance of his own behavior. In societies in which the period of dependency is extended, parental dictates guide the child's behavior for a longer period of time. The American mother who discourages dependency too early and pushes her child into growing up too fast is relinquishing in part her opportunity to control the child's actions. She may at the same time be strengthening his dependency upon his peers; the child, being too young to make his own decisions, may use his agemates as a source of guidance.

SUCCESS. Still another goal of socialization in American society is success, particularly material success. The successful American adult is one who is able to buy (or at least owe for) the "good things of life"—a car of fairly recent vintage, a house full of modern appliances, a college education for his children, some travel or vacations away from home, private music, dance, or sports lessons for his children, and wardrobes at least as good as the neighbors'. Having a great deal of money is not important; surveys of college seniors, both men and women, reveal that they want just enough "to enjoy as much relaxed time as possible at home with the family: well-roundedness, good adjustment, middling success (the tensions at the top are too great) and safety are the goals" (Lynes, 1957). "Middling" success, however, is defined as enough to ensure the material benefits of our industrial civilization for one's family.

Our emphasis upon material values has undoubtedly contributed to an easier way of life for us, but at a cost. We have become a society in which all kinds of products are judged not so much by their beauty or by the creativity that they manifest as by the dollar sign they bear. The "hero" of a recent television drama was an investment broker who won an award for writing poetry. He was immediately suspect—indeed, he lost his chance of promotion and almost his job—until he wrote a rhyming couplet that brought him $25,000 in an advertising contest. This made him "successful" as a poet, for his poetry had earned him money. Similarly, the "successful" singer is one whose records top the million mark, and the "successful" writer is one who makes the best-seller list.

Like our other goals, this goal of success has some concomitants. One of these is industry. In order to achieve success, one must be industrious; one must be willing to work hard to get ahead. Training for this aspect of the goal begins early in the child's life. He is given jobs to develop responsibility; his "work habits" are graded on his report card; he is expected to use his time wisely. Among the middle class it is not uncommon for parents to encourage their children to work outside the home, peddling papers, mowing lawns, baby sitting, and the like. The money earned is often set aside for college, for summer camp, or for a bicycle or other sports equipment. In this way the child learns to associate work with getting ahead and to measure getting ahead in terms of some material gain.

Again, we should point out the importance of the degree of emphasis upon the goal. The ability to live without the products of modern industry is hardly a desirable goal of socialization—but should the goal of success be measured in purely material terms? Perhaps the college seniors who want only "middling" success represent a welcome trend away from the excessive materialism that has characterized our society and the accompanying emphasis upon working hard to get ahead. Some mental hygienists have pointed out that our strong drive for success may be partly responsible for the great increase in mental illness in modern America. Perhaps the more relaxed attitude of the oncoming generation will prove to be a better approach from the standpoint of mental health.

PURITANISM. Puritanism, a term derived from the attitudes and behaviors of the Puritans of colonial days, refers not only to rigid inhibitions with regard to sexual behavior but also to a general tendency to deny the body and its nature. Today we see its effects in the prudery which is characteristic of the successfully socialized American. It is reflected in our child-training practices. Children are early taught modesty with respect to revealing certain parts of the body; they are taught to associate shame with the processes of elimination and wickedness with such practices as masturbation.

There has been a tendency in recent years to recognize the naturalness of body processes and to relax some of these pressures upon children. Mothers have been encouraged to tell their offspring the proper physiological names for parts of the body and its functions, to teach children to regard the processes of elimination as natural rather than shameful, and to recognize themselves that it is natural rather than evil for the young child to handle his genitals to some extent. These trends are commendable, but the general problem of regulating the sex drive still remains in our society as in all others. We continue to try to solve it by repressing it or ignoring it, but this drive is so strong that such solutions cannot be wholly successful. In Chapter 7 we shall examine some of the consequences of these mechanisms of adjustment.

These themes of getting along with others, with its concomitant emphasis upon friendliness and conformity, of independence, of success and industry, and of puritanism permeate American society. No one who grows up in American society can help but be influenced by them. Together—with all their consistency and inconsistency—they constitute the social character of the "typical" American.

Variations in the American Character

As we have recognized from the outset, nothing that we can say about *the* American character will fit all Americans equally well. There are almost as many variations in character as there are Americans. But we assume that all these variations are based on the same themes.

It may be legitimate, for example, to claim that all Americans are friendly. But the way in which that friendliness is manifested—even the degree to which it is manifested—varies from person to person or from subgroup to subgroup of Americans. We think of New Englanders and Southerners as being friendly in different ways, and of Midwesterners as being friendly in a still different way. We think of New Englanders as reserved, of Southerners as dignified but gracious, and of Midwesterners as "open" and informal, even "breezy." These are stereotypes, of course, but they exemplify the fact of variation. In just one aspect of the American character, we see marked differences from one section of the United States to another.

But the American character varies with other factors besides geography. Being an American if one is six years old, male, and a member of the upper class is quite different from being an American if one is twenty-six years old, a female, and a member of the middle class. If we are to understand the socialization of the child in American society, we must discuss, at least briefly, some significant differences in expected behavior associated with age, sex, and social status.

VARIATIONS WITH AGE. Both the nature and the strength of our expectations of children's behavior are functions of the age of the children. Socialization scarcely begins in infancy. But in early childhood we expect the child to learn to conform to simple rules and regulations, to acquire certain skills, such as walking and talking, to develop friendly attitudes toward adults and other children. We expect him to show some signs of independence. For example, we are pleased when he can button his clothes, manage the zipper on his snow suit, and tie his shoes

We expect him to acquire bowel and bladder control and associated toilet habits. He must learn to like certain foods and to eat them in a prescribed manner. We look for him to develop a certain degree of sexual modesty.

As he grows older, our expectations—at least, in their details—constantly change. For each period of his growth and development, the child faces a somewhat different set of demands. Havighurst (1948), among others, has called these demands *developmental tasks*. The tasks he lists for the periods of middle childhood and adolescence are presented below as examples.

Developmental Tasks of Middle Childhood

1. Learning the physical skills necessary for ordinary games.
2. Building wholesome attitudes toward oneself as a growing organism.
3. Learning to get along with agemates.
4. Learning an appropriate sex role.
5. Developing fundamental skills in reading, writing, and calculating.
6. Developing the concepts necessary for everyday living.
7. Developing conscience, morality, and a scale of values.
8. Developing attitudes toward social groups and institutions.

Developmental Tasks of Adolescence

1. Accepting one's physique and accepting a masculine or feminine role.
2. Establishing new relations with agemates of both sexes.
3. Achieving emotional independence of parents and other adults.
4. Achieving assurance of economic independence.
5. Selecting and preparing for an occupation.
6. Developing intellectual skills and concepts necessary for civic competence.
7. Desiring and achieving socially responsible behavior.
8. Preparing for marriage and family life.
9. Building conscious values in harmony with an adequate scientific world picture.

VARIATIONS WITH SEX. Although we have the same general expectancies for all children in our society at a given age level, the expectancies for boys and for girls differ in interpretation and strength. For example, as Havighurst points out, boys must acquire physical skills in middle childhood to a much greater

Little men don't cry.

(Reprinted by permission of the publishers, Duell, Sloan and Pearce, Inc. Copyright 1950 by William Steig)

degree than girls. Any boy who does not do so risks the disapproval of his peers and of adults. But a girl who fails to develop such skills may experience little or no loss of prestige as a result.

All children are expected to learn to read, to write, and to calculate, but, during the elementary school years, it seems to be much more important for girls to do so than for boys. At least, boys suffer less status loss than do girls by mediocre performance or even failure in academic tasks.

Similarly, we expect both boys and girls to get along with their peers, but in different ways. In the elementary school years, a boy may greet another boy with a hearty slap on the back or with a friendly poke. These techniques do not endear him to girls, but, then, we do not expect a child of this age to concern himself with children of the opposite sex. A girl of the same age also restricts her associations largely to members of her own sex, but she demonstrates her friendliness in a much less aggressive manner. In adolescence, the boy must develop more appropriate ways of getting along with girls. The girl must also modify her social behavior if she is to be accepted by the opposite sex. She sheds some of the ladylike qualities that are expected at twelve years of age and assumes the role of a good sport—active, daring, and enthusiastic (Tryon, 1939).

The adolescent boy must begin to look ahead seriously to the responsibilities of the adult male he is to become. He must concern himself somewhat more with matters of occupational training and the eventual achievement of economic independence. But even in our society, where girls are free to prepare for careers, it is expected that most of them will be wives and mothers. Thus, during these adolescent years, they must be developing some of the skills required in domestic roles.

In American society, then, as in other societies, there are well-defined patterns of sex-appropriate behavior. Since these patterns change somewhat with age, the tasks specific to sex also change. As a boy completes each of these tasks in turn, he approaches the final status of manhood. In the same way, a girl achieves womanhood. Each of them will have the traits that we have identified as part of the American character, but they will manifest these traits in somewhat different ways—the one as a male, the other as a female.

VARIATIONS WITH SOCIAL CLASS. Societal expectations are not identical for all children or for all adults or even for all males or females at a given age level. The definition of the American character varies with the social class to which the individual belongs.

According to many sociologists, prestige and accompanying privilege are distributed on the basis of socially ranked groups, which are called social classes. Each of these social classes consists of people who associate freely with other members of that class and who do not associate freely with members of groups defined as above or beneath them. Such expressions as "They don't fit in with our bunch," "I don't allow my children to play over there," and "They run around with a different social set" express these distinctions in association and social acceptance.

Most of the sociologists who have studied the social-class systems of various communities identify three major classes, with two subclasses for each major division. Thus in "Yankee City," a small New England town, Warner and Lunt (1941) identify an upper-upper class, a lower-upper class, an upper-middle class, a lower-middle class, an upper-lower class, and a lower-lower class. However, the age and economic complexity of a community, among other factors, may affect the number of social classes. Barker and others (1950), in studying the small rural community of "Midwest," found no social-class hierarchy. Conceivably, an old community that contains members at varying economic levels might be more stratified than a new community where the good things of life are more evenly distributed. Conceivably, also, a community containing foreign-born groups might have a high degree of stratification since new Americans are typically ranked lower than old Americans.

The members of a given social class are assigned by the community to socially superior or inferior positions, according to certain socioeconomic factors. These include income, occupation, location of home, ancestors, education, and clique membership. Wealth alone is not enough; going with the "right kind of people" and "doing the right things" count far more. Living on the wrong side of the tracks, being a bank president, performing manual labor, belonging to the country club, and coming from an "old" family are factors which, together with others, determine one's social-class position.

The hypothesis that social classes differ in their goals of socialization has been borne out by several research studies.

Maccoby and others interviewed 372 mothers of kindergarten children in the Boston area, divided into two main groups: upper-middle and upper-lower. The two groups were found to differ significantly in their training procedures with respect to what we have called puritanism. These investigators report: "Upper-lower mothers are much more severe in sex training. They begin modesty training at an earlier age, and insist upon higher standards of modesty. The upper-middle mothers are likely to ignore masturbation and certain forms of sex play among the children, or seek to distract the child without making an issue; the upper-lower mothers tend to react with considerable emotion, and punish the child for such behavior" (1954, p. 395).

There are class differences also with respect to educational goals for children. In general, upper-middle-class mothers expect their children to go to college and in some cases to graduate school. Upper-lower-class mothers feel that their children should finish high school but not necessarily college. However, the upper-lowers do not rule out college for the child who wants very much to go or who shows unusual abilities.

That these and other social-class differences in expectations lead to variations in the American character has been demonstrated in a study of the attitudes of children of junior high school age (Phillips, 1950). The investigator identified certain attitudes which were more typical of children in one class than of those in any other. For example, here are some statements to which he found that most lower-class children subscribed:

> It's more fun to do things when a cop is after you for doing them.
> Boys and girls who stay in school after they are sixteen years old are usually trying to keep from going to work.
> Schools teach a lot of things that don't work out when you actually get on the job.
> Girls and women should take a "back seat" to men and boys in most things.

Here are some attitudes most typical of middle-class children:

> If you fail to do your best at school, you probably won't amount to much when you grow up.
>
> Some kids aren't popular at school because they never do things the way others do.
>
> If a person is to be a good citizen, he should support community projects and public activities.
>
> In America you can better yourself if you have the ambition.

Finally, here are some characteristic beliefs of upper-class children:

> A person should not earn his living by physical labor if he can help it.
>
> Everyone should try to make as much money as he can.
>
> One must be careful not to be seen reading certain magazines which are below his social level.
>
> It doesn't pay to try to mix people from different social classes.

There seems to be little doubt that the American character is interpreted differently in one stratum of society than in another. Just as some behavior is defined as appropriate for children of a given age or sex, so certain behavior is appropriate for children in a given social class.

    4. Do you believe that members of the lower class are less (or more) conforming, friendly, independent, and successful than members of the middle class, or equally so? In what (other?) ways do you believe that aspects of the American character are manifested differently in these two social classes?

    5. Is it possible for a lower-class child to learn according to middle-class expectancies? Is it desirable for him to do so?

    6. Are expectancies identical for all children of the same sex, age, and social class? If not, why not?

    7. In what sense is the maxim "Cleanliness is next to godliness" a manifestation of puritanism in the American character? Is the degree of cleanliness commonly maintained in America warranted by considerations of health?

    8. How would the achievement of each of the developmental tasks listed on page 186 contribute to the development of the American character?

9. For each of Havighurst's developmental tasks, indicate the differences in expectations for boys and for girls.

10. We have mentioned variations in the American character related to such factors as age, sex, and social class. Might there not also be variation with time? Is the social character of this generation identical with that of the last generation? Will the social character of the next generation be different in any respect from that which is currently accepted?

HOW METHODS OF SOCIALIZATION AFFECT BASIC PERSONALITY

Fundamental differences among children of different societies and among subgroups within the same society must be explained, not only in terms of differing goals of socialization, but also in terms of differing *methods* of socialization. It is not only what parents want their children to be but how they train them that shapes personality. Individual parents, of course, differ in their approach to child rearing, but to the extent that there are general cultural patterns followed in each society, we can expect differences in the basic personality of children from society to society.

Techniques of Child Training

The various techniques used by parents to reward or punish children influence basic personality. Studies have concentrated upon the differential effects of punishment and reward. The most ambitious attempt to find correlations between the severity and frequency of punishment in different societies and the effects upon personality has been that of Whiting and Child (1953). These investigators analyzed child-training practices in seventy-five societies, including our own, focusing on five systems of behavior, or areas of socialization, with which every society is concerned. In every society children must be weaned and taught to eat in the appropriate manner (referred to as the *oral* system of behaviors); they must be taught to defecate at the proper time and place (the *anal* system of behaviors); they must learn the rules of sexual propriety (the *sexual* system of behaviors); they must learn to be self-reliant and responsible (the *dependence* system); and, finally, they must be taught to curb their aggressive impulses (the *aggression* system). Judges were asked to rate the severity of specific child-training practices for these five systems in each of the societies under study.

The investigators classified methods of punishment as either love-oriented or punishments by physical means or ridicule. (An example of the former would be the parent's threat to the child, "Mother won't love you any more if you don't behave.") They divided the societies under study into two groups: those below the median in use of love-oriented techniques and those above the median. Then they employed a statistical analysis to see whether the exposure to love-oriented techniques of punishment was correlated with ensuing anxiety in adulthood. To measure anxiety, they analyzed the cultural customs relating to illness. For example, societies differ with respect to their views on the responsibility for illness. In some societies, a sorcerer or some other outside agent or cause is blamed for illness. In others, the patient himself is blamed for being ill; he was disobedient and played in the wet grass, or didn't wear his rubbers when it rained, or did something else which brought about the illness. Societies in which the blame for being sick is usually laid at the victim's door were rated high in anxiety.

Their findings showed a positive relationship between the two variables. Societies below the median in use of love-oriented techniques were high on patient responsibility for illness. In other words, there appears to be some relationship between the practice of punishing children by denying them love and later feelings of guilt or anxiety on the part of the children, measured in these terms.

Many other studies reveal how societies differ with respect to methods of reward and punishment. One investigator (Wolfenstein, 1955b) interviewed immigrant parents in America of Chinese, Czech, Eastern European, Jewish, and Syrian origin.

She found differences among the parents in attitude toward corporal punishment. Chinese and Jewish parents tended to be moderate in their use of punishment, whereas no moderation appeared necessary to Syrians; the only problem seemed to be to punish sufficiently.

"A Syrian informant cites a traditional paternal saying: 'I do not want my neighbors to say I have done well when I beat my son; if they say I have done too much, then I will be satisfied.' When Syrian parents bring a child to school for the first time, they are supposed to urge the teacher to beat him properly, by saying: 'The skin is for you, the bones for me' " (p. 366).

We do not know whether there is a one-to-one relationship between any of these practices and the later appearance of a specific personality trait, although some surmises have been made. Hopi children, as we have pointed out, are frightened by Kachinas once a year. Eggan (1953) attributes the anxiety and mistrust which characterize many of the Hopi tribe in part to this severe method of discipline. The child's disillusionment when he eventually discovers the identity of the Kachinas may account in part for his readiness later on to suspect any and all of witchcraft. These observations are not quite in line with the Whiting and Child finding that love-oriented punishment and anxiety tend to go together; they suggest, rather, that severity of punishment of any sort is related to anxiety.

The Socializing Agents

Under methods of child rearing, or socialization, we include the socializing agents. Is the child brought up mostly by his parents, or in an extended family? Do the mother or the father or the grandparents exert the greatest influence? How powerful an influence are the child's contemporaries?

We know that societies differ with respect to socializing agents. In one study of French working-class and middle-class parents (Favez-Boutonier, 1956), it was reported that children are reared, at least partly, by their grandparents. Stendler (1954a) found that in only ten of the seventy-five Parisian middle-class families she investigated did the children live alone with parents and siblings; the rest had one or more grandparents, aunts, or other relatives living under the same roof. In contrast, the typical American family consists of mother, father, and siblings.

The presence of an extended family appears to affect the socialization process in certain predictable ways. It may be that societies in which the grandparents have considerable responsibility for child care are more traditional and change less rapidly than societies in which parents do the bringing-up. Also, parents who lack or reject the counsel of an older generation may be less secure and less confident of their own abilities as parents, and may show a greater tendency to rely upon outside "experts." Certainly this would appear to be true in America, where the influence of grandparents is minimal. Murdock and Whiting (1951), studying the effects of an extended family upon certain systems of behavior, found that the presence of grandparents tends to make for stricter imposition of rules, particularly with respect to dependency, aggression, and sexual behavior. In other words, societies with extended families are more severe in their training for self-reliance, curbing of aggression, and bringing sexual behavior into line with the accepted mores.

In some societies, other children play a significant role as socializing agents. All societies use older children to a certain extent as baby sitters, but in our society the child's own contemporaries have great importance. Their approval or disapproval of certain kinds of behavior can exert tremendous influence. American parents and teachers want children to get along well with others, to adjust to the group. They encourage the desired behaviors by saying: "Bobby won't play with you if you do that," "What will Susie think of you if you act like that?" "Johnny is spoiling our story, boys and girls. What shall we do about children who spoil our stories?" From remarks such as these, the child learns to give great weight to what other children think of his behavior, to want to gain their approval and avoid their disapproval.

In societies in which the peer group is an important socializing agent, there may be greater conformity to age-group standards. Again we note a contrast between French and American society. In American society, the peer group first rewards for conformity (or punishes for lack of conformity) to *adult* standards. Later it builds its own standards and enforces conformity to these; at this point being different from the group brings group disapproval. A third-grader, for example, may refuse his mother's request that he wear snow pants because "the kids will laugh" at him.

In France neither teachers nor parents indicate concern for the child's adjustment to the group. "Children have nothing to learn from other children," one French mother said. "It is the family who teaches." Whereas the American parent early arranges for group experiences so that her child can begin to learn to adjust to others, the French parent is wary of the interference of other agents in her child's socialization. Wolfenstein (1955a), who observed children playing in the parks of Paris, noted that French children do not leave their parents to join other children in a communal play area. They play near their parents, who keep an alert eye open for any negative behavior and immediately take steps to correct it. In France children are not urged to play with other children, and the French parent does not try to find playmates for her young child outside the family.

Undoubtedly the use of the peer group as a socializing agent by Americans helps to account for some basic differences between the French and the American personality. As we have pointed out, it probably produces a different sense of self, a person who always pays attention to what others are doing in order to get a signal for what he himself should do. In contrast, the French system of socialization emphasizes individualism; by minimizing group influence, it also minimizes group conformity.

The Timing of Socialization

Societies also differ in the timing of socialization. Some societies are in a hurry to start training children, and adults impose certain rules and restrictions upon the child even in infancy. Other societies delay the socialization process but are quite severe once they begin. Still others indulge the child from infancy through adolescence.

What effect does age of socialization have upon the development of the child? Again we turn to the Whiting and Child study (1953) for evidence. These investigators compared societies with respect to the age at which weaning, toilet training, modesty training, sex training, and independence training were initiated. They hypothesized that transgression of the rules results in stronger feelings of guilt if training was initiated early, especially if it began while the child still greatly needed parental love, than if training took place after the child had attained a degree of independent mastery of his world. Again the investigators used patient responsibility for illness as an indication of feelings of guilt or anxiety.

In general, they found that guilt feelings decline as age of socialization increases, particularly with respect to weaning and sex training. In societies in which early weaning and sex training (though not under one year) were the rule, stronger guilt feelings were found than in societies where socialization was delayed. Early training with respect to modesty and independence also produced strong guilt feelings, but the early onset of toilet training did not. Apparently the development of strong tendencies toward guilt feelings is encouraged by early socialization.

Continuity and Discontinuity in Socialization

The factor of continuity or discontinuity in the socialization process is related to the timing of socialization. Ruth Benedict (1938), the eminent anthropologist, notes that in our culture we go to great extremes in emphasizing the contrasts between child and adult. That is, in training children, we teach them certain behaviors which they must later discard if they are to be successful adults. As children they are expected to be nonresponsible; they do not make any labor contribution to our industrial society. Yet as adults they are expected to assume responsibility for earning a living or keeping the home. In other societies, there is continuous training for a responsible role; at an early age children participate with parents in performing various essential tasks.

With respect to dominant and submissive behaviors, we find similar discontinuity in our society. We expect children to obey adults, but as adults we expect them to assume a role of dominance. Again Benedict notes a contrast with simpler societies, in which it is assumed that a child who is docile and obedient will be a docile adult.

Benedict also notes discontinuity in the sexual role expected of children and adults. The child in our society is expected to be sexless until he has matured physically; yet as an adult he must accept his sex role if he is to be a successful marriage partner. There are societies, in contrast, in which children's sexual experimentation is regarded as harmless play. Children in such societies do not grow up associating sex with wickedness and do not have to unlearn lessons taught them at an earlier age.

We do not know how personality is affected by discontinuities in the socialization process. Benedict hypothesizes that they may lead to neurotic adjustments in later life and may also be responsible for the *Stürm und Drang* of adolescence. Whether the effects will be adverse and how serious they will be depend, of course, upon the strictness and severity of the initial learning, the degree to which the child is called upon to unlearn what he has learned, and the amount of variance between the new behavior and the old.

Obviously some of the discontinuities of which Benedict writes are unavoidable in a society such as ours. But as we become more aware of such discontinuities, we can make greater efforts to bridge the gap between childhood and adulthood. We can help the child to learn the new behaviors expected of him, and we can cease blaming him for failing to show these new behaviors spontaneously.

In this chapter we have examined some of the ways in which children growing up in the same society come to resemble one another and to differ from children in other societies. Evidence from cross-cultural studies suggests that the differences are due to the fact that societies have different goals for children and employ different methods of socialization. The actual dynamics of the socialization process we shall examine in the two chapters which follow.

11. Listen objectively to your favorite dramatic series on radio or television. To what extent does the hero reflect the desires and weaknesses of the "average" man? What aspects of American personality are revealed in the program?

12. Make a similar analysis of a radio or television program designed for children.

13. If possible, attend a Saturday-afternoon matinee at your local movie theater. Describe the personality of the hero, the heroine, the villain. What behaviors held the greatest appeal for the audience as judged by their reaction?

SUGGESTED READINGS

BENEDICT, RUTH. *Patterns of Culture,* Houghton Mifflin, 1934. This classic description of three primitive cultures illustrates how members of a society conform to the cultural ideal of their society.

MARTIN, WILLIAM E., & STENDLER, CELIA BURNS (eds.). *Readings in Child Development,* Harcourt, Brace, 1954. Part 2, "Society and Culture," contains a number of papers by anthropologists and sociologists which will enrich the reader's understanding of this chapter.

MEAD, MARGARET, & WOLFENSTEIN, MARTHA (eds.). *Childhood in Contemporary Cultures,* University of Chicago Press, 1955. Most of the papers in this collection deal with socialization, not in primitive cultures, but among the American, Russian, German, and French.

RIESMAN, DAVID. *The Lonely Crowd,* Yale University Press, 1950. A fascinating study of the changing American character.

WHITING, J. W. M., & CHILD, I. L. *Child Training and Personality: A Cross-Cultural Study,* Yale University Press, 1953. The advanced student of child development will benefit from this very original although complex study of cross-cultural differences in socialization and their effects upon personality.

7

a psychoanalytic
view of
socialization

A DYNAMIC POINT OF VIEW

We began our discussion of the process of socialization by describing its goals, as they are defined by a culture. By observing children at various stages of socialization in several different societies, we began to see something of the nature of the process. But a mere description does not provide enough understanding of the process to enable us to manage and modify it. Socialization takes place whether we understand it or not. Only by being able to manage and modify this process can we help the child to develop in directions defined as "good" by the society in which he lives. To satisfy this objective, we need to make a more searching analysis of socialization. Not only must we describe the process; we must also study it from a dynamic point of view.

In order to understand what we mean by a "dynamic point of view," let us consider an analogy. Let us assume that we are concerned, not with the socialization of the child, but with the operation of an automobile. More particularly, we wish to understand the process by which an automobile moves from one point in space and time to another. We might begin as we did with the socialization process, by describing some examples of this particular mechanism in operation. We could point out that the first step in initiating the process is to turn on the ignition. After completing this act, we proceed to operate the starter mechanism and, in some way, feed gasoline to the engine. Descriptively, we note at this point that, under the right conditions, the engine "starts."

We then manipulate the clutch and gear mechanism, perhaps by merely pushing a button, step on the accelerator, and move off toward our destination. Of course, there are other details to be considered, such as steering straight ahead or around corners or curves, using the brake when we wish to halt the forward motion of the automobile temporarily, and knowing how to change speed or reverse direction. This description contains the very minimum of facts about an automobile that are needed in order to operate it. Probably, there are many people who know little more.

But such drivers are completely helpless when they are confronted with unusual or unexpected factors, either in the environment through which the car is passing or within the mechanism of the automobile itself. Have you ever seen an inexperienced driver "flood" his engine to the point that the car will not start and then proceed to make matters worse by forcing even more fuel into the carburetor?

Only a person who understands something of the principles underlying the operation of the gasoline engine, especially as they apply to the automobile, can deal with such emergencies. In order to be able to manage and modify the behavior of the automobile, the operator must know, not only that the car "starts," but also what happens when it starts and why it starts. Only with this knowledge will he know what to do when the car doesn't start or doesn't start properly. Without it, man is at the mercy of the machine; he is not its master.

But there are many other operations that a person must understand if he is to have control of his automobile. He must know something of the way in which power is generated through the controlled explosion of a mixture of gasoline and air and of the way in which the energy resulting from this explosion is transformed into the mechanical energy that moves the automobile. Only a person who has this knowledge can start his car on a cold morning, or keep his automobile moving in heavy city traffic or on a muddy country road. In summary, the driver of an automobile is in command of the situation to the extent that he understands the nature of the forces involved in the behavior of that automobile and the details of the structure by means of which the productive use of a given amount of energy is realized in desired ways.

In this sense, even the best-informed automobile operator rarely understands this dynamic process completely. Ordinarily, he knows only enough to manage the machine well under normal circumstances and to make minor adjustments in emergency situations that enable him to continue operation until more expert help and advice are available. In the case of the process of human socialization, where the energy system is much more complex and not so well understood, it would be futile to expect that even the best-informed person could do more in emergency situations than take temporary measures until experts of various kinds can be called in. But most parents and teachers can understand enough of the dynamics of the process of socialization—the forces involved, their interaction, and the pertinent structures— to guide children through that process under normal conditions so as to obtain the best possible results, both from the standpoint of society and from that of the individual.

Because our knowledge and understanding of the process of human socialization are still incomplete, we can expect to find not one, but several, dynamic points of view or explanations. We shall concern ourselves here with but two of these: one based on psychoanalytic theory; the other, to be discussed in Chapter 8, on learning theory.

Commonly, the term "psychoanalysis" refers to a theory and method of treatment for individuals with some form of behavioral abnormality. These abnormalities often seem to be no more than exaggerations, distortions, or caricatures of normal behavior; they frequently appear to be the result of a developmental process which has been warped or arrested. Therefore, from explanations of abnormal behavior development, we may infer the nature of normal development from a psychoanalytic point of view. Paradoxically, we may arrive at a better understanding of normal development through a study of abnormal development.

Unfortunately, there is no one theory of psychoanalysis. If we are to use a psychoanalytic approach, we must specify which one. For our purposes, we shall discuss psychoanalytic theory as originated, developed, and tested by Sigmund Freud. But since Freud himself changed his views throughout his lifetime, we must further specify that we are considering—unless otherwise noted—his views as they are set forth in an almost completed summary written shortly before his death and published in America as *An Outline of Psychoanalysis* (1949). Freud's purpose in writing this work was, in his own words, "to bring together the doctrines of psychoanalysis and to state them, as it were, dogmatically—in the most concise form and in the most positive terms" (1949, p. 9). In the following pages, we shall consider these aspects of psychoanalytic theory: (*1*) structure, (*2*) energy, (*3*) types of mental activity, (*4*) mechanisms in mental activity, and (*5*) the developmental process.

STRUCTURE

Psychoanalysis, as a theory of behavior, is concerned with mental as distinct from physical existence and activity. This statement should not be taken to mean that the two must necessarily be divorced from each other, but merely that the emphasis is upon the former. When we talk about physical activity, it is clear that we are always concerned with some kind of structure. If the physical activity that we wish to understand is walking, we must know something of the skeleton, or that part of the skeleton that is involved in walking. Similarly, to understand mental existence and activity, we must identify the structure involved.

Since it is difficult enough to capture mental activity for examination and study—actually we study it only indirectly by observing its results—it is that much more difficult to conceive of a structure through which and by which mental activity takes place. Nevertheless, psychoanalytic theory has found it useful to postulate a kind of structure underlying mental life. This structure, which Freud called the "psychical apparatus," is made up of three parts: the id, the ego, and the superego. These parts of mental structure can best be described in terms of their functions.

The Id

As one might suppose, the structure underlying the mental life of the newborn child is very simple. It appears to consist of but a single part. To this structure, as it exists at birth, Freud gave the name "id." The id, he said, "contains everything that is inherited, that is present at birth, that is fixed in the constitution . . ." (1949, p. 14).

This structure underlies mental activity that is devoted solely to obtaining satisfactions of those needs which the child possesses from birth, if not from the beginning of life itself. All activity governed by the id is in the service of the pleasure principle—that is, the seeking of pleasure and the avoiding of pain. This form of existence and activity is, of course, primarily animal. At this stage, the child demands satisfaction of his basic needs, without any thought of the reasonableness of those demands or of the extent to which sources of satisfaction are available.

For a time, most societies tolerate existence at this level. But a point is reached when, for the child's own good—that is, so that he may develop a more mature form of existence—and for the convenience of adults and other children in the society, his demands must be countered by demands from the external world. A dog which forever remains a puppy is unthinkable. We tolerate the seemingly imperious behavior of the child only because we know that this state of affairs will not long continue.

For the child's good and for our own good, we do not allow it to continue indefinitely.

The Ego

Once the child is confronted with demands from the external world, especially demands which are not consistent with those arising within him, the simple structure of mental life which is the id no longer suffices. The young child wishes to play with the beads that his mother is wearing, but she thinks them too valuable to be used as a plaything and therefore takes them away from him. The young child sees no reason not to urinate or defecate whenever and wherever he feels the urge; his mother attempts to impose some kind of system upon him whereby elimination takes place in an appointed place and under prescribed conditions. In other words, toilet training is begun. Thus there arrives a time in the young child's life when parents begin to set limits to his activities and his demands.

To the extent that there is inconsistency between the child's needs and the demands imposed upon him, there is conflict. It is a conflict between unequal powers. For the child soon learns that he cannot ignore these external demands upon him or revolt successfully against them. As an organism, he must strive to make the best of the situation. He learns that, if he accedes to these demands, he may expect some satisfaction of his basic needs, if not now, perhaps later. He learns that, in order to receive satisfaction, he must adjust his demands in both kind and amount in accordance with external conditions. Hal is hungry. He will be given food, he learns, but only of a particular kind in a particular time and place. With increasing experience, he gains confidence in obtaining satisfaction of his own needs and yet adapting to external conditions.

Such a development requires some changes in the structure of mental life. Some part of that structure previously assigned completely to the satisfaction of the individual's needs now takes on the job of acting as an arbitrator between inner needs and external demands. Physiologically, this structure can be located in the outer layer, or so-called gray matter, of the brain (Freud,

1949). To the extent that this structure develops or is potentially capable of developing, the organism may be said to have an ego.

Freud has delineated the major characteristics of the ego:

It has the task of self-preservation. As regards *external* events, it performs that task by becoming aware of the stimuli from without, by storing up experiences of them (in the memory), by avoiding excessive stimuli (through flight), by dealing with moderate stimuli (through adaptation), and, finally, by learning to bring about appropriate modifications in the external world to its own advantage (through activity). As regards *internal* events, in relation to the id, it performs that task by gaining control over the demands of the instinct, by deciding whether they shall be allowed to obtain satisfaction, by postponing that satisfaction to times and circumstances favorable in the external world, or by suppressing their excitations completely [1949, p. 15].

It can be seen that a major part of growing up is the development of an ego. Like the id, the ego seeks pleasure, but somewhat more wisely and more effectively. The ego represents the reality principle, not necessarily opposing, but certainly limiting the pleasure principle, represented by the id. Mary doesn't always do what she wants to do; she sometimes does— or is under pressure to do—what she must do. What she must do is defined by the conditions of her existence. That definition is essentially realistic.

Only to the extent that ego development takes place can a person hope to attain the degree of maturity and independence that characterizes adulthood. It is on the basis of the degree of competence he has developed at any given point that the child evaluates himself. It is on the basis of this managerial ability that the child develops a concept of self. He considers himself worthy to the extent that he is able to obtain certain satisfactions for himself and, at the same time, retain the approval of others. He need not reject his basic needs. They can be satisfied, at least in part, but he must go about satisfying them with full recognition of external conditions. The ego sometimes says

"No." More often, it says "Later" or "Under different circumstances." The development of a strong, healthy ego is an essential part of growing up.

The Superego

Over a period of time, the child learns that certain kinds of external demand persist. From his point of view, then, the problems with which his ego must deal are recurrent. As he gains in experience, he learns to identify socially acceptable solutions to these recurring problem situations. He learns from his parents that they, together with other members of the society, have expressed these solutions in the form of rules and regulations.

No matter how angry he may become, a twelve-year-old American boy is very unlikely to strike his mother. He does not even have to consider whether or not to strike her. He automatically refrains from so doing. To him, it is "wrong." He has learned other ways of handling his feelings of anger. He may count to ten. He may go to his room until he cools off a bit. He may sulk. He may slam the door as he leaves. These means of managing anger are not equally acceptable socially, but they are all less likely to meet with disapproval than direct physical attack upon the object of his anger.

A normal nine-year-old girl sees a doll in the toy department of a store. She may want it very much. The thought of stealing it may occur to her. But she does not consider the idea seriously. The injunction "Thou shalt not steal" automatically prevents her from pursuing that particular means of obtaining the doll. Instead, she asks her mother to buy it for her. Or she saves money so that she may purchase it for herself. In either case, she may have to tolerate a delay in attaining her objective. By so doing, however, she gets the doll eventually without violating a social regulation.

A part of the individual's mental structure gradually takes over the function of indicating these socially acceptable solutions to problems. A person does not need to stop each time and think through a course of action. The decision is made for him.

These social regulations have become incorporated into his psychic structure. This particular structure, which we commonly refer to as the conscience, Freud named the "superego." When we are tempted to do things that we know are "wrong," or when we actually commit "wrong" deeds, we say that our conscience "hurts" us.

If the id is the biological inheritance of the child, the superego is his social inheritance. As the child lives and develops, he learns the nature of these inheritances. By developing—but only by developing—an ego to manage these bequests and to realize their potentialities, he makes them his own.

Freud has pointed out that ". . . in spite of their fundamental difference, the id and the superego have one thing in common: they both represent the influences of the past (the id the influence of heredity, the superego essentially the influence of what is taken over from other people), whereas the ego is principally determined by the individual's own experience, that is to say, by accidental and current events" (1949, p. 17).

The process of socialization is most closely identified with superego development. But the superego and its development and functioning cannot be considered in isolation. The divisions of mental structure are interdependent. We are more concerned with how harmoniously the whole system works than with the functioning of any one part.

From this point of view, the ego plays the main role. It is the integrator. It must handle simultaneously demands from the id, the superego, and the outside world. Considering that these demands are often conflicting, juggling them successfully is no mean accomplishment. Josselyn has described the nature of the ego's job in a simplified example:

> On a dark night one walks down a street passing a jewelry store. No one is around. In the window showcase is a beautiful diamond ring. The id says: "I want that diamond. I want it because I love myself, because it would make me beautiful and would thus make other people love me, because I am angry at

others having what I have not, and because I am uncomfortable under the tension of wanting what I do not have." The superego says arbitrarily, "No, you can't break the window and take it." The ego solves the impasse by advising, "But you shall have it if you will save your money until you can buy it" [1948, p. 24].

The superego defines what the individual should want to do and what he should not want to do. Those primitive impulsive forces that constitute the id may oppose the superego. The individual wants to do what is "right." Yet he is tempted to do what is "wrong." The situation in which he finds himself may also encourage the seeking of pleasure without regard to the consequences to himself and others. It is the ego's task to bring about harmony among these forces. On the one hand, it must deny the demands of a too inflexible and strict superego. But it must also deny the demands of an equally inflexible id. In the example above, the superego gives no hope to the individual that he will ever have the pleasure of owning the ring. The ego, although certainly not supporting completely the primitive impulse to take what one wants, points out a way in which satisfaction can eventually be obtained.

Neither the superego nor the id is realistic. It is the ego that constructs an intelligent bridge between man's nature and the nature of the society in which he lives. It is the ego that knows what the individual must do, how and when he must do it. It is the ego that identifies and recognizes rewards. The ego is the reasonable and reasoning conscious part of man. Man as a *rational* animal is ego.

The major task of socialization is the development of a balance of forces between the id—primitive unreasonable man—and arbitrary society—represented in part by the superego and in part by the demands of the outside world for which the superego defines no rules or regulations. The task is best accomplished by the development of a strong ego and a reasonable superego, together with the recognition of the nature of the id.

1. What are some signs of early ego and superego development that you might expect to observe?

2. Give some common examples of id-dominated behavior in children and adults. Of superego-dominated behavior.

3. What are some characteristic behaviors of a person with an overdeveloped superego?

4. What is the difference between society's definition of "right" and "wrong" and the organism's definition? At what point in development is this difference greatest?

ENERGY

We have described the structure underlying mental activity in terms, not of its form, but of its function—what it does. When we talk about individual behavior and development, we are talking about a dynamic system. When we describe the structure of that system, we are describing a structure that does something. To do something requires energy.

Freud regarded the human being as essentially an energy system—a point of view consistent with that taken earlier in this book. Freud concerned himself with the problem of how the energy in that system was directed. He saw that it could be used in two basically different ways. On the one hand, it could be used in constructive activities, or, as Freud said, "to establish ever greater unities and to preserve them thus—in short, to bind together . . ." (1949, p. 20). This basic predisposition of the energy system he referred to as "Eros," or the love instinct.* Energy applied in this way he defined as "libido."

But energy can be used in a second way: "to undo connections and so to destroy things" (Freud, 1949, p. 20). The latter tendency Freud called the "destructive instinct."

Energy pervades the whole mental structure of the individual and every part thereof. It can be directed from any one

* Instinct is the common English translation of the German word *trieb,* which Freud used to describe a *potentiality* or predisposition within the human being. He was not describing a precise and well-defined behavior which is laid down in the nervous system and which the individual inevitably manifests without previous learning and development. But this latter meaning is the one that American psychologists have assigned to the term "instinct." It is unfortunate that the same term is used in translations of Freud to mean something quite different.

of these parts and in the service of any one of these parts. For example, all the energy available might be used in attempting to meet the demands of the id. Insofar as a healthy ego dominates the mental life of the individual, we can expect energy to be directed and applied in the service of the ego. A person with a healthy ego uses most of his energy to perform the tasks assigned to the ego.

According to Freud, all behavior of the individual can ultimately be ascribed to the operation of either or both of the basic tendencies. But we should be cautious in labeling, in any absolute sense, the constructive application of energy as good and the destructive application of energy as bad. A person may build or he may destroy. He may destroy in order to build. The reformer, for example, must demolish the old in order to establish the new. The child destroys food in order to assimilate it and to make constructive use of it. Mechanically, with his teeth, he first destroys the form of that food. Chemically, in his digestive system, he then destroys the original nature of that food, changing it into substances from which the body can realize directly both nourishment and energy.

The creative person is encouraged to make constructive use of his energy. He is given maximal opportunity to realize his potentialities for constructiveness. He has an ego so strong that it need not dissipate its energy in unsuccessful attempts to resolve conflicts between the id and the superego. Correspondingly, he has a superego whose demands are not insatiable. In such circumstances, energy is freed with which the ego can build constructively from the materials of the individual's physical and social environment. Again, we are faced with the implication of a psychoanalytic point of view that ego development is of central concern in the process of socialization.

5. Is the Freudian theory of instincts compatible with our discussion of primary drives in Chapter 2?

6. Observe, with one of your fellow students, the behavior of a young child. To what extent do you agree as to the destructive and constructive aspects of that behavior?

TYPES OF MENTAL ACTIVITY

In investigating the behavior of a child, we are likely to assume that the child knows what he is doing, that he is aware of the reasons for his responses, that his behavior is *conscious* behavior. We recognize, of course, that the very young child may cry when he is hungry without recognizing the reason for his crying. But he learns very quickly that crying behavior is an effective reaction to his need for food. It often gets him food. Thereafter, when he cries, he knows that he is crying because he wants food.

Most of us like to think that all our mental activity is consciously planned and executed and that we are generally aware of the reasons for behaving as we do. But it was Freud who pointed out that some behavior is brought about by unconscious factors. We are aware of the behavior but unaware of the reasons for it.

For the most part, we are unaware of these reasons because to admit them would be painful to us. The admission would be painful in the sense that it would reveal something in our nature—literally, in our id—that is not acceptable to and in the society in which we live. Influenced by a superego representing that society, we, as ego, refuse to recognize in certain situations the true nature and source of our motivation. We turn from truth to fiction. What we admit *both* to ourselves and to others are only those explanations of behavior that have become identified as "acceptable."

There is that relatively rare mother, for example, who actually dislikes her child. In modern American society, however, she cannot reveal her feelings toward her child in any direct way. In fact, she cannot reveal them even to herself. Therefore, she may be very severe in her treatment of the youngster but claim that her actions are "for his own good." She may point out in apparent sincerity that he needs close and strict supervision and frequent punishment. These reasons are acceptable in some degree both to the mother and to the society in which she lives. The real reason, her dislike for the child, is literally not recognized by her. We shall have to defer discussion of the process by which the dislike has been made unconscious; suffice it to say at this point that the process, as well as the feeling of dislike, exists on an unconscious level.

There is the young adolescent boy who does not mind telling you how much he dislikes girls. His behavior toward particular girls is consistent with his stated opinions. The naïve observer might conclude that this boy's behavior emanates from conscious mental activity. The boy acts as if he dislikes girls because he *does* dislike girls, and he knows he dislikes girls. The more experienced observer is considerably more skeptical. The very intensity of the boy's dislike, as stated and as manifested in his behavior, arouses his suspicions. He asks himself whether the same behavior could not issue from a basic *liking* for girls. Perhaps the boy cannot admit this liking for girls at his age level without incurring considerable criticism from his peers and from his parents. Therefore, he attempts to deal with the conflict between what he would like to do and what he can safely do according to the standards of his social group by becoming hypocritical. That is, he pretends that he dislikes girls and says that he dislikes girls, but admits to himself that he likes them. But the boy may not be hypocritical; he may truly believe that he dislikes girls. Unconsciously he has refused, even in his private mental life, to recognize the existence of the opposite feeling.

The explanation and understanding of human behavior would be a great deal simpler if we could assume that we are all aware of the true reasons for our behavior. Yet most students of behavior today, whether or not they agree with the principles of psychoanalysis, recognize the existence of unconscious motivation. Most normal individuals get along fairly well in life despite the fact that they are not always aware of their reasons for behaving as they do. When behavior becomes sufficiently abnormal to be troublesome to the individual and his society, however, and it becomes necessary to change that behavior, the change can usually be accomplished only if the reasons for the present behavior become known to the individual. Bringing motives from the unconscious into the conscious level of activity is a process that can be accomplished only with the help of a psychologist. The individual alone cannot hope to deal with something which, in the beginning, he is unable to admit.

Of course, no one can be conscious of everything that is happening at any given moment. In attending to one matter, he must neglect or "forget" another. He is, for the time being, unaware of it. By definition, it is unconscious material. But it may be a particular kind of unconscious material in that it is always "capable of entering consciousness" (Freud, 1949, p. 38). It may be something that is "subject to recall at will" (Goodman, 1947, p. 284). Once it becomes conscious, the individual not only recognizes it but also accepts it. Freud called such material "preconscious" to distinguish it from that which cannot so readily become conscious. It is the latter that is more precisely termed "unconscious" and that we have thus far been discussing.

Although it may be inevitable that even a normal person must remain unconscious of some of the reasons for his behavior, we should not forget that to make something unconscious, as well as to keep it so, requires work. Work requires energy. If we are to help the child to keep the maximum amount of energy available for rational and constructive behavior, we must make it possible for him to admit freely his motives at all stages in the process of socialization. If we can furnish an accepting environment, we make it unnecessary for him to "cover up." We keep his mental activity an open book to him and to those who train and teach him. So long as those motives are there for us and him to examine, we have a better chance of helping him to change them when such a change seems advantageous for the individual and the society.

Parents and teachers who urge us to recognize the fact that the young child indulges in sexual activity, and finds pleasure in it, are not arguing that this behavior and this pleasure are good or bad. They are saying that so long as we accept them we can deal with them at the conscious level. We preclude the need for either inhibiting the behavior or repressing the desire to indulge in it. We do not achieve desirable development in a child by inhibiting his behavior and condemning his motives; we achieve most progress by taking the behavior for granted and then attempting to help the child control it to the extent made necessary by existing mores and regulations.

The importance of Freud's insistence upon the nonconscious character of a sizable share of human behavior cannot be overemphasized. Like an iceberg, much of an individual's mental activity is submerged below the surface of consciousness. Recognition of this fact has wrought a social revolution. Once it was believed that merely describing behavior was all that was necessary for understanding it. A mother who indulged in loving behavior toward her child was naturally assumed to love the child. An adolescent boy who indulged in disliking behavior toward girls obviously disliked girls. We now know that, in at least some instances, what seems most obvious may be least true.

Today we give most of our attention not to what a person does but to why he does it. Largely because of Freud and the development of psychoanalysis, we no longer assume that a knowledge of the first affords a reliable basis for predicting the second. W. H. Auden, the eminent contemporary poet, has observed:

> When two people today engage in an argument, each tends to spend half of his time and energy, not in producing evidence to support his point of view, but in looking for the hidden motives which are causing his opponent to hold his. If they lose their tempers, instead of saying "You are a fool," they say, "You are a wicked man" [1948, p. 190].

7. Legally, do we assume that an individual is always aware of his behavior and the reasons for it?

8. How would we classify material which an individual has completely forgotten? Is it preconscious? Is it unconscious?

MECHANISMS IN MENTAL ACTIVITY

Freud was not content merely to describe the dynamic forces that underlie individual behavior and the conditions under which they operate. He tried also to delineate some common mechanisms in mental activity, methods used by individuals to solve the problems they face.

Repression

One common solution is to relegate material to the unconscious level. The question remains: How does it become unconscious? Freud described the mechanism—repression—by which the individual makes and keeps material unconscious.

Let us consider the example of a young girl who has been punished by her mother. Her immediate reaction is dislike for her mother. That dislike she is very much aware of at that point. But she also recognizes the danger in disliking her mother. For she depends upon her mother in so many ways. She could scarcely live without her. And if her mother knew that her daughter disliked her, she might desert the girl—or so the child believes.

The solution to this problem seems to lie in making unconscious what is now conscious. The girl refuses to admit to herself the fact that she dislikes her mother. She represses the whole idea. Over a period of time, then, this youngster can repress—thrust into the unconscious—ideas or thoughts which, for one reason or another, she cannot accept. By this means, she continues to maintain a positive, affectionate, liking attitude toward her mother. Attitudes of dislike and predispositions to behavior consistent with that dislike of her mother no longer need to be managed on a conscious level.

Thus it is that children generally like their parents despite the unlikelihood that they have always received perfect justice at their parents' hands. To the extent that repression is successful, the problem is solved. It is true that this repression requires energy, energy which cannot be used in more productive ways. But it is sometimes worth the price. To the extent that repression is only partially successful—as it often is—we find individuals who have what we call ambivalent attitudes toward their parents. At the completely conscious level they like their parents. But there is also an element of dislike which appears once in a while and which causes the children to attack and grieve those whom they ostensibly love. Thus we see that one way of handling material which is repugnant to the individual is to repress it, to push it into the unconscious recesses of mental life.

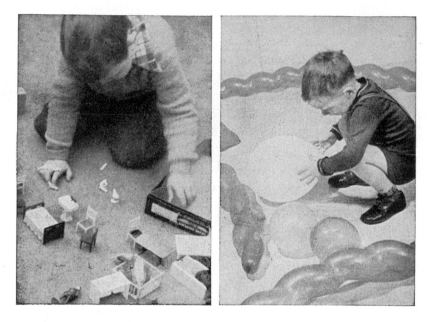

FIGURE 7-1. Projective play techniques. By observing the child as he plays with "miniature life toys" (*left*) or even simple balloons, the trained analyst can arrive at many revealing insights. In his dramatizations and in his arrangement and handling of the toys, the child may reveal some of his attitudes, fears, and concepts.

(From L. J. Stone & J. Church. *Childhood and Adolescence,* Random House, 1957)

Projection

Repression is only one of a number of ways that are available for meeting problem situations. Another is projection. A child may attack or wish to attack another. But having been taught by his parents and his teachers that aggressive behavior is not acceptable and will be punished, that one may attack only when one has been attacked, the child may not wish to face or admit any perception of himself as aggressive. He suppresses that internal perception and distorts its contents so that it becomes an external perception (Freud, 1911). It is not he who is aggressive; instead, it is the other child. He literally projects his impulses onto the other person. He attributes his motives to the other. As a result of projection, he no longer runs the risk of punishment; he even has an excuse to indulge in attacking behavior. He can always say that he did it only because the other child was going to attack him.

Many children give excuses of this kind for behavior which is disapproved. In some cases, the child may recognize that he is not speaking the truth. But projection is an unconscious process. To the extent that he has projected his behavior and motives onto others, he is completely sincere in his disavowal of any reprehensible intentions. Again, it must be noted that sometimes only a trained psychologist can tell the difference between hypocrisy and sincerity in what individuals report of their behavior. Those who study children sometimes have an advantage in that the young child does not have the means of concealing his hypocrisy that adults possess. In play situations particularly, he may reveal much of his feelings toward people and things (see Fig. 7-1).

Sublimation

Freud described a third kind of mechanism, that of sublimation. From the standpoint of observable behavior, this process involves seeking and finding substitute satisfaction. To understand what is being substituted for what, we must recall the individual's basic predisposition to use his energy for constructive purposes. One of the most important of such purposes is to establish positive affectional relationships. In this connection, we immediately think of friendship and love. Certainly we recognize the importance of love and affection, even in the infant. He seems to seek fondling and petting. In fact, he seems to seek and find pleasure in himself. He is his first love. Later, of course, he selects others as receivers and givers of pleasure.

These pleasures are erotic. They are localized in certain parts of the body, which are called erotogenic zones. Freud spoke of three such zones: the oral, the anal, and the genital. In the early years of life, pleasure is experienced primarily in the first and second of these zones; only later does the genital zone become the primary source. But, even then, it is not the only source of gratification and satisfaction. The oral and anal areas persist as erotogenic zones, although they lose much of their relative strength in the course of normal development. Freud considered all constructive uses of energy as libidinal or sexual. The early period of life, during which erotogenic zones other than the genital are paramount, he called the period of pre-genital sexuality. The later years, during which the genital zone is the most important but not the only source of pleasure, he named the period of genital sexuality.

Growing up requires, therefore, that an individual localize more and more of his pleasurable impulses in the genital zone and fewer and fewer of them in the other erotogenic zones. He must substitute satisfactions originating in the former for those originating in the latter. The increasing sensitization of the genital zone that results from biological maturation impels him to make this exchange. But, in addition, he is under some external pressure to substitute for these infantile ways the more adult ways of gaining gratification. He must divert the energy previously utilized in pregenital gratification to more mature and socially approved aims. It is this process—an unconscious one—of finding and effecting substitute satisfactions that Freud called sublimation.

Freud did not consider genital sexuality the only substitute satisfaction. In fact, he believed that sublimation underlies some artistic and creative activity (1905). In such cases, the source of the energy involved can be found in pregenital impulses which have been sublimated.

Sublimation is one of many Freudian concepts that are widely used in modern mental hygiene, even by those who could hardly be considered sympathetic to psychoanalytic theory. In such a context, sublimation often acquires a broader, if not a different, meaning than Freud originally gave it. For example, one textbook defines it as "the process whereby a primitive impulse or drive finally is converted into a socially acceptable form" (Redl & Wattenberg, 1951, p. 447).

Using this broader definition, we can say that sublimation of the destructive instinct is also required of the individual socialized in our culture. As we have already pointed out in our discussion of the American character, aggressive attacks upon other individuals and upon property are discouraged from a very early age.

Mike and Jimmy are playing together in a corner of the kindergarten room, sharing a set of building blocks. As we observe them, they complete an impressive-looking tower and stand back to inspect it, with obvious satisfaction and pride. But suddenly, without warning, Mike, with a single sweep of his hand, destroys the structure and sends the blocks flying across the room. One of them overturns and breaks some jars of finger paint standing in another corner of the room. When Jimmy objects to this behavior, Mike takes a healthy swing at him, too.

This is a not-too-uncommon example of destructive behavior in the five-year-old. It is difficult to explain such a reaction. Freudians postulate a predisposition to destructive behavior as a part of the original nature of the child. Therefore, they consider it only natural that such reactions should appear from time to time. In fact, there is some basis for arguing that outlets should be provided for such behavior occasionally. In line with this point of view, some psychologists prescribe "smash-box therapy" for children who exhibit destructive tendencies. When such a child wants to be destructive, he is given a box and a mallet and allowed to "destroy" to his heart's content.

Although such therapy may be beneficial in special cases, we should recognize that it represents a complete capitulation to the primitive unsocialized nature of the child. Most children will grow up and reach maturity in a world which does not always provide opportunities for acceptable destruction. In fact, they will live among individuals who expect them to be able to substitute constructive for destructive tendencies. It is the essence of growing up that a child surrenders a "primitive form of satisfaction in favor of a more cultivated or socially acceptable one" (Redl & Wattenberg, 1951, p. 67). Thus the society demands that he sublimate his predisposition to destroy.

The degree of sublimation required is only partial, however. The child may destroy something which a number of individuals consider "bad." He may defend himself by counterattack. He may defend his honor and that of his home, in certain circumstances. He may be rewarded if he is "aggressive" in learning. Society commends those who "attack" their jobs with vigor and spirit. But all these behaviors are in the nature of exceptions. The individual cannot turn the full force of his destructive tendencies upon others or even upon himself. Although the "murderer" may be within all of us, we are able, through sublimation, to hide that fact from each other and from ourselves. Other responses, of a more socially acceptable nature, are substituted. An original aspect of our nature becomes a stranger to us. It remains so except when we are faced with an unusually critical set of conditions. Then we may discover new resources within us to meet these special conditions.

9. Select an introductory text in psychology or in mental hygiene. Are the terms "projection," "repression," and "sublimation" used in the book? How are they defined? Do the definitions differ from Freud's as explained in the foregoing pages?

10. Can a teacher or parent identify these adjustment mechanisms when they are used by children? Of what value might a knowledge that such mechanisms do exist be to a parent or teacher?

THE DEVELOPMENTAL PROCESS

We have described the psychic structure, the nature of the energy which operates within that structure, the types of mental activity, and some of the mechanisms which characterize mental life, all as delineated in psychoanalytic theory. We have still to take up the subject which is of greatest concern to us, namely, the process by which the individual changes from infant to adult, from an asocial to a social person. How does the individual develop an ego that supports the kind of existence and behavior required by the society in which he lives? By what process does he develop a superego that will enable him to satisfy the moral requirements of his society?

The starting point of this developmental process is fairly clear. We have already seen that the infant is a creature without ego, without superego; he may be considered pure id and therefore completely asocialized. The endpoint of the process cannot be so clearly described, but it is clear that it is the level at which the individual has developed sufficient ego and superego, as well as an adequate working relationship of those two parts of his psychic structure to each other and to the original id.

Freud saw the process as a series of fixed stages, fixed in the sense that every individual, regardless of society, culture, and specific environmental conditions, attains maturity as a socialized person only by moving from one stage to another in an inevitable sequence. The basic differentiating characteristic of these stages is the object with which the individual affiliates at each stage. As we have pointed out, Freud postulated an impulse on the part of the individual to use his mental energy in constructive ways. In this sense, the maturity of the individual can be evaluated in terms of the kind of object to which he directs this constructive affiliative energy. Thus object choice, or what Freud calls "cathexis," is of central importance in the transition of the individual from child to man.

But the individual not only has the predisposition to like someone; we see as development proceeds that he also wants to *be* like someone. He makes up for his own immaturity and his own inability to solve problems by trying to be like someone who is relatively mature and able to solve problems. We say that he has identified with that person. We have all at times felt that the accomplishments of others were our own;

that is, we have identified so much with an individual that we have shared in his success. It is not uncommon for parents thus to experience a feeling of success as a result of the achievements of their children, to the extent that they are one with them. We can understand the development of the individual, then, only as we see the nature of his object choices and the identifications which take place at each of the several stages of development. But object choice is of more significance in Freudian theory than is identification. It is in terms of the former that Freud described individual development.

In the beginning, of course, the individual has chosen neither to like someone nor to be like someone. He is concerned only with attaining the most simple pleasures, pleasures already defined as such by his nature. He seeks sucking experience. He obviously enjoys being fed, warmed, petted, and rocked. He clearly displays the pleasure that comes with elimination. For a time, at least, these pleasures are made available to him freely and without hesitation. He is the center of attention. Everyone is his servant. He is the master, but, of course, he does not realize it at this very early stage.

Infantile Omnipotence

The child cannot long continue to be treated like a master without feeling like a master. He thus enters a stage of development that is characterized by a feeling of omnipotence He now differentiates between himself and the outside world. He sees himself now as an individual manipulating the people and objects of his environment for his own purposes. He has but to suggest or beckon and the world moves.

This is the beginning of ego development. The individual now has an "I." But this ego spends no energy in management of the self; its efforts are directed to the management of others in the service of self. It is at this time that the first object choice is made. The choice is a natural one: the child falls in love with himself. Remembering Greek mythology, Freud labeled this period the "narcissistic stage."

At this point, the child is a tyrant. But tyrants are tolerated for only a limited time. Sooner or later, parents begin to refuse to accede to all the child's demands, and, even more significantly, they begin to make demands upon him. The process of socialization is begun. No longer does he always eat exactly what and when he wants to eat. He may be under some pressure to take a nap even when he isn't tired. He is soon forced to face the sad fact that he is not really omnipotent. He begins to realize the degree of his dependence upon other people, especially adults.

In order to make sure that he continues to receive as much gratification as possible, the child transfers his libido from himself to his parents. In return for his demonstrated love for his parents, he can, in simple justice, expect certain favors and privileges.

The Oedipus Complex and Identification

The particular object choice at this stage depends upon the sex of the child, according to Freud. Because of their sex, the girl seeks to establish an object relationship with her father, the boy with his mother. "Oedipus complex" is the term applied to this tendency in the boy; "Electra complex" is used to refer to it in the girl.

Such cross-sex choices within the family group approximate, at least by implication, incest, a practice not tolerated by any human society. Neither the male nor the female child is allowed to make such a choice except as it is clearly nonsexual and thus, in a sense, essentially impersonal. There is, however, a way of establishing this choice indirectly. To the extent that the girl is like her mother, identifies with her mother, she can enjoy vicariously an affectionate relationship with her father. Like the mother, or as the mother, she can love the father. The boy, similarly, can identify with the father and to the degree that he is like the father can love his mother.

The Latency Period

These indirectly established object choices are not completely satisfactory. They are too much like those that have previously been prohibited. For a time, the child seeks relationships that do not hold so much danger of being disapproved. A new stage of development, which Freud called the "latency period," results and lasts for approximately the period of the elementary school years. During this time, the instinct to love goes underground, as it were. Because of the traumatic experience of having his desired object choices prohibited and shamed, the child places a restraint, for the time being, upon overtly affectionate relationships. Such relationships as he does enjoy are relatively superficial and transient.

His ego continues to develop in the sense that he becomes more and more capable of dealing with the impulses originating in the id and the demands made upon him by persons and events in the outside world. His identification with the appropriate parent persists. The standards of conduct exemplified in what his parents say and do become incorporated into the child's own mental life. In other words, he develops a superego. Thus the elementary school child ordinarily develops a sense of right and wrong, makes some attempts to behave in accordance with that sense, and feels shame and guilt when his actions are inconsistent with the demands of his superego.

Puberty

The biological changes associated with puberty bring the latency period to a dramatic end. The intensity of the sex drive is such that it can no longer be ignored. The child seeks some kind of gratification. But it is even more unacceptable now for the boy to enjoy any kind of sexual relationship with his mother or the girl with her father. The relationships that are formed during this period are as unlike those desired as possible. The child enters a homosexual stage of development in that he seeks to establish, as object choices, persons of the same sex and approximately the same age.

These relationships need not be and usually are not of an overtly sexual nature. Nevertheless, the intensity of affection is at a high level. At this time friends of the same sex are virtually inseparable. Parents often succeed after considerable effort to get their daughter to stay at home for an evening only to find that she spends the entire time on the telephone in conversation with her best friend. Friends and peers usurp the place of parents in determining appropriate behavior. To a certain extent, new and different identifications take place. Some revisions in standards of conduct ensue. But the residue of childhood experience with adult standards, especially those of parents, remains. That original part of the superego retains much of its strength throughout life. Therefore, new and later incorporations into the superego bring about conflict. "Do I do as my parents say or as my friends say?" is a question that every adolescent faces.

But the types of object relationship formed during the homosexual stage of development do not and cannot bring complete satisfaction, for both biological and social reasons. Sooner or later, the normal individual wishes and society expects him to establish some affiliation with a member or members of the opposite sex. Ultimately, of course, that affiliation is a more or less permanent one, legalized by marriage and ordinarily eventuating in offspring.

Even this final and relatively satisfactory state of affairs cannot be divorced from previous stages. The girl's tendency to choose a husband with her father's characteristics and the boy's tendency to choose a wife who resembles his mother demonstrate that the affiliations of early periods of development leave their mark upon the individual (G. V. Hamilton, 1948). The fact that the most happily married man or woman still enjoys and, indeed, requires continued affiliations with members of the same sex is a residue of the so-called homosexual period. Such friendships hold their attraction and value throughout the lifetime of almost every individual. And, of course, everyone continues to have some affection for himself; he never ceases to be, to some degree, his own object choice. While the individual succeeds in attaining the final stage of maturity, the effects of all the preceding stages remain. What he is at that point is the product of those past experiences.

INTERFERENCE WITH
NORMAL DEVELOPMENT

We are concerned primarily with the process of normal development. But it may help us understand that process better if we consider two types of interference with normal development. Freud called them fixation and regression.

Fixation

The first term, "fixation," describes the situation of a person who does not move from one stage to another but remains at an immature level. The child may become fixated at what might be called the parental stage of development. He cannot affiliate with persons other than his parents. He may be able to indulge in only the most casual and superficial of friendships with other adults and with his peers. Later on, in adolescence and young adulthood, he is unable to transfer his love and dependence on his parents to love for a person of roughly the same age and the opposite sex. Since marriage is the most common resolution of the problem of the heterosexual stage of development, we may view the confirmed bachelor or spinster as a person who has become fixated at an earlier stage and is therefore unable to complete the developmental sequence. The existence of a tragic love affair or of restrictive parents in that individual's life history may explain the fixation that we observe to exist.

Regression

There is also the individual who finds himself able to move from one stage to another but who, after an unsuccessful attempt to meet the problems of the more mature level of development, returns to an earlier and easier stage of existence. As Freud put it, he regresses. There are young people who attempt to establish the mature relationship expected in the adult phase of the heterosexual period but who, for one reason or another, are not able to cope with the demands of such a relationship. It is not uncommon to find such individuals regressing, at least for a time, all the way back to the parental stage. The unhappy bride who goes home to mother, vowing never again to love anyone but her parents, has done just this. The child who is unable to maintain healthy relationships with his peers will sometimes regress to the stage where all his love and affection and attention go to his parents. He refuses to grow up.

Josselyn again provides us with a vivid analogy to illustrate these psychoanalytic concepts:

> A man plans to eat the main part of his dinner at home and to eat his dessert at the corner drugstore. Upon finishing his meal, he may find that the serving was too small and he is not yet ready for his dessert. He, therefore, remains at home, seeking more of the same food rather than leaving to obtain his dessert. Or he may find the meal quite satisfactory but, as he is about to leave, he finds there is a blizzard outdoors. It is not worthwhile to face the storm in order to obtain the dessert, of whose merits he is not certain. Therefore, he remains at home, satisfying the remnant of his hunger with food similar to that which he has already consumed. This is "fixation." In contrast to this man's experience, another man, after adequately satisfying his hunger for more substantial food, decides to go to the corner drugstore for his dessert. Having reached the drugstore, he finds the dessert is strange and does not appear as good as he had anticipated. Instead of eating his dessert, he returns home to satiate his appetite with familiar food. He has "regressed" [1948, p. 48].

CHARACTER DEVELOPMENT ACCORDING TO FREUD

Not only does a person turn out to be relatively normal as a result of having passed successfully through these various stages of development; it is this succession of experiences that provides him with his character. For his character is based upon the object choices and identifications which he makes at any stage of development. As he grows older, he makes new choices of friends and associates and may also make more realistic identifications. In this sense, his character changes. But the extent of the change is limited. A person's character is largely a function of early and primary experiences.

More particularly, then, character is a result of specific experiences in each of the stages of development. According to Freudian theory, the child whose demands for simple pleasure in infancy and early childhood have been gratified to too great an extent will turn out to have a character entirely different from that of the child who had insufficient gratification during the same period. The first child will expect too much of others; the second will expect too little. In fact, he may even have developed considerable distrust of the world and the people who live in it. These are, of course, oversimplifications. But they indicate something of the way in which Freudian theory might explain the determination and formation of character.

The Castration Complex

We find a more detailed example of a psychoanalytic theory of character development in Freud's explanation of the psychological differences between adult males and females. In the pre-Oedipal stage, the girl establishes some kind of affectionate relationship with her mother as a result of the mother's satisfaction of her basic needs. At some point during this period, however, she observes or learns of the anatomical differences between boys and girls, especially in the external genitals. As a result, she develops a castration complex: she feels that she has been emasculated. She experiences penis envy. According to Freud, her reaction is immediate. "She makes her judgment and her decision in a flash. She has seen it and knows that she is without it and wants to have it" (1925, p. 191).

There are three possible outcomes of penis envy. The first is the suspension of sexual life, which may persist into adulthood. The second is an overemphasis on masculinity, the masculine complex, the maintenance of the hope of someday "becoming like a man." The girl may even refuse to admit to herself her lack of a penis. The third possibility is that the girl will take the first steps toward femininity. She develops a sense of inferiority together with feelings of jealousy. Her affection for her mother tends to diminish—first, because she considers her mother as insufficiently equipped as she is, and, secondly, because she suspects that her mother is responsible for her (the daughter's) inferior anatomy. As the primary object of her affection, she substitutes her father for her mother. "The mother becomes the object of her jealousy. The girl has turned into a little woman" (Freud, 1925, p. 195). The castration complex and the associated penis envy lead to the Oedipus complex—sometimes called the Electra complex—in the girl.

In the boy, early genital masturbation becomes associated—originally, quite by coincidence—with his growing feelings of affection for his mother, and thus with the Oedipus complex which is developing at this time. His culturally induced feelings of guilt over the masturbation and, more particularly, over the kind of relationship he instinctively seeks with his mother bring about a fear of aggression, specifically of castration. At this time, he remembers the appearance of the genitals of the girl, which was previously of only passing interest. That recollection only adds to the reality of the threat. The castration complex results.

The only way of escaping this threat is by eliminating all hope or desire for sexual alliance with the mother. The boy abandons incest and institutes "conscience and morality" (Freud, 1925, p. 196). This act of self-denial is the first step in the development of a strong character.

According to psychoanalytic theory, we see, then, a very significant sex difference in the course of events during these early years. The Oedipus complex and the castration complex exist in both boys and girls, but in different sequences with different outcomes. In boys, the Oedipus complex occurs first and succumbs to the castration complex; in girls, the castration complex occurs first and makes possible, even leads to, the Electra complex.

The development of the appropriate sexual character becomes a function of the manner in which the individual enters and leaves the period of the Oedipus (or Electra) complex. As a result of differences between the sexes in this respect, the female "superego is never so inexorable, so impersonal, so independent of its emotional origin as we require it to be in men" (Freud, 1925, p. 196). On this basis Freud explains the fact that women "show less sense of justice, are less ready to submit to the great necessities of life, are more often influenced in their judgments by feelings of affection or hostility" (p. 197).

Readers who belong to the so-called weaker sex may not accept Freud's view of their character. But they will admit differences in character between females and males. Boys grow up to be men; girls grow up to be women. Orthodox psychoanalytical theory attempts to explain the origin and the development of these differences. According to this explanation, the sexual character is not innate, but it seems to be almost inevitable.

11. We did not mention, in our discussion of the process of development, the process of sublimation. At what point(s) do you think it might be involved?

12. What behavior do we commonly observe in normal individuals that we might consider the residue of the narcissistic stage in development?

CRITICISMS OF PSYCHOANALYTIC THEORY

Objections to psychoanalytic theory have been both numerous and spirited. To present them in detail and to assess their validity would require a book in itself. However, a brief account of the kind of criticism to which Freud's view of human development has been subjected will serve to highlight the salient points in his thinking.

What has been most disturbing, perhaps, to students of human behavior and development is the claim that the developmental sequence described by Freud is universal and inevitable. Although it is not unlikely that some children achieve maturity via the stages that Freud has described, it is argued that other children experience normal growth through different routes. Specific circumstances determine the exact sequence of events. That sequence is not predestined for every individual.

For example, if a child grows up in a society in which little or no restriction is placed upon sexual behavior in children, the latency period does not seem to exist. There is no time when the child submerges his interest in intimate affiliation with other persons. Furthermore, the evidence of sexual activity in childhood, already noted in Chapters 2 and 5 is taken by some to mean that the latency period is not necessarily a phase of normal development, even in a society which, like ours, represses overt sexual behavior during the formative years. Thus the latency period, rather than being a fixed stage, must be the result of a particular set of conditions existing within a particular society.

On the basis of his studies of preliterate societies, Malinowski (1927) challenged the validity of many other psychoanalytic concepts. To cite one example, he concluded that the Oedipus complex may or may not manifest itself; whether it does or not depends upon the nature of the family group, as defined by the society and the culture. Among the Melanesians, for example, he found that the true father of the child was not recognized as such. Conception was not known to be the outcome of sexual intercourse. The mother's brother assumed the social role of the father. It was he who demanded, who punished, and who provided instructions and models of appropriate behavior. The father was merely a consort of the mother and a kindly adult playmate of the child. He played the role often attributed to uncles in American society. The Melanesian girl did not seek her father as an object choice, nor did she consider her mother a rival for his affections. The position of the father was such that the Melanesian boy could scarcely consider him a rival for his mother's affections. Rather, his resentment was typically directed against his uncle and his authority. His father was an ally, although perhaps not a strong one. Thus it appears that no particular pattern of object relationship and identification is inevitable. What happens is a function of the particular family pattern in which the child develops.

Freud's attempt to formulate a universal explanation of the male and female characters is also disputed on the same grounds. According to psychoanalytic theory, a male is a male because of his reaction to his possession of a penis and its absence in the female; a female is a female, psychologically, because of her reaction to her lack of a penis and its possession by the male. Since this particular sex difference in anatomy is found in every society, it might be presumed that the same psychological differences between male and female exist in every society.

The observations of cultural anthropologists challenge this presumption and therefore the explanation itself. Most of the various peoples of the world assign somewhat different roles to men and women, it is true. But the particular behavior and temperament expected of the male in one society may differ significantly from that expected of the male in a second society. We, growing up in our culture and having our ideas of appropriate masculine behavior, find surprising the "convention of one Philippine tribe that no man can keep a secret, the Manus assumption that only men enjoy playing with babies, the Toda prescription of almost all domestic work as too sacred for women, or the Arapesh insistence that women's heads are stronger than men's" (M. Mead, 1935, p. xix). Since the roles assigned to male and female, respectively, change with the social milieu, we might suspect that sex-appropriate behavior is learned. No particular role seems to be ineluctably associated with a particular sex. The Manus male does not necessarily enjoy playing with babies; he learns to enjoy that activity if he grows up in Manus society. The male in Western society does not necessarily develop a superego which is relatively "inexorable" and "impersonal"; he may acquire those characteristics under the specific conditions presented by his society.

Another criticism of Freudian theory concerns its emphasis upon the primitive, irrational, negative aspects of human motivation and behavior. Critics claim that there is too much attention given to man's striving for infantile pleasures and gratifications, his experiences of pain and frustration, the unconscious origins of his actions, and his failures to solve the conflict between the demands of his biology and those of his society.

There is too little attention given to man's attempts to be rational, to face up to problems; to his ability to postpone—even to abjure—gratification of impulses and to endure frustration; and to his ofttimes successful efforts to surmount the restraints imposed upon him. Freud thus demeans the human being, it is claimed.

Finally, one of the most perplexing aspects of Freudian theory to the modern scientist is the fact that it is so difficult to test and verify the hypotheses which constitute it. The very nature of the theory necessitates dealing with material that exists only at the unconscious level. We can study such material only indirectly, using signs that exist in conscious and overt behavior and inferring from them the nature of unconscious and covert behavior. Our present difficulty is lack of agreement on the meaning of signs. A given sign may signify one thing to one observer and another to a second observer. We have not yet reached accord upon what it is that we see when we observe behavior. We are still further from agreement on what we may infer from these observations of overt behavior with regard to its causes and antecedents.

There is an element of truth in all these criticisms. Freud was indeed concerned with the universal. Like the scientist in quest of a universal law governing physical phenomena, he sought an all-embracing explanation of human development. There was no keener observer of the idiosyncratic; his reports of clinical investigations disclose an amazing sensitivity to every detail and fragment of behavior and experience. But he was concerned always with generalizing from the particular. He was interested in *man,* rather than in *men,* at least in his theoretical formulations. He was engrossed in the main theme of human existence; he used the variations, of which he was certainly not unaware, to illuminate and enrich that theme.

Presumably as a result of his training in the biological sciences, Freud emphasized the influence of biological factors in man's nature. He was impressed with the power and persistence of these biological characteristics. He was a constitutional psychologist. He believed that development might—and, in fact, does—follow a relatively fixed pattern. In such concepts as regression and fixation, he recognized that environmental events could be involved in departures from this pattern. But he was convinced that constitutional differences, particularly in strength of the instinctual, or primary, drives and in sex, were basically responsible for the impact of these environmental events. Man's biological nature made certain stages in development and a certain ordering of these stages almost inevitable. How could the male avoid the castration complex, the female, penis envy? How could either sex avoid the impulse to seek object relationships with the parent of the opposite sex or, after the biological changes associated with puberty, some kind of sexual gratification, most naturally with the opposite sex? Although it is true that society is responsible for the restraints and frustrations that influence and even interfere with "normal" development, it must be remembered that man has created that society and thus limits himself.

Freud's view of man was pessimistic (Trilling, 1950; Adelson, 1956). Confronted with strong and conflicting biological and societal demands, man is essentially a tragic figure. Being human is his problem. There is no real solution. He must admit to the necessities of the human condition. What little freedom he possesses he can maintain only to the extent that he differentiates between the necessities that actually exist and those that only seem to exist. It is this differentiation that is the basic goal of therapy. Freud did not underestimate the difficulty of attaining and maintaining such differentiation. In a paper on whether or not there could ever be an end to psychoanalytic treatment, he observed, with characteristic candor and humility: "If the patient who has made such a good recovery never produces any more symptoms calling for analysis, it still, of course, remains an open question how much of this immunity is due to a benevolent fate which spares him too searching a test" (1937, p. 321).

Freudian theory poses difficulties for the investigator of human development, difficulties of which its author was painfully aware. But to describe a theory as complex is not to render it invalid. We do not reject the theories of modern physics because they are more complex than classical physics, with its mechanical view of the universe, and thus make experimentation and verification more difficult. Science seeks truth, not simplicity; it can only hope that the truth is simple. The worth of a theory lies in what it will explain and predict. The crucial tests of psychoanalytic theory are yet to come.

13. Refer to the discussion of human nature in Chapter 1 (pp. 5-6). Did Freud view the individual as an "empty organism"?

14. Is it possible to argue for the existence of the Oedipus complex in Melanesians despite Malinowski's observations (p. 233)?

15. To what extent does evidence from cultural anthropology invalidate the Freudian explanation of differences between the male and the female characters?

For the present, we cannot ignore Freudian theory. Some aspects of that theory are now accepted by every social scientist, even though the terminology may have been changed somewhat. And even in instances where he was wrong or may be found later to be wrong, Freud's very pronouncements have forced us into the discovery of new dimensions of human behavior. James Joyce's words are apropos. "A genius makes no mistakes. His errors are the portals of discovery." The understanding of individual development will forever bear the marks of Freud's influence.

But neither can we ignore alternative approaches to the process of socialization, which emphasize the influence of environmental factors and the plasticity of the human organism and take a more optimistic view of man and his perfectability. It is to one of these alternatives, the conception of socialization as learning, that we turn our attention in the next chapter.

SUGGESTED READINGS

BARUCH, DOROTHY WALTER. *New Ways in Discipline,* McGraw-Hill, 1949. A presentation, written for parents and teachers, of a modern concept of child discipline, based on psychiatric theory.

ERIKSON, ERIK H. Eight stages of man. In William E. Martin and
Celia Burns Stendler (eds.), *Readings in Child Development*,
Harcourt, Brace, 1954, pp. 213-20. Working within the psychoanalytic framework but using insights gained from cultural
anthropology, the author presents a view of human development that stresses the importance of a strong and healthy ego.

HALL, CALVIN S. *Primer of Freudian Psychology*, New American
Library, 1955. A paperbound edition of a concise, scholarly,
simply written account of Freudian theory as it applies to the
development of normal personality.

HALL, CALVIN S., & LINDZEY, GARDNER. *Theories of Personality*,
Wiley, 1957. Chapter 2, "Freud's Psychoanalytic Theory," and
Chapter 3, "Jung's Analytic Theory," provide an opportunity
to contrast the formulations of the founder of psychoanalysis
with those of one of his early followers who ultimately developed his own theory.

JONES, ERNEST. *The Life and Work of Sigmund Freud*, New York:
Basic Books, 1953, 1955, 1957. This three-volume work by one
of Freud's close friends and colleagues, himself a distinguished
psychoanalyst, may well be the definitive biography of Freud.
It offers an authoritative account of the origin and development
of psychoanalytic theory.

JOSSELYN, IRENE M. *Psychosocial Development of Children*, New
York: Family Service Association of America, 1948. A psychia-
trist's view of child development, written for social workers but
of interest and value for educators and psychologists.

SEARS, ROBERT R. Survey of objective studies of psychoanalytic concepts. In Martin and Stendler, *op. cit.*, pp. 221-26. A summary of a critical review of experiments testing the validity
of Freudian concepts, together with an evaluative statement on
psychoanalysis as a science of personality.

STOKE, STUART M. An inquiry into the concept of identification. In
Martin and Stendler, *op. cit.*, pp. 227-39. An explanation of
identification that does not require the concept of the Oedipus
complex. Included are a delineation and discussion of ten
factors which influence the formation of identifications.

8
socialization as learning

A SOCIOPSYCHOLOGICAL APPROACH

One of the fundamental limitations of a psychoanalytic explanation of the process of socialization, as we saw in the last chapter, is its neglect of the significance of the influences of society and culture. The approach we examined in that chapter is primarily psychological in that it places its emphasis upon the individual—his nature and his behavior. We cannot, of course, eliminate the individual from consideration. He represents the resources which are shaped by the process of socialization, the content of this process.

According to Freud, not only the content but the end of the process is found in the individual and his nature. It is inevitable that every boy will desire his mother. It is inevitable that every girl will desire her father. It is inevitable that every human being will pass through a period in which he seeks affectional relationships with persons of the same sex and age as himself. It is inevitable that the adult male will differ psychologically from the adult female in given ways. Of course, Freud acknowledged that extra-individual conditions may inhibit or delay or distort these various stages of development. But they do so in certain inevitable ways. Progress or lack of progress, under given conditions, is defined by the nature of the individual. He is what he must be.

Thus the dramatic interplay of forces that underlies the change from infant to adult takes place within the individual. The production is a monologue. The society and culture provide only the backdrop. The lines are already written. The individual may speak them clearly and proceed without error to the end of the script, or he may flounder and stammer and stutter. As prompters, we may help him, but only to speak the lines that he must speak.

This point of view concerning the socialization process in one sense robs the individual of all freedom. Under given conditions, his reactions are predetermined. In another sense, this approach bestows complete freedom upon the individual in that it considers him irresponsible. If his reactions are predetermined, he cannot, in all fairness, be held liable for them.

Study of a variety of societies with differing cultures, however, reveals that the individual does not make predetermined responses to given environmental conditions. To the same set of conditions, the child in the United States responds in one way, the child in Bali in another. Martin, living in Kansas City, smiles and laughs and kicks up his heels to show his good spirits. Marti, living in the village of Bajoeng Gedé, Bali, outwardly expresses little of his inward feeling of pleasure (M. Mead, 1954; Mead & Macgregor, 1951).

Why and how do such differences become established? They must emanate from differences among the societies in which these youngsters grew and developed. Although they may have had approximately the same potentialities, their respective societies shaped them differently. The basic materials with which the socialization process concerns itself are everywhere the same. The direction or ends of that process are defined by a particular society and vary from one kind of society to another.

A child may be competitive or he may not. Potentially, he is both. The particular culture surrounding him in his formative years determines which is to be the eventual characteristic. A boy may be dominant in his relationships with members of the opposite sex; he may be submissive. Potentially, he is both. His social environment dictates which potentiality is to be realized—and to what extent.

A full explanation of the process of socialization requires consideration, not only of the individual, but also of the society in which he grows and develops. Not only do we need to examine the nature of the child and the nature of the society, as we have already done in previous chapters, but we must also investigate the interaction between them. This approach to the socialization of the child we term "sociopsychological" (Fromm, 1949).

In this interaction, we cannot look upon the individual and society as antagonistic and foreign to each other. The individual is not something apart from society; he is *in* society. That society has been created by individuals; its form, functioning, and development continue to be under the influence of individuals. It is true that society modifies the individual, but so does the individual modify society. Each person, in fact, leaves his mark on society, albeit, in most cases, that mark is a small one. But, over a period of years, even the most stable of societies change in reaction to these infinitesimal but cumulated influences. Thus we must avoid the mistake of concluding that the individual is one system of forces in constant conflict with or absolute subjection to another system of forces, the society.

Nevertheless, we recognize that the individual does adjust his behavior to meet the expectations of society. These expectations are constantly changing during the developmental years. What is appropriate behavior for the individual when he is three years of age is not appropriate behavior when he is thirteen. At three, he may express anger by screaming and kicking and throwing himself on the floor. At thirteen, he is very unlikely to exhibit such behavior. Society expects different behavior on the part of a child when he is three than when he is thirteen. In response to such changes in societal expectations, the child modifies his behavior.

But how does he modify his behavior? He does so most often through learning. Society is the teacher; the child is the learner. The interaction between the individual and the society that constitutes the process of socialization is a learning process. This definition may seem to be an obvious one. But notice how far we have come from a psychoanalytic explanation of socialization, in which learning received little, if any, attention. From a sociopsychological point of view, learning is the crucial activity.

But society is not *a* teacher; it is a great many teachers. It is mother and father, classroom teacher, brother and sister, athletic coach, Boy Scout leader, friend, Donald Duck, Space Cadet, and Cheyenne or Wyatt Earp, along with many others. All these are agents of the society; they speak for it. But they don't always speak the same lines. The individual must learn different responses to different social agents. He must become a very versatile character indeed if he is to take part in all these various and separate kinds of interaction. To respond to a father as he would to a friend might be disastrous; it would certainly be, in most cases, inappropriate. Thus the child must learn not only the right responses but when to make them.

Since society's part in the interaction is actually played by individuals, the interaction which concerns us takes place between people. We are not interested only in learning. We are interested in learning that involves people in interaction. We are interested in *social learning*. The forces represented by the nature of the child and the nature of society are no longer abstractions. They have become personified. We deal with people.

But doesn't all learning involve people? Isn't all learning social learning? It is true that most learning is social. But most discussions of learning neglect this very important fact. Much of the educational psychology that prospective teachers study concerns such impersonal matters as methods of presenting learning material, listening *versus* reciting, massed *versus* spaced practice, retention and forgetting, transfer of training, and motivation. These are, of course, all very important matters. But they neglect the essence of the process of social learning, which is the interaction between people.

Albert generally tends to learn more in school when practice in a given skill is distributed over a period of time than when practice is concentrated. However, Albert learns more with Miss Beaver, who concentrates drill, than he does with Miss Owens, who spaces it. Assuming that all other conditions of the two learning experiences are the same, we can understand the difference only if we know something of the nature of the two human interactions, that between Albert and Miss Beaver and that between Albert and Miss Owens. (Of course, we would expect that Albert would learn even more with Miss Beaver if she knew the advantages of spaced practice.)

Teachers—and all social agents, in general—are more than technicians; they are persons. We cannot describe their influence on the child unless we study them as persons interacting with the child, who is, of course, another person. In a sociopsychological approach to the process of socialization, then, we place great emphasis upon the matter of *interpersonal relationships*.

The child not only learns the right responses to make but also develops experience in and attitudes toward interpersonal relationships. Whether he learns to trust or distrust people, to cooperate or compete with them, to be independent of or dependent upon them, to be generous and helpful or to exploit others for his own benefit—all these attitudes toward people are outcomes of the socialization process, as important as any behavioral outcomes—manners, rituals, laws, and customs. The way in which the child has learned to relate himself to other people will determine the ways and the circumstances in which he employs these behaviors. The mark of the socialized individual lies ultimately in the nature of his interpersonal relationships. This is determined by the kinds of human interaction he enjoys in the process of being socialized.

It is one thing to state the importance of social learning. It is another to describe such learning. It is to that task that we now turn. But there may be one last question to answer. Why does the child submit to the influence of society and its agents? Why is he willing to learn new behavior to meet new expectations in these social agents?

We have already answered this question by pointing out that the individual is not something apart from society. He is *in* society. Even the young child recognizes his dependence upon others. He realizes that his existence depends upon the extent to which he is a member of society and abides by its rules and regulations. The three-year-old, on occasion, may attempt withdrawal by running away from home. But he returns in a very short time, on his own initiative, recognizing his helplessness. Older children and adolescents seldom withdraw voluntarily from the influences of agents of socialization. On the contrary, they seek them out. They have learned the necessity of remaining within the society.

Individuals do resist some socializing influences at times, but, on the whole, they are strikingly amenable and docile learners. They offer only token resistance to the demands of society. Each of them soon finds that he has certain problems to solve which he can solve only with the help of society. He is born dependent upon society. He depends upon that society to meet his biological needs.

Society does meet those needs. In fact, it is organized for that very purpose. But it does so only on certain stated terms. Those terms are that the individual undergo a process of social learning, a process of socialization. By so doing, the individual not only finds that his needs are met to some degree, but he is ultimately rewarded with adult status in the society. He receives an invisible diploma which states that he has been socialized. So prepared, he can now assist the society—of which he is a member in good standing—to solve its problems. Its problems are basically those of meeting the needs of individuals—not only biological needs, but needs which the society itself has created in individuals.

1. Did Freud completely neglect learning as a part of the developmental process? Where do you think he might have

found a place for it if he had not been more interested in analyzing other phenomena?

2. What are some typical ways in which children express their resentment against the demands of society? Do adults also resist some of their responsibilities in social situations?

3. Can you think of some situations in which learning is not "social"?

4. José Ortega y Gasset, the Spanish philosopher and writer, once said: "Man has no nature. He has only a history." How does this statement conflict with the point of view taken in this chapter and in preceding chapters?

In this chapter we shall first consider a laboratory model of the process of socialization, then the nature of learning in general, and finally the special features of social learning. Throughout the chapter we shall concern ourselves with the content of learning, which we have already defined as the goals of the socialization process (see Chap. 6). The child must learn what to want to do; that is, he must acquire new needs or drives. He must learn what to do and when to do it; that is, he must acquire knowledge and learn discrimination. He must learn how to do whatever he must do; that is, he must acquire skill and competency. Finally, he must learn the signs of being successful; that is, he must learn to recognize rewards and punishments.

A MODEL OF THE
SOCIALIZATION PROCESS

How can we capture the essence of the process of socialization? Can we find a common denominator among all the various examples of this process taken from an almost infinite variety of societal settings? As is often the case, it seems necessary to turn for the moment to a description of animal behavior.

The reader may wonder how observations of subhuman life can bring much understanding of or insight into the socialization of the human being. Perhaps Dollard and Miller, in justifying their study of the learning of albino rats as a way of studying how human beings learn fear, have presented the best rationale of experiments on animals:

> In using the results from an experiment of this kind we are working on the hypothesis that people have all the learning capacities of rats so that any general phenomena of learning found in rats will also be found in people, although, of course, people may display additional phenomena not found in rats. Even though the facts must be verified at the human level, it is often easier to notice the operation of principles after they have been studied and isolated in simpler situations so that one knows exactly what to look for. Furthermore, in those cases in which it is impossible to use as rigorous experimental controls at the human level, our faith in what evidence can be gathered at that level will be increased if it is in line with the results of more carefully controlled experiments on other mammals [1950, p. 63].

To this statement we might add that in the case of animals we can control the extent and kind of previous experience. In fact, we can establish a zero point. We can select as subjects of observation animals which have learned nothing, at least nothing related to the experimental task. There are no such "empty" human organisms, for the demands of the society begin at birth. Therefore, even with the most carefully designed controls, we can never be absolutely sure whether the behavior of humans is a result of exposure to the particular conditions of the experiment or of some previous experience of which we are unaware and the results of which are not apparent to us at the beginning of the experiment.

How Rats Were "Socialized"

An experiment on maze learning by the albino rat (Whiting & Mowrer, 1943) furnishes a prototype of the socialization process. The maze employed is shown in Figure 8-1.

An animal placed in the maze at the starting point (S) can reach the goal (G) by four different routes: (*1*) from S to G via O; (*2*) from S to G via A_s; (*3*) from S to G via A_I; (*4*) from S to

G via A_L. The maze is so constructed that S-A_s-G, S-A_I-G, and S-A_L-G, the longer routes, can be barred to the rat.

The goal in the experiment is food, in the form of a pellet of Purina Dog Chow, placed at G. It should be noted that this is a real or "natural" goal to the rat, at least when it is hungry. It does not have to learn to want food and then to behave in

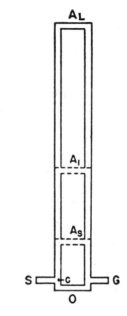

FIGURE 8-1. Diagram of the elevated maze (viewed from above) employed in the investigation by Whiting and Mowrer. The removable bridges, represented by dotted lines, were so constructed as to bar entrance to the parts of the maze lying beyond them.

(Reproduced by permission from *The Journal of Comparative Psychology,* Vol. 36, p. 231. Copyright 1943 The Williams and Wilkins Co.)

such a way that it will obtain that food. The need for food and the predisposition to put forth energy in the pursuit of it is part of the biological nature of the rat. The goal is not one arbitrarily defined by the experimenters.

In the first part of the experiment, the maze was so arranged that the rats were confronted with only two paths, the shortest, most direct route (S-O-G) and one of the alternatives. Each animal subject was given seventy-five trials in this maze; at the end of this period, all had established a preference for the shorter path as a means of getting to the goal. The experimenters concluded that by its nature, the rat not only seeks food when hungry but tends to use the quickest, most direct method of obtaining that food.

But let us assume that the rat must learn to live in a society in which taking the shortest, most direct path to food is not approved. The rat must develop a "second nature," one which continues to involve the seeking of food but requires that the seeking be accomplished only in certain prescribed ways. Can the rats in this particular experiment be taught to abandon the shortest path in favor of one of the alternatives?

Whiting and Mowrer utilized three techniques of thus "socializing" the rat. In one group of rats, the animal found food at G only if it reached that point via the prescribed alternative path, A_s, A_I, or A_L. If it took the short path, it found no pellet of food at the end. In similar fashion, parents teach their children that they may obtain food only if they sit properly at the table, use the prescribed utensils, and are neat. These conditions constitute the longer alternative path prescribed by society as the only one which will lead to the satisfaction of hunger.

A second group of rats found the short path blocked by a piece of window glass; the only way in which they could reach the food was via the longer route. Similarly, Johnny rushes in from outdoors, ready to proceed immediately to the kitchen and food. But his mother blocks his forward progress and tells him that only when he has gone to the lavatory and washed his hands will he be given his lunch.

The remaining rats were allowed to take the shorter path, but, if they did so, they received an electric shock from a grid set into the floor of that path midway between the starting point and the goal. Similarly, Johnny's mother may not block the entrance to the dining room, but, if he attempts to pass the threshold without having first washed his hands, she thumps him on the head.

Which was the most effective of these techniques of teaching rats to take the longer path to the goal? Which group of rats learned most quickly to abandon the original path? Those subjects which received the electric shock (punishment) were the ones which most rapidly accepted the alternative route. The most ineffective technique (that is, the most time-consuming) was the first, deprivation of reward. In addition, it was found that, regardless of the method of teaching used, the longer the alternative path, the longer the time before the rats learned to accept it as the means to the goal.

By one means or another, the rats in this experiment were "socialized." But were they socialized too well? If the conditions were to change, would they be able to modify their behavior to meet new conditions?

When the child is very young, we must teach him to depend upon adults. We say, "Don't try to do that by yourself. Let Mother and Daddy help you. Otherwise you'll hurt yourself." But, as he grows older, we wish him to become more independent of adults. Then we may find that we have done too good a job in our earlier teaching. We may find that, despite changes in our expectations, the child remains dependent upon us. We then ask ourselves: What techniques could we have used to discourage independence early in life that would not have blocked the development of independent behavior in later years? The efficacy of teaching method from this long-run point of view is of crucial significance.

Whiting and Mowrer considered this problem in a further development of their experiment. They re-established the experimental conditions prevailing at the beginning of the investigation, using the same rats as subjects. The rats in the first group received food even when they took the short path; those in the second group were not barred from the original path; and those in the third group received no shock when they reached the goal by means of the shortest path. Which group of rats displayed the most "intelligent" behavior in the sense that it was best able to adjust to conditions actually present in the environmental setting?

The first (nonreward) and second (barrier) groups learned most quickly that the original (and shortest) path was no longer proscribed and was now a possible way, if not the preferred way, of obtaining food. The rats in the punishment group found it extremely difficult to modify their behavior and tended to persist in taking the longer route, even though nothing now prevented them from reaching the goal more quickly. It appears that what seemed to be the most effective technique— punishment in this case—is actually the least effective if we value learning which does not deprive the individual of flexibility in adjusting to changes in societal demands. On the basis of this particular study, then, the efficacy of punishment can be questioned, even without regard to its humaneness or its possible aftereffects. In a sense, punishment is almost too effective; stereotypy results; behavior is static although conditions change.

Rat "Socialization" and Child Socialization

Elsewhere, Mowrer and Kluckhohn (1944) discuss the significant features of this study as they might be identified in a similar process among humans. First, they note that socialization takes place only because the animal, by reason of its nature, needs something—in this case, food—and, further, only because it is dependent upon the experimenter for that food. If the rat were not hungry, or if it could obtain food without the help of the experimenter, it could not be made to run any maze or any path in that maze. Thus we return to something we pointed out as significant in the child as a biological organism: the fact that he is already predisposed to behave, and to behave so as to satisfy certain needs. We take advantage of this characteristic in socializing the child. The child needs food and acts to obtain it. We say, in effect, that we shall help him to obtain food, but only if he behaves in certain socially approved ways. To the rat, we "say" that food will be made available only if the animal takes a certain path to the goal.

In the case of the child, we can use instructions. We can tell him what he must do if he is to be successful in satisfying his needs. Even before the child is able to use language, he can understand it. He can recognize such signs as facial expressions as indications that he is on the "right path." But the rat must learn by trial and error. We cannot prepare him for what is to come. He must learn by his own experience; unlike the child, he cannot profit from the experience of others.

For this reason, the problem is more difficult for the rat than for the child. But, on the other hand, the alternatives are much clearer in "rat society." There is this path or that path. For the child, there are innumerable paths. He finds it difficult to know exactly which is the most approved path. Others cannot always tell him. In fact, they may disagree as to which is the "right" path. His father may indicate one as best; his mother another; his playmates another; his teacher still another. The best path in one situation is not necessarily the best path in a second situation. The grooming that makes a boy presentable at the dinner table and therefore deserving of food would be completely out of place at a wiener roast in the community picnic grounds. This distinction is so simple that we forget that we must have learned it once.

In the process of human socialization, other persons are very important; that is, the process is very personal. Presumably, the rat does not care much what the experimenter will think of it. If it can obtain food with a minimum of delay and discomfort, it is satisfied. The experimenter would accomplish little by indicating that he liked or disliked the animal.

The child, on the other hand, becomes extremely sensitive to the presence and behavior of other human beings, especially adults. He soon learns to accept them as signs that satisfaction of his basic needs is forthcoming. In other situations, he learns to recognize the presence of adults as a sign that his needs are *not* going to be satisfied. Ultimately, the approval of others, originally only a precursor to need-satisfaction, becomes a satisfaction in and of itself. The child not only wants food; he wants the approval of adults, especially of those who have become associated with need-satisfaction. He learns to like other people. Because of this fact, the technique of punishment as applied to humans cannot be evaluated except by considering some of its consequences. If adults punish children in order to get quick results in the training program, the children will necessarily lose some of their tendency to like those adults. Although they may continue to answer the demands of adults, they will do so, not to seek the approval of these adults, but to avoid their disapproval. Whether or not optimal development can be based on fear and avoidance of punishment is somewhat doubtful. For this reason alone, it could be recommended that adults avoid punishment and disapproval as much as possible and as long as possible (Mowrer & Kluckhohn, 1944).

This prescription should not be interpreted as a recommendation for indulgence of the child. He must be made to learn, but in such ways that the emphasis is upon seeking the approval of adults rather than avoiding their disapproval. It is a question of accentuating the positive, stressing what the child can and should do rather than what he cannot and should not do. In this connection, it is interesting to note that Radke (1946), in a study of young children's perceptions of their parents, found that the children looked upon parents in general as essentially interfering, prohibiting people—people who say "No." Individual parents, however, were sometimes seen as helpful, facilitating people—people who say "Yes."

Thus it happens that new and secondary needs arise. In certain instances, the satisfaction of these "social" needs may become more important than the satisfaction of original needs. As might be expected, social needs do not develop in the rat, at least not to such an extent that they override its original needs in importance and strength. To the end of the rat's life, its basic, physiological needs remain preëminent.

For the child in the process of socialization, adults become— or may become—models. Not only can they instruct the child prior to an experience, but they can demonstrate exactly what responses are desired. The child then behaves in such ways that he is "like" the adult model. Not only does he learn to seek the approval of other adults; he learns to want to be like them. Even if it were possible for the experimenter to demonstrate to the rat exactly how the maze is to be run, it is doubtful that the animal would be much impressed or influenced. There is no evidence that any rat has ever wanted to be like any "rat psychologist."

Because the child learns to seek the approval of adults, he

may experience what we call feelings of guilt when he takes the wrong path or seeks socially disapproved goals. In the vernacular, we say that the child's conscience hurts him. "Conscience," so used, is something that "stem[s] from the indeterminancy but inevitability of punishment for forbidden acts" (Mowrer & Kluckhohn, 1944, p. 111). These feelings of guilt arise particularly when the child has done something which an adult whose approval he values has forbidden. Often the adult may punish or threaten punishment in such a way that the child learns to avoid, not only socially disapproved means to the right goal, but the right goal itself. Specialists in child care and training point out, for example, that overemphasis upon neatness in eating—the means to a goal—sometimes results in avoidance of the goal itself. Thus the child whose somewhat immature efforts to convey food to his mouth are strongly disapproved often becomes an eating problem. Punishment has become attached to eating as well as to the means by which that eating is accomplished.

To these comments by Mowrer and Kluckhohn we need make but one addition. In the experiment we have reported, the rats learned that by taking the "right" path they received the reward, food. In neither quality nor quantity was this food any different from the food they had obtained previously by taking the short path. In human socialization, the reward or goal changes. The child, by learning socially approved behavior, obtains not only the food, his immediate goal, but something more. He receives the approval of his parents and, later on, that of other adults, as well as of his peers. He not only continues to like food, but he learns to prefer those ways of obtaining it which elicit approval. What was formerly the means to an end becomes an end in and of itself.

Thus raw steak would not satisfy the hunger of a socialized adult in American society, for his drive is no longer a simple biological one—it has become socialized. Food, as such, is no longer an adequate reward. Only when it is prepared and served and eaten under given conditions will his hunger be satisfied. The rats' behavior, in contrast, at the end of the experiment as at the beginning, is an attempt to satisfy biological needs, no more, no less.

From an examination of this experimental analogue of socialization, we have derived some notion of the important factors in the process. Somehow, children not only learn socially approved ways of satisfying primary drives, but they also develop secondary drives. They not only learn what to want to do and how to do it, but they also learn attitudes, particularly toward other human beings. They learn to avoid some persons and to seek the approval of others. They learn to want to be like other persons. They learn to recognize in the behavior of others the signs of their success or failure; they learn to expect certain things from adults. They learn to use and understand language as a method of utilizing the experience of others, and they learn the value of seeing a demonstration of a performance before an actual trial.

    5. Can you give some examples of situations in which adults teach and children learn lessons too well?

    6. What do you think would have happened in the rat experiment if the "right" path had changed repeatedly from one trial to the next? Is this situation more analogous to the one that the child faces than the situation used in the experiment?

    7. Can we say of the rat that it learns *only* by experience? Can we say this of the child?

    8. We have said that rats do not seem to acquire social needs, at least not ones that are comparable in importance to their biological needs. Can we say this of other animals—of dogs, for example?

    9. Can you think of other situations in which parents and teachers confuse children by not making it clear that they are punishing "means" rather than "ends"?

    10. Is hunger the only drive operating in the rat experiment?

    11. When the child, in the process of learning, models his behavior after that of an adult, is he identifying, in a psychoanalytic sense, with that adult? Is there a difference between imitation and identification?

12. Can a child feel guilty without being fearful? Can he be fearful without feeling guilty? Are both fear and guilt attributable to the superego? Might the method of discipline used by a parent determine which is the more characteristic reaction of the child to his own misbehavior (see pp. 193-94)?

LEARNING

Before we investigate the nature of the learning process which is so important a part of socialization, we need to clarify what we mean by the term "learning." Perhaps we can best do this by looking at a specific example.

Henry receives a tricycle for Christmas. Although he has seen the older children in the neighborhood riding their tricycles, he has never actually ridden one himself. Once he was allowed by the proud possessor of such a vehicle to sit on the seat for a few minutes. But his legs were too short to reach the pedals. All he could do was sit there, feeling rather hopeless about the whole thing.

If we look in on Henry a few weeks later, we are not surprised to find him an accomplished performer on his three-wheeler. He guides it skillfully through doorways and around corners. He can go forward or backward. He can go fast or slow. We say that he has learned something; specifically, that he has learned to ride a tricycle.

What do we mean? First, we are recognizing the fact that Henry has acquired a skill. He can now do something that he could not do before. His behavior has changed. More importantly, it has changed rather permanently. He will continue to be able to ride a tricycle. Time alone has not brought about this change in his behavior. Henry learned how to ride a tricycle not just by growing older but by practicing. During our absence from the scene, he has spent many hours in the activity. At first, he gave so much attention to making the wheels go round by pedaling that he forgot to watch where he was going. Then he found that if he concentrated on steering, he did a poor job of pedaling. But finally, after a few accidents to himself and other persons and objects in the household, he became able to integrate these two important parts of the activity. Henry has learned something in the sense that he has undergone a change in behavior, a change which is more or less permanent and which has resulted from practice or activity of a particular kind.

Let us examine a slightly more complex example of learning. When Mary first goes off to school, she knows how to count. But if you ask her "How much are two and two?" she is not able to tell you. In the first grade, however, she learns many new things about numbers. If we ask the same question again at the end of the year, she will answer "four" with little or no hesitation. She has changed her behavior. She has acquired knowledge. The chances are that, if we repeat that question at intervals in the years to come, she will continue to be able to give the same answer. That is, she will be able to do so to the extent that she has really acquired the knowledge. In one sense, this is a permanent change in her behavior. We will not expect ever to see Mary again quite as she was on the day she entered school.

She did not acquire this knowledge as she did her teeth or those extra pounds of weight or inches of height. She acquired it, just as Henry acquired his new skill, through some kind of activity. That activity was probably not nearly so apparent as it was in Henry's case. If we had observed her during this practice period, we might have seen her only sitting at her desk and looking at some words and numbers on a page of a textbook. For Mary's practicing involved not so much overt movement as carrying "in her head" certain symbols—words and numbers—which replace overt movement. We could see Henry's legs move, his hands grip the steering wheel, and the tricycle move. There is no less movement in Mary's practicing, but it is concealed from our observation. Mary has learned, like Henry, in that she has undergone a permanent change in behavior as a result of activity.

Having examined these two rather simple examples of learning, we can state a more precise definition: "Learning may be said to occur whenever behavior undergoes incremental modification of a more or less permanent nature as a result of activity, special training, or observation" (Munn, 1954, p. 374).

13. Can you think of some changes in behavior commonly observed in children—and adults, as well—which are not the result of learning? What about the loss of efficiency we experience at the end of a long day's work? Is that change in behavior "learning"? Is the change in what we see after we have been in a dark room for a few minutes "learning"? Do we acquire the ability to walk through "learning"?

Munn's statement defines learning in terms of outcomes, or changes in behavior as a result of learning. We have still to examine the particular sequence of events or the particular combination of factors which constitutes the *process* of learning. As a result of learning, Henry is able to ride a tricycle; as a result of learning, Mary is able to add two and two. But what actually took place in these learnings? What were the significant aspects of the respective processes? We can identify at least four fundamentals of the learning process, regardless of what is learned: (*1*) drive, (*2*) cue, (*3*) response, and (*4*) reward. As Miller and Dollard (1941) put it, in order to learn, you have to *want* something, you have to *notice* something, you have to *do* something, you have to *get* something. Let us look again at the learning of Henry and Mary and analyze it according to these four fundamentals.

Drive

We have already discussed the nature of drives in an early part of this book (Chap. 2). From the standpoint of the individual, these drives are needs, originating within the various tissues and structures of the body—muscles, glands, nerves—or aroused in those same tissues and structures by events and conditions external to the individual. In all cases, regardless of the locus of the need, a general state of tension is a sign that some need exists. That tension is eliminated or reduced only when the need is satisfied. The tension associated with hunger disappears only when the individual obtains food. The tension accompanying fatigue is reduced only by rest or change in activity. A drive, then, is some stimulus or group of stimuli which brings about activity—activity which the individual hopes and expects will eliminate that drive.

In our earlier discussion, we were speaking only of drives, or needs, which are a normal part of the biology of the individual. These are drives which lead to activity to some degree in all individuals. Neither Henry's learning nor Mary's was initiated by any such drive. What was it that Henry wanted in this situation? Presumably he wanted to be able to ride a tricycle. The fact that he wanted to do so and could not led to the building up of a tension—just as if he wanted food or water. That tension was manifested in a constant pleading with his parents to get him a tricycle and in crying and displaying of temper when they refused.

But precisely why did Henry want to be able to ride a tricycle? We can only guess. Was it because his friends could, but he could not? Was it because learning to ride a tricycle would be a sign that he was growing up? Is there such a drive as wanting to be like others and to do the things they do? Is there such a drive as wanting to be "grown-up"? If so, these drives are not a part of the biology of the individual. In some way, they have been acquired. An examination of how this may have been accomplished is too large a task to undertake here. For the moment, we have to assume the existence of "acquired," as well as "native" or "basic," drives.

The important thing to note is that a drive, "native" or "acquired," is a necessary forerunner to learning activity. Unless Henry wanted, for some reason or other, to learn to ride a tricycle, he would not do so. In order to learn, one must first want something.

Why did Mary learn the answer to the question "How much are two and two?" What did she want? Again, we have to point out that no basic need existed. No child in the world wants to know the answer to such a question by reason of his nature. Many children, however, somehow acquire the desire to solve the problem. But just what is this drive? It is probably more than wanting to answer this particular question. Perhaps

Mary wants to please her teacher and believes that this wanting can be satisfied by getting the right answers to the teacher's questions. Mary's learning activity may be initiated by her wish to get good grades and her realization that the only way in which to get good grades is to learn the right answers. Perhaps Mary is afraid of being punished if she doesn't succeed in solving problems presented to her in the schoolroom. At any rate, Mary wants something in this situation. That is the only reason she learns.

Mary displays the tension that accompanies this "wanting" by chewing her pencil or her fingernails as she tries to work out the examples or by casting apprehensive glances at the teacher standing nearby. These are not the behaviors of learning. Rather, they are signs of the existence of tension which is motivating or bringing about behaviors designed to reduce or eliminate that tension.

Cue

In order to learn, it is necessary to do more than want something. One must notice something. Henry would not learn much about riding a tricycle if he practiced in the bathtub or at the dinner table. He practices *with* the vehicle in certain situations. That is, he cannot learn unless he is able to identify the situations in which the activity called forth by his drive is appropriate. Activity is appropriate which serves to reduce the tension associated with the drive.

Henry then looks for certain signs to tell him when to practice, what to practice, and even how to practice. In this very simple situation, the most important sign is the tricycle. But the parts of that structure are also important. He must notice the pedals, the wheels, the handlebars, and so on. The drive to learn to ride the tricycle is within the individual. The cues that tell him that the conditions are appropriate and that certain behaviors are appropriate lie outside the individual.

Similarly, it is not enough for Mary to want to learn how to add two and two. She must notice "two and two." She must be able to discriminate between "two and two" and "three and three." She must be able to tell the difference between the "number" situation and a "reading" situation. She would not get very far in learning to read if, when the teacher asked her to read the first sentence in a story, she responded with "four" or any other number. Likewise, she would be blocked in her arithmetic if, when the teacher asked her for the answer to a number problem, she responded by spelling the first word she sees on the blackboard. The actor in the learning situation must not only want to learn to give the right or the best performance; he must know his cues. The best performance in the world would be in vain if it took place on the wrong stage in the wrong theater at the wrong time. He learns best, all other things being equal, who notices most.

Response

Thus far, our learners want something and they notice something. In other words, they are stimulated by needs, or drives, within and by cues without. Now it is time to act. One learns only by doing something, only by responding to these stimuli. Henry must practice riding his tricycle. Mary must practice manipulating numbers.

But what kind of response do they make? Of course, each of them wants to make the response that will achieve his or her goal or satisfy his or her need. But, in the beginning, they do not know exactly what these responses are. At first, they may try all sorts of responses. Henry pushes forward with his feet on both pedals. But the wheels do not seem to go around as they should. He pushes down on both. That does not work very well either. After much experimentation, he learns just how to distribute the push between the pedals and between the "forward" and the "down" movements to get the tricycle going. He still has to learn to steer. He wants to turn the corner. What responses does he make? He turns the handlebar one way and goes in the opposite direction. Sooner or later, with practice and experience, he learns that to turn one way, he makes this response; to turn another, he makes that response.

What does Mary do? She tries one answer and then another. She may even forget the abstract numbers for the moment and get out some blocks. She very carefully counts out "two" of them, puts them to one side, and counts out another "two." Then she puts her two groups of blocks together and counts them all. Perhaps Mary does not have these kinds of response available. She can react to the present situation only with the behavior she has learned from the past. So she asks her neighbor. Or she looks in a book for the answer. Or perhaps she even guesses.

This is learning behavior. It is responding to given drives and cues. For obvious reasons, it is very often what we call trial-and-error behavior. The child tries this response and then that one, always looking for something that "works." Our examples are somewhat artificial because, as you may have noticed, there is no teaching. Usually, when children learn, they have help, either from formal teachers or from individuals who behave like teachers. Thus Henry might respond in a way that his father describes for him. Or perhaps his older brother gets on the tricycle and shows him how to ride it. In the same way, Mary gets direction from her teacher.

We have eliminated the teacher from the description for several reasons. First, we wanted to give all our attention to the learner and what he did. Secondly, the introduction of a teacher into these situations would not affect the fundamental nature of the learning process, although it might well facilitate that process. Thirdly, we want to reserve consideration of the role of the teacher until we discuss social learning (pp. 269-76).

For the moment, then, it is important to see that a child learns only by doing something. Learning is an active process. The learner is an active agent. He not only must want something and notice something, but he must do something.

Reward

Of all the responses they make, why do Henry and Mary learn some and not others? What determines whether Henry learns those responses that facilitate tricycle riding rather than those that will interfere with the activity? What determines whether Mary learns to respond "four" or "three" to the problem presented to her? These youngsters make those responses that lead to reward. They make those responses that lead to their getting something.

What was it that Henry wanted? We guessed that it might be to be "grown-up" or to be like other youngsters. When he makes those responses that constitute riding a tricycle, he has succeeded in showing himself and others that he is grown up or that he is able to do things that his playmates and even older children do. All this hard work of learning a motor skill has led to reward. Those responses that do not contribute to obtaining that reward are not learned.

What was it that Mary wanted? She wanted a good grade or she wanted to please her teacher or she wanted to avoid punishment. By learning the "right" answer—so identified by her textbook and her teacher or by some other authority in arithmetic—she *does* get a good grade or please her teacher or avoid punishment. In other words, she is rewarded. But since she is not so rewarded if she learns some answer other than "four," she tends not to learn any other answer.

Thus we see the distinguishing characteristic of those responses that lead to reward: they are those that bring about a reduction of the tension asssociated with the original drive. If wanting something is tension-producing, then getting something must be tension-reducing. It is the reduction of tension that constitutes the reward. It is the responses leading to reward that are learned.

Mary and Henry have learned more than responses, however. They have learned that when certain drives are operating and when certain cues are present, certain responses will result in reward. They learn to make such responses whenever such conditions exist. Each time they make these responses and are rewarded, the tendency to make these responses again in the future under the same conditions is strengthened. Learning therefore requires reinforcement of the tendency to respond in a certain way to certain cues when under the influence of a certain drive. Because the *effect* of the responses which the individual makes determines whether or not those responses will be repeated in the future, the process which we have been discussing is called "learning by reinforcement," or "effect learning." A law of effect becomes the basic principle underlying learning. Simply stated, such a law might read: An individual tends to repeat those responses which, in the past, have brought about a reduction of the tension produced by the drive which originally initiated the activity.

14. Select some situations in which you can observe children learning. For each of these situations, describe the drives, cues, responses, and rewards which constitute the fundamentals of learning.

15. Are all motives or drives within the individual? Or can he be motivated extrinsically? What relevance does the old saying, "You can drive a horse to water but you can't make him drink," have in this connection?

16. In his novel *Bread and Wine,* Ignazio Silone tells the following story:

One Sunday morning a donkey just bought at market was christened outside Matalena Ricotta's inn. A young man held it by the halter while an old man beat it with a wooden cudgel. After each blow the two shouted, "Garibaldi!" into the beast's ear at the top of their lungs.

Garibaldi was to be the donkey's name. In the minds of the peasants it stood for strength and courage. As the two men wanted to be absolutely sure the donkey knew it, the christening naturally lasted a long time. The old man beat the animal on the crupper, without anger, without impatience, without resentment, but with emphasis, as though he were beating a mattress, and shouted "Garibaldi!" after every blow.

The donkey looked at the two men, and each time the stick descended it shook its head. The old man aimed each blow at a different rib, and when he had been all around he started again. The heroic name of Garibaldi resounded dozens and dozens of times across the little square of Pietrasecca, alternating with the thudding of the stick against the poor donkey's ribs. This went on until the old man grew tired.

"That'll do," he said. "He knows it now."

To make sure, the young man tried an experiment. He took
a handful of hay, walked over to the wooden bridge, held up the
hay, and called out:
"Garibaldi!"
The donkey trotted towards him.
"Yes, he knows it," the young man said [1937, p. 54].

How would you analyze this account as a learning experience
for the donkey? Would your analysis differ from that of the
two Italian peasants? If so, how?

17. What happens in the learning situation when more than
one drive is operating? Suppose, for example, that a boy wants
to please his parents by being successful in his school work, but
also wants to avoid the disapproval of his friends that might
result from academic achievements.

18. What obstacles do children commonly face in their learning? Does learning ever take place in the complete absence of
obstacles? How do obstacles to tension-reduction affect the
fundamental aspects of learning which we have discussed? What
happens in the learning situation when obstacles persist? What
happens when they are insuperable?

Through effect learning, the child acquires knowledge and
discrimination, skill and competency, and the ability to look for
and recognize certain external signs of success and achievement.
Can this picture of the learning process also explain how a child
acquires new drives? For we have seen that socialization involves
learning to want various "somethings." Mary and Henry are
examples of youngsters who have somehow acquired drives that
were not a part of their biological nature. Where did they get
these drives? Were they learned? If so, were they learned according to the model we have just been discussing? Are new drives
acquired as a result of learning by reinforcement?

If we remember that drives are tension-producing and that
the crucial step in learning by reinforcement is tension-reduction, it is rather difficult to see how a child could acquire new
drives or new needs in this way. Why would any youngster learn
to be afraid, when fear itself is tension-producing? Why would
any child learn to want good grades, when a desire for good

grades is tension-producing? Why would any child learn to want material goods—money, fine clothes, expensive toys—when wanting them is, in a very real sense, upsetting? We have been speaking thus far as if the fundamental principle of behavior, especially learning behavior, were the avoidance or the reduction of tension.

To explain the learning of new drives, we shall describe a second kind of learning. We thereby are assuming that the first kind—learning by reinforcement—cannot explain all learning.

ANOTHER KIND OF LEARNING

As an approach to this second kind of learning, let us try to answer the question: How does a child learn to be afraid? Earlier we said that fear is not a basic drive in the human being. In the beginning, the child is not afraid of anything. He learns to be afraid. He learns to fear many things.

In terms of his original nature, we cannot explain why a child is afraid of the dark. Similarly, we cannot explain why girls scream at the sight of a snake, why all students to some extent fear poor grades and worry over the possibility of getting them, or why young children refuse to go into a dark room.

To answer such questions, we consider, first, an experiment on rats carried out by Miller and described by Dollard and Miller (1950, pp. 63-68). The apparatus used consisted of two compartments, identical except that one was black, the other white. A door connected the two compartments. At the start of the experiment, the rat showed no fear of either room. Placed in the white room, it exhibited no tendency to go into the black room; placed in the black room, it showed no disposition to go into the white room.

Thereafter, when the rat was in the white room, it received electric shocks. It experienced pain. But pain, or the desire to escape from pain, is a basic drive. It automatically brings about activity designed to stop the pain. The "shocked" rat learned to escape the pain by going into the black room through the open door.

Thus far in the experiment, we can explain everything that happened by reference to learning by reinforcement. The rat wanted something: escape from pain. It noticed a certain cue: pain is experienced in the white but not in the black compartment. It did something: it left the white room and went into the black room. It got something: cessation of pain and the reduction of tension associated with pain.

But something else happened, as revealed by the behavior of the animal when the conditions of the experiment were changed. Shock was no longer administered to the rat when it was in the white compartment. But although the rat ceased to experience pain in that compartment, it continued to run from the white into the black compartment. It did so even when the door was closed and it had to learn to open the door by rotating a wheel or pressing a bar. We cannot now explain the rat's behavior by saying that it was escaping from pain, for pain was no longer inflicted in the situation. Pain, as such, could not have been the drive which initiated its behavior.

What did bring about withdrawing or escaping behavior in the rat? It was not pain. It was *fear* of the white compartment. Somehow, during the progress of the experiment, the rat learned to be afraid of the white compartment. It acquired a new drive. Learning which involves tension-production rather than tension-reduction had taken place.

What is the nature of this learning? First, we should note that the rat made an old response—the one it made to the original stimulus, pain—to a new stimulus—in this case, a white room. Why did it do this? Because it associated the stimulus "pain" with the stimulus "white room." They were equivalent stimuli in the sense that the rat made the same response to both. It made this association because the two stimuli occurred together repeatedly. The one became the sign for the other. As a result of learning, the white room elicited the same response as pain alone did formerly. To this form of learning we give the name "conditioning." Through conditioning, the child learns to want to do what he must do, a kind of learning which is fundamental in socialization.

We could hardly carry out this same experiment using children rather than rats as subjects. But the way in which the rat learned to be afraid is not too different from the way in which children learn to be afraid. Do we not sometimes punish children to make them afraid of potentially dangerous situations? Every time Ernest runs out into the street, his mother spanks him. If she does this often enough, Ernest will learn not to run out into the street. He may shy away from the street long after he has been punished in such a situation. Originally, he was escaping from pain. Now, he has learned to be afraid of the street insofar as it has become a sign of spanking, or pain.

Such acquired fears are amazingly permanent. The fears which we have as adults can often be traced back to our association of pain with particular situations or objects. They presumably retain their strength because we tend not to re-examine these situations or objects to find, in repeated instances, that they are no longer associated with pain. These situations or objects continue to be signs of pain.

Children also become afraid of situations, not because they associate pain with them, but because they are warned of possible danger by their parents or teachers. But how do parents and teachers gain such influence over children? How does wanting to please them or to avoid their displeasure become a drive? It is not a primary drive. Therefore, it must have been acquired. Can we explain its acquisition by reference to learning by conditioning?

If we look at the very young child, we see that one of the basic needs or drives that spur his activity is hunger. When he is in that particular state of tension, he does all sorts of things in trying to get food and reduce tension. Certain figures, especially the mother, repeatedly appear in situations associated with reduction of hunger tension. It is food he seeks, but mother becomes a sign of that food and the pleasure which ensues. Over a period of time, he learns through conditioning to give the same responses to his mother as he did originally to his bottle. The stimulus "bottle" and the stimulus "mother" become equivalent stimuli. But these are not drive stimuli. They are cues. We have still to explain how the child acquires a wanting to please his mother or to avoid her displeasure.

Even the most solicitous of mothers cannot always feed the child immediately upon call. Sometimes the baby must cry and toss and turn for some minutes before his mother can get his food prepared and delivered to him. The tension originally associated with hunger becomes associated with absence of the mother or with a delay in her appearance. What was originally a wanting for food now becomes, through association, a wanting for mother. The baby welcomes her now as he originally welcomed his food. He is employing an old response to a new stimulus. Mother is no longer just a cue. She—or a wanting for her—has become an acquired drive. To get her in the situation and to keep her there, the child will learn all sorts of behavior. He will try to do as she says. If she warns him that certain situations are dangerous, that they will hurt him, he accepts her as his authority. Doing so is one way of showing his respect for her and of keeping her attention. So behaving is a way of reducing the tension associated with wanting her presence.

Thus we see another example of how a child acquires new drives through learning by conditioning. He then proceeds to learn by reinforcement ways of behaving which will obtain for him what he has learned to want.

19. What are some drives that children commonly acquire as they grow and develop? Can you outline the steps by which they are learned?

20. In our examples of learning by conditioning, we began, in each case, with a "basic" drive and then traced from that point the development of an "acquired" drive. But it is also possible to move from an existent acquired drive to a new acquired drive via learning by conditioning. Can you think of an example?

21. To what extent do acquired drives replace basic drives? How could you use Freud's concept of sublimation in answering this question?

In view of our discussion of two types of learning, we can now look at the process of socialization in this way. The child, from the beginning, is confronted with certain problems—

problems that arise in his nature as a human being. He needs food; he needs rest; he needs activity. He must learn to develop the responses that will alleviate the tension associated with these problems. But solving these problems is only the beginning. Society, because of its nature, requires modification of human nature. To get the child to behave, not as he would, but as he must, society inculcates in the child new drives. These drives, in turn, make it necessary for him to learn still more responses which will reduce the tension associated with the drives. The child then faces two sets of problems, one inherited, the other defined for him by society and learned by him. He must proceed to find solutions to all these problems which will maintain his integrity as a human being and his acceptance as a member in good standing of his society.

SOCIAL LEARNING

Learning does not often take place in social isolation. The learner is usually surrounded by other persons, some of them acting as teachers, others as fellow-learners, and still others as mere observers. In previous examples of learning, it has been almost impossible to avoid mentioning such persons. Henry did not learn to ride his tricycle in solitude. Mary was only one of many children perplexed by the problem of "two and two." The infant learned under the watchful eyes of his mother.

What effect do the presence and activities of these other persons have upon the learning process? In order to answer that question, let us consider one further example of a child's learning. This time we shall give our attention, not exclusively to the individual learner, but also to his relationship with another person in the learning situation. We shall refer to this other person by the term R. R. Sears (1948, 1951) has used in his analysis of social learning, the "social person."

Learning Skills Through Reinforcement

Tommy Aldrich is a seven-year-old boy, the only child of his parents. His father holds a responsible position as foreman in a local factory. Mr. Aldrich has had little formal education but, over the years, has advanced in his work through a rather systematic program of self-teaching. The fact that this effort has resulted in tangible benefits to him has given him a tremendous respect for education and for individual initiative. He is determined that his son, by taking better advantage of educational opportunities than he himself did as a boy, will gain even greater benefits. His ambitions for Tommy have led him to spend more time and take more interest in his son than many fathers do. As systematically and methodically as he shaped his own development, he is now proceeding to guide Tommy's growth and development. But his ambition is tempered with a deep affection for his son. Over the years, a close personal bond has been established between the two.

Tommy, like many other seven-year-olds, is sometimes disobedient. He is sometimes difficult. But, on the whole, his affection for his father and the fun he has with him make Mr. Aldrich a strong positive influence in his learning. In other words, he has learned to want to please his father and obtain his praise; he is disturbed when there is a delay in or a blocking of that praise, especially when the absence of praise is a result of his misbehavior.

Tommy's task is to learn to behave in a way that will gain his father's approval. Mr. Aldrich's task is to communicate to Tommy, in one way or another, the kind of behavior that will please him and also to help Tommy learn that behavior. Both are involved in learning. For each of them, success in learning will depend not only on what he does but also on what the other person does.

The strength of Tommy's drive will depend upon his father's behavior. If it is clear that the father is pleased, then, at that moment, there is little need to seek his approval. If the father is obviously displeased, then, at that moment, there is great need to seek his approval. Tommy learns to be sensitive to these cues in his father's behavior, for they tell him whether further learning is appropriate at the time.

Whether Mr. Aldrich's ambitions are at a high or a low level depends in large degree upon his son's behavior, especially his progress in learning. The greater that progress, the greater the reduction in the father's drive. (This may be but a momentary reduction, of course, if Tommy's achievements lead to greater ambitions in his father.) In Tommy's activity lie the cues which determine the extent to which his father is driven to induce learning activity. There is a positive relationship between the level of tension in Tommy and that in his father. When the father's drive is strong, the son's drive is strong. Conversely, when the father's drive is weak, the son's drive is also weak.

When Mr. Aldrich is feeling very ambitious for his son, he is driven to act in such a way as to elicit certain kinds of behavior from Tommy. For example, he believes that every boy ought to develop skill in handicrafts. He therefore takes Tommy on a tour of his basement workshop, pointing out the various tools and telling him what can be done with them. He asks his son: "How would you like to help me make a kitchen stool for your mother?" Tommy is enthusiastic about the project. But his original enthusiasm is not so much a sign of interest in the proposed activity as it is a sign of his recognition that his father is asking for something. There is something Tommy can do that will please his father. Until he does that something, his father will continue to lack this pleasure.

The two of them then begin the project. Mr. Aldrich teaches Tommy the uses of certain tools. Sometimes he does this by telling Tommy about them. At other times he says: "Now watch me. See how I hammer a nail so that I don't hit my finger." When Tommy catches on, his father smiles and pats his son on the head. When Tommy makes a mistake, his father does not get angry but clearly indicates that Tommy is not listening or watching or being as thoughtful and careful as he should. As a beginner, Tommy, of course, is all thumbs. His mistakes sometimes set the project back quite a bit. But his father's patience is great enough to encourage Tommy to keep trying out ways of pounding nails, sawing boards, sandpapering, and the like.

During their work on the project, Tommy shows obvious improvement. His father is pleased. The tension associated with his desires for his son has been temporarily alleviated. The outspoken approval of the father constitutes reward for the son. Having wanted to please his father, Tommy has done so. For the moment, this particular drive in Tommy has been reduced.

What, precisely, has been learned in this situation? Tommy has learned some rudimentary carpentry. In the future, he will tend to repeat the responses that turned out to be successful, those that gained the approval of his father. He will tend not to repeat those responses that ended in failure, those that did not please his father. But he learned other things as well. For example, in imitating his father's handling of the tools, he also imitated, at the same time, his father's saying, when *he* made a mistake: "Damn it all to hell!" We also see that Tommy, like his father, is very careful to have a pencil tucked in his shirt pocket while he is working. He steps back and looks at the results of his work for a moment before continuing the job, again like his father. Some of these responses Mr. Aldrich may not have intended to teach the child. But, to Tommy, they were a part of the total behavior pattern, the learning of which brought approval from his father.

Learning New Drives Through Conditioning

Tommy learned still more. In the beginning, he had little or no interest in woodworking; he wanted only to please his father. But the repeated association of "pleasing father" with "woodworking" resulted in some learning by conditioning. At the end of the project, we find that "woodworking" itself has become rewarding to Tommy. In other words, he has acquired a new drive. He wants to engage in this sort of behavior, not only because it pleases his father, but because he finds it pleasant in and of itself.

Has Mr. Aldrich learned? He has certainly learned something about teaching a young boy to be an amateur carpenter. In the future, he will tend to repeat the teaching techniques and behaviors that he has found to be successful. He will tend to eliminate those that did not seem to help Tommy to learn and that therefore were not rewarding to him.

The Salient Features of Social Learning

Even this one example reveals the salient features of social learning:

1. In the behavior of the social person, the learner reads what is expected of him. Tommy continually looked to his father with the unspoken question, "What am I supposed to do?" Some of these expectancies originate in the character of the social person as an individual. Mr. Aldrich demanded certain behavior because of the kind of father he was. But, insofar as the social person is a representative of the society, a social agent, the expectancies originate in the society. They are cultural expectations. Mr. Aldrich wanted to develop skill and initiative in Tommy, not only because he was the kind of person he was, but because of the kind of society in which both he and Tommy lived. As a social agent, the other person in the learning situation is acting to develop socially appropriate behavior in the learner.

2. The social person is a problem-maker. In this sense, he adds to the problems of the learner rather than reducing their number. Tommy's introduction to his father's workshop set up new tasks for him to solve.

3. The social person is also a problem-solver. We see that the "other person" is a kind of Jekyll-and-Hyde character. On the one hand, he makes problems. Then he steps into the situation in a new role and offers the learner his help in solving those problems.

4. The social person is a model for the learner. His behavior is a guide for the learner to follow. If imitating some aspects of the behavior of the social person brings the learner success, he will proceed to copy other aspects of that behavior, whether or not they are germane to the particular learning situation. Thus Tommy, in accepting his father as a model, not only imitates his woodworking behavior but also copies his swearing and other traits incidental to the situation.

The learner needs a model. Otherwise, the chance that he

will hit upon responses that will be rewarded is very much smaller. Learning is not nearly so efficient. Through imitation, Tommy learns more than the various kinds of behavior we have mentioned. He also learns attitudes toward people; he acquires certain predispositions to react to them. Because his father is patient, loving, and kind, Tommy will tend to expect patience, love, and kindness from other adults. He will expect them to behave in certain ways. He will also learn attitudes toward learning itself. Because he has found learning fun, he will not be averse to more of it in the future. As a matter of fact, in Tommy's case, we saw that he actually acquired a new or increased drive to learn as a result of this particular process of social learning. We should not be surprised to find him seeking to learn more and more about woodworking. The nature of the model—not only his behavior but also the permissive, encouraging, and rewarding kind of atmosphere he established—has had profound effects on Tommy's behavior.

5. The social person is a learner as well as a teacher. We saw that Tommy's father learned in the process of teaching his son. Because the learner is not only influenced by but also influences the other person, it is incorrect to regard him as a helpless creature at the mercy of forces too powerful for him to control. He is a very active agent in the learning process. The expectations of the social person are not only a function of that individual and his society; they are also a function of the learner's reaction to those expectations. Tommy's father, for example, found that in some cases he was expecting too much. He decreased his demands. In other cases, he found that Tommy was far ahead of him. Then it was necessary to modify his expectations in the other direction.

If we refrain from perceiving the learner as a completely dependent factor, our understanding of the learning process and its outcomes is considerably enhanced. At least, we analyze that process somewhat differently. For example, a study of leadership in high school youth concluded: *"Leaders* come from homes in which they have early been given responsibility, in which the parents participate in community affairs, and in which leadership is expected. . . . *Followers* come from homes where little responsibility has been given children . . ." (J. E. Anderson, 1949, p. 356). This statement does not contradict anything that we have said, but it does suggest that leadership is a reaction to forces outside the individual. Might it not also be appropriate to conclude that those youngsters with potentialities for leadership, whatever their source, produced expectations of leadership in their parents, and that the parents then reacted accordingly? Those youngsters who seemed to have few if any potentialities for leadership produced expectations of no leadership in parents, and those parents then reacted accordingly. Parents in the first group were necessarily predisposed to give responsibility to their demanding youngsters. Parents in the second group were necessarily predisposed to give little responsibility to their undemanding youngsters.

These interpretations of leadership development are not necessarily conflicting. They do demonstrate, however, that learning involving more than one person is a very complex affair. We may be neglecting some crucial information if we investigate the process with any notion that the learner is a completely passive element in the interaction. We shall see how ineluctable an association exists between the learner and the teacher in our next and last point on social learning.

6. The learner ultimately reduces the tension associated with a drive, not through his activity, but through the *effect* of his activity upon the behavior of the social person. The social person reduces the tension associated with a drive, not through his activity, but through the effect of his activity upon the behavior of the learner. Tommy learned the responses that pleased his father. Mr. Aldrich pursued that activity which produced changes in Tommy's behavior. In social learning, there is an exchange of rewards. Thus, as a result of social learning, the individual grows up to look for indications, in the behavior of others, that he has been successful. He grows up to be socially sensitive. No person who lives in a society can escape this form of dependence on others. Once he has learned, as an infant and young child, that he is forced to depend upon other people, the mature individual finds that it is necessary for him to continue to depend upon others as they must depend upon him.

22. How would you explain the attitudes toward learning and teachers which youngsters display on first entering school?

23. What relationship do you see between the concept of "model" as we have used it and Freud's definition of "identification"?

24. Summarize the fundamental differences between socialization from a psychoanalytic point of view and socialization considered as social learning. As a teacher or parent, what would you do differently if you adopted one point of view rather than the other?

On the basis of these features, how would we explain the development of a given individual according to a sociopsychological point of view? We would try to answer these questions:

1. What is the nature of the society in which the child lives?

2. How have the agents of that society—the child's parents, siblings, teachers, and friends—interpreted the society to the child? In other words, what have been their expectations? Are these expectations consistent with the nature of the society?

3. How have those expectancies been adjusted to the nature of the individual? Have they changed as he has changed? Are they realistic? Is more demanded than the child can possibly give? Has the child been subjected to conflicting expectancies?

4. What drives has the child learned? Out of what kinds of interpersonal relations has such learning been accomplished? What kinds of expectancy has the child developed?

5. What knowledge, skills, and competencies has the child acquired? Under what conditions has he acquired them? What kinds of model were furnished him? Were they well defined? Were they consistent?

6. How was the child rewarded and punished for his learning behavior?

The answers to such questions as these would constitute an explanation of the socialization of the child. To discover this, obviously, would be no easy task. There is no inevitable sequence of development. Almost anything can happen. We can understand what does happen only to the extent that we understand the nature of the child, the nature of the society, and the process through which the former is modified to meet the demands of the latter. We do not now have all the information we need. But, at least, we know the kinds of evidence we need to seek.

SUGGESTED READINGS

CRONBACH, LEE J. *Educational Psychology,* Harcourt, Brace, 1954. Chapter 11, "Identification and the Learning of Attitudes," discusses the role of models in the formation of social attitudes and values.

DOLLARD, JOHN, & MILLER, NEAL E. *Personality and Psychotherapy,* McGraw-Hill, 1950. A clear exposition of the basic principles of learning may be found in Chapter 3, "Four Fundamentals of Learning," Chapter 4, "Significant Details of the Learning Process," and Chapter 5, "Learned Drive and Learned Reinforcement."

MILLER, NEAL E., & DOLLARD, JOHN. *Social Learning and Imitation,* Yale University Press, 1941. A thorough analysis of the ways in which individuals learn from one another.

MOWRER, O. HOBART. On the psychology of "talking birds"—A contribution to language and personality theory. In William E. Martin & Celia Burns Stendler (eds.), *Readings in Child Development,* Harcourt, Brace, 1954, pp. 280-90. Mowrer's *autistic* theory of early language development, as illustrated in the teaching of talking birds, emphasizes the role of the social person, or trainer.

WHITING, JOHN W. M. *Becoming a Kwoma,* Yale University Press, 1941. In Chapter 7, "The Process of Socialization," Whiting uses learning theory to explain the transmission of Kwoma culture. Many concrete examples of teaching techniques and situations are given.

WOLFE, JOHN B. Effectiveness of token-rewards for chimpanzees. In Martin & Stendler, *op. cit.,* pp. 262-79. An extract from a report of a successful attempt to train chimpanzees to value poker chips much as human beings value money, demonstrating certain important principles in the learning of drives and rewards.

9

the effects
of early
experiences

Whether the socialization process is viewed from a Freudian point of view or from the standpoint of learning theory, the early experiences of the child are considered to be of paramount importance in influencing his later development. According to psychoanalytic theory, interference with normal development during the preschool years, more than at any other period of development, is likely to produce an adverse effect upon personality which may persist into adulthood. For example, too early and too strict toilet training during the period of development when the anus is a source of gratification to the child is said to result in an "anal character" in the adult. This may be manifested in one of two ways: the individual may express withholding through constipation, stinginess, or constricted personality; or he may express expelling by sloppiness and disorderliness. Evidence of the effects of early experiences has been derived by the psychoanalytic school from the reports of patients in psychoanalysis.

Learning theory also attaches tremendous significance to early experiences, but the evidence comes from a different source and the reasons offered for the importance of these early experiences are also different. This school of thought has drawn heavily upon animal research for its data; obviously, controlled experimentation on human beings is rarely feasible or desirable. Indeed, investigation of early learning is very difficult even with animals, as Beach and Jaynes (1954) point out in an extensive review of the research, because the animals are exposed to many different variables, only some of which can be recognized and controlled. For example, the later development of rats can be affected merely by the fact that they have been handled. In one experiment, rats which were handled by the experimenter during the first twenty days of life were found to be superior in ability to learn a task to rats which had not been handled, and even to rats which had learned a task through conditioning by shock (Levine *et al.*, 1956).

Although much of the currently available evidence is contradictory and inconclusive, three generalizations regarding the effects of early learning have emerged. These will be discussed below.

THE PERSISTENCE OF EARLY LEARNINGS

One generalization, stemming from animal research, is that habits formed early in life tend to interfere with later learnings and to persist into adulthood. The reader will recall the experimental evidence reviewed by Beach and Jaynes (1954) and discussed in Chapter 4. In one experiment referred to there, chickens were kept in the dark and fed artificially from a spoon for two weeks. When they were later put into a pen with grain and grits, they starved to death because they had never developed the pecking response. The chicks had apparently learned their lesson so thoroughly that it was impossible for them to unlearn the old responses and develop new ones. From this experiment and others, we conclude that learning the "wrong" responses and repeating them often enough (with reinforcement) can interfere with new learnings. Human beings are, of course, much more flexible than chickens; nevertheless, we can find illustrations in human behavior of this same generalization. It is difficult for Americans, for example, accustomed to look from left to right in crossing the street, to learn to look from right to left in countries like England, in which cars drive on the left side of the road. We have repeated the left-to-right response for so long that it has become second nature to us, and it can be reversed only with difficulty.

Personality characteristics learned early in life are also difficult to change. For example, children have a characteristic way of reacting to thwarting. Some give up too easily when they are blocked in trying to meet a goal; some persist blindly and stubbornly; some get very angry. Such behaviors appear at an early age and are difficult to change, doubtless because adults who are guiding the child's development reinforce them countless times before the behaviors are finally recognized as undesirable.

The strength of the motivation may be another factor in the persistence of early learnings. It may be that certain physiological needs are felt more intensely in infancy than later in life. Adult rats which had been partially starved in infancy showed a somewhat greater tendency than their controls to hoard pellets of food (Hunt *et al.*, 1947). To reach food, younger rats will cross a grid which administers shock many more times than will older rats tested after a similar period of food deprivation (Margolin & Bunch, 1940). The explanation generally proffered for these differences in behavior is that hunger is experienced more intensely in infancy.

Hunger pangs are undoubtedly felt more acutely in the very young human infant also, but, in all likelihood, this is because of the absence of competing stimuli. A five-month-old infant can forget his stomach—at least momentarily—because other things in the environment command his attention. He can be distracted if someone playfully bangs pans together or waves rattles before him or bounces him up and down or plays finger games with him. This is not true of the neonate; he will cry lustily until food is produced. But few human infants experience the extreme deprivation which the rats underwent in the Hunt study. We would expect the principle to hold true that semistarvation in infancy will have more lasting effects upon later development than semistarvation late in life. We would hope, however, that empirical evidence on this point will never be available.

Other drives may also be experienced more intensely in infancy. Fear may be one of these, perhaps because, as Beach and Jaynes (1954) point out, the young lack both familiarity with the environment and a repertoire of learned fear-reducing responses. What seems to an adult to be a relatively minor change in the stimulus properties of a person or object may therefore produce a fearful response in the infant. "Lady-wearing-hat" may be fear-inducing to an infant who has experienced only "lady-without-hat"; a shift in the living room furniture may move the two-year-old to frightened tears. Such fears as these, of course, are not strong enough to produce persistent reactions, but it is generally accepted by psychologists today that a sufficiently intense fear-producing experience in early childhood can be traumatic. Some of the stimuli associated with the early fear may be generalized so that the relation between the later behavior and the early fear is not easy to detect. The fearful child shut in a dark closet to meditate on his sins may not fear the dark later on, but he may fear elevators and other enclosures.

Because early learnings do persist, although sometimes in modified form, some popular treatises on how to rear children have overemphasized the possibility of trauma. Many a mother has worried unnecessarily that her young child might have a traumatic experience and has been overprotective in her zeal to cushion him against possible shocks. Only rarely is a *single* event of sufficient intensity to be traumatic, and even then sympathetic handling on the part of the adult in charge can counteract possible ill effects. And regardless of the intensity of the experience in infancy, repetition of the experience with reinforcement is generally necessary to guarantee the persistence of certain behaviors.

THE EFFECTS OF PARTICULAR
TYPES OF EARLY LEARNING

The infant in a normal environment is continually bombarded with stimuli from the outside world. Strange objects and strange events are perceived by seeing, hearing, smelling, touching, and mouthing. As a result of this perceptual experiencing, the infant learns the properties of each object or event, what the consequences of experiencing it will be, and how to react to it. A foot is to be chewed; a burning cigarette is to be avoided; a popping balloon will not hurt; a cat's claws can scratch; foods like jello have a texture which is different from that of spinach.

Young animals also are exposed to a great many perceptual stimuli, and the effects of these stimuli upon their later behavior can be studied under controlled conditions. According to Hebb (1949), who has directed many studies on animals, animals which have had much perceptual experience early in life prove to be better learners than animals which have had little such experience. To test this theory two groups of rats were reared, one in a small room and one in a cage (Bingham & Griffiths, 1952). Then the two groups were compared in adulthood on the basis of their responses to a problem which neither group had experienced before: running a maze. Which group would learn the maze faster? Does having richer experiences early in life affect the kind of learner one becomes? Apparently it does, at least in rats. The rats which had had wider perceptual experience—those reared in a room—were found to be superior in maze learning in their adult life. Similarly, rats reared as house pets showed superiority in certain learning activities over animals reared in laboratories.

Additional evidence of the importance of early perceptual learning comes from the work of Thompson and Melzack (1956). These experimenters worked with Scottish terriers, divided into two groups. Animals in the control group were farmed out to families (after weaning at four weeks), where they lived the normal lives of household pets. Those in the experimental group were confined to individual cages, so constructed that no animal could see outside, and had no contact with their keepers. This group lived without any social stimulation for seven to ten months.

At the end of the experimental period, the two groups were brought together and exposed to various strange phenomena: a slowly swelling balloon, an umbrella being opened, and the like. The dogs in the restricted group were highly agitated; their behavior was described as diffuse and undifferentiated. The control group displayed avoidance behavior, running away from the strange objects, but without much excitement. A year later, when the trial was repeated, the control dogs attacked the strange object, while the experimental group, after twelve months of "normal" living, showed the avoidance behavior characteristic of the control dogs when they were a year younger (see Fig. 9-1). Apparently, emotional responses which normally appear at a particular point in the developmental timetable are delayed and altered by restricting early perceptual experiences.

To test the problem-solving ability of the two groups of dogs, changes were made in feeding procedures. First the dogs were trained to get food in a particular spot in a room in a particular way. Then the food was placed in a different corner while the dogs looked on. The "normal" dogs immediately went to the new position, but the restricted dogs returned to the old corner. Similarly, in other test situations, the dogs reared in families were able to learn more readily than those reared in the restricted environment. The investigators concluded that animals need sensory stimulation for optimal development and learning. Intellectual as well as emotional responses appear to be affected by early perceptual experiences.

The *kinds* of early perceptual experience available to the subject appear to affect later learnings. Forgus (1955) was interested in studying the relationship between the quality of earlier experience and performance on a task to be solved in later life. He reasoned that early experience could be a hindrance or an aid in later problem solving, depending upon the nature of the

FIGURE 9-1. When the irrational fears of a normal and a restricted dog were compared by exposing the animals to an opening umbrella, an emotion-evoking object, the normal dog (*background*) soon accepted the object, but the restricted dog continued to be frightened by it.

(From W. R. Thompson & R. Melzack. Early environment. *Scientific American,* Jan. 1956, *194:* 42)

experience and the requirements of the problem. Not just any perceptual experience would be helpful, he hypothesized, but only those experiences that have some relation to the demands of the problem. He compared two groups of rats, one reared in a complex environment which offered many opportunities for normal visual and motor experiences, and the other reared with rich opportunities for visual experiences but few opportunities for motor experience. As adults, the rats were tested to see how well they could run a maze, first with many visual cues present and then with few. The rats which had had only an enriched visual environment did well when there were visual cues present, but they were handicapped when the visual cues were reduced and they were exposed chiefly to cues originating in one of the senses other than sight. Those that had had both visual and motor experiences, however, were still able to perform when visual cues were reduced. A complex perceptual environment is probably better in the long run since we cannot predict the kinds of perceptual challenge that will have to be met in adulthood.

Some of the effects of restricted perceptual experiences can be observed in a homely example of human behavior. All of us know some adults who have difficulty in learning the names of strangers unless they see the names in print. If the names are spelled orally, the learner may even try to form a mental image of them in order to fasten them upon his memory. Perhaps early visual experiences in learning to read and spell account for this attempt to find visual cues in new situations. These persons have learned to depend upon their eyes for learning more than upon their other senses.

The results of experimental work on restricted animals as compared to "normal" animals raise the interesting question of what might happen in an enriched environment. Suppose that, instead of providing merely a normal amount of stimulation, we were to step up enormously the opportunities in learning. What would be the result?

Some evidence with respect to the effects of an enriched environment is provided by the report on Viki, a chimpanzee reared by two psychologists in their home (Hayes, 1951). Viki, reared like a human child, was exposed to a tremendous variety of learning situations which would not be available to a laboratory-reared animal. Among many other things, Viki learned to sew, to use facial tissue in blowing her nose, to wash dishes, and to operate a number of household gadgets. Would this enriched environment have any effect upon Viki's ability to solve problems by imitation?

To find the answer, the Hayeses gave some learning problems to Viki, to human children of the same age, and to a laboratory-reared chimpanzee, nine months older than Viki. (The latter had not experienced a restricted environment but had not had the benefit of an enriched environment.) The problems involved getting a toy or a piece of candy out of a box by performing such tasks as pulling levers in a certain sequence, burning a string with a candle flame, and using a stick to strike a distant string. In each test, the experimenter demonstrated to the subjects how to open the box. Viki and the children solved all the problems about equally well and without much difficulty; the laboratory-reared chimpanzee solved only one. Part of this chimp's difficulty appeared to be that he lacked the manipulative skills necessary for solving the problems.

THE EFFECTS OF SOCIAL CONDITIONS

Early social experiences have been found to affect the aggressive behavior of some animals. King and Gurney (1954) discovered that male mice reared together with other mice, either male or female, tend to be more aggressive than males reared in isolation. The explanation they offer for this behavior is not that mice learn aggression from their early social associations but that the social conditions aggravate the natural tendency of the mice to compete for food. Participating in the same social situation does not result in identical learnings on the part of different participants, however. Skinner (1958) has pointed out that when two young children are left alone in a room with a few toys, conditions are almost ideal for the onset of aggressive behavior, but that *who* is reinforcing *whom* with *what* and to *what effect* must be noted. Aggression as a drive is learned as aggressive responses are found to be satisfying (see pp. 576-81).

Some rather weighty claims have been made for the effects

of social factors upon the well-being of an organism. According to some investigators, infant mammals depend upon their parents not only for nutrition but also for stimulation, which apparently triggers certain necessary responses or produces certain conditions necessary for life. When social conditions are such that this vital stimulation is not provided by the parents or an adequate substitute, the organism may die.

Spitz (1945, 1946) reports a most dramatic contrast between children reared under conditions of social stimulation and children reared under conditions of social impoverishment. One group, composed chiefly of infants whose mothers were unable to support them, lived in a foundling home; the other, in a nursery attached to a women's prison. Both groups received excellent medical and physical care, but they differed with respect to the amount of association they had with other human beings. The babies in the foundling home were kept in cribs all day, each crib in a separate cubicle so that the occupant saw only the ceiling directly above the crib, three walls, and a corridor. The busy nurses fed and cleaned the children but had no time to play with them. Few toys were provided for them. Mothers in the prison were permitted to spend a few hours each day with their children, during which time the babies received a great deal of affection and care. These children had many more social experiences than the babies confined to cribs.

According to Spitz's report, 19 of the 123 babies reared in the foundling home developed a behavioral syndrome during their first year which he called "anaclitic depression." This is characterized by mourning, negative emotions, inability to act, and loss of appetite, sleep, and weight. In later stages, the decline becomes more severe; there is a general deterioration of muscle tone and body reflexes accompanied by extreme lethargy. Spitz named this extreme condition "hospitalism." Among the children he studied, the depression became so severe in some cases that 37 per cent died during a measles epidemic; *all* the children in the prison nursery, exposed to the same epidemic, survived. According to Spitz, the significant factor in the development of anaclitic depression and hospitalism is the lack of a "close and balanced" mother-child relationship. Ribble (1943) has also written convincingly of the disorganizing effects upon infant personality of a lack of "mothering."

A careful evaluation of the Spitz and Ribble findings by Pinneau (1950, 1955) did not substantiate their conclusions. Pinneau examined evidence from controlled physiological and psychological studies bearing on Ribble's points and found that the evidence refuted every one of them. He has also been critical of the Spitz research on the ground that it did not meet the standards of acceptable experimental design and procedures, which require that the groups be matched as nearly as possible in all respects except the variable being tested, and that observer reliability be carefully controlled to make sure that each observer labels a particular behavior in the same way.

The research by Spitz was a pioneer study, and, like many first studies in a particular field, it undoubtedly suffered from faulty design and execution. His unqualified attribution of anaclitic depression and hospitalism to the lack of a close and balanced mother-child relationship and his descriptions of the dramatic recovery of the babies when their mothers reappeared are skeptically received today. But although we discount the effects of a socially impoverished environment upon viability, Spitz also reported shocking effects in certain areas of development which have been substantiated by additional studies. Spitz found that the babies reared in a foundling home could not walk at a normal age, they were markedly retarded in speech, and at four years of age not a child was toilet trained and only one could dress himself without help. Even though the children were later removed from their cribs and allowed to play about on the floor with other children, they still showed significant retardation in development.

In an experiment using a control group, Goldfarb (1945) tested one of the findings more precisely; namely, the effects of a highly impoverished environment upon later learning. He compared the mental development of children brought up for three years in an institution and then placed in foster homes to be reared with that of children whose major life experience from early infancy had been in foster homes. The foster homes for the two groups were similar when compared both objectively and subjectively. Mothers of the institution-reared children were superior in intelligence to mothers of the foster-home group. Yet, when the children were tested in later childhood (ten to fourteen years of age), striking differences were found between those who had spent their first three years in the institution and those who had not. The children reared in homes under conditions of normal social stimulation with normal opportunities for perceptual experiences were brighter, superior in school achievement, and had a greater ability to conceptualize. This last, of course, is very important since it affects other learning abilities.

The institution-reared children, on the other hand, revealed the following characteristics (among others):

1. *Absence of a Normal Inhibitory Pattern.* In fourteen of the fifteen cases there is a history of extremely difficult behavior. The problem appears to have been not so much one of focused hostility or conflict as of crippled or defective maturation and a primitivization of the total personality. Hyperactivity and disorganization are the major symptoms. The children are described as unmanageable and undisciplined, with no control over their actions, frequently flighty in their association, and unable to concentrate. Some are enuretic through the latency and adolescent periods. Severe temper tantrums are common. In the early years of school, a majority of the group is regarded as among the most unmanageable in their respective classes. Teachers were particularly impressed with disregard for rules, inability to sit in one place, and general lack of organization. There is a diffuse, random discharge of body energy. When strong external controls are introduced, strange body movements and grimaces appear. . . .

There was extreme curiosity regarding the environment, yet an inability to grasp its meaning so that there was a constant unsatisfied drive to test and try out. The result was continuous movement and distractibility. During psychological examinations administered in the preschool and preadolescent periods, behavioral descriptions mentioned that children opened and

closed drawers and closet doors constantly, had difficulty in keeping their hands off psychological materials, and were easily
distracted by everything about them. Some asked innumerable
questions but paid no attention to the answers. . . .

2. *Affect Hunger.* In these children one observes exaggerated
illustrations of the outcomes of unmitigated affect hunger. All
indiscriminately demanded affection and attention. . . . [His]
foster mother stated that Irving made such demands constantly
and was excessively demanding of affection. "All he wants is to
hug and kiss." Constance's teacher felt that her outstanding
characteristic was her demand for attention. If, in a particular
period, the teacher happened to be too busy to give her attention, Constance would cease working and attempt to attract
attention by misconduct. . . .

3. *Emotional Imperviousness and Superficiality of Relationship.* The insatiable demand for affection did not significantly
enrich the capacity of the children to form ties. In adolescence,
most were described by their case workers as removed, emotionally isolated, and cold. . . .

4. *Absence of Normal Tension and Anxiety Reaction.* This
tendency to meagerness of feeling for other humans is comple-
mented by the absence of normal anxiety display following acts
of hostility, cruelty, or unprovoked aggression. In addition,
focused tension in specific situations normally calling for tension
responses is frequently not observed . . . [Goldfarb, 1945, pp.
250-52].

It should be pointed out that the total number of infants
in the Goldfarb study was small (fifteen in each group). Not
every child who experiences institutional care becomes a flighty,
immature, conceptually deficient adolescent. This writer had
the experience of visiting a nursery home in a Midwestern community which years ago had kept babies in cribs, in tiers of
three, each tier enclosed in sheets, until the babies were almost
two years of age. One of the members of the board of directors
of the now modernized nursery was reared in the institution
before its reform. He is today a successful professional man,
father of a fine family, and an outstanding community member.
He notes two effects of his early experience: an ardent desire

to provide a warm family life for his wife and children, and a zeal to do what he can to improve conditions in institutions for children. Although, in general, conditions of traditional institutional care produce unfortunate consequences, there are undoubtedly constitutional differences in ability to withstand social and psychological deprivation. Further, merely because a child is reared in an institution, deprivation should not be taken for granted. Nurses frequently have "pets" upon whom they lavish a good deal of care and attention; some children reared in institutions may have been fortunate in this respect.

It has been claimed that such studies as those of Spitz and Goldfarb demonstrate the importance of "mothering" babies, of giving them much affection. Proponents of this school of thought have argued that the actual physical contact involved in rocking a baby, for example, contributes to his future development. We are not arguing against giving affection to babies (indeed, we are for it); however, we recognize the importance of discovering precisely what it is in the mother-child relationship that makes a difference to the growing organism.

One variable in the early socialization process which is now recognized as important is the need for caretaking from a single person. In an interesting experiment, Rheingold (1956) explored the effects upon institutionalized infants of having one person care for them rather than several. Eight controls were cared for by different hospital personnel (seventeen in all), in the customary fashion; the children in the experimental group were cared for by only one person each. All children were tested every two weeks on responses to the person who cared for the experimental group and to the examiner who administered the tests. After a period of eight weeks, the social reaction of both groups of babies to the presence of a stranger was tested. Although all babies in both groups responded positively to the approach of the stranger, the babies who had been cared for by one individual were more responsive. A significant difference in responsiveness to the experimenter was also noted; babies in the experimental group made a social score of 37.2 as compared with 24.2 in the control group.

In a normal family environment, an infant may be cared for by many individuals, but generally one person is the chief caretaker, and the child has a chance to establish a continuing relationship with this one person. Under a system of multiple mothering or caretaking, such as prevails in most institutions, the opportunity to establish a continuing relationship with a single individual is absent; also, each caretaker has less opportunity to build up feelings of love and affection for every child.

The warm nurturing environment which a single caretaker can provide furnishes the infant with many opportunities to learn. Consider, for example, the act of bathing a baby. An impersonal caretaker, particularly if the child is one of many whom she must tend, will make short work of this chore, dispensing with it as quickly as possible. A warm, affectionate mother uses this opportunity to present all kinds of stimuli to the child. She plays games with the baby and she permits him many new experiences; he finds out how soap tastes and how it feels in the eyes; he sees some toys float on the water and others submerge; he hears a continual stream of conversation directed at him. The affectionate mother wants to spend more time with the baby (within limits, of course) and wants to be doing more things with him and to him during this time. She is providing him with a wealth of learning experiences, although she does not think of her "play" in this way.

Indeed, it may well be, as Beach and Jaynes (1954) point out, that one of the universal conditions affecting human development is the impact of a considerable amount of stimulation from the environment. Note the needs of the infant during his first year as observed by Gesell and Ilg:

> *Four weeks.* The infant stares at lights and windows. . . . He may become angry if turned on the side away from the light. He quiets as he is shifted toward the light. This desire for light and brightness, apart from sunlight to which he makes a violent negative response, is later shown at eight to ten weeks in an interest in red and orange colors. Intense crying may be controlled by having a bright-colored cretonne pillow to gaze upon.
> Visual experience with light and bright colors is important to

the child as well as is the food in his stomach. The baby stares at faces that are close by. If he cries in the evening—which is his way of asking for social stimulation—he quiets if he is picked up and held or if he is allowed to lie naked on a table where he can hear voices and look at lights for an hour or two. This demand is most frequent from six to eight weeks. . . .

Sixteen weeks. There is at this age an increased demand for sociality. . . . Demand for social attention is especially strong toward the end of the day, around 5 P.M. The infant likes to be shifted from his bed for this social period. . . . He likes to have people pay attention to him, talk to him, sing to him. . . . By twenty weeks he so much enjoys being talked to that he may cry when people leave. . . .

Forty weeks. Though the infant will play by himself for relatively long periods, he is quick to articulate his desire for a shift of toys or company. He particularly likes to be with the family group from 8 to 10 A.M. and in the later afternoon (4 to 6 P.M.), and happily stays in his crib, play pen, or chair at these times. He also likes a carriage ride in the late morning or early afternoon—depending on his naptime.

Social activities which he enjoys are peek-a-boo and lip play (which consists of patting his lips to induce singing), walking with both hands held, and being put prone on the floor or being placed in a rocking toy. . . .

One year. Fifty-two weeks is the heyday of sociality. The baby enjoys social give and take, and social occasions are apt to come about spontaneously, without planning. . . . Most of his sociality, other than in relation to regular routine, occurs in the afternoon. He enjoys his carriage ride—enjoys standing up in his harness, and is especially interested in moving objects such as automobiles or bicycles. His playthings no longer absorb his attention . . . [1943, pp. 99, 106-07, 122, 129-30].

In these behavior profiles, we see the baby's demands for stimulation, as well as his obvious pleasure in it. And, like the puppies reared in families, babies learn from the perceptual experiences provided in the normal home environment. But, unlike the puppies, who are mobile and can find stimulation for themselves, young infants are dependent upon other human beings for the perceptual stimulation which they sorely need.

For optimal development, a single caretaker with whom the baby can have a close and continuing relationship is important—but it is not enough. The baby must also be provided with a considerable amount of perceptual stimulation from this caretaker.

But can we give a baby too much stimulation? The reader is probably familiar with home environments in which babies are continually confronted with stimuli, sometimes by anxious mothers who want to "develop" their children as fast as possible and so provide them with the latest and most advanced "educational" toys, or by overactive families who bounce and jostle and "amuse" the baby for hours on end. We do not have evidence from controlled experiments on the effects of "overstimulation" (if it could be defined), but Gesell and Ilg note that at "around thirty-two weeks, though the baby enjoys the company of others, he may easily become overexcited. Instability of emotional make-up at this time is expressed in the close interplay of crying and laughing" (1943, p. 115). If properly interpreted, these danger signals may deter those who are playing with the baby from further stimulating him. Occasionally, of course, fatigue sets in, and sleep protects the baby from overexcitement.

Perhaps the baby's best protection against overstimulation is a mother who loves and appreciates the child for himself, not because he can meet her own unfulfilled needs. The mother who wants her baby to be a high achiever so that she can compete with the neighbors, or for some other personal reason, will force stimuli on the baby and will persist in her efforts to train him to respond. The accepting mother, on the other hand, may expose her baby to the same stimuli, but she will permit him to ignore them if he wishes to do so. She does not need the baby's achievements to add to her own sense of adequacy—although, of course, like any doting parent, she will enjoy the baby's progress.

We need to consider, too, the possibility of enriching the environment for children by providing various kinds of stimulation. Because of their own personal interests and tastes, parents tend to limit the kinds of perceptual experience they offer their children in the preschool years. For example, the parent who is interested in books will read to the child and build up a good library of children's books, but he may fail to provide enough experiences in other areas. We need to have considerably more research on the effects of various kinds of stimulation upon later development.

1. On the basis of your observations of young children in a family environment, what is your reaction to each of the following hypotheses:

 a. Middle-class parents provide more stimulation in the form of reading materials than do lower-class parents.

 b. Most parents, regardless of socioeconomic class, provide less musical stimulation than stimulation through books.

 c. The kinds of perceptual experience provided in the preschool years influence the child's interest in and liking for certain subjects in the elementary school.

2. Observe a mother taking care of a baby less than fifteen months of age. If possible, observe the bath, a meal, and playtime. What does the mother say to the baby during these activities? What is the baby having a chance to learn?

3. Observe children in an elementary classroom. What kinds of sensory stimulation are present? How does the stimulation differ, in amount and kind, from what is offered in a nursery school or kindergarten?

CRITICAL PERIODS IN SOCIALIZATION

Another significant generalization with respect to the importance of early learnings is that there may be critical periods in the socialization process during which future development can be crucially affected in a way not possible at any other time. The analogy to the prenatal period is tempting. The reader will recall the description in Chapter 5 of periods during which disturbances in the fetal environment might affect the particular organs being developed at the time. The discussion pointed out that such disturbances would affect *only* those organs being developed at the time, not those already formed or those to come, and that the effects would be permanent.

The intriguing question is whether or not there are similar danger periods in postnatal life, periods when disturbances of a *psychological* nature can occur more easily and with greater consequences than at other times. This question has been explored in several studies using animals. One investigator (Lorenz, 1955), who studied the early social behavior of birds, has reported what happens when there is a disturbance in the imprinting process. (Imprinting is a process of object-fixation with respect to a single function which occurs in many animals. Lambs, for example, become fixated on, or imprinted to, the mother sheep in respect to the following-the-mother response soon after birth, and thereafter follow after her "like sheep." Goslings similarly become imprinted to the mother and follow after her in a pattern that is very evident to the observer.) From experimental work by Lorenz and others, it is clear that there is a critical period during which the imprinting response can be altered so that the young animal becomes imprinted to a different species, with respect to a particular response. Goslings removed from the nest soon after birth, so that they never saw the mother, never became conditioned to following a goose, but instead followed after their human keeper. Parrots, cockatoos, Andean geese, and many other birds have also been imprinted, with respect to one or more functions, to other species. In all cases, it was found that *the fixation can occur only during a relatively short period after the animal is born.* Once imprinting occurs, the process is irreversible. One human-imprinted male bittern in the Amsterdam Zoo would chase its mate out of the nest when the director of the zoo appeared and ceremonially invite the director to sit on the nest with him (Lorenz, 1955). The earlier conditioning process, during which he had become fixated on a human being, produced a stronger fixation than the secondary conditioning to a normal object.

The concept of critical periods has also been demonstrated in experiments with dogs. Scott and others (1951) have de-

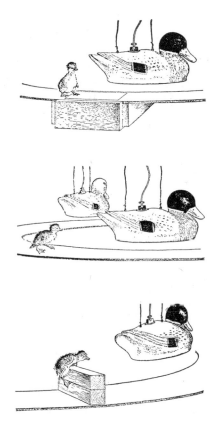

FIGURE 9-2. Imprinting in a duckling. The duckling is imprinted by being placed in a runway behind a model of a male duck which is wired for sound. Below the duckling is a trap door through which it is removed.

The duckling is tested for imprinting by being placed between the male model and a female model which emits a different sound. If it follows the male, the response is scored positive.

The duckling scales an obstacle in the runway in an experiment to determine whether the effort it expends during imprinting is related to its score when tested.

(From Eckhard H. Hess. "Imprinting" in animals. *Scientific American,* March 1958, *198*:82)

scribed five distinct periods in the social development of dogs, as follows:

> *Period 1:* the neonatal period. The principal activities of the puppy are nursing, defecation, urination, crawling, and whining.
> *Period 2:* the transition period. At the end of this period, the puppy can perform most adult patterns of behavior and can be

conditioned very easily. . . . The puppy suddenly becomes very vulnerable to environmental changes. . . .

Period 3: the period of socialization. This is a critical period with regard to the development of social relationships. Adjustment to human beings is important. Dogs who do not have human contacts during this period become "pathologically" shy. The evidence suggests that disturbances occur more easily at this time and have definite effects on later adjustments.

Period 4: the juvenile period. This period is marked by growth, increasing physical skill, and increasing independence.

Period 5: the adult period. Adult patterns of sexual behavior appear, occurring as early as seven months in some breeds.

From experimental work by these and other writers, it appears that there are special times in the development of dogs which are more important for certain learnings than other times. Period 3 appears to be most critical for social relationships, probably because of the vast change in the capacity for associative learning which occurs at this stage.

MATERNAL DEPRIVATION

What of human development? Are there also critical periods during which the future development of humans can be influenced in an important and irrevocable way? We cannot generalize to man from findings derived from studies of goslings, bitterns, sheep, and dogs, and, obviously, carefully controlled experimental work cannot be done on humans. There are unfortunate instances, however, of infants who do suffer disturbances; the later development of these infants can be studied and possible consequences of the disturbance noted.

One kind of disturbance which might conceivably affect later development occurs when a young child is deprived of his mother. The consequences of maternal deprivation have been inferred from observations by many investigators (such as those of Spitz and Goldfarb already reviewed), and Bowlby (1952) has summarized their findings. Maternal deprivation may be said to have occurred when the child is completely deprived of his mother, or of an adequate substitute, over an extended period of time, whether the deprivation is brought about by protracted hospitalization, divorce, death, or any other form of separation.

During the first three years of life, the child establishes a very close and important relationship with the mother; he learns that he can depend upon her for the satisfaction of his needs. Many writers agree that if this relationship is disturbed, serious consequences will result. According to them, three kinds of experience can have highly adverse effects: (1) lack of any opportunity to form an attachment to a mother-figure during the first three years; (2) deprivation for a limited period—at least three months and probably more than six—during the first three or four years; and (3) changes from one mother-figure to another during the same period. Although there are probably differences in the effects of these three types of experience upon later development, early investigations showed the over-all results to be the same. Children who experienced a severe degree of maternal deprivation developed into persons who seemed to have no real feelings for anyone and could establish only superficial relationships; a deficiency in conceptual and language development also resulted.

Later research by Bowlby and others (1956), using controls, has caused Bowlby to modify some of his earlier statements on the effects of maternal deprivation. He studied sixty children aged seven to thirteen who, as tubercular patients, had been separated from their families before the age of four, and who had spent from a few months to two years in a sanitarium. Comparing these children with their schoolmates, teachers reported more symptoms of maladjustment in the experimental children, particularly apathy or rough behavior. However, the contrast was not great, and the experimental children did well on such items as ease in making friends. Bowlby concludes, ". . . Statements implying that children who experience institutionalization and similar forms of severe privation and deprivation in early life *commonly* develop psychopathic or affectionless characters are incorrect."

Although a warm, close, and continuing relationship with one person during the first three or four years of life is something we would wish for all children, it appears that disruption of this relationship is not inevitably shattering to the developing personality. Certain variables need to be sorted out for more careful attention. One writer (Gewirtz, 1957) suggests a number of turns that such a relationship might take and hypothesizes about the consequences. Some of the variations he suggests, with the hypotheses they imply, are as follows:

1. The mothering may be inadequate in the sense that the caretaker does not furnish reinforcement that is clear enough or frequent enough. The child learns to seek attention but fails to learn when and how to seek it and so may become an indiscriminate attention-seeker.

2. Caretaking may be on a group basis, as in an institution, and not in response to a particular child's needs. Hence the child may not learn which of his behaviors are valued by his culture and may develop an asocial behavior pattern.

3. Mothering may be so incompetent that the infant suffers. The child may then exhibit withdrawal, antisocial behaviors, or ambivalence in the presence of caretakers.

4. If the infant has learned that the presence of an adult usually brings other reinforcing stimuli (like food), and if the environment is such that the adult is too busy to supply the reinforcers frequently enough, an emotional (often "angry") pattern of responses may be produced.

5. An abrupt, extreme, and continuing change accompanied by a situation in which substitute persons do not supply the proper stimulus conditions may bring about progressive withdrawal and apathy.

From the research on the effects of early experiences, it would appear that the preschool years are highly important for later development. Investigators have begun to explore some of the factors in the social and perceptual environment which might be significant. Findings from previous studies are being carefully analyzed, and their hypotheses are being translated into learning theory and rigorously tested in controlled situations. From this tremendous amount of research, some important implications can be drawn for child care in both homes and institutions.

4. Is it possible for maternal deprivation to occur without the physical separation of mother and child? Explain your answer.

5. Ask a local veterinarian or the manager of a kennel how old a dog he thinks it best to buy. What are his reasons? Evaluate them from the point of view of this chapter.

6. On the basis of your reading of Chapter 3, do you think that maternal deprivation might work greater hardships on some children than on others?

SUGGESTED READINGS

BEACH, FRANK A., & JAYNES, JULIAN. Effects of early experience upon the behavior of animals. *Psychol. Bull.,* 1954, *51,* 239-63. A comprehensive review of the literature to date on the effects of early experiences.

BOWLBY, JOHN. *Maternal Care and Mental Health,* World Health Organization Monograph Series No. 2, Geneva, 1952. Chapter 3 reviews the evidence on effects of maternal deprivation.

GESELL, ARNOLD, & ILG, FRANCES. *Infant and Child in the Culture of Today,* Harper, 1943. The accounts of "behavior days" at various intervals from birth to five years contain interesting material for study from the standpoint of the time when babies seem to be most dependent upon their mothers.

socializing agents

10

the child
in the family

An American child is like all other
American children, but he is also an individual. He acquires
his distinctly American characteristics by being brought up in
American culture; he acquires his unique characteristics because of his unique life history. Every American child is molded
by the culture, but each is molded in a different way. This
process of molding begins in the family; the child's parents are
his first socializing agents. In countless interactions with their
child each day, the parents teach him their own interpretation
of how a child should behave; in learning the parental version
of cultural behavior, a child develops his unique personality.

It is not difficult to find and to analyze behavior incidents
that illustrate the process by which parents socialize their children. When a mother slaps a two-year-old for crumbling her
food on the table and says admonishingly, "Patty's a pig. Messy
Patty," she is teaching the child that there are certain accepted
ways of eating and that anything parents might describe as
messy is not an accepted way. When a father shouts to his four-
year-old who is engaged in a brawl, "Hit him back, Mike. Don't
let him get away with it. Attaboy! Sock him good," the parent
is obviously trying to encourage aggressive behavior in certain
situations. It is equally clear that he is trying to *discourage*

passive acceptance of others' aggression in those same situations. Slowly but surely, as the child interacts with his parents in situations which bring him pleasure and in situations which bring him pain, he grows to understand that certain forms of behavior are acceptable and that others are not.

There are, however, more subtle ways in which parents influence the socialization process. Consider the case of Randy:

> Randy was led by his young mother to a seat on the train, where he was installed near the window. He was an attractive boy, big for his four years. His mother kept up a rapid flow of conversation; she explained about the diesel engine, commented on the number of cars, encouraged him to count cars with her as the train rounded a bend. Then she lectured on the kinds of car—Pullman, dining, mail, coach, tender. As the train rode alongside the Mississippi River, she commented on the excursion boat in detail. The child asked a question or two, but for the most part he was a fascinated listener to the mother's interesting discourse.
>
> At this point the sandwich man came through the train. Said Randy, "I want something, Mother." "You keep looking out the window, Randy. You can see food any time, and you might miss something." Eventually the sandwich man arrived, and Randy was asked what he wanted to eat. "I want candy, Mother, and a coke."
>
> "You may have what you like, dear, but perhaps a sandwich would be better."
>
> "I think I'd rather have the candy and coke."
>
> "All right, dear," and the mother ordered.
>
> Randy began eating and spilled some coke on his clothes.
>
> "Oh, Mother, I'm so sorry. I've spilled."
>
> "That's all right, dear. It was an accident. It will dry quickly."
>
> Following lunch, train blocks were brought out and the child played. "This diesel (block) can go faster than a jet," he said. His mother corrected him gently.
>
> "This truck can go faster than a train or a taxi." Again his mother corrected him.
>
> Eventually Randy tired of his game. Before it petered out completely, the mother asked, "Would you like me to read you

a story now?" She produced a book about trains and read with much expression.

The pillow man came through and Randy asked for a pillow. Although they were but an hour from their destination, the mother rented a pillow and settled Randy in the seat with her raincoat over him. He had trouble with his legs. "Where shall I put them, Mother?" She put them on the seat behind her, which forced her to sit on the very edge of the chair. Randy fell asleep. When the train stopped, the small 110-pound mother lifted up her 50-pound boy and carried him, still sleeping, from the train.

This behavior incident is much more difficult to analyze than the two we have described earlier. Randy is being socialized in much more subtle ways than Mike or Patty, yet his development is being carefully guided, even dominated; in some ways, it is being guided more carefully than the development of children whose parents use more direct techniques. Randy's mother gave the appearance of being a very permissive parent: she allowed him to choose his food; she did not scold when he spilled his drink; she gave up most of the seat space to him; she did not pressure him into going to sleep. But the mother did guide the child in that she selected from the environment those experiences that *she* thought would be good for him; in the incident we have described, she emphasized intellectually stimulating experiences involving the immediate environment. Other children of Randy's age on the train experimented with levers on the seats, ran up and down the aisles for water, and chatted with other passengers; that is, they made the train ride a socially stimulating experience *of their own choosing*. Randy's mother did not have to punish him for straying outside the framework that she had set up; she made her lectures so fascinating that he never lost interest. Further, she had planned in advance—providing herself with train blocks and a book about trains—so that the situation could be wrung dry of its intellectual content. The intellectual stimulation, plus the fact of having his mother's undivided attention, made the situation so rewarding for Randy that he was not tempted by the usual childish delights of a train ride (running up aisles, etc.).

It is safe to predict that Randy and his mother will have few serious incidents of friction in the next few years. Because she is an intelligent, quick-witted woman who is able and willing to spend a major portion of her time with her son, she will be able to outthink and outplan Randy. She will make what she wants him to do so interesting, so rewarding, that he will rarely protest, and there will be few occasions in which punishment is necessary. How Randy will turn out we cannot predict. We have not had enough studies of socialization-by-mother-selected experiences to be able to forecast his future. It would seem, however, that limiting a child's choice of action so narrowly, even by highly desirable methods, might have restrictive effects upon his personality development.

1. What kind of behavior might a teacher expect of Randy in the classroom?

2. How might Randy's social relations with other children be affected by this type of maternal care?

INFANT DISCIPLINES

The incidents we have described are illustrations of situations in which parents interact with young children and of the decisions parents make as socializing agents. Some decisions are made immediately or soon after birth, such as those which have to do with feeding schedules, toilet training, picking baby up when he cries, weaning, and the like—the so-called infant disciplines. Should a mother feed her baby when he seems hungry, or should she keep to a schedule even though he cries? If she picks him up when he cries, will she spoil him? If she doesn't pick him up, will she ruin his personality? What should she do if baby sucks his thumb?

Parents have always had to contend with such problems as feeding and weaning babies, but it is only in recent years that emphasis has been placed on the relationship between infant disciplines and personality development. A study of women's magazines (Stendler, 1950) reveals that two extreme schools of thought have prevailed since about 1920. Beginning in the 'twenties and continuing through the 'thirties, a philosophy based upon Watsonian "behaviorism" was widely popular. J. B. Watson, a psychologist, had contended that each act of behavior is caused by a particular stimulus which sets up a connection in the nervous system leading to a particular response. According to this view, scheduling is important as a way of conditioning the baby to feeding or sleeping or toileting at a particular time. Parents in the 'twenties and 'thirties were told that picking up a crying baby just once would be enough to "condition" him; that is, he would learn that the stimulus, crying, produced a particular response, being picked up, and a bond between the two would be set up in his nervous system. The result would be a "spoiled" baby who had learned that he need only cry in order to receive attention. On the other hand, if left to cry it out a few times, the baby would soon learn that he could not manipulate adults and would not be continually demanding attention.

The baby could also be "conditioned" to toilet training early. In the words of one expert: "If you can, start training your infant to have a bowel movement in the chamber each morning at the age of one month. . . . Fix upon a definite time . . . place the chamber on your lap . . . and hold the infant over it. Insert a tapered soap stick about two inches into the rectum, keep it there from three to five minutes. . . . If you keep this up with regularity, a daily bowel movement will probably result" (Bartlett, 1933, pp. 231-32). Early weaning was also advocated; the sooner infants were trained to give up the breast or bottle, the more praiseworthy it was considered.

In the 'forties, however, a revolutionary new doctrine took over. Freudian psychology had earlier emphasized the importance of a permissive, indulgent attitude toward infant disciplines, and this attitude was strengthened by such writers as Margaret Ribble. Ribble (1943) noted a connection between an infant's physiological well-being and the amount of "mothering" he received; she also pointed out that permanent damage could be done to a child's personality by lack of adequate mothering.

Breast feeding was deemed preferable to bottle feeding because, so the argument goes, the baby derives security from physical contact with his mother; cuddling the baby was advocated on the same ground. Infants should be fed when they are hungry to spare them undue frustration: "When a baby cries on, trying

"But there's an even newer theory out, dear—
you're supposed to hit them!"

(Reproduced by permission. Copyright *The Saturday Review*)

in vain to tell his wants, he may even come to feel, 'The world is against me.' " Mothers were also advised to delay toilet training and never to reprove a child for toileting accidents, lest the reproof arouse in him feelings of guilt or hostility which might be damaging. In every area of infant discipline, a permissive attitude was advocated—letting the child set the pace for feeding, for weaning, for toilet training—in place of a regimented system under which the socialization process was speeded up.

Yet there appears to be considerable question as to whether the newer doctrine is any sounder than the old. Orlansky (1949) examined experimental and semiexperimental investigations on the relationship between infant disciplines and personality development. From his review of the extensive studies on breast feeding *versus* bottle feeding, self-demand *versus* scheduled feeding, weaning, thumbsucking, mothering, sphincter training, and early-childhood conditioning, he concluded that the assertion that breast-fed babies are invariably better off than bottle-fed babies has not been proved; that the connection between self-demand feeding and a secure, well-adjusted personality remains to be shown; that mothering or lack of mothering, early toilet training or late, may or may not affect personality.

More recent evidence also leads to the conclusion that no technique of feeding has the same effect for all children (Sears *et al.,* 1957). A child's early feeding experiences can, of course, affect his later development, but the effects are specific to the individual. Children who had been breast-fed (40 per cent of the 379 whose mothers were interviewed) did not differ in personality from those who had not been breast-fed, as judged by the mothers' descriptions.

3. Would a mother's reluctance to breast-feed her child have the same meaning in the Victorian era as in the 1930's? Explain the source of the reluctance in each case.

Another disciplinary problem of great interest to parents and research specialists is that posed by thumbsucking. There are currently three theories in vogue. According to all of them, thumbsucking is a response to an oral drive. One theory, however, states that habitual thumbsucking results from insufficient opportunity to suck while feeding (Levy, 1937). That is, infants who have been weaned abruptly or too early, or who have not had a long enough sucking time during any one feeding, might begin thumbsucking to satisfy their oral drive. According to psychiatric theory, thumbsucking persists because of insecurity or frustration. Adjustment to a new sibling or environment or difficulties in the parent-child relationship may cause the child to seek comfort in thumbsucking. The third view, based on learning theory, holds that thumbsucking results from a reinforced oral drive, strengthened by a relatively long period of feeding through sucking (Sears & Wise, 1950). In a study of children under six, grouped according to time of weaning, investigators found that the middle- and late-weaned groups showed a slightly greater tendency toward thumbsucking than the early-weaned group. Babies who were fed from a cup at birth showed a weaker sucking reflex after ten days than babies in a breast-fed group (H. V. Davis *et al.*, 1948).

Although the first and third theories seem to conflict, it may be that both are partly right. Constitutional differences are undoubtedly reflected in the varying sensitivity infants exhibit toward disturbing stimuli in the environment. These differences may cause some infants to seek more comfort in sucking than others—and the more sucking that is done, the stronger becomes the drive to reduce tension by sucking.

Present-day writers, then, would hesitate to make extravagant claims for a permissive approach to infant disciplines; but neither would they urge parents to return to the heartless methods of the 'thirties. They advise, rather, that we apply any new theory with caution and with regard for individual differences in the personalities of babies and mothers. There are "martyr" type mothers who derive satisfaction from meeting babies' excessive demands. Such mothers need help, not in becoming more permissive, but in setting reasonable limits to demands. Warmhearted mothers may schedule feedings or begin toilet training early for very practical reasons, but their children may nevertheless feel loved and wanted.

4. What factors should a mother keep in mind in making a decision with regard to a specific infant discipline?

FAMILY CLIMATES

Parents, then, need not be concerned about the effects of a specific infant discipline upon a child's personality. The sum total of the child-training practices they adopt, however, will make a difference, for parent behavior creates a climate or atmosphere in the home which has an influence upon the child's development. According to some studies, each home has a "personality" of its own. Whether that "personality" is warm, harsh, indulgent, or democratic, it is determined by the parent-child interactions. Parents continually have to make decisions about how to handle child behaviors. They have to decide what to do, if anything, when the infant throws his cracker on the floor, breaks his father's best ashtray, smears food on his face, tells his mother he hates her, plays in mud, refuses to stay in bed, and the like. They will make their decision in each case in the light of what they know about growth and development and the kind of person they want their child to be.

In a series of studies conducted at the Fels Institute, Baldwin, Kalhorn, and Breese (1949) have attempted to establish a relationship between certain types of parent behavior and the behavior and personality of children who have been exposed to them.

First they rated each home on the Fels Parent Behavior Rating Scales. These consist of thirty variables which describe parent behavior in terms of "General babying," "Coerciveness of suggestion," "Democracy of regulation and enforcement policy," "Severity of actual penalties," and other factors. For each of the thirty variables, each parent was rated on a five-point scale. With respect to the variable "Babying," for example, a parent's behavior might be rated as 5, "Withholds help," or as 1, "Overhelps." Then the ratings were analyzed. The investigators discovered that homes might be classified according to three major syndromes: (*1*) democracy, (*2*) acceptance of the child (or warmth), and (*3*) indulgence.

A comparison of the ratings of parents' behavior with ratings of their children's nursery school behavior suggests that the degree of democracy practiced by parents at home is by far the most important factor in accounting for differences in their children's nursery school behavior. Children from homes rated as democratic were found to be more active and more socially outgoing. Some expressed their "outgoingness" in friendliness; others, in hostile, domineering behavior. In the case of the latter children, however, aggressiveness and bossiness were successful group techniques. Children from democratic homes also were judged high on intellectual curiosity, originality, and constructiveness. Children of highly indulgent parents, on the other hand, were rated low in both large- and small-muscle skill and showed a relatively great amount of physical apprehensiveness (Baldwin, 1949).

According to these studies, then, we should expect children who come from democratic homes to be relatively active and outgoing, although at times their outgoingness may take an aggressive turn. We should expect children from indulgent homes to be relatively cautious and unskilled in motor activities. However, family climates are not always "purely" democratic or indulgent. There were some parents in the Fels group who loved and accepted their children but still were fairly strict in their standards of child behavior. There were democratic homes in which parents nevertheless put pressure on their children for achievement. We also know that children reared in the same family may have quite different personalities. Since parents are seldom "pure" in their treatment of children, it may be the child's *perception* of his parents as loving or indulgent or rejecting or democratic that affects his development. This perception, of course, may not be the same as that of a visitor who rates the home objectively.

The work of Gough and others sheds additional light on the problem of home atmosphere and socialization. In studying children's ethnic attitudes, they found that these attitudes are part of the total personality structure. A child who is relatively intolerant is also "more constricted, cynical, fearful, less confident and secure, and more suspicious and more ethnocentric than children of greater tolerance" (1950, p. 91).

Harris, Gough, and Martin (1950) hypothesized that authoritarian child-training practices might be related to ethnic bias in children. They reasoned that a child whose parents are authoritarian will be more prejudiced against certain ethnic groups than will a child from a more democratic home atmosphere; that the way in which the parents handle a child, particularly in disciplinary matters and in affectional relationships, might affect the child's personality structure; that, if parents fail to meet the child's organic and social needs, ethnic prejudice might result.

Interesting differences between the mothers of prejudiced and unprejudiced children were revealed by comparing results of a questionnaire on child-training practices filled out by mothers with the incidence of prejudice in children as revealed by attitude scales. It was found that mothers of prejudiced children favor more authoritarian training patterns. They expect prompt and unquestioning obedience from children; they believe that obedience is the most important thing a child can learn, and that it is wicked for children to disobey their parents.

Not only do mothers of prejudiced children expect instant obedience; they are also seen by their children as more punitive (Lyle & Levitt, 1955). Fifth-grade children who showed a strong antidemocratic tendency viewed their parents as punitive and were also more inclined to be punitive themselves. Apparently, the syndrome of ethnocentrism has its origin in the kind of family climate in which the child is reared.

5. Can you offer an explanation for the finding that authoritarian child-rearing practices might result in ethnic prejudice in children?

6. Would it be possible for children from homes characterized by democratic child-rearing practices to be prejudiced? How might prejudice be learned in such homes?

7. List the traits that you would expect to find in youngsters from homes characterized by acceptance, affection, and respect for children as individuals. Does your list include only positive traits? If not, what factors might account for the negative ones?

Radke (1946, p. 103), summarizing her own findings and the previous findings of others, has developed certain constellations of child behavior associated with certain conditions of insecurity. The characteristics of children from inharmonious, rejective, and restrictive homes are as follows:

Inharmonious *Homes*	*Rejective* *Homes*	*Restrictive* *Homes*
Aggressive	Submissive	Unpopular with
Hyperactive	Aggressive	other children
Neurotic	Adjustment	Nonrivalrous
Lying	difficulties	Passive, colorless
Jealous	Sadistic	
Delinquent	Nervous	

Radke also found that two other variables in the parent-child relationship may be accompanied by certain behavior constellations in children:

Dominating Parents	*Autocratic Parents*
Quarrelsome	Doesn't get along with
Uncooperative	other children
Tense	Noncompliant
Bold	Unstable emotionally
Disinterested	Uninhibited
Dependable	Inconsiderate
Shy, submissive,	Insensitive
polite	Nonrivalrous
Self-conscious	Unpopular

The sum total of the evidence supports the statement that family climates influence socialization, but that there is no invariable relationship between a particular kind of home atmosphere and the child's personality. The same atmosphere may produce very different children; we need to look beyond family climate to explain such differences.

MOTHER-CHILD RELATIONSHIPS AND SOCIALIZATION

In our society, child rearing is largely the mother's responsibility during the early years of childhood; the mother-child relationship therefore deserves special consideration. As Levy has pointed out:

It is generally accepted that the most potent of all influences on social behavior is derived from the primary social experience with the mother. If a mother maintains toward the child a consistent attitude of, let us say, indifference and hostility, the assumption is made that the child's personality is greatly affected thereby. His outlook on life, his attitude toward people, his entire psychic well-being, his very destiny is presumed to be altered by the maternal attitude. Life under a regime of maternal indifference develops a psychic pattern of quite a different mold than under a regime of maternal overprotection. Psychiatrists regard the difference as great as though the children concerned lived in entirely different worlds. Indeed, two children of the same parents, whose mother exhibits a different attitude toward each, manifest on that basis alone profound differences in personality [1943, pp. 3-4].

We need to remember that every child is reared in a situation in which the mother-child relationship is only one of many variables. A boy might be the only child of a mother who dotes on him and a father who rejects him. The dynamics would be quite different if he were a girl; if there were other children in the family, one of whom was a girl whom the father preferred; if the father accepted him and the mother rejected him; or if both parents rejected (or accepted) him. The dynamics will differ, too, depending upon the resiliency of the child's personality, which might in turn depend upon his constitution, the prevalence of rejection in his culture, whether the rejection is a constant factor in his life, and the age at which it is strongest.

Despite the fact that many other factors affect the child's development, it might be helpful for us to describe as accurately as possible two extreme types of parent-child relationship: overprotection and rejection. It is hoped that the presentation of these types in "pure" form may enable the student of child development to identify other elements in parent-child relationships which are not so clear-cut.

The Overprotected Child

Levy defines maternal overprotection as excessive maternal care which is manifested in three ways: (*1*) by excessive contact

("the mother is always there; hates to let him out of her sight");
(2) by infantilization ("he's fourteen but she treats him like a kid
of five; she won't let him grow up"); and (3) by prevention of
independent behavior ("she won't let him cross the street by
himself, although he's eight; she won't take any risks") (1943,
p. 37).

Excessive contact reveals itself in many ways. Overprotective mothers typically spend a relatively great amount of time
in the company of their children, give them prolonged nursing
care when they are ill, fondle them excessively, and permit or
encourage their children to sleep with them long past infancy.
In a group of twenty overprotected children (nineteen boys and
one girl) six of the boys, ranging in age from eight to thirteen,
still slept with their mothers. In this same group, there were
twice as many illnesses and three times as many operations as in
a control group. Levy interprets this finding to mean that overprotective mothers are more likely to seek and act on medical
advice than a control group of mothers. It does not mean that
the children were less healthy than their peers. Not a single
serious accident was recorded for the overprotected group.

The most common symptom of infantilization among overprotected children is the prolongation of breast feeding. Levy's
group averaged fourteen months of breast feeding as compared
with four to nine months in five check groups.* One mother
breast-fed her baby for three years, despite the criticism of
doctors and neighbors. Infantilization is also revealed in the
practices of feeding, dressing, bathing, and punishing children
beyond the normal time. A thirteen-year-old in Levy's group
was still being dressed by his mother; another thirteen-year-old
was put to bed in the afternoon as a punishment.

Prevention of social maturity is generally accomplished by
restricting the child's social contacts. In twelve of the twenty

---

* It should be noted that infantilization must be defined culturally. A
fourteen-months' nursing period in some primitive societies, and not so
long ago in our own society, would not be considered abnormal. A survey
of today's practices would probably reveal breast feeding continuing longer
than four to nine months and bottle feeding continuing for two to three
years in many situations.

cases, the formation of friendships by children was discouraged or prevented. All twenty of the children had special problems in forming friendships.

Levy has distinguished between two types of overprotective parent—the indulgent type and the dominating type. The indulgent type caters to the child and indulges his every whim. The child of this parent is rebellious and aggressive. He is frequently disrespectful and disobedient; he spits, hits, and kicks the mother, throws food on the floor, and may even make her sleep in a particular bed. The dominating mother, on the other hand, produces a child who is submissive and dependent. Typically, he is timid and seclusive in school, clean, neat, obedient, and polite; he does not fight with other children and is sometimes regarded as a "sissy."

Overprotected children are rarely "problems" in school. The dominated child is as submissive in school as he is at home. Even the indulged type, although defiant and brutal at home, is usually a model of deportment in school. Both types are conscientious students and, according to Levy, do well in school subjects, particularly reading.

The two case histories presented below summarize these data. The first is that of an overindulged child; the second, of a dominated one.

CASE 1 (*Male, Eight Years*)

Excessive contact: When he was an infant, mother could never leave him for an instant. When he was two years old, she had moods of despondency because she could not get away from him. She feels worried and unhappy when patient is out of her sight. Has been sleeping with him the past six months because he has called her. Lies down with him at night. Extra nursing care has been required because of his frequent colds. Mother says they are attached together like Siamese twins.

Prolongation of infantile care: Mother dresses him every day, takes him to school every morning, and calls for him every afternoon. When at school in the morning, she pays the waiter for his lunch and tells waiter what to give him. Breast-fed thirteen months. Mother fed him the first five years. Mother still goes to the bathroom with him and waits for him. Mother insists on holding his hand when they walk together. Resents his walking alone.

Prevention of independent behavior: He has one friend whom mother takes him to see every two weeks. Mother does not allow him to help in housework for fear he'll fall and break a dish, and so on.

Maternal control: Mother must have a light burning for him until he falls asleep. He goes to bed at 10 P.M. Mother always gives in to him, does everything for him, is dominated by him. He spits at her and strikes her [Levy, 1943, p. 28].

CASE 5 (*Male, Thirteen Years*)

Excessive contact: Mother has slept with him the past three years. Up to age seven, she never let him go out with any adult (even father) except herself.

Prolongation of infantile care: When the patient is disobedient, she puts him to bed in the afternoon, even now. She still prepares special food for him when he refuses to eat. She still sits by and coaxes.

Prevention of independent behavior: Mother delayed his schooling until he was seven because she did not like him to leave her. She blocks the plan of sending him to boarding school. She kept him from having friends or learning bad things from other children. When he was sent to camp . . . the mother visited him on the second day, found that his feet were wet, and took him home.

Maternal control: General obedient, submissive response to maternal domination. Uses aggressive methods to maintain his dependency on the mother, insisting she walk to school with him, and so on [Levy, 1943, p. 30].

8. Does overprotective behavior manifest itself in the same way in all societies? Might either of the foregoing examples be considered "normal" behavior in other societies? Which?

The Rejected Child

The rejected child is more difficult to identify. It is assumed in our society that all parents love and accept their children; to hate one's own child, not to want him, is less than human. Therefore, extreme rejection, when it exists, is very likely to be disguised. The rejecting mother may dress her child beautifully, look after his physical well-being most solicitously, and appear, to the casual observer, to be a very good parent. Yet she may be denying the child what he needs most—wholehearted acceptance and affection. It should also be pointed out that certain types of overprotection may be due to guilt feelings arising from actual rejection of the child.

Maternal rejection reveals itself in a number of ways. Excessive punishment, either corporal or verbal, may indicate the underlying hostility of the parent. Continually expecting more of a child than he is developmentally or intellectually able to give and holding up standards which the child cannot possibly attain may be a parent's way of refusing to accept a child. The child is never quite good enough for the rejecting parent, regardless of how hard he tries.

Relatively few intensive studies of rejected children are available, and detailed descriptions of the behavior of the rejected child are consequently difficult to find. However, it is clear that since the ego depends for its strength upon wholehearted and consistent recognition of real accomplishment, the egos of rejected children undoubtedly suffer severe damage which will be expressed in their behavior. We do know that sometimes the rejected child refuses to grow up; his speech even in the primary grades is unintelligible and his mannerisms infantile. Sometimes the rejected child becomes hostile and over-aggressive. Symonds (1949), summarizing studies on the rejected child, describes him as rebellious, jealous, attention-seeking, hyperactive, annoying in school, and aggressive. He may lie, steal, and take perverse satisfaction in upsetting mother and teacher.

Rejection and overprotection are only two of a wide range of possible mother-child relationships that might be fruitfully explored. They are discussed here with the reservation that most mother-child relationships are not of these extreme types but, rather, are modified or mixed. As we have already noted, it is possible for a child to be rejected by one parent and not by the other, or to be overprotected for a short time but not continuously. Factors such as these undoubtedly affect the socialization process.

The Mother's Warmth

Perhaps the most important factor in the mother-child relationship is its warmth. Mothers who rate high in this characteristic might be described behaviorally as follows:

1. Much affectionate interaction with the baby.
2. High affectionate demonstrativeness toward the child.
3. Finds ample time to play with the child.
4. Reacts acceptingly to child's dependency.
5. Praises the child when he shows good table manners.
6. Uses reasoning as a method of training [Sears *et al.*, 1957].

Warmth of the mother toward the child appears to be pervasive in its effects. Presumably, children get more satisfaction from such mothers and so are more amenable to socialization with the result that there are fewer behavior problems among this group. By contrast, the children of "cold" mothers are more likely to be feeding problems, bed-wetters, aggressive, and slow in development of conscience.

Mother-Child Interaction

To understand how factors such as "warmth" and "coldness" affect socialization, we turn next to a study by Merrill (1946). Merrill was interested in finding out, among other things, whether individual differences in the stimulus properties of mothers could be related to differences in child behavior. Her study gives us a glimpse of how maternal attitudes are actually reflected in behavior and how the children respond to this behavior.

A play session was set up to which nursery school children were invited one at a time, accompanied by their mothers. Each mother was told that the child might play with the equipment provided while the mother looked on, behaving much as she would if the child were playing at home. This play session was observed and analyzed by the experimenter. Then a second play session was set up, during which half the group of mothers and children carried on as before. The experimental group of mothers was told that the child's previous play performance had not been a satisfactory sample of his potentialities.

Merrill hypothesized that mothers are usually consistent in their behavior toward their children; even inconsistent parents are likely to be consistent in their inconsistency. Indeed, the control group behaved in much the same way in both sessions, since the sessions were identical in plan. But, as might be expected, the experimental group behaved in a markedly different way in the second play session. Merrill reported a significant increase in directing, interfering, criticizing, and structurizing the activity during this session.

Naturally, one would expect a mother to want her child to appear to the world in the best possible light and to do what she can to facilitate his success. But some interesting individual differences appeared in the Merrill study. One mother in the experimental group, the most extreme, attempted even in the first session to have her child perform well. Remarks such as "Build a beautiful bridge like you do at home" and "But you build such lovely things at home; why don't you do it here?" were characteristic. At the second session, she made almost desperate attempts to force the child to show what he could do. When the bewildered child performed badly, she became very much annoyed. This child understandably showed extreme dependence on the mother, turning to her with questions such as "Mother, how would *you* build this bridge?" and "But don't you want me to make what you want?"

A second mother, by contrast, was genuinely interested in and enjoyed her child in his own right. She allowed the child autonomy, yet she was always ready to help him when he indicated a desire for help. She changed somewhat in the second session, but her increased interfering was primarily of the structurizing type. Her child showed a high level of constructive play. His behavior toward his mother was characterized by respect and enjoyment.

A third mother in the experimental group vacillated between a friendly, playful relationship with the child and a domineering, annoyed reaction when he deviated from her standards. The boy's response was indifference; he seemed staunchly determined to continue doing things in *his* way. He responded to his mother's uncertainty and inconsistency by turning his back upon her.

In countless interactions like these throughout the day, mothers mold their children's personalities. They provide stimuli to which children react. When particular reactions are satisfying to a child, they tend to become his characteristic way of reacting to the same or similar stimuli. A study of the interaction process is most rewarding for those who seek to understand the socialization process.

Obviously, an "accepting" mother-child relationship is most desirable if a child is to develop a sufficiently strong ego to function effectively in life. Some writers go so far as to say that regardless of social, economic, physical, or intellectual status; regardless of whether he is very thin, undersized, or crippled; regardless of whether he has a high or a low intelligence quotient, a child will be a happy, outgoing, constructive member of his group if his parents accept him as he is.

Working Mothers

It is becoming increasingly common in America for mothers to work. In 1950 about 15 per cent of all children under eighteen years of age were in families in which both parents were employed (Bernert, 1958). About 2 million working mothers had children under six years of age, and 3.2 million had children of school age.

The effects of a mother's employment upon the child are very difficult to assess. Two of the factors which must be taken into account are the age of the child when the mother begins work and the nature of the substitute child care she is able to provide. In some families this care is divided between husband and wife; the husband, for example, might work a 7:00 A.M.-3:00 P.M. shift and hurry home to relieve the mother, who works from 4:00 to 11:00 P.M. A peculiar pattern of family living ensues, with husband and wife visible as a team to the children only on weekends. We can only speculate on the effects of such an arrangement. One beneficial effect might be that the father has more contact with his children than the average and can exert a positive influence upon their behavior. And many a mother, bored with housework and small children, is glad to get out "into the world" when 4 P.M. arrives. Such mothers may return to child care in a better frame of mind after a respite from household routines. On the negative side is the possible fatigue of each parent, trying to do two jobs each day—a fatigue which may be manifested in lack of patience with the children. Also, the husband's self-esteem may be challenged; he may feel inadequate in his role as family provider or degraded at having to do housework.

When the mother must turn the job of child care over to a person outside the family, different problems arise. Unfortunately, in some lower-class homes in particular, such care is often haphazard. Preschool children may be left with a neighbor, an untrained person who may care for six or eight children in the vicinity in her home. School-age children may be left to roam the streets without supervision when school is out. Some preschool children are taken to day-care centers each day, where standards for child care are at least minimal; however, this arrangement often entails long hours of separation of mother and child and long hours of group care, when the young child must share a substitute with too many other children. In some countries, the government provides financial assistance to families so that mothers of preschool children do not have to work, but similar legislation has not yet been passed in the United States.

Many middle-class mothers are financially able to hire a caretaker to come to the home, at least during the years when their children are of preschool age. Such an arrangement is easier for children than being cared for outside the home, but its success depends, according to one writer (Maccoby, 1957), on the similarities between the caretaker's methods and those of the mother when she is at home. The very young child finds comfort and security in routine. If his mother always puts on the left leg of his pajamas or play suit first, he may resist vigorously when the caretaker starts with the right leg. He may be confused if his mother lets him suck his thumb and the caretaker does not. When he is older (four or five years of age), he can adjust to such differences; but when he is very young, the child is often confused and unhappy under such circumstances.

The abruptness of the mother's departure from the home may also be upsetting to very young children. Four-year-olds can be prepared in advance for a change in caretaker; they can be reassured that the mother will return at a certain time. But a two-year-old may suffer a separation anxiety when he is suddenly left with a stranger. A transition period during which mother and caretaker are together in the home and the mother disappears for increasingly long periods of the day eases the adjustment. There will be an initial disturbance, but the child will quickly adjust to the new routine.

Provided that the substitute care is adequate, there are some circumstances in which separation of mother and child is highly desirable (Maccoby, 1957). If the mother has certain neurotic needs, if she encourages dependency or is extremely punitive or rejecting, her young child will be better off with a reliable caretaker during the day. Not all mother-child relationships are desirable, as we have seen.

> **9.** List some behaviors that an accepting mother might show in her interactions with a three-year-old son. Contrast these behaviors with those of a rejecting parent.

COMPOSITION OF THE FAMILY AND SOCIALIZATION

Not only family climate and mother-child relationship but composition of the family may affect socialization. A typical American child has a small immediate family; unlike children in some other societies, he lives alone with his father, mother, and siblings. The typical Trobriand household may bulge with relatives of the mother who find their rightful place in her household, but the American child depends for his security only upon his parents. Does it make a difference with whom the child lives?

Family Size and Ordinal Position

From recent research, it appears that the size of the family and the ordinal position of an individual child within the family also influence the socialization process. The only child receives his parents' undivided attention, whether it be positive or negative. The first-born has his parents to himself for a year or more, but then must learn to share them with one or more siblings. The social grouping to which the youngest child in the family is exposed provides learning experiences quite different from those which the middle or first-born child has. What differences do these various social groupings make to the child?

Koch (1956) has reported on some behavioral correlates of ordinal position in two-child families. She took into account, not only the position of the children as the first- or second-born, but also their sex and the time elapsed between their births. One of the most significant findings is that all these variables must be studied in interaction; they cannot be considered independently. That is, the first-born child develops differently depending upon the age difference between him and the younger sibling and upon his and his sibling's sex.

Specifically, she found that second-born males with an older sister tend to be more dependent and "sissyish" than first-born males with a younger sibling of either sex—particularly when the boy is much younger than his sister. Apparently, the older sister takes on the job of mothering the boy so that he has less opportunity to learn independent and boylike behavior.

She also found that boys or girls with an older or younger brother are more competitive, ambitious, and enthusiastic and less wavering in their decisions than are children with a sister. Koch attributes the influence of the male sibling to an "alerting" factor. The male child typically receives more attention from the mother than a female child in the same family. Because he is so favored, he presents a challenge to his sister to be on her mettle. When both children are boys, each competes with the other for the mother's favor and so serves to stimulate the other.

Koch cautions against sweeping generalizations about the effects of a single factor, such as birth order, sex, age difference, or sex of sibling. This same caution would extend to applying her conclusions to families with more than two children. The birth of each child changes the family environment, and the impact of that change upon each individual depends upon the complex relationships already existing within the family.

Contrary to popular opinion, the only child and the "baby" in the family are not necessarily indulged, at least with respect to certain infant disciplines. Sears and others (1957) report that these children were least indulged with respect to breast feeding and weaning. Also, the only child is subject to more restrictions on his freedom; his mother is likely to supervise his activities more closely than the mother of two or more children.

Fatherless Children

We have pointed out that in America the immediate family is numerically small and includes only two socializing agents—mother and father. We should also note that there are many families in the United States in which there is only one parent or none at all. In 1950 there were more than four million children under eighteen years of age who lived in families which had been broken by widowhood, divorce, or separation (Bernert, 1958). Loss of a mother typically affects family life differently from loss of a father. When a father is left with preschool children, he usually continues in his role of breadwinner and brings in a new socializing agent to take over housekeeping duties and care of the children. This new agent is, in effect, a substitute mother. When a father is missing from a family, however, the mother may become both breadwinner and homemaker, with no adult male figure introduced into the house. The absence of such a figure has certain effects upon socialization.

In order to understand what it means to grow up without

a father, we need to consider what a father means to a growing child. Actually, he means different things to children at different stages of development. Ideally, the young child sees him as a person who can accomplish prodigious tasks and who represents strength and security. To the growing boy, a father becomes a model to copy and hence an important source of learning sex-appropriate behavior. Sears, Pintler, and Sears (1946) point out that the learning process depends upon the existence of such models. The child must be in close contact with someone who has *practical* knowledge of right and wrong sex-typed behavior. When the father-son relationship is good, when the father is perceived by his son as a highly rewarding, affectionate person, the boy is more likely to identify with the father (Payne & Mussen, 1956). Sometimes, indeed, he *is* the father in his own mind. A five-year-old playing at driving the family car is not just mimicking father in his behavior—signaling for turns, shouting at other drivers and pedestrians, and so on—he is *being* father. The following observation by Sharpe illustrates the point:

> On the seat in front of me in a bus one day was a boy between the ages of six and seven, and beside him his young mother. I noticed him get up suddenly, walk to the exit platform, and ask the conductor to stop at the next "Request" halt. The bus stopped, the boy jumped out on the pavement and waited for his mother who followed him. As she got down, he held out his hand to help her. He then waited until she crossed to the inner side of the pavement and he walked beside her on the outer side.
>
> No words had been spoken by either of them, but, as they passed out of sight, he was striding along and talking gaily to her, and she was smiling. The little boy wore a cap at a rakish angle on his fair head. It was a replica of an airman's. Something of what both mother and father meant to this young boy is clear.
>
> The mother did not suggest to her boy that he should ask the conductor to stop the bus. She did not caution him to be careful or to wait till the bus stopped. He had formed a habit; he trusted himself, and she trusted him. She took his offered

hand as she stepped down as if he were of real assistance to her. She dropped his hand again, as if he were a man, and took the inside of the pavement in the same way. Both were quite unself-conscious.

One knew certain things about this boy and about his father. One knew father was an airman, that he thrust his head forward, clasped his hands behind his back, and took long strides. One knew how he treated his wife, not on one occasion but habitually. The little boy obviously thought and felt his father was a wonderful man. He had absorbed certain of his characteristics and was "being father" [1945, pp. 23-24].

Not all father-son relationships are so fortunate. Relatively masculine mothers tend to inhibit strong father identification in their sons (Payne & Mussen, 1956). When this is true, boys rate lower on masculinity of attitudes. A boy who is rejected by his father will have difficulty in adjusting to being a man. If the father prefers a daughter, the boy may develop feminine ways of behaving as a means of winning father's acceptance. And if the father is absent during the crucial years of his son's development, the boy may be slow in learning his masculine role.

To the growing girl, the father serves as a reinforcer of her femininity; he admires her hairdo, comments on her clothes, teases her, and in general treats her differently from her brother. Thus he teaches her what it means to be a woman. The girl also observes the relationship that her father has established with her mother; where there is marital harmony, the girl tries to be like mother so that father will love her, too. On the other hand, by admiring his daughter's tomboyishness, a father can subtly encourage her to be boylike, which will make her task of becoming a feminine woman far more difficult. Absence of the father or rejection by the father may create an unsatisfied need in the girl, so that she goes through life continually seeking a father in the men she meets.

Isaacs (1945) points out other ways in which the loss of a father can influence a child's development. Often guilt feelings arise as the child comes to feel in some way responsible for the father's death. Sometimes the guilt feelings come because the

child resents his father's being dead; daddy *ought* to be alive
and is a bad daddy not to be there to take care of mother. The
child then feels that his hostile wishes have killed the father
and feels responsible for and guilty about his absence or death.

The attitude of the mother toward the absent father is a
significant factor in determining the child's attitude toward his
missing parent. Bach (1946) studied the effect on the fantasies
of school-age children of the absence of the father from the
home. His report revealed that the children of mothers who
were antagonistic toward or contemptuous of their spouses
showed more aggression toward the father doll in their doll
play than did children of mothers who were affectionate toward
and longing for the absent father.

Fatherless children may develop a number of problems.
Sometimes they become excessively dependent upon the mother;
sometimes they grow rebellious and defiant, difficult for the
mother to control. Antisocial behavior in the form of stealing
may also break out following the loss of a father.

It is interesting to note that boys from fatherless homes
show less aggression in general than do boys from homes in
which father is present (Sears, Pintler, & Sears, 1946). This was
not true of girls in the same study. In explaining their findings,
the authors reason that during the preschool years the father
contributes heavily to the sex-typing of boys in respect to their
expression of aggression. They also reason that the parent of
the same sex provides greater frustration and more rigid controls, which might result in greater aggression on the child's
part. In other words, fatherless boys are less aggressive because
it is the father's job to teach a boy to be aggressive, and also
because the male parent is a greater frustrater than the mother
for male children.

Fatherless children can be helped, Isaacs believes, if they
can be made to feel that they need not choose between destroying the father by denying their memories or feelings for him
and putting the whole of their energies into an effort to keep
him alive in their minds. They should be encouraged to turn
to other people and other interests. Father should not be pre-

sented to these children as a perfect image; his name should be brought into conversation as normally as possible. Contact with other men should be provided for the bereaved children, so that they do not feel isolated and overdependent upon the mother.

Absentee Fathers

A special problem arising out of the tensions of war is that of the adjustment of the soldier-father to his children and vice versa. During World War II, it was almost as common for young children to grow up with the father absent from the home as it was for them to have the father present. Sometimes the father was away when the baby was born and the child was many months old before the father's return. Sometimes the father had to leave children who were accustomed to his presence and too young to comprehend where or why he had to go. To some extent, absentee fatherhood still persists in many young families in which the first baby arrives while the father is putting in his years of military service.

The father relations of warborn children has been the subject of a comprehensive study by L. M. Stolz and others (1954). They were especially concerned with how the return of the father might affect the behavior and personality of first children born while he was at war.

The returning father, according to this study, faces many areas of stress. First he must adjust to being the head of a family; he must assume the status of breadwinner and cope with the many anxieties connected with earning a living for himself and his family. Next he must adjust to a wife and to re-establishing love relations with her. Then he faces problems in accepting routines of living, in becoming accustomed again to living with a person whose habits might differ markedly from his own. Related to all these problems are the problems arising from adjusting to a child. All but one of the men in the war-separated group felt that the baby interfered in some way in their relations with their wives. They resented the baby's intrusion upon their privacy; they resented having to share the wife's attention with the baby; they resented the close bond that had developed between mother and child. They took out their resentment both by criticizing the child-rearing methods used by the mother and by punishing the child. If the child wouldn't eat or be toilet trained or be quiet or sleep in his own bed, it was the mother's fault for spoiling the child, and the father set about to remedy this situation. Typically, the mothers responded by standing up for the child—in front of him, too—which added to the father's anger and resentment. The problem was further aggravated in some cases by the child's shyness with the father, or outright rejection of his advances. Even after many months at home, the father and his first-born were distant, and the child and his mother continued to be very close. Children in this situation were found to be less competitive and more compulsively obedient than average, and had more difficulty in their relations with other children. Many of the fathers compensated for their relatively poor relationship with their first-born by establishing a warm, intimate relation with the second child, born after the father's return.

This study highlights the importance of the first year or two for the establishment of satisfactory relations between father and child. As one father put it, having the opportunity to see a baby develop from birth, to watch him learn to eat, walk, and talk, helps the father to know what to expect of a child and to avoid the typical mistake of the returning father: expecting too much. Helping to guide the baby's development also makes the father feel closer to the child, more involved in his development. When he has had a large share in child-rearing decisions, he feels that he has shaped the child's personality and is more understanding and less critical of him. When the father feels left out, he is more likely to be critical of the child and the mother, and interpersonal relations within the home are endangered. The modern trend toward having the father participate in the routines of baby care, in the feeding, even diapering and training of the child, would seem to be a wholesome one.

SUBCULTURAL DIFFERENCES
AMONG FAMILIES

Thus far we have looked at the setting of the socialization process within the family. We have seen that the socialization of a particular American child will differ from that of other American children because his parents use certain child-training practices rather than others, because they establish a certain kind of relationship with him, and because of the interaction of the child with various members of his family.

The socialization process, however, varies with subgroups within this American frame. A child from a lower-class home will have many things in common with other lower-class children and will differ in important ways from upper-class children; the American-born child of Polish parents will learn ways of behaving unique to his subcultural group and different from those of fourth-generation Americans in his community and of his social class; a girl growing up in rural America will resemble other rural children and differ from urban children in certain mores and values.

Social-Class Differences

In recent years, there have been numerous studies devoted to social-class differences in our society. Many of these have focused on social-class differences in socialization. Results indicate that social classes differ in the methods they use to train the young and in the ways of behaving they teach their children.

Different investigators, however, have reported different—sometimes conflicting—results. In a report of research published in 1947, Davis and Havighurst claimed that middle-class parents were much stricter with their children, trained them earlier and more severely, and in general caused their children to suffer greater frustration than did lower-class parents.

In 1954, however, Maccoby and Gibbs published a report on child-rearing practices which contradicted the Davis-Havighurst findings. These later investigators found the middle-class group to be generally more permissive than the lower. The groups did not differ significantly in infant-feeding practices, but the upper-lower-class mothers were more severe in toilet training and in sex training. They employed physical punishment, deprivation of privileges, and ridicule as techniques of controlling their children, in contrast to upper-middle-class parents, who were more likely to use reasoning and praise and who were warmer and more demonstrative toward their young children. Upper-middle-class parents also allowed their children more freedom to show aggression toward the parents than did upper-lower-class parents. More recently, Schaefer and Bell (1958) report that, in general, well-educated mothers are more likely to have approved attitudes toward child rearing than mothers from lower educational levels.

From his review of recent research on this subject, Bronfenbrenner (1958) attempted to explain this variation in findings. He concluded that both findings may be correct for the time period during which the studies were made. Prior to World War II, when Davis and Havighurst gathered their data, working-class mothers *were* more permissive than middle-class parents with respect to feeding, weaning, and toilet training. However, as we have pointed out, a revolution in child-training practices began in the 'forties; literature directed toward mothers, especially the bulletins of the U.S. Children's Bureau (Wolfenstein, 1953), began to advocate more permissive practices. And, Bronfenbrenner suggests, child-rearing practices may change most quickly in those segments of society which have closest access to child-training literature, physicians, counselors, and other agents of change—i.e., the middle and upper classes.

One additional explanation is in order. The relative freedom that the lower-class parent permits his child may to some extent reflect, not a less restricting attitude, but a rejecting attitude (Maccoby *et al.,* 1954). The lower-class mother may be less willing to be "bothered" by the child; she may permit him later hours and more time away from home by himself as a way of getting rid of him.

One factor about which there seems to be agreement is that the middle-class parent, even when he is tolerant of his child's impulses, has higher expectations for the child (Bronfenbrenner, 1958). This is particularly true with regard to progress in school. When middle-class parents of first-graders are asked how far they expect their children to go in school, the parents will reply that they want their children to get as much education as possible and that of course they expect the children to go to college, perhaps even beyond. Lower-class parents, too, want their children to get as much education as they can, but they add that they hope their children will finish high school. Undoubtedly, the higher expectations that middle-class parents have for their children affect the children's own level of aspiration.

Social-class differences also appear in the area of learning the appropriate sex role. There is some evidence of social-class differences in the content and timing of the teaching of sex-appropriate behavior. Rabban (1950) compared 150 working-class children between the ages of thirty months and eight years with 150 middle-class children of the same age range. Results indicate that the lower socioeconomic group became aware of sex-role patterns earlier than the middle-class group, that they were given more clear-cut concepts of what sex-appropriate behavior involves, and that sex-appropriate behavior was more rigorously enforced by the parents. In middle-class families, the father is away from home for a large part of the child's waking hours, which means that the mother becomes the sole authority and model. Middle-class families also permit the children greater leeway with regard to behavior and do not define sex-appropriate behavior so rigidly as do working-class parents.

To give the reader a clearer picture of the process by which children learn sex-appropriate behavior, two "child-in-the-family" cases, one working class and the other middle class, are presented below (Rabban, 1950, pp. 130-32).

"Danny"

Toy choices: Six boys' toys at each session.
Sex awareness: All correct.
Age period covered: 49-51 months.
Siblings: Sister, 20 months.
Father's occupation: Welder's helper.
Mother's occupation: Charwoman and factory operative.

The family lives in a three-room railroad flat in a street of uniform three-story frame houses. There is no yard.

On a weekday the mother usually is with Danny from 6:00 to 7:30 in the morning. She calls for him at the Day-Care Center at 4:30 P.M. and he goes to bed at 8:00 P.M. The father is home from work at 5:30 P.M.

The only things he does alone with his mother are to hold the hose when she is washing clothes, and to dry the silverware.

The entire family is together on the weekends. Saturdays all four will go shopping in the morning. In the afternoon the father works on the car and has Danny with him. He shows him how to take the car apart and now Danny knows all parts of an engine. He proudly tells the nursery school children that he knows all about his father's car. Danny and his father are together all Sunday morning. His mother says: "They sit for hours on the back porch together. His father calls him his shadow." On Sunday afternoon they all go out visiting to the grandmother, go out for a drive, and usually end up in a drive-in movie.

Danny imitates his father's manner of talking, his stance and walk. His interest in cars spreads to those he sees on the street, and to his play.

His father never participated in routine baby care. He was in the Army until Danny was thirteen months old.

Danny's only playmates are the children in the Day-Care Center.

Both father and mother offer praise and rewards. There is no need to punish because he "follows all the rules now that his father set down from the time he was an infant." He does not leave the table unless the father excuses him. He must always say "May I?" The mother also says: "Danny's father can be very stern when he wants him to act a certain way. All he has to do now is give a look—and Danny knows what to do." But even that is not very frequent, for Danny understands all the rules and knows how to behave. He looks to his father when he is uncertain.

He is especially affectionate with his father and enjoys rough-housing with him.

When asked her attitude toward a boy's interest in girls' games and association with them, she replied she would tell Danny: "Dolls are for girls, not for boys. Everybody will think you are a sissy. You should play with cars and trucks." And directly to the interviewer, she said: "We bought him a truck for Christmas."

The factors most active in this boy's sex socialization are: (*a*) clear-cut definition of appropriate behavior by both parents; (*b*) close affect relationship with the father, who also strictly defines the rules; child follows the rules so as not to lose status with him; (*c*) active induction into masculine interests by the father; (*d*) clear-cut identification with the father, promoted by mother's attitude.

"Norman"

Toy choices: 1st session, four girls' toys; 2nd session, four boys' toys.

Sex awareness: All correct.

Age period covered: 58-61 months.

Siblings: Brother, 36 months.

Father's occupation: Architect.

Mother's occupation: Housewife.

The family lives in a six-room house set in a quarter-acre plot. The boys have a slide, sandbox, and rubber pool back of the house.

On a weekday, the mother usually spends about one-and-a-half hours with Norman in the morning before nursery school. After nursery school he has his lunch, naps, and then plays with other children in the neighborhood. On rainy days he likes to help his mother cook. He spends a great deal of time building with his blocks. His mother will often listen to phonograph records with him or read to him.

The father is not at home during the week. His work takes him away a good deal. On his weekends at home the father takes walks with the children. Norman follows him about as he gardens or does carpentry chores about the house. He resents any time the father spends out of his sight. The father participated a great deal in all aspects of routine baby care. . . .

He imitates his father in pretending that he is shaving in the morning. He remarks that when he grows up he is going to have a "scratchy face like daddy."

The mother commented that Norman imitates his younger brother's behavior more than that of his father. He has always been very jealous of him.

She also remarked that Norman doesn't seem to recognize boy and girl differences in activities. He would just as soon cook as do carpentry. He has not played with the typically boy things. Recently, however, for his fifth birthday his grandmother gave him a gun. With this new plaything, he has achieved a new status with his playmates and with it, new awarenesses. He seemed to reveal this in the choices he made in the second session, which took place after his fifth birthday.

When asked about her attitude toward his participation in girls' activities, Norman's mother said she would do nothing. She didn't think it important. . . .

The factors most active in this boy's sex socialization are: (a) considerable father absence with only a minimal sense of identification; (b) mother, nursery school teachers, and older girl playmates as the predominant behavior models; (c) parents who are not concerned with early or strict definitions of sex-appropriate behavior; (d) evidence that he is only now, after his fifth birthday, becoming aware of the status value of a gun. There are incipient signs of a new system of sex-appropriate responses.

These studies indicate that there are social-class differences in the teaching and learning of sex-appropriate behavior. In the models with which he is furnished, the expectations that his parents have for him, and the activities and toys that are permitted him, the middle-class child appears to differ from the lower-class child, and his behavior is affected by these differences.

10. Do all middle-class families permit as much leeway in the matter of sex-appropriate behavior as do Norman's? Can you cite some evidence to substantiate your answer?

Rural-Urban Differences

Early childhood experiences of rural children have received little attention in child-development literature. Yet, as Levinger and Murphy (1947) report, there are certain important differences in child training between rural and urban children, and it is erroneous to assume that findings from research on city children also apply to farm children. On the basis of their observations of children in Westchester County, New York, and in Southern Ohio, these two writers have described some important differences between the two groups. However, it should be pointed out that many of these differences are hypotheses rather than facts; we need considerably more data on both farm and urban children in order to generalize with more conviction.

The basic early experiences of farm children would appear to be freer from pressure than those of middle-class urban children. Toilet training is casual and delayed, breast feeding is prolonged, and less value is placed upon cleanliness and orderliness. The farm child also is spared the rather arbitrary commands to which the urban child is subjected; the things that he is asked to do or not to do make more sense. As these authors point out, if a city child doesn't close a door he may be punished for it, but may not quite know why shutting a door is important; if a farm child leaves a gate open, he sees young turkeys head for the highway, so that the punishment which follows has meaning for him.

The relative importance of a baby in the household may be different for farm children and urban children. The pressure of work on the farm mother means that the baby is relegated to the sidelines and is not the center of the household as he is in middle-class urban life. For the farm child this may mean that he is spared the responsibility of measuring up to standards that sometimes results when a baby is the center of the household. Further, because farm families tend to be larger than urban families, older children frequently take over the baby's care. The older farm child can be more demonstrative toward the baby because he isn't restricted, as is his city cousin, by admonitions such as "Don't touch baby with dirty hands!" and "Don't get the baby too excited!" Because older farm children participate more directly in the care of babies and because the baby occupies a relatively minor role in the household, sibling rivalry may be reduced.

Age-status relationships would appear to be more closely defined for the farm child than for the city child. Whereas growing up for the city child is defined in terms of going to school, being able to cross streets alone, and the like, for the farm child there are much more varied and concrete bases for age status. He sees older children doing important chores about the house and barn, and when he is "big enough" he is given the run of the farm and responsible jobs to do. Because so much of the work is connected with animals and is related to the farm economy, the jobs gain in prestige. Emptying garbage can never seem so important to a young child as feeding chickens or letting cows out to pasture.

The father is much more a part of the household in farm families than he is in urban communities. Also there is a sharper distinction between the roles of men and women. These two factors may combine to make the job of learning to be a man or a woman easier for the farm child.

11. The differences in socialization presented here favor the farm child. Can you suggest possible advantages in the socialization of the urban child?

Ethnic and Other Differences

The socialization of a white upper-lower-class Protestant boy of German descent may resemble in many respects the socialization of American boys of the same social stratum but with an English, Dutch, French, Italian, Polish, or other nationality background. Not even the child's race necessarily makes for differences in the socialization process. Davis and Havighurst (1947) found that middle-class Negroes resemble middle-class whites much more closely than they resemble lower-class Negroes, and that lower-class whites and lower-class Negroes resemble each other more than they do middle-class groups of their own color.

However, there are some subcultural groups which are slow to assimilate the prevailing cultural values. Assimilation is slow among immigrant groups in which the original differences between "American" culture and the immigrant culture are great, particularly with regard to color, language, and religion. French-Canadians who are Catholic and who speak a foreign language have established a stronger subcultural group than English-speaking Protestant Canadians. Similarly, Latin-Americans, Chinese, Japanese, and Filipinos are not assimilated so rapidly as Scandinavians and Germans (Warner & Srole, 1945). There are also certain religious groups that live apart from the mainstream of American culture and that perpetuate strong subcultural differences. These groups maintain themselves as ethnic or religious islands and socialize their children in ways quite different from the socialization of the majority group. Only a few of these subcultures have been studied intensively. One of them, a separatist sect known as the Amish, illustrates some of the ways in which a subcultural group, maintaining its own identity and resisting encroachment of mores and values prevalent in the larger cultural group, passes on its own way of life to its children (Kollmorgen, 1942).

Amish children are brought up to believe that all behavior must be based on the "Bible standard." Worldly ostentation is frowned upon; Amish boys wear broadfall trousers with plain, homemade suspenders. Jackets have no lapels, no outside pockets, no buttons. Broad, flat, black felt hats are worn in winter and broad, flat straw hats in summer. Girls wear long dresses of solid color with full skirts and long sleeves. Hair must be parted in the center and curls and fancy hairdos are forbidden.

Children have no contact with the world outside the Amish community except for occasional shopping trips to town with their parents. The radio and motion pictures are frowned upon, and social contacts are permitted only with other Amish children. Relaxation comes in the form of Sunday church meetings, visiting between families, and Sunday evening "sings."

The Amish disapprove of consolidated schools because they do not want their children to mix with "outsiders"; Amish children therefore go to one-room schools scattered about the countryside. In these schools, they learn to read both English and German. They speak a German Rhenish dialect at home. An eighth-grade education is thought sufficient, for once an individual has learned to read the Bible, no further education is considered necessary.

Successful agriculture is one of the major Amish objectives, and children are inducted into the workaday world very early in life. Work activities are sharply differentiated for men and women, and boys and girls learn what are sex-appropriate activities at an early age.

Amish families are patriarchal; all decisions are made by the husband and father. The authority of the father is absolute. Fear of social ostracism and threats of eternal damnation keep children in line.

The details of socialization within the Amish family are difficult to get at, for these people disapprove of outsiders seeking information. It is possible, however, to see how, in this kind of setting, a different way of life can be perpetuated. Children have no opportunity to learn competing customs, and they are taught to be *proud* of being different, since the Bible approves of it. They are also prepared to be ridiculed by outsiders; since they have no doubt that they are right and outsiders wrong, the ridicule does not affect them. Furthermore, rewards for practicing the group culture are very great; the community aids an individual in trouble, and Amish farmers are prosperous, with incomes upwards of $4000 a year in 1942. Punishment in the form of "shunning" is severe, and future punishment in Hell seems very real.

Here, then, we have an illustration of how a group of people, by setting themselves off from the mainstream of American culture, can perpetuate their different values and customs in the socialization process. While a "typical" American child may be learning conformity, materialism, and a belief in education, an Amish child will be learning to reject those values and to accept others.

ADOPTIVE CHILDREN

The child in modern American society holds a unique position. More so than children of any earlier era, he is valued for himself. Whereas children were once considered highly desirable as future contributors to the family economy, the child today, although he is an economic liability, is regarded as a precious commodity. Most married couples want children. When they cannot have a child, they may initiate steps to adopt one. The increasing number of requests received by agencies for adoptive children is a reflection of the intrinsic value that our society places upon the child.

Social-welfare agencies have developed elaborate procedures to ensure the placement of the right child in the right home. These include some type of developmental examination of the child and an evaluation of his future home. Since most children are adopted early in life, the question of how well infant examinations predict future development is an important one to consider. The infant-examination procedure is based upon observation of the infant's responses to a series of standard situations. Like individual tests of intelligence (see Chap. 15), these examinations vary in content with the age of the child. They have been considered particularly valuable for assessing the developmental status of babies between twelve and forty weeks old. Motor, linguistic, personal-social, and adaptive aspects of infant development are evaluated, and the infant's developmental status is determined in comparison with norms established on many infants. Then the infant is classified as superior, high average, average, low average, dull, or even borderline and moron. Children who perform well on the tests are recommended for adoption; others are classified as "not adoptable," although they may be retested at a later time.

Recent research, however, has failed to uncover evidence that the infant examination has a useful predictive validity. Wittenborn (1956) did a follow-up study of several adoptive children, one group of five- and six-year-olds and a second group of eight- and nine-year-olds, all of whom had been tested in infancy on the Yale Developmental Examination of Infant Behavior. Some of the children had been confidently classified as adoptable on the basis of the infant examination; some had either not been examined at the optimal age (and in fact had been adopted before the infant examination) or had not been confidently classified as a result of their first examination.

Because of the age of the children at the time of the follow-up, it was possible to obtain a great deal of information regarding their intellectual, motor, personal-social, and other aspects of development. A comparison of scores made by the children at the time of the study and their earlier classification on the infant examination failed to reveal statistically significant correlations. The only exception occurred in a subsample of children who had apparently had the benefit of selective placement on the basis of their infant examination; the later evaluation of these children, who had been placed in superior homes, was in keeping with the early evaluation. The study "offers no encouragement to those who would depend upon an *infant* examination as a basis for anticipating the subsequent development of adoptive children" (p. 114). It also "strongly suggests that many aspects of the development of children, particularly those we might call personal or social, emerge at least in part as a result of differences in the child's environment, particularly those differences which have to do with the values of the home and its child-rearing practices" (p. 114).

From this review of some of the factors in the family that affect the socialization of the child, it is readily apparent that bringing up children in American society is a complex matter.

Fortunately, it is an experience that is more often rewarding than not; the satisfactions that accompany parenthood are greater by far than the dissatisfactions (Jersild *et al.*, 1949). Nevertheless, parents face many problems for which they cannot find answers. More information about child rearing is needed. Perhaps, as Jersild has suggested, we need a more realistic approach to child rearing which takes into account the practical details of everyday living.

SUGGESTED READINGS

BERNERT, ELEANOR H. *America's Children,* Census Monograph Series, Wiley, 1958. Every ten years the Bureau of the Census collects a tremendous mass of data on the American people. This volume presents important information about the children of America and their families, based upon 1950 census figures.

MARTIN, WILLIAM E., & STENDLER, CELIA BURNS (eds.). *Readings in Child Development,* Harcourt, Brace, 1954, Part 4, "Socializing Agents." The papers by Orlansky, Baldwin, Merrill, Harris *et al.,* Bach, Maccoby *et al.,* and Goldfarb are especially relevant to the problems discussed in this chapter.

MILLER, D. R., & SWANSON, G. E. *The Changing American Parent,* Wiley, 1958. Based on research by the authors, this book provides new and much-needed insights into the values and practices of the modern American parent.

SEARS, R. R., MACCOBY, ELEANOR E., & LEVIN, H. *Patterns of Child Rearing,* Evanston, Ill.: Row, Peterson, 1957. This volume reports on how 379 mothers in the Boston area actually brought up their children from birth to kindergarten age. Chapters 1-4 and 9-13 are particularly pertinent to this chapter.

WITTENBORN, J. R. A study of adoptive children. *Psychol. Monogr.,* 1956, *70,* 1-115. An investigation of the development of children living in adoptive homes by Wittenborn and his collaborators at the Yale Clinic of Child Development.

11
the child
in school

For most of the children in our society, a new and important socializing agency is introduced into their lives at five or six years of age. This agency is the school. That school entrance does have an impact upon the socialization process was reported by mothers of first-grade children interviewed two months after their children had begun school (Stendler & Young, 1950). Of 212 mothers who were asked whether or not their children had changed with school entrance, 170 answered in the affirmative, and 78 per cent of these reported improvement in child behavior. Particularly, they thought their children had improved with respect to such traits as responsibility, helpfulness, good humor, and independence.

These changes may be due to a change in the child's self-concept; there is a cultural importance attached to first-grade entrance which is communicated to the child and which may make him see himself differently. From the way in which adults discuss school entrance ("So you're going to *first grade* in the fall!"), from remarks of adults and other children concerning future school activities, even from his new haircut and new clothes for the event, the young child gets a feeling of participating in a great and important adventure in which older children, whom he recognizes as having age status, are already participating. Furthermore, it is an adventure in which all six-year-olds share; our culture says that at six one leaves home and goes to formal school. It may bring with it feelings of increased self-importance, self-esteem, and ego-identity. Indeed, it might be likened to the initiation ceremonies at puberty in some primitive tribes. Entrance to junior high or high school may have similar effects.

Eighty-one per cent of the mothers interviewed in the Stendler-Young study said that their children gave indications of increased feelings of self-importance. Their answers included such comments as: "He acts inflated now. Comes home and says, 'Boy, we sure had some hard work today!' "; "Considers kindergarten children quite babyish. He acts big at home and is proud of his reading. He never showed pride before"; "She thinks going to first grade and learning her letters is the best thing that has ever happened to her"; "Feels she isn't playing any more. Feels important because she brings home so many papers."

The child's need for stimulation and the satisfaction of this need by entrance to school may also account for changes in the child's behavior. School is stimulating; it provides a host of new experiences which may come as a welcome relief to a home situation which has ceased to be challenging to the growing intelligence of the child. And, of course, there is always the possibility that the child is not really improved; he may only seem improved to the mother because he is away for a larger part of the day and there are fewer opportunities for behavior difficulties to occur.

Like the family, the school seeks to induct children into culturally accepted ways of thinking and behaving. Just as the parent is the socializing agent in the family, so the teacher acts as socializing agent in the school. In the process of socializing, he rewards and punishes certain kinds of behavior, he acts as a model for children to imitate, and he selects experiences or materials for children which emphasize certain values and play down others. These methods of socializing we shall now examine.

HOW THE TEACHER SOCIALIZES

Rewards and punishments are continually used in the classroom to make some ways of behaving pleasurable and other ways painful. Rewards, of course, are not limited to gold stars, good marks, or prizes; nor are punishments limited to staying after school, being excluded from the group, or writing "I won't fight" two hundred times. Both punishment and reward can be defined as something the teacher does or gives to a pupil in response to a particular pupil behavior; reward, however, is something that gives the pupil pleasure. Punishment is whatever brings him discomfort or pain. Thus a nod of approval, a reassuring smile, and a frown are subtle ways in which the teacher rewards or punishes a particular act.

Consider Miss A, a third-grade teacher.

Miss A's class is writing letters to Tony, who is ill at home. Miss A walks up and down the aisles, supervising the children's work. She stops at Pete's desk and picks up his paper.

"Boys and girls," she says to get the attention of the group. "May I have your attention? That means you too, Matilda.

"This is Pete's paper. I want you to notice how carefully Pete has followed my directions. See? He has left margins at both sides and has written the heading exactly right. See how neat and clean his paper is, too?"

Miss A returns Pete's paper with a beam of approval and goes on. She stops at Raymond's desk. Raymond does not fare so well.

"Boys and girls." Again the heads go up.

"Look at Raymond's paper. Raymond needs some help. See the smudges and spots on his paper? What can we tell Raymond to help him improve?"

"He should wash his hands before he starts and not erase," say the children.

The teacher returns the paper to Raymond with a look of disapproval.

"It will have to be done over, Raymond, and that's wasting paper, you know."

Some of the children finish their letters and must wait for the others to finish. Several sit and do nothing. Miss A comments to the class.

"I like the way some people are finding jobs to do when they finish. I saw two children studying spelling and one boy doing his workbook. That's using time wisely, isn't it, boys and girls? You'll have five more minutes to finish and I expect all of you to be done, if you haven't been dawdling."

Making Behavior Pleasurable or Painful

Miss A did not distribute gold stars as rewards or spankings as punishments. Yet she made certain ways of behaving pleasurable to the children and other ways painful by her approval and disapproval of their actions. In the short space of five minutes, she indicated her liking for children who obeyed her requests for attention, followed her directions, did neat, clean work, kept obviously busy, did not waste supplies, and finished work on time. The children in Miss A's class did not learn obedience, respect for authority, neatness and cleanliness, avoidance of waste, and the importance of time in this one lesson, but when day after day, school year after school year, teacher after teacher, the same kinds of action are rewarded and punished, these responses become reinforced in the child.

If behavior is to be effectively modified, rewards must be used more often than punishments. This implies that teachers must work *with* pupils rather than against them. Evidence of the importance of working positively with children can be found in studies of the relationship of teachers' classroom personalities to pupils' behavior. Anderson and Brewer (1946) studied sixty-four third-grade children in two classrooms, observing the behavior of both teachers and pupils in the fall and again in the winter. Three types of dominative and three types of integrative behavior on the part of the teachers were identified.

1. Domination with evidence of conflict.
2. Domination with no evidence of conflict.
3. Domination with evidence of working together.

1. Integration with evidence of conflict.
2. Integration with no evidence of working together.
3. Integration with evidence of working together.

In the fall, it was found that both teachers worked against the children more frequently than they worked with them, and that both rooms were low in the number of instances of child behavior which the writers assumed to be representative of good mental hygiene—i.e., spontaneity and initiative, problem-solving behavior, social contributions by the child, and lack of domination of other children. Both teachers were again low in the winter in their group contacts, but in contacts with individual children, it was found that one of the teachers had a decided advantage. More integrative contacts and fewer dominative contacts on his part produced, in the individual children, behavior which had a higher mental-hygiene rating. In other words, the more the teacher worked with a child in an integrative way, the higher the child's scores in spontaneity and initiative tended to be. When the teacher used domination in conflict, nonconforming behavior was the result.

The Teacher as a Model

Teachers also help to socialize by serving as models for children. Sometimes children pick up rather superficial mannerisms as they imitate the teacher. For example, they may adopt certain of the teacher's favorite words or phrases. More important, however, is the fact that children tend to copy some of the teacher's attitudes. When a teacher rejects a pupil overtly, the other pupils may follow his example. When a teacher indicates his disgust for pupils who are dirty, the rest of the class may do likewise. And when a teacher accepts ethnic and religious differences among pupils and indicates his acceptance by his actions, children may learn similar attitudes toward differences.

In connection with the question of the influence of the teacher, we need to consider the impact of the teacher's own adjustment upon pupils. Do maladjusted teachers cause maladjustment in their pupils? If a teacher's personal adjustment is poor, will his pupils also show signs of poor adjustment? Gladstone's (1948) analysis of available data indicates that this does not necessarily follow. Both the adjusted teacher and the maladjusted teacher, as rated by pencil-and-paper tests, can harm the mental health of pupils. More important than general adjustment is the teacher's knowledge of children and acceptance of them. Some maladjusted teachers may be particularly effective with certain maladjusted pupils because their own experience gives them insight into the pupils' difficulties and makes it easier for them to accept these difficulties. A maladjusted teacher may be especially sensitive to the needs of very dependent children, for example, and more successful in helping them than a better adjusted teacher, who might reject them. However, maladjustment needs to be defined more clearly and on some basis other than pencil-and-paper tests before firm conclusions can be drawn. Degree and kind of maladjustment also need to be considered; a person who has lost touch with reality or whose contacts with others are suspicious and hostile might conceivably be more capable of harming children's mental adjustment than a person whose maladjustment takes another form.

Selection of Experiences and Materials

The experiences and the materials that teachers make available for children also influence the socialization process. Children must read what the school requires, and such reading becomes a source of guidance for role behavior. A boy or girl can find out from books what behavior is appropriate for his or her age and sex, for heroes and heroines in our culture, for a particular occupation or a particular social class. This is not to say that *choice* of role is influenced by reading. It is extremely doubtful that small fry want to be cowboys because they read cowboy books. However, children *can* find in cowboy books samples of the kind of behavior the authors think appropriate for cowboys, and the behavior pictured there can become a model for the would-be cowboy to imitate.

1. Observe a teacher at work with his class. Record everything he says or does in a half-hour period. Do you find any instances in which he acts as a socializing agent?

CONDITIONS FOR EFFECTIVE SOCIALIZATION BY THE SCHOOL

Whether the teacher's approval or disapproval actually operates to reward or punish the child, whether the model of behavior he sets will be imitated, whether the experiences he provides will effectively modify behavior depend upon several factors. One of these is the extent to which the relationship between teacher and pupil is one of mutual acceptance and respect. As we have frequently pointed out, in order for the child to learn from the socializing agent, he must be getting something from that agent; the learning situation must be rewarding for him. The acceptance that children need in order to learn is sometimes denied them, however. Some teachers find it hard to accept pupils whose cultural background is markedly different from their own. Factors in the emotional make-up of other teachers may influence their readiness to accept certain children.

When significant differences exist between the value systems of teacher and pupils, the school can expect difficulties as a socializing agent. Erikson reports on the ideological chasm existing between white teachers and Indian children in government schools, and the resulting difficulties:

"They are without initiative," the exasperated white teachers would say; and indeed the wish of an Indian boy to excel and to compete, while fully developed under certain circumstances, may disappear completely under others. The members of a running team, for example, may hesitate at the start of a race. "Why should we run?" they say. "It is already certain who is going to win." In the back of their minds there may be the reflection that he who wins will not have too good a time afterwards. For the story of the little Boy-Whose-Father-Has-Money has its parallels in the fate of all those Indian boys and girls who show signs of actually accepting the demands of their educators and of finding delight and satisfaction in excelling in school activities. They are drawn back to the average level by the intangible ridicule of the other children [1950, p. 114].

If teachers are culture-bound to the extent that they find the ways of other cultures irritating and exasperating, they will be unable to give children who are different the acceptance and respect they need for effective socialization.

2. If possible, observe children at play in a lower-class neighborhood. What kinds of behavior do you find that might be difficult for American teachers to accept?

Conflicts in values are not confined to different ethnic groups; they can be found between social classes as well. As a member of the middle class, the teacher may try to inculcate a way of life which differs in important respects from the way of life of lower-class children. Middle-class teachers may try to teach the virtues of thrift, nonaggression, care of property, respect for authority, cleanliness, and getting ahead to children who come from families with quite different values. They may teach their pupils that "nice" people don't swear, whereas the child from the slums may count among his friends and relatives many with a rich and pungent vocabulary. They may punish children for fighting who are taught at home to stick up for their rights. In *Father of the Man,* Davis and Havighurst (1947) illustrate the conflict in values between two children from the same family:

Mary, who is praised by her middle-class teacher for being quiet and anxious to please, is criticized by most of her family for the same behavior. Her softness and compliancy are regarded by Hazel and all her sisters as traits of a schemer and of

an "apple polisher." Most of her family believe that she is de-
signing [p. 14].

> Paulette's aggression, on the other hand, seems to her mother
> and Hazel to prove her honesty. . . . In her slum community,
> where a curse and a blow—and a readiness to "tell people off"
> and let them "like it or lump it"—are highly admired, Paulette
> is popular [p. 15].

Mary, it is safe to predict, will get along well in school;
that is, her behavior is such that she can be accepted by her
middle-class teacher. This acceptance may be so rewarding for
Mary that she will be motivated to please the teacher and learn
other things the school has to teach.

Paulette, on the other hand, is not in so favored a position
as far as the school is concerned. The very things that make her
accepted at home will be a cause of trouble in school. Her
middle-class teacher may reject her for her language, her fighting, and her disrespect for authority. Paulette will not find the
school situation a rewarding one; she may outwardly conform,
but chances are that she will not change her ways and that her
socialization will continue to be influenced mainly by the home.

3. *Should* the school attempt to change Paulette? If so, what
should be changed?

4. Suppose that Mary comes to accept more and more of the
middle-class ways the school teaches. What difficulties will she
face outside the school? How are such difficulties to be resolved?

5. Is Mary or Paulette the better adjusted? Explain your
answer.

Sometimes, however, a teacher finds it difficult to accept a
child for reasons that lie within the personality of the teacher
himself. Consider the case of Lawrence:

> Lawrence is a large, overweight boy in the first grade. He
> stands out, not only because of his size, but also because of his
> actions. During an observation lasting one hour, Lawrence
> stuck a pin into the boy in front of him and pretended he knew
> nothing when the boy squealed with pain; he "accidentally"
> knocked against a neighbor's crayons as he swaggered down the

aisle, and then proceeded to step on them when they fell to the floor; he used Bobbie's miniature projector against Bobbie's better judgment and held on to it for ten minutes, although four boys were lined up waiting for it; he snatched a film from one of the boys and kept it until the boy appealed to the teacher; he crowned his accomplishments by spilling a jar of paint on the floor.

At this point the group turned on Lawrence and poured out their wrath to the teacher. Terribly angry, the teacher told Lawrence that he couldn't be trusted, that he was a "mean person," that nobody liked a mean person, and that he'd have to work in a corner by himself until he learned to get along with other children. Lawrence stared straight into the teacher's face; unashamed and apparently unmoved by his tirade, he insolently and noisily moved his seat into the corner and sat facing his peers with a look of defiance, indeed, almost triumph on his face.

This anecdote illustrates the behavior of a child who gets satisfaction in perverse ways. Lawrence enjoyed the effects of his misbehavior because it was his way of triumphing over the teacher who wished to control him. The teacher had yet to learn that calling Lawrence names, excluding him from the group, and becoming angry with him did not constitute punishment for Lawrence in the usual sense of the word.

The teacher is not responsible for Lawrence's characteristic way of dealing with adults in control. But he cannot influence the child's behavior at present because he rejects him. Admittedly, it may be difficult to like and accept *all* children. Each of us in growing up has acquired an attitudinal structure which makes us react positively or negatively, to a greater or lesser degree, to the behavior of others. Some teachers respond negatively and some positively to the clinging, overdependent child; some teachers accept and others reject the overbearing, bullying, aggressive child; some teachers find it easy and some difficult to like the shy, timorous pupil. Blos (1941) has pointed out that teaching very young children and teaching adolescents may make the greatest demands on the maturity of the teacher, since in these age groups emotional stability as adults define it is lacking or is easily upset. As teachers grow in self-awareness, as they become sensitive to the kinds of child behavior to which they react emotionally, they may also grow in ability to deal with all kinds of behavior objectively and to accept all their pupils.

    6. Observe a classroom in action. Are there certain pupil behaviors that you would find it difficult to tolerate if you were a teacher?

    7. Compare your list with those of your classmates. What explanations can you give for any similarities and differences that you find?

WHAT VALUES DOES THE SCHOOL TEACH?

Thus far we have been considering how the teacher socializes and what the conditions are for effective socialization. We also need to consider the goals the teacher has in mind as he socializes and the direction in which he is trying to influence the behavior of his pupils. We can get some indication of the kind of product the school wants by examining the values the school attempts to teach.

Teachers as Middle-class Members

Although we do not have empirical data on this point, sociologists who have observed school practices report that the schools encourage what they call middle-class values—responsibility, honesty, respect for authority and property, and conformity—and frown upon aggression and sex-suggestive behavior. Some support for this position is found in the study of character and personality development by Havighurst and Taba (1949). These investigators first defined character as a composite of five moral traits: honesty, responsibility, loyalty, moral courage, and friendliness. Then they proceeded to study a high school population in a Midwestern community in relation to such problems as the influence upon character development of the value systems of social groups (family, church, school, friends, community) and the influence upon character development of certain emotional and intellectual factors in the individual. Their findings show that the school tends to perpetuate middle-class values, particularly responsibility and honesty. They found that students accepted familiar stereotypes without question. With regard to responsibility, students believed that school rules must always be obeyed, regardless of what they are; that one should do dull jobs, if the school needs them done, in order to be a good citizen; that coming to school on time, finishing jobs, and helping one's family financially are adequate ways of defining responsibility. Confused and uncertain beliefs were found in regard to loyalty, moral courage, and friendliness, and the school was found to be even less effective in instilling these three traits. With regard to loyalty, most students saw their first duty as to their own success; it was not considered wise, generally, to sacrifice this value to any demands that might be made for the general school welfare. When faced with the problem of defending a position in opposition to their peers, few students were willing to take a stand that might jeopardize their popularity, regardless of their professed beliefs as to moral courage. Friendliness was rather narrowly defined as being nice to people. All in all, the reader gets a picture of a rigid but superficial code of conduct to which students think they should conform.

Havighurst and Taba make many recommendations. Two in particular are worth noting here: (*1*) that pupils should learn "to make distinctions between the lesser mores of eating, drinking, amusement, clothing, and marriage customs, which differ from one social group to another, and the more basic moral qualities, such as honesty, loyalty, kindliness, and courage, which are very nearly universal"; and (*2*) that the school should train children systematically to study moral problems so that they learn to generalize intelligently and build up a code of values which protects them against moral provincialism (p. 201).

Values in Traditional and Modern Schools

The Havighurst-Taba investigation is the most thorough study focusing directly on the school's part in teaching values. Other studies also provide information on the school as a socializing agency; although somewhat indirectly. One of these, a study of what young children expect from their teachers, gives us insight into how the child perceives the teacher and what kinds of behavior the pupil thinks have teacher approval. Biber and Lewis (1949) presented thirteen pictures to first- and second-graders in two schools. Included among the pictures were the following, with the investigator's remarks to the children:

> *The Good Girl:* "Here is a teacher in school, and here is a little girl in school. The teacher is telling her she's been a good little girl. See how she's smiling, and how happy she looks? Now you guess what she did that was good."
>
> *The Praise Card:* "Here's a little boy getting a praise card, isn't he? What do you think he did to get the praise card?"
>
> *The Gold Star:* "Here are some children getting ready to go home. See, they have their hats and coats on. And the teacher is giving them some gold stars—see [pointing]? But this little girl is crying. She didn't get one. Why didn't she get one?"
>
> *Boy in the Corner:* "Here's a little boy who has to go and sit off in the corner because he did something bad. What do you think he did?"

The children's responses to the pictures reveal the kinds of behavior that children think teachers approve or disapprove. Notable differences appeared between the traditional school (North School) and the more modern school (South School). Compliant, obedient behavior was mentioned more often by pupils in the traditional school, while children in the progressive school attached more importance to social relations in the classroom. Some quotations from the study give specific illustrations:

> The South School children see the little girl's goodness in terms of behaving, doing good school work, and helping the teacher. . . .

By and large, at the North School, it appears that the little girl is good when she behaves, keeps quiet, and does her lessons. . . .

The little boy (North School) is given a praise card because he is good, does what the teacher says, sits still and folds his hands, and, less importantly, because he does good work, keeps quiet, and plays nicely with other children. . . .

The little girl (North School) fails to get a gold star because she is bad, and she is bad because, chiefly, she doesn't do what the teacher says; she talks and she sometimes hits (and possibly makes faces). . . .

There are some notable differences between the Bad Boy at the North School and the Bad Boy at the South School. If we try to boil down to very brief terms what the boy at the North School did, we can say that he fought and disobeyed. On the contrary, at the South School he fights and *disturbs,* and does something wrong in relation to his school work. Disobedience in terms of not doing what the teacher says, or talking, is much *less* important. Social relations in terms of getting along with others without grabbing, bothering, and disturbing are much *more* important [pp. 33-46].

Thus it appears from the Biber-Lewis study that schools may differ in what they consider good and bad behavior, if the children's perceptions are correct. It also appears that traditional schools may be overemphasizing quiet, compliant behavior at the expense of emphasizing behavior based upon independent, responsible decisions. Children learn to conform for conformity's sake instead of learning to make decisions regarding their own actions in the light of fundamental moral principles and to take responsibility for their decisions.

Values in Textbooks

A third study (Child, Potter, & Levine, 1946) also reveals some shortcomings in the teaching of values in the schools. The investigators classified the contents of third-grade readers according to a set of motivational categories. They found that behavior involving the seeking of information, help, or friendship was rewarded in the majority of the stories, but that behavior involving attempts to avoid blame or to act aggressively or independently was punished. The cumulative effect upon the pupil is to convey the notion that it is safe to be compliant; that when a child disobeys adults, disaster always results.

The authors also point out that the stories are characterized by unrealistic optimism. Good behavior in the stories is always rewarded, and children are rarely pictured as having to adjust to failure. "Yet from the point of view of contribution to the solutions of problems of everyday life, failures ought to receive a larger proportion of attention, for it is they that pose problems" (p. 45).

Although these studies reveal deficiencies in the values that the schools are teaching, it should be pointed out that the source of the difficulty may lie partly in our culture. If confusions, inadequacies, and inconsistencies are present in the culture, they will be reflected in various cultural settings, including the school. Success, for example, is valued in our society; so is concern for the rights of others. Sometimes one can be achieved only at the expense of the other. Respect for property is a value; so is respect for the dignity of man. Sometimes these are not compatible. The school may be an agent of change in society in certain limited ways, but in the last analysis it cannot be much more moral than the society of which it is a part.

> **8.** From your observations of children in school, make a list of classroom and playground situations that could be utilized for the teaching of values. Analyze each situation in terms of the values that can be taught.

GROUP CLIMATE AND SOCIALIZATION

Democratic, Laissez-faire, and Authoritarian Climates

Studies of groups working together have revealed that the climate or general feeling tone of a classroom may influence the behavior of pupils. The conditions which help to establish a group climate have been analyzed by a number of writers.

Early experimental work in this area showed that the kind of leadership the teacher exercises may be an important factor in determining group climate (Lewin, Lippitt, & White, 1939). In the experiments a boys' club of five members was exposed successively to a democratic-type leader, a laissez-faire leader, and an authoritarian-type leader. The interactions of members under each type of leader were carefully recorded. Results indicated that group morale was highest under democratic leadership, even in the absence of the leader. Under democratic leadership, the group, held together by common goals, continued to work while its leader was gone. The amount of social interaction in the group also differed according to the type of leadership. Autocratic leadership had the effect of inhibiting free and easy sociability among the boys. The number of child-to-child conversations was almost twice as great in the democratic atmosphere as in the autocratic.

Although these studies are thought-provoking, they do not support sweeping generalizations regarding leadership and group climate. A boys' club does not duplicate a classroom group. What is true in a clubroom might not apply in a classroom. The school in a sense has a culture of its own. There are certain kinds of behavior that are appropriate in school and expected of pupils; the actions of children are modified as they perceive these expectations. Thus a child soon learns that crying on the playground is not an appropriate school behavior; that the child who cries can expect to be laughed at by his peers. Even in democratic classrooms, pupils may not behave themselves when the teacher is out of the room simply because misbehavior is expected and is therefore appropriate in these circumstances.

9. Are there situations in which autocratic leadership is more desirable than democratic leadership? What might these be?

Other studies carried out in actual classroom situations have extended our knowledge of how the role of the teacher sets the stage for group behavior. In one study (Cunningham *et al.,* 1951), five patterns of interaction were identified, as were group reactions to the particular patterns:

1. Where teachers give the orders and children are expected to obey without question, two divergent types of reaction may occur: docile obedience and open hostility. Pupil reaction, in the opinion of the writers, depends upon the experience or expectation of the group. Compliance to teacher rule is most likely to be manifested by children of middle-class communities, while hostility to such a pattern is demonstrated by children in lower- or upper-class groups. This finding is to be expected when we realize that the middle-class parent supports the school and insists that the child conform to school regulations, right or wrong, whereas the lower-class parent is more likely to be openly critical.

2. Where there is no attempt by the teacher to control or organize the group, confusion and insecurity result. As many mental hygienists have emphasized, children need limits and are bewildered when adults do not provide them. There were teachers in the study who suddenly substituted a planless, catch-as-catch-can pattern for adult-rule—child-obedience under the mistaken notion that they were being democratic. In these situations there was keen competition for control of the group, among individual pupils and between pupils and teachers.

3. Where teacher-pupil planning is on an individual basis—i.e., where each pupil plans a course of action with the teacher—some degree of individual initiative results but no favorable group interaction.

4. Where there is adult-directed group planning—i.e., where the children are permitted to plan but within an area designated by the teacher—constructive group reaction results in some instances. This method is particularly successful when the teacher has sufficient insight to determine progressive degrees of difficulty in planning. In situations in which the planning opportunities provided for pupils are neither too hard nor too easy, the result will be maximum cooperation among group members.

5. Where there is group self-management through group planning, where the group has unlimited opportunities for developing and achieving goals, maximum group learning and growth result. However, this pattern of control is not always suitable for immature children or children who are lacking in group skills. Such children need practice in self-management in limited areas, and other patterns of control must be used instead.

The most effective teachers, in the eyes of the observers, were those who used the widest range of patterns, suiting the pattern to the situation. An emergency situation may demand the autocratic pattern 1; the permissive pattern 2 may be helpful at times; and the individualized pattern 3 may be necessary for teachers and pupils who are unskilled in group processes. *It is only when one of these patterns is used consistently that we can predict a nonconstructive group reaction.* The patterns described above, however, must be regarded as hypotheses at present; we lack sufficient evidence to prove their existence.

The reader must not interpret the emphasis upon group planning as a blanket endorsement of this method for achieving all the goals of education. When there is a group task to be done, such as planning a class outing, group planning is indicated. But certain goals can best be achieved *only* if the teacher plans with individual pupils, or if two or three children work together. In his concern for the group, the teacher must not overlook the importance of individual spontaneity and creativity.

> **10.** Teacher A has inherited a sixth-grade class accustomed to a very autocratic teacher. He wishes to move in the direction of more group planning of goals. What principles should he follow? What pitfalls must he avoid?

Competitive and Cooperative Climates

The competition-cooperation factor has also been studied to determine its possible influence upon group interaction. This factor is defined in terms of the accessibility of the goal to members of the group. The problem might be posed briefly as follows: What is the effect upon group atmosphere when conditions are such that in a given group all (or none) can receive a prize (reach the goal) upon completion of a task in a satisfactory manner? How does this compare with group atmosphere when conditions are such that only one (or no) person in a group can receive a prize?

A study of children working under cooperative and competitive conditions throws some light on the problem (Stendler, Damrin, & Haines, 1951). Second-grade children were asked to paint a mural cooperatively; if the mural met certain standards, each of the children would be awarded a prize. It was made clear that all or none of the participants would receive a prize. A competitive situation was then set up by asking the group to paint a second mural, with the stipulation that only the child who painted the very best part of the picture would be given a prize. Observations were made during the painting sessions, during the evaluative sessions, and during the free-play periods which followed, when the children played with blocks or with miniature housekeeping equipment. Results showed that when the children worked for an individual prize, there was less positive behavior and more negative behavior than when the same children worked for a group prize. Under cooperative conditions (in which all or none of the children could reach the goal), the children made more friendly remarks, shared materials, and helped one another more often than under competitive conditions. However, it was also noted that merely setting up a cooperative situation does not guarantee that all children will work constructively together all the time. Some children competed even in the cooperative situation. There were children who worked to have the group win but who also wanted to be best in the group. The reverse was also true: there were children who cooperated in the competitive situation. Children whose level of aspiration with regard to painting was low might help a friend by cornering the market on a particular color of paint for him. The writers concluded that whether children compete or cooperate depends only partly on the structure of the group situation. Children bring competitive attitudes with them to school as part of the cultural conditioning that they have received from their parents. Schools that discourage situations in which rewards are limited to a very few may not be able to eliminate competitive attitudes, but they can expect more positive interaction in a group than if they emphasized competition.

Competition between groups does not appear to be more desirable than competition within a group. A report of an exploratory study of group relations (Sherif, 1951) throws light on this aspect of competition and group atmosphere. An attempt was made to test the following hypotheses:

1. When individuals having no established relationships are brought together in a group situation to interact in group activities with common goals, they produce a group structure with hierarchical positions and roles within it. The group structure tends in time to generate by-products or norms peculiar to the group, such as common attitudes, positive in-group identifications, nicknames, catchwords, etc.

2. If two in-groups thus formed are brought into functional relationship, positive or negative out-group attitudes and appropriate friendly or hostile actions in relation to the out-group and its members will arise, depending upon the harmony or friction between the goals of the two groups [p. 398].

In order to test these hypotheses, twenty-four boys of about twelve years of age, from a lower-middle-class income group, were brought together at a summer camp site for eighteen days. After being divided into two experimental groups to split budding friendships, the two groups worked and played separately for five days. During this time the Red Devils and the Bull Dogs, as they called themselves, formed well-defined in-group organizations, complete with secret hideouts, insignias, nicknames, songs, and the like. These symbols helped members of each group to develop strong in-group feelings of loyalty and solidarity within the group and feelings of antagonism toward the out-group. Thus some Red Devils who were friendly toward Bull Dogs were branded as traitors; preferred songs in each group included some with derogatory phrases about the other group. Competitive feelings toward the other group developed rapidly.

At the end of five days, the two groups were brought into functional relationship in competitive situations. The effect of the competitive games was to create considerable group friction. To the losing Red Devils, the Bull Dogs were "cheaters" and "dirty players." Bull Dogs eventually retaliated with such names as "dirty bums," "jerks," and "pukes." Expressions of hostility rapidly increased to the point where an intense intergroup conflict broke out, with fighting, shouting, throwing of utensils, and the like. Boys who were low in status in the group were more intense in their manifestations of intergroup hostility than were members who were higher in status.

This experimental situation has its counterpart in many school situations in which competition between classrooms or between schools is fostered as a "wholesome" outlet for competitive feelings. The experiment indicates that the consequences of such competitive situations will be a solidifying of in-group belongingness, an enhancement of in-group democracy, and a strengthening of in-group friendships, *but* at the cost of generating out-group hostility, in the manifestations of which the rudiments of prejudice can be seen. In-group democracy and cooperation do not guarantee democracy and cooperation with the out-group, if two groups are working for conflicting interests.

11. Are there some kinds of competition which are undesirable in themselves?

12. What kinds of home condition would produce highly competitive children?

Group Contagion

Other studies of group functioning are needed. One fascinating area which has only begun to be explored is that of group contagion. All teachers are familiar with this classroom phenomenon, but only recently have any attempts been made to explain why a particular act of bad behavior spreads like wildfire on one occasion, while on another occasion the same act goes unnoticed. Redl (1949) describes an incident in a summer camp when a boy hurled his tin plate across the mess hall. Immediately the room was in an uproar as tin plates flew about wildly. Yet a tin plate had been hurled previously without any group reaction.

Why the difference? According to Redl's analysis, the following conditions might determine whether a particular act of behavior will spread among a group of children:

1. The group status of the initiator. A boy who ranks high in leadership among a group of children is much more likely to be imitated than a child who is not accepted by the group.

2. Affinity of behavioral area to the group code. If what the child initiates is a kind of behavior that "counts" with the group—as any reference to eliminative processes does among young children—the teacher can expect the behavior to spread.

3. Commonality of basic expressional trend. Suppressed wildness in a group may flare up if a behavior incident occurs which appeals to a latent wildness in individuals.

4. Size, structure, and organizational pattern of the group. If there are no subgroups, contagion is more likely to occur. If a class is organized into small groups working around tables, contagion is less likely to occur than if the whole group is in a circle.

5. Group atmosphere. A disturbed child is less apt to be noticed in a democratic atmosphere, although a particular group, no matter what the atmosphere, can absorb only so many volatile or disturbed children.

The alert teacher, knowing these conditions, will plan to avoid group contagion of a destructive nature. By knowing his pupils, by intelligently planning group organization, and by paying careful attention to group and subgroup organization, he can keep to a minimum occurrences of the tin-plate-throwing variety.

13. How can a teacher tell when a group is about to blow up? What signs will he look for? What specifically can he do to avoid the outburst?

We have been discussing various aspects of the socializing role of the school, paying particular attention to the influence of the teacher and the atmosphere of the classroom. As we have indicated, the school can and does affect the socialization process. The teacher, by both what he teaches and how he teaches, influences the behavior of his pupils chiefly in the direction of middle-class mores. Thus far we have concentrated mainly on the school's influence upon socialization in terms of changes in the behavior of pupils. Socialization, however, also includes the skills and subject matter which the child must learn in order to be a member of his society. For American children it means reading, writing, and arithmetic, as well as history, geography, science, and other formal subjects. We turn our attention now to the relationship between the socialization of the individual and the learning of these subjects.

SOCIALIZATION AND
SCHOOL LEARNING

It is obvious, even to a casual observer in the classroom, that there are individual rates in learning what the school has to teach. Some children master the initial stages of reading with ease and are independent readers before they leave first grade; others are still struggling with the beginning stages as second- or third-graders. Some children will remember that $9 \times 7 = 63$ after only one exposure to the fact; others will still have difficulty after countless repetitions. Why these differences in individual learning rates?

We have already noted one source of individual differences: the constitution of the child. Some children inherit a potentiality for more intelligence than others. The average classroom includes pupils who range from below to above normal in intelligence. And, as we indicated in Chapter 4, some children mature physically faster than others; this differential rate of maturation may also apply to intellectual abilities. Boys, for example, are slower to mature physically than girls; they are also slower in learning to read. Thus it is conceivable that two children of equal intelligence will still differ in their learning achievement in school because one is faster maturing than the other. George, a fast-maturing boy, may learn to read faster than Roy, a slow-growing child, but if his intelligence is similar and if other things are equal, Roy will eventually catch up with George in reading ability.

Children's learning ability, however, is not predictable solely on the basis of their intelligence and rate of maturation. As every classroom teacher knows, there are bright, fast-maturing children who become reading problems while less bright and slower maturing children do not. Although the explanation for some of these peculiarities in development may lie in instructional method, more often it lies in the personality of the child. In the process of socialization, the child builds up certain concepts about himself which affect the way in which he learns. The child who feels good about himself, who has built up a strong ego, who looks upon himself as a worthwhile person is more likely to utilize his intelligence effectively than the child who lacks self-confidence.

One writer has hypothesized that a child's feelings about himself are directly related to parental attitudes (Ausubel, 1949). The child who is accepted and valued by his parents is willing to accept a dependent position in the family; he is motivated to learn what the parents have to teach because in return he is guaranteed security and feelings of adequacy. Such a child, when he comes to school, regards the teacher as a substitute parent. If he receives the same acceptance from the teacher as he does at home, he will readily accept his teachings. He enters into new learning situations, confident in his ability to master them eventually, and he is not emotionally disorganized by failure. The great danger with such children, as Ausubel points out, is that they will blindly accept what they are taught; the teacher needs to encourage active critical and independent habits of thinking in them.

Both rejected and overvalued children are likely to suffer in the school situation. Since they lack inner feelings of security and adequacy, they are frightened by new learning situations and tend to resist change. They are particularly reluctant to enter into situations which could end in failure, and when they do experience failure they find it difficult to take. Similarly, such children have a strong reaction to teacher criticism; the teacher's disapproval has a disruptive effect upon them. Their self-esteem is injured and their feelings of inadequacy are increased.

The overvalued child carries an additional burden. When he fails to measure up to parental expectations, he may undergo a sudden and severe devaluation both at home and at school. A doting mother who thinks that she has a genius and then discovers that she hasn't may turn against her child and substitute rejection for overvaluation. The rejected child, on the other hand, does not run such a risk. If he does not do well at school, he suffers the same rejection at school that he has already experienced at home. If, however, he happens to be a bright child, he may find school a source of ego-satisfaction, although he will always want more prestige, more attention, and more success than he has.

What we are saying is that the child learns a self-concept in early socialization, and that this early self-concept will influence his goals and level of aspiration. Since children have different self-concepts, they will learn to want different things; some children learn to want prestige and have an insatiable desire for it; some children learn to want to please everybody; some children learn to want attention even of a negative sort; some children learn to want success at any cost.

In terms of these wants, children set their sights. They set certain standards for themselves which they must reach if they are to attain ego-satisfaction. A task has to be not too difficult and not too easy, but easy enough or difficult enough so that success or failure is something of a gamble. Children whose ego-development has suffered because of early socializing experiences may set their sights very low because they are afraid of failure. These are the children who do not try very hard and who give up easily. Other children set their sights so high that they continually push themselves to achieve success. And if such children lack the ability to compete successfully, the resulting failure to reach their goal may be a severe blow to their egos.

These differences in approach to learning are illustrated in the following five-minute observations of three children at work in a first-grade classroom. The teacher has given the children an assignment to do in their workbook.

SANDRA

Sandra takes out her workbook and crayons and turns to the correct page.

She selects a crayon thoughtfully and begins to color the grass.

She finishes the grass, replaces her crayon methodically, looks the box over carefully, and chooses blue.

She colors the sky, staying nicely within the lines.

She replaces blue and chooses yellow.

One by one, she carefully colors a row of ducks.

She looks up when a neighbor interrupts and lends him the crayon he has asked for.

She glances up to the front of the room where the teacher has a reading group and then goes back to work again.

CLARA

Clara takes out her workbook and begins turning the pages.

She looks across at Ann to see what the correct page is. She turns to Bill on her other side and asks a question.

She takes out her pencil and goes to the pencil sharpener to sharpen it.

She returns to her seat and takes out her crayons.

She looks at Ann's book for guidance and finally selects the same color Ann is using.

She colors two of the ducks and looks at Bill.

She checks to see what her neighbor behind her is doing.

She is attracted by what is going on in the front of the room and listens attentively.

She looks at Ann's work and resumes her coloring of the ducks.

SHARON

Sharon takes out her workbook and crayons and turns to the correct page.

She chooses a yellow crayon and begins to color the ducks. She holds the crayon very tightly and colors in hard, determined strokes.

She goes outside the outline with one stroke and erases the slip with her eraser.

She finishes coloring the ducks, alternating between crayons and eraser whenever she makes an error.

She goes up to the teacher and presents her book for approval. The teacher motions her back to her seat with a gesture of disapproval for interrupting.

She sits down and glances around to see if anyone has observed this interaction. No one looks her way.

She puts the eraser end of the pencil in her mouth and begins to suck on it dejectedly.

These three pupils are exposed to the same teacher and the same classroom environment, but they approach this learning situation in very different ways. Sandra appears to be confident and at ease; she works well at the assigned task. Clara seems unsure of herself and uses other pupils as models for behavior. She is easily distracted and does not accomplish much. Sharon works hard and is finicky about her work, so finicky that she gets little done. She needs the teacher's approval and finds disapproval hard to take.

We cannot generalize about children's approaches to learning on the basis of one observation, but when we see the same behaviors repeated again and again, we are able to describe a number of patterns, differing according to the individual's previous socializing experiences. Sandra, Clara, and Sharon have different goals and set different sights for themselves because different things have happened to them in the process of growing up.

The school has a remedial job to do with some children. If the child's early socializing experiences have been such that he has a very low or unrealistic concept of himself, teachers can help him to build a stronger and more realistic ego. Special coaching in certain skills, careful planning of goals, work assignments geared to individuals, and provision of opportunities for need-satisfaction will help some children in their adjustment problems. For others expert help in child-guidance clinics or the like may be needed.

Classroom and Teaching Conditions That Affect the Child's Motivation

As we have pointed out, what children want for themselves affects the way in which they accomplish the tasks required by the school. But we have not as yet had systematic studies that would enable us to predict exactly how the differences among children in motivational systems are likely to affect their school behavior, or exactly what can be done to modify motivation and behavior. An interesting beginning has been made by P. Sears (1957) in a pilot study of sixth-grade children. Instead of setting up a laboratory situation under controlled conditions, she studied children in the classroom, where behaviors occur spontaneously, in an attempt to determine what classroom and teaching conditions modify the child's behavior. In particular, she was interested in conditions that maximize his talents and potentialities.

The problem of underachievers in the classroom is a very real one. Again and again, teachers report that one of their major problems is to encourage some children to work at a level commensurate with their ability. Successful techniques for accomplishing this purpose are not easy to plan.

In the Sears study, eight sixth-grade children were selected for intensive study, and their behavior in September was analyzed for apparent needs for change. The child's own perception of his need for change was included in the analysis. Then goals were set up, consisting of improved forms of behavior. For example, for one of the boys, an excellent student with an intelligence quotient of 144, the following objectives were sought:

1. Leadership skill in facilitating the ongoing activity.
2. Followership role in relation to teacher or peers.
3. Positive personal overture or response toward other pupils.
4. Careful written work.
5. Less dominance; less seeking of social status, attention, or recognition.
6. Less anxiety when social status is challenged.

During the school year, changes in the children's behavior were evaluated, using materials produced by the pupils themselves, teacher anecdotes, ratings made by the teacher or an observer covering a day's activity, and a sampling of the child's behavior by observers in the classroom.

If improved behavior does occur, what is responsible for the change? In some cases, Sears discovered, new behavior is instigated by the teacher, perhaps playing one of the following roles:

1. The *wise-adult* role, in which the teacher serves as the source of knowledge, or provides encouragement and support, or sets standards for performance, or serves as a referee.

2. The *counsellor* role, in which the teacher draws out children, lets them discover things for themselves, clarifies or interprets children's behavior when necessary.

3. The *group-member* role, which may involve "kidding" relationships, agreeing with or sharing students' enthusiasm for accomplishment and discovery.

According to the Sears study, other children also influence the motivational structure of a given pupil. Some pupils are concerned—indeed, unduly so—with the opinions of their classmates and will modify their behavior so as to improve those opinions. For example, if clowning is frowned upon by the group, a pupil may restrain his desire to clown in an attempt to avoid group disapproval. Social stimuli emanating from peers also modify behavior. Sears tells of a quiet, too serious pupil who was seated by the teacher among a lively group of sixth-graders and who finally loosened up to the point of wanting and enjoying the social interaction of the group.

The classroom is an enormously influential but enormously

complex social milieu. From such studies as the one by Sears will come more information on the significant variables affecting motivation and specific hypotheses for testing. Eventually, as knowledge becomes available, it should be possible to guide the socialization process more effectively, so as to maximize pupil potentialities.

SUGGESTED READINGS

BARKER, ROGER G., & WRIGHT, HERBERT F. *One Boy's Day: A Specimen Record of Behavior,* Harper, 1951. In an effort to learn more about the psychological habitat of the child, eight observers followed a seven-year-old and observed his behavior for one day, from the time he got up until he went to bed. The section describing Raymond in the school situation (Parts 3 and 5) might profitably be analyzed from the standpoint of socializing experiences.

DAVIS, ALLISON. *Social Class Influences upon Learning,* Harvard University Press, 1948. This short but powerful statement of how social class influences learning raises interesting and important questions regarding the motivation of lower-class children and the shortcomings of present-day curricular practices for this group.

JERSILD, ARTHUR T., *et al. Child Development and the Curriculum,* Teachers College, Columbia University, 1946. A critical analysis and interpretation of child-development materials as they relate to the curriculum.

FULLAGER, WILLIAM A., LEWIS, HAL G., & CUMBEE, CARROLL F. *Readings for Educational Psychology,* Thomas Y. Crowell, 1956. Section 3, "The Learning Situation," contains a number of papers on the school as a socializing agent.

12
the
peer group

It is clear from the discussion thus far that parents and teachers are powerful socializing agents. Moreover, they tend to reinforce each other in their influence upon the socialization of the child. That is, parents *generally* support teachers and the objectives and practices of the school, while teachers *generally* support parents and the objectives and practices of the home. This mutual reinforcement is especially evident in middle-class society. It is not surprising that the child finds it almost impossible to resist or escape the influence of this more or less united group of adults.

But the youngster also faces demands and expectations that come not from adults—his superiors—but from other children, approximately his own age—his equals. These "other children" constitute the peer group, another socializing agent and one whose influence grows stronger and stronger as the child advances in age. In this chapter, we give our attention to this peer group and the part that it plays in the socialization process.

We shall describe some of its significant characteristics, the nature of its influence in the socialization of the child, and the kind of learning it fosters. In addition, we shall consider a particular kind of peer group, the childhood or youth organization, for which adults may provide the formal leadership and objectives. But, as a preliminary to this discussion, perhaps we need to renew our acquaintance with children as they constitute a peer group. Let us therefore look first at a group of peers in action.

A PEER GROUP IN ACTION

Five seven-year-old children are gathered together in George Andrews' back yard. No one is in charge of the group. No one has issued a call for this meeting. But it is Saturday afternoon. There is no school and home responsibilities are taken care of. The children are "free."

Tommy had dropped by to see what George was doing, and the two of them had ended up by climbing a tree in front of George's house. At about that time, Mike, who lives just across the street, had joined them. For a while, the three of them had talked of going down to the Rialto, where the latest Jerry Lewis picture was showing. But no one had any money, and that plan was, of necessity, abandoned.

Next door Bernice Elston and her friend Betty, dressed up in some of Mrs. Elston's old clothes, were having a make-believe tea party on the front porch. The temptation was too much for the boys, especially when George suggested that they could slip around the house, kneel at the far side of the porch, and, with a loud whoop, scare these young matrons silly.

The plan, as carried out, worked to perfection. The girls screamed and upset their tea table. A cup in Betty's tea set was broken. After they had recovered from the shock, the girls were very properly indignant, as young matrons of society must be. But more than that, Betty cried when she saw what had happened to her cup and threatened to go and tell Bernice's mother.

The boys, having had their fun, now sought a way to avoid adult intervention. They disclaimed any intention of causing damage and tried to convince the girls it was only a joke. Then Tommy had the idea that they should play "pioneers and Indians." With the girls, they could have a pioneer family and also a band of bloodthirsty Indians to attack the white settlers.

The others suddenly forgot the incident of the interrupted tea party in their enthusiasm for this plan. The five of them moved to George's back yard, where there is room enough for their game. This is as we find them.

Casting is the first problem. Who is to be what? Betty says, "I'll be the wife of the family." But Bernice objects, "What can I be?" Betty thinks a moment and says, "You could be the baby." But Bernice will have none of that and finally decides that she will be the grandmother.

An even more difficult problem now arises: Who is to be the head of the family? Each of the boys wants to be an Indian brave. The thought of participating in an attack on this pioneer family is a heady one indeed. No one volunteers to be Betty's "husband." How does the group solve this problem? In this case, George nominates Mike for the job. Everyone endorses the nomination—except Mike. He is told by George that either he is the husband or he is nothing. Mike does not like this, but no one else supports his objections and he finally gives in. He is willing to pay the price for staying in the game. But George does suggest that Mike change places with one of the Indians on the next round of the game. Everyone agrees to this and the casting is completed.

Betty, Bernice, and Mike select a spot for their cabin and proceed very quickly to set up housekeeping. In the meantime, Tommy and George have withdrawn to make their plans for the attack. It is not long before they begin to make their way stealthily across the lawn while the "white settlers" studiously ignore their obvious presence. When a certain point is reached, the Indians suddenly rise up and, with ersatz tomahawks flying and loud war whoops, move in on the defenseless family.

The attack is too much for the settlers. While Mike puts up some resistance, he is quickly subdued by the combined efforts of George and Tommy. The mother and grandmother surrender. But the worst is yet to come. For the Indians decide to scalp their victims. Mike and the two girls had not bargained for this, and they resist. The scalping operation involves some hair pulling and the girls are soon in tears. They run home as

George and Tommy yell, "Crybabies! Crybabies!" Mike is angry too. He succeeds in holding back his tears, but he decides that he wants nothing more to do with his "friends" and follows the girls across the yard. For as long as they can see him, George and Tommy mock Mike with the words, "Mike's a sissy. Going to play with the girls. Ya! Ya! Sissy Mike."

Then they are alone. There is an awkward moment or two before Tommy decides that it is time to go home. George goes into the house and the back yard is deserted. The game is ended. The play is over.

Here is a rather typical picture of the peer group in action. It is a particular form of peer-group activity, which we call "free" or "informal" play. No one would deny the importance of such play activity. It is a normal outlet for energy and sheer "animal spirits." Children need to have their work periods interrupted from time to time with play. From this point of view, play seems to meet certain basic needs of children—such as the need for activity—and is therefore essential. But this implies a rather sharp distinction between play and work. Work accomplishes something: children learn as a result of work. But play is only a reward for good behavior or for having learned.

But we take a somewhat more serious view of play and peer-group activity in general. For us, peers, like parents and teachers, are socializing agents. But what do they do? What does a child learn from them? We can see rather clearly the functions of these other socializing agents and the content of the learning which they foster. The school has a curriculum or a course of study; the home has a training program, the details of which can be elicited from parents. We can observe parents and teachers in their respective jobs of training and teaching. They have methods and techniques. We can trace the results of their efforts in children's learning. But what part does the peer group play in the socialization of the child?

It is difficult to answer this question. In most activities involving peers, there do not seem to be programs and methods and techniques, all carefully formulated to meet stated ends. Nevertheless, careful students of peer-group activity claim that learning does take place in these situations and that that learning is a very significant part of the total socialization process. Before we examine the learning itself, let us point out some of the characteristics of the peer group as a socializing agency.

CHARACTERISTICS OF THE PEER GROUP

The Peer Group Is a Society in Embryo

Today's children, as peers, will constitute tomorrow's adults, as peers. But societies do not spring into being fully formed. The adults of tomorrow will be able to work together to achieve their common purposes as a society to the extent that they have learned in the past to work together as peers.

These potential adults, of course, can and do learn many of the needed skills and competencies in the home and in the school. But in the home they learn how to live and work with other persons with whom they enjoy a very intimate relationship. In the peer group, except in the case of close friends, we are dealing with much less intense kinds of interaction. They are less intimate and less personal; they are not nearly so crucial to the young child as are his relationships with adults. He learns to behave differently with people outside the home. There are many things that he does not say or do in the presence of people whom he knows only casually and sees infrequently. What children learn in the home, then, is not enough to prepare them for the adult society in which they will eventually take their places.

Perhaps an example will convince the reader that the child cannot learn everything that he must learn solely from the interpersonal relationships available in the home. How does a boy learn to behave like a boy? He does not inevitably act "like a boy" merely because he *is* a boy. The appropriate behavior varies with the society and even with the specific situation within the society. A father can be his son's model for the man the boy is to become, but not for the boy he is now. Father does not catch tadpoles or beg to be allowed to wear long pants or ask for a chemistry set for Christmas. The son must seek models elsewhere—in the peer group. Father sometimes helps by pushing the boy out in search of that model; he says: "You're a boy. Why don't you act like one?" (Courtney, 1949).

Wise parents, realizing that they cannot supply all the necessary learnings, see to it that early in life their children begin to have opportunities for social interaction outside the home. The nursery school has been one answer to this problem. Here a child finds himself thrust into a group of his peers with new adjustments to make and new skills to learn. But what the nursery school tries to accomplish under careful supervision is not unlike the outcomes of unsupervised play in the peer group.

The school does offer an opportunity for experience in the kinds of social skill in extrafamily group relationships which the child will eventually require as an adult. But school for most children comes relatively late in life. Six years have already passed. By that time, the typical child has learned much about getting along with his peers. He has already given more time to such learning than he will give, in the next few years, to arithmetic or reading or spelling.

There is still another reason that the school cannot accomplish this particular requirement of socialization, learning to get along with one's peers. The school has other objectives to fulfill; these objectives are primarily individualistic. The school must teach the child, *as an individual,* to look up words in a dictionary, to express himself clearly, to "think," and so on. Even when the learning of these skills and abilities takes place in a group situation, the emphasis must be on the skills and abilities rather than on the functioning of the group. The latter is only a means to an end.

No school can possibly provide group activities that, in number or variety, represent all those in which the individual normally participates as a member of society. The classroom cannot be a microcosm of society. Nor should it try to be. The school is but one of many socializing agents. As such, we cannot expect it to do the whole job.

It is the peer group that furnishes the best opportunity for the child to develop the requirements for living with his fellow men, not only now but, more importantly, in the future. Play, as one of the most important forms of peer-group activity, is an integral part of the process of socialization. It is more than relief from work. It is more than an activity designed to keep Jack from being a dull boy. It is actually necessary to make Jack a full man. In the larger view, it is not an escape or vacation from reality. It is a rehearsal for reality—the reality of the future.

It is in this sense that we must look at the example of children's play with which we began this chapter. Concerning George, for example, we ask: How does he get along with other children? But an even more important question is: What is George learning in this particular play situation that will affect his getting along as an adult with other adults? Why is he learning some skills and not others? How is he being rewarded? What is motivating his learning? We want now only to point out some important questions; we shall defer the answers for later discussion.

The Peer Group Is a Crucial Testing Ground for What Has Been Learned Elsewhere

Ultimately, the child retains those learnings which he can use profitably among his peers. A teacher may labor for an entire year to develop both arithmetic and reading ability in his pupils. He may be quite satisfied with the results of his efforts at the end of that time. But when he tests the same children after their summer vacation, he finds that although they can read as well as they did in June—if not a little better—they seem to remember few or none of the many things that they presumably had learned about number.

Reading is instrumental to peer-group activity. Arithmetic is not. Youngsters read books, talk about the books they read, exchange books, and use information and ideas gained from reading in their various activities. Number, in so far as it is associated with "arithmetic in school," is used very little.

Each child, then, uses the peer-group situation as a test of the "worth" of an idea, a skill, or an act. In this respect, he does not differ from adults, who use the same kind of situation in the same way. Traditional ways of behaving are passed on from one generation to another by this means. Children observe their parents. They then try out the same behavior on their peers. But the behavior changes as the actor changes. Bernice and Betty are copying their mothers. But it is no longer "mothers acting like mothers"; it is "daughters behaving like mothers." New touches are added. Some features are eliminated. Experimentation takes place. If traditions are not too firmly entrenched and enforced by adult authorities, then each succeeding peer group modifies and makes innovations.

The days have long passed since a boy's graduation from childhood was marked by his receiving his first pair of long trousers. This change was not promoted by parents or teachers. It was promoted by the peer group. Slowly but surely, such dress became a necessity for younger and younger boys—and for girls as well: blue jeans are now *de rigueur* for both sexes from an early age. As women dictate to each other in some mysterious way that this skirt length is stylish and that one is not, so children arrive at standards which are more rigid and inexorable than any formulated for them by adults.

A child's severest critics are his peers. They grow ever more severe and powerful with advance in age. In adolescence, the pressure for conformity to peer-group standards becomes so great that it constitutes one of the major forces in the individual's life.

Some years ago, as one of the projects of the Motion Picture Research Council, children and adolescents were asked to report some of the influences that movies had had upon them. Two examples of these reports will demonstrate the "testing" function of the peer group and also its power as critic:

One fifteen-year-old high school girl wrote this:

> I remember one movie star, Mabel Normand, who had large eyes, and from admiring them I gradually began to stare at

others with wide eyes. My friends thought there was something wrong with my eyes [Forman, 1933, pp. 144-45].

Another high school girl reported:

I simply adore Greta Garbo. She wears her clothes so sporty, and the way men fall for her! Boy! I'll bet every girl wishes she was the Greta Garbo type. I tried to imitate her walk. She walks so easy, as if she had springs on her feet. But when I try to copy her walk, I am asked if my knees are weak. How insulting some people are [Forman, 1933, p. 145]!

The Peer Group Is Also the Setting for New Learning

The peer group is not only a mirror of society as it is; it is also a reflection of a society as it is to be. If we knew enough about what was going on in the peer group now, we could make some good guesses about what the attitudes, motives, behaviors, and customs of the next adult generation would be.

We have already suggested that, in the process of trying out a behavior learned in the home or school, some modification is generally made in that behavior both by the child and by his audience of peers. This in itself constitutes innovation and invention.

But we also find mutations in this process of social inheritance. Behaviors not found anywhere else suddenly arise and are adopted in the peer group. They are originated within that peer group. Many of these new behaviors are transient and specific to the age level. Again, we can find some of our best examples among adolescents.

A few years ago (1948), *Life* magazine ran a feature article on "Teenagers" with the subtitle, "They are still changing their customs to suit themselves." Pictured were the results of a nationwide survey of teenage behavior. The pages made for some strange reading and looking. A new vocabulary had been originated and adopted, probably by youngsters whose teachers were despairing of their ever learning English. How would a parent or teacher define these words: geek, mole, pine, tweet, snook, tube, scurb? It is doubtful that any adult would know that they were synonyms, that year's "fashionable word[s] for a jerk, square, or schmo." A survey this year might find that all these terms are passé. But if any one of them is retained in the language, some future etymologist is going to understand its origin only as he delves into some of the mysterious goings-on within the peer group.

The same article reported that some football players in Seattle were wearing hair curlers at night, while "in Atlanta on Thursday the boys have nothing to do with the girls and the girls have nothing to do with the boys." In Des Moines one day a week every high school boy wore GI boots, which he referred to as "my old lady's Army shoes."

It is doubtful that these customs will be retained as part of American culture. But the fact that they appear at all is striking evidence of the learning that takes place within the peer group. Surely, the discontinuities in social history can often be explained by innovations and changes made by this group. Why are beards rarely worn by men today? One generation of adolescent boys must have not used adults as models and instead must have adopted a different model which they developed themselves. Clean-shaven men became the rule, not the exception.

As adults, we become so interested in the learning for which we are responsible in the home and in the school that we tend to neglect the transformation in children's behavior brought about by the peer group. We must try to understand the particular part that this group plays in the socialization of the child.

1. Can you recall some new kinds of behavior that appeared in your peer group in early childhood? In adolescence? Who introduced them? Why were they accepted? How long did they last?

2. Do you think that the modern school, with its emphasis upon group activity, is taking over some of the functions of the peer group? In what ways? To what extent can it do so? To what extent *should* it do so?

3. Would you recommend nursery school experience for

every child? Should it be a part of our program of public education? Explain your answer.

4. Erikson, in *Childhood and Society*, says: "I propose the theory that the child's play is the infantile form of the human ability to deal with experience by creating model situations and to master reality by experiment and planning" (1950, p. 95). Restate this theory in your own words. How does it agree with or differ from what we have said of play? How would you apply the theory to the play situation described on pages 378-80?

5. How does adult recreation differ from children's play?

6. What behaviors or attitudes have you ever taken from movies, radio programs, or your reading and tried out with your peers?

THE INFLUENCE OF THE PEER GROUP

It is one thing to say that the peer group plays an important part in the socialization of the child. It is another to explain why. In some way, we must identify what it is that the child gets from his peers. For, if he is to learn, he must get something; he must be rewarded. The peer group must help the child in some way to reduce the tension which impels him to activity. How does the peer group help a child to meet his needs, basic or acquired?

The Peer Group Provides Models

In the first place, as we have already suggested, the peer group provides models which are not available in any other place, in the home or in the school. Other socializing agents may set the goals and define in general what is expected. But it is left to the child to define those goals and expectations in terms of specific behaviors at his level of maturity.

A parent may expect his child to be successful. He may specify the area or areas in which success is to be sought. It may be school achievement or popularity among peers or consideration for others. But how does the child learn to be successful in school? The teacher can help him by providing the right cues, by guiding him in making the "right" responses, and by providing rewards at the proper moment. He sets standards or goals. But it is very difficult for him to be a model. When he works out an example for a pupil, he is a model of an adult solving the problem. But a ten-year-old child is not expected to solve a problem as an adult; he is expected to be successful only as a child. A more appropriate model is found among his peers.

Where does a child get a model for popularity? He cannot be popular in the sense that his father or his mother is. He cannot win friends and influence people by inviting his friends in for cocktails or by entertaining them at a pleasant evening of bridge. He must learn how to be popular as a child, not as an adult. He accomplishes that end by observing other children in action and by observing their reactions to him as he tries out various means and methods of becoming popular.

In the play situation we have described, each child was trying out various social techniques with the purpose, among others, of making and keeping friends. No child was completely successful. George lost, temporarily, his popularity with everyone but Tommy. Mike found himself reduced to playing with the two girls. We can assume that, in some small way, each child learned something in the situation. To the extent that having friends and participating in group activity is important to him, each child will behave a little differently the next time he is with the others. The children have learned from one another.

The Peer Group Provides Rewards

But peers are more than models and reflectors in the learning of a child. They also have the power to reward or to withhold reward. The price of group acceptance is learning the ways of the group. So long as a child is expected by adults to be accepted by his peers, he has no choice but to pay that price. Within the group, of course, he can attempt to modify expectancies. But he must be adroit in his reform. The threat of expulsion is always present.

A child joins a group and learns its ways originally because only by this means can he satisfy the expectancies of his parents. But, once in the group, he finds that he develops new needs.

He acquires new drives. What was originally a means to an end—the learning of certain behavior to gain approval of adult social agents—becomes an end itself. He learns to seek the approval of his peers. The group goals become his goals. Just as Tommy Aldrich, whom we spoke about in Chapter 8, originally took up woodworking only to please his father and then learned to like the activity for its own sake, so the child originally joins a group to meet parental expectancies and then learns to enjoy and seek out group activity as a goal in and of itself, often regardless of whether parents continue to approve.

The Peer Group Provides an Identity

The peer group also helps the child to develop a more and more mature self-concept. The young child identifies himself as being Mr. and Mrs. Jones's little boy. He is a minor member of the family. He lives in a house which belongs to his parents. They buy his food and his clothes. The money is furnished by the father.

As he becomes older and joins his peers, his identity undergoes expansion. He is now more than Mr. and Mrs. Jones's little boy. He is a six-year-old. That term, to him, not only means that he is that many years old but also refers to all the things that six-year-olds, their friends, and their associates do—things that two-year-olds and twenty-year-olds do not do. Successively, he adds to his identity by becoming a first-grader, a Cub Scout, a member of the Twelfth Street gang, a Sigma Nu, and a Mason. Adolescents recognize, value, and verbalize such group identifications.

Hollingshead, after interviewing representatives of the high school population in "Elmtown," a Midwestern community, described three peer groups:

> 1. *The elite.* The elite is composed of leaders in extracurricular student activities, as well as in church work, in the youth groups, and in social affairs. The teachers, ministers, and adult leaders rely upon them for help in the formation and promotion of organized adolescent activities. These students conceive of themselves as leaders. Students who do not belong to this

group view them as those who do things and think they are somebody.

2. *The "good kids."* In adolescent language the "good kids" are "never this or never that." They come to school, do their work, but do not distinguish themselves with glory or notoriety. Some two thirds of the students are in this category.

3. *The "grubby" gang.* "Grubbies" are set off from the other students for many reasons—unfortunate family connections, personality traits, lack of cooperation with teachers, living in the wrong part of town. Boys and girls identified as grubbies are "nobody" in the eyes of the nongrubbies. To be rated a grubby is comparable to being blacklisted. According to student beliefs, grubbies have no interest in school affairs; besides, they are troublemakers. They are not believed to be clean personally; certainly they are not well groomed. Some are alleged to be cheaters, school skippers, and sassy and uncooperative . . . [1949, p. 221].

Any adolescent attending high school in Elmtown would presumably have membership in one of these groups. He would have an identity, derived from that membership, which supersedes in importance identities of earlier years and of former groups. To maintain that identity, he would behave in accordance with the patterns approved by that group. If a grubby, he would behave like a grubby. If part of an identity as a grubby lies in not taking any interest in school affairs, then he would cultivate such a lack of interest.

Does this mean that an individual must always conform to the group mores? So long as he continues to derive his identity from that group association, he must. He can change groups if he is willing to forsake the old identity and take his chances on finding a new one. Unless he is willing to take that risk, his only recourse is to conserve the old identity by appropriate behavior in the group. (An individual, of course, derives identity also from his achievement as an individual.)

The Peer Group Provides Support

Another source of influence of the peer group over the child lies in the fact that there is strength in numbers. The individual child may get nowhere in his request for a pair of cowboy boots.

But if he says, "All the other boys on the block have them," he is in a much stronger position. Parents can withstand the importunings of one child; they may find it much more difficult to refuse the demands of many. The peer group says, in effect, to each prospective member: "Join us, do as we do, and you can speak in behalf of all of us." The dependent child manages to gain gradually more and more independence from his parents by greater and greater affiliation with his peers. This may seem like exchanging one form of dependence for another. But there is a difference; in his new group memberships, he is a peer. True, he is subject to many expectations and demands, but he complies as a sovereign, not as a subject. The peer group, then, not only meets needs of children and helps them to develop more and more mature identities; it also, through its strength in numbers, constitutes a bridge from a dependent to an interdependent status. For most children, conformity to behavior patterns in that peer group is a small price to pay for such self-enhancement.

The Peer Group May Have Adverse Effects

In stressing the influence of the peer group upon the socialization of the child, we have undoubtedly given the impression that this influence is all positive, all to the good of both child and society. We need to correct any such impression before we move on to a discussion of learning in the peer group.

REJECTION. We should first note that all groups are characterized by a measure of exclusiveness. Some individuals belong to a group; other individuals do not. Very often, we define a particular group in terms of the kind of person who is excluded, as well as the kind of person who is admitted, to membership. The peer group, and especially subgroups within the larger group, present no exception to this observation.

There are always children who find themselves excluded from the various groupings in the peer society. They may be rejected because of their race, their religion, the neighborhood in which they live, their size, their age, or certain personality characteristics. We cannot always determine the effects of such peer-group rejection. For some children, it means a stunting of psychological development. Lacking the opportunity to achieve status as a peer, they are forced to continue a dependency status in adult society. They develop an adult orientation. They accept adult expectancies. In adult society, they may appear to be very mature, even precocious. It is only when we see them among their peers that we observe their social deficiencies. They speak the language of adults, not of children; they find it difficult to communicate with other children. They do not know the games that other children play. They do not possess the skills that are highly valued in their age group. They do not know how to behave when in a group of their peers.

Fortunately, it is only as children grow older that exclusiveness becomes a very significant characteristic of their group life. During the years of childhood, the individual shows little discrimination in his choice of associates. It is true that a child may be excluded from a group, but that exclusion is usually for the most arbitrary and transient of reasons. Under such conditions, the child who is excluded today may be the most highly accepted tomorrow, *within the same group*. Children have not developed up to this time stable preferences or prejudices. They do not care how a child is dressed, how clean he is, who his family is, or how much money his father makes. It is in adolescence, when peer groups become more highly structured and organized, that acceptance and rejection play an important part in group activity.

NEGATIVE INFLUENCE UPON MEMBERS. But rejection of some children from membership is not the only negative aspect of the peer group. The peer group may have a negative influence upon its members, the children it does accept. It may provide a model, but the wrong kind of model; it may provide reward, but the wrong kind of reward; it may provide an identity, but the wrong kind of identity; it may provide support, but support in the wrong kind of activity.

Certain terms that we apply to peer groups carry a negative connotation, at least to adults. For example, consider the terms "gang," "clique," even "crowd" (although the latter is often further identified explicitly as "good" or "bad"). The gang is a relatively small group, usually with about five members, of the

FIGURE 12-1. Five boys, all clad in dungarees and identical tee shirts, stand before the booking officer in juvenile court. They were among some ninety persons picked up by New York City police in a drive on juvenile delinquents and "generally undesirable characters."

(Photograph from Wide World)

same age and sex. It flourishes in the preadolescent period, beginning at about ten years of age. Its activities may enhance but they may also retard individual growth and development. A gang may be constructive, but it may also be destructive. In some cases, gang activity of the latter type may be the first step along the road to delinquency and criminality (see Fig. 12-1).

The clique is a grouping not commonly found until adolescence. It is made up of relatively few individuals, sometimes of both sexes, and it is distinguished chiefly by its exclusiveness and stability. It is usually a subgroup within a larger group. Its members give their loyalty to this subgroup rather than to the larger group. Highly organized and numerous cliques can make the functioning of the total group almost impossible. As a result of such extreme differentiation within the total group, many children find themselves isolated and ignored with no part to play in the social life of the peer group.

The crowd differs basically from the clique only in size and in the fact that it is more likely to include both boys and girls. The term usually refers to a larger group that is necessarily less well organized and whose membership is somewhat less stable. Individuals come and go. Others remain on the fringe, only partially identified with the group. Its effects are therefore not likely to be so disintegrative of the total group as are those of the clique.

PARENT-CHILD CONFLICT. It should not be surprising to find that the individual child is often torn by simultaneous and conflicting loyalties to the gang, clique, or crowd, on the one hand, and to his parents, on the other. Neither should we be surprised to find that parents are often suspicious and resentful of these other-group loyalties. Parent-child conflicts can hardly be avoided as the child transfers his allegiance, even in part, from home to various kinds of peer group. If the peer groups are such that they necessitate a rejection of parental expectations, then the intensity of the parent-child conflict becomes great enough to affect seriously the further socialization of the child. At its best, the peer group as it relates to other socializing agents should not be an opposing but rather a supplementary influence.

It is clear that we must recognize the importance of the peer group as a socializing agent and the nature of its influence upon its members. But we cannot conclude that the influence is for good or for bad except as we consider a particular peer group and a particular individual.

7. How would you evaluate the adolescent peer groups in Elmtown High School? Can you state some probable outcomes which are positive? Can you state some which are negative?

8. The three peer groups in Elmtown are defined in terms of the reputations of their members. How do you think the members of each of these groups look upon themselves? Which is the more significant kind of definition for understanding the behavior of the group members?

9. Observe in an elementary school classroom for a few weeks. Can you identify the subgroupings? Can you identify some isolated children in the group? Does the structure of this group change from one observation to another? Are the same children always the isolated ones? Evaluate the group structure that you find.

10. What circumstances may deprive a child of needed peer-group experience? In what sense can such a child develop an identity?

11. Make a list of the peer groups to which you belonged as a child and adolescent. Then try to set down the influences— good and bad—that these group memberships had upon you and your development.

12. Many students of modern society are alarmed by the increasing pressure upon the individual—and by the growing predisposition of the individual, as well—to conform to the standards of the group in both thought and action (Riesman, 1950; Whyte, 1956). In the light of our discussion of the influence of the peer group, how would you explain this cultural development? Does group membership make some loss of individuality inevitable? How serious is this loss for the individual and for society? Have you observed or experienced instances in which conformity was imposed upon or sought by children and youth?

LEARNING IN THE PEER GROUP

Acquired Drives

We have already said that the child learns to seek the approval of the group, first as a means of meeting the expectations of adults, but later as an end in and of itself. As he acquires this particular drive, he develops certain subsidiary motives which we must recognize if we are to understand the socialization of the child. There are at least three: (*1*) wanting the attention of one's peers; (*2*) wanting to be successful in the eyes of one's peers; (*3*) wanting to get along with one's peers.

The child acquires the need to have the attention of his parents—other persons—early in life, because getting that attention becomes a sign that his basic needs are going to be met. The need to gain the attention of his peers is of a slightly different nature. He holds membership in a group because of his conformity to group ways; but it is not enough to conform, he must make others aware that he is conforming. They must notice him. He seeks to be visible in the group. He seeks *social visibility*.

Much of the behavior of the child in the group is devoted to satisfying this particular need. He must make others aware of him. He must accomplish this by remaining just so much of an individual but no more. If he is too much of an individual, too obviously different from the others, he automatically loses membership in the group.

This is the problem that the group leader faces. He seeks the attention of his followers. In so doing, he sets himself off as an individual from the group, but only to a limited extent. He cannot lose communication with them. It is not surprising that studies of children's groups find that the most intelligent youngster is seldom chosen as leader (Hollingworth, 1926, 1942). It is not that he lacks social visibility; it is that he has too much. So long as he does not represent the group in the function of leader, his individuality, to a point, is tolerated and even appreciated by his fellow members.

As a Boy Scout, the child must attempt to retain his individuality in the group in order that he may be recognized as *a* member of that group. But he cannot cultivate it to the point that he is no longer a Boy Scout. Wanting the attention of one's peers is a somewhat delicately structured drive. The child must want some attention, but not too much.

Wanting to be successful in the eyes of one's peers is based upon an earlier acquired wanting to be successful in the eyes of one's parents. But again there is a difference. In the home, the child must strive to be successful as a dependent member of the family group. In childhood society, the child must seek to be successful as an interdependent member of the peer group. In the first situation, he often trades on his innocence and immaturity; in the second situation, he must at all times seek to be the sophisticated grown-up, equal to any one of his peers. Mother's little girl is a quite different individual when we see her in the company of her friends. Because a somewhat different pattern of responses is required to satisfy the need to be successful in the peer group, we are justified in referring to it as a newly acquired drive.

In the home, the child learns to want to get along with others. But he learns to want to do so as an inferior, at least in terms of age and experience. That is, by learning to respect the authority and wisdom of his superiors, he has obtained rewards of various types. Getting along with them has become rewarding in and of itself; it has become an acquired drive.

Similarly, in the peer group, the child learns to want to get along with others, but now as an equal, at least in terms of age and experience. Responses he learned in the home no longer suffice, for the drive has been somewhat modified. Authority rests no longer in individuals but in the mores of the group. The child wants to get along with others, not as authorities, but as fellow group members who share with him responsibility for carrying on the activity of the group. The future citizen in a democratic country learns to want to do what he must do to be a citizen, not as a subordinate member of a family group, but as a sovereign member of the peer group. It is in the latter group that he learns to want to get along with others by obeying laws, not men.

Knowledge

The nature of the drives acquired in the peer group suggests the types of skill and competence and discrimination that the child learns as a member of this group. From his peers, the child acquires a great body of information, some of it accurate.

much of it inaccurate and distorted. Henry, who does not seem to absorb anything from his sixth-grade science class, can tell you the current batting averages of the leaders in the major leagues. You might think that he studies the sports page, but he reads it only casually. However, one of the most popular boys in his crowd *does* follow the fortunes of these sports figures and passes the information along to his friends.

A group of boys for whom the teacher has given up all hope hold in their heads the most detailed information about modern planes. They are authorities on maximum speeds, specifications in design and structure, performance, and fire power. Youngsters, interested as peers in airplanes, acquire a great amount of information over a relatively short period of time and without formal instruction.

Consider also the things that adolescent girls know about motion-picture and television stars: their ages, the names of the pictures in which they have appeared, the number of times they have been married and to whom, their hobbies, their interests, and the kind of clothes they wear!

There have been few investigations of the amount and kind of knowledge that children acquire in the peer group. Too often we assume that the child has learned whatever he knows in school or at home. But there is one kind of information for which the home and the school have frequently taken little responsibility, that concerning sex. In this area, then, we can measure the amount of information that children can and do acquire from one another. Boys in particular have been given little instruction in this area until recent years. What facts they have, most of them acquired from their peers. In a typical study, Ramsey found that by the age of fourteen years, more than 95 per cent of his group of some three hundred boys were acquainted with the origin of babies and knew the meaning of intercourse, masturbation, and prostitution. More than 85 per cent of them knew what contraceptives were. The primary source of sex information was found to be male companions: "Approximately 90 per cent of the first information that boys receive [is] acquired from male companions or their own experience." (1943, p. 350).

Sex information is, of course, of a very special type. But other areas are equally neglected, although for different reasons, by other agents of socialization. The peer group becomes a valuable source of knowledge for the child. We need only imagine what a child would know if he learned only in the home and school to realize how much he acquires from his peers.

Social Sensitivity

If the child is to behave in accordance with the demands and expectations of his peers, he must learn to be responsive to cues in the reactions of those peers to him and his behavior. The young child, who has not yet learned to seek group acceptance, pays no attention to what others think of him. But with greater experience and maturity, he becomes increasingly sensitive to what they say and do with relation to him.

Children are quite frank in their reactions to one another. They can hardly be called subtle. When Mike does not behave in accordance with the standards represented by George and Tommy, the latter make their opinions of that behavior crystal-clear: "Mike's a sissy. Going to play with the girls. Ya! Ya! Sissy Mike."

As a child grows older, the cues which inform him that his behavior is acceptable to the group become more and more subtle. Rather than a plain outspoken opinion, such as was rendered by George and Tommy, the cue may consist of nothing more than a slight change in expression, a turning away, or a very polite "brush-off." To maintain acceptance among his peers, the child must learn to become more and more sensitive to these cues, so that he can take advantage of them.

In this sense, as Riesman (1950) has so vividly described in his discussion of the process of socialization, the child learns to take on the characteristics of radar. He learns to send out signals, to bounce them against targets—his peers, in this case—and, by the way in which the signals are reflected, to judge the degree of acceptability implied in those signals. In the process of learning, these are trial signals. The child evaluates them in terms of others' reactions to them. The reactions of others determine or reveal whether the child is "on the beam." In the peer group, he learns to read the reactions of others. Of course, he has already learned to read the reactions of his parents, but in so far as peers provide more appropriate models *and* judges, development of sensitivity to them becomes a much more compelling and crucial need.

Awareness of Group Expectations

It is not enough for the child to learn to be sensitive to the reactions of his peers; he must also become aware of what the group expects of him as a member. In a well-organized peer activity, those expectations are clearly defined. If a boy is assigned to play third base, certain behaviors are expected of him by his peers. A girl who is elected secretary of her class is expected to carry out certain duties. Before the baseball player and the class secretary can begin to learn their responsibilities, they must be aware of what those responsibilities are. When these expectations vary from one person to another and from one situation to another, the learning required is considerable.

In the informal play group, especially among young children, these expectations are much more diffuse and lacking in detail. But they are no less real. The inability of young children to carry on a sustained group activity is, in large part, a result of their poorly developed sense of whatever expectations exist and their lack of agreement about these expectations. Tommy and George were expected by the other members of their play group to behave like Indians. But those expectations were very poorly defined and understood. Tommy and George perceived them differently than did Bernice, Mike, and Betty. But the latter three children were not completely aware of what the "Indians" expected of them. They had not anticipated being the rather passive victims of an Indian scalping.

As children grow older, they facilitate awareness of group expectations by making explicit rules and regulations. Already, by late childhood and early adolescence, peer groups make elaborate codes of conduct and constitutions to govern their members' activities. While the expectations of a group undoubtedly become more demanding with advance in age of its members, they also become better defined and more explicit. At the same time, there is less and less tolerance for ignorance of those expectations. For the adolescent, as well as for the adult, "ignorance of the law is no excuse."

Roles

It is one thing to know what the group expects of you; it is another to meet those expectations. The child must learn a role—that is, the particular behavior that the group expects of him. A third baseman has one role to play; a pitcher has another. In hide-and-seek, the seeker plays one part, the hider another.

How do children learn these roles? Generally speaking, they learn them as they learn anything else. They try this behavior and that until they hit on the particular responses which bring group approval or, to put it in another way, which meet group expectations. Through repetition of those responses with continuing approval, they become more and more skilled, gaining ever greater commendation from the group. For those activities which are similar for children and adults, youngsters utilize adults as models. The baseball player of the sand-lot game has had his father demonstrate the correct way of catching a fast-rolling ground ball. The Mickey Mantles and the Willie Mayses of tomorrow find models in the newsreels and on television. Those pioneer settlers whom we saw being attacked by Indians were copying the behavior of characters in a movie that they had seen the previous Saturday afternoon.

For many of the peer group's activities, the children have only one another as models. How do children learn to play hide-and-seek or run-sheep-run or pom-pom-pullaway? A girl new to the neighborhood may have played it once before and introduces it to her new friends. She does not remember all the details, but the idea is enough. The children work out the rules and regulations and define the pertinent roles as they go along.

Each new generation of peers seems to develop some of the traditional games and to play them as their parents did; but they also develop new ones.

A seven-year-old boy in our neighborhood has set up a miniature Cape Canaveral during the past year. Quite a large staff has been assembled, with well-defined and differentiated duties. Some children gather the required materials. Some are engineers. Some are guards. At intervals, the participants have announced that a new and formidable missile is virtually completed. Each time, however, technical difficulties have arisen and the neighborhood breathes a sigh of relief.

This same group of children will suddenly discard old roles and assume new ones. Last week's engineer is this week's county sheriff, with a large posse at his command. What was once a highly respectable rocket expert has now become a despicable cattle rustler with a huge price on his head.

Casual observation does not reveal the intricacies and details of this group process. There are all kinds of unanswered questions. How does the group decide on this activity rather than another? How does it define the necessary roles? Where do the members obtain their ideas? Who are their models?

In spite of our lack of knowledge, we recognize that the children are learning. They are not only learning specific roles in specific activities; they are learning the necessity, as well as the ways, of meeting the expectations of their peers. They are developing and defining those group expectations. As they learn, they become able to participate in peer activities at higher and higher levels of organization and differentiation. They become more and more specialized in the roles they take. Any child can be "it" in a game of hide-and-seek at seven years of age; only the one who has adequately learned the role of left tackle can satisfy the group in that role in a football game at seventeen years of age.

The Rules of the Game

The child must not only learn to play the right role, as defined by his peers; he must learn to integrate his role-playing with that of others. He must learn team play. He must learn the rules of the game.

The role that a member of the group plays must always be subordinate to the total activity. A batter can learn to play his part too well; he may become so intent on getting hits that he loses sight of the group goal. At times, it may be more important in winning the game for him to make a sacrifice bunt or accept a walk that a wild pitcher gives him.

The ability to subordinate his personal interests to those of the group is something that the child learns well in the peer group. It involves the development of behavior that we might call social responsibility or loyalty to the group. To the extent that he learns such behavior as a child among his peers, he will be able, as an adult, to sacrifice his welfare, when necessary, for the general good. He will pay taxes to support armies, old-age pensions, schools, parks, and the like. He will have learned to follow the rules of the game in that largest of peer groups, the citizenry.

Discipline

One of the most important learning outcomes of peer activity is group discipline. In the home and in the school, the child learns discipline, but he learns it often as an inferior bowing to the superiority of adults who make the laws or at least enforce them.

In reaction to this forced kind of obedience, the youngster, in his first peer-group experiences, is likely to demand his rights as an equal. He is predisposed to obey no one who is not older and bigger than he is. The play of young children at its worst is therefore a rather good example of anarchy. Since that anarchy is usually a completely disruptive force, it is not long tolerated by children. Sooner or later, they develop rules and regulations which not only have to do with roles and integration of roles within the group but which also pertain to the group activity in general. They also develop enforcement machinery.

The same children who, in the home and in school, have

no part in making or enforcing rules will have developed, in their peer groups, an exceedingly rigorous code of conduct and also methods of enforcing that code. Long after a child has participated in legislating laws and in passing judgment on transgressors of those laws among his peers, adults will still consider him too young to assume such weighty responsibility. If it were not for such experiences in the peer group, it is difficult to see where each succeeding generation would learn the skills involved in judging and being judged as a member of a democratic society.

Reward

The peer group rewards the child by meeting his basic and previously acquired needs, as well as by satisfying the needs he has acquired as a group member. This reward is essentially group acceptance, as we have already pointed out. But the child must learn certain external signs of this reward. He must learn to recognize that he is being approved or disapproved.

Every group develops a system of rewards which are learned by all its members as signs of its approval. It defines positions of honor. For example, a whole staff of officers may be elected periodically. In some youth and adult organizations, there are almost as many officers as there are members. Some of these positions are necessary for the carrying on of the group's activity. As such, they are power positions. The bestowal of power as well as the honor makes election to such positions doubly rewarding.

The other positions are, at least to an observer, designed only for the purpose of rewarding group members. The second assistant doorkeeper, the fifth vice president, the fifth-ranking imperial wizard will find it somewhat difficult to identify their duties. But they have gained social visibility. There is clear evidence of group acceptance.

Children's groups do not ordinarily have so elaborate a system of rewards. Nevertheless, they learn to recognize assignment and election to positions of honor and responsibility within the group as an indication that they are approved by their peers. Later on, they will be happy, at least for a time, with positions which have honor but little responsibility.

The leaders of the group must be careful to show that they appreciate and value the services of those members of the group who do not hold office of any kind. They must point out that "They also serve who only stand and wait." Then, there always remains the possibility of later accession to higher duties. George was successful in retaining Mike as a member of the play group for the moment by saying: "You be the husband this time. Next time you can be one of the Indians."

13. Do children differ in the strength of their need for the approval of the group? Give some examples from your own observation. How would you explain such individual differences?

14. Describe in detail how a child might acquire a new drive in a peer-group situation.

15. Should some kinds of information be left to be learned in the peer group? Or should the school and the home be responsible for transmitting all knowledge? Can you think of some information which is particularly well suited for acquisition in the peer group?

16. Why do children sometimes seem to acquire information more easily and retain it longer in the peer group than at home or in school?

17. Can a child develop too much social sensitivity? What might explain such "excess learning"?

18. What new kind of activity was originated in a play group to which you belonged as a child? How was it developed?

19. To what extent do adults teach children games? How else do children learn the games which seem to be played in each successive generation?

20. Is there a difference between self-discipline and group discipline? Explain.

THE PEER GROUP AND OTHER SOCIALIZING AGENTS

It is virtually impossible to determine with any precision the relative importance of a given social agent. But it is clear that, in the last generation, the peer group has come to exert more and more influence in the total socialization process.

In a stable society, the home, with the help of the school, is the major influence; the peer group is a relatively unimportant agent which serves as a bridge from childhood to adulthood, without introducing any significant changes in the nature or direction of that development. By a stable society, we mean one in which there is only one set of values, in which the great majority of adults accept those values for themselves and for their children. Each child learns them in his home with later reinforcement in school. The peer group in such a society is a collection of children who have had similar, if not identical, histories of socialization. There is nothing for them to learn except how to work out for the future a society which duplicates the present one. The truth is known to all. Scattered revolt is not uncommon but is looked upon as a symptom of immaturity. Youth is not disallowed its proper share of follies and foolish notions because time alone will reveal them for what they are.

Observers of modern society tell us that we no longer live in such a stable social world. When the emerging society no longer seems to be a replication of the past, a new factor is introduced into the process of socialization, one which gives new and increased prominence to the peer group as a socializing agent.

Children must not only practice what they have already learned in the home (indeed, they practice home learning to a lesser extent) but also learn the new ways of behaving demanded by the society which is emerging. The peer culture is the agent for this new learning. Parents represent a society and culture to which the child is exposed only in the home. They are no longer completely appropriate models. They expect of him much as their parents had earlier expected of them. It is to his peers that the child turns.

The school, as a socializing agent, finds itself in a very difficult position. It is supported by an adult society with one system of values, but it is trying to teach members of a child-

hood society in which the old values are undergoing modification. If it sympathizes with the old society, it loses its influence
over its pupils. If it sympathizes with the evolving society, it
loses the support of parents.

The peer group also has its difficulties. Too often, it revolts
against the old values without having developed new values to
replace them. Its members then have the tremendous task of
existing and developing without the help of direction or tradition. To a considerable degree, it must go through a process of
developing its own set of values by trial and error. In the absence of tradition, each member must look to the others. "Am I
doing right?" can be answered only by reference to another
person.

Riesman (1950) describes this transition as one from a
"tradition-directed" or "inner-directed" character to an "other-
directed" character. Having discarded the "eternal truths" or
the "lessons at mother's knee," the child must turn to the other
person, especially his peer. Seeking approval from peers becomes a very significant way of preserving his psychological
stability in a changing society.

This transition has been one of evolution rather than of
revolution. The home and the school are still among the primary agents of socialization and show every sign of retaining
their importance. But we must recognize the increasingly influential role that the peer culture plays in the socialization
process.

Many adults have recognized this growing influence, and,
instead of fighting it, they have joined it. In the twentieth century, we have seen the development of youth organizations
which, while they are often directed by adults and have a program formulated by adults, nevertheless are designed to meet
the peer group on its own terms. Adults who participate in such
activities reason: if we, as adults, are losing some of our influence in the home and school situations, we can perhaps regain
it by offering our services to the peer group. In the early 1900's,
a movement began which has resulted in the formation of the
Boy Scouts, the Girl Scouts, the Campfire Girls, the Brownies,

the Cub Scouts, the Bluebirds, Hi-Y, and Four-H Clubs—to give but a few examples. Although these organizations were originally planned for older children and adolescents, their success has led to the formation of similar groups for younger and younger children. An examination of one of these—the Cub Scouts—will not only show the influence that such adult-directed organizations have in socializing the child but also illustrate the important aspects of peer-group learning that we have already discussed.

In view of what we have said about the function of such organizations, it is interesting first to note the statement for parents in the first of three Cub Scout manuals:

> "I wish there were some way in which I might get a little closer to my son. I try my best to understand him, but the gap between his viewpoint and my more mature viewpoint is a wide one. I need a bridge to span that gap."
>
> Have you ever said something like that? Don't be too concerned about it, because almost every parent has that problem. Cub Scouting is the sort of bridge of understanding which you have been seeking [*Wolf Cub Scout Book,* 1952, p. 2].

In an earlier day, most parents would have scoffed at such an appeal, although they might not have objected to the organization itself. They felt that they understood their offspring only too well.

What are the distinctive features of the program of the Cub Scouts? First, it is a system of successive goals related to age. Age is a basic dimension. The organization is age-graded. To join it, a boy must be at least eight years old but not yet eleven.

As an eight-year-old, he is first a Bobcat. By learning the Cub Scout Promise, the Law of the Pack, the meaning of Webelos, and the Cub Scout Sign, Handclasp, Motto, and Salute, he becomes a full-fledged Cub Scout.

But this is only the beginning. In his first year, he follows the Wolf Trail. A series of achievement tests, for each of which he receives certain credits, leads him along this trail. They involve such tasks as tying knots, keeping a scrapbook, making a collection, or accomplishing "feats of skill." These are not home activities or school assignments; they are peer-group activities. To a child, they are fun; but they are also pointed to the future. By completing them, he becomes a Wolf Cub Scout.

Is he finished now? No. He finds himself on the Bear Trail, with another set of tasks before him. At the end of that trail, he is made a Bear Cub Scout. This is his second year. The next year, he follows the Lion Trail and attempts a new series of tests. His goal is now to become a Lion Cub Scout. After that he has only to achieve the highest rank, that of Webelos, at which time he is qualified to join the Boy Scouts. One thing leads to another; that is the underlying principle. The attainment of one goal only serves to bring a new one into focus. The child enters a system. It is the system, as such, that provides direction and authority; the adults who may be involved are there only to keep the system working.

A second feature of the Cub Scouts, which is characteristic, to some extent, of all forms of organized peer-group activity, is that the goals themselves are realistic. They are realistic in the sense that they are related to the interests and capabilities of the child. If only the child tries, he is assured of success. There are no impossible tasks. Task difficulty is very carefully graded. Each successive goal is set just a bit beyond the last one. What a contrast with the home and the school, where, in spite of the best of intentions and planning, some children find it almost impossible to be successful!

A third important characteristic of organized peer activity is the offering of frequent and tangible rewards. As soon as he finishes his training period as a Bobcat, the child becomes a Cub Scout. His new status is made clear to all who see him, for he now wears the Cub Scout Uniform and Cap Badge. The outward signs of his success are evident to all.

By completing the achievement tests of the Wolf Trail, not only does he become a Wolf Cub Scout; for each of the tests that he completes beyond the requirement, he is given arrow points—a gold one for ten credits of electives, a silver one for each ten additional credits of electives. And so it goes at every stage.

Fourthly, we see in this program an appeal to character and values that have already been developed in the home. Consider the Cub Scout Promise: "I, _____, promise to *DO MY BEST* to do my *DUTY* to *GOD* and my *COUNTRY,* to *BE SQUARE,* and to *OBEY* the Law of the Pack." What does it mean to *BE SQUARE?* According to the *Wolf Cub Scout Book,*

> *BE SQUARE* means be fair to everybody. Sometimes this is not easy. But a Cub Scout will try to be square. He wants everybody to be fair to him, so he is fair to everybody [p. 5].

What is the "Law of the Pack"?

The Cub Scout Follows Akela.

Who is Akela?

> Akela is a Cub Scout name for a good leader. A leader is someone you follow. Some of the people you may call Akela are your father or mother, your teacher, your Den Chief, Den Mother or Cubmaster, or anybody who is a good leader.
>
> Most good leaders first learned to follow. That's why the first part of the Law of the Pack asks you to learn to follow. Follow good leaders. Follow Akela [p. 8].

Let us consider one additional example of this appeal to previously developed values. The child is told:

> "The Cub Scout Gives Good Will."
> You will find that if you smile at your friends, they will smile back at you. If you are friendly to them, they will be friendly to you.
> Look for things to do for other people. They need not be big things, but just little things that help.
> Smile and help—these are two fine Cub Scouting words [p. 9].

The organization makes clear to the child that he can grow up, achieve, and have fun with his peers without coming into conflict with previous learnings. At the same time, it utilizes these previous learnings to motivate activity and achievement.

Finally, we should note that the Cub Scouts develop in-group feeling. Many of the rewards are designed to inform the

"*Well, I did and I didn't. I was helping an old lady across
the street, but she was sideswiped by a taxicab.*"

(Reproduced by permission. Copyright 1951 The New Yorker Magazine, Inc.)

individual that he is successful; they also inform others that he
is one of them. There is the uniform and badge that he has
earned. He is authorized to give the Cub Scout Sign and the
Salute. With another Cub Scout, he can use a special handclasp.

There is a code so that he can write a letter to a fellow Cub Scout that only the sender and the recipient (or other Cub Scouts) can read. There are words that only Cub Scouts know, such as Webelos and Akela. As a Scout, the child *belongs*. He gains an identity. He has learned some skills; he has acquired some knowledge; he has earned various insignia that make him one with the others.

Adults who build such programs as this do so on the basis of a canny insight into the ways in which children learn. They understand peer-group activity. Such a program is not fundamentally different from what was going on in the free-play situation with which we began this chapter. The activity has become highly organized and formalized. The content and direction is predetermined by adults. But it is, in all essentials, peer-group activity. As such, it is a significant part of the socialization of the child.

21. We have discussed the Cub Scouts by direct references to the published manuals. This might be called the theory of Scouting. How well does actual practice correspond to the theory? Answer this question by observing, if you can, a den of Cub Scouts in action, or by interviewing a Den Mother.

22. We have mentioned one way in which learning in an organized peer group differs from that in the classroom: each child can succeed if only he tries. What other differences can you point out?

23. Select another youth organization and analyze its program as it relates to the socialization of the child.

24. Would you recommend that every child belong to the Scouts or some similar organization?

25. Does a youth organization tend to preserve the values of the present social order? Compare the values implicit in Scouting with those which we described in Chapter 6 as constituting the American character. Are new or modified values ever developed? In what ways? In what circumstances?

SUGGESTED READINGS

BALDWIN, ALFRED L. *Behavior and Development in Childhood*, Dryden Press, 1955. In Chapter 9, "Social Controls over the

Behavior of Children," Baldwin discusses social rules, roles, and compliance in childhood.

BLAIR, ARTHUR WITT, & BURTON, WILLIAM H. *Growth and Development of the Preadolescent,* Appleton-Century-Crofts, 1951. A review and interpretation of research on the period of late childhood which clearly reveal the importance of the peer group.

BOSSARD, JAMES H. S. *The Sociology of Child Development* (Rev. Ed.), Harper, 1954. Chapter 23, "The Role of the Peer Group," presents a thorough analysis of this important socializing agency.

FREUD, ANNA, & DANN, SOPHIE. An experiment in group upbringing. In William E. Martin and Celia Burns Stendler (eds.), *Readings in Child Development,* Harcourt, Brace, 1954, pp. 404-21. This report of six refugee children, deprived from an early age of maternal care, demonstrates how the peer group may, in extreme circumstances, assume the socializing responsibilities of the family.

HARTLEY, RUTH E., FRANK, LAWRENCE K., & GOLDENSON, ROBERT M. *Understanding Children's Play,* Columbia University Press, 1952. Some suggestions for training classroom teachers to study children through their play activities, based on systematic observation of children at play.

HOLLINGSHEAD, AUGUST B. *Elmtown's Youth,* Wiley, 1949. Chapter 9, "Cliques and Dates"; Chapter 12, "Recreation and Tabooed Pleasures"; and Chapter 15, "Leisure Hour Activities," will be of particular interest in this report of a study of adolescents.

JONES, HAROLD E. *Development in Adolescence,* D. Appleton-Century, 1943. In this study of an individual from sixth grade to college, the attitudes and judgments of the peer group were carefully considered. The results are reported in Chapter 3, "John as Seen by His Teachers and Classmates," and Chapter 4, "John as a Member of Social Groups."

POLANSKY, NORMAN, LIPPITT, RONALD, & REDL, FRITZ. An investigation of behavioral contagion in groups. In Martin and Stendler, *op. cit.,* pp. 493-513. The susceptibility of children to the influence of their peers is strikingly illustrated in this study of the "spreading of a mood, an attitude, a behavior from one person to another, or through a whole group." On the basis of their observations in a summer-camp setting, the authors identify the factors which seem to determine the extent of such behavioral contagion.

SPIRO, MELFORD E. *Children of the Kibbutz,* Harvard University Press, 1958. The *kibbutzim* (collective settlements) of Israel, with their emphasis upon group living and peer relationships from birth through adolescence, provide a natural laboratory for the study of a unique pattern of socialization. This book presents an analysis of the effects of collective education upon personality development, based upon the author's participation in and systematic observation of life in a *kibbutz*.

13
the child
in the
community

Thus far in this book we have taken the position that a child learns a particular pattern of behavior as he interacts with other people; that he becomes what he is as a result of his interrelations with such socializing agents as parents, teachers, and peers. The question we must now consider is whether there are other influences upon the child which affect his behavior. To answer this, we must turn to the wider community setting and analyze the forces in operation there. Aside from the school and the peer group, what influences are there in the community that might conceivably affect the child?

THE PHYSICAL SETTING
OF BEHAVIOR

We might begin by raising the interesting question as to the kind of physical setting that is most conducive to healthy growth and development. Does the child's habitat affect his behavior, and if so, how? Wright and others (1951) have pointed out that we need to know a great deal more about the naturally occurring behavior of children, *and the situations in which it occurs,* in order to answer these questions. In the field of agriculture, if we want to find out how to raise livestock, grow flowers, run a fish hatchery, or raise corn, we can go to specialists who know how livestock, flowers, fish, and corn "behave" in a variety of natural habitats. We can read concrete and detailed descriptions of the necessary conditions of life for whatever we want to raise—except children. These authors emphasize our need for more ecological information in psychology. Just as biologists study the naturally occurring biological homelands or habitats of plants and animals, so, these writers say, we need to study the habitat in which children behave. For the setting of behavior can affect the behavior, at least indirectly.

Some children in slum areas of our large cities grow up knowing alleys strewn with broken glass and garbage as play areas. It is obvious that such settings are not appropriate for growing flowers or for wiener roasts or square dancing or hiking. There are some behaviors that children reared in such an environment never have a chance to learn, and there are some behaviors that such an environment promotes. An alley strewn with broken glass is more likely to appear to children as a setting for the breaking of glass than as a setting for a picnic. Certain behaviors which appear in a poolroom are recognized by adolescents as inappropriate in a classroom. In the process of socialization, children learn what is appropriate in certain settings. They may not always act accordingly, but, depending upon how well socialized they are and how familiar they are with the setting, a particular habitat may be more conducive to one kind of behavior than to another. Furthermore, some children never have the opportunity to learn certain behaviors—good or bad—because they have never been exposed to the appropriate setting. In "Midwest," for example, a small community studied by Barker and Wright (1954), children could not visit an aquarium, ride a subway, eat pizza in an Italian restaurant, or attend an opera. Opportunities for certain cultural experiences were nonexistent for them.

1. Select a behavior setting in your own community. List the behaviors appropriate in such a setting for a high school boy. Might there be age and sex differences in the behaviors appropriate in this particular setting?

Some writers would argue that cities are a bad physical habitat in which to rear children and that smaller communities are better. From the standpoint of the child's physical freedom, there would appear to be justification for this line of reasoning. A small child in New York City, particularly if he belongs to the middle or upper class, can go outdoors only if he is accompanied by an adult. When he needs fresh air or exercise, he must be taken out for a walk by an adult, and his play must continually be supervised. He rarely has the chance, before he begins school, to strike up spontaneous friendships, to have the fun of exploring a back yard by himself, to know the blessings of self-imposed solitude.

In a community such as Midwest, by way of contrast, the child has considerably more physical freedom. In the opinion of Barker and Wright, Midwest is a "good" place for children; among their reasons for this statement are the facts that children can roam the community at will, and that adult restrictions can be kept to a minimum. The child's curiosity and zest for exploration can be given rein in a fashion that the city child never knows, hemmed in as he is by admonitions such as "Keep off the grass," "Please deposit all trash in this container," "Cross at street crossings only," "Wait for the green light." The child in Midwest can know the thrill of the first spring days, of searching for the first violet, of a secret place in the woods, of having the world to himself.

We should note here a distinction that some writers have drawn between lower- and middle-class child-rearing practices in a city environment. Lower-class children have the freedom of the streets at a much earlier age; they are protected, not by parental supervision, but, rather, by being warned of the danger spots in their environment. The young child in a middle-class family does not need to know that the world is dangerous, for his mother's presence protects him; the lower-class child, however, is protected by knowing what he must avoid: "Keep away from Avenue A. It's the red-light district." "Don't go in that store by yourself if you're a girl. The guy in there's got itchy fingers." "Don't get into cars with strangers." Eight-year-olds in slum areas know these admonitions.

THE GOOD COMMUNITY

Physical freedom, or a minimum of adult restraint, will hardly suffice as the sole criterion of the good community; nor will experiences with nature, rewarding as they may be. The "good" community for children offers much more. The physical setting of behavior is important, but even more important are the social interrelations within that habitat. The "good" community, through its members, takes over the job of socialization where the family leaves off. As Hart puts it: "In the good community no family ever brought up its own children. After they were six or seven years old, they were the responsibility of the whole community" (1951, p. 72). Through interaction with others outside the family, the child learns the wider community. He is exposed to a complexity of interests and activities, to diversities of economic conditions, religion, education, social conditions, and politics. Through exposure to the problems and conflicts of the community, his social and intellectual development is enriched.

The community, in other words, provides a laboratory of human relations for the child; within this laboratory he can learn that people are different, that these differences make for conflict, that man must ever search for better ways of resolving conflict. It is Hart's contention that shielding children from conflict, depriving them of their right to live and have experiences, stunts their development; rather, he argues, children must be permitted to participate in the varied life of the community as a means of attaining a personal share in the larger world.

Today many adults—particularly in the middle class—take the opposite point of view. They argue that children should be shielded from life; that they must not know slums or community conflicts or the seamy side of life until they are young adults. The conflict between these two beliefs is dramatically illustrated in an incident that happened on New York's East Side many years ago. A young settlement-house group leader tells the story:

> When I was a boy, growing up in this very neighborhood, the fire laws were very inadequate and the ones that existed were poorly enforced. One year—I was nine at the time—we had a terrible fire. A whole tenement burned to the ground, and many families died horrible deaths. We kids heard our pals inside that house screaming to get out before they died, but the only exit was the first part of the building to go up in flames because it had never been fireproofed. All of us were pretty upset about it. Then the director of the settlement house organized a march on City Hall. All the kids in the neighborhood, even some of the five-year-olds, paraded with placards and banners, yelling slogans at the crowds that gathered to see us. Some of the newspapers took a dim view of the whole affair; they said kids shouldn't be mixed up in anything like that— that it was "exploiting" us. But we felt the kids who died were the ones who had been exploited and that we had done some good (for new laws were passed and tenements improved) and that it was a relief for us to be able to get into the thing and do something.

It is tragic that such things happen to children; whether children should engage in a program of action to improve social conditions is open to question. But the fact remains that children cannot be shielded from reality, and that community conflicts as they impinge upon their lives should not be treated in a "hush-hush" manner but should be considered important for them to know.

> **2.** Give examples of community conflicts with which a fourth-grader might be concerned; a sixth-grader.

There is some evidence that in small communities, at least, children do enter into a wide range of community settings and engage in a great diversity of behavior. In their study of Mid-

west, Barker and Wright (1954) found that the range of activities available to children was only a small part of the total
American culture, but that nevertheless the children entered
freely into the settings that were available. Although the population of Midwest was only 721, the investigators found 585
community-behavior settings during a single year, including
food sales, parades, paper routes, town elections, funeral services, banquets, club meetings, the jail, restaurants, and school
classes. Because there was a great variety of settings available
and a small population, there was pressure on all residents to
enter many settings; because there were not enough adults to
man the various settings, Midwest children engaged in a number of diverse activities. In fact, about a fourth of all performances in Midwest were by children.

The settings into which the children entered were not
created primarily for them; more than half involved adult activities essential to the community. Children, therefore, were
not a luxury in Midwest. They were vital to the functioning
of the community and, as a result, had the opportunity to
perform in situations that had considerable prestige. In many
small communities, without the children papers would not be
distributed, soda fountains manned, prescriptions delivered,
babies tended in the evening, lawns mowed, corn detasseled,
or tomatoes picked.

Barker and Wright have noted some of the effects of the
participation of children in community life. Because their participation was so widespread, Midwest children had the opportunity to know people of varying ages, socioeconomic back-
grounds, intelligence, personality, and political beliefs. Thus
they were required from an early age to adjust to a wide range
of individual differences. Such a psychological setting is in
sharp contrast to that in our modern large-scale housing developments, inhabited by people similar in age, color, and social
class. We can assume that children growing up in a homoge-
neous setting in which their participation is restricted will be
different in some respects from the children of Midwest, al-

though we do not yet know enough about the effects of the former setting to describe the differences.

We can only guess at the other possible effects of childhood participation in community life upon later development. For many children reared in communities like Midwest, these experiences undoubtedly foster industriousness and responsibility. Because they are placed in situations in which they must deal with meaningful problems, they may also develop independence, versatility, resourcefulness, and ingenuity. Some unfortunate consequences have also been noted, however. In Midwest, the accomplishment of children was usually at a lower level than their capabilities. Because they were under pressure to take part in so many activities, the children did not attain maximal competence in most of them. Also, there was no specialized training at an advanced level available to them. The child growing up in a small community is fortunate if, like the pianist Van Cliburn, he has a mother who can and does teach and encourage him, for such communities ordinarily provide neither encouragement nor opportunity to excel in a special field.

3. List some criteria for evaluating a community's attitudes toward its children. Will you include recreational facilities for children? For-rent ads in newspapers which say, "No children or pets"?

Thus we see that the community impinges upon the socialization process in several ways, once the child extends his horizons beyond the immediate family. The physical environment provides the setting for behavior and thus sets certain limits upon the possibilities for learning. These learnings include not only knowledges and skills (e.g., how to run a paper route or how to board a subway) but also personality characteristics. We are what we are partly because of the kind of community in which we have been reared.

The community also affects the socialization process in that it mirrors a bit of American life for the child. Through wider participation, he may learn that the values held dear in his family are the same as (or at variance with) values in the community at large. He can learn from others cultural ways of behaving which are not taught in his family. We turn now to a discussion of some of the media through which these are taught

THE CHURCH

A community institution which merits special consideration is the church. To what extent does it operate as a socializing agent? Since its special function is to deal with problems of good and evil, we should expect to find that the church significantly affects the moral development of children. It is conceivable that when the moral teachings of the home are reinforced by spiritual sanction, the internalization of controls of conduct will proceed very efficiently.

Indeed, the church is so much a part of our American tradition that "churchgoer" has become part of the definition of "respectable citizen"; character reputation is dependent upon church participation (Havighurst & Taba, 1949). Those who attend church have better character reputation than those who do not; those who do not attend are either so secure that they don't care about character reputation or are at the bottom of the scale, with a poor character reputation anyway. Reputation varies, however, with the church that one attends. In Prairie City, a Midwestern community studied by Havighurst and Taba, the Lutherans had the highest morals-reputation score. They were known for their strict views; they frowned upon dancing, card playing, drinking, and attending movies. The Federated Church was the most liberal in town. It permitted its members activities frowned upon by the Lutherans. The character reputations of Federated Church members were not so high as those of the Lutherans. Apparently, the stricter the church, the higher the rating.

But while church membership may influence character *reputation*, the question still remains as to whether it influences *character*. Prairie City residents, like many of us, may have a certain stereotype for those who attend church regularly and another for those who do not; they may rate people in terms of the stereotype rather than in terms of actual behavior. Thus Johnny Jones may be rated a good boy by the community because he goes to Sunday School every week, whereas those who know Johnny intimately might not rate him so high. Or Johnny may be rated high because he's a Lutheran, and his church is known to be strict; but whether Johnny has earned the rating is still open to question if we judge in terms of reputation alone. And even if we knew that Johnny deserved his good reputation, we would not know whether his religious education had contributed to it.

A different approach to the problem of the extent to which the church is a socializing agency is to study the relationship between religious education and behavior. This was done in a limited way in the Character Education Inquiry completed some years ago by Hartshorne and May (1928). In conducting their inquiry, these authors devised some ingenious tests of performance for the measurement of such traits as honesty, self-control, and cooperativeness. Among them was a series of tests that a child could pass only if he cheated. They found that 31 per cent of the children in a group of Sunday School goers cheated as against 40 per cent of the children in a group which did not attend Sunday School. On a second sampling, the percentages were 38 and 43, respectively. No tests of significance were applied, however, and so we do not know whether this difference occurred merely by chance or would be found in the total population.

Unfortunately, the problem of measuring the effects of religious education is extremely complex. It is difficult to control all the variables affecting socialization. In comparing a group of children who have had religious instruction with a group of children who have not, it is difficult to know whether the differences that appear (when they are statistically significant) are due to home influence, intelligence, peer-group influ-

ence, superiority of instruction, or other factors in addition to
Sunday School attendance.

4. Many Sunday Schools concentrate on coloring and construction activities for young children. What suggestions would
you make for other kinds of activity in order to meet the
"social, ethical, or religious needs of children"?

MEDIA OF MASS COMMUNICATION

Thus far we have been considering the child in the local
community only. The wider community—indeed, the whole of
his society—impinges upon the child through the media of mass
communication. Today, as never before, the child is exposed
to a barrage of ideas and models of behavior in books, comics,
newspapers, magazines, radio, movies, and television. These
media have been subjects of thousands of investigations which
have sought in the main to answer two questions: (*1*) are children influenced by these media; and (*2*) if so, is this influence
good or bad?

Reading and Comics

In our culture, voluntary reading tends to compete unsuc-
cessfully with other media of communication. In the study of
Midwest, the amount of time children spent in reading was
compared with that spent on other activities (Wright *et al.*,
1951). The results showed that "reading" had a temporal weight
of 73 hours per year per child under twelve, as compared with
a temporal weight of 193 hours for "radio program." What the
children read was not reported, but, judging by sales records,
a large part of the 73 hours per year devoted to leisure-time
reading was probably spent in reading comics.

However, children do spend a considerable portion of the
school day in reading both fiction and nonfiction. The precise
influence of this reading is not known, but it is safe to assume
that it is an important source of guidance for role behavior. As
we have indicated earlier, children learn the role patterns that
are approved by society as they read again and again that cer-

tain kinds of behavior are rewarded and certain kinds punished. This is not to say that they will accept the role pattern thus defined for them, but at least they will be familiar with it. They learn from their reading how children are expected to act at different age levels, what kind of person boys are expected to be and what girls should be and do. By the middle grades, some sex differences appear in reading choices. Boys prefer books with such themes as "display of strength, independence, self-control, making a team at the expense of an unfair rival, saving a person's life, and gaining mastery in physical combat when the opponent is despicable" (Reed, 1938, pp. 123-24). Both boys and girls are interested in science, although more boys choose to read about astronomy, geology, and space travel (Rudman, 1955). Girls prefer themes of "kindliness to others, wearing beautiful clothes, holding a high social position, being honorable and unselfish, being useful in the home," and the like (Reed, 1938, p. 124). They express more interest than boys in reading stories about mythology, mysteries, teenagers, famous people, and boy-girl relationships (Rudman, 1955).

5. How would you assess the influence of reading upon your own development? Are there some books that stand out in your memory as being particularly influential? What was the nature of their influence?

6. If possible, poll the children in an elementary class regarding their three favorite books. Analyze these books from the standpoint of the themes they contain.

The medium of comics and comic strips has been explored by many investigators, particularly in recent years. All agree that comics have a tremendous appeal; in 1944, Zorbaugh found that 93 per cent of children between eight and fifteen years of age read comic books. Although interest gradually declines, particularly after the sixth grade, nevertheless, 44 per cent of men in the Army in World War II read the comics regularly.

Investigators generally agree that there are some comics which are socially undesirable, but they also seem to agree that some comics represent the folk literature of modern America.

Comics have been criticized for portraying fantastic situations, for emphasizing violence, and for excessively using vulgarisms and slang; yet these are the very characteristics that endear them to children, and many students of children do not find them objectionable. Indeed, recent developments in science have brought much of what was once fantastic in the comics into the realm of possibility, even probability. Rocket ships to the moon are not yet a reality, but in these days of atomic energy, rocket-propelled missiles, jet planes, earth satellites, and the like, this suggestion and others in the comics no longer seem so far-fetched. Although it is true that some comics do emphasize blood-and-thunder, it has been pointed out that many Bible stories, folk tales, and myths are no less gory, and that, in comic books, right always triumphs in the end. And language specialists generally agree that children's language habits are not significantly altered by the comics.

But when a child's reading of the comics is confined to the variety based entirely upon crime and sex, a serious problem is raised. A boy or girl who feeds on a steady diet of horror, terror, and sex is sometimes a child who is poorly socialized or unsocialized. In such cases the school has a responsibility to procure psychological help, if it is available, and also to guide the pupil's reading into more desirable channels.

7. Give some concrete suggestions for ways in which the school can guide children's reading away from comics exclusively into more desirable channels.

Television

The comics, because they offer an inexpensive way of filling a need that children obviously feel, will undoubtedly be with us until another medium appears that fills this same need more effectively. There are indications that television is doing just that. In a middle-class school district in Brooklyn, a survey of 1208 school-age children in the first eight grades revealed that 60 per cent of the boys and 50 per cent of the girls preferred television to books, motion pictures, radio, and comics as a leisure-time activity. Comics was the least popular of the five choices the children were given, with only 7 per cent of the boys and 4 per cent of the girls preferring them (Fogler, 1950).

Although we do not have before-and-after figures, it is safe to assume that, before the advent of television, the population of this Brooklyn community behaved more nearly like the population Zorbaugh reported with respect to comic-book reading. Although Zorbaugh studied the percentage of children who read comics rather than those who preferred them, it seems likely that the competition of television had something to do with the discrepancy between his figure (93 per cent of children read comics) and the Fogler figure (7 and 4 per cent, respectively, of boys and girls prefer comics to other mass media).

Writers are finding it fascinating to speculate about the impact of television upon children. Articles in professional journals and popular magazines are appearing by the score, but most of them are devoted to what the writers *think* will be the influence of television rather than to results of research on the actual influence. All the writers agree that it is a tremendously effective medium of communication. It combines both eye and ear appeal, is available at the flick of a switch, and represents no financial outlay for the child. Whether it will be an effective medium for good or for evil is, however, a matter for debate. Almost all the writers agree that television will affect family living. Some of them take a gloomy view, predicting the decline of family discussions and conversation as even mealtime is spent in front of the screen. Others see television as a force that will keep the family together for shared recreation. Some worry about the effects of television on children's eyesight and about the effects of so much sedentary activity on their general health. Others are concerned about the effects of trashy programs on children's tastes and of programs emphasizing violence on their mental health.

Actually, we know little about the possible effects of television upon children's physical, social, and emotional development. It is clear, however, that television is a powerful force which can exert tremendous influence, positive or negative.

Right now we need more research, not on what people think of television or on whether or not they approve of it, but on what values are being disseminated and perpetuated through this medium.

8. Study a current television program for children. Make a list of the kinds of behavior that are rewarded on the program and the kinds that are punished.
9. What values does the hero of the program represent?

Motion Pictures

Although television has cut down movie attendance in areas in which it is available, movie going is still a regular pastime for many of America's children. Earlier studies revealed that children prefer movies that are thrilling, exciting, and funny (Seagoe, 1931). From the present popularity of Westerns and cartoons, it would seem that these same characteristics still appeal.

Just as adults today are concerned about the effects of television upon the youth of America, so twenty years ago there was considerable concern about the effects of motion pictures. This concern resulted in three types of study. In one category were efforts to discover what, if any, were the effects of movies upon children's physical well-being. By means of an instrument used to measure sleep, the sleeping patterns of 163 children were studied over a period of two and a half years. Results showed that many boys and girls slept more restlessly after seeing night movies; others were so emotionally fatigued that they slept as if in a stupor. Studies of pulse rates and skin moisture, both of which increase with excitement, corroborated the finding that movies can have an intense emotional effect upon children. Indeed, children's reactions were three times as intense as those of adults (Renshaw et al., 1933).

Few people would argue that occasional intense excitement is physically harmful for most children. But it is questionable whether frequent nighttime viewing of exciting films, on either the motion-picture or the television screen, should be permitted to children who react so negatively to them.

A second group of studies concentrated on the effects of motion pictures upon children's ethnic attitudes. Children were questioned with regard to their attitude toward the Chinese before and after seeing a film in which the Chinese were depicted favorably. An improvement in acceptance of Chinese was noted after they had seen the film. Similarly, a film which depicted Negroes unfavorably produced negative attitudes in children that still persisted after eight months (Forman, 1933). Considering the fact that Hollywood in recent years has produced many fine films designed to combat prejudice, such studies are very encouraging. However, the reader will recall our discussion in Chapter 10 of more recent studies which showed that ethnic attitudes are part of total personality development. It is extremely doubtful that deep-rooted prejudices can be altered by seeing a film. However, if negative attitudes toward an ethnic group are the result of misinformation or of an unfavorable climate of opinion, some changes might reasonably be expected to follow the viewing of a film in which that group is presented in a favorable light.

Perhaps of most concern to educators is the question of the possible effects of movies upon children's moral development. From time to time, newspaper accounts appear of a boy or girl who has committed a murder or a robbery "because I saw it done in the movies." Most students of juvenile delinquency, however, would caution against interpreting the fact that one event follows another as evidence that the first event is the cause of the second. Rather, they would look to the early socialization of children and to the environment in which they live for the roots of delinquency. A child is exposed to many models of behavior on the screen. If he chooses to pattern his behavior after the model of the villain, he can learn the details of such behavior from the movies; but his original choice of villain as model stems from causes other than the film itself.

Undoubtedly, the influence of the movies upon socialization is much more subtle than studies to date show. We need careful analyses of the values to which children are exposed in films, as well as studies of children's acceptance or rejection of these values. One provocative analysis of Hollywood Westerns, although not statistically documented, has been made by Elkin (1950). He finds the appeal of the Western in action and simplicity; the typical film is a continual series of chases, daring rescues, galloping horses, gun battles, and fist fights. There are no complex characterizations; the hero is all good, and goodness is defined as honesty, loyalty, sympathy for the oppressed, and respect for just law. The villain is unequivocally bad, which means that he is treacherous, ruthless, and contemptuous of the underdog. The right of the individual to mete out justice when the law fails to do so, man's righteous aggression against dishonesty, the achievement of victory through struggle and merit —all these themes recur in Westerns.

As Elkin points out, Western themes extol typical American values. Except for the fact that human life is not always held up as sacred, the child is exposed to a moral influence that follows along traditional American lines. There is a question, however, as to whether the values emphasized in Westerns are as well suited to modern American life as they were to frontier society. Extreme individualism, "taking the law into one's own hands," and emphasis upon achievement as the inevitable accompaniment of merit may not be desirable or realistic in present-day society.

Radio

Although radio listening suffers a sharp decline when television is introduced into an area, studies made in the 'forties, when children were spending from one to three hours daily with this medium (Jersild, 1947), reveal certain information about age changes in children's tastes which are probably reflected in other media as well. Fairy tales and juvenile stories and songs become less popular as children grow older, while sports broadcasts, quiz programs, news broadcasts, and dramas increase in popularity. Certain adult comedians appeal to children at all age levels. Older girls' preferences run to soap operas, whereas boys' choices, more so than girls', lean toward stories of action and violence.

Studies of the possible effects of listening to radio programs upon children's physical status corroborate the findings
of investigations in other media. Studying photographic records
of changes in pulse rate, blood pressure, and respiration,
De Boer (1939) found that children respond intensely to many
situations in radio programs. Indeed, violent action is not even
necessary to raise the blood pressure; children will react intensely to any situation in which a character is trying to overcome a barrier to his goal. It is conceivable that television,
which presents visual as well as auditory stimuli, produces an
even more intense reaction.

Soap operas, so popular on both daytime television and
radio, have received attention in the research literature. One
analysis of radio soap operas indicated that the solutions to
problems offered in these serials are so unlifelike that they can
have only the negative effect of building up romantic visions
that can never be realized (Warner & Henry, 1948). The fact
that soap operas are so appealing to high school girls makes this
finding especially significant. Again, the matter of degree is
important. Occasional escapes from reality are good and necessary, but a steady diet of fantasy might be harmful.

Mass Media: Their Total Effects

The total impact of mass media upon children is even
greater than a consideration of each medium separately would
indicate. For one thing, these media are at present absorbing
a large portion of children's leisure time. This fact in itself can
be deplored, for it means that children are devoting more and
more of their time to passive leisure pursuits and less and less
time to active and creative forms of behavior. Whether this will
eventually have an effect upon the basic personality structure
of American children remains to be seen.

Since there is considerable similarity in the content offered
by the various media, their cumulative effect upon children is
likely to be great. Superficial effects upon dress, play, grooming,
language, and the like can easily be noted. Zorros and Wyatt
Earps abound in every community; Hollywood hairdos and

sweater girls, in every high school. Through the mass media, children are exposed to the whole gamut of models of behavior and standards of living which exist in America, and some of these models influence their dress and manners.

The subtler influences upon social and moral development are more difficult to measure. Many adults deplore the preponderance of comics, films, and radio and television programs which are devoted to crime and violence. Some believe, as we have mentioned, that in general this preponderance is not serious because right always triumphs in the end, and because the child may use the media as an outlet for his own aggressive feelings. Nevertheless, at least one critic questions whether so much exposure to violence and crime, and so little to anything else, does not influence the tastes of young children adversely (Jersild, 1947). Violence and crime, of course, appear in good literature too, but only the modern child has been exposed to so much of it in unadulterated form. More research on the values exemplified in the mass media, as well as on the possible influences of these values upon children, is needed.

In recent years, there have been attempts to apply principles derived from learning theory to a study of the impact of mass media upon the socialization process. Presumably each comic book, motion picture, or television program contains a communication or "message." Under what conditions does this message have an impact upon the child? If the message is an aggressive one, is it likely to foster aggression in the child? Do children become juvenile delinquents as a result of repeated exposure to stories of crime and horror? These questions are of interest, not only to the research psychologist, but to all concerned with the welfare of children.

The learning theorist thinks of aggression as an acquired drive which arises in response to frustration. Tension built up in the organism as a result of frustration is discharged in an aggressive act. Some of the children who are exposed to aggression in the mass media already have strong aggressive drives, learned as they were socialized. (Chapter 16 will deal with this learning in some detail.) They have learned to release tension through aggression. Are these children more likely than other children to be affected by an aggressive message in a motion picture, comic strip, or television program?

As a way of studying the differential effects of a movie with high aggressive content, Maccoby and others (1956) first "frustrated" groups of fifth- and sixth-grade pupils by giving them too-difficult tasks in a spelling bee. Then the pupils were shown a movie with a high aggressive content. The children were tested a week later on the content of the film, and their test scores were compared with those of a control group of children who had also participated in the spelling bee, seen the movie, and taken the test, but who had been given very easy words to spell.

Results showed that the nonfrustrated children remembered the total content of the movie somewhat better, but that the frustrated children remembered more of the aggressive content. At the same time, the latter remembered less of the neutral content. The emotional arousal effected by the frustrating spelling bee apparently caused the frustrated group in this experiment to concentrate on the aggressive content and to fail to notice the nonaggressive material.

But, as an illustration of the complexity of research on the impact of mass media, a repetition of this experiment on other groups of children failed to confirm these findings (Maccoby *et al.*, 1956). There are undoubtedly other variables at work which must be taken into consideration in planning experiments. We can speculate about what some of these might be. The extent to which the child identifies with the aggressor, whether the aggressive act is punished as well as how it is punished, whether it is used for good purposes or bad—these and other variables might conceivably influence the effectiveness of a particular message for a particular child (Brodbeck, 1955).

The studies by Brodbeck and by Maccoby and others have been concerned with the possible effects of mass media upon the motivations of children. However, cognition, as well as motivation, undoubtedly influences what a person does; that is,

what a child considers to be the realities of social life may influence his behavior. In particular, according to one investigator
(Siegel, 1958), cognition helps to determine the child's role
expectations; he learns to expect certain behaviors from a person having a particular status in our society, and he learns what
he himself is expected to do when he holds that status. These
role expectations in turn help to shape behavior. If the child's
concept of his own role calls for aggression, he may be aggressive; if he perceives the other person's role to be an aggressive
one, he may modify his own behavior accordingly. Siegel tested
the hypothesis that the role expectations held by children are
modified by the content of dramatic presentations in the mass
media and found that the data supported her hypothesis. An
experimental group, exposed to a story in which a taxi driver is
very aggressive, attributed more aggression to a taxi driver in a
supposedly real-life situation than did a control group. Apparently, the message contained in a dramatic presentation, at
least with respect to role behaviors, gets across to children,
although we still cannot predict exactly how a particular child's
knowledge of role expectations will affect his behavior. Motivation *and* cognition together contribute to behavior.

American children are being exposed to mass media as
never before. Witty (1956) reported, on the basis of a survey
made in 1955, that the elementary school child averaged twenty
hours of television viewing alone. What did he see during those
hours? The National Association for Better Radio and Television surveyed television programs in Los Angeles for a week
and discovered that programs viewed before nine o'clock showed
223 deaths, 161 of them murders; 192 attempted murders; 83
robberies; 15 kidnappings; and 24 other instances of violence.
Research on the impact of these programs is sorely needed.

The adaptability of the mass media for propaganda purposes is frightening to contemplate. Where access to the juvenile
mind is so readily available, there is always the danger that
forces of evil will attempt to seize control. Our only safeguard
against such a danger lies in intelligent listeners. Only if children receive help and practice in analyzing the values and tech-

niques in mass media can we be assured of such a safeguard. One communications expert charges the schools as follows:

> What can the schools do about it? They can orient their pupils toward the real world we live in to a greater degree than is now done. A conspicuous opportunity lies before teachers in the humanities, especially in the field of English. Our curricula in these fields are heavily weighted with literature—prose and poetry—and with drama. But our population, once it leaves school, pays precious little attention to such material. Instead, we find that reading rates low on all studies of how people spend their leisure time. . . . The "literature" and "drama" of our present culture are thus predominantly composed of what is heard over the radio (and, to a lesser degree, what is seen in movies and read in magazines and newspapers). Increasingly, our "literature" and "drama" will grow to consist of what is seen over TV.
>
> The schools of our democracy have the obligation to serve its needs. In the field of English, these needs are for the development and practice of standards of criticism as applied to the popular "literature." This is not the occasion for a discussion of what such standards should be. Knowledge and experience in criticism of art forms already exist which may be adapted. The objectives are simple. Selective use of the media should be encouraged, based ultimately on respect for the dignity of man. And the pupils should be encouraged to make known to the stations (or movie-makers or publishers) their considered judgments on the program fare they are offered. They should learn their rights and responsibilities toward TV (and radio generally) in their capacities as future citizens and co-owners of the radio channels which they, through their federal agencies, license to private persons for use in the "public interest, convenience, and necessity." It goes without saying that before they can teach such things, teachers should practice such rights and responsibilities themselves [Smythe, 1950, p. 52].

SUGGESTED READINGS

BARKER, ROGER G., & WRIGHT, HERBERT F. *Midwest and Its Children*, Evanston, Ill.: Row, Peterson, 1954. Chapter 1 presents the general problem and methods of psychological ecology; Chapter 13 summarizes the findings of the Midwest study.

DEWEY, RICHARD, & HUMBER, W. J. *The Development of Human Behavior,* Macmillan, 1951. Chapter 25, "The Good Society," takes to task those sociologists who are reluctant to evaluate any society or culture. The authors provocatively discuss the concept of "the good society" and propose an evaluation in terms of the basic needs of mankind.

HIMMELWEIT, HILDE T., OPPENHEIM, A. M., & VINCE, PAMELA. *Television and the Child,* Oxford, 1958. Three British sociologists report on the impact of television upon English children. The book suggests some interesting contrasts between British and American habits and tastes in television; although the English child, like the American, prefers exciting stories with a good deal of action, children's programs in England show less realistic scenes of violence than the programs designed for American children.

LAZARSFELD, PAUL F., & STANTON, FRANK N. (eds.). *Communications Research 1948-1949,* Harper, 1949. Part 1, "American Mass Media in Action," is an analysis of the comics from the standpoint of content, types of comic fan, and child and parental attitudes toward comics.

PACKARD, V. O. *The Hidden Persuaders,* McKay, 1957. A popularly written book which analyzes the drives in the consumer to which advertisers try to appeal in the mass media and also describes how they try to create new drives. Chapter 15 deals with "The Psycho-Seduction of Children."

the course of normal
development

14
physical and motor development

Having examined the influence of biological factors and the impact of society and culture upon the individual, we are now prepared to describe the outcome of these two influences, the course of normal development. In this chapter we shall return again and again to facts, principles, and generalizations introduced in our earlier discussion of the biological nature of the child.

PHYSICAL DEVELOPMENT

No student of the developmental process is or can be completely indifferent to the physical aspects of that process. Some, however, are relatively incurious about the details of physical development or about its relationship to behavioral and personality development. Most studies of physical growth give little or no attention to the psychological concomitants of that process; similarly, most studies of psychological development ignore the physical characteristics of their subjects. Despite the belief that only interdisciplinary investigation can unravel the tangled web of the developmental process, specialization of research and knowledge continues to increase. One investigator, who has attempted to relate physique and temperament, has recently complained that "the social sciences . . . [are] dominated by a curiously motivated group of people—really a sort of lunatic fringe so devoted to a one-sided approach to psychologic dynamics that even the mention of physical structure has been considered an infuriating intrusion if not a heretical subversion" (Sheldon, 1957, p. 125). And Helen Thompson has reminded us that:

> Just as child behavior cannot be understood apart from the cultural forces impinging on it, so it cannot be understood apart from the internal stimuli in effect and the physical body through which it perceives, reacts, and functions, and to which others react. It is the child's physical maturity that governs, limits, and to a large extent determines his physical and social environment [1954, p. 292].

Fortunately, evidence of concomitant variation in physical and psychological factors does exist, permitting not only a description of the process of physical development and the factors which influence it but also some conclusions about the relationship between developmental status and physique, on the one hand, and behavior and temperament, on the other.

The Measurement of Growth

As physical growth is complex, so is its measurement. Since growth is a form of motion (Tanner, 1955), two questions arise: How *much* has an individual grown? How *fast* is he growing? The graphic answer to the first question is a *distance* curve; the answer to the second is a *velocity* curve.

Two types of study provide answers to these questions. (See also p. vii.) In a *cross-sectional* study, no child is measured more than once; the subjects at any one age level, then, are different from those at any other age level. In a *longitudinal* study, each child is measured at each age level; the subjects are the same at all age levels. A cross-sectional study of growth over the entire developmental span can be done in the time it takes to do the measurements. A longitudinal study requires as many years as there are in the period to be covered; the investigation grows with the youngsters and is ended only with the completion of the growth of its subjects.

Cross-sectional data provide distance curves of growth; they tell us how much growth is achieved on the average at any particular age level. Such data provide only relatively crude estimates of growth velocity unless the number of subjects is large. In fact, if they are to result in estimates of average growth increments as accurate as those derived from longitudinal studies, cross-sectional studies require more than twenty times as many subjects (Shuttleworth, 1937). If we are interested in the variability of growth velocity from one year to another, longitudinal data are essential (Tanner, 1955).

The Growth Cycle

The cycle of growth may be described most simply as two periods of rapid growth with an intervening period of steady slow growth. The first phase of growth takes place in the months before birth and in the years of infancy and early childhood. As impressed as we are—and rightfully so—with changes in size in the child after birth, we must take note of the fact that the greatest increments (relative *and* absolute) are found in the prenatal period. The highest velocity of growth in length (or height) is recorded near the end of the second trimester of pregnancy; the most intense spurt of growth in weight occurs in the third trimester, the gain being at the rate of over 200 grams (or almost a half pound) a week by the middle of the trimester (Stuart & Stevenson, 1954). The second period of rapid growth is, of course, adolescence. Moderate increases characterize the intervening years of childhood.

Within this general pattern there are significant variations in the quantity and timing of change from one part or tissue of the body to another. Scammon (1930) has identified four types of postnatal growth, as illustrated in Figure 14-1. The curves indicate the percentage of adult size attained at each chronological age level. (Size at birth is 0; size at age 20 is 100 on the vertical scale.)

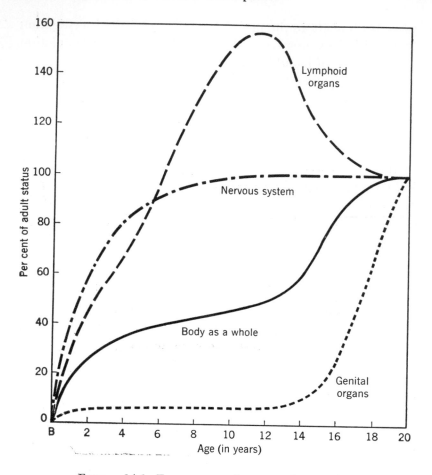

FIGURE 14-1. Four types of postnatal growth.

(After M. L. Faegre & J. E. Anderson. *Child Care and Training,* 7th Ed., University of Minnesota Press, 1947, p. 24)

Although only postnatal growth is depicted, the successive periods of acceleration, deceleration, and acceleration that constitute the general pattern are apparent in the curve for the growth of the body as a whole. The components of this curve include all external dimensions (except those of head and neck), respiratory and digestive organs, musculature as a whole, and skeleton as a whole. But the nervous system, including the brain, participates in only the first and second of these growth periods.

In the first year of life, the brain attains almost half its adult size; by the age of 6 years, it has completed 90 per cent of its growth. In contrast, genital growth is slow in infancy and childhood, rapid in adolescence. The lymphoid tissues and organs grow very rapidly in childhood, reaching a peak at puberty, and actually decrease in size thereafter.

Growth of the Body as a Whole

The most common measures of growth concern changes in size, particularly in height and in weight, and changes in body form and proportion.

CHANGES IN SIZE. Distance and velocity curves for height, male and female, are presented in Figure 14-2. The curves for weight are shown in Figure 14-3. The data are based on measurements made of children at 3, 6, 9, and 12 months of age, then at six-month intervals through the fifth birthday and at annual intervals until and including the seventeenth year. The subjects were free of gross physical and mental defects; their parents were above average in socioeconomic status and in education and were of North European ancestry; all were white. A total of 999 children, 515 boys and 484 girls, was examined. The data are *mixed longitudinal* (Tanner, 1955), in that some of the children entered the program after it was begun and some left before it was completed; therefore, the subjects were not the same at all age levels, although there was considerable overlap from one age to the next.

As these graphs show, growth in height and weight is most rapid in earliest infancy. If the rate were maintained through childhood and adolescence, the average adult would be 200 feet tall and would weigh 10 tons; actually, height increases only fourfold and weight twentyfold in the period from birth to maturity (J. E. Anderson, 1949).

The decrease in rate of growth is particularly marked during the first 2 years. At 3 months, length has increased by 20 per cent over that at birth; at 1 year, by 50 per cent; and at 2 years, by 75 per cent. Not until the age of 4 will the infant double his birth length. Similarly, it requires only 5 months for the infant

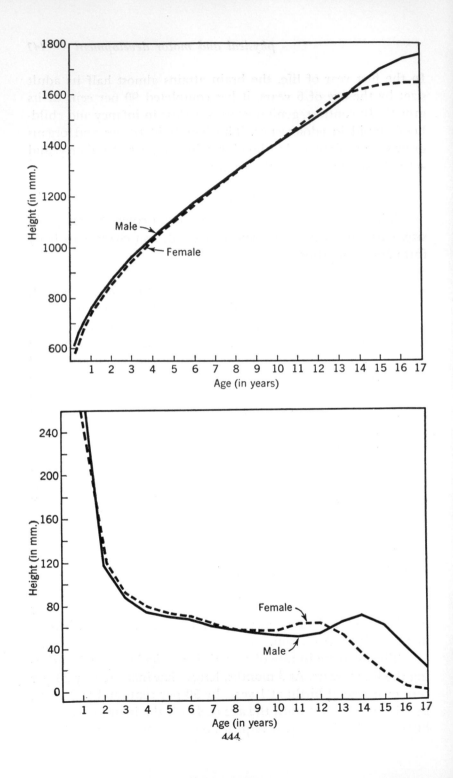

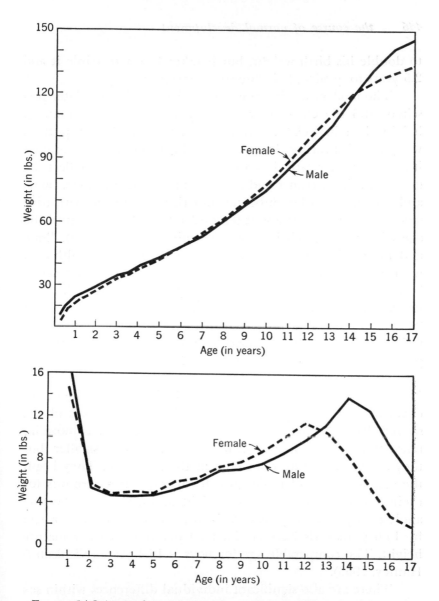

FIGURE 14-2 (*opposite*). Means of standing height (*top*) and mean annual standing-height increments (*bottom*), 3 months to 17 years, Brush Regular Series, male and female.

FIGURE 14-3. Means of weight (*top*) and mean annual weight increments (*bottom*), 3 months to 17 years, Brush Regular Series, male and female.

(After K. Simmons. The Brush Foundation study of child growth and development. II. Physical growth and development. *Monogr. Soc. Res. Child Develpm.*, 1944, 9:1, 41, 43, 44) to double his birth weight, but it takes 1 year to triple it and 2.5 years to quadruple it (Stuart & Stevenson, 1954).

The moderation in growth that characterizes the later pre-school and the elementary school years is more apparent in height than in weight. Furthermore, the adolescent spurt in weight begins earlier than the spurt in height, and the annual increments are relatively greater. Changes in weight reflect the growth of many tissues and organs, among them muscle, bone, and subcutaneous fat. Subcutaneous tissue increases in relative amount from birth to about 9 months, then decreases until the age of 6, after which it increases again (Tanner, 1955). Bone and muscle increase throughout the growth period, although with generally decreasing velocity. Mature stature is reached before the skeletal musculature is fully developed; the develop-ment of the heart muscle may be even further delayed (Stuart & Stevenson, 1954). Muscles constitute 20 to 25 per cent of body weight at birth, 30 to 35 per cent in early adolescence, and 40 per cent at maturity (Breckenridge & Murphy, 1958).

Males are generally larger than females, except for the years 11 to 13 in height and the years 6 to 14 in weight. The differ-ences become particularly significant in the latter half of the second decade, chiefly because the adolescent spurt is more in-tense and more prolonged in males. Girls may be smaller, but they are more mature than boys of the same age. They begin the second period of rapid growth earlier, which accounts for their temporary advantage in height and weight in the pre-adolescent years. They also reach adult status at an earlier age; by 14.6 years girls have attained 99 per cent of their mature height. The comparable age for boys is 16.4 years (Nicolson & Hanley, 1953).

There are also significant individual differences within sex groups in growth in height and weight. These differences be-come marked in the second decade, with wide variation from child to child in the timing of the beginning, the peak, and the end, as well as in the magnitude and intensity, of the adolescent growth spurt. Using longitudinal data from the Harvard Growth Study, Shuttleworth (1939) classified more than 1500 subjects by age at maximum growth. Figure 14-4 shows the growth trends in average height and in the average annual increments in height for nine groups of girls and ten groups of boys having different maximum-growth ages.

The average age at maximum growth for the total of 711 boys included in the analysis was 14.8 years; for the total of 747 girls included, it was 12.6 years. The range for the groups of boys was from 12.5 to 17.0; for the groups of girls, from 10.5 to 14.5. The actual range was, of course, greater, since the maximum growth ages of the girls in Group A fell between 10.25 and 10.74 years and those of the girls in Group I between 14.25 and 14.74 years, making the range from 10.25 to 14.74. The corresponding range for boys was 12.25 to 17.25 years. Furthermore, some girls experienced maximum growth even earlier than 10.25 years, and some boys, earlier than 12.25 years. Shuttleworth eliminated these relatively infrequent cases from his analysis.

In the velocity curves (Fig. 14-4, *bottom*) the grid lines at the left marked "SLG" and "2 SLG" provide a measure of the intensity of the adolescent growth spurt. They denote, respectively, "straight-line growth" and "twice straight-line growth" from ages 8 to 17 for girls and from ages 10 to 19 for boys. That is, if average growth in height during these periods proceeded by constant annual increments, the points would fall on the "SLG" line; if growth took place at a constant rate but was twice the average amount for the periods indicated, the points would fall on the "2 SLG" line.

Boys not only grow more; they grow more intensely. However, the increments for the fastest growing girls exceed those for the slowest growing boys. Within both sexes, the earlier the age of maximum growth, the more intense is the increment in height. That is, the individual who begins his adolescent growth early is relatively short in stature and has more to grow if he is to reach an adult height not significantly different from that of his late-maturing peers, as is probable in the case of males. Although early maturers tend to be advanced at all ages during the growth cycle, it is unlikely that any boy in Group E would

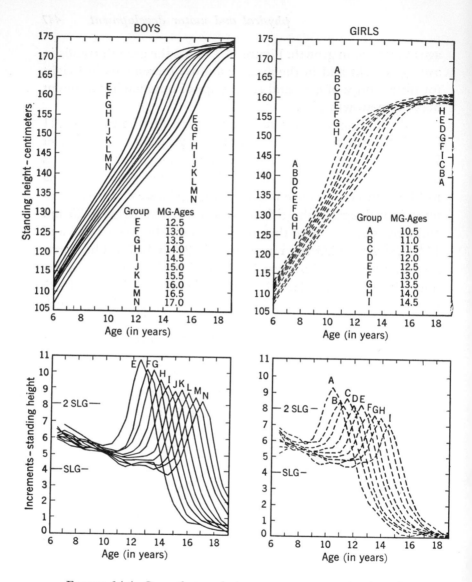

FIGURE 14-4. Growth trends in average stature (*top*) and annual increments of stature (*bottom*) for ten groups of boys and nine groups of girls, classified by age of maximum growth.

(Adapted from F. K. Shuttleworth. The physical and mental growth of boys and girls age six to nineteen in relation to age at maximum growth. *Monogr. Soc. Res. Child Develpm.*, 1939, 4:3) be so tall at his age of maximum growth (12.5 years) as any boy in Group N at *his* age of maximum growth (17.0 years).

By ignoring chronological age and superimposing the curves for the several groups in each sex so that the maximum growth ages are in the same vertical line, Shuttleworth (1939) demonstrated that the patterns of growth of early maturers and late maturers are similar in many respects. Yet the differences in timing, associated as they are with differences in the intensity and magnitude of growth, make the experience extremely dissimilar from one individual to another.

CHANGES IN BODY FORM AND PROPORTION. Differences among the various parts or tissues of the body in the magnitude, intensity, and timing of growth bring about changes in body form and proportion. From birth to adulthood, the head doubles in size and the trunk trebles; the upper extremities quadruple in length and the lower extremities increase fivefold (Krogman, 1955). These differential rates are reflected in changes in the ratio of sitting height (or stem length) to total height: at birth, this index is about .70; at 3 months, .65; at 3 years, .57; at 13 years in girls and at 15 years in boys, .52, rising somewhat thereafter (Bayley, 1956b; Stuart & Stevenson, 1954). These figures indicate that much of the growth in height during childhood is due to the increase in length of the lower limbs; increase in length of trunk accounts for more of the spurt in height during adolescence, when the ratio of trunk length to leg length increases significantly (Tanner, 1955). The head contributes less and less to total body length, from one fourth at birth to one twelfth at maturity.

In adolescence the order in which the various dimensions reach their greatest intensity of growth is as follows: leg length, hip width and chest breadth, shoulder breadth (in boys), trunk length, and chest depth; growth in height reaches its peak midway in the one-year period between the maximum growth velocities in leg length and trunk length (Tanner, 1955). Increases in bone, fat, and muscle tissue during adolescence cumulate to make weight gain relatively greater than height gain.

The result of these differential growth patterns is a progression in body proportions from the chubbiness of infancy to the long-legged, flatter body of childhood to the heavier and stockier adolescent. These changes are illustrated in Figure 14-5, which shows the same subject at six ages from 15 months to 18 years, all adjusted to the same height.

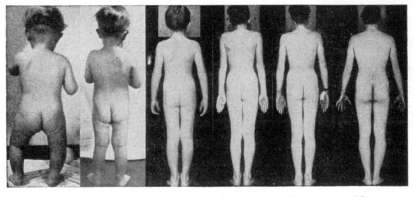

15 mos.   30 mos.   6 yrs.   11 yrs.   14 yrs.   18 yrs.

FIGURE 14-5. Changes in body proportions with growth, from 15 months to 18 years. The photographs are of the same boy at six ages, all adjusted to the same height.

(From N. Bayley. Individual patterns of development. *Child Develpm.*, 1956, *27*, 45-74)

Sex differences in body proportions and form exist throughout the growth cycle. The skelic index—that is, the ratio of lower-limb length to sitting height—differentiates between boys and girls as early as 8 weeks, with girls having relatively longer legs. The difference disappears between 5 and 6 years, reappears at 7 years, and continues through the ninth year (Meredith & Knott, 1938).

There may be small sex differences in subcutaneous fat from birth. At any rate, girls lose fat less rapidly than boys in the first 6 years and gain it more rapidly thereafter. In adolescence there are large gains in bone and muscle tissue and a loss in fat in boys; in girls there is little acceleration in bone growth but a great deal in fat. It is possible to determine the sex of adults with 95-per-cent accuracy from the relative amounts of fat and bone in X rays of the calf; similar X rays of children between the ages of 7 and 8 reveal sex with only 60-per-cent accuracy (Tanner, 1955). The fact that sex differences in fat gain are particularly marked in the legs explains a characteristic difference between males and females in the shape of the legs, particularly in adulthood. With the ankles placed together, there is space between the thighs and even more between the calves of the male; there is only a small space just below the knees and above the ankles of the female.

More striking sex differences in shape become apparent in adolescence, when the male is characterized by broader shoulders, narrower hips, and longer legs and arms (especially forearms). Tanner (1955) identifies three sources of these differences: (*1*) differential growth rates operating only in adolescence (hip and shoulder breadths); (*2*) later adolescent spurt in males, which prolongs for them the effects of differential growth rates that are responsible, from birth onward, for changes in body proportions in both sexes (lower and upper extremities relative to trunk lengths); (*3*) sex differences in growth rate existing from birth or before (relative forearm length).

In their study of growth in the first 3 years of life, Bayley and Davis (1935) used the ratio of weight to the square of height (or length) as a measure of body build. Bayley (1956) has published age curves of body build based on this index for 40 children, all of whom were examined through at least the age of 18 years and some through the age of 25 years (Fig. 14-6). The changes in lateral-linear tendencies in build are in accordance with the facts already cited.

Sheldon and his colleagues (1940) developed a system for describing body build based upon inspection and measurement of the nude standardized photographs of some four thousand male college students. They identified three major components:

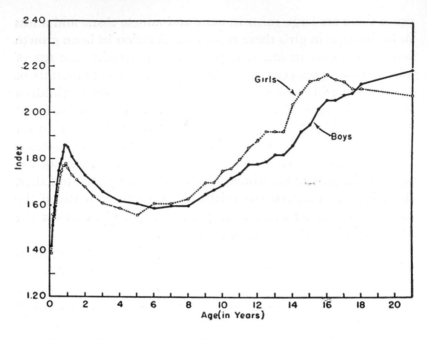

FIGURE 14-6. Age curves of body build for boys and girls, as expressed by the index $\dfrac{\text{weight}}{\text{height}^2}$.

(From Bayley, Individual patterns . . . , *op. cit.*)

endomorphy, mesomorphy, and *ectomorphy.* Endomorphy refers to fatness, roundness, thickness, relatively large viscera but poorly developed extremities; mesomorphy, to muscularity, heaviness of skeleton, and breadth; ectomorphy, to linearity and fragility, relatively large skin area and nervous system. Each photograph was rated on a seven-point scale on each component in turn; the result was a three-digit number representing the somatotype of that individual. The extreme endomorph is represented by the number 711 and is as spherical as it is humanly possible to be; the extreme mesomorph, a 171, is a Hercules; the extreme ectomorph has a somatotype of 117 and looks something like a caricature of an egghead (see Fig. 14-7). A completely average person would be a 444.

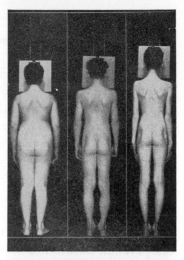

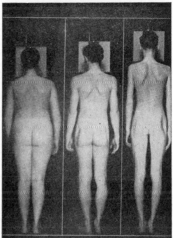

FIGURE 14-7. An extreme endomorph
(5½-3½-2), an extreme mesomorph
(1½-7-1½), and an extreme ectomorph (1-3½-5½), shown at 11.8
years (*top*), 15.0 years (*center*), and
18.0 years (*bottom*). These represent
the most extreme of the 90 subjects
in the California Growth Study,
somatotyped by Sheldon at their
terminal ages, for whom complete
photographic records are available.

(From F. K. Shuttleworth. The adolescent
period: a pictorial atlas. *Monogr. Soc. Res.
Child Develpm.*, 1949, *14*:2)

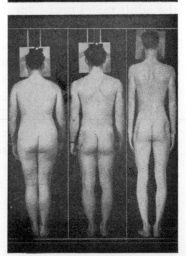

By definition, the somatotype does not change with age or circumstance. It is the best measure that can be made of what is primarily a constitutional characteristic which, of course, becomes completely manifest only at maturity. The system of classification and the claims made for it have been the subject of controversy. Bayley's data indicate that changes in body build, however measured, are not uncommon (1956b). Stuart and Stevenson (1954), although they admit that in cases in which one component is dominant the body type may be apparent from early childhood, conclude that too little research of a developmental nature has been done to permit precise description of body build among children. At the other extreme, Tanner does not believe that the adolescent spurt, regardless of its timing, has any significant effect on body build:

> It adds only the finishing touches to a physique which is recognizable years before. Anyone who has looked at serial pictures of children followed from infancy to adulthood must be impressed chiefly by the similarity the child shows from one age to another. So great is this that *there is little doubt that someone used to looking at children's photographs could predict with accuracy the adult somatotype from a picture taken at age 5 or even earlier* [1955, p. 78; italics added].

Only further research can determine whether the somatotype is indeed permanent and whether it is applicable to male children and to females, both children and adult, as well as to the adult males on whom it is based. At present, it can be said that the Sheldon typology represents the most promising approach available to the study of body build.

Differences in physique are related to rate of maturation. Early maturers among males tend to be high in mesomorphy and low in ectomorphy, while late maturers, both male and female, are inclined to linearity. The suggestion that early-maturing girls are relatively high in endomorphy is still to be confirmed (Tanner, 1955). A comparison of the growth from ages 2 to 17 of 26 ectomorphs and 28 mesomorphs, all males, somatotyped at about age 21, revealed the following: (*1*) the ectomorphs were taller on the average at all age levels from age 4 and grew in height over a longer period of time; (2) the mesomorphs were heavier on the average at all age levels, reached their peak of growth in both height and weight about one year earlier than the ectomorphs, and grew faster in the sense that they reached a higher percentage of adult height at each age level (Dupertuis & Michael, 1953). The writers conclude, not only that boys of different physique have different growth patterns, but also that the somatotype remains fairly constant.

The Assessment of
Physical Growth and Maturity

The discussion thus far has concerned such questions as these: How much does a child grow? How fast does he grow? What is his pattern of growth? The answers to such questions lead inevitably to another: How well is he growing? We sometimes need to evaluate as well as to measure growth. The extent of individual differences in amount, rate, and timing of growth is such that chronological age is an unsatisfactory index of physical maturity. Among the more adequate indicators are *morphological age, skeletal age,* and *sexual age.*

MORPHOLOGICAL AGE. Perhaps the most obvious indicator of developmental status is size. We determine the height of a given child and compare it with the values obtained for children at different chronological age levels. For example, we may find that at 7 years of age Robert is 50.2 inches tall. Using the height-age tables provided by Stuart and Stevenson (1954), we see that Robert is taller than three fourths of his fellow 7-year-olds; in fact, he is slightly taller than the average boy at 7.5 years. It is clear that he is advanced in his growth in stature; at least, he is taller than average for his age. But is he more mature? He may be accelerated in his growth and therefore more mature. Or he may be just a larger-than-average child (who will be a larger-than-average adult) whose greater height at 7 years is normal *for him;* that is, his relative rate of growth may be average.

Weight is also a morphological index of maturity. Sarah is 10 years old and weighs 70.3 pounds, exactly what the average girl of her age weighs. Is Sarah growing normally with respect to weight? She is like other girls of her age in weight. But, if she is taller than average, she may weigh too little; if she is shorter than average, she may weigh too much.

A useful morphological index of maturity would seem to require, at the least, a simultaneous consideration of height, weight, chronological age, and perhaps body build over a period of time to differentiate maturity from size. Consistency over time and between measurements is perhaps a more important indicator of normality of growth than is mere size, for it enables us to distinguish between the consistently small or consistently large child and the child who is irregular in growth (Stuart & Stevenson, 1954). It is the latter whose developmental status may be of some concern.

Methods have been devised for determining morphological age in terms of chronological age, weight, and height. Among the most widely used is the Wetzel grid (1941, 1943, 1946). The grid is a double graph. In the first graph, height is plotted against weight at various age levels to determine a child's "body size" and "physique." The latter is located in one of nine "channels," ranging from "obese" to "very thin." In the second graph, age is plotted against "body size" to arrive at a measure of rate of development. Under normal conditions, the growth of any given youngster tends to follow the same physique channel and to maintain the same relative rate (fast, slow, or average). A shift in channels or a change in rate of growth may indicate malnutrition, disease, or emotional disturbance. The grid has also been adapted for infants (Wetzel, 1946).

The Wetzel grid has been criticized on at least two grounds: it is claimed that normal growth does not necessarily follow a channelwise progression (Garn, 1952; Sontag & Garn, 1954); further, the grid appears to give too much importance to weight, so that obesity may erroneously be taken as a sign of developmental advancement (Stuart & Stevenson, 1954; Tanner, 1955). Nevertheless, the Wetzel grid is perhaps the most imaginative of the morphological indicators that have been offered. Its defects and limitations are those which are common to all such indicators, especially its confounding of size and maturity.

SKELETAL AGE. In the study of human growth, the most common and the most useful method of assessing developmental status over the entire period is skeletal age. The skeleton first appears as a model in cartilaginous tissue early in prenatal life. As we have mentioned in Chapter 3, bone gradually replaces this tissue, the process beginning at ossification centers and spreading concentrically. As replacement proceeds, a given bone increases in width. In the model for a long bone, in addition to the primary center of ossification (the diaphysis, or bone shaft), one or more additional centers (epiphyses) appear at the ends. These additional centers also enlarge and eventually fuse with the shaft, completing the formation of the bone.

The sequence of development is remarkably constant; only the rate varies from individual to individual. In the prenatal and infancy periods, the presence or absence of ossification centers is of greatest significance (see pp. 70-72). In early childhood the relative size of the centers, together with the shape and contour of the bone model, provides a basis for determining skeletal maturity. The process of fusion between epiphyses and diaphyses becomes the significant indicator in later childhood and adolescence. Roentgenograms record this process of development at every stage. Although any part of the body could be used, the hand and wrist are the most convenient since they contain so many centers and bones in a relatively small area (Tanner, 1955). Skeletal-maturity standards, consisting of radiographs representing average status at each of several age levels, are available. Figure 14-8 shows the development of the hand and wrist for the average girl from birth to maturity. The stages we have described are clearly apparent in these X rays.

Sex differences in skeletal development necessitate separate standards for boys and girls. Girls are more advanced in this respect than boys at all ages, slightly so at birth (see Table 3-2, p. 72), by a year at the beginning of the elementary school period, and by two years upon entrance into high school

Birth

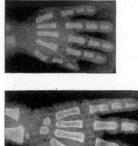

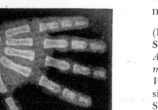

1 year

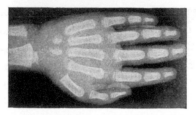

2 years

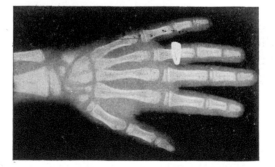

5 years

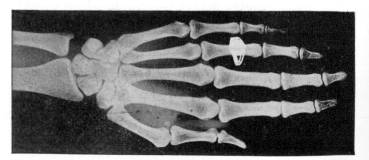

18 years

(Thompson, 1954). Again we see that, although girls are generally smaller than boys, they are more mature at all ages during childhood and adolescence. These differences reflect the two processes involved in physical growth: the multiplication of cells, associated with size; and the differentiation of cells, associated with maturity (Tanner, 1955).

SEXUAL AGE. The physical characteristics associated with sexual maturity appear in a relatively orderly sequence, differing from one individual to another within a sex group only in time of appearance. Thus they provide a third index of maturity, which is especially useful in later childhood and adolescence.

Tanner (1955) recommends separate ratings of genital and pubic-hair development for boys and separate ratings of breast and pubic-hair development for girls. The two ratings for each sex can be averaged if a composite measure is desired.

The five stages of pubic-hair development, applicable to both sexes, are as follows:

Stage 1. Preadolescent. The vellus over the pubes is not further developed than that over the abdominal wall—i.e., no pubic hair.

Stage 2. Sparse growth of long, slightly pigmented, downy hair, straight or only slightly curled, appearing chiefly at the base of the penis or along the labia.

Stage 3. Considerably darker, coarser, and more curled. The hair spreads sparsely over the junction of the pubes. It is at this stage that pubic hair is first seen in the usual type of black and white photograph of the entire body; special arrangements are necessary to photograph Stage 2 hair.

Stage 4. Hair now resembles adult in type, but the area covered by it is still considerably smaller than in the adult. No spread to the medial surface of the thighs.

Stage 5. Adult in quantity and type with distribution of the horizontal (or classically "feminine") pattern. . . . Spread to medial surface of thighs but not up linea alba or elsewhere above the base of the inverse triangle [Tanner, 1955, pp. 25-26].

The typical boy reaches Stage 2 after his twelfth birthday and Stage 5 just before his sixteenth birthday. The normal range for Stage 2 is from age 10 to 15; for Stage 5, from 14 to 18. The average age at which girls reach Stage 2 is slightly over 11 years, with a normal range of from 8 to 14 years; Stage 5 hair appears on the average at about 14 years.

The earliest sign of sexual maturation in the male is, however, the acceleration of genital development. The five stages, again from Tanner, are as follows:

Stage 1. Preadolescent. Testes, scrotum, and penis are of about the same size and proportion as in early childhood.

Stage 2. Enlargement of scrotum and of testes. The skin of the scrotum reddens and changes in texture. Little or no enlargement of penis at this stage. . . .

Stage 3. Enlargement of penis, which occurs at first mainly in length. Further growth of testes and scrotum.

Stage 4. Increased size of penis with growth in breadth and development of glans. Further enlargement of testes and scrotum; increased darkening of scrotal skin.

Stage 5. Genitalia adult in size and shape. No further enlargement takes place after Stage 5 is reached . . . [1955, p. 25].

Testicular growth begins on the average at about 12 years, thus signaling the approach of puberty; the range is from age 10 to 13.5. Growth is completed at about 16 years on the average, with a range from 14.5 to 18 years. The period of penis growth is somewhat shorter; the average age at the beginning of growth is 13, with a range from 11 to 14.5 years; average age at the end of the growth period is 15, with a range from 13 to 17.5 years.

Five stages in breast development, identified by Reynolds and Wines (1948), are as follows:

Stage 1. Preadolescent: elevation of papilla only.

Stage 2. Breast bud stage: elevation of breast and papilla as small mound. Enlargement of areolar diameter.

Stage 3. Further enlargement and elevation of breast and areola, with no separation of their contours.

Stage 4. Projection of areola and papilla to form a secondary mound above the level of the breast.

Stage 5. Mature stage: projection of papilla only, due to recession of the areola to the general contour of the breast [Tanner, 1955, p. 30].

The appearance of the breast bud (Stage 2) is the forerunner of adolescence in the female, typically occurring at about 11 years, just prior to the appearance of pubic hair (also Stage 2); it may appear as early as 8 years and as late as 13 years. Breast development is ordinarily completed between the ages of 13 and 14, after the age of menarche (first menstruation).

INTERRELATIONSHIPS OF MATURITY MEASURES. How well do these various measures of developmental status agree? Is a child who is considered advanced according to one index also advanced according to other indicators? Nicolson and Hanley (1953) undertook a study of various measures of physiological maturity, using data from a longitudinal study of 180 boys and girls examined annually from 1 to 8 years of age and semiannually thereafter until 18 years of age. They found a relatively high degree of agreement. Early-maturing girls tended to be advanced in all respects—appearance of sex characteristics, skeletal development, and attainment of mature height. The same may be said of boys, although the intercorrelations were not so high as in girls. The best single measure of maturity for both sexes was found to be age at reaching 90 per cent of mature height.

There seems to be a tendency for an individual to be advanced or retarded as a whole. But it is only a tendency. More than one measure is always advisable. Tanner (1955) recommends the use, when it is available, of the unweighted average of the ages at which the following are attained: 90 per cent of mature height; skeletal age of 12.75 (girls) or 14.75 (boys); pubic-hair Stage 3; and breast or genitalia Stage 3.

Bayley (1956a) has published growth curves of height and weight for boys and girls, scaled according to physical maturity, as measured by hand and knee X rays and by percentage of adult stature attained. These curves are based on measurements of some three hundred healthy California children examined repeatedly from birth until 18 to 21 years of age. In each height chart, distance and velocity curves are presented, together with the percentages of mature height reached at each age level by youngsters who are advanced, average, and retarded in their development (see Figs. 14-9 and 14-10). Similar curves are presented for weight, with tables of mean weights for height by age for each of the three maturity groups (Figs. 14-11 and 14-12).

The central-distance curve in each case (C) represents the growth of an average-sized child. The curves just above (or below) this central curve depict the growth of an individual who is large (or small) only because he is fast (or slow) in maturing. The top and bottom curves (A and E) represent the growth of children who are both constitutionally large (or small) *and* accelerated (or retarded) in developing. It should be noted that only when constitutional differences in size are present do we find significant differences in adult stature. Rate of maturing seems to have somewhat more relation to adult weight, particularly in girls. In Figure 14-11, separate velocity curves are shown for boys in the three maturity groups. In Figures 14-9, 14-10, and 14-12, the maximum annual increments of the early and the late maturers are noted by dots. In normal growth, the child's weight and height curves should be in the same channel and should follow the same general pattern of yearly increments. Any disparity in magnitude or direction can be taken as an indicator of nutritional status.

1. Tuddenham and Snyder (1954) have published growth records for 66 males and 70 females on the following measures obtained seriatim from birth to 18 or more years of age: weight, height, stem length, shoulder width (biacromial), hip width (bi-iliac), leg circumference, and strength. For each subject, the age of attaining skeletal maturity and the somatotype at that age are given. In addition, for each girl, age of menarche is given. To what extent do these data (or any other longitudinal data to which you have access) confirm the following generalizations:

a. The greatest increments of postnatal growth in height and weight are found in infancy and early childhood.
b. Adolescent increments in height and weight are greater for boys than for girls.
c. The earlier the age of maximum growth in adolescence, the more intense is the velocity of height growth.
d. The ratio of stem length to total height decreases from birth to a minimum in late childhood and rises in adolescence.
e. Early-maturing boys tend to be more mesomorphic than late-maturing boys.
f. Girls tend to reach skeletal maturity earlier than do boys.
g. Age of menarche follows or is the same as age at maximum growth in height in adolescence in girls.

Factors Influencing Physical Development

The complex sequence of events in physical development, together with the marked differences in magnitude, intensity, and timing among individuals and between the sexes, suggests that the determinants of the process must be complex and multiple. But the orderliness of the sequence from individual to individual strongly implies a high degree of internal regulation and control, with external factors having but limited influence. The nature of the growth cycle also indicates that genetic influences on the rate and timing of growth are exerted somewhat independently of those on amount of growth and final size attained (Tanner, 1955). It is probable that all growth influences, whether hereditary, constitutional, or environmental, are mediated by the glands of internal secretion (Stuart & Stevenson, 1954). Changes in size and maturity and sex differentiation are correlated with complex changes in the nature and amount of hormones secreted by these glands and in the sensitivity of various tissues and organs to hormonal stimulation (Tanner, 1955). Disturbances or dysfunction, whatever their origin, in this intricate endocrinological mechanism result in disturbance in the growth cycle.

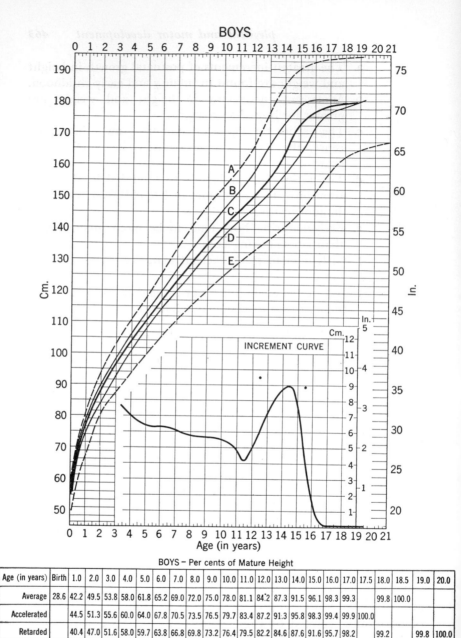

BOYS

Age (in years)	Birth	1.0	2.0	3.0	4.0	5.0	6.0	7.0	8.0	9.0	10.0	11.0	12.0	13.0	14.0	15.0	16.0	17.0	17.5	18.0	18.5	19.0	20.0
Average	28.6	42.2	49.5	53.8	58.0	61.8	65.2	69.0	72.0	75.0	78.0	81.1	84.2	87.3	91.5	96.1	98.3	99.3		99.8	100.0		
Accelerated		44.5	51.3	55.6	60.0	64.0	67.8	70.5	73.5	76.5	79.7	83.4	87.2	91.3	95.8	98.3	99.4	99.9	100.0				
Retarded		40.4	47.0	51.6	58.0	59.7	63.8	66.8	69.8	73.2	76.4	79.5	82.2	84.6	87.6	91.6	95.7	98.2		99.2		99.8	100.0

BOYS – Per cents of Mature Height

FIGURES 14-9 and 14-10. Growth curves of height by age
and annual-increment curves for boys (Fig. 14-9, *above*)
and girls (Fig. 14-10, *opposite*).

464

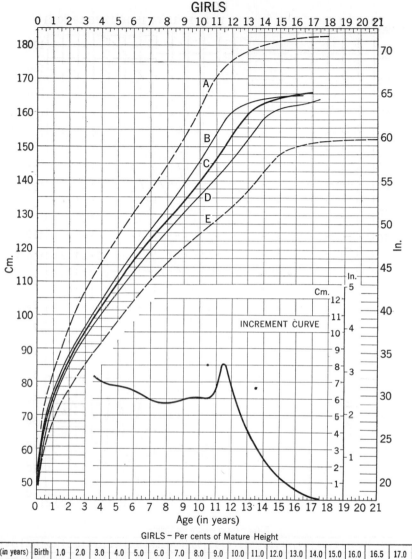

GIRLS

(After N. Bayley. Growth curves of height and weight by age for
boys and girls, scaled according to physical maturity. *J. Pediat.*,
1956, *48*, 187-94)

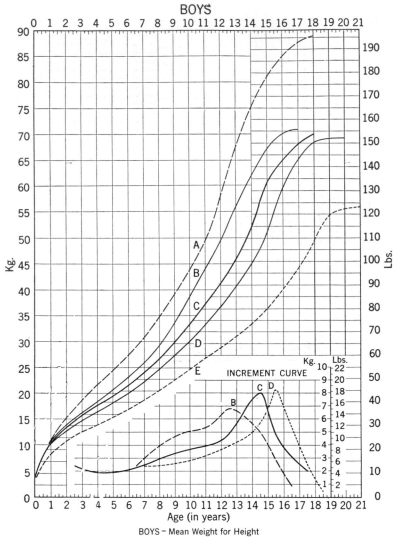

BOYS – Mean Weight for Height

Age (in years)		Birth	1 0	2.0	3.0	4.0	5.0	6.0	7.0	8.0	9.0	10.0	11.0	12.0	13.0	14.0	15.0	16.0	17.0	18.0	19.0
Average	Height, in.	19.8	30.7	34.6	38.0	40.8	43.7	45.8	48.7	50.9	53.1	55.3	57.5	59.1	61.4	64.6	68.1	70.1	70.5	70.9	-
	Weight, lbs.	8.4	22.9	29.3	34.6	39.0	42.8	47.6	52.9	58.2	66.8	74.1	82.2	91.3	101.4	116.0	133.8	142.6	149.7	154.1	-
Accelerated	Height, in.	-	30.9	35.2	38.6	41.5	44.5	47.2	50.0	52.5	54.9	57.3	59.6	61.8	65.6	68.5	70.7	71.7	71.7	-	-
	Weight, lbs.	-	23.8	31.1	35.5	41.4	45.9	51.8	56.9	65.0	74.5	86.0	97.2	109.8	124.8	134.5	147.9	154.1	155.9	-	-
Retarded	Height, in.	-	29.3	32.8	36.2	39.6	42.3	44.9	47.0	49.4	51.8	54.1	55.8	57.7	59.4	61.7	64.2	67.7	69.5	70.5	71.3
	Weight, lbs.	-	23.4	27.3	30.6	35.7	40.3	44.1	48.5	54.7	60.2	66.1	73.4	80.7	90.2	100.1	112.2	131.0	143.1	150.8	151.7

FIGURES 14-11 and 14-12. Growth curves of weight by age and annual weight increments for boys (Fig. 14-11, *above*) and girls (Fig. 14-12, *opposite*).

GIRLS

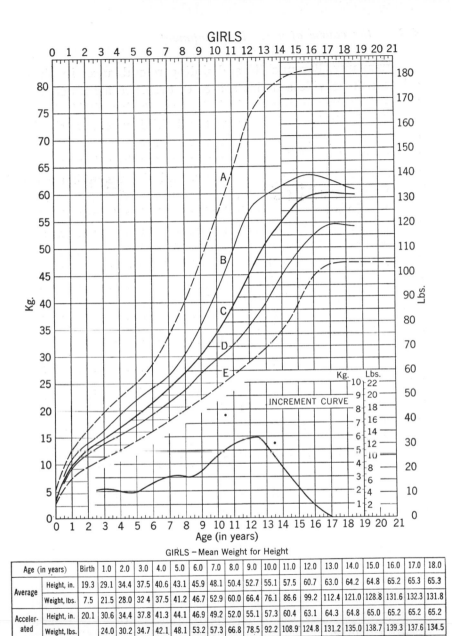

GIRLS – Mean Weight for Height

Age (in years)		Birth	1.0	2.0	3.0	4.0	5.0	6.0	7.0	8.0	9.0	10.0	11.0	12.0	13.0	14.0	15.0	16.0	17.0	18.0
Average	Height, in.	19.3	29.1	34.4	37.5	40.6	43.1	45.9	48.1	50.4	52.7	55.1	57.5	60.7	63.0	64.2	64.8	65.2	65.3	65.3
	Weight, lbs.	7.5	21.5	28.0	32 4	37.5	41.2	46.7	52.9	60.0	66.4	76.1	86.6	99.2	112.4	121.0	128.8	131.6	132.3	131.8
Acceler-ated	Height, in.	20.1	30.6	34.4	37.8	41.3	44.1	46.9	49.2	52.0	55.1	57.3	60.4	63.1	64.3	64.8	65.0	65.2	65.2	65.2
	Weight, lbs.		24.0	30.2	34.7	42.1	48.1	53.2	57.3	66.8	78.5	92.2	108.9	124.8	131.2	135.0	138.7	139.3	137.6	134.5
Retard-ed	Height, in.		28.3	33.3	36.7	39.4	41.7	44.5	47.2	49.2	51.5	53.3	55.5	57.7	59.8	62.4	63.8	64.5	64.8	64.9
	Weight, lbs.		21.2	25.9	30.6	33.7	37.9	43.0	47.6	51.1	59.7	64.8	69.9	78.0	86.9	99.0	108.5	114.6	119.3	119.0

(After Bayley, Growth curves of height . . . , *op. cit.*)

HEREDITY. Parent-child and sibling resemblances in physical growth provide a major source of evidence for a belief in the predominance of genetic influence. Bayley (1954) found that the similarity between parent and child in relative size increased with age. The resemblance in relative size between parent and child of the same sex was greater than that between parent and child of opposite sexes, and the resemblance between mother and daughter was greater than that between father and son. A moderately high correlation (about .40) has been found for age of menarche of mothers and daughters, and of sisters; a much higher one, between identical twins (Tanner, 1955). The correlation coefficients for times of appearance of ossification centers during the period from birth to age 6.5 years for identical twins (.71), siblings (.28), first cousins (.12), and unrelated persons (−.01) also support the hypothesis that growth is controlled genetically (Reynolds, 1943).

NUTRITION. As we have noted (p. 79), a person does not inherit any response or characteristic; he inherits a genotype which responds in a given way to a given environment. Although that genotype may exert a powerful influence, as it seems to do in physical development, the outcome, whether it be stature or rate of maturation, may vary somewhat with the environment.

"Nutritional factors, both in health and in illness, undoubtedly constitute the most common group of causes of retarded growth and development in childhood" (Stuart & Stevenson, 1954, p. 44). Realization of hereditary potential requires adequate nutrition. Retardation in growth is the inevitable result of malnutrition. How severe and prolonged that malnutrition must be before growth is permanently stunted is not known. Tanner emphasizes the recuperative powers of animal and human organism:

> During a short period of malnutrition, the organism slows up its growth and waits for better times; when they arrive, growth takes place unusually fast until the animal has returned to its genetically determined growth curve, along which it then pro-

ceeds as before. . . . Adolescence under these circumstances simply waits until the body has grown, however slowly, to approximately its normal adolescent size or, more probably, to its required maturity [1955, p. 85].

He cites Wolff's study of the effects on Berlin children of nutritional deprivation during World War I. The study showed the children to be retarded in height and weight at age 5 but no longer so at adolescence.

An excess as well as a deficit in the dietary may have consequences for physical growth, particularly in weight. Bruch (1939, 1940, 1941) and Bronstein and others (1942) found that obesity in children was more commonly due to overfeeding than to faulty endocrine function.

As we examine the influence of other factors on physical development, we shall see that nutrition is probably involved, directly or indirectly, in every case, whether it be a matter of climate, secular trends, socioeconomic status, or ethnicity.

CLIMATE AND SEASONAL EFFECTS. The relationship between season of the year and rate of growth is such that the average velocity of growth in height in the Northern Hemisphere in April, May, and June is two to two-and-a-half times that in October, November, and December; increase in weight in October, November, and December is as much as five or six times as great as that in April, May, and June (Tanner, 1955). Tanner suggests that variations in hormone secretion may explain these seasonal variations.

Transcending the seasonal variations are the effects of climate and, more particularly, temperature. Mills (1949), generalizing from animal experimentation, stresses the retarding effects of high temperatures and the accelerating effects of lower temperatures on metabolic activity and consequently on growth and behavior. He would thus explain the slow growth, late maturation, smaller adult size, and generally poorer health of those who live in tropical and semitropical areas. Despite a certain logic in this explanation, it is impossible to disentangle the influences of climate and nutrition. For peoples of the high-temperature zones of the world generally have an inadequate dietary; those of the moderate zones are more likely to be adequately nourished.

SECULAR TRENDS. Increases in adult size from generation to generation have occurred not only in stature but also in weight. Moreover, there has been an increase in the rate of growth over time so that children of today are larger than children of the same age fifty years ago, the differences becoming particularly marked in adolescence (Tanner, 1955). American boys of today are 6 to 8 per cent taller and 12 to 15 per cent heavier than those of a half century ago (Stuart & Stevenson, 1954). This advancement over time can also be seen in the decrease in age of menarche from 1850 to 1950—from one third to one half year per decade (Tanner, 1955). The average age at menarche for American white girls is now between 12.5 and 13.0 years (Nicolson & Hanley, 1953); a hundred years ago it was more nearly 16 or 17 years.

Similarly, the greatest increment in height in the adolescent years is occurring at an earlier and earlier age, as is the age at which adult height is attained. Tanner (1955) estimates that fifty years ago adult height was not attained until the age of 26, as contrasted with the present ages of about 18 in boys and 16 in girls.

Again, nutrition is generally considered the most potent factor underlying these secular changes. Since increases in both size and rate of growth have been experienced at all socioeconomic levels (Meredith, 1941), it cannot be only a matter of increase in caloric intake; it must also involve changes in the quality of diet (Tanner, 1955).

SOCIOECONOMIC STATUS. At all age levels, there are significant differences in size and in rate of growth between children of high and low socioeconomic status. Infants from poor homes weigh less and are shorter than those from good homes, "good" and "poor" being defined primarily in socioeconomic terms (Bakwin & Bakwin, 1931). In the middle-childhood years,

"North American boys of the indigent class probably are more than two inches shorter and five pounds lighter than those of the wealthy class" (Meredith, 1951, p. 709). Nutrition is one cause of this differential. So is the quality of care, including regularity in feeding. Bakwin and Bakwin (1936) found that supervision in a pediatric clinic restored infants from poor homes to normal levels of height and weight. To the extent that there is a relationship between constitutional inferiority and low socioeconomic status, the genetic factor may also be invoked as a partial explanation.

There is some evidence that individuals from upper socioeconomic levels tend to be more linear, or ectomorphic, in build (Tanner, 1955). If we recall that early-maturing youngsters tend to be mesomorphic and that nutrition is given credit for the fact that maturation is taking place earlier and earlier, this socioeconomic differential in body build appears to be a somewhat unexpected result, indicating how complex and how multiple the causation of physical development is. We are also reminded that the growth process itself is very complex; the variables of magnitude, rate, and timing at any age operate independently of one another to a large degree and result in variable outcomes of size and build.

ETHNICITY, NATIONALITY, AND GEOGRAPHY. Differences in size, rate of growth, and physique have been established among groups of differing culture, nationality, and region. Shuttleworth (1939), for example, found significant differences, which increased with age, between American boys of North European extraction and those of Italian stock. At 6 years, the former were 1.73 centimeters taller; at 19, they were 4.09 centimeters taller.

The layman is prone to assume from such data the existence of racial differences. The conclusion is unwarranted, even when the term "racial" is used properly—i.e., to refer to a group united in blood or heredity. So-called racial characteristics may actually be due to differences in pattern of living, including the dietary, that are cultural in origin and related to circumstances of geography and climate. If a change in that pattern of living produces changes in the magnitude and rate of growth, one can be certain that race is not the significant variable.

Greulich (1958) has reported the results of a study comparing the physical growth of 898 American-born Japanese children in California with that of children of the same sex and age in Japan. At every age level, the American-born Japanese boys were taller than the boys in Japan by an amount greater than the secular change in Japan since 1900. The American-born Japanese girls were superior to the girls in Japan at all ages and to the same degree until the age of 14. Furthermore, the skeletal development of the American-born Japanese youngsters compared favorably with that reported for American white children from the Brush Foundation study (see pp. 443-46) who were from families of higher than average socioeconomic status. Greulich concludes that the smaller average stature, the relatively shorter leg length during childhood, and the retardation in skeletal development of children in Japan are not racial characteristics but, rather, the result of environmental conditions which are not so conducive to growth as those found in America. On the other hand, the fact that the ratio of sitting height to stature in the American-born Japanese was not significantly different from that in children in Japan in the postpubertal period, despite the more rapid growth rate of the former, suggests that this ratio may be a valid racial characteristic.

2. Does the fact that similarity in relative size between parent and child increases with age cast doubt upon heredity as an explanatory factor in physical growth?

3. Why cannot the differences in size between American boys of North European and those of Italian extraction be considered racial differences? Is the advanced skeletal status of the Negro at birth (Table 3-2, p. 72) a racial characteristic?

The Relation of Physical Development to Behavior and Personality

Behavior and personality are related both to rate of development, or developmental status, and to physique and size.

Early-maturing boys are more likely to be chosen as leaders in athletic and social activities in school (Latham, 1951). They are, of course, larger at any given age during the adolescent period, stronger and more masculine in build, and more accomplished in athletics; they are rated by their peers and by adult observers as more attractive in physique, better groomed, more relaxed, more matter-of-fact, less affected, more interested in the opposite sex, and better natured (M. C. Jones & Bayley, 1950). In terms of personality, the late maturers show the adverse effects of retardation in physical growth; they are more likely to have negative self-conceptions, feelings of inadequacy, strong feelings of being rejected and dominated, prolonged dependency needs, and rebellious attitudes toward parents (Mussen & Jones, 1957).

Although the early-maturing boy seems to occupy an advantageous position with respect to his late-maturing peer, the reverse is found in girls. The early-maturing girl is seen as submissive, listless in social situations, and lacking in poise (H. E. Jones, 1949). It is the early-maturing girl who has little status or influence among her peers (M. C. Jones, 1958). However, M. C. Jones and Mussen (1958) were unable to confirm these observational findings with data from the Thematic Apperception Test on the same subjects. This suggests that developmental status is of greater social significance among males than among females. The boy who is still a child when his peers have become men faces a serious challenge in his psychological development; the girl who becomes a woman while her peers remain children experiences less difficulty.

Stone and Barker (1939) found that in maturity of interests postmenarcheal girls were approximately a year in advance of premenarcheal girls of the same chronological age. In children who are accelerated in their endocrinological development, Sanford and his colleagues (1943) observed a stronger manifest need to avoid blame and more intense covert antisocial needs, with fear of retaliation. These authors offer the following explanation: "Onset of puberty . . . stimulates the individual toward expression of instinctual biologic urges; as these latter become stronger, the forces for inhibiting and controlling them become stronger . . ." (p. 102).

PHYSIQUE AND TEMPERAMENT. Sheldon has defined three major components of temperament, each of which, like those of physique, are rated on a seven-point scale (Sheldon & Stevens, 1942). The first, *viscerotonia,* is characterized by relaxation, love of physical comfort, sociability, and dependency; the second, *somatotonia,* by assertiveness, adventurousness, and impulsivity; the third, *cerebrotonia,* by restraint, inhibition, secretiveness, and social withdrawal. The correlations for some two hundred subjects between ratings on these temperamental components, based on clinical-interview data, and somatotypes were approximately .80 for viscerotonia and endomorphy, somatotonia and mesomorphy, and cerebrotonia and ectomorphy. These results are almost too good to be true and have been criticized, "though more on the grounds of incredulity than of conflicting evidence" (Tanner, 1953, p. 757).

Sheldon's results are given some confirmation in a longitudinal study of 48 children between the ages of 5 and 14 years on a variety of physiological, psychological, and environmental variables (Sanford *et al.,* 1943). The subjects with a tall, narrow build tended to show signs of "pronounced inner life or inner emotional conflict"; the short, wide subjects tended to be "either socially responsive or placidly immobile" (p. 526).

Glueck and Glueck (1956) found a high relationship between physique and delinquency in their study of 500 delinquent youths and 500 controls (nondelinquent youths). Among the delinquents, 60.1 per cent were somatotyped as mesomorphs; 14.4 per cent, ectomorphs; 11.8 per cent, endomorphs; and 13.7 per cent, the remainder, balanced. The corresponding percentages for the controls were 30.7, 39.6, 15.0, 14.7. It is clear that mesomorphy is associated with delinquency potential and with whatever personality and behavior characteristics may be involved in such a potential.

A further aspect of the relationship between temperament and physique concerns the sex-appropriateness of body build.

To the extent that early maturation is associated with a pre-dominance of mesomorphy in boys and of endomorphy in girls (Bayley, 1943), early-maturing boys have an advantage and early-maturing girls a disadvantage. This may account for the relationships already cited between developmental status and personality and behavior.

To attempt to explain the relationships between physical development and behavior and personality would be to repeat our inconclusive and speculative discussion of the biological basis of individual differences in Chapter 3. Certain behavior and personality patterns may require a certain size or maturity or physique. It is on this basis that the Gluecks explain the relationship they found between mesomorphy and delinquency proneness. To be a mesomorph is not necessarily to be a delinquent; but to be a delinquent, there is a certain advantage in being a mesomorph. Similarly, we would find a greater proportion of mesomorphs participating in any type of activity calling for mesomorphic characteristics. Why is a mesomorph assertive, adventurous, and impulsive? Perhaps, because he can be. Perhaps, because he is expected to be. In the same way, we could explain why early-maturing boys exhibit the behavior and personality and attain the high social status they do. Despite the logic of such arguments and the relationships that have been demonstrated to exist, one note of caution must be sounded: *there is no inevitable relationship.* Certainly, no one individual with any particular physical characteristics must be any particular kind of personality. The relationships are group trends. Not all early-maturing boys are All-American boys; not all late-maturing boys are social outcasts. It is not impossible to be ecto-morphic *and* sociable; it may just take a little more effort. There are some grouchy endomorphs. There are some mesomorphic Caspar Milquetoasts.

    4. How could you explain the fact that it is the *late*-maturing girl but the *early*-maturing boy who possess the more positive behavioral and personality characteristics and the higher social status? Why is developmental status less important in its consequences for girls than for boys?

5. Would grouping children for educational purposes by developmental age rather than by chronological age tend to eliminate, or at least reduce, the psychological consequences of differences in rate of maturing?

MOTOR DEVELOPMENT

From birth, as we have seen, the human being is a very active organism. The activity of the young infant is a combination of mass movement, related primarily to internal factors, and specific reflex acts—searching, sucking, blinking, grasping, Moro, and startle, among others—elicited by both internal and external stimulation (Pratt, 1954). This early sensorimotor behavior is largely involuntary; the organism responds as it must to stimulation over which it has no control. Except in a very limited sense, the baby cannot move toward or away from situations. He can only *be* moved.

With advance in age and maturity, voluntary acts emerge to replace or supplement reflex behavior, and the acquisition of postural-locomotor skills enables the child to move about in his physical world. Increasing ability to reach, to grasp, and to manipulate make it possible for him to manage and control the contents of that physical world. Multiplication of specific skills, together with their integration or patterning in the accomplishment of more and more complex acts, results in a steady advancement in motor ability.

Locomotion

The sequence of development from the prone position of the neonate to standing and walking alone is illustrated in Figure 14-13, which is based on Shirley's careful observation of 25 babies during their first two years of life. The ages given in the chart are those at which each phase of the developmental sequence typically appeared. Individual differences were marked from the beginning and varied in magnitude from stage to stage. Although the average child first lifted his chin up at 3 weeks, one fourth of the group did so before the age of 2 weeks, and another fourth did not do so before the age of

7 weeks. Sitting alone for one minute was characteristic of the 31-week-old child, but the range of ages for the middle 50 per cent of the group was from 27 to 34 weeks. The corresponding range of variation for walking alone was 8 weeks.

Shirley (1931) obtained a graphic record of the walking of each of her subjects at weekly or biweekly intervals from the age of about 4 months. Olive oil was applied to the soles of the feet so that the infant, when he walked or was walked on a white unglazed paper strip, left his marks behind him. Dusting these oil footprints with black powder produced a clear picture of the walking pattern of each of the infants. From this picture it was possible to determine the number of prints, the total distance traversed, the print sequence, the stepping width, and the angles. In each of these measurements, there were individual differences at all age levels. These, together with more subtle differences, difficult to measure but clearly apparent, accounted for the individuality in walking pattern observed: Carol was light on her feet; David was pigeon-toed; Fred stamped; Peter and Patricia both took short, wide steps; and so forth.

Walking alone is, of course, not the end of the process of locomotor development. In the second year, Shirley found evidence of increasing skill as indicated by these changes: increase in speed of walking, increase in length of step, decrease in width of step, decrease in angle of step, and increasing tendency toward straight steps.

Prehension

One of the marvels of early infant behavior, as we have pointed out earlier, is the grasping reflex. Light pressure of an adult's finger upon the palm of the baby's hand will elicit closing of the hand about that finger; withdrawal of the finger results in gripping or clinging. The strength of that clinging is great. Halverson (1937) found that nearly a third of his infant subjects, all less than 24 weeks of age, could support their own weight with both hands when pulled toward suspension.

After the age of 16 weeks, reflexive closing and, at 24 weeks, reflexive clinging disappear and are replaced by volun-

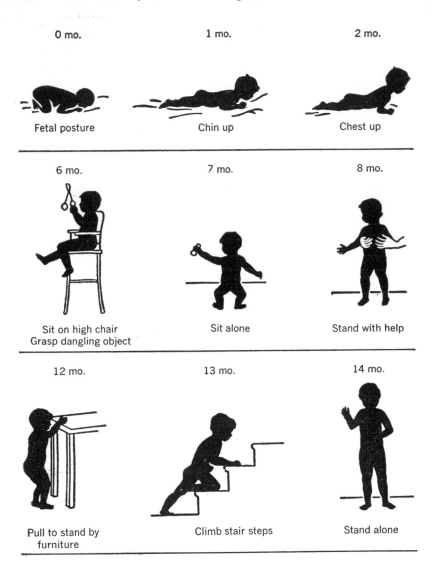

0 mo.	1 mo.	2 mo.
Fetal posture	Chin up	Chest up

6 mo.	7 mo.	8 mo.
Sit on high chair Grasp dangling object	Sit alone	Stand with help

12 mo.	13 mo.	14 mo.
Pull to stand by furniture	Climb stair steps	Stand alone

tary reaching, grasping, and manipulation. At this time thumb opposition begins to function (Halverson, 1932). During the remaining weeks of the first year, prehensile development is rapid. By the end of the period, "In accuracy of reaching and

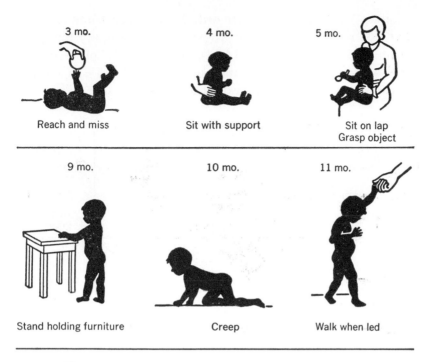

FIGURE 14-13. The motor sequence.

(Adapted from M. M. Shirley. *The First Two Years*, II. Intellectual Development, University of Minnesota Press, 1933)

Walk alone

in precision of grasping, infants . . . rank on almost equal terms with adults in prehension of objects of regular form and of average size" (Halverson, 1932, p. 61). On the basis of careful cinematographic records, Halverson (1931) identified ten types of grasp which appear in an orderly sequence from "no contact," most characteristic at 16 weeks, to "superior-forefinger grasp" at 52 weeks (see Fig. 14-14). Halverson also observed that at first grasping is "enveloping and forceful," while at the end of the year it is "precise and delicate" (1932, p. 61).

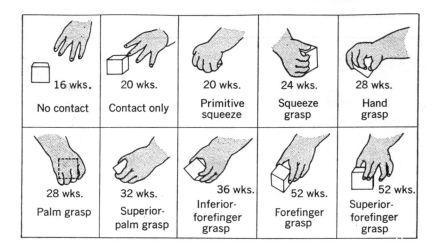

16 wks. No contact	**20 wks.** Contact only	**20 wks.** Primitive squeeze	**24 wks.** Squeeze grasp	**28 wks.** Hand grasp
28 wks. Palm grasp	**32 wks.** Superior-palm grasp	**36 wks.** Inferior-forefinger grasp	**52 wks.** Forefinger grasp	**52 wks.** Superior-forefinger grasp

FIGURE 14-14. Types of grasping behavior in the first year of life.

(Adapted from H. M. Halverson. An experimental study of prehension in infants by means of systematic cinema records. *Genet. Psychol. Monogr.*, 1931, *10*, 107-286)

Handedness

In our discussion of the nature of the child (Chap. 1), we noted the bilateral symmetry of his structure, the asymmetry of his early posture as seen in the tonic neck reflex, and finally the appearance of symmetry, after the age of 3 months, in both his voluntary posture and his behavior in general. From this point, over a period of years, he develops lateral dominance, particularly in the use of his hands. In manipulative acts in which both hands are used, he learns to coordinate them so that one is dominant; in acts in which one hand or the other may be used, he acquires a preference. In other words, he becomes left-handed or right-handed.

During the latter part of the first year, the beginnings of a preference may be seen; by the age of 3 years, the preference is pronounced. That preference is a matter of degree or tendency; there are no "purely" right- or left-handed people. (In some cases, the degree of preference is so slight that we call the person "ambidextrous.") But, in the preschool years, the tendency to prefer the right hand increases; less than 15 per cent of children of this age show a preference for the left hand. The percentage falls to 7 or 8 per cent in the elementary school years and to 5 per cent in adolescence and adulthood. All investigations of handedness indicate that the degree of preference varies with the task, skill, or act. In using a spoon or fork, for example, there is a pronounced preference; in eating with the fingers or in rolling a toy car, there is little or none. The difference between the two types of situation is that some training is involved in the former, but little or none in the latter. There is a significant sex difference in handedness. There are more left-handed males than females, perhaps because males, being more active, have more experience in the use of both hands, but particularly the left (Hildreth, 1949).

There is no agreement on the origin and significance of handedness (G. G. Thompson, 1952). Unimanual dominance is, of course, an advantage, and its development would seem inevitable. But why the world should be right-handed rather than left-handed is not so easy to explain. Although the failure to find a genetic or constitutional basis for handedness has resulted in the increasing popularity of a social-learning theory, the presumed universality of right-handed preference casts some doubt on this theory. Few such socially arbitrary customs have been maintained for so long in so many groups in so many parts of the world.

In any event, it is a right-handed world. Left-handedness is a problem, or at least an inconvenience. Nevertheless, the concern that parents and teachers once showed for such a display of individuality has been largely dissipated in recent years. Few of them spend much energy now in trying to change a child's hand preference once it has been established.

Motor Development in
Childhood and Adolescence

In the preschool and early elementary school years, play activities are essentially motor activities, and children exhibit a steady increase in the level and number of skills they have mastered. On the basis of observations of nearly two thousand children between the ages of 2 and 7 years, Gutteridge (1939) established norms for such common activities as sliding, skipping, climbing, jumping, and tricycling, and ball-throwing, bouncing, and catching. The nature of improvement in a motor skill is exemplified in throwing a ball: at first, it involves the whole body and the use of both hands; by 5 or 6 years of age, nearly three fourths of the children throw well, using only one hand in a pattern of specific movements. Girls, Gutteridge found, were more skillful than boys in hopping, tricycling, galloping, and catching and bouncing balls; boys were superior in ball-throwing, climbing, jumping, sliding, and skipping.

Espenschade (1940) has reported the results of tests of motor performance administered to 80 girls and 85 boys at six-month intervals over a period of three and a half years for the girls and four years for the boys, from the ages of slightly less than 12 to more than 16 years. The tests included distance throw, target throw, standing broad jump, jump and reach, Brace test, 50-yard dash, and dodging run. The mean scores on all tests for boys increased steadily and markedly over the entire age period. The increases were less in girls and, after the age of 14 years, there was a decline in dash and broad-jump records. Sex differences, which increased with age, were all in favor of the boys; they were particularly marked in the broad jump and the distance throw. In general, individuals tended to maintain their group standing from one test period to another.

Components of Motor Skill

STRENGTH. Increases in strength are highly related to increases in weight, particularly in boys. From 3 to 11 years, strength of grip doubles for both boys and girls, the boys being consistently stronger (Metheny, 1941). Figure 14-15 shows the age changes in grip strength of each hand for boys and girls in late childhood and adolescence. Sex differences are in favor of boys throughout the entire age period from 11 through 17 years,

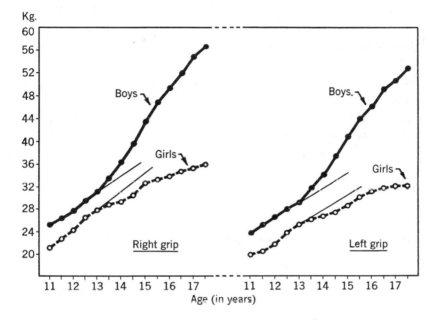

FIGURE 14-15. Age changes in strength of right and left grip of boys and girls.

(From H. E. Jones. Sex differences in physical abilities. *Hum. Biol.,* 1947, *19,* 12-25)

but the superiority becomes especially great after the age of 13. At the end of the period, boys are approximately 60 per cent stronger than girls. This increased discrepancy is, of course, related to the differential adolescent spurt in strength; the earlier sex difference is presumably due in part to the superior length and breadth of the forearm in the male, which exists prior to puberty. It is important to note, however, that the adolescent boy does not attain the strength of a young adult of the same size and body type until about a year after he has completed his physical growth (Tanner, 1955). Stolz and Stolz (1951) report that the greatest increment in strength is experienced some 18 months after the greatest intensity in height growth in adolescence.

SPEED. One measure of speed is reaction time, the interval between the presentation of a signal and the individual's response. It is sometimes a crucial factor in motor performance; an advantage of as little as one hundredth of a second can make the difference between an expert and an average performer. Reaction time decreases with age (Goodenough, 1935); the average time in reacting to a sound is about .5 second at 3.5 years and about .2 second at 9.5 years. In younger children, the sex difference is in favor of boys.

A similar measure of speed was obtained in a longitudinal study of children between the ages of 11 and 15 (H. E. Jones & Seashore, 1944). The results, expressed in standard scores, are shown at the left in Figure 14-16. It appears that a limit of growth is reached at about 14 years of age, at which time the average score is .15 second, equal to that achieved by individuals of college age. There are no significant sex differences.

Speed can also refer to the time required to complete an act or movement. On the right in Figure 14-16 are the results of repeated measurements of the same subjects on the time consumed in inserting a metal stylus in a hole, involving eye-hand coordination. Age changes are similar to those noted for reaction time in these same individuals; sex differences are persistent but not significant.

Atwell and Elbel (1948), using a combined measure of speed—the time needed to move the hand to press a switch after hearing a bell—found a decrease in reaction time in boys over the period from age 14 to age 20.

COORDINATION. Coordination refers to such qualities of motor performance as accuracy, ease, poise, smoothness, and rhythm, all characteristics that separate the champions from the dubs. It can be measured in tests of agility and balance, such as the Brace test (see Espenschade, 1940, p. 126). There is a steady increase with age in scores on the Brace test, especially in boys, sex differences becoming marked after puberty. These steady increases belie any concept of the adolescent as awkward. Longitudinal data indicate, rather, that a clumsy adolescent was prob-

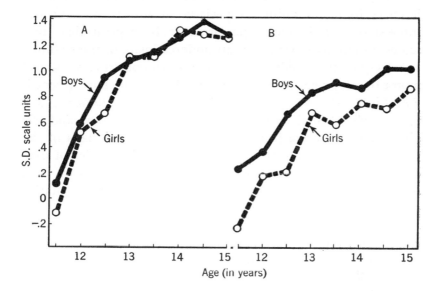

FIGURE 14-16. Age changes in reaction time to sound (A) and in speed of spatial eye-hand coordination (B) of boys and girls.

(From H. E. Jones & R. H. Seashore. The development of fine motor and mechanical abilities. *Yearb. Nat. Soc. Stud. Educ.*, 1944, *43*(I), 123-45)

ably a clumsy child, and, unless special training is given, will probably be a clumsy adult (Tanner, 1955).

The Assessment of Motor Ability

Several difficulties lie in the way of arriving at an over-all measure of general motor ability as it varies from person to person, from age level to age level, and with sex. In the first place, motor skills (unlike intellectual skills) are only slightly related, and what intercorrelations there are decrease as development proceeds. In addition, it is difficult to find tests or tasks for which the experience background of all subjects is comparable—that is, tests or tasks that are equally familiar or unfamiliar to all subjects. Finally, there is the problem of motivation, which is particularly important in determining sex differences in motor ability. Especially in adolescence, the disinterest of girls in motor performance is so great that their scores undoubtedly represent an underestimate of their ability.

Despite these difficulties, attempts to construct a scale of motor development have been made. Among the most recent is *The Lincoln-Oseretsky Motor Development Scale* (Sloan, 1955). Oseretsky's original 85 items were given to 380 boys and 369 girls, ranging in age from 6 to 14 years. On the basis of the results, 36 items were retained and arranged in order of difficulty, an objective scoring system was established for each item (the number of points varying with performance), and tentative norms were determined for each sex at each age level.

Examples of the easier items (in order of increasing difficulty) are: walking backward, standing on one foot, jumping over a rope, closing and opening the hands alternately. The more difficult items (also in order of difficulty) include: tracing mazes, jumping and touching heels, balancing on tiptoe. An inspection of the items indicates that, of the three components of motor skill, strength is least involved in this scale.

Total score on the scale is highly related to age (.87 for males, .88 for females). It appears to be highly reliable and differentiates among children in motor performance at all age levels, except at 14 years for girls. This suggests a leveling off in motor performance, supporting the Espenschade data (see p. 482). Males exceed females in average total score at ages 7 through 11; females are superior to males at age levels 6 and 13; there is no difference at ages 12 and 14. The apparent superiority or equality of females at the later ages is probably due to the sex difference in rate of physical development and to the fact, already noted, that the component of strength is not present to any great degree in the items of this scale.

Factors Influencing Motor Development

SIZE, PHYSIQUE, AND MATURITY. Physical development is highly related to motor development, but the nature of the relationship varies with the motor skill or task. Size may be a disadvantage in locomotor development. Shirley found that the "thin, muscular babies and small-boned babies . . . [walked] earlier than short, rotund babies and exceedingly heavy babies" (1931, p. 126). On the other hand, a 17-year-old boy who weighs 160 pounds and is 70 inches tall would have an advantage in playing tackle over his peer who weighs 120 pounds and is 65 inches tall. The advantage would again be reversed if potential jockeys rather than football players were being considered. The optimal size and physique is specific to the skill. Nevertheless, within limits, the larger (and presumably stronger) the person and the more athletic (mesomorphic) his build, the more proficient he is likely to be in most of the common motor activities. In tests of motor ability, the correlations with height and weight, especially the latter, are significant for boys in adolescence (Espenschade, 1940).

It is to be expected, then, that early-maturing youngsters, particularly boys, will generally have an advantage over their late-maturing age peers. Espenschade (1940) found a generally significant relationship between motor performance and measures of physical maturity in boys, even with chronological age held constant, but not in girls. On specific tests, the influence of maturity varied greatly; skeletal advancement was quite important in the broad jump and the distance throw, but not in the Brace test.

LEARNING AND MATURATION. Our earlier discussion of principles of growth and development (Chap. 4) gave particular attention to the relative contribution of learning and maturation to the development of motor skills. As children grow older and tasks grow more difficult, differences in learning and practice play a larger and larger part in the determination of individual differences.

Even in those instances in which a delay in training until greater maturity has been attained significantly reduces the time required for acquiring a skill, early training may still be desirable. Childhood is the optimal period for the development of motor skills in that more time is available for practice, and even minor successes can be an important source of personal satisfaction and a major determinant of group status. How many youth complain that they did not have the opportunity, or were not encouraged, to learn to swim, skate, play tennis, and the like when they were young! Now it is too late. Some motor abilities acquired in childhood are retained throughout life and are a significant element in the pattern of living and adjustment. The tendency in some educational circles to advise that all training be delayed until success is assured (until the child is "ready") would seem to be of questionable validity. If the child is interested, if time is available, and if his physical status makes an activity appropriate, let him by all means be encouraged and helped.

This is not to endorse the growing practice of looking upon elementary and junior high schools as potential "farm clubs" for the early recruiting and training of children in contact sports, such as football and basketball, in the hope of producing winning teams at the high school and college level. In view of the nature of physical growth, such a practice must be deplored. Strength and endurance lag behind stature and weight in their adolescent increments; a boy may be big enough for football and yet not old enough. The fact that the final spurt in the growth of the heart does not come until the end of the period of adolescent acceleration suggests that highly competitive athletics should be avoided before the age of 15 (J. E. Anderson, 1949).

CULTURAL OPPORTUNITIES AND EXPECTATIONS. Man's biological nature sets limits on his motor development; so does the society, with its culture, in the opportunities it offers for practice and experience. American boys would not compare very favorably with English or West Indian boys in cricket; they would probably excel both these groups in basketball and, to a lesser extent, in baseball. Within the United States, many differences in motor skill can be attributed to differential opportunity. The quality of tennis is much higher in California than in Maine or Minnesota; swimming is a more common skill in Florida than in Arizona (although the growing number of public and private pools in inland areas will probably serve to reduce this differential). The explanation lies in customs which reflect variations in geography, particularly climate. The popularity of basketball in certain states is difficult to explain; yet it exists as a part of the culture in those areas. For many people at all age levels, the annual state basketball tournament is the highpoint of the year.

To the extent that there is emphasis upon team or individual competition in athletic performance, opportunities for learning may be restricted to relatively few children and youth. The remaining youngsters serve as spectators; their participation is limited to "physical education" as a part, often a very minor part, of the school program. Although available data do not permit a definitive statement, it is claimed that the result is a decreasing level of physical fitness for the mass of American children as compared with children of nations which emphasize physical training for all.

As a professional group, physical educators are keenly aware of this situation and its consequences. But the combination of the sound of the band on a sunny afternoon, the smartly marching drum majorettes, the roar of the crowd, the click of the turnstiles, and the thrill of championship performance is a powerful and perhaps irresistible social force. For many it is the one link between school and society.

The ever-increasing mechanization of American society would seem to lead inevitably to some diminution in the physical fitness of the population, both children and adults. We are a people on wheels. Along with the log cabin, the walk of several miles to school and back every day through rain, sleet, snow, and every other kind of weather—associated or not with the development of character—is a part of the past, never to return. Many a mother has become a part-time chauffeur, taking her children to school, to music lessons, and to social events, and bringing them home again. Car pools and station wagons have become an essential part of the American way of life. Moreover, the task of operating automobiles, and other devices as well, in this age of the push-button grows ever simpler. Golfmobiles have taken much of the activity out of golf; the appearance of their counterpart on the tennis court should not be dismissed as an impossibility.

Opportunities for participation in motor activities and for the acquisition of motor skills mirror cultural expectations, not only as concerns the classification of specific sports or recreational activities as "major" or "minor" in importance, but also with reference to sex differences. If physical prowess has much importance for the male, it has little or none for the female. Thus the adolescent girl is not strongly motivated to develop whatever capacities she may have for excellence in motor performance. However, there does appear to be some limited cultural change in this respect. The emancipation of women, the concept of the female as a "good sport" as well as an object of love and attention from the male, the emphasis upon marriage as a partnership—all these relatively recent developments in the definition of the role of the female, wife, and mother have tended to encourage the active participation of women in activities that might earlier have been restricted largely to men. No longer are the golf courses and bowling alleys the purlieu of men only; in fact, women, with their greater amount of leisure time, may constitute the larger part of the clientele. In a single generation, women have left the washboard and the hot stove for the golf greens and tennis courts. It is likely that they will challenge men in other areas of athletic skill. For the moment, football would seem to remain a man's game.

INTELLIGENCE. The once-held belief that there was a significant negative relationship between intelligence and motor ability has been thoroughly disproved. Bayley (1935) found a *positive* correlation of about .50 at 15 months, but this finding is probably due to the fact that so-called infant intelligence tests are heavily saturated with motor items. In childhood and adolescence the relationship is close to zero, although a comparison of extremely gifted and extremely retarded children has shown the former to be generally accelerated in both physical and motor development (Miles, 1954).

It must be assumed that the precise relationship, while positive and low, varies somewhat with the particular skill. If brawn is almost the only factor involved, then performing ability would seem to be completely independent of intelligence. However, if there is an element of judgment or timing or accuracy in the activity, mental ability should be more highly related; in such cases, it is difficult to differentiate between motor and mental components of the performance. Perhaps such overlap can be found only in the champion. Among individuals in general, no relationship of any significance exists between motor and mental ability.

Motor Development and Personality

Much of our previous discussion on the relationship between personality and physical development applies to motor development as well. For the differences between early- and late-maturing boys in behavior and personality are in part the consequences of rate of maturing for motor performance. Although in girls and, to some extent, in boys a more crucial element may be the sex-appropriateness of physique, the importance of excellence in motor performance among males cannot be overemphasized. For better or worse, high peer-group status is ineluctably related to such achievement. Evidence is lacking on the point, but we can assume that the consequences for personality development are also positive. Yet the ritual surrounding the performing of these relatively few youth is such that a much larger number of individuals can share and benefit from the glory of their achievements. The champion belongs to the school and the spectators. His triumphs are theirs as are his failures. Victory infects everybody; defeat is a social disaster.

At less lofty levels of performance in younger children, no systematic investigation of the relationship between personality and motor skill has been undertaken. Such understanding as we now have of the interrelatedness of motor development and various aspects of adjustment has been discussed in Chapter 4.

6. How well does the motor sequence as defined by Shirley in Figure 14-13 agree with the California Infant Scale of Motor Development (Table 4-1, p. 109)? What is the nature of the discrepancies? How might they be explained?

7. Does the development of the ability to throw a ball, as described by Gutteridge, follow the laws of developmental direction discussed in Chapter 4?

8. J. E. Anderson (1949) states that one reason for the superiority of boys in throwing a ball is a slight sex difference in the shoulder joint which makes throwing awkward and uncomfortable for girls. What other differences in physical characteristics might explain the sex differences in motor skill and activity observed by Gutteridge in young children? What cultural factors might be influential?

9. Observe young children at play. What part do motor skills have in their activities? How important is motor ability in social interaction among these youngsters? To what extent is physical size important in successful performance? What sex differences do you note?

10. List the motor skills which you think are essential for adequate functioning and adjustment in the elementary school years.

11. Examine the physical-education program in an elementary school. What kinds of motor skill does it emphasize? Is its primary purpose to provide recreation, to develop motor ability, or to build physical fitness?

SUGGESTED READINGS

Jones, Harold E. *Development in Adolescence,* D. Appleton-Century, 1943. This report of a longitudinal study of John Sanders, a late-maturing boy, offers a striking example of the interrelationships of timing, magnitude, and intensity of physical growth, motor development, and social and personality development. It also provides examples of the many methods and techniques utilized in the study of growth.

SHUTTLEWORTH, FRANK K. The adolescent period: A graphic atlas. *Monogr. Soc. Res. Child Develpm.,* 1949, *14:*1 (Serial No. 49). A reference work containing 453 charts from a variety of sources in the scientific literature relating primarily, but not exclusively, to adolescent growth and development.

———. The adolescent period: A pictorial atlas. *Monogr. Soc. Res. Child Develpm.,* 1949, *14:*2 (Serial No. 50). A collection of standardized nude photographs illustrating sexual maturation and physique in the adolescent period.

TANNER, J. M. *Growth at Adolescence,* Springfield, Ill.: Charles C Thomas, 1955. The many references in the text to this book indicate the authors' high opinion of its value for the study of human development. The coverage is much broader than the title indicates; preadolescent events are discussed whenever appropriate.

———. Growth and constitution. In A. L. Kroeber (ed.), *Anthropology Today: An Encyclopedic Inventory,* University of Chicago Press, 1953, pp. 750-70. A summary statement on constitutional psychology, the fundamental differences among individuals and their origins.

THOMPSON, HELEN. Physical growth. In L. Carmichael (ed.), *Manual of Child Psychology* (2nd Ed.), Wiley, 1954, pp. 292-334. A review of the literature on physical growth, with particular emphasis upon morphological changes. Selected references on growth norms are listed.

15
cognitive
development

The child lives, behaves, and develops in a world of other persons and things. He himself is a part of that world. It is the source of the satisfactions he seeks. He will be successful in his strivings to the extent that he learns to know that world. He will learn to know it to the extent that he experiences it.

From the beginning, the child is aware of his physical and social environment; as he grows older, he becomes increasingly aware of it. But awareness is not enough. He must learn to identify objects, both physical and social, and their properties and to recognize their similarities and their differences; in other words, he must learn to perceive, to abstract, to generalize, and to discriminate. He must discover the relationships among these objects, in part by observation, in part by manipulation. He may deal with them directly or through symbols, such as words, that represent objects. To the degree that he develops some symbolic system, some language, he magnifies his ability to explore and to experiment with the contents of his environment. He can manipulate symbols rather than the objects themselves. He can think.

Through a process of cognitive development, the child thus comes to know his world. He learns to recognize order and significance in his environment as they are represented in "natural" laws; he learns to attribute order and significance as they are prescribed in social conventions.

As we have already seen in Chapters 1 and 3, the potentialities for cognitive development are a part of the biological nature of the child, the limits varying from child to child. But both the content and the course of this development are profoundly influenced by environmental factors. Climate and geography make some experiences impossible for some children: the child in the tropics does not see snow; the child in an inland region does not hear the roar of the ocean. Society and culture make some otherwise possible experiences improbable for some children: for example, few youngsters in the United States taste eels. As we shall see, society and culture also play a part in determining how a child learns to identify whatever experiences he does have and what meaning he attributes to them.

The several aspects of cognitive development are so interrelated that only for the purposes of discussion are we justified in treating them separately. We shall first examine the process by which the child acquires his language. Then we shall see how he learns to generalize and to abstract, and thus to form concepts. Next we shall trace the increasing ability of the child to use these concepts in thinking. Finally we shall consider the composite of these verbal, conceptual, and reasoning abilities which we commonly call intelligence.

LANGUAGE DEVELOPMENT

One of the most remarkable and distinctively human characteristics of man is his ability to transform experience symbolically by means of language. Wherever man has lived with man, even among the most primitive tribes and the most remote societies, language exists. Furthermore, every society, regardless of how backward or advanced it is in civilization, has a complete and well-ordered language, possessing (by definition) both vocabulary and grammar; no society has ever been found whose members did not possess the ability to communicate with one another by means of a language. And, prejudice to the contrary, primitive peoples are not evolving toward "higher" type languages. As Langer points out: "People who have not invented textiles, who live under roofs of pleated branches, need no privacy and mind no filth and roast their enemies for dinner, will yet converse over their bestial feasts in a tongue as grammatical as Greek, and as fluent as French!" (1942, pp. 83-84).

Our concern, of course, is with children. But in developing a theory of how children acquire language, investigators have also considered the question of whether animals have language. Their discussion of this question has resulted in a more adequate concept of what language is, and of the conditions that are necessary for its acquisition.

Do Animals Have Language?

Man differs from other animals in his possession of this remarkable characteristic. As every reader knows, it is possible to teach some birds to talk. Mynah birds, crows, parakeets, parrots, and magpies are especially trainable. In one household, a parrot would call out to the iceman as he approached, "Fifty pounds today, please"; in another neighborhood, a mynah bird created considerable consternation (and a reputation as quite a rake for its hitherto respectable owner) by practicing a wolf whistle and yelling "Oh you kid!" at female passers-by. Through conditioning, birds can learn to reproduce sounds and to make the appropriate response in certain situations. But they cannot take the words and put them together in a different way to form sentences (Mowrer, 1950). Nor are they able to use words as abstractions, for they lack the primary requisite for speech: the ability to transform experience symbolically.

Animals do appear to communicate with one another; they respond to signals of danger, food, and sex. A dog will "answer" the bark of another dog; colonies of howler monkeys establish "lookouts" whose cries alert the colony to flight or to approach. But it is unlikely that such sounds are made with any *intent* to communicate; they probably express simply the emotional state of the animal at the time. Probably, too, the listening animal responds in terms of the state expressed, since the sound is similar to the sound that he himself makes in the same circumstances (Osgood, 1953). Communicating, however, with or without intent, does not necessarily imply the possession of language; again, symbolic transformation of experience is necessary.

Even when investigators have attempted to teach animals near the top of the evolutionary scale to talk, their efforts have met with a singular lack of success. Furness (1916) was successful in teaching a young orangutan to use two words appropriately—"papa" and "cup"—but it took six months of extensive training, including manipulation of the lips of the ape, before the first word was mastered.

More recent evidence comes from the report by Hayes (1951) on the experiment to which we referred in Chapter 9, in which a newborn chimpanzee was taken into the home and reared as a human infant, in an effort to find out, among other things, the limits of animal intelligence. Like Furness with his orangutan, Mrs. Hayes spent long hours trying to teach Viki, the chimpanzee, to talk. By nature, a chimpanzee can make thirty-two different speech sounds (called "reflex sounds"), which is a sufficiently varied repertoire for the development of speech. These sounds, however, are usually made only when the animal is emotionally excited. Viki, like other chimps, had no "urge to talk." The Hayeses decided to try to make Viki speak for her supper by placing food before her but delaying feeding until Viki spoke. Mrs. Hayes reports the first trial:

> She looked at the milk, and then at me, and of course said nothing. I waited for fifteen minutes and then rose to leave. As I moved away, worried little "oo-oo's" broke the silence, and I quickly rewarded her for making the sound. The milk tasted good, and Viki sputtered food barks which earned her a few more portions. Then as her appetite wore off, we spent long moments gazing at the food and each other. I kept saying "Speak" and Viki kept saying nothing, but each time I rose to leave, she cried, and thus she earned her supper [pp. 64-65].

But, as Mrs. Hayes points out, Viki did not speak when *commanded* to do so; in the situation described above, Viki was merely making certain noises characteristic of chimps in similar emotional states. The first new sound appeared five weeks after training began, a "rasping, tortured, loudly whispered 'ahhh!' " Mrs. Hayes attributes Viki's difficulty in learning to speak to the fact that chimpanzees ordinarily do not make any sounds at all *on purpose;* the noises that they make, as we have mentioned, are *reflex* sounds and therefore are beyond their conscious control. It is probable, too, that the "ah" sound was especially difficult for Viki because chimpanzees do not have expired vowel sounds in their vocal repertoire; this strange sound could be made only with great effort. After the appearance of the "ah" sound, Mrs. Hayes, by manipulating Viki's lips, taught her to say "mama." Later "papa" was learned, and by three years of age, "cup."

A parrot, of course, can learn many more words in a short space of time than a chimpanzee. But one gets the impression from Mrs. Hayes's account that something had dawned on Viki that never occurs to a parrot—the *idea* of the spoken word, a primitive concept of the use of language to *denote* something. The most dramatic account of the dawning of this great concept comes from Helen Keller (1936). Most of us acquire the notion of the use of language so early in childhood that we cannot recount how we acquired it. Helen Keller, however, was six years old before she learned that there are symbols that stand for objects in the environment, that everything has a *name* by which it can be mentioned, conceived, remembered. In the story of her life, she tells us that her teacher had been spelling words into her fingers, but that they were only finger play to the child. Then one day,

> She brought me my hat and I knew I was going out into the warm sunshine. This thought, *if a wordless sensation may be called a thought,* made me hop and skip with pleasure.
>
> We walked down the path to the well-house, attracted by the fragrance of the honeysuckle with which it was covered. Someone was drawing water and my teacher placed my hand under the spout. As the cool stream gushed over my hand she spelled into the other the word *water,* first slowly, then rapidly. I stood

still, my whole attention fixed upon the motion of her fingers. Suddenly I felt a misty consciousness as of something forgotten—a thrill of returning thought; and somehow the mystery of language was revealed to me. I knew then that w-a-t-e-r meant the wonderful cool something that was flowing over my hand. That living word awakened my soul, gave it light, hope, joy, set it free! There were barriers still, it is true, but barriers that in time could be swept away.

I left the well-house eager to learn. Everything had a name, and each name gave birth to a new thought. As we returned to the house, every object which I touched seemed to quiver with life. That was because I saw everything with the strange, new sight that had come to me [pp. 23-24; italics added].

Miss Keller has given us a dramatic and exciting account of how she discovered the concept of lanugage. Perhaps Viki was making a primitive beginning toward the acquisition of this concept when she first uttered "ah," but the description of her efforts to learn language lends credence to the belief that the capacity for language is a peculiarly human characteristic. For the acquisition of this capacity, three conditions would seem to be necessary: (*1*) sufficiently elaborate physiological equipment; (*2*) enough intelligence to make many fine discriminations; and (*3*) a stable cultural organization which standardizes, elaborates, and transmits specific, distinctive symbolic reactions (Osgood, 1953). Research on animals supports the need for these first two conditions; we turn to theories on the origin of language in human beings to find support for the third.

Theories on the Origin of Language

There are several theories on the origin of language, which for obvious reasons remain highly speculative. One of these, the *onomatopoetic* theory, attributes the beginnings of language to the imitation by our primitive ancestors of sounds in the natural environment. "Buzz," "rumble," and "bark" (or their foreign equivalents) are cited as examples of symbols which might have developed in this fashion.

According to the *interjectional* theory, the automatic ejaculations of primitive man might have been the origin of speech. Sounds like "ow," "mmm," "oh," and "ugh" might have become standardized responses to certain stereotyped situations. A third theory, the *ding-dong* theory, is mystical in nature. It assumes that various objects in the environment elicit certain sounds from man; that is, the objects stimulate man to produce certain unlearned vocalizations, in the same way that a bell will produce a certain sound when a stimulus is applied. Still another theory, the so-called *yo-he-ho* theory, states that communication by language might have originated in the rhythmic vocalizations of primitive men as together they pulled or lifted heavy objects. Thorndike's theory (1949), the *"babble-babble"* or *"lucky-chucky"* theory, as he facetiously called it, emphasizes associations that might have been formed by chance between the babbling sounds of man and certain objects or experiences. He describes an imaginary situation as follows:

> Consider a child of early man playing with a large shell. . . . Let us take the state of affairs least favorable to connecting the sound *ug* with that shell. . . . Let his prattling possibilities consist of a thousand syllables all equally likely to occur in any one situation or in any other. Then the chance that he will utter *ug* as he puts a pebble in the shell is 1 in 1000 if he prattles at all [pp. 286-87].

The child's play does not stop at this point, however. Enjoyment of the act makes him repeat both the manual and the vocal play and so strengthens the connection between the situation and the utterance. "The probability that the child will drop a second pebble is substantial, and the probability that he will utter *ug* therewith if he utters anything is far above 1 to 1000," says Thorndike.

All these theories with respect to the origin of language assume that primitive man chanced upon or invented a certain term and then used it to represent an object or an experience. Unless he could teach others to use it, however, the invention was purely personal. Even today we often find that very young children happen upon a particular sound and use it to symbolize an experience; often, too, fond parents adopt the word into the family vocabulary. In one family, for example, "fiscus," the invention of a three-year-old, became the symbol for lunch served at the kitchen bar-counter. Such inventions do not become

"Here we yell 'Dismissed,'
not 'Fall out' "

Meanings become associated with words as a result of experiences.

(Reproduced from *Esquire* Magazine, July 1958, © 1958 by Esquire, Inc.)

adopted by society at large, for we can use conventional phrases such as "lunch-at-the-bar-counter" to symbolize the experience and have no need for the new term. Judd (1926) points out, however, that when the world was young opportunities for inventing (or for "happening upon") new words must have been unlimited. Yet, he adds that before the inventor can regard his task as complete, he must induce his neighbors to use the sound as he had used it. Such transmission of knowledge became possible only when human beings began to live together in society; society provided the means whereby the inventions standardized in one generation could be passed on to another.

The Developmental Process

THE REFLEXIVE STAGE. With a lusty, robust cry or a thin, reedy wail—for some infants are depressed at birth and their cry is feeble—the newborn comes into the world. This first vocalization is a reflex. Sometimes it is uttered as soon as the head emerges into the air; sometimes it waits upon the completion of delivery; sometimes it is delayed until the umbilical cord is severed or even until the traditional pat on the rump or on the feet is administered. This vocalization is part of a sequence of homeostatic adjustments to the cutting off of the neonatal oxygen supply, to an increase of carbon dioxide in the blood, and even to the stimulus of birth itself. In the course of these adjustments, the first gasp of air is drawn into the lungs, rapidly expanding as the neonate leaves the cramped environment of the uterus. As the air passes rapidly over the vocal cords, the birth cry is produced. External stimuli, such as the drying of the skin and its cooling, are also important in causing the first gasp.

Also reflexive are the speech sounds (phonemes) made during the first few months of life. The vocal apparatus is part of the body's muscular system and is exercised just as the rest of the body is (Osgood, 1953). The infant moves his arms, legs, and head in random fashion; he likewise exercises his jaws, lips, tongue, and vocal cords. As air passes through the oral cavity during these exercises, sounds are produced, varying according to the chance alignment of various parts of the vocal apparatus.

Most experts agree that, during the first year of life, the infant uses all the speech sounds that are basic for language— any language. Some of these sounds he will later drop, if the particular language of his society does not use them. Thus American infants, like infants the world over, have the German *umlaut* and French vowels and trills, but these disappear with disuse as English is learned, to be painfully reacquired in later years by students struggling to learn these foreign languages.

Irwin and Chen (1943) report that a great expansion in the mastery of sounds occurs in the first six months of life; by the time he is six months of age, the infant has acquired most of the vowels and about half the consonants. During the first month, in contrast, he knows only half the vowels and few consonants. Their studies, continued through the first thirty months of life, show increasing diversity in speech sounds as the baby matures. However, according to another investigator (Osgood, 1953), all the speech sounds that the human vocal system can produce may be found during the first two months of life. This finding refutes earlier reports that the infant gradually "becomes capable" of making various sounds. A more accurate statement, according to Osgood, would be that the comparative *frequencies* of various speech sounds change as development proceeds. Osgood attributes the contradiction between his finding of a complete repertoire in the first two months and the results of earlier experiments to the fact that he used a different research technique. He recorded, by electrical transcription, a sample of ten minutes of vocal activity each week, including both spontaneous vocalization and responses to standard stimulus situations. Other investigators have used the technique of sending observers into the home to take down, in the International Phonetic Alphabet, the sounds the infant utters during a specified number of breaths (thirty in one study). As Osgood points out, this technique has at least two drawbacks: the sounds cannot be reproduced for later study and verification, and the sampling is too brief to reveal the full range of infantile speech potentiality.

THE BABBLING STAGE. The stage during which infants vocalize using reflexive sounds is followed by the babbling stage. It should be noted, however, that in speech development one stage does not disappear completely, to be supplanted by a new one. As in other areas of development, each new stage overlaps the earlier; only gradually, and after occasional reversion to the earlier stage, is each new one firmly established.

In the babbling stage, the infant makes a sound and then repeats it over and over again. His "da" is followed by "da-da-da-da," and his "ga" by "ga-ga-ga-ga." Many specialists believe that babbling appears in all infants without training and that therefore it must be due to an internal factor. However, Mowrer (1950) argues that it is *learned*. He reports the observations of an educator in a deaf-blind school that the congenitally deaf do not babble; they make only "weird sounds." According to Mowrer's theory, the normal infant makes a sound and hears it; it gives him pleasure, and so he repeats it. Since a deaf child cannot hear the sounds he makes, repeating them cannot give him pleasure. This explanation of babbling is the foundation for a widely accepted explanation of how children learn to talk.

HOW CHILDREN LEARN TO TALK. In order to shed some light on the first stages of language learning, Mowrer attempted to teach birds to talk. He rejected the theory that the development of language is due to an "instinct of imitation," but proposed, rather, that babies and birds learn to reproduce words "because these words *sound good to them*." As the mother takes care of the baby's needs, she makes gentle noises over him. The infant comes to associate attention to his needs with vocalization; because of the association, he learns to like vocalization. Thus when he hears his own voice it has a satisfying effect upon him; he is rewarded "for his own first babbling and jabbering, without any necessary reference to the effects they produce on others" (1950, p. 699). Later, the infant hits upon a sound that is recognizably similar to a sound that his mother makes. This seems especially "good" to him because of its association with need-reduction, and so he says it again and again in an effort to reproduce a perfect sound.

Work with talking birds substantiated Mowrer's hypothesis. Bird fanciers had long agreed that in order to teach a bird to talk, the trainer must behave toward it "like a good mother." Loving care of the bird makes the appearance of the trainer a rewarding event to the bird. This is the first condition that must be met for effective speech learning. Mowrer spelled out what this means in detail. Specifically, the trainer must feed the bird exclusively by hand, at the same time repeating the word to be learned. Thus the trainer says "water" when he offers a drink to the bird or "bread" when bread is offered. The bird thus builds up an association between the word and hunger or thirst reduction. Eventually, the trainer can withhold the water or food, merely saying the word until the bird repeats it, and then give the water as a reward.

The same conditioning process also works with human infants, although it is unnecessary, of course, to supply food and water to reinforce their spontaneous vocalizations. Rheingold and others (in press) have shown that an infant's vocal output can be increased if adults make social responses immediately following the infant's vocalization. The subjects they used were three-month-old babies living in an institution. When an experimenter leaned over the crib, each baby had a tendency to vocalize. The investigators found that they could increase the vocal output of the babies by responding immediately to each such sound with a broad smile, three "tsk" sounds, and a light touch on the infant's abdomen. The number of sounds recorded for the infants increased by 39 per cent the first day and by 34 per cent the second day. Removing the reinforcer depressed the rate. In other words, it appears that the everyday behavior of adults can function as reinforcement when it is contingent upon an infant's vocalizing. Why these responses reinforce vocalization is not clear; it may be that they provide a change in stimulation to which the increase in vocalization is a response. Or it may be that the smiles, sounds, and affectionate pats of the adult are pleasing to the infant because of his association of them with caretaking acts in the past.

Mowrer's work also suggests that the factor of age may be important in language learning. Just as older birds are difficult to train, so children who have not learned to speak by the time they are six or seven rarely learn to speak normally. So-called "wolf" children, who are lost to civilization in their formative years and then recovered, do not acquire language; nor does the occasional child who makes newspaper headlines because his rejecting mother has kept him in a closet almost since birth. Being treated like a baby is important in learning speech; this kind of treatment is difficult to give when the child is six or seven years of age. No woman, as Mowrer points out, will lavish the same loving care and unconditional acceptance on an older child as on a young baby.

Language in the first year, then, is learned in connection with reduction of the primary drives discussed in Chapter 2. As the good mother tends to her baby's needs, as she feeds him, relieves his pain, helps him to be comfortable, and at the same time talks to him, the sound of her voice and then the sound of any voice, including his own, acquires a secondary reward value for the child. Thus the baby is motivated to make sounds because such sounds have become satisfying to him.

1. Observe or read descriptions of the work of a speech therapist. According to Mowrer's theory, what might be an important factor in determining the success or failure of speech-correction work?

2. What might Mowrer's theory of language learning imply for the classroom teacher's handling of speech-retarded children?

Between the onset of babbling and the first recognizable word, there are a number of interesting speech developments. Some of the language items reported by various investigators, with age in months for appearance of each item, are listed below, as summarized by McCarthy (1954). The reader will note that although the investigators occasionally differ with respect to the timing of appearance of an item, these differences are small.

THE FIRST WORD. It is difficult to establish a norm for the time of appearance of the first word because observers do not always agree on whether the infant's vocalization is really a word or not. Students of language development do not recognize the infant's use of the mere phonetic form of a word as language

Table 15-1

Age at Which Selected Language Items Appear *

	Age (in months)				
	Bayley [a] (1933)	Shirley [a] (1933a)	Buhler [b] (1930)	Gesell & Thompson [b] (1934)	Gesell [b] (1925)
Vocalizes displeasure	5.9			5	
"Talks" to a person		6			
Distinguishes between friendly and angry talking			6		
Imitates sound re-re-re— immediate or delayed response			6		
Imitates sounds			6		
Vocalizes satisfaction	6.5				
Makes singing tones		7.3			
Gives vocal expression to recognition				8	
Utters single consonants		8			
Makes vocal interjections	8.1				
Listens to familiar words	8.5				
Waves "bye bye" or says it					12
Imitates syllables—e.g., mama, papa, dada			11		
Imitates words	11.7				

* Adapted from D. McCarthy. Language development in children, 1946. In L. Carmichael, *Manual of Child Psychology,* Wiley, 1954, pp. 499-502.
[a] Strictly longitudinal studies.
[b] Principally cross-sectional studies.

unless he can use it in an appropriate situation. (The infant may vocalize "ma-ma" or "da-da" as early as seven months.) Only when the infant can use "mama" to refer to his mother can he be said to have this word in his vocabulary. Generally, the first word is said to appear shortly before the end of the first year of life. It is almost always of the duplicated-monosyllable type because, the experts explain, frequently occurring syllables which are part of the child's babble are picked up by adults, who use them in talking to the child. The child then learns to use the syllables with meaning. By his first birthday, the infant may have two or three words of this type.

DEVELOPMENT DURING PRESCHOOL YEARS. The language de-velopment of most children from the first to the second birthday is slow in comparison with development between the second and the fifth birthday. Shirley (1933a, 1933b) reports that by two years of age, each baby in her group averaged 36.9 words, with the range from 6 to 126 words. It is generally agreed that a rapid increase in vocabulary waits upon the mastery of walking, and that when the child begins to walk there is a plateau in language development (McCarthy, 1954). Thus the baby may say a few words at twelve months and then, when walking begins, show little or no progress in speech until eighteen months of age or later, when he has mastered walking. The child puts all his eggs into one basket, as it were; he does not dissipate his energies but appears to concentrate on one developmental task at a time.

The first words the child uses are nouns. Often they are used as generalized terms; "daddy" may be applied to any man from salesman to postman. However, the names that the child uses may first be applied to objects which belong to a totally different class. Thus one child learned the word "door," but he applied it to the noise made when his bricks tumbled to the floor; "door" to him was not the door seen, but the door heard! (Watts, 1944).

For the first eighteen months of life, the wants of the infant are simple and his linguistic needs are correspondingly few and easily satisfied. Toward the end of this period, an interest in continuous vocalization appears. At first, the infant pours forth a stream of gibberish, perhaps in imitation of the continuous vocalization which he hears adults produce (Watts, 1944). Then he begins to put words together conversationally. Apparently, he realizes that objects do not stay put, so he adds a word or two to the simple noun to indicate what the subject is doing or what he would like it to do. These free expressions are open to various interpretations; "Daddy bye-bye" may mean "Daddy is going bye-bye" or "Daddy has gone bye-bye" or "Is Daddy going bye-bye?" or even "I wish Daddy would clear out of here—fast!"

Gradually, the child's two- or three-word free expressions become modified as he realizes that they *can* be modified according to the circumstances. By three-and-a-half years, he lengthens his sentences to four words, and at entrance to first grade, the five-word sentence is most prevalent (McCarthy, 1954).

The great child psychologist Jean Piaget (1926) reported that young children are egocentric in their speech—that is, that they speak without regard for the point of view of their audience. The child does not trouble to make himself understood. Piaget believed that this kind of speech is typical of young children and that not until seven years of age is there much evidence of socialized speech. However, in summarizing the data on egocentricity in speech, McCarthy (1954) notes that egocentric speech is characteristic even of adults, and she and other workers report a smaller percentage of egocentric remarks among preschool children than did Piaget.

At three or four years of age, 85 per cent of all children show a hesitation in speech; they may stutter and stammer as they attempt to talk. For the great majority of these children, the defect disappears within a year or two. The cause of this phenomenon is generally attributed to the fact that the child's hearing vocabulary grows faster than his speaking vocabulary. His relative limitation in speaking resources may produce tension as he tries to communicate, and stuttering results. Many experts believe that the continuance of stuttering indicates emotional difficulties, and that "true" stuttering may develop during this period if undue attention is called to the child's difficulty.

At three years of age an outcropping of "Why" questions develops. Piaget's theory was that the child asks these questions not so much for information as for the pleasure of asking. Sometimes the child is apparently seeking not a detailed explanation of why the sky is blue, if that was the question asked, but, rather, an affirmation of his observation that the sky *is* blue.

LATER SPEECH DEVELOPMENT. Once the plateau in language development is passed, command of vocabulary and ability to communicate in longer and more complex sentences develop at a phenomenal pace. Girls are usually reported as more advanced than boys, and bright children as more advanced than the average. Because different methods of analyzing vocabulary yield different results, experts differ in their estimates of the number of words the typical child knows at a given age. One investigator (M. E. Smith, 1926) tested children on a sample from the 10,000 words in Thorndike's *Teacher's Word Book* (1921) and reported a vocabulary of 2562 words for six-year-olds. However, Seashore and Eckerson (1940) report a much greater number. They devised a special vocabulary test for Grades 1 through 12, based on a sampling from an unabridged dictionary. They found that for Grade 1, the average number of words in the total vocabulary was 23,700, with a range of 6000 to 48,000; for Grade 12, it was 80,300, with a range of 36,700 to 136,500. Despite the discrepancy in results of investigations, it is safe to say that the child's vocabulary grows slowly at first and then undergoes a rapid increase after his third birthday.

Comprehensibility of speech also increases with age. McCarthy (1930) found that only 26 per cent of the responses of eighteen-month-old children were comprehensible. At two years, 67 per cent could be understood, at three years 93 per cent, and virtually all responses from three and a half years on. Investigators generally report that the speech of boys is not so comprehensible as that of girls.

The most marked increase in the accuracy of articulation of all types of vocal sound appears between two and three years of age (McCarthy, 1954). Ninety per cent of the child's vowel production is correct by thirty months of age, but the child is six or six and a half before he has mastered all twenty-three consonant sounds. Eight years is given as the upper age limit at which time it is expected that the normal child will be able to articulate all speech sounds correctly.

As might be expected, there are differences in the ways in which the school-age child uses language in writing and in speaking. In comparing the development of oral and written language in elementary school children, Harrell (1957) discovered that children's use of written language is more mature than their speech. He reports that children use subordinate clauses, particularly adverbial clauses, more freely in their writing, and that the tendency to use subordinate clauses is more marked for brighter pupils and for those from higher socioeconomic groups.

Influences upon Speech Development

SOCIOECONOMIC STATUS. Study after study reports that language development is significantly related to socioeconomic status. Children from upper socioeconomic levels have larger vocabularies, use longer sentences, and use more mature sentence forms than do children of the same age from lower socioeconomic levels. These differences begin to manifest themselves early in life; Irwin (1948) found that after eighteen months of age, children of parents in the upper occupational groups forged ahead both in types of phoneme used and in frequency of phonemes. The differences are undoubtedly due in part to the more restricted environment usually experienced by children from lower classes. Their experiences with books and with travel are more limited; their parents offer poorer models of language and also less verbal stimulation. At mealtimes, for example, a child from the middle- or upper-income group usually has the benefit of family conversation, whereas the lower-class child often eats alone, helping himself to food already prepared on the stove and rarely engaging in discussion with other family members. Innate differences in intelligence in favor of the upper socioeconomic groups probably also contribute to social-class differences in language development.

MOTHER-CHILD RELATIONSHIPS. Investigators also agree in their findings that children reared in institutions are retarded in language development. Several factors explain the deficiency. We have previouly pointed out that the normal mother-child interaction is ideal for facilitating language development, with the mother babbling back to the baby, encouraging him to say "ma-ma," "da-da," and "bye-bye," and approving his successful vocalizations. In countless interactions throughout the day, the baby in a normal home environment learns to want to vocalize and is in fact exposed to a variety of stimuli to which he responds with vocalization. Also, he learns from the parent what to say and how to say it. The institution-reared child too often spends long periods lying passively without any external stimulation. He also lacks the intimate type of instruction available in the home. Consequently, he has less opportunity to learn to want to talk and less exposure to satisfactory language models. At the same time, he has more contacts with other children who understand his speech, incomprehensible though it may be to adults, and so has little incentive to improve. As a result, children reared in institutions are deficient linguistically at all stages. They vocalize less frequently and use fewer phonemes during the first six months than do infants living with their families (Brodbeck & Irwin, 1946). Three-year-olds reared in institutions are deficient in speech sounds, intelligibility of speech, and level of language organization as compared with children reared in foster homes (Goldfarb, 1946). Older children in orphanages compare unfavorably with nonorphanage children, even when mental ability is held constant (Moore, 1947).

Other studies also point up the importance of close and continuous contact with a mother or mother-substitute during the early stages of language development. It is commonly observed that when siblings are born close together—when a baby is supplanted during the latter part of his first year or the first half of his second—the first child is often retarded in speech development. Conversely, Koch (1954) found that a first-born boy with a sibling two or more years younger is superior to his sibling and even to first-born girls, presumably because the child has undivided maternal attention for a relatively long time and presumably also because, being a boy, he is shown special devotion by the mother (Sears *et al.*, 1953). Retardation may occur when the normal course of the mother-child relationship is interrupted because of illness, return to work by the mother, or some other reason.

Lessened opportunity for close contact with an adult undoubtedly explains also why second- and later-born children are less advanced in speech than the first-born. Further, such children associate more with other children, who are not likely to furnish so good a model as adults. Twins are markedly retarded as compared with singletons (D. M. Davis, 1937), and triplets have been found to be even more retarded. Howard (1946), for example, found that a five-year-old triplet had a mean length of sentence of only 2.98 words, which is about equal to that of a four-year-old twin and a two-and-a-half- to three-year-old singleton.

EFFECTS OF SPECIAL TRAINING. If, as we have suggested, the relatively rich environment of children from upper socioeconomic levels contributes to their superiority in language development, then, presumably, providing enriched experiences for deprived children should improve their language. Dawe (1942), in an experiment involving two groups of orphanage children, found this to be the case. The experimental group of children listened to stories and poems, looked at and discussed pictures, went on excursions, and had both individual and small-group training in understanding words. In three months, the training group was significantly advanced over a control group in all respects except comprehensibility of speech and complexity of sentence organization. Similar training experiences are part of the readiness program in kindergarten and first grade; they are particularly needed in schools which draw their population from low socioeconomic groups.

BILINGUALISM. In these days, when more and more stress is being placed upon the learning of a second language, the possible effects of bilingualism upon language development are receiving more and more attention. Unfortunately, however, research on this problem is difficult to control. The socioeconomic factor, the nature of the child's relationships with the persons who teach him the two languages, the consistency with which the child hears the same language from the same person, and the values the family supports, all must enter into any evaluation of the effects of bilingualism.

Among lower socioeconomic families in which the parents are foreign-born, it is common practice for children to learn the foreign language in the home and pick up English outside the home. This was true of early immigrant families years ago and is true today of Puerto Rican Americans, Mexicans, and other foreign-speaking groups. These children, of course, are handicapped on all tests involving the English language; frequently, they spend their first year or two in school learning English, and the teaching of reading and other subjects must be postponed beyond the first grade. It is not uncommon for such a child to drop the foreign language completely once he enters school. As an adult, he may retain his ability to understand the foreign language, but not to speak it. It is not clear whether discarding the foreign language is symbolic of a rejection of the parents' foreign ways or represents an attempt to simplify the learning situation. Obviously, this situation is not good; the child is handicapped in English—at least for the first few school years— a loss which is not compensated by competence in a second language.

In some cases, the child attempts to forge a new language from the two to which he has been exposed. If social conditions are favorable, this new language will be passed on from generation to generation and become part of the culture. This has happened to a considerable extent on the islands of Hawaii; pidgin English is commonly used among those bilingual groups which are low in socioeconomic status. The use of pidgin is a serious language handicap to many Hawaiian children; they learn neither a foreign language nor English and are at about the three-year-old level linguistically when they enter school (M. E. Smith, 1939).

But what of children who learn two languages under more favorable circumstances, and what constitutes more favorable circumstances? Smith (1935) advises that it is better for young children to receive their two languages from separate sources. Informal observations of American children being reared abroad lend support to Smith's advice; American children growing up in Paris who from infancy have heard English from their parents and French from a nurse develop bilingually with happy results.

When bilingualism proceeds under favorable circumstances, the child's vocabulary development in either language will be below average, but when the two vocabularies are totaled, the child will exceed the norm. Smith (1949) tested bilingual children in both English and Chinese and found that two fifths of them had total vocabularies above average for their age, although in either language taken alone they were below average. Apparently, a parent who is rearing a child bilingually can expect that the child will make slower than average progress in English, at least in the early years. Whether this handicap will be overcome and at what age it will be overcome are not known. Although it is sometimes asserted that the bilingual child is handicapped intellectually, it is not hard to find, on a university faculty, examples of brilliant adults who were reared bilingually. Puerto Rican children studied by Anastasi and Cordova (1953) tested low intellectually, but social-emotional attitudes rather than bilingualism *per se* apparently contributed to their low scores. Whether the initial handicap in English *can* be compensated by achievement in another language depends partly upon the values of the parent.

Speech Problems

Some speech problems have a physiological basis. A child with a cleft palate, a harelip, or some other malformation involving organs of speech will obviously be handicapped in his speech and may need special training if he is to learn to talk. Hearing-handicapped children are also at a disadvantage in speech since they do not have speech models available to them. Because of the conditions necessary for the learning of speech, it is advisable to begin this special training as early as possible. In some states special classes for the deaf and hard-of-hearing begin even before three years of age.

Mentally retarded children are backward in all aspects of language development. For example, one nine-year-old girl with an intelligence quotient of 40 was capable of only animal-like grunts and a gibberish which was not intelligible even to her parents. After two years of training, she could make herself understood and had progressed to roughly a four-year-old level, her maximum. Although an occasional child of superior intelligence is slow to talk, the research generally shows a correlation between intelligence and language development. One of the ways in which mental deficiency manifests itself is in speech retardation.

Some children of normal or superior intelligence, however, enter school still using an incomprehensible speech often referred to as "baby talk." Many laymen believe that these children have been babied and indulged, that they do not speak comprehensibly because they get what they want from doting parents or grandparents without it. Research findings do not substantiate this belief. Rather, they show that there is a language-disorder syndrome; that is, that various forms of language disorder—delayed speech, stuttering, articulation defects, reading disabilities—may appear in the same person as a result of emotional insecurity (McCarthy, 1954). The cause of the insecurity, and hence of the syndrome, is usually a disturbed parent-child relationship. Rejection by a parent, impossibly high standards set by a perfectionist parent, unfortunate discontinuities in the parent-child relationship during critical stages in language learning, intense sibling rivalry—any one of these, if severe enough, can produce personality disturbances which will be reflected in speech. In fact, speech is a good indicator of the state of both emotional and physical health; the reader may have noted in himself occasional speech hesitation, hoarseness, or inability to express ideas when he is in a state of emotional stress or great fatigue. Stutterers in particular have been carefully scrutinized. A summary of the research (McCarthy, 1954) shows that these children, most of whom are boys, exhibit several symptoms of maladjustment in addition to stuttering. In some cases, therapy has been helpful in effecting an improvement.

Language learning is one of the most important tasks to be accomplished in the socialization process. There are still many unanswered questions about it, but research has shed much light on the normative aspects of language development, as well as on the factors that influence development. Parents and teachers can facilitate language learning by taking these factors into account.

3. If possible, observe a speech therapist at work with a young child. How does the therapist attempt to establish rapport with the child?

4. Interview a friend or neighbor who has tried to teach a bird to talk. Analyze his training procedures to find possible explanations for his success or failure. To what extent are the successful methods like those described in this chapter?

5. Arrange for a two-hour observation of a baby between nine and twelve months of age, during his waking hours. Record as well as you can the sounds that he makes, the times or occasions for his vocalizations, and what the mother does to encourage vocalization. (Do not tell the mother in advance that you are interested in language development.)

6. The problem of changing a child's language habits is one that many teachers face. What principles can you set forth to guide a teacher who is attempting to teach lower-class children to speak differently?

CONCEPT FORMATION

Conceptual Development

The child becomes acquainted with himself and the external world through his sensations. Early in life, he is aware of sound, light, odor, taste, pressure, and movement—his own and that of other objects. The content of this awareness must remain something of a mystery; it may be that the world for him is a "big blooming buzzing Confusion" (James, 1890). But these primitive perceptions, which we presume to be vague, diffuse, and undifferentiated, furnish the material out of which the individual slowly creates his view of reality.

Originally, sensations are primarily the by-products of reflexive acts. By the end of the first month, however, there is clear indication of self-stimulation. The infant acts spontaneously to continue and to enhance sensations—for example, by putting out his tongue and sucking his finger. Piaget (1952) calls these and other reactions, such as looking, listening, and moving the hands and fingers, *primary circular reactions*. The child thus creates awareness of himself. Later, by the age of four months, *secondary circular reactions* emerge which seem designed, not to prolong a self-stimulating activity, but to maintain an event in the external environment (Piaget, 1952). The following observation of an infant at four months, twenty-eight days, illustrates this kind of behavior:

> Lucienne . . . is lying in her bassinet. I hang a doll over her feet. . . . Her feet reach the doll right away and give it a violent movement which Lucienne surveys with delight. Afterward she looks at her motionless foot for a second, then recommences. There is no visual control of the foot, for the movements are the same when Lucienne only looks at the doll or when I place the doll over her head. On the other hand, the tactile control of the foot is apparent: after the first shakes, Lucienne makes slow foot movements as though to grasp and explore. For instance, when she tries to kick the doll and misses her aim, she begins again very slowly until she succeeds (without seeing her feet). In the same way, I cover Lucienne's face or distract her attention for a moment in another direction: she nevertheless continues to hit the doll and control its movements [Piaget, 1952, p. 159].

At this point the child has extended awareness and exploration to include not only himself but also the world around him *as it is related to him*. With repetition of experience, he begins to show signs of recognition of objects and persons. He will note their appearance and disappearance. There will even be efforts to produce absent or hidden objects, as in the following observation of Jacqueline at eight months, fourteen days:

> . . . Jacqueline is lying on my bed beside me. I cover my head and cry "coucou"; I emerge and do it again. She bursts into peals of laughter, then pulls the covers away to find me again. Attitude of expectation and lively interest [Piaget, 1954, p. 46].

Such behavior indicates that the child remembers. Research with young children, using the delayed-reaction test, demonstrates that memory is present in the first year (Munn, 1954). In a test developed by Buhler (1930), the infant was given a ball containing a mechanical chicken which popped out when he squeezed the ball. After he had played with the toy for a while, the ball was taken away and some other activity was substituted. Later, another ball, which looked exactly like the first one but did not contain a chicken, was given to the subject. If he looked astonished or puzzled or searched for the chicken when it did not appear, he was assumed to have remembered. At the age of ten to eleven months, children showed evidence of memory after a delay of as long as one minute after the original experience. By the end of the second year, the maximum delay was seventeen minutes.

With recognition, there comes discrimination of perceptions; the child becomes able to tell being cold from being hungry, me from not-me, mother from not-mother (Sullivan, 1953). Ling (1941) found that ability to discriminate form was present as early as six months of age. His subjects were fifty children, six to fifteen months of age. The forms used were colored circles, crosses, and triangles. Two different forms, pegged into a gray board, were presented to a child at a time. One form on each trial was sweetened with saccharine and could be removed and sucked; the "incorrect" form was fastened down. The subjects were able to learn to choose the right one, even when, from trial to trial, size and orientation of the forms were varied. These findings not only demonstrate that infants can discriminate; they also suggest that they can conceptualize.

Ling's subjects identified and isolated a property of an object—its triangularity, for example—which served to differentiate it in form from some other object. In other words, they abstracted. They then ascribed that property to other forms (triangles), where appropriate, even when those forms were larger or smaller than the first, or upside down. In other words, they generalized. They possessed at least a primitive concept of form.

Presented with two blocks, one thirty-two square inches and the other sixteen square inches in area, three-year-old children can be trained to choose the smaller; when they are then presented with two blocks, sixteen and eight square inches in area, respectively, they will tend, with a frequency greater than could be expected by chance alone, to choose the eight-inch block; if tested with two blocks, eight and four square inches in area, they will show a tendency, less strong but still significant, to choose the four-inch block (Stevenson & Langford, 1957). They seem to have learned the relational concept of "smaller than," even though they cannot verbalize it. Thus young children learn to respond to relationships between objects rather than to the absolute properties of the objects. They are said to *transpose*. Transposition behavior increases with age (Alberts & Ehrenfreund, 1951), in part because of the development of language. Once children have developed skill in the use of language and can verbalize their concepts, they are able to transpose equally well whether the test objects differ little or greatly from the training stimuli (Kuenne, 1946).

It appears that concept formation does not await the appearance of names or labels that language development provides. Language serves only to facilitate a process that has already begun on the nonsymbolic level. Yet, we should not underestimate the power of language in advancing conceptualization. Providing a name or even a nonsense syllable (the same one consistently) for a number of objects will increase a child's tendency to respond similarly to each of the objects; conversely, providing different labels for different objects will increase his tendency to respond differentially (Spiker, 1956). But there is also a danger in labeling. The same word can be attached to a number of objects to suggest an identity or similarity among them that does not really exist; different words for objects may obscure an identity among them. Propaganda, through skillful use of appellations and slogans, leads adults to overgeneralize and stereotype or to overdiscriminate. Similar behavior is found in young children when they apply the word "doggie" to anything that is furry or reject some familiar article because an adult refers to it, quite incidentally, by an unfamiliar name.

Social Influences on Conceptualization

The language that a society provides to the child shapes his perception of the world. Casagrande (1956) suggests that the tendency for English-speaking children to discriminate objects first on the basis of color and size may be a function of their particular language. In contrast, he points out that the Navaho-speaking child might be expected to attend earlier to properties of form or shape because his language requires that he select a particular verb form depending on the formal properties of the object to which he is referring. Thus he must use one verb stem to ask for a long flexible object (a piece of string, for example), another for a long rigid object (e.g., a stick), and still another for a flat flexible object (a piece of cloth).

Even within a society with a common language we may expect to find differences among children in their conceptualization. Each child must, at least in the early stages of conceptual development, look to his parents to provide names for the things in his environment. The choice of what to label and how to label is largely the parents', not the child's. In a sense, he perceives the world through their eyes. Thus "parents unwittingly transmit their own cognitive structures" to the child (R. Brown, 1958, p. 17).

Concepts of self and of other persons arise out of social interaction. The child builds a concept of self out of self-awareness *and* awareness of the reactions of others to him; similarly, he comes to understand others and the social roles they play to the extent that he can assume those roles and thus experiences awareness of them (G. H. Mead, 1934). Playing house, so common a game among American children, reflecting perhaps their intense striving toward independence, provides opportunities for discovering what it is like to be Daddy or Mommy or even Baby. Also arising out of social interaction are such abstract concepts as justice. The child need not experience just (or unjust) treatment as such in order to develop the concept; he may learn from experience in situations in which just treatment is necessary or desirable or possible. Every social situation requires rules; if none are provided, the participants establish them. That the process of establishing justice through rules is not without its difficulties is indicated by the plaintive, and sometimes even outraged, cry that rises from many a back yard, vacant lot, or playing field: "Come on, play fair!"

Experience is personal. Words serve to objectify and generalize experience and to make it communicable to others. To the extent that children learn to use the same words, they come to share a common view of the world. Yet personal factors continue to influence perception. The value which the child places on an object affects his perception of that object. A hungry person is more sensitive to food than is a satiated individual (Levine, Chein, & Murphy, 1942); the poor child estimates the size of coins as larger than does the rich child (Bruner & Goodman, 1947); the youngster sees an object belonging to him as larger than an identical object not belonging to him (Blum, 1957).

The Formation of Concepts

Older children and adults arrive at concepts both inductively, from the particular to the general, and deductively, from the general to the particular. Rover may successively be classified as a collie, a dog, a quadruped, and an animal; at the same time, it may be inferred that he has the attributes of any class of objects to which he is assigned. Piaget has suggested that younger children proceed from the particular to the particular, or transductively: "A is like B in one respect; therefore A must be like B in other respects" (Berlyne, 1957, p. 6).

Since there is a tendency to stress the vagueness and diffuseness of perceptions and concepts in infants and young children, this particularity in children's responses is worthy of some emphasis. A young child's attentiveness to detail is often a source of astonishment, annoyance, and embarrassment for his parents. Jane points to the quite inconspicuous mole on a visitor's face and loudly asks, "Mommy, what is that?" Randy refuses to eat a certain cereal because the picture on the box is different from the usual one. Investigators of discriminative behavior in preschool children must take care that no smudges of dirt appear on any of the stimulus objects, for frequently the subjects will attend to them rather than to the properties intended.

A young child who is shown a drawing of a large number of circles may respond, when asked what he sees, that they are all balls. But he is equally likely to point to each circle in turn and say "Ball," continuing to do so, even though there may be as many as ninety-six of them, until he finishes naming all of them or until he is stopped (Martin, 1951). His responses may be specific to certain objects or persons, particularly himself. Stern describes the four-year-old boy who, when his grandfather asked him, "How many fingers have I got?" answered, "I don't know. I can only count my own fingers" (1924, p. 382).

It must be presumed that the conceptual process involves both the differentiation of impressions which are originally diffuse and the integration of impressions which are originally detailed and fragmentary. Abstraction, discrimination, and generalization are thus utilized at all age levels.

Formal education is largely a process of teaching concepts. What concepts of size, space, time, number, life, self, and other persons children possess at various age levels have been rather thoroughly established (Russell, 1956). Such information has been utilized in determining age norms for various concepts in intelligence tests. According to the 1937 Revision of the Stanford-Binet (Terman & Merrill, 1937), the average child at two years of age should be able to identify the hair, eyes, feet, and nose on a paper doll and to name at least four of the following objects: kitty, button, thimble, cup, engine, spoon. At three-and-a-half years, the typical child is expected to identify the larger of two balls; at four years, he is expected to answer the question "How many?" when presented first with two blocks and then with two beads. By five years, he should know the concept of "three"; by six years, the concept of "six" or "seven." At the nine-year-old level, he will be asked to tell how the objects in each of the following pairs are alike and how they are different: honey and glue, pencil and pen, banana and lemon, shoe and glove. By the age of eleven, he is expected to define such abstract words as "connection" and "obedience."

Although we know a great deal about the conceptual abilities of children at various age levels, we are far from an adequate understanding of the process by which concepts are acquired and what we, as adults, can do to facilitate that process. (Witness the never-ending controversy over methods of teaching in our public schools.) To say that intelligence is a factor explains little or nothing, since one measure of intelligence is the ability to conceptualize. (The fact that chronological age, with mental age held constant, is highly related to concept formation suggests that experience is a crucial factor.) This we might have anticipated, since the basic ingredients of concept formation are sensory impressions. The child who is deprived of experience, whether because of an impoverished environment or because of a physical handicap, such as deafness or blindness, will necessarily be retarded in his concept formation. For such deprived children, and for normal children who have difficulty in conceptualizing, rich experience in concrete activities involving the active participation of the learner must be provided (Werner & Carrison, 1943). Jeffrey (1958) tested the ability of young children to discriminate between a stick figure pointing right and another stick figure pointing left by labeling one figure "Jack" and the other "Jill." Those subjects who received preliminary training on the simple motor response of pressing a button on the left or right, corresponding to the direction in which the stick figure was pointing, learned the labeling task much more easily than those who received no such training. The effect of the preliminary training was to add to the variety as well as to the quantity of sensory impressions out of which the required discrimination emerges. The child experienced "left-right" not only visually and auditively but also kinesthetically.

Conceptualization requires rich and intimate experience with a variety of objects through the various sense modalities. "Knowledge *about* a thing is knowledge of its relations. Acquaintance with it is limitation to the bare impression which it makes" (James, 1890, p. 259). With adults as well as with children, what is sometimes considered knowledge might often be better termed acquaintance.

7. Can the circular reactions observed by Piaget be seen as manifestations of the principle of adience discussed in Chapter 1?

8. Analyze the conceptualization of the child who calls a strange man "Daddy."

9. James wrote that we know the meaning of a word "so long as no one asks us to define it" (1890, p. 225). Can a person have concepts without words? Can he have words without concepts?

10. Is direct experience with an object essential in forming a concept of that object?

11. Do parents and teachers emphasize some sense modalities more than others in the training and education of children?

12. What kinds of experience might you provide to help a child to develop time concepts?

13. Why is transposition essential in concept formation?

14. At what points in the learning process, as discussed in Chapter 8, would conceptualization be involved? In what ways?

15. How might the goals of socialization in a society color the percepts and concepts of children growing up in that society?

16. To what extent do both children and adults "see" what they want to see?

17. What symbols other than words are used to name properties of objects?

THINKING

Our discussion of concept formation may have implied that the world is there to know if only the child will attend to it and assimilate his experiences of it; that he need only be a camera. Not so! The world is not so apparent as all that. The child must sometimes manipulate the contents of his world, not merely to enhance his awareness of them, but to construct and reconstruct and thus to explain his experiences. He must solve the problems presented to him by his environment.

Problem Solving and Thinking

Infants can and do solve problems. In a situation in which they are hungry and no food is present, they reconstruct that situation by simple addition, by crying and thus summoning mother *and* food. A study by Richardson (1932) demonstrates problem-solving ability early in life. He presented a series of problems to infants at intervals over the age period from twenty-eight to fifty-two weeks. On a table was a toy attached to a string; the end of the string was within the child's reach; the toy was not. At the earliest age level, only the single-string situation was presented. Gradually, the other situations—A, B, C, and D, in order of difficulty—were added (see Fig. 15-1). The settings were always arranged behind a screen. The experimenter then removed the screen and called the infant's attention to the toy. These reactions were noted: (*1*) interest in the string rather than in the toy; (*2*) interest in the toy with contact, perhaps accidental, with the string; (*3*) awareness of both string and toy, but not of the relation between them; (*4*) experimentation with both objects; (*5*) use of the string to bring the toy within reach. Only the last of these responses represents a successful solution to the problem. It requires perceiving a means-end relationship. It constitutes insight.

Alpert's (1928) investigation illustrates more clearly the reconstructive aspects of problem solving. Working with preschool children, she used situations devised by Köhler in his

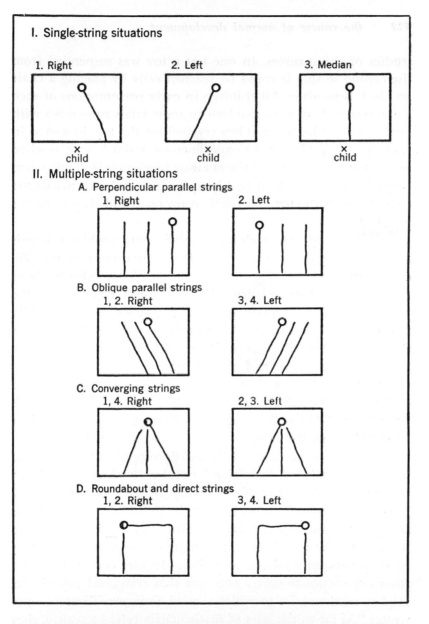

I. Single-string situations

1. Right   2. Left   3. Median

×
child   ×
child   ×
child

II. Multiple-string situations
    A. Perpendicular parallel strings
       1. Right   2. Left

    B. Oblique parallel strings
       1, 2. Right   3, 4. Left

    C. Converging strings
       1, 4. Right   2, 3. Left

    D. Roundabout and direct strings
       1, 2. Right   3, 4. Left

FIGURE 15-1. Representative string problems used with infants. The arabic numbers above the situations indicate the order of presentation in each category.

(From H. M. Richardson. The growth of adaptive behavior in infants: an experimental study of seven age levels. *Genet. Psychol. Monogr.*, 1932, *12*, 195-359) studies of chimpanzees. In one test a toy was suspended from the ceiling so that it could be reached only by placing a chair or block beneath it. All children in early presentations of such situations and younger children in most trials responded with trial-and-error behavior. They reached for the toy, looked at it, backed away, looked at the experimenter, walked away, reached again; they rarely noticed the chair or block nearby. Only when they did and saw its relationship to the lure *and* then placed the chair beneath the toy and climbed up on it did they solve the problem.

Infants and young children solve many problems at this relatively simple perceptual level. With situations that are difficult or unfamiliar, older children and adults are also likely to revert to direct experience with the object elements of the problem; they manipulate, feel, and rearrange. But we usually reserve the term "thinking" for problem solving that involves the manipulation of *concepts*. The child can solve the problem "How much are two and three?" perceptually by combining two things and three things and counting them, pointing to each in turn, saying what may be to him the meaningless words "one," "two," "three," and so on. Without the objects he might be unable to do the sum.

Only when the individual has developed the concepts of "two," "three," and "addition" can he *think* quantitatively. Concepts free him from the necessity of manipulating objects. He does symbolically what he once had to do concretely. He is no longer bound to any particular situation. He is more free to reconstruct the world; he can actually create a world that may be only tenuously related to reality. He uses concepts derived from experience to create concepts that transcend experience. Higher mathematics provides a good example. Einstein once wrote: "As far as the laws of mathematics refer to reality, they are not certain; and as far as they are certain, they do not refer to reality."

Thinking is the crowning achievement of man, as James pointed out in his characteristic style:

Without abstract concepts to handle our perceptual particulars by, we are like men hopping on one foot. Using concepts, along with the particulars, we become bipedal. We throw our concept forward, get a foothold on the consequence, hitch our line to this, and draw our percept up, traveling thus with a hop, skip, and jump over the surface of life at a vastly rapider rate than if we merely waded through the thickness of the particulars as accident rained them down upon our heads. Animals have to do this, but men raise their heads higher and breathe freely in the upper conceptual air [1909, pp. 246-47].

The way in which children explain physical events provides one measure of their ability to think. Following Piaget's (1930) earlier investigations, Deutsche (1937) studied causal thinking in children in Grades 3 through 8. In the first part of her test, she demonstrated familiar phenomena and then asked her subjects to explain them. For example, she lit a candle and covered it with a jar and then asked, "Why does the candle go out?" Or she dropped a wooden block on the table and asked, "What makes the noise when the block falls?" Then she posed such questions as these: "What makes the wind blow?" "Why do balloons go up in the air?" "What causes thunder?" "How is it that you can see yourself when you look into the mirror?" The adequacy of answers, as rated by several judges, increased consistently with age, with the greatest one-year difference occurring between eleven and twelve years, perhaps reflecting the formal introduction of science into the school curriculum at about that time. The explanations of boys were superior to those of girls. There was little or no relationship between ability in causal thinking and intelligence or socioeconomic status. Within age groups, there was a relationship between scores on the test and school grade.

Inhelder and Piaget (1958) have reported the results of some ingenious experiments to assess the thinking ability of children and adolescents. In one experiment, involving conservation of motion, each one of a set of balls varying in size and weight could be propelled by a spring device onto a horizontal plane. The subject was asked to predict the stopping point for each ball and to explain why that point varied with the size and weight of the ball. The explanations of the six-year-old were contradictory, utilized a concept of animated force, and were not based upon observation. He predicted that a small ball would go far because it was smaller and that a large one would go far because it was larger. When he did attempt to verify his predictions, he might explain the result by saying, "It didn't get very far because it didn't have a flag" (p. 126). The quality of response of the fourteen-year-old is illustrated in the following protocol:

> "*If you send them off with a push of the same strength, it* [the resting point] *depends on weight, friction, and volume.*" Next, he doubts that volume plays any role, but in comparing a small and a large ball, he says: "*The small one will go better because it has less friction, less air resistance.*" "That's all?" "*If it's truly horizontal*" [Inhelder & Piaget, 1958, p. 130].

Factors in the Thinking Process

Not all symbolic activity is thinking. Daydreaming, fantasy, and even imagination, to the extent that they are free-flowing, uncensored, and undirected, do not ordinarily lead to solutions of problems. They may, of course, be essential to creative activity, be a necessary preliminary to productive thinking, and serve a useful purpose in personality function. But thought would seem to require a combination of fertility of ideas and self-criticism or self-control (J. E. Anderson, 1949). Fertility of ideas reflects, in part, the richness of experiential background. Deutsche's findings, as we have pointed out, suggest that training and experience are more influential in the development of causal thinking than is intelligence.

More specifically, the nature of past experience in problem-solving activity is related to level and quality of thinking. Experience of success has the effect of increasing the range of responses to a problem situation and the persistence of attack upon the situation; failure has the contrary effect (Lewin, 1954). Success defined in terms of one's own past performances also tends to result in a raising of level of aspiration, as measured by the difficulty of the next task undertaken; failure, similarly defined, is followed by a lowering of aspiration level (Lewin *et al.,* 1944). Success and failure defined in terms of the performance of some group to which the individual belongs may have the opposite consequences (Festinger, 1942). Success also seems to have the effect of making the individual more realistic in his aspirations (P. Sears, 1940). The factor underlying the relationships of success and failure to aspirational level seems to be the desire on the part of the individual to maximize the probability of success on future performances. P. Sears and Levin (1957) found this concern with being successful present in four- and five-year-old children. The emphasis which the culture places on being successful may well explain this desire to ensure success.

These findings indicate the desirability of providing, in the interests of encouraging and eliciting productive thinking in youngsters, a history of successful experiences with problem solving. Yet success has its disadvantages. Undiluted and uninterrupted, it takes the challenge out of the task; it jades the intellectual appetite. Wright (1937) found that children in a choice situation selected the toy which was more difficult to reach, provided that the difference in accessibility was not too great and the toys were not identical. However, in making the choice between two tools with which to get the toy, children chose the one which was easier to reach. It appears that the principle of least effort does not generalize to the selection of the easiest goal. It is as if the problem-solver were saying: "I want to do the best possible job [in this case, get the more inaccessible toy], but I want to do it in the best [easiest] possible way." He thus maximizes the possibility of success *and* at the same time maximizes his feeling of accomplishment.

It might also be presumed that some experience of failure is necessary if the child is to develop any ability to evaluate, to censor his own thinking, and to establish some standards of excellence. A case in point is the story of the three-year-old who, after finger painting for some days in a nursery school and being told by his teacher that each of his paintings was good, asked his father one day, "How do you make a bad painting?"

The problem for the parent and the teacher is not an easy one. Tasks must be difficult enough to challenge and engage the interest of the learner. But they must not be so difficult that the child is discouraged from even trying or is constricted in his approaches to a solution.

18. Does the child need to be able to think quantitatively in order to compute?

19. In the Deutsche study, judges were asked to rate each answer on a scale from 7, correct and complete, to 1, entirely incorrect. What rating would you give to each of the following answers to the question, "Why does the candle go out?" (Deutsche, 1937, p. 32):

> Oxygen necessary to burn, and it's all used up.
> Hydrogen in jar.
> Smothered.
> Heat can't get out.
> Air used up.

20. Why do you think girls gave less adequate explanations than boys in the Deutsche study?

21. How might you explain the fact that the effects of success or failure on aspirational level depend upon whether that success or failure is defined in terms of the individual's past performances or in terms of the performance of a group to which he belongs?

22. Can there be a feeling of accomplishment without some experience of failure?

23. Is there no place for thinking in creativity? Is it all imagination?

24. Observe children in a school classroom. What evidences of thinking do you find? What is there in the situation that encourages (or discourages) thinking?

25. Are not conceptualization and thinking essentially the same process? How might you differentiate between them?

26. Hanfmann (1941) has suggested that some individuals approach a problem perceptually, maintaining close contact with the material objects in the situation; others utilize a conceptual approach, paying relatively little attention to the objects as such. In observations of children, can you differentiate between problem-solvers in this way?

INTELLIGENCE

The Growth of Intelligence

Intelligence is a property of behavior which is associated with the successful adaptation of organisms to their environments. As we have already seen (in Chap. 1), it is particularly characteristic of man's behavior. Tests of human intelligence are largely measures of conceptualization and problem solving, especially as these require the use of language or some other symbolic system, since such behavior tends to differentiate the successful from the unsuccessful individual.

As in the case of physical characteristics, we can describe the growth of intelligence by determining at any age level either how much an individual has grown or how fast he is growing. Unfortunately, we cannot measure intelligence as well as we can a physical characteristic, such as stature, for example. Part of the difficulty lies in the fact that units of mental measurement, unlike those of physical measurement, are not comparable from one age level to another. The most commonly used measure of intellectual growth in children is mental age (M.A.), defined as the average chronological age of a representative group of subjects performing at a given level on a test of intelligence. Thus a child whose test performance is like that of four-year-olds, whatever his chronological age, is said to have an M.A. of four years. As he grows in intelligence, his M.A. increases by so many months or years. In growth in height, an increase of six centimeters in any year is exactly equivalent to an increase of six centimeters in any other year. But an increment of six months in M.A. at one age level is not necessarily equal to an increase of six months at another age level.

Another difficulty that confronts us in the assessment of intellectual ability is the fact that what we measure changes with age not only in amount but in nature. The only difference between stature at five years and stature at fifteen years is that there is more of it at the latter age level. But intelligent behavior in a five-year-old differs both in amount and in kind from intelligent behavior in a fifteen-year-old. Hofstaetter (1954) analyzed intelligence-test scores from the Berkeley Growth Study obtained on the same subjects from birth through eighteen years. The predominant characteristic in the first two years was what he named *sensory motor alertness;* in the years from two to four, it was *persistence;* and in the period after four years of age, it was *manipulation of symbols.*

Moreover, at any one age, the intelligence level of an individual as measured by one test may differ significantly from the level as measured by another test. We have no one yardstick.

It should also be pointed out that the state of the subject at the time of testing influences his score on an intelligence test. To the extent that he is disturbed, disinterested, distracted, or ill during the administration of the test, he behaves less intelligently than he might. The resulting score may be an underestimate of his actual intelligence.

These and other sources of measurement error make any description of the growth of intelligence only an approximation. The results of Bayley's careful analysis of longitudinal data for the period from birth to twenty-one years of age (Fig. 15-2) provide as good a picture as is now available. She expressed the score of each individual at each age, not as an M.A., but as a deviation from the 16-year average for the group, labeling it a 16-D score. Not only does the average intelligence of the group increase with age, as might be expected; so does the amount of variability of intelligence within the group. What is not indicated in this graph is the fact that growth in intelligence does not cease at twenty-one years; it continues to the age of twenty-five and perhaps beyond (Bayley, 1955, 1957).

Intellectual and physical development are positively related, as indicated by correlations of about .40 between height and 16-D intelligence scores (Bayley, 1956b). Further analysis of these same data suggests that although the more able youngsters tend to be larger and to develop physically at a more rapid rate, they approach mental maturity somewhat more slowly than do the less able subjects (Bayley, 1956b).

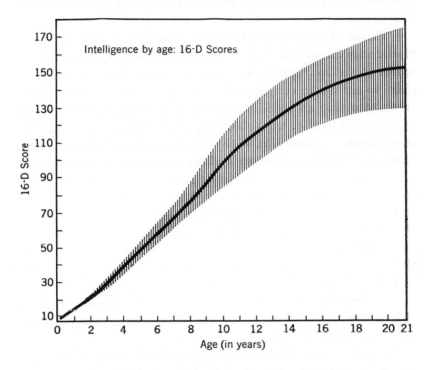

FIGURE 15-2. Curves of means and standard deviations of intelligence by 16-D units, birth to 21 years.

(From N. Bayley. On the growth of intelligence. *Amer. J. Psychol.,* 1955, 805-18)

The lack of a stable unit of measurement makes it virtually impossible to construct a velocity curve for intellectual development such as we saw for physical development. Instead, rate of mental growth is expressed as a ratio of mental age to chronological age (multiplied by 100), or the familiar intelligence quotient (I.Q.). Changes in I.Q. with age are discussed on pages 538-41.

Individual Differences in Intelligence

Within any one age group, children differ markedly in the amount of intelligence they exhibit. The source of this varia- tion has been the subject of much investigation and even more discussion.

Errors of measurement already discussed account for some of the individual differences observed. The fact that any test varies in its appropriateness as a measuring instrument from child to child also contributes to the range of scores obtained. In constructing an intelligence test, it is assumed that answers to the items in that test reflect "general training in a common environment" (Sandiford, 1938). When an intelligence test asks, "In what way are a baseball and an orange alike, and how are they different?" (Terman & Merrill, 1937), it is assumed that all children have had equal experience with both objects and that any differences in answers given will be a result of differential ability in abstraction and discrimination. Even with such com- mon objects as a baseball and an orange, the assumption is not always a valid one. The child who has never seen them because he is blind, the child who has not heard and cannot hear the words, the child from another culture who has neither seen the objects nor heard of them—for these the item is inappropriate as a measure of intelligence.

Children may also, through exceptional and specific train- ing, experience, and stimulation, develop facility in language, concept formation, and problem solving which gives them an advantage in performance on certain test items not anticipated by the maker of the test. Thus differences in environment, even within the same culture, are associated with differences in intel- ligence. Several indexes of the quality of environment, includ- ing education of parents, paternal occupation, socioeconomic status, and residence (rural vs. urban), have been found to be significantly correlated with scores on mental tests (H. E. Jones, 1954).

These environmental differences are not unrelated to the intelligence of the parents of the children. The more intelligent parents tend to provide the more stimulating environment and thus to produce the more intelligent children. To the degree that genetic factors contribute to individual differences in intelligence, the more able parents also tend to produce, in a biological sense, the more able children. Evidence of a genetic influence on individual variation in mental ability comes from a comparison of the degree of resemblance in intelligence of individuals of differing degrees of genetic similarity. Identical twins are identical in genetic composition; children of the same parents but singly born are similar; children of different parents are relatively dissimilar. To the extent that the degree of resemblance in mental ability is greater in twins than in siblings and greater in siblings than in unrelated children, hereditary influence is implied. But it still can be argued that twins resemble each other to the degree that they do, not only because they have an identical inheritance, but also because they have a virtually identical environment. Likewise, siblings can be expected to be more alike in intelligence than unrelated children because they develop in a more similar environment. Thus the more crucial test of genetic influence comes in the comparison of identical twins (or of siblings) who are reared together with twins who are reared apart. If the resemblance persists despite the separation, then an inherited predisposition to intelligent behavior is established. The following correlations, reported by Burt (1958), provide the evidence for this argument.

Identical twins reared together	.925
Identical twins reared apart	.876
Siblings reared together	.538
Siblings reared apart	.517
Unrelated children reared together	.269

A further measure of the genetic contribution to intellectual variation is the resemblance of parent and child. In the first two years, there is little or no relationship. By the age of four years, a significant resemblance appears and is maintained thereafter, as represented by a correlation of about .50 (H. E. Jones, 1954). Again, it can be claimed that it is impossible to infer from this relationship that heredity is an influence, since a common environment could explain the resemblance. Again, circumstances make a further test possible. Some children are reared by their parents; others are reared by foster parents. If the relationship between parents and children is attributable to environment rather than to heredity, we should find a resemblance in intelligence between children and the persons who rear them, whether or not they are the true parents. The fact is that adopted children resemble, not their foster parents, but their true parents; furthermore, there is a significant relationship between the intelligence of children, whether adopted or not, and the educational level of their true mothers and fathers, but not between the intelligence of adopted children and the educational level of their foster parents (Honzik, 1957).

It is impossible to determine experimentally the relative contribution of heredity and environmental factors to variation in intelligence. On the basis of a statistical analysis of data on almost a thousand pairs of siblings and their parents, and, when available, their grandparents, uncles, aunts, and first cousins, Burt (1958) has concluded that about 88 per cent of the total variance for assessments of intelligence is due to genetic factors, 7 per cent to environmental factors, and the remaining 5 per cent to errors of measurement.

Age Variability in I.Q.

Arguments concerning the constancy of the I.Q. were once the favorite pastime of social scientists, particularly those who identified themselves either as hereditarians or as environmentalists. The latter emphasized the modifiability of the I.Q.; the former, its immutability. The zeal of the hereditarians in this controversy is somewhat difficult to understand in view of the fact that an appreciation of the influence of genetic factors would not seem to demand constancy in rate of development. We are agreed that heredity plays a large part in physical development, and yet we recognize significant variability in the rate of a child's growth from one age period to another; we

Table 15-2

Interage Stanford-Binet Correlations *

Form	Age	M 4	M 5	M 6	L 7	M 8	L 9	M 10	L 11	M 12
M	3	.83	.72	.73	.64	.60	.63	.54	.51	.46
M	4		.80	.85	.70	.63	.66	.55	.50	.43
M	5			.87	.83	.79	.80	.70	.63	.62
M	6				.83	.79	.81	.72	.67	.67
L	7					.91	.83	.82	.76	.73
M	8						.92	.90	.84	.83
L	9							.90	.82	.81
M	10								.90	.88
L	11									.90

* From L. W. Sontag, Charles T. Baker, & Virginia L. Nelson. Mental growth and personality development: A longitudinal study. *Monogr. Soc. Res. Child Develpm.*, 1958, *23*:2 (Serial No. 68), Table 7, p. 28.

suspect that this variability itself is under the control of genetic factors.

Now that the heat of the battle has diminished, it is clear that both change and constancy characterize rate of mental growth. Individuals do tend to maintain the same I.Q. Table 15-2 shows the correlations among I.Q.'s of fifty children tested annually from three through twelve years of age on different forms of the 1937 Revision of the Stanford-Binet.

As the table reveals, the shorter the period between tests, the higher the relationship. Yet we can predict with better than chance accuracy the score of a twelve-year-old from a knowledge of his I.Q. at three years of age ($r = .46$). The size of the correlations increases with age when the interval between tests is held constant. Predictions from eleven to twelve years ($r = .90$) are more accurate than predictions from three to four years ($r = .83$) or from four to five years ($r = .80$). If different tests were administered at different age levels under conditions less favorable than those under which the data reported in Table 15-2 were collected, the relationships would be considerably lower, and predictions therefore much more hazardous.

Scores on so-called infant tests of intelligence are related negatively, if at all, to later measures of mental ability, and thus have little or no predictive value (Bayley, 1955). The later relationship between parent and child in intelligence indicates that the mental ability of the infant's parents provides the best measure for predictive purposes at the earlier ages (Bayley, 1958).

The rate of mental development also changes with age. In an analysis of Stanford-Binet scores from 140 subjects tested annually from infancy through at least ten years of age, Sontag, Baker, and Nelson (1958) found that in the interval from three to ten years of age (*1*) 62 per cent of the group changed in I.Q. by more than 15 points; (2) the median change was 17.9 points; (*3*) the greatest change recorded was 58 I.Q. points; (*4*) increments decreased in size with increase in age; and (*5*) acceleration was more typical of boys than of girls, particularly in the elementary school years.

To determine the personality correlates of these changes in rate of mental growth, the investigators selected for special study those children who gained the most and those who gained the least during each of two age periods: from four to six years, and from six to ten years. On the basis of records on each child in the files of the Fels Research Institute for the Study of Human Development, these investigators then obtained ratings of personality as of six years and again as of ten years. They then compared the ratings of their accelerated and decelerated groups. One personality scale, independence, clearly differentiated the two groups at six years; those children who were more emotionally dependent on their parents tended to experience losses in I.Q. during the preschool years. The following personality variables, rated at ten years of age, were associated with an accelerated rate of mental development in the elementary school years: independence, aggressiveness, self-initiation, problem solving, anticipation, and competitiveness. Moreover, those children who at age six were rated high on aggressiveness, self-initiation, and competitiveness were more likely to show increases in I.Q. in the years thereafter. The fact that ratings on the scales discriminating the gainers from the losers were highly interrelated suggested to these investigators that the underlying factor is a positive orientation toward achievement or an achievement motive. The discussion of the development of such an orientation we shall reserve for Chapter 16. Suffice it to say here that the process of socialization is involved.

Both Bayley (1954) and Kagan and Moss (1959) have reported that maternal education is a better predictor of a child's I.Q. than is paternal education, and that it is also a better predictor of the I.Q. of girls than of boys. This suggests that the mother's handling of a child, especially as it concerns intellectual interests and activities, influences significantly the rate of mental growth.

The findings of these several investigations cast some light on reported increases in I.Q. associated with nursery school attendance (Wellman & McCandless, 1946). To the extent that the experience of nursery school lessens the emotional dependence of the child on his parents and encourages autonomous achievement and initiative, the Fels results would lead us to predict some acceleration in intellectual development.

It is clear that impoverishment and deprivation of experience may retard intellectual development, and that enrichment of experience and the development of achievement motivation may accelerate mental growth. What is yet to be determined is whether these induced changes in the rate of intellectual development have any significant effect upon the eventual intellectual level attained by the individual.

Special Abilities

Throughout this discussion we have referred to intelligence as though it were a unitary trait, implying that children differed only in the amount of that characteristic which they exhibited at any age level. This implication is only a half-truth. Approximately 50 per cent of variability in intelligence is due to differences in what we call general intelligence (Burt, 1958), thus accounting for the fact that a child who does well on one item will tend to do well on another item in any test of intelligence. But he only *tends* to do so. He may manifest special abilities which enable him to do particularly well on some tasks.

Such specific characteristics of intelligent behavior as these have been identified and measured: reasoning, vocabulary, verbal fluency, memory, space perception, and quantitative ability. Intelligence seems to become more and more differentiated with age; that is, with age, special abilities account for more and more of the variability (Burt, 1958). In older youngsters we may therefore expect to find significant differences in the quality, as well as in the quantity, of intelligence.

There are no sex differences in general intelligence or in total scores on tests of intelligence; there are differences in special abilities: boys tend to be superior on quantitative and spatial problems, and girls on verbal problems (Terman & Tyler, 1954). The origin of these differences has yet to be determined. But it might be suspected that sex differences are in part the result of differential treatment of boys and girls, which in turn reflects different cultural expectancies for male and female behavior.

27. Can we judge a person's intelligence without observing his behavior or without some record of his behavior?

28. Intelligence is a concept. What abstraction and generalization are involved in its formation?

29. Examine the items on a standardized intelligence test. To what extent do they assume a common experiential background?

30. How could you account for the absence of relationship between intelligence-test scores of parents and those of children in the first two years?

31. What kinds of maternal behavior might serve to encourage intellectual curiosity and activity in a child?

32. Why might boys show a greater degree of acceleration in mental development than girls in the elementary school years?

33. What differences in the experiences provided for boys and girls might explain sex differences in special abilities?

SUGGESTED READINGS

BERLYNE, D. C. Recent developments in Piaget's work. *Brit. J. educ. Psychol.,* 1957, 27, 1-12. A useful introduction to current research and theory on cognitive development as formulated by Piaget.

BRUNER, JEROME S., & GOODMAN, CECILE C. Value and need as organizing factors in perception. In William E. Martin and Celia Burns Stendler (eds.), *Readings in Child Development,* Harcourt, Brace, 1954, pp. 310-18. A classic demonstration of the role of behavioral determinants in perceptual development.

CRONBACH, LEE J. *Essentials of Psychological Testing,* Harper, 1949. The student who wishes to know more about the measurement of intellectual development will find this book both interesting and informative.

ESCALONA, SIBYLLE. The use of infant tests for predictive purposes. In Martin and Stendler, *op. cit.,* pp. 95-103. An insightful discussion of the nature of infant intelligence and its measurement.

KIRK, SAMUEL A. *Early Training of the Mentally Retarded,* University of Illinois Press, 1958. A report of a longitudinal study on the effects of special nursery education on the rate of intellectual development of young mentally retarded children, with significant implications for developmental theory and educational practice.

LANGER, SUSANNE. *Philosophy in a New Key,* New American Library, 1942. Chapter 5 is a very provocative section dealing with the symbolic rather than the developmental aspects of language.

McCARTHY, DOROTHEA. Language development in children. In L. Carmichael (ed.), *Manual of Child Psychology* (2nd Ed.), Wiley, 1954, pp. 492-630. A scrupulously complete review of research on language development, of particular interest to the more advanced reader.

PIAGET, JEAN. *The Language and Thought of the Child,* Meridian Books, 1955. A paperback edition of a work, first published in 1926, describing research which Piaget conducted on child logic in the first seven years.

RUSSELL, DAVID H. *Children's Thinking,* Ginn, 1956. A definitive summary of research findings concerning all aspects of cognitive development.

SAPIR, EDWARD. *Language,* Harcourt, Brace, 1921, 1949. This classic work combines the points of view of linguistics and anthropology in presenting concepts basic to a study of language.

WATTS, A. F. *The Language and Mental Development of Children,* London: D. C. Heath, 1944. Chapter 2, "Growth in Vocabulary," and Chapter 3, "Continuous Speech," are highly readable accounts of early speech development.

16
motivational development

Most teachers describe Tom as a good all-around American boy. Big for his eleven years and strong, an early maturer, he excels in sports and is a leader on the playground. For the most part he is a good leader; he is fair, he avoids being "bossy," he sees to it that even poor players get a chance to play. However, he is a poor loser. When his team is trailing, he may pull its members off the field, angrily charging the other side with unfairness. When he strikes out in baseball, he may go off to a corner of the field and sulk, to be coaxed back only with difficulty by the other players.

The principal says that he couldn't run the school without Tom. He is president of the student council and can be counted on to do many tasks reliably and well. If folding chairs need to be put in place for a school assembly, Tom will be at school in plenty of time to get the job done. If the school is sponsoring a paper drive, Tom sees to it that it is well planned and well run.

Tom is a bright student, too. He shows no special abilities except, perhaps, in music, but his grades in all subjects are at or near the top. However, these grades are based on a comparison of Tom's work with a grade standard; they are not an evaluation of what he might do in the light of his ability. His teacher is concerned because she regards him as an underachiever; with an intelligence quotient of 150, he should be doing more advanced academic work. Tom does his assignments, but he doesn't read as widely as he should; nor does he follow up some of the classroom work with special projects or delve as deeply into a topic as he might when he prepares a special report. He lacks strong intellectual interests and an achievement drive commensurate with his ability.

Tom is the only child of middle-class parents, who are proud of and affectionate toward their son. He has been a fairly easy boy to rear. The father is obviously the preferred parent, and the mother reports some concern because Tom occasionally speaks rather disrespectfully to her and of her. Both parents would like to have Tom overcome his sulkiness, which he displays at home as well as on the playground. When Tom is losing an argument with his father or when his father "razzes" him, Tom heaps verbal abuse upon his father before retiring to his room to brood. For the most part, however, he is a good-tempered boy, pleasant, rather serious, yet with a nice sense of humor and a natural friendliness that endears him to all.

Tom is an individual. There is no one else in the world exactly like him. How did he become what he is? In a sense that is what this whole book has been about. In Part One we discussed the fact that the predisposition to develop some individual characteristics was Tom's by inheritance; his physical characteristics, his intelligence, the tempo at which he functions, his energy level, and his rate of maturation, all have been influenced by the genes. In Part Two we described the impact of society and culture upon children, and the process by which Tom's inheritance was modified by the demands of society. The influence of socializing agents in the process and the way in which they help to shape a child's individuality was explained in Part Three; as Tom interacted with his family, his peers, his teacher, and other community forces, he was exposed to stimuli, made responses, and received reinforcement in a way quite unlike that experienced by any other person.

But we still have to explain the development of those

drives which Tom learned in the process of socialization and which underlie most of his behavior. It is obvious that Tom has developed some systems of behavior that cannot be attributed to primary drives. He does not "boss" the other boys around because he is hungry or cold or thirsty; he does so because he has acquired a new drive—to dominate—which motivates him to act, and certain response tendencies—"Take the bat, Richards. I'm saving that one for Golden." . . . "You're out in the field, Parker." . . . "Drive around that way, Dad"—associated with that drive. In this final chapter, we turn to the problem of motivational development to find the factors that influence the learning of these very important aspects of personality.

TRENDS IN EMOTIONAL DEVELOPMENT

The term "emotion," as applied to an individual, means that "the subject's motivation is somehow in a special state" (Hebb, 1958, p. 156). That is, the organism is in a "stirred-up" or aroused condition, which may be mild or intense. The special state may be what we call distress, anger, delight, fear, joy, jealousy, or any of a number of other conditions, all of which affect the individual's behavior, as do all drives or motivational states. Early investigators were interested in fixing the timetable for the appearance of these various emotions in the young child.

Emotional Development in Early Childhood

Before a theory of learning was formulated to explain motivational development, investigators were interested in the problem of whether emotional behaviors are part of the child's "human nature." According to one team of writers (Watson & Morgan, 1917), emotional responses which might be labeled love, rage, and fear are unlearned. They believed that love might be provoked in response to stroking, rage in response to physical restraint, and fear in response to loud noises and loss of support. This theory has been subjected to empirical test, however, and results have not confirmed its assumptions. Although clothing is a kind of restraint, Irwin and Weiss (1934) found that infants are quieter when clothed than when unclothed, and anthropologists have failed to turn up evidence of rage in response to swaddling. Irwin (1932) reported that only two out of eighty-five infants showed fear when dropped a distance of two feet at an age of less than one month. Clarke, Hunt, and Hunt (1937) found that the noise of a revolver shot produced a startle response in every young infant tested, but it did not induce crying.

What emotions, then, is the infant born with? Bridges (1932) proposed, on the basis of her observations of babies, from newborns to children more than two years old, that the newborn infant is capable only of an "undifferentiated state of excitement" and that, from this initial state, emotional behaviors which adults identify as distress, anger, delight, and the like become differentiated. According to her theory, the process of differentiation begins during the neonatal stage, and, as weeks and months go by, the responses take on more clear-cut form in relation to specific situations. Distress is the first emotional behavior to appear and is present at the end of the first month; from distress, anger is differentiated. Delight also appears early (by the end of the second month), and, from delight, elation is differentiated. Other emotional responses are differentiated during the first two years, as Figure 16-1 indicates.

Investigations by Sherman (1927) also support the theory that emotional responses which can be precisely labeled are not present at birth. He found that psychology students and nurses were unable to identify correctly the emotional reactions of newborn infants unless they knew the stimulating circumstances. A hunger reaction, for example, might be called grief, irritation, discomfort, or even fear or pain by observers who did not know that the infant was hungry. Sherman concluded that observers who claim to find differentiated emotions present in the infant are merely reading into the infant's behavior an interpretation based upon their own experiences.

When an attempt is made to label the expressions of older infants, however, the results are surprisingly accurate. Goodenough (1931b) showed a group of students several photographs of a ten-month-old child exhibiting eight emotional expressions. The students were asked to match each expression with a verbal description of one of twelve situations. She reported an accuracy almost six times greater than chance expectancy. Goodenough's procedures do not duplicate Sherman's, but the

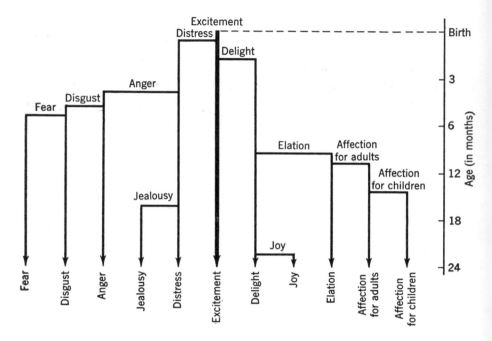

FIGURE 16-1. The approximate ages of differentiation of emotions in early childhood.

(After K. M. B. Bridges. Emotional development in early infancy. *Child Develpm.*, 1932, *3*, 340)

relatively high reliability of interpretations of the expressions of an older infant, in contrast to Sherman's failure to elicit accurate judgments about newborn babies, may be indicative of the differentiation that occurs during the first year.

One of the difficulties involved in interpreting the results of these early investigations is semantic. Each investigator tended to develop his own classification of emotional responses, and responses that one investigator grouped under one general category might be divided by another investigator into several categories. Furthermore, some investigators used overt reaction as the basis for classification, while others used the stimulus eliciting the reaction. From the studies reviewed above, therefore, we cannot generalize accurately about motivational development during the first year of life. We can state, however, that during the first year the number of different responses to aspects of the environment increases, and we can infer from some of these responses that the development of certain powerful secondary drives has begun.

The Role of Maturation

The role of maturation in the development of emotional responses has also received attention in research studies. It is always difficult to isolate the maturational factor, but several studies have achieved some success. In one, Goodenough (1932) observed and took motion pictures of the emotional reactions of a ten-year-old girl, totally blind and deaf from birth. Here was a child who was unable to perceive the emotional behaviors of others through sight or hearing, who had never been punished so that she had not experienced strong emotional reactions of adults directed against herself. Yet Goodenough observed responses that could be interpreted as indications of delight, rage, timidity, and other emotions, reactions essentially similar to those observed in normal children. She concluded that "the primary forms of expressive behavior are determined by native factors," although we learn to disguise these primary forms with a veneer of socially accepted forms of behavior. Other observers of human behavior agree with Goodenough that there are overt characteristics of some emotions which are unlearned.

One of the overt characteristics that has been studied by a number of investigators is smiling. The first smile appears at two months; it may be evoked by smiling or unsmiling faces, or even by a nodding puppet head (Spitz & Wolf, 1946). During the second half of the first year, indiscriminate smiling disappears; the child will smile at some faces and not at others. Laughing first appears at twelve weeks, in response to a chirruping sound made by the experimenter (Washburn, 1929); it may be elicited in a sixteen-week-old baby by peek-a-boo games.

Studies of crying show that the infant does not cry with tears until the second month (Lund, 1930). Crying in the neonate is closely associated with hunger; thus, we find, babies on a four-hour feeding schedule cry more than those on a three-hour schedule. Wrapping the newborn in a receiving blanket appears to reduce crying (Aldrich, 1946); the explanation offered is that close wrapping approximates the confinement of prenatal life and thus reduces the adjustments the neonate must make to the outside world. Crying due to colic decreases with age (Bayley, 1932), while crying in response to other factors, such as strange persons, places, and activities, tends to increase during the first year.

Age Changes in Emotional Reactions

A number of studies have been made of the changes in emotional responses that occur with age. For the most part, investigators have given more attention to expressive behaviors stemming from such strong motivational states as fear, aggression, and jealousy than to those motivated by more positive emotions. Some attention has been given to the development of affection, but chiefly as a part of the development of emotional dependency. We shall reserve discussion of affective development, therefore, for the section of this chapter in which we discuss the dependence drive (pp. 563-69).

FEAR. Perhaps the most thoroughly investigated emotional response is fear. Studies of the growth and decline of children's fears show some interesting changes with age. Jersild and Holmes (1935) found that in younger children, any intense, sudden, or unfamiliar stimulus will produce a fear reaction, whereas the fears of older children appear to be related to past experiences. Fears due to strange objects, noises, falling, unexpected movement, and the like decline during the preschool

years, but fears of the dark, of being alone, of imaginary creatures or robbers increase and, in fact, show a sharp upturn
during this same period (see Fig. 16-2).

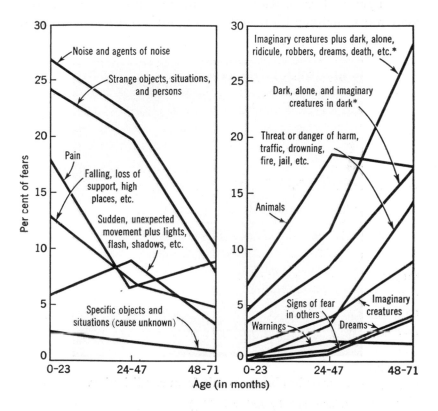

FIGURE 16-2. The relative frequency of children's fears in
response to various situations. Starred items represent the
cumulative tally of two or more items that are depicted
separately.

(After A. T. Jersild & F. B. Holmes. Children's fears. *Child Develpm.
Monogr.*, 1935, *20*, 358)

Fear is a very powerful drive and one which may serve an
important function in the survival of the organism. As we
pointed out in Chapter 2, fear enables the body to produce
extra energy to meet an emergency situation. But many of the

situations that are fearful to the young child do not require an extra output of energy. Fear of the dark or fear of a dog cannot be resolved by running. Children need to be helped to get over their irrational fears. Ridiculing the child for his timidity is a poor way of helping him; so is forcing him to meet the dreaded

Fear or its absence result from conditioning.

(Photograph by Esther Bubley)

situation by himself. Explanations sometimes help, and so does the example of another child.

Direct conditioning is the most effective means of eliminating a fear. Just as fear of something is learned by associating that thing with an unpleasant event, so fear can be unlearned by associating the feared object or place or person with something pleasant. Watson and Raynor (1920) demonstrated that a nine-month-old baby could learn fear of furry animals if the investigator struck a bar with a hammer at the same time that the baby was shown a white rat. Although the infant had not previously been afraid of rats, rabbits, a Santa Claus mask, or other furry objects, the association of the rat with the sudden loud and fearful noise caused the baby not only to fear the rat but to generalize his fear to all furry things. To overcome fears of this kind, M. C. Jones (1924) tried presenting a feared object —a rabbit in this case—to a two-year-old boy, while the child was engaged in a pleasant activity—eating. At first the rabbit was kept at a safe distance. Gradually, it was moved closer, until finally the child played with the rabbit while he ate. The association of the rabbit with a pleasant experience reconditioned the child and eliminated his earlier fear. Parents and teachers will find this method more effective with children than scolding or shaming them.

ANGER AND HOSTILITY. The young child responds to frustration with an explosive display of temper. His first attempts to use anger to reduce tension may do little to remove the frustration. A nine-month-old baby may fling his bottle away in a rage when the nipple gets stuck—an act which may relieve his feeling of annoyance but will not satisfy his hunger. Goodenough (1931a), studying the development of expressions of anger, found that these expressions become less explosive as the infant matures and more directly aimed at the enemy or obstacle. Gradually, the child learns that he must express his anger not physically but in subtler fashion. One of the three-year-olds studied by Goodenough sucked his thumb when angry—an act which was sure to provoke his mother. Some children refuse to eat; others will "accidentally" damage a cherished possession of the frustrator. Some children find that holding their breath or banging their heads against the floor is an excellent retaliating measure. Older children learn to call names, to criticize, or to exclude others from the group as expressions of hostility.

JEALOUSY. The most common form of jealousy in young children is sibling rivalry. The first-born child who has enjoyed the undivided attention of his parents for a year or more may resent the newborn baby, whose arrival threatens his position of prestige. These feelings may be so intense that the first-born will physically attack his rival; many a horrified mother has seen her older child pinch, poke, slap, and bite the younger sibling. When overt aggression is discouraged, the older child may resort to more subtle means of attack. He may cough his germs in the baby's face or smash one of the baby's toys or wake the sleeping baby with a loud whoop.

Often children try regression as a way of coping with their rivals; they go back to babyish ways of behaving which they may have long since outgrown. They want to drink from a bottle, to be fed by the mother, and to be bathed and dressed like a baby. Negativistic behavior and temper tantrums may reappear in what was formerly a pleasant, easily managed child (Sewall, 1930).

Jealousy is not confined to the first-born. The second-born and those to follow may resent the child who is the mother's favorite or the father's favorite, or the child who appears to be getting special treatment. Younger children may envy the privileges that go with being the oldest child in the family. Siblings of any birth order will compete among themselves for parental approval; many of the petty squabbles that arise in the course of daily living are due, at least in part, to competition for parental attention. In fact, mothers frequently remark that their children are better behaved when the mother is out, that bickering begins when the mother returns.

Sibling rivalry, however, is not inevitable. Among the seventy children she studied, Sewall found that only thirty-nine appeared to be jealous of their siblings. We do not know specifically what parents can do to prevent or "cure" jealousy in their children, but logic suggests that they should try to make the first-born feel loved and wanted, that they should give him a part to play in caring for the new baby so that he does not feel excluded, and that they should recognize and deal with the problem, when it appears, as jealousy, not as disobedience or "badness."

TRENDS IN SOCIAL DEVELOPMENT

Additional information on motivational development is derived from studies of the social behavior of children. As a child interacts with others, we can make some inferences about what is motivating him to behave. Early studies, descriptive in nature, provide us with a picture of developmental changes in social behavior.

The Preschool Years

During his first year, the infant learns to recognize various members of his family and to distinguish them from strangers. His social contacts are limited, however, and his play is in the main solitary. He treats other children as play materials and explores them as he might a toy (Maudry & Nekula, 1939).

After the "other children as toys" stage, the young child engages in parallel play (Parten, 1932). During this period, he does not play *with* another child in a give-and-take relationship but engages in the same kind of play as the other at the same time. Thus a two-year-old may seize a broom and sweep the floor when he sees another two-year-old performing this activity, or he may push a miniature truck on the floor when his friend does so. Later, he will swap trucks with his playmate, and still later in the preschool years, he may engage in cooperative activity involving both trucks.

"Engaging in cooperative activity," however, is not so peaceful as it sounds. The social life of the preschool child is marked by many quarrels, most of them centering around possession of property. The young child has not learned how property rights are defined in his culture and he takes—sometimes forcibly—what he wants, apparently operating on the theory that possession is nine tenths of the law.

In an extensive investigation of conflicts among nursery school children, Jersild and Markey (1935) found that conflicts occurred as often as once in every five minutes! With younger children, the conflicts are of very short duration; with older children, they are more prolonged. Older children, however, are less inclined to resort to physical aggression. Instead, they use their greater facility with language to call names.

Patterns of ascendance-submission have also been studied. Most American mothers want their children to be ascendant—at the top of the pecking order among their peers—rather than submissive. Yet, in a study of the behavior of preschool children in a play situation in which the supply of toys was limited, Jack (1934) found wide individual differences in the children's tendency to be ascendant. Special training with toy materials built up feelings of confidence in the submissive children and enabled them to assert themselves more forcefully than before. Page (1936) and Mummery (1947) also found it possible to build up children's ascendance scores by increasing their self-confidence through special training.

Not all ascendant behavior is socially desirable. H. H. Anderson (1937) described two types: dominative and integrative. Dominative behavior is intended to satisfy the child's own needs without regard for others; integrative behavior takes the needs of others into account and is planned to satisfy both the child and his playmates. As might be expected, the young child returns what he receives in kind; dominative behavior elicits dominative responses, and integrative behavior is met with integrative responses.

Can dominative children be helped to become less dominative? Chittenden (1942) found that when an experimenter role-played social conflicts for children, using dolls, and then helped the children to analyze the play situation in terms of the possible consequences of behavior, dominative behaviors were reduced. Classroom teachers have found this technique helpful also; as the child learns the kind of behavior he can expect from other children in response to certain behaviors on his part, he is less likely to resort to bullying and other undesirable tactics.

Another area of preschool development that has been explored involves the young child's perceptions of racial, religious, and nationality differences. For years it was believed that young children were not aware of such differences and that consequently they had no prejudices. More recently, investigators have found negative intergroup attitudes in children as young as five years. In a study in Philadelphia, research workers used a series of pictures depicting social episodes involving children of various races and religions. One picture, for example, shows several white children playing together, with a Negro child standing in the foreground. He may be interpreted as part of the play group or as isolated from it. Children were shown each picture and asked questions such as, "What is happening in the picture? Tell me about this little boy." Children who responded that the Negro boy was not playing with the others were asked, "Why isn't he playing?" Findings revealed that attitudes toward racial and religious groups are learned early in childhood. Even five-year-olds have learned to some extent such stereotypes as "Negroes are dirty" and "Italians like to fight" (Radke, Trager, & Davis, 1949).

The Elementary School Years

Most children in our society begin their school careers at approximately six years of age and, with entrance to first grade, leave their early childhood behind. Approximately six more years will elapse before the onset of puberty. During this time important changes occur in the developing child. These are different in nature from the changes occurring in the preschool years; the "middle-aged child," as he has been called, faces different developmental problems.

During the elementary school years, the sexes begin to segregate in their play. In early childhood boys and girls commonly play together. This trend persists through the first few years in school, when the child is pretty much under the thumb of his teacher and his mother. But by the time children reach the fourth grade, the lines are clearly drawn between the boys' group and the girls' group, and after-school activities as well as in-school play are organized on a single-sex basis. There are individual opposite-sex preferences, but these do not affect the play groups.

The reasons for the segregation in play groups is not quite

clear. This cycle of development does not occur in all societies, and so we cannot explain it in terms of the child's nature. With the Manus, for example, age groups are not so important or so distinct; at all ages, children of both sexes may play together.

"Boy! What a stinker I'm going to be
next *year!"*

(Drawing by Whitney Darrow, Jr. Copyright © 1953 The New Yorker Magazine, Inc.)

The phenomenon in our society may occur because school practices encourage segregation. There are boys' "basements" and girls' "basements" (as the toilet rooms are euphemistically called in some schools). Boys form in line and girls form in line. Boys are assigned one side of the playground and girls are assigned another. The boys compete with the girls in races of various kinds. Boys are expected to play certain games and girls are expected to play others. Over and over again, the cultural ways of the school encourage boys and girls to form separate groups.

The elementary school child grows in his ability to work in groups. This is evident in classroom discussions as the child grows older. In the primary grades, a give-and-take discussion is difficult for the child; he is apt to go off on a tangent and to make many remarks that are beside the point. Should the teacher attempt to lead a discussion on snakes, the child might volunteer the information that his uncle had paid him a visit on Saturday. In the middle grades, however, he begins to concentrate on a topic and to participate more effectively in discussion. He also shows a greater capacity for organization. He can participate as a committee member in choosing a leader, helping to plan and to carry out plans, and setting up the rules governing the enterprise.

With the child's growing ability to work as a team member come a liking for and a respect for rules. Indeed, in the middle grades, the child sometimes appears to be compulsive about rules. Three nine-year-olds, for example, decide to jump rope. They spend several minutes in serious discussion. "Let's have two misses and out," one proposes. "Everyone has to run in," says another. "Rotten turning and you lose a turn to jump," says the third. Baseball games, jumping contests, jacks games, and many others are organized in similar fashion, and each child constitutes himself a referee to see that the rules are followed. With increasing maturity, and with guidance in group living, children come to see the necessity for rules and sometimes set up much stricter regulations governing their own activities than those established by adults.

Toward the latter half of the elementary school years, as we have noticed, the child begins to substitute the standards of the peer group for those of parents and teachers. According to Havighurst (1953), this development in later childhood helps the child to achieve an appropriate dependence-independence pattern. In the process of growing up, the child must free himself from parental domination and learn to stand on his own feet; he takes an important step in that direction when he begins to realize that adults can be wrong. As his social relationships with other children are extended, he is exposed to varying points of view and comes to see that his parents are not infallible. The stage is then set for identification with agemates and for substitution of their standards for parental ones. The peer group, in effect, becomes a socializing agent; it is such an important one that we have devoted a whole chapter to it.

The Adolescent Years

Adolescence in our society is generally regarded as a period of storm and stress. In his desire to be grown-up, the adolescent in our society may run into conflict with parents, teachers, and other adults who still regard him as a child. Thus the use of cosmetics, late hours, driving the family car, spending money, or out-and-out rebellion against adult authority may be the cause of bickering in the home or conflict at school. In our culture, the discrepancy between the increased physical maturity of the adolescent and his childhood status in society contributes to the difficulty of the period. However, Mowrer (1952) points out that keeping the adolescent a child may be the only course of action possible in a society such as ours, in which an extended period of education is necessary if young people are to reap their just share of material benefits. The adolescent may be biologically ready for manhood, but in our technological civilization he must spend additional years in a dependent status in order to prepare himself to make a living. A disturbed adolescence may be the price we pay for living in a culture which, because of its complexity, makes a long period of dependency necessary.

The adolescent period is accompanied by marked changes in social and emotional behavior. Interest in the opposite sex creates an interest in personal appearance; the child who formerly had to be urged to wash behind his ears now may spend hours primping. A boy may even, on occasion, discard sloppy gear for a white shirt; a girl, for a sophisticated dress. The adolescent likes fads and indulges in a wide variety of them—from eating goldfish to wearing socks that don't match to getting lipstick imprints on his sweat shirt. He adopts a peculiar slang which also sets him apart from other age groups. He is likely to be compulsive about conforming; being different from his peers may be a source of anxiety, particularly for early- and late-maturing youngsters. Thus a boy may worry if his pals develop fuzz on their chins, hair on their chests, or a deepening of the voice before he does. A girl may worry if she lags behind her friends in beginning menstruation or developing breasts. Similarly, the youth who matures much earlier than his peers worries about his development. Physical defects and deformities—warts, pimples, and birthmarks, as well as more serious ones—which may not have been of much concern during later childhood assume great importance with the adolescent because they may mark him as different or make him less attractive to the other sex.

Statements by college students (Kuhlen, 1952, pp. 72-73) illustrate some of the concerns they felt as adolescents:

Adolescence was certainly the unhappy period in my life. My physical features were probably the cause of it. It seemed to me that I was so fat, I was square, and clothes hung on me like a bag. My face looked as though it still belonged in the baby buggy and not even a permanent wave made my hair curl. I was also very touchy about a birthmark on my leg. It is a big brown one on my leg, and everyone asks me if I've hurt myself or if it's dirty. During my adolescent period, I felt ready to crawl into a hole and die every time these questions popped up. I refused to wear socks and usually got into terrifically awkward positions in order to cover it up. (Now I'm attached to it, and have good come-backs for the inquisitive ones.) However, the results of these physical handicaps made me a prize wallflower. Night after night my friends would be taking their first steps into the field of romance, while this poor lonesome child sat at home. No one who hasn't experienced a late maturation can understand or appreciate such a condition. Not until I was sixteen did I blossom into an attraction for the opposite sex—just three or four years after my friends.

Another girl wrote:

> I didn't have "adolescent skin," I was neither too fat nor too thin, not too tall nor much too short, *but I did wear glasses.* I, along with other girls of my age, read many romantic stories, and I, along with the same girls, often tried to visualize myself in the heroine's part. It was rather hard to see myself at a college prom with my glasses on. In fact, I think for a while I was convinced that I should be an old maid—and a very unpopular one at that. My mother, suspecting my mental anguish, wisely encouraged my leaving my glasses off for social functions. I went to my first assemblies with a new party dress and minus my glasses. I don't think I looked any better, but I *thought* I did!

Concern about "adolescent skin" and other aspects of physical development may result in feelings of inadequacy, which can seriously affect other areas of development. A hitherto amiable child may become quarrelsome and critical; a bright student may lose interest in school work to the detriment of his grades. In such cases, the difficulty is caused, not by the physical changes accompanying adolescence, but by the social pressure to have the same developmental status as one's peers.

1. Observe a two-year-old and make a note of any resistant behavior that you notice. What is the immediate occasion for this behavior? Should a parent or teacher try to avoid all such occasions? What is the best way of dealing with the behavior? What is your criterion for "best"?

2. Observe first-grade and sixth-grade children at play during outdoor recess. How do they differ in social behavior? In emotional behavior?

3. Would you expect to find nine-, ten-, and eleven-year-olds in all societies substituting age-sex standards for parental ones? Explain your answer.

4. In some primitive societies youth are initiated into adulthood with appropriate ceremonies, without having to endure a long transitional period of being neither children nor adults. Would you expect that such a practice would completely eliminate the storm and stress of adolescence?

LEARNED DRIVES

In the course of growing up, as we have pointed out, the child acquires certain drives which form the basis of his relations with other people. These drives are learned in the course of interaction with other human beings; they then become a motivating force in behavior. The reader may have been exposed to various lists of such drives. Some authors speak of the need for security, for status, for recognition, for affection. Often the terminology is vague; the need for "security," for example, might be satisfied in some children by more independence and in others by less. Murray, in his *Explorations in Personality* (1938), formulated a widely used classification system, listing such needs (or drives) as autonomy, aggression, construction, dominance, recognition, and succorance. In recent years, however, many investigators have chosen to concentrate their research on four learned drives: dependency, independence, achievement, and aggression. Each of these terms embraces several of the more specific drives listed by Murray. We shall consider dependency first, for the dependency drive is learned early in life and exerts considerable influence upon the child's social development.

Dependency

During the first months of life, few demands are made upon the infant. He leads an irresponsible existence, in which his every whim is gratified and he need do nothing in return— except grow and develop as a normal healthy baby. He cries and sooner or later he is fed; he sleeps when he is sleepy; he evacuates at will; he is indulged and waited upon by loving relatives who make him the center of the household. As a result, the child first conceives of himself, not as a helpless infant, but rather as an omnipotent being whose mother, father, and other relatives are at his beck and call. Freud, as we have pointed out in Chapter 7, described this stage as the period of "infantile omnipotence."

Yet even though from the infant's standpoint this period

may be one of omnipotence, actually he is learning, during this time, to be dependent, not all-powerful. He is not born with dependency needs but acquires them in accordance with certain known principles of learning. When the baby is hungry or in pain, he cries, and his mother (or some other socializing agent) helps him. Soon he learns to depend upon his mother for reduction of his hunger drive or alleviation of his pain. Whiting describes how dependency learning occurs in Kwoma society:

> Kwoma infants are cared for almost exclusively by their mothers. For approximately the first three years of his life, a Kwoma infant sits in the lap of his mother during the day and lies by her side at night. It is the Kwoma mother's duty to care for all the needs of her child during this period. When, despite this constant care, Kwoma infants suffer frustration, crying is the response which becomes most firmly fixed. A Kwoma mother, whenever her infant cries, does her best to comfort him. If he is hungry she feeds him; if he is cold she warms him; if he is sick or in pain she tries to soothe him. Thus, by removing the source of frustration or pain, the Kwoma mother rewards crying as a response to these conditions. Toward the end of infancy, when the child begins to talk, he responds to frustration or pain by asking for help, and his mother complies with his request whenever it is possible for her to do so. Thus during infancy a frustration-dependence sequence is established [1944, p. 115].

Actually, the child may learn to be dependent upon his mother without prior frustration. The mother can acquire secondary reward value simply because the child comes to associate her with reduction of his hunger drive and elimination of pain. Gradually he builds up a conception of mother as the giver of love and approval and becomes dependent on her for emotional succorance as well as for satisfaction of his physical needs (Sears, 1950).

A THEORY OF DEPENDENCY LEARNING. The infant, as we have learned, is born with a hunger drive. He must have food in order to survive; when his stomach is empty, the need for food gives rise to a drive state which typically takes the form of restless or crying behavior. We may say that the infant has a hunger drive which motivates his behavior. This restless or crying behavior will cease when food is swallowed and the hunger drive is reduced.

The infant, however, is capable of learning. Through a process of conditioning, he comes to respond to certain cues by ceasing to cry and thrash about, even before the food is swallowed. Probably the first cue he learns is the feel of the nipple in his mouth. Because this sensation is invariably followed by reduction of the hunger drive, it quickly becomes the cue to which he responds by stopping his crying.

The next step in the learning of dependency takes place when the infant stops crying and begins to make sucking noises upon being picked up. A new cue has been added to his repertoire. It is no longer necessary for food to begin its way to the child's stomach or for him to feel the nipple in his mouth in order for his tension to decrease. The cue of being picked up has become the signal for reduction of the hunger drive. Gesell and Ilg (1943) note that cessation of crying upon being picked up can occur as early as four weeks of age.

The next step in learning dependency occurs, according to Gesell and Ilg, at sixteen weeks, the age at which the infant quiets when his mother enters the room. Tension-reduction now occurs, not on being picked up, not on oral sensation, not on food in the stomach, but with the presence of the mother. As her presence becomes more and more closely associated with the good things of life, it comes to have reward value for the infant.

Throughout the first year of life, the infant shows increasing awareness of the value that he attaches to his mother's presence. At twenty-eight weeks he can distinguish his mother from other people and demands more of her than of others. These demands continue as the infant approaches his first birthday; he may cry when she leaves the room or when she gives him to a stranger to be held. By his demands upon her, he indicates his own recognition of his need for her. When his perception of his need for mother's presence has reached this stage, we may safely say that he has a dependency drive. Now when he is faced with a problem that gives rise to tension—whether it is a toy that lies just beyond his reach, a strange visitor, or hunger, cold, and thirst—the infant turns to his mother to solve the problem and reduce the tension. He has a need or drive for her presence and for her help.

The next step in the learning of dependency occurs when the child learns to seek the approval and avoid the disapproval of others. Again, this occurs through a process of conditioning. Typically, when the mother is trying to soothe the infant, she talks to him in comforting tones. Reduction of his primary needs by feeding, rocking, or warming is accompanied by verbal "approval." Eventually the words of others in themselves come to seem "good" to the child. He is also eventually conditioned to distinguish between verbal approval and disapproval. If reduction in tension is accompanied by verbal approval, the child learns to seek this approval as a means of reducing tension. In similar manner, he learns to want to avoid disapproval. When the mother decides *not* to comfort the child, she will tell him so, frequently in sharp, "disapproving" tones. These tones come to have a negative value for the child, since they signify that his primary wants will not be cared for; thus they come to mean a painful, rather than a pleasurable, state of affairs.

Not all children have the opportunity to learn dependency. When the child does not have a continuing relationship with one person, the kind of conditioning process we have described does not occur. A study by Wittenborn (1956) has produced some evidence on this point. He compared adoptive children who had previously been institutionalized for some months with children who had been adopted almost immediately after birth. He found, in interviewing parents, that the children who had spent some time in the institution showed less dependency at the age of five than those in the other group.

Children who have learned only a very weak dependency drive are very difficult to socialize because they have never learned to want the approval of others. They are driven by inner impulses which demand immediate satisfaction. They alternately cling and react in very independent fashion. Threats have no effect upon them. According to Bowlby (1952), the behavior of such children can best be explained in terms of a failure to learn dependency. In societies such as ours, which place much emphasis upon independence as a goal of socialization, the importance of first learning dependency is not always recognized (Stendler, 1954b).

A number of studies have focused on some of the antecedents of the dependency drive. These have attempted to discover what produces a strong dependency drive. Is it repeated demonstrations of affection? Or does a lack of love and attention cause the child continually to seek them?

Some answers to these questions have come from the Sears, Maccoby, and Levin study (1957) to which we have referred earlier. On the basis of interviews with 379 mothers in the Boston area, these investigators established a measure of dependency and then searched for possible antecedents. They summarize their findings as follows:

> Mothers who repeatedly demonstrate their affection for children are providing many supports for whatever actions the children have performed in order to obtain such demonstrations. These actions often involve following the mother around, touching her, smiling at her and talking, and keeping some kind of contact with her. These are the actions, of course, that we have labeled dependency.
>
> Once the child has developed these habitual ways of acting—and all children develop some—he may be expected to use them as devices for reassuring himself that his mother does love him. That is to say, if she shows signs of rejection, if she uses withdrawal of love to discipline him, and if she is punitive toward his aggression, he may be expected to double his efforts to secure her affection. This will simply increase the frequency and persistence of the acts we have defined as dependent, and hence the mother will describe more of them.
>
> The influence of affectionate demonstrativeness, if we may suggest a theoretical point, is an influence on the *learning* of dependent behavior. The effect of withdrawal of love, punish-

ment of dependency and aggression, and other behaviors that threaten the child's security is an effect on performance or *action*. Therefore, the actual amount of dependency observed and reported by a mother is a product of both factors. It follows that the most dependent children should be those whose mothers express openly their affection for the child but repeatedly threaten the affectional bond by withholding love as a means of discipline and by being punitive toward his displays of parent-directed aggression [pp. 174-75].

Investigators are now beginning to turn the experimental spotlight on some of the enormously complex variables associated with the learning of dependency. One study in particular (Gewirtz & Baer, 1958) deserves note. The authors have isolated the influence of brief social deprivation on the effectiveness of adult approval as a social reinforcer. Learning to want adult approval, as we have noted, is a most important part of learning dependency. The question Gewirtz and Baer attempted to answer was: If children are deprived of a particular adult for a time, will his approval mean more to them when he returns? Just as food and water are stronger reinforcers when the individual is hungry or thirsty, so, it was reasoned, the approval of a given adult will be a stronger reinforcer if the child has been deprived of social contact with that person than if deprivation had not occurred. Two groups of nursery school children, aged forty-six to sixty-three months, were compared. Each child in the experimental group was subjected to a twenty-minute wait before playing a game, during which time the experimenter left the room (supposedly to repair a toy). Then the game was played, and the experimenter indicated approval of the right moves by saying "Good!" "Fine!" and the like. Other details were carefully controlled, and the frequency of correct moves by each child was noted. The scores of the experimental group were compared with those of the control group, which had not been subjected to isolation before playing the game. Results showed that the effectiveness of adult approval as a reinforcer was reliably enhanced by a preceding period of social isolation (deprivation); in other words, the child will apparently try harder to win adult approval following a period of deprivation. The degree to which adult approval was an effective reinforcer to individual children in the social-deprivation group was shown to be related to the degree to which each child characteristically sought approval in other settings. It was also related to age; the reinforcers were most significant for the older children. Later research by Gewirtz, Baer, and Roth (1958) found that the child will engage in more attention-seeking behaviors in a situation of low social availability on the part of the adult (e.g., he sits at a desk engrossed in paper work while the child plays) than when the adult is continually available.

The results of these researches are in accord with the observations of mothers, who find that they are much more effective in socializing their young children after a brief absence from the home. Teachers, too, find themselves enthusiastically greeted by the class after a day's absence and note that never are the children so good! Occasional deprivation, then, is not in itself undesirable; in fact, as these investigations show, *brief* deprivation might conceivably have constructive effects in some circumstances.

Independence

Independence has not been studied so extensively as dependency, and therefore we know less about its origins and subsequent development. Presumably, dependency needs build up first and fast, while independence begins later and develops at a much slower tempo. Presumably, also, independence is learned through a conditioning process in association with some primary drive. The infant's striving for autonomy over his own body—in turning over, sitting up, standing, and later walking by himself—may derive from his activity needs. Infants who hold their own bottles may be rewarded by being able to regulate their intake of milk more satisfactorily than when the bottle is held by an adult. Similarly, a nine-month-old baby may get satisfaction from finger-feeding himself because it can appease his hunger drive more readily than feeding by an adult.

Paradoxically, the need for parental approval (dependency)

may motivate some children to act independently ("You can do it; that's a good boy; let's see you climb the steps all by yourself") or may reinforce independent behavior which the child initiates ("Just look at my big boy carrying that big heavy package all by himself!"). (In fact, it has been suggested that most secondary drives stem from the dependency drive.) As the proud mother exclaims over the baby's independent behavior, he eventually finds enough reward in her approval to want to repeat it.

But independence, like dependency, must be culturally trained. It is not enough for the child to be independent in areas that he chooses for himself; he must learn to be independent (and dependent) in ways which the culture sanctions. Therefore the early period of indulgence must end and child training begin. Typically, parents in our society begin to make demands upon the child when he is old enough to be dangerous to himself or destructive to objects in his environment. Sometimes these demands take the form of restrictions on new behaviors; thus the nine-month-old infant is restrained from standing in his carriage, and the fourteen-month-old toddler is not permitted to climb stairs unless accompanied by an adult. They may also take the form of interference with former habits; thus the eighteen-month-old baby must eat with his spoon and not with his fingers, and the two-year-old must tell his mother when he needs to go to the bathroom. As Dollard and others put it:

> [The child] must learn to walk where it has formerly been carried; . . . it learns not to be picked up when it has experienced some small disaster. It must give up much of the cuddling, holding, and petting which is the prerogative of the smallest darling. Childish approximations of table manners and etiquette must be altered in favor of the customs preferred by adults. The child must learn to wait for its food, to keep its face clean, to submit to having its hair combed, to eat in the regular stages designated by our table techniques. At some time or another, all of these lengthened sequences invoke frustrations and elicit protest from the child [1939, pp. 64-65].

During this early period of child training, and particularly between the second and third year, much resistant or negative behavior appears. In this stage of negativism, children who were formerly quite tractable become very difficult to manage. The child says "no" to almost every demand made upon him; in fact, he sometimes says "no" from habit when he really means "yes"! By three, the child is past this stage and is once more a delight to his parents. From one standpoint, the period of negativism may be regarded as a time when the child is learning culturally accepted ways of being dependent and independent, when dependent behavior begins to wane and independent behavior is on the rise. At this point conflicts may arise because the child's conception of independent behavior is at variance with that of his parents; the child may want to be independent in ways which his parents do not or cannot approve, or the parents may want the child to give up his dependency in certain areas, and the child rebels. A satisfactory resolution of the crisis results when the child has learned in which areas he is expected to be dependent and in which he is to be independent (Stendler, 1954b).

But dependency and independence do not represent opposite extremes of behavior. Beller (1955) identified the components of dependency as seeking help, physical contact, proximity, attention, and recognition; he identified the components of independence as taking initiative, trying to overcome obstacles in the environment, trying to carry activities to completion, getting satisfaction from work, and trying to do routine tasks by oneself. He found that children aged three and a half to five and a half years differed significantly from one another when compared in their composite dependency scores and their composite independence scores.

That both dependency and independence can be encouraged at the same time is not difficult to see. Whiting and Child (1953) found that American middle-class parents tend to be indulgent with respect to dependency in the infant, and that they punish disapproved dependency behaviors much less severely than transgressions of toilet training and aggressive behaviors. However, our society also values independence, and parents therefore encourage children to stand on their own feet, to do certain things for themselves, at an earlier age than children in many other societies. We pointed out in Chapter 6 some of the many ways in which the independence training of French children differs from that of American children, and some of the consequences of these differences for the socialization of the children (Stendler, 1954a). Swiss children, too, differ from American children in respect to the development of independence. Boehm (1957) compared Swiss and American children, ranging in age from six to fifteen years, by means of a projective technique which involved telling each child a story and then asking him questions about it. She found that the American children showed independence from adults earlier than did the Swiss; the latter were more likely to believe in the omniscience of adult authorities and to rely on adult judgment. The children's answers also revealed that the American child seems to transfer his dependence upon his parents to dependence upon peers at an earlier age. Whereas the Swiss child lacks confidence in the judgment of his peers, the American child is likely to prefer peer advice to advice from adults.

Growth in physical independence is not so difficult to achieve as satisfactory growth in emotional independence. As the child slowly develops emotional maturity, he must develop a greatly increased capacity for self-help, accompanied by an increasing degree of psychological self-support. More research is needed on the progressive stages in this development, on how much independence is desirable at various stages, and on how various techniques of child training affect growth in independence, both adversely and positively.

Achievement

A child growing up in our society not only must learn to want to stand on his own feet (independence motivation); he must also learn to want to meet certain standards of excellence in areas of behavior deemed important by the society. We call the drive to meet these standards the achievement motive. The strength of this drive varies with individual children. Some have very high achievement motivation; in others the drive is weak. One child may work very hard at almost everything he tackles, even doing more than the required amount of work; another makes virtually no effort, works at a level far below his ability, and appears not to care about how well he does. What factors in the socialization process explain these individual differences?

According to McClelland and others (1953), independence training is closely related to achievement training. The child who is forced to stand on his own feet and to give up his dependency on adults learns to master his own problems. Further, parents who stress independence are likely to stress self-reliance and achievement as well. Using ethnographic materials in the Human Relations Area Files, these investigators examined age of beginning independence training and severity of training in eight Indian tribes. They correlated their findings with independence ratings previously made on these same tribes by Whiting and Child (1953; see p. 192). Results showed that the tribes that initiate training earliest and train most severely with respect to nursing, toileting, sexual behavior, and aggression have the highest ratings in independence.

It would seem, then, that very early demands for achievement in certain areas coupled with severe training will strengthen the independence drive, although not necessarily the achievement drive. A child so treated will learn to want to do things for himself, but not necessarily to do them well. And, as we have pointed out, too strong an independence drive is not desirable in children.

A more direct test of the cause-and-effect relationship between achievement and independence training has been made by Winterbottom (1953). She asked a group of boys aged eight to ten to tell stories about the following situations:

1. A father and son talking about something important.
2. Brothers and sisters playing. One is a little ahead.
3. A young man alone at night.
4. A boy with his head resting on his hands.

Their stories were analyzed and achievement scores assigned. An independence score was obtained for each boy from interviews in which his mother was asked at what age she expected her son to have met certain independence demands: to be able to undress and go to bed by himself, to earn his own spending money, and the like. When achievement scores and independence scores were correlated, the following conclusions were drawn:

1. Mothers of sons with high achievement motivation expect their children to have met independence demands much earlier in life than do other mothers.

2. Mothers of sons with low achievement motivation tend to demand less in the way of independent achievement at an early age.

3. Mothers of sons with high achievement motivation impose more restrictions upon the child's freedom *initially*.

4. Mothers of sons with low achievement motivation tend to continue restricting children beyond the age at which other mothers relax restrictions.

5. Mothers of high achievers reward children both for meeting the demands for independence made upon them and for observing the restrictions initially placed upon their independence.

Apparently, then, mothers of sons with high achievement scores follow the procedure of urging the child to master a skill early, restricting him until he succeeds, and then letting him alone. These mothers also reward the child more often and more intensely both for independent behavior and for acceptance of early restrictions upon independence. The early restrictions protect the child from experiencing failure in his first attempts at being independent; the parent waits until the child is old enough to accomplish a task successfully before urging him or permitting him to undertake it.

Further information on how high achievers are developed comes from an ingenious study by Rosen and D'Andrade (1957). These investigators obtained achievement scores for nine- to eleven-year-old boys on a Thematic Apperception Test. An experimental situation was then set up for the twenty highest achievers and the twenty lowest achievers. Each boy was required to perform five experimental tasks: stacking blocks while blind-folded, working anagrams, making patterns with special blocks, playing ring toss, and building a hat rack. These tasks were performed in the home, in the presence of both parents, who were told the kind of help they would be permitted to give their boy in each task. Investigators were interested in seeing how much autonomy parents allowed their boy to have, and whether their behavior might be characterized as warm, rejecting, or pushing.

Rosen and D'Andrade found that parents of high achievers tended to show more involvement and seemed to take more pleasure in the problem-solving experiments. They also tended to have a higher regard for their boy's competence in problem solving, and higher expectations: they set up standards of excel-lence for their son even when none was given and expected their boy to do "better than average" at any of the tasks. They tended to react to their son's performance with approval and warmth.

Interesting differences were found between mothers and fathers of high achievers. Fathers tended to give hints to their boys, rather than telling them how to do it; they were less likely to push. The fathers appeared to be competent men who were willing to take a back seat while their sons were performing. Mothers, on the other hand, were likely to be more dominant, to have higher aspirations for their boys' achievement, and to be more emotionally involved in their success. They were more likely than fathers to reward success with approval, but also more likely to punish failure with hostility.

A reasonably high achievement drive is a desirable goal of socialization. Too high an achievement drive may make an individual dissatisfied, unhappy, and compulsive, perhaps sub-ject to various psychosomatic complaints. However, an individ-ual whose achievement motivation is too weak will never fully realize his potentialities.

In this connection, the relation between parental level of aspiration for children and the achievement drive of the chil-dren needs investigation. When permissive parents allow their children to have many independent experiences without restriction, they are in effect providing opportunities for failure, and repeated failures may result in a weak achievement drive. Permissive parents who interpret "accepting the child" to mean accepting his performance without regard for his capabilities may also have low achievers. The children of overrestrictive parents may be weak achievers because they don't have enough opportunity to do things well by themselves and to be rewarded for doing them. And parents who set standards so high that the child too often experiences failure may also have a child who is a low achiever. The formula for developing an achievement drive that is neither too strong nor too weak would seem to be to restrict the child from doing things by himself when he is likely to experience failure, but to have enough faith in the child's competence and to give him enough instruction on how to handle himself so that restrictions are not imposed too long. He should be rewarded for his successes in behaving independently and also for accepting early restrictions.

Aggression

Like sex, aggression is an extremely powerful drive. However, it is stronger in some children than in others. Constitutional differences undoubtedly predispose some children to have a stronger aggressive drive than others. But what environmental influences account for the drive and contribute to its strength? And what are the effects of attempts to control or inhibit the tendency to be aggressive? These are the kinds of question to which investigators have directed their attention.

Aggression means behavior that is intended to hurt or injure someone (Sears, Maccoby, & Levin, 1957). The young child uses very direct means to express this intention: he may hit, bite, pull hair, kick, or scratch, using every part of his body that has potentiality as a weapon, or he may injure someone by destroying his favorite possessions. As he grows older, he develops less direct techniques of expressing anger. He taunts, ridicules, calls names, insults, or assassinates character in a manner intended to hurt another person, not physically, but by attacking some social drive—need for status, for affection, for belonging, for approval, for achievement. He also learns to hurt others by ignoring them, withholding his affection, or rejecting them.

Sears, Maccoby, and Levin explain how aggressive behavior is learned:

> One thing he discovers during the first couple of years is that when his mother wants his cooperation, he can give it or not as he chooses. If he does not choose, his mother will make continued efforts to ensnare him. Some of her acts are good to have happen: she may pick him up, cajole him with little murmurs and kisses, talk to him lovingly, offer him food or a toy, or tickle him. As he gets older, and proud of his skills, she may urge him to walk a little more or build a little higher or say another word. He learns that he has the power to require that a price be paid for doing what his mother wants. This is extremely important for the development of aggression, for by learning what things he can withhold from his mother, he has learned how to cause pain without using his impotent fists. . . .
>
> It is difficult for parents to realize, sometimes, how often a young child achieves some relief from an uncomfortable state of affairs via aggressive actions. The mother may not know how tired, or how frustrated, he is until she sees signs of a temper tantrum, at which point she realizes that something must be done and goes into action. Even if she is irritated with him over his show of temper, she will put him to bed, or feed him, or open the sticking door, or somehow change the situation so that the source of trouble has been removed. Thus, even if she scolds the child for being aggressive, she simultaneously solves his problem and hence strengthens his aggressive behavior. Many a child has learned that his busy mother pays little attention to him so long as he is getting along all right, and that it is primarily when he screams or otherwise makes his mother uncomfortable that she will turn her attention to his difficulties and help him solve them. Understandably, a child is especially likely to learn to get attention by aggressive action during the stage of his life when he cannot yet talk clearly, for the more "rational" process of telling his mother specifically what is wrong is not yet possible [1957, pp. 223-24].

Aggression, then, may be regarded as one possible response to frustration (Dollard *et al.,* 1939). Sometimes the aggressive act is followed by a relief of discomfort administered by the socializing agent; sometimes it is not. The aggressive act in itself is tension-reducing; although it may be accompanied by guilt feelings, there is also a relief that comes from "blowing off steam." Presumably, when the aggressive act is followed by removal of the frustration, tension-reduction is even greater. As Sears points out, even though a mother may scold a child for being aggressive, she will, inevitably, at the same time solve his problem, *thus strengthening his aggressive drive.* This paradox explains why aggression is so hard to deal with. The mother cannot let the baby beat his head in temper against the floor; he *might* injure himself. She must act; she must give him some attention or change the situation for him. Her doing so teaches the baby that aggressive behavior, even when it hurts, has its rewards.

Does the amount of frustration the child encounters in infancy affect the strength of his aggressive drive in later childhood? In some aspects of the parent-child relationship, it apparently does. Radke (1946) found, in reviewing the research, that aggressive tendencies are positively correlated with parental rejection, overprotection, and disharmony, all of which can be frustrating to the child. More recently, Lesser (1952), in a study of aggression in ten- to thirteen-year-old boys, found a "very marked positive relationship to parental rejection." A similar finding is reported by Wittenborn (1956), who discovered in interviews that mothers who, by their own evaluation, were rejecting produced more aggressive children.

The mother's attitude toward the child's aggression against herself and others appears to affect the child's tendency to behave aggressively. Since the mother is often a source of frustration to the young child, it is only natural that at times he should want to vent his anger upon her—by striking at her physically, raging at her vocally, or attacking her in fantasy. Some adherents of the psychoanalytic view have advocated permissiveness on the part of parents toward the child's aggression. Repressing the aggression, they contend, might create anxiety within the child which could find expression in more undesirable behaviors. They argue, therefore, that parents ought to be prepared to accept a certain amount of aggression from the child—at least to the extent that they do not punish his aggressive behaviors or teach him that they are "bad" so that he acquires guilt feelings. If the child does acquire feelings of guilt about his aggressive impulses, these may in turn strengthen his hostile feelings and make him truly aggressive.

The findings of Sears and his colleagues do not support the argument that permissiveness is a way of producing a nonaggressive child. They suggest, rather, "that the way for parents to produce a nonaggressive child is to make it abundantly clear that aggression is frowned upon, and to stop aggression when it occurs . . ." (p. 266). A mother who believes that aggression is undesirable and who, under no circumstances, permits the child to express it toward her is more likely to have nonaggressive children than a permissive parent—*provided* that one other condition is met.

The other condition has to do with punishment for aggression. Many mothers have the firm conviction that the only way in which to stop aggression is to punish it. Sometimes the punishment takes the form of aggression by the mother, even to the point of an eye-for-an-eye code of behavior. Thus, if the child bites, the mother bites him back; if he pinches, she pinches him back—but harder than he, so that he will know how his action hurts others. As Sears and his colleagues point out, punishing the child is satisfying to the mother; the child's aggression hurts her physically and emotionally, and produces the desire to retaliate, to be aggressive in return. However, aggression toward one's own child is not tolerated in our society, and so she justifies the punishment on the ground that it is a good training procedure. "Spare the rod and spoil the child" is an axiom that has long been sanctioned.

But does it work? The Sears group reports that punishment has complex effects; it can stop a particular form of aggression, but it builds up more hostility in the child which will spill over later. Also, when the parents use physical punishment, they are setting an example of aggression for the child which may be reflected in his behavior in the future. Severe punishment of aggression interferes with the development of nonaggressive children. "The homes where the children show angry, aggressive outbursts frequently are homes in which the mother has a relatively tolerant (or careless!) attitude toward such behavior, or where she administers severe punishment for it, or both" (Sears *et al.*, 1957, p. 266).

Some investigators have used indirect methods of studying aggressive impulses in children. Kagan (1956), for example, analyzed children's fantasies as expressed in the stories they tell about specially devised pictures. Others have studied children's play behavior, on the theory that children may permit themselves aggressive acts during private play which are inhibited at other times. Some investigators have used a doll-play technique—setting up a play house with dolls representing various family members, and encouraging the children to play freely with the dolls (see pp. 218-19). Hollenberg and Sperry (1951) found some indications that punishment for aggression at home is positively related to the amount of aggression children express in doll play. These findings lend credence to the theory that severe socialization of aggression does not eliminate hostility but, on the contrary, increases *latent* hostility.

How, then, are parents and other socializing agents to deal with aggression? How can we prevent a child from becoming so aggressive that he is a threat to his own happiness and the happiness of others? How can this be done without increasing latent hostility which may sap the child's creative energies and manifest itself in other undesirable ways? Should parents be permissive or not with respect to aggression? Sears, Maccoby, and Levin offer some sound advice:

> A child is more likely to be nonaggressive if his parents hold the value that aggression is undesirable and should not occur. He is more likely to be nonaggressive if his parents prevent or stop the occurrence of aggressive outbursts instead of passively letting them go on, but prevent them by other means than punishment or threats of retaliation. If the parents' nonpermissive-

ness takes the form of punishing the child (and thus leading the child to *expect* punishment) for aggressive behavior, then nonpermissiveness will not have the effect of reducing the child's aggression. On the contrary, the instant that punishment enters, all the consequences of punishment that have been discussed earlier may be anticipated, including that of increasing the child's level of aggression.

One cautionary point: we are not suggesting that parents should band together in omnipotent suppression of every justifiable angry response the child makes. The right to be angry without fear or guilt is as inalienable as any other, and more important than some. But since anger interferes with constructive action in the face of many, if not most, problem situations that the child and his family face, parents are understandably anxious to keep it within reasonable bounds; and our interest has been in showing what parental actions are likely to have the desired effects and what actions are likely to have undesired side-effects [1957, pp. 268-69].

5. In terms of learning theory, how would you explain the fact that extreme parental permissiveness may result in a low achievement drive in a child?

6. Can you explain how a child may learn to be aggressive in an extremely permissive home?

7. Which of these behaviors would you practice if you were interested in building a strong achievement drive in your child?

    a. Buy him a bicycle with a 24" wheel for his fifth birthday.

    b. Leave a dinner party at ten o'clock because your twelve-year-old boy is alone in the house.

    c. Arrange for archery lessons for your nine-year-old son, who has enjoyed an interest in archery for the past two years.

    d. Throw your seven-year-old son into the deep end of the swimming pool when he is learning to swim.

Explain your reasons for accepting or rejecting each alternative.

SUGGESTED READINGS

CARMICHAEL, L. (ed.). *Manual of Child Psychology*, Wiley, 1954. The reader who is interested in an exhaustive review of the research will find Chapter 14, "Emotional Development," and Chapter 19, "Social Development," excellent sources.

GESELL, A., & ILG, FRANCES. *Infant and Child in the Culture of Today,* Harper, 1943.

————. *The Child from Five to Ten,* Harper, 1946. Gesell and Ilg postulate that the child, because of his nature, is "in and out of focus" from year to year. At three he is very good; at four he is difficult; at five he is an angel again; and at six he is extremely difficult to live with. Although their theory of development differs from the one presented in this book, the reader will find their accounts of a "behavior day" at various age levels rewarding reading.

SEARS, PAULINE. Levels of aspiration in academically successful and unsuccessful children. In William E. Martin & Celia Burns Stendler (eds.), *Readings in Child Development,* Harcourt, Brace, 1954, pp. 437-59. This paper reports research on achievement motivation.

SEARS, R., MACCOBY, ELEANOR, & LEVIN, H. *Patterns of Child Rearing,* Evanston, Ill.: Row, Peterson, 1957. This report of research on how mothers bring up their children contains excellent chapters on dependency and aggression.

WATTENBERG, W. *The Adolescent Years,* Harcourt, Brace, 1955. For the reader who is especially interested in the adolescent, Part C, "Problem Areas," discusses many problems in the social-emotional area pertinent to this chapter.

bibliographical
index

Acknowledgment is made to authors and publishers for permission to use the following quotations. References are listed alphabetically by date of publication. The boldface numbers following each entry identify the pages of the text on which the reference is cited.

ADELSON, J., 1956. Freud in America: some observations. *Amer. Psychologist, 11,* 467-470. **236**

AINSWORTH, M. *See* Bowlby *et al.,* 1956.

ALBERTS, E., & EHRENFREUND, D., 1951. Transposition in children as a function of age. *J. exp. Psychol., 41,* 30-38. **520**

ALDRICH, C. A., 1946. The crying of newly born babies. *J. Pediat., 28,* 665-670. **152, 550**

———, & ALDRICH, M. M., 1954. *Babies are human beings,* (2nd Ed.) Macmillan. **43, 44, 45, 49, 61, 81-82, 88**

ALDRICH, C. A., SUNG, C., & KNOP, C., 1945. The crying of newly born babies. *J. Pediat., 26,* 313-326; *27,* 89-96, 428-435. **73**

ALDRICH, M. M. *See* Aldrich & Aldrich, 1954.

ALPERT, A., 1928. The solving of problem-situations by preschool children. *Teach. Coll. Contr. Educ.,* No. 323. **526**

AMATRUDA, C. S. *See* Gesell, 1945.

ANASTASI, A., & CORDOVA, F. A., 1953. Some effects of bilingualism upon the intelligence test performance of Puerto Rican children in New York City. *J. educ. Psychol., 44,* 1-19. **515**

ANDERSON, H. H., 1937. Domination and integration in the social behavior of young children in an experimental play situation. *Genet. Psychol. Monogr., 19,* 343-408. **556**

———, & BREWER, J. E., 1946. Effects of teachers' dominative and integrative contacts on children's classroom behavior. *Appl. Psychol. Monogr.,* No. 8. **350**

ANDERSON, J. E., 1949. *The psychology of development and personal adjustment.* Holt. **11, 19, 274-275, 443, 488, 492, 530**

AREY, L. B., 1946. *Developmental anatomy.* (5th Ed.) Saunders. **136, 137**

ATKINSON, J. W. *See* McClelland *et al.*, 1953.

ATWELL, W. O., & ELBEL, E. R., 1948. Reaction time of male high school students in 14-17-year age groups. *Res. Quart. Amer. Ass. Hlth, 19,* 22-29. **484**

AUDEN, W. H., 1948. Yeats as an example. *Kenyon Rev., 10,* 187-195. **216**

AUSUBEL, D. P., 1949. Ego development and the learning process. *Child Develpm., 20,* 173-190. **370**

BACH, G. R., 1946. Father-fantasies and father-typing in father-separated children. *Child Develpm., 17,* 63-80. Reprinted in Martin & Stendler, 1954, pp. 368-379. **331**

BAER, D. M. *See* Gewirtz & Baer, 1958; Gewirtz *et al.*, 1958.

BAKER, C. T. *See* Sontag *et al.*, 1958.

BAKWIN, H., & BAKWIN, R. M., 1931. Body build in infants: II. The proportions of the external dimensions of the healthy infant during the first year of life. *J. clin. Invest., 10,* 377-394. **470**

———, 1935. Body build in infants: growth of the cardiac silhouette and thoraco-abdominal cavity. *Amer. J. Dis. Child., 49,* 861. **70**

———, 1936. Growth of thirty-two external dimensions during the first year of life. *J. Pediat., 8,* 177-183. **471**

BAKWIN, R. M. *See* Bakwin & Bakwin, 1931, 1935, 1936.

BALDWIN, A. L., 1949. The effect of home environment on nursery school behavior. *Child Develpm., 20,* 49-61. Reprinted in Martin & Stendler, 1954, pp. 337-345. **314**

———, 1955. *Behavior and development in childhood.* Dryden. **412**

———, KALHORN, J., & BREESE, F. H., 1949. The appraisal of parent behavior. *Psychol. Monogr., 63,* No. 4. **313**

BALINT, M., 1948. Individual differences of behavior in early infancy, and an objective method for recording them: II. Results and conclusions. *J. genet. Psychol., 73,* 81-117. **75-76**

BARKER, R. G., KOUNIN, J. S., & WRIGHT, H. F. (eds.), 1943. *Child behavior and development.* Mc-Graw-Hill. **123**

BARKER, R. G., & WRIGHT, H. F., 1951. *One boy's day.* Harper. **376**

———, 1954. *Midwest and its children.* Row, Peterson. **416, 417, 420, 435**

———, NALL, J., & SCHOGGEN, P., 1950. There is no class bias in our school. *Progressive Educ., 27,* 106-110. **189**

BARKER, R. G. *See also* Stone & Barker, 1939.

BARTLETT, F. H., 1933. *Infants and children: their feeding and growth.* Farrar & Rinehart. **309**

BARTRAM, J. B., 1954. Feeding of infants. In W. E. Nelson (ed.), *Textbook of pediatrics.* (6th Ed.) Saunders. Pp. 95-124. **42**

BARUCH, D. W., 1949. *New ways in discipline.* McGraw-Hill. **30-31, 237**

BAYLEY, N., 1932. A study of the crying of infants during mental and physical tests. *J. genet. Psychol., 40,* 306-320. **550**

———, 1935. The development of motor abilities during the first three years. *Monogr. Soc. Res. Child Develpm., 1,* No. 1. **109, 490**

———, 1943. Size and body build of adolescents in relation to rate of skeletal maturing. *Child Develpm., 14,* 47-90. **119-120, 475**

BAYLEY, N., 1954. Some increasing parent-child similarities during the growth of children. *J. educ. Psychol., 45,* 1-21. **468, 541**

———, 1955. On the growth of intelligence. *Amer. Psychologist, 10,* 805-818. **534-535, 540**

———, 1956a. Growth curves of height and weight by age for boys and girls, scaled according to physical maturity. *J. Pediat., 48,* 187-194. **116, 117, 451, 461-462, 464-467**

———, 1956b. Individual patterns of development. *Child Develpm., 27,* 45-74. **77, 116-117, 449-450, 452, 454, 534-535**

———, 1957. Data on the growth of intelligence between 16 and 21 years as measured by the Wechsler-Bellevue Scale. *J. genet. Psychol., 90,* 3-15. **534**

———, 1958. Value and limitations of infant testing. *Children, 5,* 129-133. **540**

———, & DAVIS, F. C., 1935. Growth changes in bodily size and proportions during the first three years: a developmental study of 61 children by repeated measurements. *Biometrika, 27,* 26-87. **70, 451**

BAYLEY, N., & PINNEAU, S. R., 1952. Tables for predicting adult height from skeletal age: revised for use with the Greulich-Pyle hand standards. *J. Pediat., 40,* 423-441. (Erratum. *J. Pediat., 41,* 371.) **77**

BAYLEY, N., & STOLZ, H. R., 1937. Maturational changes in rectal temperatures of 61 infants from 1 to 36 months. *Child Develpm., 8,* 195-206. **50**

BAYLEY, N. *See also* M. C. Jones & Bayley, 1950.

BEACH, F., & JAYNES, J., 1954. Effects of early experience upon the behavior of animals. *Psychol. Bull., 51,* 239-263. **104, 279, 281, 292, 301**

BELL, R. Q. *See* Schaefer & Bell, 1958.

BELLER, E. K., 1955. Dependence and independence in young children. *J. genet. Psychol., 87,* 25-35. **571**

BELO, J., 1949. The Balinese temper. In D. Haring (ed.), *Personal character and cultural milieu.* (Rev. Ed.) Syracuse Univer. Press. Pp. 148-174. **170-171**

BENDA, C. E., 1949. Prenatal maternal factors in Mongolism. *J. Amer. med. Ass., 139,* 979-985. **142**

BENEDICT, R., 1934. *Patterns of culture.* Houghton Mifflin. **199**

———, 1938. Continuities and discontinuities in cultural conditioning. *Psychiatry, 1,* 161-167. Reprinted in Martin & Stendler, 1954, pp. 142-148. **197-198**

BERLYNE, D. C., 1957. Recent developments in Piaget's work. *Brit. J. educ. Psychol., 27,* 1-12. **523, 542**

BERNERT, E. H., 1958. *America's children.* Wiley. **324, 328, 346**

BIBER, B., & LEWIS, C., 1949. An experimental study of what young children expect from their teachers. *Genet. Psychol. Monogr., 40,* 3-97. **359-360**

BINGHAM, W. E., & GRIFFITHS, W. J., JR., 1952. The effect of different environments during infancy on adult behavior in the rat. *J. comp. physiol. Psychol., 45,* 307-312. **282**

BLACK, G. H. B. *See* Swan *et al.,* 1947.

BLAIR, A. W., & BURTON, W. H., 1951. *Growth and development of the preadolescent.* Appleton-Century-Crofts. 413

BLOMMERS, P., KNIEF, L. M., & STROUD, J. B., 1955. The organismic age concept. *J. educ. Psychol., 46,* 142-150. 122

BLOS, P., 1941. *The adolescent personality.* Appleton-Century-Crofts. 356

BLUM, A., 1957. The value factor in children's size perception. *Child Develpm., 28,* 3-14. 522

BOEHM, L., 1957. The development of independence: a comparative study. *Child Develpm., 28,* 85-92. 572

BOSSARD, J. H. S., 1954. *The sociology of child development.* (Rev. Ed.) Harper. 413

BOSTON, M. *See* Bowlby *et al.,* 1956.

BOWLBY, J., 1952. *Maternal care and mental health.* WHO Monogr. Ser. No. 2. **298, 301, 567**

———, AINSWORTH, M., BOSTON, M., & ROSENBLUTH, D., 1956. The effects of mother-child separation: a follow-up study. *Brit. J. med. Psychol., 29,* 211-247. **299**

BOYD, J. D. *See* Hamilton *et al.,* 1952.

BRECKENRIDGE, M. E., & MURPHY, M. N., 1958. *Growth and development of the young child.* Saunders. **50, 446**

BREESE, F. H. *See* Baldwin *et al.,* 1949.

BREWER, J. E. *See* H. H. Anderson & Brewer, 1946.

BRIDGES, K. M. B., 1932. Emotional development in early infancy. *Child Develpm., 3,* 324-341. **547, 548**

BRODBECK, A. J., 1955. The mass media as a socializing agency. Paper read at Amer. Psychol. Ass., San Francisco, September. 433

———, & IRWIN, O. C., 1946. The speech behavior of infants without families. *Child Develpm., 17,* 145-156. **512**

BRODBECK, A. J. *See also* H. V. Davis *et al.,* 1948.

BRODY, S., 1956. *Patterns of mothering.* International Universities Press. 43

BRONFENBRENNER, U., 1958. Socialization and social class through time and space. In E. E. Maccoby, T. M. Newcomb, & E. L. Hartley (eds.), *Readings in social psychology.* Holt. **335, 336**

BRONSTEIN, I. R., WEXLER, S., BROWN, A. W., & HALPERN, L. J., 1942. Obesity in childhood. *Amer. J. Dis. Child., 63,* 238-251. 469

BROWN, A. W. *See* Bronstein *et al.,* 1942.

BROWN, R., 1958. How shall a thing be called? *Psychol. Rev., 65,* 14-21. 521

BRUCH, H., 1939. Studies in obesity in childhood: I. Physical growth and development of obese children. *Amer. J. Dis. Child., 58,* 457-484. 469

———, 1940. Studies in obesity in childhood: III. Physiologic and psychologic aspects of the food intake of obese children. *Amer. J. Dis. Child., 59,* 739-781. 469

———, 1941. Obesity in childhood and personality development. *Amer. J. Orthopsychiat., 11,* 467-474. 469

BRUNER, J. S., & GOODMAN, C. C., 1947. Value and need as organizing factors in perception. *J. abnorm. soc. Psychol., 42,* 33-44. Reprinted in Martin & Stendler, 1954, pp. 310-318. **522, 543**

BUHLER, C., 1930. *The first year of life.* Day. 519

BUNCH, M. E. *See* Margolin & Bunch, 1940.

BURKE, B. S., STEVENSON, S. S., WORCESTER, J., & STUART, H. C., 1949. Nutrition studies during pregnancy. Relation of maternal nutrition to condition of infant at birth: a study of siblings. *J. Nutrition, 38,* 453-467. 141

BURT, C., 1958. The inheritance of mental ability. *Amer. Psychologist, 13,* 1-15. 537, 538, 541, 542

BURTON, W. H. *See* Blair & Burton, 1951.

CANNON, W. B., 1929. *Bodily changes in pain, hunger, fear and rage.* D. Appleton-Century. 60, 63

——, 1939. *The wisdom of the body.* Norton. 9

CARMICHAEL, L., 1951. Ontogenetic development. In S. S. Stevens (ed.), *Handbook of experimental psychology.* Wiley. Pp. 281-313. 96, 97, 100

——, 1954. The onset and early development of behavior. In L. Carmichael (ed.), *Manual of child psychology.* (2nd Ed.) Wiley Pp. 60 185. 21, 129, 135, 138, 139, 154, 581

CARRISON, D. *See* Werner & Carrison, 1943.

CASAGRANDE, J. B., 1956. The Southwest Project in comparative psycholinquistics: a progress report. *Soc. Sci. Res. Council Items, 10,* 41-45. 521

CHEIN, I. *See* R. Levine *et al.,* 1942.

CHEN, H. P. *See* Irwin & Chen, 1943.

CHERASKIN, E. *See* Langley & Cheraskin, 1958.

CHEVALIER, J. A. *See* S. Levine *et al.,* 1956.

CHILD, I. L., POTTER, E. H., & LEVINE, E. M., 1946. Children's textbooks and personality development: an exploration in the social psychology of education. *Psychol. Monogr., 60,* No. 3. Introductory and final chapters reprinted in Martin & Stendler, 1954, pp. 479-492. 360-361

CHITTENDEN, G. E., 1942. An experimental study in measuring and modifying assertive behavior in young children. *Monogr. Soc. Res. Child Develpm., 7,* No. 1. 556

CHOW, K. L. *See* Nissen *et al.,* 1951.

CHRISTIE, A., 1949. Prevalence and distribution of ossification centers in the newborn infant. *Amer. J. Dis. Child., 77,* 355-361. 72

CLARK, R. A. *See* McClelland *et al.,* 1953.

CLARKE, F. M., HUNT, W. A., & HUNT, E. B., 1937. Incidental responses in infants following a startle stimulus. *J. genet. Psychol., 17,* 298-401. 547

COGHILL, G. E., 1929. The early development of behavior in Amblystoma and in man. *Arch. Neurol. Psychiat., 21,* 989-1009. 96-97

CORDOVA, F. A. *See* Anastasi & Cordova, 1953.

COSTIN, F., 1958. The effect of child psychology on attitudes toward parent-child relationships. *J. educ. Psychol., 49,* 37-42. vi

COURTNEY, P. D., 1949. Identification and learning: a theoretical analysis. Unpublished doctoral dissertation, Harvard Univer. 382

CRONBACH, L. J., 1949. *Essentials of psychological testing.* Harper. 543

——, 1954. *Educational psychology.* Harcourt, Brace. 277

DOLLARD, J., & MILLER, N. E., 1950. *Personality and psychotherapy.* McGraw-Hill. **245-246, 265, 277**

DOLLARD, J. *See also* N. E. Miller & Dollard, 1941.

DOOB, L. W. *See* Dollard *et al.,* 1939.

DUNN, L. C., & DOBZHANSKY, TH., 1946. *Heredity, race, and society.* Penguin Books. **79, 80, 81**

DUPERTUIS, C. W., & MICHAEL, N. B., 1953. Comparison of growth in height and weight between ectomorphic and mesomorphic boys. *Child Develpm., 24,* 203-214. **455**

ECKERSON, L. D. *See* Seashore & Eckerson, 1940.

EDWARDS, M. *See* Gough *et al.,* 1950.

EGGAN, D., 1953. The general problem of Hopi adjustment. In C. Kluckhohn, H. A. Murray, & D. M. Schneider (eds.), *Personality in nature, society, and culture.* (2nd Ed.) Knopf. Pp. 276-291. **194**

EHRENFREUND, D. *See* Alberts & Ehrenfreund, 1951.

ELBEL, E. R. *See* Atwell & Elbel, 1948.

ELKIN, F., 1950. Psychological appeal of the Hollywood western. *J. educ. Sociol., 24,* 72-86. **430**

ERIKSON, E. H., 1950. *Childhood and society.* Norton. Chapter VII, Eight Stages of Man, reprinted in Martin & Stendler, 1954, pp. 213-220. **43, 46, 115, 238, 353-354, 387**

ESCALONA, S., 1950. The use of infant tests for predictive purposes. *Bull. Menninger Clin., 14,* 117-128. Reprinted in Martin & Stendler, 1954, pp. 95-103. **543**

———, 1953. Emotional development in the first year of life. In M. J. E. Senn (ed.), *Problems of infancy and childhood.* (Transactions of the Sixth Conference) Josiah Macy, Jr., Foundation. Pp. 11-92. **75, 93**

———, LEITCH, M., *et al.,* 1952. Early phases of personality development: a non-normative study of infant behavior. *Monogr. Soc. Res. Child Develpm., 17,* No. 1. **84**

ESPENSCHADE, A., 1940. Motor performance in adolescence. *Monogr. Soc. Res. Child Develpm., 5,* No. 1. **482, 485, 486, 487**

FAVEZ-BOUTONIER, J., 1956. Child development patterns in France (II). In K. Soddy (ed.), *Mental health and infant development: Vol. I, Papers and discussion.* Basic Books. Pp. 25-33. **194**

FESTINGER, L., 1942. Wish, expectation, and group performance as factors influencing level of aspiration. *J. abnorm. soc. Psychol., 37,* 184-200. **531**

FESTINGER, L. *See also* Lewin *et al.,* 1944.

FOGLER, S., 1950. Prometheus or Frankenstein? *J. educ. Sociol., 24,* 154-166. **426-427**

FOREST, I., 1954. *Child development.* McGraw-Hill. **13**

FORGUS, R. H., 1955. Early visual and motor experience as determiners of complex maze-learning ability under rich and reduced stimulation. *J. comp. physiol. Psychol., 48,* 215-220. **283-285**

FORMAN, H. J., 1933. *Our movie-made children.* Macmillan. **384-385, 429**

FRANK, L. K., 1951. *Nature and human nature.* Rutgers Univer. Press. **35**

FRANK, L. K., 1954. *Feelings and emotions.* Doubleday. **64, 65**

FRANK, L. K. *See also* Hartley *et al., 1952.*

FREDERICSON, E. *See* J. P. Scott *et al., 1951.*

FREUD, A., & DANN, S., 1951. An experiment in group upbringing. *Psychoanal. Stud. Child, 6,* 127-168. Reprinted in Martin & Stendler, 1954, pp. 404-421. **413**

FREUD, S., 1905. Three contributions to the theory of sex. (4th Ed.) *Nerv. ment. Dis. Monogr. Ser.,* 1930, No. 7. **220**

———, 1911. Psychoanalytic notes upon an autobiographical account of a case of paranoia (dementia paranoides). In *Collected papers,* Vol. III. Hogarth Press, 1925. Pp. 387-470. **219**

———, 1925. Some psychological consequences of the anatomical distinction between the sexes. In *Collected papers,* Vol. V. Hogarth Press, 1950. Pp. 186-197. **222-226, 228, 230, 231, 232**

———, 1937. Analysis terminable and interminable. In *Collected works,* Vol. V. Hogarth Press, 1950. Pp. 316-357. **236**

———, 1949. *An outline of psychoanalysis.* Norton. **204, 205, 206-207, 209, 211, 212, 213, 215, 217**

FROMM, E., 1941. *Escape from freedom.* Rinehart. **180**

———, 1949. Psychoanalytic characterology and its application to the understanding of culture. In S. S. Sargent and M. W. Smith (eds.), *Culture and personality.* Viking Fund. Pp. 1-12. Reprinted in Martin & Stendler, 1954, pp. 207-212. **241**

FULLAGER, W. A., LEWIS, H. G., & CUMBEE, C. F. (eds.), 1956. *Readings for educational psychology.* Crowell. **376**

FULLER, J. L. *See* J. P. Scott *et al., 1951.*

FURNESS, W. H., 1916. Observations on the mentality of chimpanzees and orangutans. *Proc. Amer. phil. Soc., 55,* 281-290. **497**

GARN, S. M., 1952. Individual and group deviations from "channelwise" grip progression in girls. *Child Develpm., 23,* 193-206. **456**

GARN, S. M. *See also* Sontag & Garn, 1954.

GATEWOOD, M. C., & WEISS, A. P., 1930. Race and sex differences in newborn infants. *J. genet. Psychol., 38,* 31-49. **75**

GERARD, M. W., 1946. The psychogenic tic in ego development. *Psychoanal. Stud. Child, 2,* 133-162. **113**

GESELL, A., 1954. The ontogenesis of infant behavior. In L. Carmichael (ed.), *Manual of child psychology.* (2nd Ed.) Wiley. Pp. 335-373. **20, 21, 99, 100, 152**

——— (in collaboration with C. S. Amatruda), 1945. *The embryology of behavior.* Harper. **46, 47, 48, 67**

GESELL, A., & ILG, F. L., 1937. *The feeding behavior of infants.* Lippincott. **153**

———, 1943. *Infant and child in the culture of today.* Harper. **110-111, 125, 150, 156, 292-293, 294, 301, 565, 582**

———, 1946. *The child from five to ten.* Harper. **viii, 125, 582**

GESELL, A., & THOMPSON, H., 1929. Learning and growth in identical infant twins: an experimental study by the method of co-twin control. *Genet. Psychol. Monogr., 6,* 1-124. **100-101**

GEWIRTZ, J. L., 1957. Social deprivation and dependency: a learning analysis. Paper read at Amer. Psychol. Ass., New York City, September. **300**

——, & BAER, D. M., 1958. The effect of brief social deprivation on behaviors for a social reinforcer. *J. abnorm. soc. Psychol., 56,* 49-56. **568**

——, & ROTH, C. H. A note on the similar effects of low social availability of an adult and brief social deprivation on young children's behavior. *Child Develpm., 29,* 149-152. **569**

GEWIRTZ, J. L. *See also* Rheingold *et al.,* in press.

GIBBS, P. K. *See* Maccoby *et al.,* 1954.

GILLIN, J., 1948. *The ways of men.* Appleton-Century-Crofts. **25-26, 29**

GLADSTONE, R., 1948. Do maladjusted teachers cause maladjustment? A re-review. *J. except. Child., 15,* 65-70. **352**

GLUECK, E. *See* Glueck & Glueck, 1956.

GLUECK, S., & GLUECK, E., 1956. *Physique and delinquency.* Harper. **93, 474-475**

GOLDBERG, M., 1955. What makes us grow as we do? *J. Amer. med. Women's Ass., 10,* 110-116. **119**

GOLDENSON, R. M. *See* Hartley *et al.,* 1952.

GOLDFARB, W., 1945. Psychological privation in infancy and subsequent adjustment. *Amer. J. Orthopsychiat., 15,* 247 255. Reprinted in Martin & Stendler, 1954, pp. 397-403. **288-290, 298**

GOODENOUGH, F. L., 1931a. *Anger in young children.* Univer. of Minnesota Press. **40, 553**

——, 1931b. The expression of the emotions in infancy. *Child Develpm., 2,* 96-101. **547-548**

——, 1932. Expression of the emotions in a blind deaf child. *J. abnorm. soc. Psychol., 27,* 328-333. **549**

——, 1935. The development of the reactive process from early childhood to maturity. *J. exp. Psychol., 18,* 431-450. **484**

GOODMAN, C. C. *See* Bruner & Goodman, 1947.

GOODMAN, P., 1947. Glossary. In S. Katz (ed.), *Freud: on war, sex, and neurosis.* Arts and Science Press. Pp. 277-287. **215**

GORER, C., 1948. *The American people.* Norton. **179-180**

GOUGH, H. G., HARRIS, D. B., MARTIN, W. E., & EDWARDS, M., 1950. Children's ethnic attitudes: I. Relationship to certain personality factors. *Child Develpm., 21,* 83-91. **314**

GOUGH, H. G. *See also* Harris *et al.,* 1950.

GREULICH, W. W., 1950. Rationale of assessing the developmental status of children from roentgenograms of the hand and wrist. *Child Develpm., 21,* 33-44. Reprinted in Martin & Stendler, 1954, pp. 42-47. **123, 126**

——, 1958. Growth of children of the same race under different environmental conditions. *Science, 127,* 515-516. **78, 472**

——, & PYLE, S. I., 1950. *Radiographic atlas of skeletal development of the hand and wrist.* Stanford Univer. Press. **458**

GRIFFITHS, W. J., JR. *See* Bingham & Griffiths, 1952.

GURNEY, N. L. *See* King & Gurney, 1954.

GUTTERIDGE, M. V., 1939. A study of motor achievements of young children. *Arch. Psychol., N. Y., 34,* No. 244. **482, 492**

HAINES, A. C. *See* Stendler *et al.,* 1951.

HALL, C. S., 1938. The inheritance of emotionality. *Sigma Xi Quart., 26,* 17-27. Reprinted in Martin & Stendler, 1954, pp. 59-68. **93**

———, 1955. *Primer of Freudian psychology.* New American Library. **238**

———, & LINDZEY, G., 1957. *Theories of personality.* Wiley. **238**

HALL, G. S., 1904. *Adolescence.* D. Appleton-Century. **155n**

HALPERN, L. J. *See* Bronstein *et al.,* 1942.

HALVERSON, H. M., 1931. An experimental study of prehension in infants by means of systematic cinema records. *Genet. Psychol. Monogr., 10,* 107-286. **479-480**

———, 1932. A further study of grasping. *J. gen. Psychol., 7,* 34-64. **478-480**

———, 1937. Studies of the grasping responses of early infancy. *J. genet. Psychol., 51,* 371-449. **477**

———, 1940. Genital and sphincter behavior of the male infant. *J. genet. Psychol., 56,* 95-136. **51, 151, 154**

———, 1941. Variations in pulse and respiration during different phases of infant behavior. *J. genet. Psychol., 59,* 259-330. **51, 151, 154**

HAMILTON, G. V., 1948. *A research in marriage.* Lear. **227**

HAMILTON, W. J., BOYD, J. D., & MOSSMAN, H. W., 1952. *Human embryology.* (2nd Ed.) Williams & Wilkins. **132-133, 136, 137, 141**

HANFMANN, E., 1941. A study of personal patterns in an intellectual performance. *Charact. & Pers., 9,* 315-325. **532**

HANLEY, C. *See* Nicolson & Hanley, 1953.

HANSEN, A. E., 1954. Nutritional requirements. In W. E. Nelson (ed.), *Textbook of pediatrics.* (6th Ed.) Saunders. Pp. 79-95. **43, 44, 45**

HARRELL, L. E., JR., 1957. A comparison of the development of oral and written language in school-age children. *Monogr. Soc. Res. Child Develpm., 22,* No. 3. **511**

HARRIS, D. B., GOUGH, H. G., & MARTIN, W. E., 1950. Children's ethnic attitudes: II. Relationship to parental beliefs concerning child training. *Child Develpm., 21,* 169-181. Reprinted in Martin & Stendler, 1954, pp. 358-367. **314-315**

HARRIS, D. B. *See also* Gough *et al.,* 1950.

HART, J. K., 1951. *Education in the human community.* Harper. **418**

HARTLEY, R. E., FRANK, L. K., & GOLDENSON, R. M., 1952. *Understanding children's play.* Columbia Univer. Press. **413**

HARTSHORNE, H., & MAY, M. A., 1928. *Studies in the nature of character: I. Studies in deceit.* Macmillan. **423**

HAVIGHURST, R. J., 1948. *Developmental tasks and education.* Univer. of Chicago Press. **186-187**

———, 1953. *Human development and education.* Longmans, Green. **559**

———, & TABA, H., 1949. *Adolescent character and personality.* Wiley. Excerpts reprinted in Martin & Stendler, 1954, pp. 460-472. **357-359, 422**

HAVIGHURST, R. J. *See also* A. Davis & Havighurst, 1947.

HAYES, C., 1951. *The ape in our house.* Harper. **35, 285-286, 497, 498**

HEBB, D. O., 1949. *The organization of behavior.* Wiley. **63-64, 282**

——, 1958. *A textbook of psychology.* Saunders. **546**

HENRY, W. E. *See* Warner & Henry, 1948.

HESS, E. H., 1958. "Imprinting" in animals. *Sci. Amer., 198,* 82. **297**

HILDRETH, G., 1949. The development and training of hand dominance: II. Developmental tendencies in handedness. *J. genet. Psychol., 75,* 221-254. **481**

HILGARD, J. R., 1932. Learning and maturation in preschool children. *J. genet. Psychol., 41,* 31-56. **101**

HIMMELWEIT, H. T., OPPENHEIM, A. N., & VINCE, P., 1958. *Television and the child.* Oxford Univer. Press. **436**

HOFSTAETTER, P. R., 1954. The changing composition of "intelligence": a study of *t*-technique. *J. genet. Psychol., 85,* 159-164. **534**

HOLLENBERG, E., & SPERRY, M., 1951. Some antecedents of aggression and effects of frustration in doll play. *Personality, 1,* 32-43. **580**

HOLLINGSHEAD, A. B., 1949. *Elmtown's youth.* Wiley. **389-390, 413**

HOLLINGWORTH, L. S., 1926. *Gifted children.* Macmillan. **396**

——, 1942. *Children above 180 IQ, Stanford-Binet.* World Book. **396**

HOLMES, F. B. *See* Jersild & Holmes, 1935.

HONZIK, M. P., 1957. Developmental studies of parent-child resemblance in intelligence. *Child Develpm., 28,* 215-228. **538**

HOOKER, D., 1952. *The prenatal origin of behavior.* Univer. of Kansas Press. **135, 138**

HORNEY, K., 1937. *The neurotic personality of our times.* Norton. **61**

HOWARD, R. W., 1946. The language development of a group of triplets. *J. genet. Psychol., 69,* 181-188. **513**

HOWELLS, W., 1944. *Mankind so far.* Doubleday. **22, 23, 24, 26-27, 31**

——, 1954. *Back of history: the story of our own origins.* Doubleday. **35**

HUGHES, B. O. *See* Olson & Hughes, 1943.

HUMBER, W. J. *See* Dewey & Humber, 1951.

HUNT, E. B. *See* Clarke *et al.,* 1937.

HUNT, J. McV., SCHLOSBERG, H., SOLOMON, R. L., & STELLAR, E., 1947. Studies on the effects of infantile experience on adult behavior in rats. I. Effects of infantile feeding-frustration on adult hoarding. *J. comp. physiol. Psychol., 40,* 291-304. **280-281**

HUNT, W. A. *See* Clarke *et al.,* 1937.

ILG, F. L. *See* Gesell & Ilg, 1937, 1943, 1946.

INGALLS, T. H., 1950. Dr. T. H. Ingalls describes tests on mice indicating heredity and environment overlap as determining factors. *New York Times,* December 20. **140**

INHELDER, B., & PIAGET, J., 1958. *The growth of logical thinking.* Basic Books. **529-530**

IRWIN, O. C., 1930. The amount and nature of activities of newborn infants under constant external stimulating conditions during the first ten days of life. *Genet. Psychol. Monogr., 8,* 1-92. **82**

IRWIN, O. C., 1932a. The amount of motility of seventy-three newborn infants. *J. comp. Psychol., 14,* 415-428. **82, 547**

——, 1932b. The distribution of the amount of motility in young infants between two nursing periods. *J. comp. Psychol., 14,* 429-445. **82**

——, 1932c. Infant responses to vertical movements. *Child Develpm., 3,* 167-169. **547**

——, 1942. Can infants have IQ's? *Psychol. Rev., 49,* 69-79. **87**

——, 1948. Infant speech: the effect of family occupational status and of age on the use of sound types. *J. Speech Hearing Disorders, 13,* 224-226. **511**

——, & CHEN, H. P., 1943. Speech sound elements during the first years of life; a review of the literature. *J. Speech Disorders, 8,* 109-121. **503**

IRWIN, O. C., & WEISS, L. A., 1934. The effect of clothing on the general and vocal activity of the newborn infant. *Univer. Iowa Stud. Child Welf., 9,* 149-162. **546**

IRWIN, O. C. *See also* Brodbeck & Irwin, 1946.

ISAACS, S., 1945. Fatherless children. In *Fatherless children.* New Education Fellowship. **330-331**

JACK, L. M., 1934. An experimental study of ascendant behavior in preschool children. *Univer. Iowa Stud. Child Welf., 9,* No. 3. **114, 556**

JAMES, W., 1890. *Psychology.* Holt. **518, 525**

——, 1909. *The meaning of truth, a sequel to "Pragmatism."* Longmans, Green. **528-529**

——, 1911. *Memories and studies.* Longmans, Green. **5**

JAYNES, J. *See* Beach & Jaynes, 1954.

JEFFREY, W. E., 1958. Variables in early discrimination learning: I. Motor responses in the training of a left-right discrimination. *Child Develpm., 29,* 269-275. **524**

JERSILD, A. T., 1947. *Child psychology.* (3rd Ed.) Prentice-Hall. **430-432**

——, *et al.,* 1946. *Child development and the curriculum.* Teachers Coll., Columbia Univer. **126, 376**

JERSILD, A. T., & HOLMES, F. B., 1935. Children's fears. *Child Develpm. Monogr.,* No. 20. **550-551**

JERSILD, A. T., & MARKEY, F. V., 1935. Conflicts between preschool children. *Child Develpm. Monogr.,* No. 21. **555**

JERSILD, A. T., WOODYARD, E. S., & DEL SOLAR, C., 1949. *Joys and problems of child rearing.* Teachers Coll., Columbia Univer. **346**

JONES, E., 1953, 1955, 1957. *The life and work of Sigmund Freud.* Basic Books. **238**

JONES, H. E., 1930. The galvanic skin reflex in infancy. *Child Develpm., 1,* 106-110. **76**

——, 1943. *Development in adolescence.* D. Appleton-Century. **413, 492**

——, 1947. Sex differences in physical abilities. *Hum. Biol., 19,* 12-25. **483**

——, 1949. Adolescence in our society. In *The family in a democratic society.* Columbia Univer. Press. Pp. 70-82. **473**

——, 1954. The environment and mental development. In L. Carmichael (ed.), *Manual of child psychology.* (2nd Ed.) Wiley. Pp. 631-696. **536, 537**

JONES, H. E., 1958. Problems of method in longitudinal research. *Vita humana, 1,* 93-99. 86

——, & SEASHORE, R. H., 1944. The development of fine motor and mechanical abilities. *Yearb. nat. Soc. Stud. Educ., 43* (I), 123-145. 484, 485

JONES, M. C., 1924. A laboratory study of fear: the case of Peter. *Ped. Sem., 31,* 308-316. 553

——, 1957. The later careers of boys who were early- and late-maturing. *Child Develpm., 28,* 113-128. 86

——, 1958. A study of socialization patterns at the high school level. *J. genet. Psychol., 93,* 87-111. 473

——, & BAYLEY, N., 1950. Physical maturing among boys as related to behavior. *J. educ. Psychol., 41,* 129-148. Reprinted in Martin & Stendler, 1954, pp. 48-58. 86, 121, 126, 473

JONES, M. C., & MUSSEN, P. H., 1958. Self-conceptions, motivations, and interpersonal attitudes of early- and late-maturing girls. *Child Develpm., 29,* 491-501. 473

JONES, M. C. See also Mussen & Jones, 1957.

JOSSELYN, I. M., 1948. *Psychosocial development of children.* Family Service Association of America. 209-210, 229, 238

JUDD, C. H., 1926. *The psychology of social institutions.* Macmillan. 501

KAFKA, F., 1948. *The diaries of Franz Kafka, 1910-1913.* Schocken Books. 19

KAGAN, J., 1956. The measurement of overt aggression from fantasy. *J. abnorm. soc. Psychol., 52,* 390-393. 580

——, & Moss, H. A., 1959. Parental correlates of child's IQ and height: a cross-validation of the Berkeley Growth Study results. *Child Develpm., 30,* in press. 541

KALHORN, J. See Baldwin et al., 1949.

KAPLAN, S. See Lyon & Kaplan, 1954.

KELLER, H., 1936. *The story of my life.* Doubleday. 498-499

KELLOGG, L. A. See Kellogg & Kellogg, 1933.

KELLOGG, W. N., & KELLOGG, L. A., 1933. *The ape and the child.* Whittlesey House. 28, 29

KING, J. A., & GURNEY, N. L., 1954. Effect of early social experience on adult aggressive behavior in C57BL/10 mice. *J. comp. physiol. Psychol., 47,* 326-330. 286

KINSEY, A. C., POMEROY, W. B., & MARTIN, C. E., 1948. *Sexual behavior in the human male.* Saunders. 52

KIRK, S. A., 1958. *Early training of the mentally retarded.* Univer. of Illinois Press. 543

KLUCKHOHN, C., 1947. Some aspects of Navaho infancy and early childhood. In *Psychoanalysis and the social sciences,* Vol. 1. International Universities Press. Pp. 37-86. Reprinted in Martin & Stendler, 1954, pp. 177-193. 153

KLUCKHOHN, C. See also Mowrer & Kluckhohn, 1944.

KNIEF, L. M. See Blommers et al., 1955.

KNOP, C. See C. A. Aldrich et al., 1945.

KNOTT, V. B. See Meredith & Knott, 1938.

KOCH, H. L., 1935. An analysis of certain forms of so-called "nervous habits" in young children. *J. genet. Psychol., 46,* 139-170. **52**

———, 1954. The relation of "primary mental abilities" in five- and six-year-olds to sex of child and characteristics of his sibling. *Child Develpm., 25,* 209-223. **512**

———, 1956. Attitudes of young children toward their peers as related to certain characteristics of their siblings. *Psychol. Monogr., 70,* No. 19. **327-328**

KOLLMORGEN, W. M., 1942. The old order Amish of Lancaster County, Pennsylvania, *U.S. Dept. Agr., Bur. agr. Econ., Rural Life Stud.,* No. 4. **342**

KOPPE, W. *See* Wright *et al.,* 1951.

KORCHIN, S. J. *See* S. Levine *et al.,* 1956.

KOUNIN, J. S. *See* Barker *et al.,* 1943.

KROEBER, A. L., 1948. *Anthropology.* (Rev. Ed.) Harcourt, Brace. **22**

KROGMAN, W. M., 1955. The physical growth of children: an appraisal of studies 1950-1955. *Monogr. Soc. Res. Child Develpm., 20,* No. 1. **449**

KUENNE, M. R., 1946. Experimental investigation of the relation of language to transposition behavior in young children. *J. exp. Psychol., 36,* 471-490. **520**

KUHLEN, R. G., 1952. *The psychology of adolescent development.* Harper. **561**

LA BARRE, W., 1954. *The human animal.* Univer. of Chicago Press. **35**

LANDRETH, C., 1958. *The psychology of early childhood.* Knopf. **151**

LANGER, S. K., 1942. *Philosophy in a new key.* Harvard Univer. Press. **496, 543**

LANGFORD, T. *See* H. W. Stevenson & Langford, 1957.

LANGLEY, L. L., & CHERASKIN, E., 1958. *The physiology of man.* (2nd Ed.) McGraw-Hill. **49**

LATHAM, A. J., 1951. The relationship between pubertal status and leadership in junior high school boys. *J. genet. Psychol., 78,* 185-194. **473**

LAZARSFELD, P. F., & STANTON, F. N. (eds.), 1949. *Communications research, 1948-1949.* Harper. **436**

LEEPER, R. W., 1948. A motivational theory of emotion to replace "emotion as disorganized response." *Psychol. Rev., 55,* 5-21. **63**

LEITCH, M. *See* Escalona *et al.,* 1952.

LESSER, G. S., 1952. Maternal attitudes and practices and the aggressive behavior of children. Unpublished doctoral dissertation, Yale Univer., 1952. **578**

LEVIN, H. *See* Maccoby *et al.,* 1956; P. S. Sears & Levin, 1957; R. R. Sears *et al.,* 1957.

LEVINE, E. M. *See* Child *et al.,* 1946.

LEVINE, R., CHEIN, I., & MURPHY, G., 1942. The relation of the intensity of a need to the amount of perceptual distortion: a preliminary report. *J. Psychol., 13,* 283-293. **522**

LEVINE, S., CHEVALIER, J. A., & KORCHIN, S. J., 1956. The effects of early shock and handling on later avoidance learning. *J. Pers., 24,* 475-493. **279**

LEVINGER, L., & MURPHY, L. B., 1947. Implications of the social scene for the education of young children. *Yearb. nat. Soc. Stud. Educ., 46* (II), 15-43. **340**

LEVITT, E. E. *See* Lyle & Levitt, 1955.

LEVY, D. M., 1928. Fingersucking and accessory movements in early infancy. *Amer. J. Psychiat., 7,* 881-918. **52**

———, 1937. Thumb- or fingersucking from the psychiatric angle. *Child Develpm., 8,* 99-101. **311**

———, 1943. *Maternal overprotection.* Columbia Univer. Press. **316-320**

LEWIN, K., 1954. Behavior and development as a function of the total situation. In L. Carmichael (ed.), *Manual of child psychology.* (2nd Ed.) Wiley. Pp. 918-970. **530**

———, DEMBO, T., FESTINGER, L., & SEARS, P. S., 1944. Level of aspiration. In J. McV. Hunt (ed.), *Personality and the behavior disorders.* Ronald. Pp. 333-378. **531**

LEWIN, K., LIPPITT, R., & WHITE, R. K., 1939. Patterns of aggressive behavior in experimentally created "social climates." *J. soc. Psychol., 10,* 271-299. **362**

LEWIS, C. *See* Biber & Lewis, 1949.

LEWIS, H. G. *See* Fullager *et al.,* 1956.

LEWIS, O., 1951. *Life in a Mexican village.* Univer. of Illinois Press. **171-172**

LILIENFELD, A. M., & PASAMANICK, B., 1956. The association of maternal and fetal factors with the development of mental deficiency. *Amer. J. ment. Def., 60,* 557-569. **142**

LINDZEY, G. *See* C. S. Hall & Lindzey, 1957.

LING, B. C., 1941. Form discrimination as a learning cue in infants. *Comp. Psychol. Monogr., 17,* No. 2. **519-520**

LIPPITT, R. *See* Lewin *et al.,* 1939; Polansky *et al.,* 1950.

LORENZ, K., 1955. Morphology and behavior patterns in closely allied species. In B. Schaffner (ed.), *Group processes.* (Transactions of the First Conference) Josiah Macy, Jr., Foundation. Pp. 168-220. **296**

LOWELL, E. L. *See* McClelland *et al.,* 1953.

LUND, F. H., 1930. *The emotions of men.* McGraw-Hill. **550**

LUNT, P. S. *See* Warner & Lunt, 1941.

LYLE, W. H., JR., & LEVITT, E. E., 1955. Punitiveness, authoritarianism, and parental discipline of grade school children. *J. abnorm. soc. Psychol., 51,* 42-46. **315**

LYNES, R., 1957. *A surfeit of honey.* Harper. **182**

LYON, R. A., & KAPLAN, S., 1954. The heart and circulation in health and disease. In W. E. Nelson (ed.), *Textbook of pediatrics.* (6th Ed.) Saunders. Pp. 852-872. **71, 72**

MACCOBY, E. E., 1957. Effects upon children of their mothers' outside employment. Paper read at Nat. Manpower Council Conf., Arden House, October 20-25. **325, 326**

———, GIBBS, P. K., *et al.,* 1954. Methods of child-rearing in two social classes. In W. E. Martin & C. B. Stendler (eds.), *Readings in child development.* Harcourt, Brace. Pp. 380-396. **190, 334, 335**

MEAD, M., & WOLFENSTEIN, M. (eds.), 1955. *Childhood in contemporary cultures.* Univer. of Chicago Press. 199

MELCHER, R. T. *See* Doll *et al.,* 1932.

MELZACK, R. *See* W. R. Thompson & Melzack, 1956.

MEREDITH, H. V., 1941. Stature and weight of children of the United States, with reference to the influence of racial, regional, socioeconomic and secular factors. *Amer. J. Dis. Child., 62,* 909-932. 470

——, 1951. Relation between socioeconomic status and body size in boys seven to ten years of age. *Amer. J. Dis. Child., 82,* 702-709. 471

——, & KNOTT, V. B., 1938. Changes in body proportions during infancy and the preschool years: III. The skelic index. *Child Develpm., 9,* 49-62. 450

MERRILL, B., 1946. A measurement of mother-child interaction. *J. abnorm. soc. Psychol., 41,* 37-49. Reprinted in Martin & Stendler, 1954, pp. 346-357. 322-323

MERRILL, M. A. *See* Terman & Merrill, 1937.

METHENY, E., 1941. Breathing capacity and grip strength of preschool children. *Univer. Iowa Stud. Child Welf., 18,* No. 2. 483

MEYERSON, B. *See* Wright *et al.,* 1951.

MICHAEL, N. B. *See* Dupertuis & Michael, 1953.

MILES, C. C., 1954. Gifted children. In L. Carmichael (ed.), *Manual of child psychology.* (2nd Ed.) Wiley. Pp. 984-1063. 491

MILLER, D. R., & SWANSON, G. E., 1958. *The changing American parent.* Wiley. 346

MILLER, H. C. *See* H. V. Davis *et al.,* 1948.

MILLER, N. E., & DOLLARD, J., 1941. *Social learning and imitation.* Yale Univer. Press. 257, 277

MILLER, N. E. *See also* Dollard *et al.,* 1939; Dollard & Miller, 1950.

MILLER, V. L. *See* Renshaw *et al.,* 1933.

MILLS, C. A., 1949. Temperature dominance over human life. *Science, 110,* 267-271. 469

The miracle of growth, 1950. Univer. of Illinois Press. 130-131, 146-147

MIRSKY, I. A., 1953. Psychoanalysis and the biological sciences. In F. Alexander and H. Ross (eds.), *Twenty years of psychoanalysis.* Norton. Pp. 155-185. 73

MOHR, G. J., 1948. Psychosomatic problems in childhood. *Child Develpm., 19,* 137-142. 114

MONTAGU, M. F. A., 1950. Constitutional and prenatal factors in infant and child health. In M. J. E. Senn (ed.), *Symposium on the health personality.* Josiah Macy, Jr., Foundation. Pp. 148-175. Reprinted in Martin & Stendler, 1954, pp. 15-29. 141, 156

——, 1951. *On being human.* Henry Schuman. 35

MOORE, J. K., 1947. Speech content of selected groups of orphanage and non-orphanage preschool children. *J. exp. Educ., 16,* 122-133. 512

MORGAN, J. J. B. *See* Watson & Morgan, 1917.

MOSS, H. A. *See* Kagan & Moss, 1959.

MOSSMAN, H. W. *See* Hamilton *et al.,* 1952.

MOWRER, O. H., 1950. On the psychology of "talking birds"—a contribution to language and personality theory. In *Learning theory and personality dynamics*. Ronald. Pp. 689-707. Reprinted in Martin & Stendler, 1954, pp. 280-290. **277, 496, 504-506**

——, 1952. In *Growing up in an anxious age*. Nat. Educ. Ass. **560**

——, & KLUCKHOHN, C., 1944. Dynamic theory of personality. In J. McV. Hunt (ed.), *Personality and the behavior disorders*. Ronald. Pp. 69-135. **250, 252, 253**

MOWRER, O. H. See also Dollard et al., 1939; Whiting & Mowrer, 1943.

MULLER, H. J., 1956. Genetic principles in human populations. *Sci. Mon., 83*, 277-286. **78-79**

MUMMERY, D. V., 1947. An analytical study of ascendant behavior of preschool children. *Child Develpm., 18*, 40-81. **556**

MUNN, N. L., 1954. Learning in children. In L. Carmichael (ed.), *Manual of child psychology*. (2nd Ed.) Wiley. Pp. 374-458. **257, 519**

——, 1955. *The evolution and growth of human behavior*. Houghton Mifflin. **129, 138**

MURDOCK, G. P., *et al.*, 1950. *Outline of cultural materials*. (3rd Rev. Ed.) Human Relations Area Files. **164**

MURDOCK, G. P., & WHITING, J. W. M., 1951. Cultural determinants of parental attitudes: the relationship between the social structure, particularly family structure, and parental behavior. In M. J. E. Senn (ed.), *Problems of infancy and childhood*. (Transactions of the Fourth Conference) Josiah Macy, Jr., Foundation. Pp. 13-80. **195**

MURPHY, G., 1947. *Personality*. Harper. **14, 37, 39, 65**

——, MURPHY, L. B., & NEWCOMB, T. M., 1937. *Experimental social psychology*. (Rev. Ed.) Harper. **40, 59**

MURPHY, G. See also R. Levine et al., 1942.

MURPHY, L. B. See Levinger & Murphy, 1947; G. Murphy et al., 1937.

MURPHY, M. N. See Breckenridge & Murphy, 1958.

MURRAY, H. A., 1938. *Explorations in personality*. Oxford Univer. Press. **563**

MUSSEN, P. H., & JONES, M. C., 1957. Self-conceptions, motivations, and interpersonal attitudes of late- and early-maturing boys. *Child Develpm., 28*, 243-256. **473**

MUSSEN, P. H. See also M. C. Jones & Mussen, 1958; Payne & Mussen, 1956.

NALL, J. See Barker et al., 1950; Wright et al., 1951.

NEILON, P., 1948. Shirley's babies after fifteen years. *J. genet. Psychol., 73*, 175-186. **92**

NEKULA, M. See Maudry & Nekula, 1939.

NELSON, H. W. See Rheingold et al., in press.

NELSON, V. L. See Sontag et al., 1958.

NEWCOMB, T. M. See G. Murphy et al., 1937.

NICOLSON, A. B., & HANLEY, C., 1953. Indices of physiological maturity: deviation and interrelationships. *Child Develpm., 24*, 3-38. **446, 461, 470**

NISSEN, H. W., CHOW, K. L., & SEMMES, J., 1951. Effects of restricted op-

PINNEAU, S. R. *See also* Bayley & Pinneau, 1952.
PINTLER, M. H. *See* R. R. Sears *et al.*, 1946.
POLANSKY, N., LIPPITT, R., & REDL, F., 1950. An investigation of behavioral contagion in groups. *Hum. Relat., 3*, 319-348. Reprinted in Martin & Stendler, 1954, pp. 493-513. **413**
POMEROY, W. B. *See* Kinsey *et al.*, 1948.
POTTER, E. H. *See* Child *et al.*, 1946.
PRATT, K. C., 1954. The neonate. In L. Carmichael (ed.), *Manual of child psychology.* (2nd Ed.) Wiley. Pp. 215-291. **38, 87, 151, 152, 153, 156, 476**
PYLE, S. I. *See* Greulich & Pyle, 1950.

RABBAN, M., 1950. Sex-role identification in young children in two diverse social groups. *Genet. Psychol. Monogr., 42*, 81-158. **336-339**
RADKE, M. J., 1946. *The relation of parental authority to children's behavior and attitudes.* Univer. of Minnesota Press. **252, 315-316, 578**
———, TRAGER, H. G., & DAVIS, H., 1949. Social perceptions and attitudes of children. *Genet. Psychol. Monogr., 40*, 327-447. **557**
RAMSEY, G. V., 1943. The sex information of younger boys. *Amer. J. Orthopsychiat., 13*, 347-352. **398-399**
RANK, O., 1929. *The trauma of birth.* Harcourt, Brace. **150**
RAYNOR, R. *See* Watson & Raynor, 1920.
REDL, F., 1949. The phenomenon of contagion and shock effect in group therapy. In K. R. Eissler (ed.), *Searchlights on delinquency.* International Universities Press. Pp. 315-328. **368**
———, & Wattenberg, W. W., 1951. *Mental hygiene in teaching.* Harcourt, Brace. **221, 222**
REDL, F. *See also* Polansky *et al.*, 1950.
REED, H. B., 1938. *Psychology of elementary school subjects.* (Rev. Ed.) Ginn. **425**
RENSHAW, S., MILLER, V. L., & MARQUIS, D. P., 1933. *Children's sleep.* Macmillan. **428**
REYNOLDS, E. L., 1943. Degree of kinship and pattern of ossification. *Amer. J. phys. Anthrop., 1*, 405-416. **468**
———, & WINES, J. V., 1948. Individual differences in physical changes associated with adolescence in girls. *Amer. J. Dis. Child., 75*, 329-350. **460-461**
RHEINGOLD, H. L., 1956. The modification of social responsiveness in institutional babies. *Monogr. Soc. Res. Child Develpm., 21*, No. 2. **291**
———, GEWIRTZ, J. L., & NELSON, H. W., in press. Social conditioning of vocalizations in the infant. *J. comp. physiol. Psychol.* **505**
RIBBLE, M., 1943. *The rights of infants.* Columbia Univer. Press. **288, 309**
RICHARDS, T. W., & NEWBERRY, H., 1938. Studies in fetal behavior: III. Can performance on test items at six months postnatally be predicted on the basis of fetal activity? *Child Develpm., 9*, 79-86. **146**
RICHARDSON, H. M., 1932. The growth of adaptive behavior in infants: an experimental study of seven age levels. *Genet. Psychol. Monogr., 12*, 195-359. **526-527**
RIESEN, A. H., 1949. The development of visual perception in man and chimpanzee. *Science, 106*, 107-108. **104**

RIESMAN, D., 1950. *The lonely crowd.* Yale Univer. Press. **200, 395, 399, 407**

ROSEN, B. R., & D'ANDRADE, R., 1957. The psychosocial origins of achievement motivation. Progress Report, Research Project M1495, National Institute of Mental Health, U.S. Public Health Service. **574-575**

ROSENBLUTH, D. *See* Bowlby *et al.*, 1956.

ROTH, C. H. *See* Gewirtz *et al.*, 1958.

RUDMAN, H. C., 1955. Informational needs and reading interests of children in grades IV through VIII. *Elem. Sch. J., 55,* 502-512. **425**

RUSSELL, D. H., 1956. *Children's thinking.* Ginn. **523, 543**

SANDIFORD, P., 1938. *Foundations of educational psychology.* Longmans, Green. **536**

SANFORD, R. N., *et al.,* 1943. Physique, personality, and scholarship. *Monogr. Soc. Res. Child Develpm., 8,* No. 1. **473, 474**

SAPIR, E., 1921, 1949. *Language.* Harcourt, Brace. **543**

SCAMMON, R. E., 1930. *The measurement of the body in childhood.* Univer. of Minnesota Press. **441**

SCHAEFER, E. S., & BELL, R. Q., 1958. Development of a parental attitude research instrument. *Child Develpm., 29,* 339-361. **335**

SCHLOSBERG, H. *See* J. McV. Hunt *et al.,* 1947.

SCHOGGEN, P. *See* Barker *et al.,* 1950.

SCOTT, J. P., FREDERICSON, E., & FULLER, J. L., 1951. Experimental exploration of the critical period hypothesis. *Personality, 1,* 162-183. **297-298**

SCOTT, R. *See* J. Williams & Scott, 1953.

SEAGOE, M. V., 1931. Children's reactions to the movies. *J. juv. Res., 15,* 169-180. **428**

SEARS, P. S., 1940. Levels of aspiration in academically successful and unsuccessful children. *J. abnorm. soc. Psychol., 35,* 498-536. Reprinted in Martin & Stendler, 1954, pp. 437-459. **531, 582**

———, 1957. Problems in the investigation of achievement and self-esteem motivation. In M. R. Jones (ed.), *Current theory and research in motivation.* Univer. of Nebraska Press. **374-376**

———, & LEVIN, H., 1957. Levels of aspiration in preschool children. *Child Develpm., 28,* 317-326. **531**

SEARS, P. S. *See also* Lewin *et al.,* 1944; R. R. Sears *et al.,* 1946, 1953.

SEARS, R. R., 1943. Survey of objective studies of psychoanalytic concepts. *Soc. Sci. Res. Council Bull.,* No. 51. Chapter VIII, Conclusions, reprinted in Martin & Stendler, 1954, pp. 221-226. **51, 238**

———, 1948. Personality development in contemporary culture. *Proc. Amer. phil. Soc., 92,* 363-370. **269**

———, 1950. Ordinal position in the family as a psychological variable. *Amer. sociol. Rev., 15,* 397-401. **564**

———, 1951. A theoretical framework for personality and social behavior. *Amer. Psychologist, 6,* 476-483. **269**

———, MACCOBY, E. E., & LEVIN, H., 1957. *Patterns of child rearing.* Row, Peterson. **53, 146, 157, 311, 322, 328, 346, 567-568, 576-581, 582**

SEARS, R. R., PINTLER, M. H., & SEARS, P. S., 1946. Effect of father separation on preschool children's doll play aggression. *Child Develpm., 17,* 219-243. **329, 331**

SEARS, R. R., WHITING, J. W. M., NOWLIS, V., & SEARS, P. S., 1953. Some child-rearing antecedents of aggression and dependency in young children. *Genet. Psychol. Monogr., 47,* 135-234. **513**

SEARS, R. R., & WISE, G. W., 1950. Relation of cup-feeding in infancy to thumb-sucking and the oral drive. *Amer. J. Orthopsychiat., 20,* 123-138. Reprinted in Martin & Stendler, 1954, pp. 240-251. **312**

SEARS, R. R. *See also* H. V. Davis *et al.,* 1948; Dollard *et al.,* 1939.

SEASHORE, R. H., & ECKERSON, L. D., 1940. The measurement of individual differences in general English vocabularies. *J. educ. Psychol., 31,* 14-38. **510**

SEASHORE, R. H. *See also* H. E. Jones & Seashore, 1944.

SELYA, B. M. *See* Maccoby *et al.,* 1956.

SEMMES, J. *See* Nissen *et al.,* 1951.

SENN, M. J. E. (ed.), 1953. *Problems of infancy and childhood.* (Transactions of the Sixth Conference) Josiah Macy, Jr., Foundation. **93**

SEWALL, M., 1930. Two studies in sibling rivalry: I. Some causes of jealousy in young children. *Smith Coll. Stud. Soc. Work, 1,* 6-22. **554**

SHARPE, E. F., 1945. What the father means to a child. In *Fatherless children.* New Education Fellowship. **329-330**

SHELDON, W. H., 1957. Review of S. Glueck & E. Glueck, *Physique and delinquency. Contemp. Psychol., 2,* 125-126. **440**

——, & STEVENS, S. S., 1942. *The varieties of temperament.* Harper. **474**

——, & TUCKER, W. B., 1940. *The varieties of human physique.* Harper. **451-454**

SHERIF, M., 1951. A preliminary study of intergroup relations. In J. H. Rohrer and M. Sherif (eds.), *Social psychology at the crossroads.* Harper. Pp. 388-424. **366**

SHERMAN, M., 1927. The differentiation of emotional responses in infants: II. The ability of observers to judge the emotional characteristics of the crying of infants, and of the voice of an adult. *J. comp. Psychol., 7,* 335-351. **547-548**

SHIRLEY, M. M., 1931. *The first two years: I. Postural and locomotor development.* Univer. of Minnesota Press. **81, 476-477, 487**

——, 1933a. *The first two years: II. Intellectual development.* Univer. of Minnesota Press. **476, 478-479, 492, 508**

——, 1933b. *The first two years: III. Personality manifestations.* Univer. of Minnesota Press. **73-75, 88-89, 92, 508**

——, 1939. A behavior syndrome characterizing prematurely born children. *Child Develpm., 10,* 115-128. **144**

SHOCK, N. W., 1944. Physiological changes in adolescence. *Yearb. nat. Soc. Stud. Educ., 43* (I), 56-79. **9**

SHUTTLEWORTH, F. K., 1937. Sexual maturation and the physical growth of girls age six to nineteen. *Monogr. Soc. Res. Child Develpm., 2,* No. 5. **441**

——, 1939. The physical and mental growth of girls and boys age six to nineteen in relation to age at maximum growth. *Monogr. Soc. Res. Child Develpm., 4,* No. 3. **446-449, 471**

——, 1949a. The adolescent period: a graphic atlas. *Monogr. Soc. Res. Child Develpm., 14,* No. 1. **493**

SHUTTLEWORTH, F. K., 1949b. The adolescent period: a pictorial atlas. *Monogr. Soc. Res. Child Develpm., 14*, No. 2. 453, 493

SIEGEL, A. E., 1958. The influence of violence in the mass media upon children's role expectations. *Child Develpm., 29*, 35-56. 434

SILONE, I., 1937. *Bread and wine.* Harper. 263-264

SIMMONS, K., 1944. The Brush Foundation study of child growth and development. II. Physical growth and development. *Monogr. Soc. Res. Child Develpm., 9*, No. 1. 444-445

SIMPSON, G. G., 1950. *The meaning of evolution.* Yale Univer. Press. 19-20, 24-25

SKINNER, B. F., 1958. Reinforcement today. *Amer. Psychologist, 13*, 94-99. 286

SLOAN, W., 1955. The Lincoln-Oseretsky motor development scale. *Genet. Psychol. Monogr., 51*, 183-252. 486

SMITH, C. A., 1947. The effect of war-time starvation in Holland upon pregnancy and its product. *Amer. J. Obstet. Gynecol., 53*, 599-608. 141

———, 1951. *Physiology of the newborn infant.* (2nd Ed.) Thomas. 50

SMITH, M. E., 1926. An investigation of the development of the sentence and the extent of vocabulary in young children. *Univer. Iowa Stud. Child Welf., 3*, No. 5. 510

———, 1935. A study of the speech of eight bilingual children of the same family. *Child. Develpm., 6*, 19-25. 515

———, 1939. Some light on the problem of bilingualism as found from a study of the progress in mastery of English among preschool children of non-American ancestry in Hawaii. *Genet. Psychol. Monogr., 21*, 121-284. 515

———, 1949. Measurement of vocabulary of young bilingual children in both of the languages used. *J. genet. Psychol., 74*, 305-310. 515

SMYTHE, D. W., 1950. Television and its educational implications. *Elem. Eng., 27*, 41-52. 435

SNYDER, M. M. *See* Tuddenham & Snyder, 1954.

SOLOMON, R. L. *See* J. McV. Hunt *et al.*, 1947.

SONTAG, L. W., 1941. The significance of fetal environmental differences. *Amer. J. Obstet. Gynecol., 42*, 996-1003. 143-144

———, 1946. Some psychosomatic aspects of childhood. *Nerv. Child, 5*, 296-304. 81

———, BAKER, C. T., & NELSON, V. L., 1958. Mental growth and personality development: a longitudinal study. *Monogr. Soc. Res. Child Develpm., 23*, No. 2. 539-540

SONTAG, L. W., & GARN, S. M., 1954. Growth. *Annu. Rev. Physiol., 16*, 37-50. 456

SONTAG, L. W., & WALLACE, R. F., 1934. A study of fetal activity: preliminary report of the Fels Fund. *Amer. J. Dis. Child., 48*, 1050-1057. 145

———, 1935. The effect of cigarette smoking during pregnancy upon the fetal heart beat. *Amer. J. Obstet. Gynecol., 29*, 77-83. 143

SPELT, D. K., 1948. The conditioning of the human fetus *in utero. J. exp. Psychol., 38*, 338-346. 145

SPERRY, M. *See* Hollenberg & Sperry, 1951.

SPERRY, R. W., 1951. Mechanisms of neural maturation. In S. S. Stevens (ed.), *Handbook of experimental psychology.* Wiley. Pp. 236-280. **101**

SPIKER, C. C., 1956. Experiments with children on the hypotheses of acquired distinctiveness and equivalence of cues. *Child Develpm., 27,* 253-263. **521**

SPIRO, M. E., 1958. *Children of the kibbutz.* Harvard Univer. Press. **414**

SPITZ, R. A., 1945. Hospitalism: an inquiry into the genesis of psychiatric conditions in early childhood. *Psychoanal. Stud. Child, 1,* 53-74. **287-288, 298**

——, 1946. Hospitalism: a follow-up report on investigations described in Vol. 1, 1945. *Psychoanal. Stud. Child, 2,* 113-117. **287-288, 298**

——, & WOLF, K. M., 1946. The smiling response; a contribution to the ontogenesis of social relations. *Genet. Psychol. Monogr., 34,* 57-125. **549**

SROLE, L. *See* Warner & Srole, 1945.

STAGNER, R., 1951. Homeostasis as a unifying concept in personality theory. *Psychol. Rev., 58,* 5-17. Reprinted in Martin & Stendler, 1954, pp. 3-14. **35**

STANTON, F. N. *See* Lazarsfeld & Stanton, 1949.

STELLAR, E. *See* J. McV. Hunt *et al.,* 1947.

STENDLER, C. B., 1949. *Children of Brasstown.* Univer. of Illinois Press. **179**

——, 1950. Sixty years of child-training practices. *J. Pediat., 36,* 122-134. **309**

——, 1954a. The learning of certain secondary drives by Parisian and American middle-class children. *Marriage Fam. Living, 16,* 195-200. **172-173, 180, 194-195, 572**

——, 1954b. Possible causes of overdependency in young children. *Child Develpm., 25,* 125-146. **567, 571**

——, DAMRIN, D., & HAINES, A. C., 1951. Studies in cooperation and competition: I. The effects of working for group and individual rewards on the social climate of children's groups. *J. genet. Psychol., 79,* 173-197. **365**

STENDLER, C. B., & YOUNG, N., 1950. The impact of beginning first grade upon socialization as reported by mothers. *Child Develpm., 21,* 241-260. **347-348**

STENDLER, C. B. *See also* Martin & Stendler, 1954.

STERN, W., 1924. *Psychology of early childhood.* Holt. **523**

STEVENS, S. S. *See* Sheldon *et al.,* 1940; Sheldon & Stevens, 1942.

STEVENSON, H. W., & LANGFORD, T., 1957. Time as a variable in transposition by children. *Child Develpm., 28,* 365-370. **520**

STEVENSON, S. S. *See* Burke *et al.,* 1949; Stuart & Stevenson, 1954.

STOCKARD, C. R., 1931. *The physical basis of personality.* Norton. **140**

STOKE, S. M., 1950. An inquiry into the concept of identification. *J. genet. Psychol., 76,* 163-189. Reprinted in Martin & Stendler, 1954, pp. 227-239. **238**

STOLZ, H. R., & STOLZ, L. M., 1951. *Somatic development of adolescent boys.* Macmillan. **115, 118, 124, 126, 484**

STOLZ, H. R. *See also* Bayley & Stolz, 1937.

STOLZ, L. M., *et al.*, 1954. *Father relations of war-born children.* Stanford Univer. Press. **332**

STONE, C. P., & BARKER, R. G., 1939. The attitudes and interests of premenarcheal and postmenarcheal girls. *J. genet. Psychol., 54,* 27-71. **473**

STONE, L. J., & CHURCH, J., 1957. *Childhood and adolescence.* Random House. **218**

STROUD, J. B. *See* Blommers *et al.*, 1955.

STUART, H. C., 1944. Studies of the nutritional status of children in unoccupied France in the fall of 1942. *J. Pediat., 25,* 257-264. **8**

———, & STEVENSON, S. S., 1954. Physical growth and development. In W. E. Nelson (ed.), *Textbook of pediatrics.* (6th Ed.) Saunders. Pp. 10-66. **68, 69, 441, 446, 449, 454, 455, 456, 463, 468, 470**

STUART, H. C. *See also* Burke *et al.*, 1949.

SULLIVAN, H. S., 1953. *The interpersonal theory of psychiatry.* Norton. **519**

SUNG, C. *See* C. A. Aldrich *et al.*, 1945.

SWAN, C., TOSTEVIN, A. L., & BLACK, G. H. B., 1947. Final observations on congenital defects in infants following infectious diseases during pregnancy, with special reference to Rubella. *Med. J. Austr., 2,* 889-936. **139**

SWANSON, G. E. *See* D. R. Miller & Swanson, 1958.

SYMONDS, P. M., 1949. *The dynamics of parent-child relationships.* Teachers Coll., Columbia Univer. **321**

TABA, H. *See* Havighurst & Taba, 1949.

TANNER, J. M., 1953. Growth and constitution. In A. L. Kroeber (ed.), *Anthropology today.* Univer. of Chicago Press. **474, 493**

———, 1955. *Growth at adolescence.* Thomas. **51, 77, 78, 440, 441, 443, 446, 449, 451, 454, 456, 457, 459-461, 463, 468-469, 470, 471, 484, 485, 493**

TAYLOR, R., 1917. Hunger in the infant. *Amer. J. Dis. Child., 14,* 233-257. **152-153**

TERMAN, L. M., & MERRILL, M. A., 1937. *Measuring intelligence.* Houghton Mifflin. **524, 536**

TERMAN, L. M., & TYLER, L. E., 1954. Psychological sex differences. In L. Carmichael (ed.), *Manual of child psychology.* (2nd Ed.) Wiley. Pp. 1064-1114. **76, 542**

THOMPSON, G. G., 1952. *Child psychology.* Houghton Mifflin. **481**

THOMPSON, H., 1954. Physical growth. In L. Carmichael (ed.), *Manual of child psychology.* (2nd Ed.) Wiley. Pp. 292-334. **440, 459, 493**

THOMPSON, H. *See also* Gesell & Thompson, 1929.

THOMPSON, W. R., & MELZACK, R., 1956. Early environment; with biographical sketches. *Sci. Amer., 194,* 20-21, 38-42. **282-284**

THORNDIKE, E. L., 1921. *The teacher's word book.* Teachers Coll., Columbia Univer. **510**

———, 1949. *Selected writings from a connectionist's psychology.* Appleton-Century-Crofts. **500**

TINBERGEN, N., 1953. *Social behaviour in animals.* Methuen. **106**

TOSTEVIN, A. L. *See* Swan *et al.*, 1947.

TRAGER, H. G. *See* Radke *et al.*, 1949.

TRILLING, L., 1950. Freud and literature. In *The liberal imagination*. Viking. Pp. 44-64. **236**

TRYON, C., 1939. Evaluations of adolescent personality by adolescents. *Monogr. Soc. Res. Child Develpm., 4,* No. 4. **188**

TUCKER, W. B. *See* Sheldon *et al.,* 1940.

TUDDENHAM, R. D., & SNYDER, M. M., 1954. *Physical growth of California boys and girls from birth to eighteen years.* Univer. of California Press. **462**

TYLER, F. T., 1953. Concepts of organismic growth: a critique. *J. educ. Psychol., 44,* 321-342. **122**

TYLER, L. E. *See* Terman & Tyler. 1954.

TYLOR, E., 1871. *Primitive culture.* Murray. **164**

VAUGHAN, V. C., III, 1954. Administration of parenteral fluids. In W. E. Nelson (ed.), *Textbook of pediatrics.* (6th Ed.) Saunders. Pp. 169-174. **71**

VINCE, P. *See* Himmelweit *et al.,* 1958.

WALLACE, R. F. *See* Sontag & Wallace, 1934, 1935.

WARNER, W. L., & HENRY, W. E., 1948. The radio daytime serial: a symbolic analysis. *Genet. Psychol. Monogr., 37,* 3-71. **431**

WARNER, W. L., & LUNT, P. S., 1941. *The social life of a modern community.* Yale Univer. Press. **189**

WARNER, W. L., & SROLE, L., 1945. *The social systems of American ethnic groups.* Yale Univer. Press. **342**

WASHBURN, R. W., 1929. A study of the smiling and laughing of infants in the first year of life. *Genet. Psychol. Monogr., 6,* 397-539. **550**

WATERS, E., 1951. *His eye is on the sparrow.* Doubleday. **168**

WATSON, J. B., & MORGAN, J. J. B., 1917. Emotional reactions and psychological experimentation. *Amer. J. Psychol., 28,* 163-174. **546**

WATSON, J. B., & RAYNOR, R., 1920. Conditioned emotional reactions. *J. exp. Psychol., 3,* 1-14. **552**

WATTENBERG, W. W., 1955. *The adolescent years.* Harcourt, Brace. **582**

WATTENBERG, W. W. *See also* Redl & Wattenberg, 1951.

WATTS, A. F., 1944. *The language and mental development of children.* Harrap (London). **508, 543**

WEISS, A. P. *See* Gatewood & Weiss, 1930.

WEISS, L. A. *See* Irwin & Weiss, 1934.

WELLMAN, B. L., & McCANDLESS, B. R., 1946. Factors associated with Binet IQ changes of preschool children. *Psychol. Monogr., 60,* No. 2. **541**

WENGER, M. A., 1936. An investigation of conditioned responses in human infants. *Univer. Iowa Stud. Child Welf., 12,* No. 1. **154**

WERNER, H., & CARRISON, D., 1943. Principles and methods of teaching arithmetic to mentally retarded children. *Amer. J. ment. Def., 47,* 309-317. **524**

WETZEL, N. C., 1941. Physical fitness in terms of physique, development, and basal metabolism. *J. Amer. med. Ass., 116,* 1187-1195. **456**

WETZEL, N. C., 1943. Assessing physical fitness in children: I. Case demonstration of failing growth and the determination of "par" by the grid method; II. Simple malnutrition: a problem of failing growth and development; III. The components of physical status and physical progress and their evaluation. *J. Pediat.,* 22, 82-110, 208-225, 329-361. **456**

——, 1946. The baby grid: an application of the grid technique to growth and development in infants. *J. Pediat.,* 29, 439-454. **456**

WEXLER, S. *See* Bronstein *et al.,* 1942.

WHITE, R. K. *See* Lewin *et al.,* 1939.

WHITEHEAD, A. N., 1929. *The aims of education.* Macmillan. **7, 29**

WHITING, J. W. M., 1941. *Becoming a Kwoma.* Yale Univer. Press. **36, 277**

——, 1944. The frustration complex in Kwoma society. *Man, 44,* 140-144. Reprinted in Martin & Stendler, 1954, pp. 194-198. **564**

——, & CHILD, I. L., 1953. *Child training and personality.* Yale Univer. Press. **192-193, 194, 197, 200, 571, 573**

WHITING, J. W. M., & MOWRER, O. H., 1943. Habit progression and regression: a laboratory study of some factors relevant to human socialization. *J. comp. Psychol., 36,* 229-253. **246-249**

WHITING, J. W. M. *See also* Murdock & Whiting, 1951; R. R. Sears *et al.,* 1953.

WHYTE, W. H., JR., 1956. *The organization man.* Simon & Schuster. **395**

WILLIAMS, J., & SCOTT, R., 1953. Growth and development of Negro infants. IV. Motor development and its relationship to child-rearing practices in two groups of Negro infants. *Child Develpm., 24,* 103-121. **71**

WILLIAMS, R. J., 1953. *Free and unequal: the biological basis of individual liberty.* Univer. of Texas Press. **94**

——, 1957. *Biochemical individuality.* Wiley. **94**

WINES, J. V. *See* Reynolds & Wines, 1948.

WINTERBOTTOM, M. R., 1953. The relation of childhood training in independence to achievement motivation. Unpublished doctoral dissertation, Univer. of Michigan. (Abstract in Univer. Microfilms, Publication No. 5113.) **573**

WISE, G. W. *See* R. R. Sears & Wise, 1950.

WISHIK, S. M., 1955. *Feeding your child.* Doubleday. **65, 83-84, 85**

WITTENBORN, J. R., *et al.,* 1956. A study of adoptive children. *Psychol. Monogr., 70,* Nos. 1, 2, & 3. **345, 346, 566, 578**

WITTY, P., 1956. Sixth report on TV. *Sch. & Soc., 83,* 166-168. **434**

Wolf Cub Scout Book, 1952. Boy Scouts of America. **408-409, 410-412**

WOLF, K. M., 1953. Observation of individual tendencies in the first year of life. In M. J. E. Senn (ed.), *Problems of infancy and childhood.* (Transactions of the Sixth Conference) Josiah Macy, Jr., Foundation, 1953. Pp. 97-137. **93**

WOLF, K. M. *See also* Spitz & Wolf, 1946.

WOLFE, J. B., 1936. Effectiveness of token-rewards for chimpanzees. *Comp. Psychol. Monogr., 12,* No. 60. Reprinted with abridgment in Martin & Stendler, 1954, pp. 262-279. **277**

WOLFENSTEIN, M., 1953. Trends in infant care. *Amer. J. Orthopsychiat., 33,* 120-130. **335**

WOLFENSTEIN, M., 1955a. French parents take their children to the park. In M. Mead and M. Wolfenstein (eds.), *Childhood in contemporary cultures.* Univer. of Chicago Press. Pp. 99-117. **181, 196**

——, 1955b. Some variants in moral training of children. In M. Mead and M. Wolfenstein (eds.), *Childhood in contemporary cultures.* Univer. of Chicago Press. Pp. 349-368. **193-194**

WOLFENSTEIN, M. *See also* M. Mead & Wolfenstein, 1955.

WOODYARD, E. S. *See* Jersild *et al.*, 1949.

WORCESTER, J. *See* Burke *et al.*, 1949.

WRIGHT, H. F., 1937. The influence of barriers upon the strength of motivation. *Contr. psychol. Theor., 1,* No. 3. **531**

——, BARKER, R. G., KOPPE, W., MEYERSON, B., & NALL, J., 1951. Children at home in Midwest. *Prog. Educ., 28,* 137-145. **415, 424**

WRIGHT, H. F. *See also* Barker *et al.,* 1943, 1950; Barker & Wright, 1951, 1954.

YOUNG, N. *See* Stendler & Young, 1950.

ZORBAUGH, H. W. (ed.), 1944. The comics as an educational medium. *J. educ. Sociol., 18,* 193-255. **425, 427**

subject index

A RETOURNER

Bongrand & Cⁱᵉ - Montrouge

R 26			
DEC 28			
MAY 11			
- 4 MAI			
7 FEV. 1976			
4 JUIN. 1977			
9 NOV. 1978			
1 1 DEC. 1979			
-7 JAN. 1980			
2 8 JUIL. 1982			
-1 NOV. 1983			

B